D1270172

BORN UNDER SATURN

WILLIAM HAZLITT
A SELF PORTRAIT

BORN UNDER SATURN

A Biography of
WILLIAM HAZLITT

by

CATHERINE MACDONALD MACLEAN

New York
THE MACMILLAN COMPANY
1944

FIRST PRINTING.

To

C. M. F.

Where Hazlitt lies
By quiet St. Anne's
Old men were wont to sun themselves and children play
Under the fair and tranquil skies
Where Hazlitt lies
"Snug, out of harm's way."

Where Hazlitt lies,
On quiet St. Anne's
The Kite has dropped huge dereliction and dismay.
Yet still I hear a voice that cries:
"Snug, out of harm's way,"
Where Hazlitt lies.

Contents

ILLUSTRATIONS

To the Reader

It is hoped that this study, not only of the intellectual and emotional development of a man of genius who seemed to his contemporaries "a species by himself," but of the life-struggle in the service of Liberty of one who considered that he had passed through "an apocalyptical chapter in the history of human nature," and who was regarded in his own day not merely nor even primarily as a man-of-letters, but by his enemies as "a bigot of the Revolution," whom it was a virtue to calumniate almost out of existence and to hunt down "as a wild beast," by his friends as the spear in the hand of Democracy—may have some immediate interest for the Reader of to-day.

C. M. M.

Part One

THE CHILD AND THE BOY

These are the materials of history; and if it is not made of them, it is a nickname and a mockery. All that does not lay open the fine net-work of the heart and brain of man, that does not make us see deeper into the soul, is but the apparatus and machinery of history-painting, and no more to it than the frame is to the picture.

HAZLITT.

Chapter One

CHILDHOOD IN AMERICA (1783-1787)

"... to the north King-Oak Hill, which in winter, when covered with snow, reflected the golden and purple tints of the setting sun. Over this hill the road leading to Hingham was seen. How often have we stood at the window, looking at my father as he went up the road with William, in his nankeen dress, marching by his side, like one that never could be tired!"

MARGARET HAZLITT.

I

ON APRIL 3RD, 1783, the *Henry* set sail from Cork for the New World, bearing with it the news of the Treaty of Peace between England and America, heartily damned by the captain, as eagerly rejoiced over by some of his passengers. Of all the freight of human souls now turning their eyes towards the receding shores of Ireland we know nothing, save of one little group of emigrants on board, arresting in its corporate individuality, and each of the members of which has some touch of distinctiveness that holds the eye. The leader of this group is the Rev. William Hazlitt, the dissenting clergyman, recently of Bandon, who had drawn much unpopularity upon himself by his intervention to prevent the ill-treatment of the American prisoners at Kinsale by the officers of the regiment in charge of them, and who had been so much persecuted in consequence, that it had put him out of love with his native land. He has along with him his wife, his sons John and William, his elder daughter Margaret and the infant Harriet, attended by a servant or nurse. Sturdy, square-rigg'd, he is just a few days short of his forty-seventh birthday, and he looks more than his years, for his

9

has been a hard life. He is very definitely of the people, with no claim
to distinction except the stamp of character on his broad, square-cut
face, and no claim to beauty, except the light in the wide-set meditative
eyes. There is any amount of strength in him, yet perhaps he lacks
the something that can direct strength to any great purpose. A very
good man—one would say—but without a spark of genius, he is yet
of those out of whose strength genius is bred, of those from whose
steadfastness genius takes its flight. He had been born at Shronell,
County Tipperary, in 1737, the son of John and Margaret Hazlitt, poor
folk, who yet desired their sons to have the key to the door of knowledge, closed to themselves, and had managed to send both him and
his brother James to the University of Glasgow. Thither he had gone
to prepare for the Presbyterian ministry, but finding in himself some
scruples about accepting the tenets of Calvinism, he had adopted the
milder, and as it seemed to him, more Christlike tenets of the Unitarians, notwithstanding the pain and dissatisfaction his rejection of the
creed in which he had been brought up had given to his parents. In
1764 he had become the minister of a congregation at Wisbeach.
There he had done one of the best things he ever did for himself, had
wooed, won and wedded, on January 19th, 1766, the gentle and
beautiful Grace Loftus, daughter of an ironmonger in the town. Like
himself, she had obstinate dissenting blood in her veins. There had
followed four years in which he had ministered to a congregation at
Marshfield, where his sons John and Loftus had been born. In 1770
he had been chosen minister of the Earl Street Meeting House at
Maidstone. While there he had enjoyed the friendship of Dr. Priestley,
Dr. Price, and Dr. Kippis, as well as of many other ministers less
distinguished, had been privileged, at the house of one of his friends,
to make the acquaintance of Benjamin Franklin, and had been able to
enjoy the play of mind and the converse he most loved, on religious
and political liberty, and on disputed points of theology; but the
obstinate integrity which had led to the rift with his parents had
offended some of his congregation, and his outspokenness with regard
to the American War, about which he felt much as did Chatham and
all who loved the name and cause of Liberty, had finally caused so
much dissension that in 1780 he had led his wife and family back to
Ireland, where he had accepted the charge of a small congregation at
Bandon, near Cork. His son Loftus had died while he had been at
Maidstone, and the family, when he had settled at Bandon, had consisted of John, his eldest son, Margaret, who had been born shortly
after the settlement at Maidstone, and his youngest son William, also
born at Maidstone, and now just under five years old. The child had
been born on April 10th, 1778, just almost three months before the
death of Jean-Jacques Rousseau, and just three days after Chatham had
held the House of Lords spellbound with his last plea: "My Lords,

any state is better than despair; if we must fall, let us fall like men;" and had then sunk down, the spell broken and the fire extinguished, in the exhaustion preceding his death.

Mr. Hazlitt had accepted the ministry of the small congregation at Bandon, hoping to find peace, but this boon was denied him, for there was an iniquity close to him which pressed upon him, wounded his sense of humanity and his sense of religion, and would not let him rest. The treatment of the American prisoners by the officers of the regiment of Colonel Fitzpatrick at Kinsale was an open scandal. The shadow of Chatham's statue did not extend from Cork to Kinsale, nor did the memory of Chatham's spirit avail to protect these. Many were shocked by the matter, but refrained from intervention that might be dangerous to themselves. Not so Mr. Hazlitt! By temperament unfitted for compromise, by nature quite unable to understand the type of mind that can brand a human being as "rebel" and henceforth regard it as devoid of the elementary rights of a human being, he denounced the iniquity in private and in public, in speech and on paper; wrote to the War Office about it, and brought the matter to the notice of Lord Shelburne, through his friend Dr. Price. The result of his intervention was that a court of inquiry was held, and certain officers were censured;[1] but in a district dominated by the military element, which allowed itself far more licence than would ever have been suffered in England, life became very difficult for the one who had intervened, and for his family. It was in immediate consequence of this he was setting out to find what peace he could for a man of his political and religious views, in America. Apart from this, he had felt for some years that yearning towards America which was felt also by many of those of his contemporaries in whom the love of Liberty burned, among them Chatham himself, who almost eleven years before, wearied of the intrigue and the ineptitude and the spirit of oppression against which he had fought his long fight, had declared publicly: "Were I but ten years younger I should spend the remainder of my days in America. . . ."

Rock-rugged and rough-hewn, bearing on his face not only the marks of thought, resistance to circumstances, privation, and suffering, but the ravages left by the smallpox, the casing of the cheekbone and chin obstinate as pig-lead, this poor minister about to cross the seas to witness for what he was persuaded was eternal Truth, looked not unlike our conception of Mr. Valiant-for-truth about to cross the river. And he too might have said: "My marks and scars I carry with me."

The other members of this little group, following their brave leader in unquestioning obedience and faith, form a curious contrast to him, in that each of them has a touch of beauty, distinction, and delicacy. Mrs. Hazlitt, although nearing her thirty-seventh year, is still pretty, albeit her beauty has a slightly erased, plaintive look. Hers is the perfection of the true womanly character, in that she seems to live and have her being only in relationship to and through her affection for those most dear to her. These affections at the moment are divided. She is with her husband and children, it is true, but she has left behind her old mother in England, whom she never expects to see again. She has had to leave behind her two of her children. Loftus, who lies in English ground, is already of the fine dust of the earth. Thomas, born during the brief and troubled stay at Bandon, rests in Irish soil. The wound of this loss is still fresh; and as she thinks of the months to come, and of the child to whom she will give birth in the course of a summer spent in an unknown country, in unknown circumstances, and in unknown ways, trustful though she be in the leadership of her husband, she has more than enough to press upon her.

The children have inherited their looks from their mother rather than from their father, although in Margaret's face there is a hint of their father's strength. John, in his fifteenth year, is a handsome spirited lad, with perhaps the slightest hint of petulance about the mouth. He has had some training in art, and he means to contribute to the support of the family by portrait-painting in the New World. Margaret, a girl of twelve, bright of colouring and auburn-haired, has a delightful face. Gentleness dwells in her beautiful eyes, sweetness in the curve of her charming mouth. She has much of her mother's nature, but also some of her father's strength. Already her mother turns to her; already her father trusts, although unconsciously, in her reserves of character. Two moods struggle in her at the moment, regret for the friends she is leaving, and eager anticipation of the wider world now about to open itself out before her. She has just been reading the book she calls *The American Farmer*,[2] and her expectations have been raised so high by it that if she found before her an earthly Paradise she would hardly have been surprised. And, of course, she has gathered from her father's conversation that she is going to a perfect land, where her father will no longer meet with such difficulties as have made her heart beat fast for him in the past, a land "where no tyrants were to rule, no bigots to hate and persecute their brethren, no intrigues to feed the flame of discord and fill the land with woe," and where "nothing was to hurt or destroy in all that holy mountain."

Then we must not forget to mention, last of all, the child who had made his appearance at such a moment of crisis in English history, and whom the consequences of that crisis have flung forth across the waves of the Atlantic before he is five years old. He will be celebrating his fifth birthday in mid-ocean in exactly a week's time, the eager little bit of life that is William—small pale face, sweet-curving mouth, wide-open grey eyes which sometimes look almost blue, dark curls, a pair of active legs that he uses to keep himself as near his sire as may be!

He is sturdy on his feet now, but even before he could crawl he, who is now numbered among those seeking Liberty in the New World, had learned to know the word Liberty, oft-repeated by his father's lips. No! we must certainly not allow the *homo* William, although we confess that we have some affection for him, to overshadow the *homunculus* William, sprung from his loins, for even as Margaret is the heart of the family, this child is the living nerve of it. He among them all, the little Paleface whose life began just when Rousseau was nearing the end of his warfare, is the one whose life is destined to be a continuous fight in the battle to which poor Jean-Jacques had sounded the call to arms; the one to whose memory even, therefore, as to Rousseau's, his enemies will never grant the boon of peace. Yet he among them all is the one whom the world will not willingly let die.

2

The *Henry* reached New York on Monday, May 26th, after a voyage which had lasted eight weeks all but two days. As soon as the ship cast anchor she was invaded by British officers eager to hear the news, and violent in their denunciation of the Treaty of Peace when they heard of it; the captain joining heartily in their curses and imprecations both on Congress and on the Ministry at home. It was six o'clock in the evening before the Hazlitt family landed. The new country, naturally enough, had no welcome for these unknown folk, and it was late before they could find any resting-place. This was because Mr. Hazlitt had been given a letter of introduction to a certain Mr. Trench Cox who was very unpopular because he was pro-British in his sympathies, and whose presence, when he acted as guide in the quest for lodgings, made things even more difficult than they might otherwise have been, for people were prejudiced in advance against those who appeared to be his friends. Mrs. Hazlitt and Margaret—or "Peggy" as they all called her—the young brother who is evidently her little pet·and whom she addresses as "Billy,"[3] Harriet and the maid at last sank down to rest, while awaiting the return of Mr. Hazlitt and John, in the shelter of a porch, making such a forlorn and extinguished a little group of immigrants as might any day be seen at that time in New York. At last they all secured admission into a house where they spent two days, while waiting for their goods to be delivered from the ship.

Then began those long journeyings from place to place which Mr. Hazlitt's life in America was to become. Driven forward by his desire to spread throughout a new country the joy and peace of the doctrine in which he believed he had found an uncorrupted and undistorted Christianity that would redeem from unbelief many who had been driven into repudiation of Christianity by the harsh distortions of Calvinism, he was far more sanguine in his expectations of a welcome for himself and his family, in his pioneer mission, than would have seemed reasonable to any onlooker; he had come thus far, in spite of the dissuasion of friends, Dr. Price among them; and he was still buoyed up by apostolic zeal and by his faith. He had as yet no conception of the difficulties of his mission; while he knew that there were very few Unitarians in America, he did not know that even these did not dare to make open confession of their faith, for fear of the persecution of their Calvinistic brethren;[4] nor did he realise that the spirit of intolerance, leading to the splitting of hairs over minute points of orthodoxy and to petty enmities between those who disagreed on these points, was keener, bitterer, more probing in the New England than it had been in the Old.[5] He did not as yet know that there were many who would not listen to what he had to teach them, until they had first of all satisfied themselves that he conformed to each of the *minutiæ* of dogma on which they prided themselves, and had forced the newcomer to subscribe to them. His heart might well have failed him had he known of the difficulties that lay before him, but as yet he did not know, and nothing doubting, he went forward.

His first desire was to settle in Philadelphia, and towards it they journeyed, by way of Perth Amboy, where they rested at a fine inn, set on rising ground, with a green lawn in front sloping down to a river, and Burlington, also by a river, on the opposite banks of which stood Bath and Bristol, the very names of which brought back to Mrs. Hazlitt the recollection of the early days of her married life, at Marshfield, just five miles from Bath; of the friendly faces of the simple folk of that congregation on whom they would drop in, informally, for tea; of known ways and home and settled days. As if rejoicing in coming even upon names that were known to her, she wished her husband to settle there and to open a school; but all his heart was set on pressing forward: all his zeal was for preaching, and so they departed for Philadelphia, in a stage-wagon, and travelled for two days through the Jersey woods, then gay with the blossom of the wild peach and the apricot, and filled with the scent of the yellow blossom of the high locust trees, reminding them of laburnum, while splendid oak and ash towered over all the others.

At Philadelphia the only house they could get was both small and expensive, and housekeeping in it was difficult, for the only pantry was a shelf in the cellar, where everything had to be placed in water or it was devoured by swarms of ants. There his family remained for fifteen months, while Mr. Hazlitt sallied forth on his many expeditions, and began his course in disillusionment. He had in the course of the summer the opportunity of what they all regarded as an excellent settlement, but his scruples interfered with his acceptance of it. He had preached, among other places, at Carlisle, and had spent some time there; and his preaching had met with such acceptance that he might there and then, upon the warm recommendation of Dr. Ewing of Philadelphia, have settled with a stipend of £300 a year and the prospect of becoming president of a college then being erected; but the orthodox of the congregation made it a condition that he should subscribe to a confession of faith that they set before him. This he could not do, and he shook the dust of the town off his feet, telling them to their faces that he would "die in a ditch" rather than submit to any human authority in matters of faith.

He had in the meantime incurred the enmity of Dr. Rush of Philadelphia, who not only attacked him in the newspapers but also made a bitter attack on Dr. Ewing because being a Presbyterian he had recommended a Socinian to be pastor of a church and president of a college.[6]

Apart from this disappointment, embittered by public controversy, the summer brought grief and trouble to all of them, but especially to the mother of the family: the child Harriet, although she had survived her long journeying, perished in the heat of the town; a child Esther struggled into life only to fade out of it again quickly and without struggle. In the autumn there came a yet heavier trouble. Shortly after the death of Esther, Mr. Hazlitt set out to preach to a congregation in Maryland. They heard nothing of him for some weeks, and then came the news that he had fainted in the pulpit there while preaching, this being the first symptom of the yellow fever which had since stricken him. His wife, already shaken by the deaths of two children in what had been the country of their hopes, broke down completely under the news of this fresh calamity, and for a time she could not be persuaded that he too was not dead. The next day John set out on horseback to find his father. So desperate was the boy with anxiety that he managed to cover over a hundred miles of riding through wood and swamp in unknown country in two days. The sadly diminished family waited anxiously for news and for his return with his father. At last, on November 1st, father and son reappeared, in the midst of the first fall of snow. Somehow or other they had managed the journey, but Mr. Hazlitt was still very weak and ill, and so spent with fatigue that he had to be lifted down from his horse. Throughout the winter he was but the shadow of himself: the snow lay many feet on the ground; the cold was intense, and it seemed as if he could not get the chill out of his bones. The heat of the summer had seemed to melt them; now the cold seemed to pierce them to the marrow. Yellow of face, and wrapped in his greatcoat, he sat shivering over the fire day after day.

By the spring he was sufficiently recovered to deliver a set of lectures on the Evidences of Christianity at the College of Philadelphia.

He was invited to settle at Charleston in South Carolina, but dared not risk the climate. An invitation to settle at Pittsburg he also declined, thinking it too far back in the wilderness to give John any opportunity of exercising his art. In June he preached at Boston, and was so well liked that he would have settled there as minister of the Brattle Street Meeting-House, were it not that "the persecuting zeal of the orthodox" —as his daughter puts it—sent "one of their chosen brethren" there to report adversely against him. Especially he seems to have felt that one of the ministers 'near Boston, the Rev. William Gordon of Jamaica Plain, whom he described as "a busy bigot,"[7] was zealous in the attempt to injure his prospects.

Thus they were deprived a second time of the chance of finding rest for the sole of their foot.

Mr. Hazlitt, however, had found congenial society in Boston, and a kindred spirit in the Rev. John Lathrop, minister of the second church,[8] and had resolved to move into its neighbourhood; and so, in August, 1784, they left Philadelphia. Peggy Hazlitt probably expressed the feelings they all had towards it when she wrote many years afterwards: "We then bade farewell to Philadelphia, casting a last look at this beautiful city of William Penn, where so many events had befallen us, and where we left my two infant sisters sleeping in their early graves, the beloved and the beautiful."

And so they retraced their steps, back again through the Jersey woods, with wild peaches and apricots now on the trees instead of blossom, grapes, and every variety of nut, through Burlington to the pleasant inn at Perth Amboy, where Billy, his mother, his sister, a lady with her little girl, and a large Newfoundland dog who *snored*, all spent the night in one room. The next morning they breakfasted gloriously—"for an American breakfast is like a Scottish one," Peggy wrote afterwards—on the lawn before the door, after which they went on board a sloop for New York. At New York they again spent a couple of days, waiting for "the packet going to Rhode Island." When they arrived at Newport, they found it all disfigured and scarred by the war, for the British troops had not left a tree on the island; many of the floors of the houses had been hacked by their axes; and the mahogany furniture of the houses had been cut up for firing. The next day's journey brought them to Providence, on the banks of "the most beautiful river that ever was seen." There they spent the night. In the morning they rose early, set out for Boston in two coaches, and travelled all day once more through the heart-shaking beauty of the woods, now taking on the incredible brilliance and variety of their autumn colouring, where the scarlet and gold of the trees themselves seemed to rustle and to make wild music as innumerable birds that matched their fantastic colouring darted in and out of them, or sang their matin and vesper songs. Of the big game which these woods contained they saw nothing: bears, the tiger-cat, and the cat-a-mountain, hating the sight and sound and smell of man, driven down only by the severities of winter towards the loathed habitations of man. Of all the little townships they passed, Margaret Hazlitt afterwards remembered only the name of one, Jamaica Plain, where they passed the residence of the Dr. Gordon who had shown himself so inimical to her father.

They settled in the course of the autumn in Weymouth, a hamlet fifteen miles away from Boston, consisting of only a few houses, a meeting-house and a parsonage, a mill by the river and a meagre shop; but the house in which they lived was so finely situated as to be in itself a joy. It was surrounded on three sides by great hills that sloped down just in sight of the windows; in front a sloping green led downwards towards a lane and meadow, jewelled with fireflies on the summer evenings, and the river; and the country around was very beautiful. Here they seem to have felt that they had found at last a real home in the heart of the wilderness. The first thing they saw when they took possession of the house was a painting, reputed to be one of the early works of Copley, of the meeting of Jacob and Esau, showing the two brothers embracing, the groups of followers on either side, camels and cattle, and the background winding up between the hills. This did not make it seem less homelike to them. Nothing could have made Mr. Hazlitt feel more at home than to be greeted by "such glimmerings of patriarchal wanderings," and as for Peggy, the painting had for her a kind of enchantment. She could interest herself for hours studying the detail of the picture, marvelling the while at the way in which the artist's imagination had gone to work and in which his hand had executed its imaginings.

Winter snapped its jaws at them almost as soon as they had settled into their new home, and they felt its severity, but the younger members of the family, at least, had many compensations. It was a delight to them to climb the slippery hills and carve their names in the frozen snow, or identify the places that recently had become matter of history, the Bay of Boston or Dorchester Heights or Bunker's Hill. They marvelled at seeing the pageant of the evening sky reflected on the white expanse of the snowy heights, for they had never seen anything in the least like it before. It was a vision of such beauty as had never entered even into their dreams. The chief pleasure of all was cutting through the air in a sleigh, right over hedges and ditches that had been levelled by the snow.

But their lives on the whole were rigorous and hard. There was neither butcher nor baker anywhere near, and the one small shop in the hamlet contained only a few groceries, some remnants of linen, and some of the materials for sewing. For the most part they lived through the winter on hard sea-biscuits, cheese, butter, salt beef and

pork. Yet they were not quite without pleasant exchange of hospitalities. When neighbours came in they always saw to it that there was a
clean hearth and a bright wood fire, before which, when preparing the
tea, they would set little cakes made with Indian flour without yeast,
to bake in a pewter plate. These sweet cakes were the chief delicacies
they could offer to their guests.

It was at the beginning of this autumn that Mr. Hazlitt sent his
first letter from America to Dr. Price. No doubt he had not felt it an
easy matter to write of the difficulties he had experienced, to one who
had tried to dissuade him from his American venture. His letter is
very quiet in tone, but it is clear from it that he felt his fortunes to
have been heavy: "Dear Sir, I have wished to write to you almost
every week, since my first arrival in this country, but was restrained
by the consideration, that I had nothing satisfactory to communicate
respecting myself. The same reason might still induce me to throw
away my paper. But I can no longer deny myself the satisfaction of
addressing you. . . .

"You have been told, I presume, by others, that I lived a considerable
time at Philadelphia, and how I succeeded there, and that I was seized
with a fever in Maryland last year, which rendered me useless whilst I
was groaning under a great expense, almost six months."[9]

He spent most of his time that winter walking to and from Boston,
where he was giving again the course of lectures on the Evidences
of Christianity which he had already given in Philadelphia. No
severity of weather detained him. Often he walked through the snow.
Once John and he set out in blinding rain.

In mid-February they had a deceptive thaw, when the weather
became mild and the snow seemed to have vanished. The melted
snow flowed right into their wash-house; then the thaw was suddenly
succeeded by harder frost than ever, so that John and his father had
to cut up the ice in the wash-house with their axes, and throw it outside
in great blocks.

The gradual drawing-on of the spring and summer that year was
an unforgettable experience—first of all the ice breaking and floating
down the river, then the sheets of water covering the lower meadows
like a "glassy essence," the snow-pure scent and the marvel of the
arbutus delicately pink and white under the dead leaves, the taste of
the barberries that had lain on the hills all the winter under the snow.
Later came the singing of the birds, the gradual breaking into flower
and perfume of the locust trees that covered the hills by which the
house was surrounded on three sides, so that the white hills of winter
seemed to have been exchanged for golden ramparts; the blossoming
of pear tree and peach; the colour and strangeness of the birds—
humming-birds of five or six different kinds, the most beautiful of
them purple, green and gold, darting in and out of the peach trees, so

near to the windows of the house that once a humming-bird flew right inside; the blue bird, coloured like a pale sky; the scarlet bird; the fire-coloured bird that hangs her nest at the end of a bough; the Virginia nightingale, of a bright crimson; the red linnet; the king-bird, from which the hawk itself takes flight; the snow-bird and the Bob Lincoln, noted for its song; and the mocking-bird, who imitated the cries of all these as if he meant to dazzle the ear. Even the familiar birds were different from those named by the same name at home. There were swallows, but they were brighter than English swallows; There were robins, but they were larger than English robins. The thrush looked the same, but had a different note. Sometimes, amid all this exotic colour and stir of sound they may have longed, like Cobbett, for the sight of the birds of their native land, that take the eye less, but are loved with a familiar love, and for the simple sound of the wild wood-notes of the English countryside.

Billy found a new friend in one of their neighbours, Captain Whitman, who had been an officer in the American Army during the war, and had returned to his farm and his plough immediately the war was over, and who grew so fond of the little English boy that he liked to take him everywhere with him—to the woods, to the fields when the men were ploughing, to the milking of the cows. But loving eyes watched the child, to see that he did not overtire himself, even in his play. Within the sloping green before the door there stood a solitary pear tree. When the summer was at its height Billy was forbidden to go beyond this tree until four o'clock in the afternoon, when the sun was to some extent shaded by the surrounding hills. Even within this green a child might find sufficient entertainment in sight and sound, for the woodpeckers would sit on the poles which enclosed it, making with their bills a noise like a saw. Often he was with his father. He loved now to accompany his father when Mr. Hazlitt went to preach at villages not too far away, and would sit in the pulpit during the service, busy with his own thoughts, listening desultorily to his father's discourse, or observing the faces of the peculiarly fine old men whom this country seemed to breed. The loving eyes that watched to see that he did not overtire himself at his play would again watch him from the window as he set out on these expeditions: indeed in these days, whatever the hardships he had, the child lived his life in that element of love which afterwards, as a man, he could not win for himself, and in trying to force which he made shipwreck of his life. Once in the course of the summer his father took him on a more distant expedition, when he went to preach at Cape Cod. There was little to be seen in that desolate place but rocks, sands, and the long breakers of the ocean. The child missed the sight and the sound of the birds, and asked whether any robins or Bob Lincolns never came there. He was told that they did not. Already he always liked to have a reason for things, but unlike most children he was given to thinking out his own reason. "I suppose they do not like such an ugly place," said he in a moment, as if he had satisfied himself on the matter.

It did not endear Cape Cod to him that stepping into the boat he dropped into the sea a shoe with a silver buckle of which he was proud. Silver shoe-buckles did not rain on him in New England.

Mr. Hazlitt preached in Weymouth itself but once, for the congregation there was rigidly Calvinistic, and his family was not wont to attend the meeting-house on the hill. When he chanced to be there on a Sunday, he held a service in his own home. That summer he again left his family, this time to preach at a new settlement in the wilds of Maine, Holywell, on Kennebec river. He narrowly escaped death by drowning, in the Bay of Fundy, when returning home in the spring.

Tired of his endless walks to and from Boston, he moved his family into a house at Upper Dorchester, five miles from the town, in July; but in the course of that summer he came to feel that he was unlikely to find the settlement he wished, and that there was nothing to do but to make his way back to England, and begin his career there again. Wishing to spare his family any further vicissitudes until he had some hope to offer them, he left them where they were comfortably settled. His daughter writes of the parting: "He talked to us of our separation and the hope of meeting again, and charged me, above all things, to be careful of and attentive to my mother, and endeavour by every means in my power to keep up her spirits and soften every care."

On October 23rd, 1786, he who had come out with his family, and full of hope, returned to England, alone, with no one by him to soften any care. What were his thoughts as he sailed from the Long Wharf, Boston? Did the voices of the children he had buried in the parching heat of the Philadelphian summer cry to him from the now clay-cold ground! Did he feel a tightness at his breast as he thought of the helpless ones he had left behind him! Did disillusionment and self-distrust nag at the roots of his great courage! We do not know. His eye may have had less lustre than in earlier days; his face may have been a trifle heavier; certainly some of the fighting spirit had gone out of him, and he was less inclined in after years to trust himself to the mercies of the world; but we have no record of any complaining of his as to his fate. His daughter, we know, grieved for him, not for his labours, but that he should have done so much and that his name and effort should have been so little remembered. Almost fifty years afterwards she wrote: ". . . perhaps my father was destined to remove the rubbish and to clear the way for more fortunate Unitarians who, coming after him, entered into his labours and reaped the fruits thereof." A second time she returned to this theme: "I cannot help remarking how strange it seems that my father, who openly preached the Doctrine of the Divine Unity from Maryland to Kennebec, should have been so entirely overlooked, and the whole work ascribed to Dr. Priestley, who went there so many years after him. But it is so."

She grieved also because if he had only remained a little longer he might have obtained such a settlement as he had wished, either at Hingham, his old friend Mr. Gay, the minister there, having died, or at Jamaica Plain, which his enemy Dr. Gordon had quitted, having sailed for London to arrange for the publication of his book on the American Revolution.[10]

<h2 style="text-align:center">3</h2>

The letters which arrived from him in the course of the spring, written from the house of his friend Mr. David Lewis, in London, were full of hope, although he had not yet found a settlement. They were also full of longing. He wished them to rejoin him, and they started at once to make their preparations for departure, although they were not a little sorry to be leaving the circle of kindly, cheerful, and hospitable friends they had made since settling near Boston; Peggy and John especially looked back with regret on their sleighing expeditions and on the happy evenings spent in playing chess and whist and loo with their friends in Boston, or in games and songs after which they returned home in the moonlight over roads slippery as glass. Peggy had played more at cards that winter—whose simple gaieties she always remembered with pleasure—than during all the rest of her life.

Billy, though he too did not lack little friends and playfellows, had distinguished himself chiefly since his father's departure by almost killing himself with excessive application to Latin grammar. Possibly he had been charged by his father to study diligently under his brother John. At any rate, at the age of seven years, having outstripped his first friends *Jack the Giant-Killer* and *Whittington and his Cat*, and Mrs. Barbauld's story-books for children, from which he had learned to spell,[11] he showed for the first time in his life that passionate absorption in any pursuit in which he was interested, which afterwards turned to eccentricity or at least idiosyncrasy. Of all the letters sent to their father during the months of their separation from him, his is the only one which has been preserved. In some ways it is quaintly anticipatory of the man he was to become:

"12 of Nov.

"My dear Papa, I shall never forget that we came to america. If we had not came to america we should not have been away from one and other, though now it can not be helped. I think for my part that it would have been a great deal better if the white people had not found it out. Let the   [12] have it to themselves, for it was made for them. I have got a little of my grammar; sometimes I get three pages and sometimes but one. I do not sifer any at all. Mamma Peggy and Jacky are all very well, and I am to. I still remain

"your most affectionate Son

"William Hazlitt."

On July 4th, 1787, the anniversary of the Declaration of American Independence, Mrs. Hazlitt and her children—all that were left to her of them—embarked at Boston on the *Nonpareil*, bound for Portsmouth. Peggy never forgot the time she spent in America, and she always seems to regret that her family did not settle there; John left his impressions in his paintings; William, despite the claim made in his childhood's letter, would seem, if we judge him merely by his later writings, to have remembered little of his sojourn. As a boy of twelve, when offended by grudging and formal hospitality, he confessed to his father that he could not help thinking of the hospitality he had received in America, warm and informal, and wishing himself back there; once he wrote that after an interval of thirty years he still remembered the incomparable taste of the barberries which had hung out in the snow during the severity of a North American winter;[13] he commended Cobbett's descriptions of the gold and scarlet plumage of the American birds,[14] and referred to "the dazzling almost invisible shimmer of the humming-bird's wings," as if he remembered something of these things; his phrasing, when he wrote of Washington Irving's deficiencies as a writer, suggests some degree of reminiscence: ". . . he brought no new earth, no sprig of laurel gathered in the wilderness, no red bird's wing, no gleam from crystal lake or new-discovered fountain."[15] These are slender suggestions enough. Yet who can doubt that these days had their share in moulding him, that if they left but few sensual impressions clear enough to be called memories, they yet had affected that something in him that was deeper than memory, the something that does not remember, but that *is*; that something of the temper of the father who, when every circumstance of his life might have tempted him into compromise, had said he would "die in a ditch" sooner than submit to authority in matters of faith, remained in his under-consciousness, making it inevitable for him afterwards to side always with the oppressed, to champion the forlorn cause; that perhaps some sense of the innate malignity of man towards his fellow-man, tending to hunt down its victim relentlessly, very specially if it seem likely that such persecution will end in the destruction of human life or human personality, was bred in him, to remain couchant until the events of after years caused it to start from its slumbers and assume the terrible form of an unshakable belief in "the theoretical benevolence and practical malignity of man;"[16] that some of his father's aspiration towards Truth and integrity of thinking had passed into the roots of his being! Also there is something else to remember, something which, although he gives but shadowy indication of it, is not slight, but which, as gropingly we try to understand him, throws the first clear beam of light on the nature of the life-struggle for which he was destined. Already the thought of Liberty was blended in his childish mind with the thought of that religion which was as much part of his daily life as the air in which he breathed, which mingled indeed with the air he breathed. As he himself felt afterwards, aspiration towards Liberty might be said to have been his cradle.[17]

Chapter Two

CHILDHOOD AT WEM (1787-1790)

"He was at this time the most active, lively, and happiest of boys; his time, divided between his studies and his childish sports, passed smoothly on. Beloved by all for his amiable temper and manners, pleasing above his years. The delight and pride of his own family. William always liked this old house at Wem better than many superior ones that we have lived in since; but he liked Wem better than any of us, for it was the scene of his childhood, and where he first began to show those talents which have since shone so brightly."

MARGARET HAZLITT.

I

MRS. HAZLITT and her children disembarked at Portsmouth on Sunday, August 12th, 1787, and on the following morning they set out for London in the stage. Peggy Hazlitt, in the few words in which she describes their arrival at the inn where her father was waiting to receive them, leaves us in no doubt as to the quality of the welcome they received. Before even she had time to see her father's face she found herself clasped in his arms and being lifted out of the coach.

They spent the first few weeks in the house in Mansion-House Street of their father's friend Mr. David Lewis. Then they took lodgings at Walworth, for Mrs. Hazlitt had been tried beyond her strength during the years of uncertainty in America and was now in very poor health, and they hoped that the fresher air coming from Walworth Common would revive her. When they had been there a fortnight, David Williams, who was also numbered among their friends, told them of part of a house which was to be rented cheaply, and they moved into it. There they stayed almost three months, and Mrs. Hazlitt's mother, old Mrs. Loftus, who when they had left for America had had no hope of ever seeing her daughter again, came up to town and spent a month with them. She was now a very old lady, almost eighty-four years of age, yet she was still active, and able to walk about two miles. To the younger members of the family their grandmother seemed almost to have the character of history or antiquity about her, for she had been born at the beginning of Queen Anne's reign; she remembered well the persecution of the Dissenters, and she had one especially vivid memory of the relief and joy with which the Dissenters had gone to their prayers—for they had been afraid of having their meetings shut up—when the news of the Queen's

24

death had reached them, on the first Sunday of August, 1714. She had been at that time a girl of eleven years.

While they were in town the children enjoyed such pleasures as it was in their father's power to give them. Peggy, who was keenly interested in painting, found the windows of the print-shops a never-failing source of interest and amusement. She was delighted when one day her father took her to Boydell's in Pall Mall, and bought her a print, "The Fishstealers by Moonlight." William, after his long muring on board ship, delighted in the Montpelier Tea-Gardens, to which his father used to take him. His sister marvelled at the keenness of the joy he took in the autumn colourings, for although the weather was on the whole dry and pleasant, she could not help feeling the contrast between the English mists and the fogs that descended on them now and again, and the brilliant glory of the American fall.

But the child was well content. Perhaps, even as aonther William some few years his senior had done—of Hawkshead he!—our younger William was drinking in:

> A pure organic pleasure from the lines
> Of curling mist.

It is worth, however, recording that even as he played in careless freedom, drinking in primary impressions of shape and colour and scent, the sweet playthings devised by Nature's love, for the moulding of such as he, something of which he thought little enough, the machinery designed by the foresight of man for the moulding of such as he, was just in the process of being completed. The Committee for establishing a "New Academical Institution among Protestant Dissenters for the education of Ministers and Youth," of which Dr. Price, Dr. Kippis, and Dr. Abraham Rees had been the most active members, had succeeded, in April of that year, in taking "a spacious and eligible house in the parish of Hackney." On September 29th, 1787, it was opened for the reception of its first band of students.[18]

Mr. Hazlitt had at length found a settlement at the little market-town of Wem, ten miles north of Shrewsbury, and towards the end of the year they set out for their new home. Perhaps their feelings, or the feelings of those of them old enough to realise the risks they had taken during the past four years, are best expressed in some words in which many years afterwards William dismissed some of his own wanderings throughout the earth: "After making the grand tour, and seeing the finest sights in the world, we are glad to come back at last. . . . We have a resting-place for the sole of our foot. The flutter of hope, anxiety and disappointment is at an end. . . ."

2

At Wem Mr. Hazlitt, although he had neighbours congenial enough in the Rev. Mr. Rowe of Shrewsbury and the Rev. Mr. Jenkins of Whitchurch, felt himself to some extent cut off from many of his main interests, from the friends of his youth and maturity, and from the only kind of converse that he loved, "the talk about disputed texts of Scripture and the cause of civil and religious liberty." He had gained a haven for himself and a home for his wife and children, but he had also resigned some portion of his life when he settled there, for his was essentially a fighting questing spirit. His life is beginning to repeat itself, but more flatly than in earlier years. He is henceforth never to be in the centre of things, although his thoughts tend towards it constantly. Instead of the road from Weymouth to Boston, he now walks the road between Wem and Shrewsbury. Beyond that he seldom goes.

He must also have felt in some measure the constriction of poverty, for the annual stipend raised by the congregation at Wem for its minister was only £30. In after years William perceived something of what his father felt, realised the nature of all that had been resigned in exchange for a very modest portion of security, and the measure in which his father's life had come short of fulfilment. Perhaps even as a child he sensed it—for the sympathy between the man and the child was close—but intuitively, after the way of children, without giving a thought to the reason or inquiring more closely into it. Yet for the first few years after coming to Wem he sensed little so much as his own almost flawless joy. The small two-storied house adjoining the chapel, especially its oak-panelled parlour with the window-seat which was his own special place for study, the little garden behind in which he played or worked at his light tasks, the rather flat country bounded by high hills which seen from a distance looked dewy in their freshness, were to him but the boundaries of his allotted portion of bliss. His life was still nourished by love, untroubled and untroubling, such as it was never to be his to receive once these pure pristine years were over. The family circle was not now complete; John had been left behind in London, to practise painting and get a living by it, if he could, to study also, under Reynolds. But with all those around him the child's relationship was perfect. To his father he was "my William!" Do not these two words, from the inexpressive deep-hearted man, express all! He was his mother's delight. His sister's love for him was peculiarly understanding and tender.

"The child is a poet . . . when he first plays at hide-and-seek, or repeats the story of Jack the Giant Killer,"[19] he wrote in after years. And again: "in youth and childhood every step is fairy-ground, be-

HAZLITT'S HOME AT WEM

cause every step is an advance in knowledge and pleasure, opens new prospects, and excites new hopes. ∵ . . ."[20] Here he was drawing on his recollections of his own childhood. He was always a poet at heart. He was often a poet in words, although he did not write "in numbers;" but he was never more a poet than in his first sensitive response to the world around him. This first sensitiveness was the making of him as a man, as a writer, even as a critic. The child, "startling at" the sight of the daisy as he played at trying to leap over his own shadow, noticing it consciously for the first time in his life as a delicate thing which his careless foot had just missed destroying, becomes the grown man to whom the flower ever afterwards seems to cast "a timid upward glance" imploring him not to tread upon it. The boy, idly watching the glittering down of the thistle, "at first scarcely rising above the ground, and then mingling with the gale, borne into the upper sky with varying, fantastic motion," or observing that as he lay with his face close to the ground on a summer's day, the blades of spear-grass appeared "like tall forest trees, shooting up into the sky," becomes the critic whose eye dwelt "with a giddy delight" on the delicate detail of Van Huysum's painting, on "the liquid drops of dew, on the gauze wings of an insect, on the hair and feathers of a bird's nest, the streaked and speckled eggshells, the fine legs of the little travelling-caterpillar." In the fullness of his joy he did not crave for more than the moment offered him, or wish any thing to be other than it was. Being happy, he loved whate'er his eyes encountered. He loved the sun in its bright descent on warm summer evenings, and the "rich broken columns of light," but he was equally satisfied with watching it trying to struggle through the clouds of winter. He loved spring, and the first coming of the leaves on the trees and the crying of the lambs running over the green turf, the primroses that peeped out at him from sheltered banks; but he loved no less the massy foliage of autumn, or even the naked windswept woods of winter and the dry reeds that rustled by the streams. From all these things, he tells us, he drank pleasure as from a cup filled to the brim.[21]

These were the things to which in after years, when the life within him was in danger of becoming parched, he

> ". . . would repair, and thence would drink
>   As at a fountain."

There was at that time no cleavage in his mind between feeling and action, no cleavage even, as in most children, between work and play, for it would be difficult to say which he enjoyed the more. To thumb his Eutropius or to knuckle down at taw, to fly his kite or to pore over Livy in the window-seat, were to him equally delightful. The stirring of his blood as he played his games or jumped or ran, the stirring of his mind as he pored over his books, quickened alike "the pulse of life and joy" in him.

His own reminiscences and his sister's Diary make it easy enough to understand the manner of his from day-to-day life, during the opening years at Wem. We see him at home, in play and in study, under his father's guidance; in the garden, watering the rows of cabbage-plants his father had set in the ground, in the evening, or poring over them in solicitude the next morning, when he saw them with all their freshness faded and hanging down their heads in the sun; at the private school to which he was sent, reciting his lessons to his master, learning ciphering and spelling, making acquaintance with English literature through the medium of Enfield's *Speaker*, and arguing with his companions; attending a dancing-class taken by an "old fantastical dancing-master" who not only directed the steps of his pupils but scraped upon his kit the well-known, well-loved tunes to which they danced; picking one morning a large bunch of lilac for the little girl he had selected as his partner in the *Minuet de la Cour* which he was to go through that very morning before "the assembled taste and fashion of the neighbourhood." He was much among older people, and this, as he usually tried to follow their conversation, gave him rather a quaint, old-fashioned turn of speech. He always listened carefully to argument—nay—would argue himself, like a positive little old man, to such as would listen to him, would advance his opinion freely on such matters as the Test and the Corporation Acts, or the interpretation of a point in Scripture. Often he went visiting with his parents among the members of the congregation, and sometimes he would accompany his mother and sister to little gatherings of ladies. On these occasions he amused himself as best he could. There was one house to which he never went with reluctance. At ten years of age he had read with delight the story of John Gilpin. In this house the parlour was hung round with prints of John Gilpin and his travels. This, to the child, was sheer treasure. While the old ladies were playing at whist and the young ones were amusing themselves at forfeits, the little boy among them never wearied of his slow progress around the sides of the room, tracking down John Gilpin "from his counter to his horse, from his own door to the turnpike, and far beyond the turnpike gate and the Bell at Edmonton, with loss of wig and hat, but with an increasing *impetus* and reputation, the further he went from home." In this crawling journey round a little room he compassed the delights of two worlds—of poetry and of art. It is safe to say that of all those present the child was receiving the deepest, most ineffaceable and, at that time, most incommunicable impressions of pleasure.

Our impression of him as he was when he was nearing his tenth birthday is completed by a letter which he wrote in March, 1788, to his brother, then living and working at 288 High Holborn. Like all children's letters, it is a huddle of facts, knocking up against each other, in a way inexpressive, yet full of character. Indeed it may be said that from the opening of his life he was a true writer, in that there is nothing which he wrote which does not bear the imprint of character and the suggestion of a temperament at once critical and positive. Even the affectionate impatient scrawl he had sent to his father from America was oddly characteristic of him. His letter to his brother is like a plot of ground at which we look speculatively. It is as yet bare, but all sorts of seeds have been thrown into it, and there is no saying which of them will flourish in it and which of them it will reject. It opens with a curious touch of didacticism, often present in his early letters, and sometimes shading off into religiosity: "We were all glad to hear that you were well, and that you have so much business to do. We cannot be happy without being employed." It is clear that he is deeply interested in John's painting: "I want you to tell me whether you go to the Academy or not, and what pictures you intend for the exhibition. Tell the exhibitioners to finish the exhibition soon, that you may come and see us."[22] He tells his brother that he tries to draw a little himself: "You want to know what I do. I am a busybody and do many silly things: I drew eyes and noses till about a fortnight ago. I have drawn a little boy since, a man's face, and a little boy's front face, taken from a bust." Then he gives an eager account of his studies. He is going to begin to read Ovid's *Metamorphoses* and Eutropius the following week: "I shall like to know all the Latin and Greek I can. I want to learn how to measure the stars. I shall not I suppose paint the worse for knowing everything else." He tells of his progress in ciphering: "I shall go through the whole cyphering book this summer, and then I am to learn Euclid. We go to school at nine every morning. Three boys begin with reading the Bible. Then I and two others show our exercises. We then read the *Speaker*." In the account of what he does at school he does not omit to mention that he is almost always first at spelling. Later in the letter he corrects one of his brother's misspellings. There follows some criticism of a few of the boys, who are quarrelsome because they cannot learn, being "fit only for fighting," and some affectionate thought of and for Peggy: "We are not all well, for poor Peggy has a great cold. . . . I wish I could see all these paintings that you see, and that Peggy had a good prize."[23] He tells of his progress in jumping: "I can jump four yards at a running jump and two at a standing jump. I intend to try you at this when you come down." The last sentences of the letter hurtle against one another abruptly, and then he " gives over" suddenly: "I don't want your old clothes. I shall go to dancing this month. This is all I can say.

"I am your affectionate brother,

"WILLIAM HAZLITT."

I want to learn how to measure the stars! And what, my child, are the designs of the stars towards you!

3

One thing they are already preparing, which may either make him or break him, which may perchance do both to him, as it did to some millions of his unprepared and unsuspecting fellow-beings. In the spring-time of that year, while he was filled with the sweet hopes and happy wishes that always came to him with the unfolding of the leaves, there began to appear in France the signs of that awakening which seemed to herald the spring-time of the world, and the unfolding of the hopes and expectations of the human race in the same course as that of the pageant of Nature. It seemed as if the tears of Rousseau had at once watered and fructified the soil of human nature, so that now at last it was ready for a most fair birth. All those whom William heard discussing this awakening hoped—nay believed!—that a long night of darkness had come to an end, and they rejoiced as at the preludings of dawn. That perhaps two centuries would have to lesson the new-born democracy ere it had passed through its first stages of agonised distortion, was as yet undreamed of by any of them. They had not the shadow of a doubt that the sun would soon rise full upon the horizon. Many of them, like Dr. Price, openly

> ". . . with popular talents preach'd the cause[24]
> Of Christ and of the new-born liberty."

The child who heard their talk shared in their faith and joy. To attribute to him at that time understanding of the deeper forces that were at work, except that it was clear to him that the poor man should eat bread and not nettles, sorrel or grass, would no doubt be wrong. To minimise the effect upon his life of the shock of joy which came to him with the breaking out of the Revolution and the hope that the reign of Liberty on earth might yet come, would be equally wrong. It was by far the greatest thing that had as yet happened to him in his life, and it increased the joy he took in living. He felt as a child, but yet as a child into whom the love of Liberty and a sense of its preciousness had been instilled from his cradle, and so intense was his feeling that the memory of the experience coloured and conditioned his whole life. He has himself expressed the effect on his imagination of what he heard from day to day, in such simplicity of idiom as a child might use whose thoughts had already been saturated with Bible story. In his mind's eye he saw, quite simply, "visions of unsullied bliss . . . rising in bright successions and endless gradations, like the steps of that ladder which was once set up on earth, and whose top reached to heaven." The way to human happiness seemed to him as plain as those prints over which he pored in *The Pilgrim's Progress*, pointing the way to Paradise. When the news came towards the middle of July, 1789, of the fall of the Bastille, and it seemed to those around him that Louis Tournay smiting at the outer drawbridge chain had been smiting at all the bonds that had enslaved not only the body but the spirit of man, that the crash of each of the towers symbolised the breaking-up of a monstrous mechanism into which human life had been fed remorselessly from generation to generation until Time itself had sickened at the work, that it would hardly have been surprising if the wrath of the attackers had melted the stone walls like flax or if the dead had risen from their dungeons to assist the living, the little boy listening to the accounts of the demolition of the building put the matter to himself in his own way, in the terms of one of his own loathings. He had always hated spiders. To him it seemed as if a great ugly spider, brooding in sullen silence over those whom it had the power to ensnare and lying in wait for its accustomed prey, had suddenly been obliterated into the clean earth and the sweet young grass had closed over it.

The purity of his sympathy at that time, and his grief, rage and shame when afterwards he saw the Leviathan harpooned, as he thought, by the powerful rhetoric of Burke, and therefore weltering in frantic distortion, fouled and even poisoned by its own gore, can perhaps best be understood if we recall the confession he made towards the close of his life in a work into which he was determined that no base alloy of feeling should enter: ". . . a little child I knelt and lifted up my hands in prayer for it."[25]

4

It would seem that the spring of 1790, or the early summer, brought with it two experiences which should be noted because his later reactions to them indicate his extreme sensitiveness and nervous susceptibility. How—we do not know—possibly in the course of jumping or climbing or of some sport into which he was throwing himself with the well-attested intensity characteristic of him, he put his arm out of joint. The pain, of course, was transitory, but the shock of this, his first experience of severe physical pain, never quite passed from his nerves. The chance sight of any suffering that reminded him of it sent a quivering through them. Some fifteen years afterwards he wrote: "When a boy I had my arm put out of joint, and I feel a kind of nervous twitching in it to this day whenever I see any one with his own bound up in consequence of a similar accident."

The other impression which he records was pleasurable. It was of the life of the strolling players and the delight they brought to the children especially who watched them in the barns or the small halls of the scattered towns and villages through which they passed. The youth in Hawkshead already mentioned by us as "also named William" knew this pleasure too, and its power to quicken a boy's imagination:

> "When, at a Country-Playhouse, having caught
> In Summer, through the fractur'd wall, a glimpse
> Of daylight, at the thought of where I was
> I gladden'd more than if I had beheld
> Before me some bright cavern of Romance
> Or than we do, when on our beds we lie
> At night, in warmth, when rains are beating hard."

Hawkshead William is yet to bring some joy into the life of *our* William, is to teach him much, is also to cast upon him shadows that thicken as life thickens, that scarce forbear the porch of the grave. But these things as yet are only in the shaping. *Our* William knows only that the sight of beings who seem so happy and so free fills his heart with joy as he sees the players "glitter along the street . . . like mealy coated butterflies or insects flitting in the sun;" that he is giddy with expectation when the manager knocks on the door with his cane, leaves a play-bill, chats a good deal, tells of having supped with their friend Mr. Jenkins at Whitchurch, and hopes that at least the young lady and gentleman will come to the performance of *The West Indian*[26] at the market hall the following evening; that he is all a-quiver with mingled hope and fear until his father says that they may go; that he is as impatient as "greyhound on the slip" for the time to pass; that he is almost weeping with excitement by the time the curtain rises; that the next moment he is "up to the chin in Heav'n."

In July he made his first flight from home. There had come to Wem a lady named Mrs. Tracy, the widow of a West Indian merchant, to visit her daughters, who were at school there. She had made the acquaintance of the Hazlitt family and had made much of the bright eager little boy. She had now returned to Liverpool with her daughters, who were studying under private tutors for a year, before returning to Jamaica, and she sent an invitation for him to spend some weeks with her, and to share in the studies of the girls, especially in French, which there was no one to teach him at home. The opportunity was eagerly welcomed, and towards the beginning of July William set out on his two days' journey towards Liverpool, apparently in the company of one of his schoolfellows, George Dickin, and under convoy of a Miss Shepherd[27] who was also going to spend some time in Liverpool. The first of his letters home of which there is mention is one which was posted to his father on July 6th, but this has not been preserved. The other letters[28] written during his visit give a very clear impression both of the way his personality was developing and of the influences that were shaping it. Of these the earliest is to his mother. It is a very courteous, dutiful letter: "Dear Mother, It is with pleasure I now sit down to write to you, and it is with pleasure that I do anything, which I know will please you." It is also a curiously interesting letter in its mingling of artless childishness with alert intelligence. He tells of the doings that fill up his days, of visits and visitors, of the amusement he finds in looking at the pictures in the shops. He sympathises with his mother for her poverty—his father has evidently been telling him how straitened they are—but rejoices with her over a gift the rich Mr. William Tayleur of Shrewsbury[29] had made them. While uniting with her in hoping that his father may succeed in his efforts to get a better charge, he tries to console her by telling her that her portion will be in the next world, in spite of which, as some pocket-money is necessary even to a boy sustained by such reflections, he adds: "Be sure to tell me if I may sell my old Buckles." But what is most interesting in this letter, although somewhat astonishing, is the way in which it suddenly breaks into something like a discourse on Liberty and Slavery. This shows how keenly his ears were tuned to catch what was going on in the world around him, how keen his intelligence was, how ready he was to take his side in any conflict and pronounce judgment. Immature as it is, it has distinctly in it the suggestion of the essayist he was one day to become. What occasioned his disquisition was that he sensed on this point a certain tension within the circle of friends who were entertaining him. In the crusade against the slave-trade the Dissenters took a foremost part, and among these the Unitarians were on the whole honourably distinguished by their zeal. But Liverpool had become the chief slave-trade port; and there, as in Bristol, even among the Unitarians, there was division of opinion, so greatly against the interests of some of them who were engaged in commerce would abolition be. It was not safe for Unitarian ministers dependent for their livelihood on the good-will of the richer members of their congregations to be too outspoken. Yet the Rev. John Yates, whose chapel William attended and whose preaching he admired, and the Rev. William Shepherd, of Gateacre, in spite of this, denounced the traffic in slaves in no uncertain voice. Indeed Mr. Yates, two years before, had given very bitter offence to many of the richest members of his congregation by preaching a most outspoken sermon against slavery. It was inevitable, William being what he was, that he should choose his side in this warfare of opinions. He begins to discourse to his mother on this theme when mentioning a dinner to which George Dickin and he had been invited, at a certain rich Mr. Fisher's. There is not a word about what they ate or drank, but there is much about their host's opinions. William does not quite

approve of Mr. Fisher, because Mr. Fisher approves of slavery, and he
goes on to argue that the man who wishes to enslave others must be at
heart a slave himself. His argument is as follows: "The King, who
wishes to enslave all mankind, is a slave to ambition; the man who
wishes to enslave all mankind for his King, is himself a slave to his
King. . . . The man who is a well-wisher to liberty, wishes to have
men good, and himself to be one of them, and knows that men are not
good unless they are so willingly, and does not attempt to force them
to it, but tries to put them in such a situation as will induce them to be
good. Slavery is not a state for men to improve in, therefore he does
not wish them to be in that condition. In a state of liberty men
improve. He therefore wishes them to be in such a state."

It is perhaps worth while, by way of illustrating the remarkable
consistency and continuity of Hazlitt's opinions, to compare the
child's ingenuous argument with the following pronouncement, made
in the last of all his works: "It is not that I blame him for being what
he is, a king; but I blame those who think he can ever forget that he
was one. He is what they have made him, for the tyrant is the work of
slaves; but let them beware how they proceed, gravely and by piece-
meal, to undo their own handywork. It is no child's-play, the *un-
crowning* of a monarch." [30]

Other abuses of the day also catch his eye, during his stay in Liverpool, and he takes up his mental stand against them. He continues his
letter on Tuesday the 13th. On that day the finishing touches have been
put to the Champ-de-Mars; it is all "trimmed, buttressed with firm
masonry;" on that day Hawkshead William, now no longer of Hawkshead, or indeed of any place, for he is a wanderer on the face of the
earth, is landing at Calais, and seeing for himself:

> "In a mean City, and among a few,
>   How bright a face is worn when joy of one
>   Is joy of tens of millions;"

on that day the child William Hazlitt tells his mother that he has seen
the press-gang at work on the streets of Liverpool. His comment is:
"The world is not perfect yet." Yet his sense of the world's imperfection, although it is there, is jostled in his mind by his own preoccupations and childish interests. His arm is hurting him. Mrs.
Tracy tells him that he had better leave it alone, but he wishes that he
could "procure grains" so that he could foment it. He is going to the
play on Friday the 16th. His letter concludes: "I like my Balls very
well, and have also received the money."

It is still a child, although a quite exceptionally intelligent and
sensitive child, who falls asleep that night, the thirteenth of July,
1790, on which all France too smiled herself lightly to sleep like a

highly strung child whose rest is broken by dreams of the next day's joy.

On the following evening laughing crowds dance where once the Bastille frowned, only to leave the spot, for nothing can quite clear away the memory of the sighing that once went up from it, for the radiant glittering Champs Elysées; on the following evening the William wandering through France found:

> "benevolence and blessedness
> Spread like a fragrance everywhere, like Spring
> That leaves no corner of the land untouch'd,"

and saw beneath the Evening Star "dances of Liberty" and even during the hours of darkness, dancing under the free night-sky; on the following evening "a very respectable company, consisting of several hundreds of Gentlemen, met at the Crown and Anchor Tavern in the Strand, to celebrate the first Anniversary of the Glorious Revolution in France, Earl Stanhope in the Chair." Mr. Sheridan, "carbuncle his eyes," proposed a resolution expressive of the joy of the company in the extension of Liberty to France. Little more of him in our story! but for this one moment he leaps into our canvas—rather a sombre canvas on the whole—the light of heart and of wit, the bright and the brave, the irresistible to all creditors save the Future itself, for the Future *cannot* be bilked, the easy words of good-fellowship flowing from his lips, the vine-leaf in his hair, and *carbuncle his eyes*! Dr. Price rose to give as the toast of the evening—An Alliance between France and Great Britain:

"Thus united, the two kingdoms will be omnipotent. They will soon draw into their confederation Holland, and other countries on this side the Globe, and the United States of America on the other; and, when alarums of war come, they will be able to say to the contending nations, *Peace*, and there will be *Peace*.

"I have therefore thought that it would be worthy of this respectable company on this most animating occasion, to express its wishes of success to the proposal I have mentioned, by drinking,

"' An Alliance between France and Great Britain for perpetuating Peace, and making the world happy, Amen and Amen!'"

In after years William Hazlitt, when his life, after having known all the heat and burden of a long fight, is drawing to a close, will yield to no man in paying tribute to Richard Brinsley Sheridan, the meteoric man who yet in his politics "held out to the last, even when Charles Fox had deserted his side,"[31] to dally with coalitions. What, in the meantime, while the great men feast and hope, and his father's friend prophesies eternal Peace on earth, has the child William been doing on this day of days! Has he, too, been providing sport for the spirits sinister and ironic! Of him it is only recorded that he employed his time in learning how to find the latitude and longitude of any place, and that he can do this upon the globes with ease. Could Time but stand still with him for a little and leave him with nothing to do but to con his little task and be happy! It may not be. Leviathan is already poisoned, although as yet it knows not its hurt! Canst thou tame Leviathan? Nay—but when Leviathan is poisoned, who shall escape the stench and foul contagion that blows from it, not only towards Man but towards all his children!

5

The letters that passed between William and his father leave no doubt as to the completeness of the sympathy between father and son. It is admirable, and yet we view it with a touch of concern, for nothing is surer than that if the boy should find that the movement of his life and thought were to carry him in a direction contrary to that willed by his father, he will inevitably suffer deeply. But in the meantime all is harmony. *Homunculus* pipes to *homo*, and *homo* sends back the note deeper, more meditative, but not less sweet, in reply. The letters show a desire on the boy's part, unconscious yet passionate, to do all that will please his father. They contain such old-time moralisings on the vanity of pleasure and sin and the satisfaction of duty well performed as he knows his father loves to hear. They tell all about his studies, into which he threw himself with the intensity that was now becoming customary with him. They contain messages to be passed on to the friends he had left behind at Wem, John Kynaston and Joseph Swanwick—one of them includes a letter to be given to J. Swanwick—and accounts of his doings and conversations with the friends who were near him. In one of these, he relates an argument he has had with his friend George Dickin, over the Test Act, in a manner which anticipates the extraordinary gift he showed afterwards of remembering conversations *verbatim*, and repeating them for the entertainment of his friends; it shows, too, his whole-hearted sympathy with his father's point of view. That year, yet another attempt had been made, in the long chain of efforts of this kind made by Unitarians, to have the Test and Corporation Acts repealed. The attempt had been defeated, largely owing to the opposition of Burke. George Dickin, with a touch of what the man Hazlitt was afterwards wont to call "the malice of a friend," thought fit to inquire of William whether he was not glad that the Test Act had not been repealed. The answer was an uncompromising "No!" Then George asked why.

"Because all the people who are inhabitants of a country, of whatsoever sect or denomination, should have the same rights with others."

George replied: "But then they would try to get their religion established."

"Well! What if it should be so?"

"But the Church religion is an old one."

"Well! Popery is even older than that. Do you want to bring back Popery?"

George was not floored by this. "But the Church religion is better than Popery," said he.

"And the Presbyterian is better than that. I think so because I have reasoned the matter out, not merely because I go to chapel."

George got more than he had bargained for in the torrent of reasoning that followed. "I wish I understood it as well as you do," said he, quite overpowered at length. "You are too high learned for me."

I think so because I have reasoned the matter out! Have we not in this boyish claim the clue to what was afterwards called the "inveteracy" of his opinions, and to the scorn he never ceased to feel for those whose opinions being but echoes had all the mutability and transitoriness of echoes?

6

After this triumph, William goes on to a concert, to which he gives qualified and discriminating praise: "Meredith's singing was worth all the rest." He tells also of the whole-hearted enjoyment he had when George and he dined on Saturday the 16th at the house of a Mr. Corbett who afterwards took them on the visit to the theatre he had promised them. This is the first piece of dramatic criticism we have from his pen: "The play was ' Love in many Masks ' and the farce ' No Song, no Supper.' It was very entertaining, and was performed by some of the best players in London, as, for instance, Kemble, Suett, Dignum, the famous singer, Mrs. Williams, Miss Hagley, Miss Romanzini and others. Suett, who acted in the character of Ned Blunt, was enough to make any one laugh, though he stood still; and Kemble acted admirably as an officer. Mr. Dignum sang beautifully. . . ."

"Here's three on's are sophisticated!" No doubt he entertained his companions with his comments. Anyhow, Mr. Corbett promised to take him to the theatre again.

He is also a taster of sermons. He goes to chapel the following morning to hear Mr. Yates preach, and describes the sermon with *gusto*, having found it "a very good discourse." On the Monday morning the eager little soul is up at seven o'clock, and is writing to Mr. Yates, who has been kind about lending him books, to ask whether he might have the loan of Horace and a dictionary. Here he is not sophisticated. He is, in fact, as usual, a quaint mixture of sophistication and innocence. He puzzles his head over the form of his letter, and after sending it, consults his father anxiously as to whether he has expressed himself with propriety: "Was it right to express myself in this manner? ' Mr. Hazlitt sends his compliments to Mr. Yates, and would be obliged to him if he would send him a dictionary and an Horace.

"P.S.—Papa desired me to remember him to you.'"

We hope "Mr. Hazlitt" was suitably rewarded for this epistolary communication by Mr. Yates, and that he received both the dictionary and the Horace and perhaps a smile too into the bargain.

He tells his father of other sermons, for sermon-tasting is evidently the main business, the main pleasure too, of his Sundays. Of Sunday the 25th he writes: "I spent a very agreeable day yesterday, as I read 160 pages of Priestley, and heard two good sermons." But once he deviated into a Church of England service, and it is amusing to see the fury with which the boy, used to exercising his brains on a good argument, turns and rends the preacher for irrelevance and sheer wool-gathering. He concludes his strictures with the words: "In short, his sermon had neither head nor tail. I was sorry that so much time should be thrown away upon nonsense. I often wished I was hearing Mr. Yates; but I shall see I do not go to church again in a hurry."

Already we see that, loving as he is towards his own people, towards the outside world which he is beginning to realise, he is "nothing if not critical." While he enjoyed his expeditions with Mr. Corbett, and with Mr. Clegg, one of the tutors who attended upon the Misses Tracy, we see him developing an exceedingly critical, indeed hostile attitude to almost all of the ladies at whose houses he was entertained. If he had made only one or two of these unfavourable comments, the matter would not be worthy of remark, but he makes so many that we feel he is beginning to experience that "difficulty" in social intercourse, and in his relationship towards women, which afterwards became so marked. He dines "at Mrs. Chilton's . . . which was not very agreeable." He goes, "not willingly, to Mrs. Sydebotham's to dinner." He goes with George one Saturday afternoon to "a Mrs. Bartton's, who appeared to be an unhospitable English prim ' Lady ' if such she may be called. She asked us as if she were afraid we would accept it, if we would stay to tea." He makes a positive onslaught on another lady, whose name he has forgotten, but who, he says, must certainly be English: "I am sure she belongs to no other country than to England. . . . I had rather people would tell one to go out of the house than ask one to stay, and at the same time, be trembling all over, for fear one should take a slice of meat or a dish of tea with them."

"Such as these," he adds virtuously, "require an Horace or a Shakespeare to describe them."

Here already in this shrill note of indignation have we not the cry he was afterwards to utter so often, although in the deeper tones of manhood: "Out upon this half-faced fellowship!"

The father's answers to these letters are admirable. It is evident that he is delighted with William's intelligence, with his zest for knowledge, his skill in argument, and his piety, but he feels that his son needs some training in those social ways which make life pleasant, and this he tries to give, but without over-emphasis, indeed, in the gentlest way possible. He feels that the censoriousness requires a check, and he gives it, but this also in such a way as not to check the flow of the boy's confidences or to wound his self-esteem: "The inhospitable ladies, whom you mention, were, perhaps, treated by you with too great severity. We know not how people may be circumstanced at a particular moment, whose disposition is generally friendly. They may then happen to pass under a cloud, which unfits them for social intercourse. We must see them more than once or twice to be able to form a tolerable judgment of their characters. There are but few, like Mrs. Tracy, who can always appear what they really are. I do not say, however, that the English ladies whom you mentioned, are not exactly as you described them. I only wish to caution you against forming too hasty a judgment of characters, who can seldom be known at a single interview."

Only two of Mr. Hazlitt's letters have been preserved, both of them written towards the end of the visit, one of them on July 31st, the other on August 6th, Monday, August 9th, having been finally fixed for William's return. In these letters he gives his son guidance as to the parting courtesies he must pay. William must call on all who have shown him "any particular civilities." He is to thank his tutors for their attention, and Mr. Yates for his books, which must be returned in good order. He is also to take leave of Mr. Yates on the Sunday afternoon in the vestry. He is to be careful to leave none of his things behind, so that Mrs. Tracy will not have the trouble of forwarding them. As to the manner of thanking his hostess, that is left to the boy's own feeling and judgment: "But what must you say to Mrs. Tracy? I leave that entirely to yourself. But present her with your mamma's respect and mine, and our sincere thanks for all favours, and tell her that we wish to see her again, and also hope for this pleasure with all the young ladies, and all of them quite happy."

It is evidently a pleasure to this generous and guileless one that his own gift to Mrs. Tracy is in the course of preparation: "My sermons will soon be printed. I shall embrace the very first opportunity of sending Mrs. Tracy her copy."

He gives directions for the journey home that are clear, precise, frugal, and yet very considerate. William is again to travel to East-ham with Miss Shepherd and George Dickin, but "if the weather be blowing, or if it be not very fine, when Miss Shepherd comes upon the water" he may wait until it is just what he would like it to be before crossing the Mersey. Horses are being sent to Eastham for the boys; Mr. Dickin is sending a horse for George; William can have a white horse sent by Joe Swanwick's father, if he be not afraid to ride him. If he prefer some other mode of travelling, he is to let his father know. His greatcoat and spatterdashes will be sent to protect him from the weather. The first day he is to make his halting-place for the night some five miles on the Wem side of Chester, and spend the night at the house of an acquaintance. In one of his letters he had written to his father: "I shall have *satis pecuniae, dum tu habeas opportunitatem mittendi aliquam partem mihi.*" He is told that at Chester, if he likes, he may break his journey to buy the best hat he can get for himself for eight shillings if he has left himself sufficiently "rich" to do so.

The second day he is to stop at Whitchurch for dinner, and then ride home. He is to dine at the house of a friend, but is to call on Mr. Jenkins, if he has time, and bring back with him the last part of Dr. Priestley's *Familiar Letters*, which Mr. Jenkins had borrowed the last time he had been at Wem.

Mr. Hazlitt mentions, too, that he has decided to add to his income by taking half a dozen boys to educate, at £25 a year each. Poor Mr. Hazlitt! He did not secure the pupils. Nor did he get a better charge. His day is over before it has well begun. The hungry generations are beginning to tread him down. As Dr. Kippis told him at the end of the year, in a letter in which he also told him, however, that from various Funds he had succeeded in obtaining grants that would add £14 to the small stipend raised by the congregation at Wem: "All the vacancies go to the younger men."

That the traveller had "satis pecuniae" to buy himself the new hat, that the weather was to his liking when he "came upon the water," and that he found courage enough in himself to ride Mr. Swanwick's white horse through Chester with *panache*, we can only hope. All that we know of his return is that he received a great welcome from his father, from his mother, and from Peggy, who herself had been away in London and Maidstone during most of the time he had been in Liverpool. Since her return, although she was glad to be at home and among familiar friends, the house had not seemed quite itself to her without its happy little William, nor had her homecoming seemed complete to her until she had this dearly loved young brother by her side again.

MARGARET HAZLITT

Chapter Three

ADOLESCENCE (1790-1793)

"By the time he was twelve or thirteen he would not attend
the devotions of the family. He would not go to chapel. He
would shut himself up from the rest of the family: be seen by
no one during the day: but at night he would ramble forth no
one knew where: and in the moonlight nights he used to scamper
about the fields, like . . . any wild thing."

THE REV. JOSEPH HUNTER.

I

A YEAR has passed since Mr. Swanwick sent his white horse to take his
son's friend back to Wem. It is now midsummer, 1791, and the boy
has just taken his first step—unnoticed except by his father, the other
members of the family, and a few friends—in the career of authorship,
for he has sent a letter to the Editor of *The Shrewsbury Chronicle*.
During the year that has passed since August, 1790, the two great scene-
shifters, Death and Life, have been busy. In the beginning of April, all
France was mourning the death of Mirabeau, the man without
illusion. A fortnight later, his own circle of tried and faithful friends
were mourning the death of one whose *Observations on the Importance
of the American Revolution*, permeated with the love of Liberty, Mirabeau
had thought it worth while to translate for the benefit of his own
oppressed fellow-countrymen. This was Dr. Price, the man without
guile, by no means without illusion, but happy in this, that he died
innocent of the way in which the spirits sinister and ironic had cracked
their joke through his lips. On Sunday, May 1st, 1791, his friend Dr.
Priestley preached his funeral sermon in the chapel at Hackney, in the
course of which he reminded his audience of the words Dr. Price had
used in connection with the opening of the French Revolution: "Now
lettest thou thy servant depart in peace, for mine eyes have seen thy
salvation," and added that the death of Dr. Price might be compared
"to the death of a warrior in the moment of victory." The spirits
sinister and ironic, finding much entertainment in watching the play
and counterplay of men's passions, must have cackled over this,
although it was but a small jest compared to the one uttered through
the lips of the man without guile, for some side-play of sport is
a-preparing for them at the expense of the speaker. Drop by drop, the
passion of anger, sorrow, fear and hatred in the soul of Burke is
beginning to distil itself into the souls of others. There is no resisting

41

its sullen potency. It is getting, not only into the soul, but into the blood of his fellow-countrymen. Priestley may reply to the *Reflections*; Tom Paine may seek to apply the antidote: "He pities the plumage, but forgets the dying bird," but the phrase, though poignant as a spear, is beaten into the earth by the terrible flail-like rhetoric it assails. Nor does Mary Wollstonecraft fare better—she who has not yet learned that Woman has no rights, and Man himself very few. She is great of heart, but she cannot get the beat of her own powerful personal dynamo into her words—and she is matching herself against a Master. The friends of the People have not among them, as yet, a mind and a voice to match that of their grand adversary. And so the spirits sinister and ironic may well cackle, although, to be sure, when presently they are going to see all Europe caught in the blind tides of passion, it is only a minor jest, the wrecking of one man's house, and goods, and life too, unless his courage be stout. Yet a jest it is. Ten weeks after that first of May on which Dr. Priestley, while lamenting his friend's death, yet celebrated his triumph, a Birmingham mob crying "Church and King" will burn him out of his house, into the wide world; will burn too, the work of his hand and brain; will yet make England too hot to hold him, will not, however, be able to make the wide world too hot to hold him.

It is this, the burning of Dr. Priestley's house and the destruction of his books and papers on July 14th, 1791, the burning also of the houses of some of his friends and of two Unitarian chapels in Birmingham, together with the torrent of calumny which followed these exhibitions of mob violence, which brings into the arena for the first time the one who is yet to be more than Burke's equal. His words will one day comfort the poor man, and delight the free, will strengthen the courage of his friends like wine; but to the foes of the poor man, to the haters of the free in spirit, and to the enemies of Liberty, will seem as "Venom! venom! the very essence of prussic acid!" As yet he can only address himself to a provincial newspaper. As yet he is little more than a child. But as this letter of his to the Editor of *The Shrewsbury Chronicle* is his first known act in the long warfare against prejudice and injustice which was to be his portion throughout his life, and his first assertion of the need to appeal to principle rather than to force, it deserves recording. All he says in defence of his father's friend is perfectly consistent with all he was to teach in later years. He entered in fitting fashion upon his career as the fighting-man of the forces of Liberalism, in registering thus the protest of his spirit against the spirit of persecution and calumny in the angry summer of 1791, when persecuting fires again arose from England.

2

It seems to have been in the course of the following year that
he first made acquaintance with the country from which his mother
had sprung. In 1792 Mrs. Hazlitt paid a visit of nine weeks' duration
to her mother, now almost ninety years of age, and her friends at
Wisbeach and Peterborough, and we gather that she took her youngest
son with her.[32] It seems that his first memories of Peterborough and
Wisbeach may be referred to this visit. He took these places to his heart,
for these were among the places in which he had been happy. His
memories of them have the freshness and lustre that belonged only to
his memories of early youth, and he looked back to them with the
yearning that early memories alone awakened in him. He tells us that
as a boy he used to gaze at the monument of Mary Queen of Scots in
Peterborough Cathedral, till his mind would droop with the weight
of thought as to all that had happened since those days, for the trouble
of the past always affected him deeply. Some of his thoughts were
touched with fear; some of them were exquisite, so that they were
afterwards to take their place in the casket of memories along with
those things to whose sweetness and purity nothing could ever add—
"the first breath of spring, the hyacinth dipped in dew, the mild lustre
of the evening star, the rainbow after a storm." There was one spot
on which his thoughts loved afterwards to linger, for it symbolised
for him one of the points at which his spiritual life linked itself with
his mother's. This was the farmhouse gate where—she told him—she
used to stand when a child of ten years old and watch the setting sun.
In their feeling for such things the mother and son were drawn
together by a bond at once delicate and powerful. Indeed, it was from
his mother—as it was from her side of the family that he inherited his
love of literature and art—that he inherited this sense of affinity with
certain places and intuition of the "genius" of certain places, together
with a capacity which never deserted him for centring a world of
pleasure or pain in places where at one moment or another he had
felt with special intensity. And it is not difficult to see whence Mrs.
Hazlitt had inherited it. Old Mrs. Loftus, who when a girl had lived
at Oxford, would tell of the way in which the entrance to the botanical
gardens there had wrought upon her imagination. This spot was one
of the places which she associated specially with the fear that sometimes comes upon childhood, for it was guarded by two great yew
trees which to her had seemed necromantic—and small wonder!—
seeing that these grim and ancient guardians of the frail passing
beauty of the shrubs and flowers had been cut into the monstrous
semblance of giants.

If such memories were part of Mrs. Hazlitt's inheritance, they were also part of her son's. And are they not in their way the stuff of poetry too, such shapeless floating stuff of poetry as may one day be translated by him into the poetry of words, if he can but endure the years of penal servitude to Life that must be endured, ere it can be granted to him to fashion his endless inarticulate reverie into articulate speech!

The inheritance from his mother's side of the family was not confined to temperament. In looks, too, he resembled it, being delicately moulded rather than rugged of face and build like his father. In appearance he took somewhat after his grandmother, who when young had been slender, black-haired and very pale. She was now, of course, so frail as to seem almost a phantom, "of texture"—as it would appear —"midway betwixt life" and death. In her youth she had been beautiful. It is not seemly that we should look too closely at her now. The five years that have passed since we last saw her have made a difference to her. Her grandson John Hazlitt painted her in her extreme old age, and the portrait seems hardly less than a cruelty. The veil of flesh is almost worn through. Almost she lies "bare to the universal prick of light." But her grandson William Hazlitt! At him, for he has as yet the veil of flesh and strength about his spirit, it is fair that we should look. And it would be well if we were to look somewhat closely at him now, for never again shall we see him look just as he does at this fleeting moment of time.

Two miniatures of him, both by his brother John, were made of him about this time. One of these he kept in his own possession, and it is now lost. At the time when his life began to slope downwards towards its unquiet ending, he took it out of its case one day to look at it. It seemed to him at first, as the careless smile met his eye, as if he had retained but few traces of the face that looked out at him; yet as he looked, it became once more, to his eye, his own face in miniature: the brow, the dimpled mouth, the timid yet inquiring glance—all seemed the same as ever.

The second miniature has been kept. It is very like the one just described, except that the brow is almost covered by the curling black hair, and that the lips are not smiling. Indeed, the expression has a hint of wistfulness. The wide-set eyes are gentle yet searching in their expression. The lines of the cheek and chin are delicately modelled. The mouth is curved and very sensitive. The clasped hands are sensitive and beautiful. Altogether, the impression given is of exquisite refinement and delicacy. Although the full lines of childhood are still there, unflawed by thought or feeling, it is very much like the oil painting of him as a young man, done by his brother; very much like the wistful drawing of him by William Bewick at the age of forty-six; we can even see some connection between the look in this young untried face and the intolerable pathos of the death-mask. This miniature has far more similarity to these than it has to the round

HAZLITT AS A BOY

childish countenance depicted in the miniature John Hazlitt had made of his brother some years earlier. Already during these years, in which childhood has been left behind, the face has refined itself almost out of all recognition. There is no suggestion of joy in it now, but rather the suggestion of an extreme sensibility which can include in it the capacity for the whole gamut of feeling, from extreme joy to intense suffering.

This then, we take it, is William Hazlitt as he looked when childhood had just been left behind him, and those uncouth and, as they would appear to him, shapeless difficulties of adolescence which for a time "robbed him of himself" and "made him different from others," even from his fellow-adolescent human beings, had begun to throw their hauntings athwart his life and their shadows into his face.

3

Thus far our story has been the simple record of a child's happiness. It now becomes less harmonious, for the task that now lies before us is that of tracing the change that came over the boy at this time, and of giving some account of the first steps of the difficult journey and the "uncouth way" which transformed the happy child of 1790 in six years' time into the being who, just as he was on the threshold of manhood, felt himself to be "dumb, inarticulate, helpless, like a worm by the wayside, crushed, bleeding, lifeless."

The Rev. Joseph Hunter of Bath, who became a friend of the Hazlitt family in later years, points to the year 1790 itself as the year in which the change became visible, and connects it with the Liverpool visit. After giving an account of William's entire delightfulness in his early years, and the charm which accounted for his receiving the invitation from Mrs. Tracy, he writes: "To Liverpool he went. But he soon found that he was not made so much of there as he had been at Wem. The lady went out visiting, leaving him at home by himself; and, in short, the child . . . thought himself slighted: he became sullen: and this sullenness continued ever after, and formed the predominant feature of his character during the remainder of his schoolboy days."

There is no doubt some element of truth in this. At Liverpool William had found himself for the first time in his life in a world of which he did not feel himself the centre. Being very intelligent, he may have realised that, kind as Mrs. Tracy was, her kindness was of a different quality from his mother's and his sister's. We remember what he says to his mother as to the arm which was hurting him: "Mrs. Tracey* says I had better let my arm alone, until I come home; but I

* This is the child's spelling of the name.

wish I could tell how to procure grains, and then I would foment it in them." In some dim way he might have felt that at home his arm would not have had to wait thus upon circumstances, before receiving attention. Also, as to his being left alone, we have seen from his letters that he did not "mix" well with some of Mrs. Tracy's friends, that sometimes when invited to their houses he went "unwillingly," that he could be caustic of speech when his entertainment was not to his liking. It may well be that towards the end of his visit "the lady went out visiting, leaving him at home by himself," and that though he did not like visiting particularly, it did not raise his spirits to be left "at home by himself." It may well be, too, that on his return to Wem he seemed to those around him, after their first joy in his homecoming was over, to have changed. He was at the age when change in a child is rapid, when, as he himself said afterwards, "a year makes the difference of an age." It may have been with this visit and its interruption to the routine of his childish life, that he associated putting childish things aside, just as Rousseau dated the breaking-up of his childish joy from the moment when, at the age of twelve years, he was unjustly punished.

On the other hand, the suggestion that his development in the years that followed may be accounted for in the words: "he became sullen: and this sullenness continued ever after," is mere distortion. We shall have to go elsewhere for information if we are to understand the sources of the oppression that began to cloud his brow. The value of the sketch does not lie in its perceptiveness, but in the impression it leaves, imperceptive though it be, of the time at which the development of adolescence first began to show itself, the impression, too, of the nature of the distress, and that it was both inarticulate and deep.

It seems likely that this rough sketch was based on Margaret Hazlitt's conversation.[33] Yet such portions of her Recollections as have been published throw no light on the first difficulties of her brother's life. It may be that she touched on them, and that what she said has not been published; or it may be that in putting together her recollections of her brother's childhood at Wem, she forgot for the moment the shadows that fell across the closing years of it. This is not altogether surprising, for the period was peculiarly associated in her mind with the memory of his happiness, and it would not be until the year before he left home for London that the agitation of his nerves and spirit would express itself in any way that seemed troublesome to those around him. As Margaret turned her eyes backwards towards this time, it may well have seemed to her through the haze of years to have been altogether a period of joy.

Or it may be that she just failed to understand what was happening to him, that in her thoughts she attributed all that puzzled her in his difficult moods to a growing sullenness, and that while chance fragments of her conversation may have given this impression to this person or that, Mr. Hunter included, she did not wish to put it on record after his death.

If she were imperceptive, it was only because of those limitations of our human nature which make it difficult to see what is passing in the minds of those with whom we live from day to day, perhaps more especially if we love them dearly. If she failed her brother it was from lack of vision, not from lack of love. That he, growing up in a household where there was no one of the same age as himself or experiencing any of the conflict he felt within himself, felt himself to be little understood, seems to be indicated by some of his later words, although they are very tender words too: "We do not see the features of those we love, nor do we clearly distinguish their virtues or their vices . . . all we know is, they are *more* to us than any one else can be. . . . If any doubt arises, if the veil of our implicit confidence is drawn aside by any accident for a moment, the shock is too great, like that of a dislocated limb, and we recoil on our habitual impressions again. Let not that veil ever be rent entirely asunder, so that those images may be left bare of reverential awe, and lose their religion: for nothing can ever support the desolation of the heart afterwards!" [34]

It is not, then, to those who heard of his life casually and considered it dispassionately, nor even to those who viewed it tenderly, but yet "through a veil," that we must go if we wish to understand the road by which he travelled, but to the only being on earth who knew anything about it, the one who made the journey, although he, too, at times expresses himself but darkly with regard to that strange journey, or should we say rather, although for the most part he chooses to express himself but parabolically.

Still, he makes it credible, "though hard and rare;" and he makes his own personality credible. In doing that he does more for himself than any one else has done for him. Truly, "men see not one another, but distorted phantasms which they call one another." If we want to see the man, not the phantasm, it is to Hazlitt himself, not to any of his friends or contemporaries, that we must go, even although, since almost anything that is said of such a being is worth recording, we note at the same time what *they say.*

4

One thing at least is clear, that the world in which he had been reared was, spiritually considered, a carefully fenced and enclosed world. No division of opinion was suffered to rend it. No evil, nor even the knowledge of the grosser forms of evil, was permitted to draw nigh unto it; its enclosures were high; the south wind was not permitted to blow upon its flowers.[35] It was largely, of course, because it had been thus enclosed, that a child bred in it could draw in so much of the pure breath of happiness. Yet it was the law of Nature that happiness of this kind could not continue. Before the child William could become the man he was born to be, he must burst through the protective sheath of this first world of his consciousness, must fare forth shivering, perhaps naked, when he has cast away his first vestments, into a new hard bewildering world, must find for himself there such new raiment, if possible such armour, as he can—or perish; and once having started on this venture, must fight his way through to the end.

The first shock to his moral nature, and perhaps the first keen stimulus to his intellectual development, was—we think—the burning of Dr. Priestley's house in 1791, or indeed, we might say, the fire-deluge in Birmingham that day, and the misrepresentation and calumny which followed it, finding its way, not only into the great London newspapers, but even into the flimsiest local Journals and Chronicles. The boy who, up to this time,

> ". . . had approached, like other Youth, the Shield
> Of human nature from the golden side,"

must have been shocked, in hearing of the calamity that threatened to ruin the life of his father's friend, into realising the existence of the reverse side of the shield. Perhaps he realised then too, for the first time, the existence of other forces in the world, and of other motives of human conduct, than those which he had been trained, in his narrow world, to recognise as good. This may have been his first experience of "that domain which we call the Passions," which he was afterwards to explore so thoroughly. No doubt he worked off some of the passion of the moment in his letter to *The Shrewsbury Chronicle*. Certainly he must have felt some of the joy of battle, and perhaps some pride in his own phrasing, when he stigmatised Dr. Priestley's opponents as being less "like the wren pecking at the eagle," than like the dim-eyed owl, "attempting by the flap of her wings" to dislodge Mount Etna. But he was of a brooding temper, and the sense of an injustice which he could attack but not rectify, would tend to rankle. The sense of being ranged against forces, powerful, inimical, and blind, would remain with him. "Where I see a spirit of intolerance, I think I see the great Devil,"[36] was to him at that time literal truth. He had had his first glimpse of "the great Devil."

Although, as we have seen, his friends seem to indicate 1790 as the year in which he began to change markedly, and although we have the evidence of his letter to the Editor of *The Shrewsbury Chronicle* to prove the stirring of his mind by the events of 1791, it is to the year

1792 that he himself points, as the year in which the spell of his child-hood was first broken. This year brought with it development in two ways. During it he began to find his way out to literature which could satisfy his curiosity as to the world beyond the enclosed world in which he lived, which could show him creatures not "' of the element' but of the earth, not ' living in the clouds '" but living very much as he hoped one day to do himself. Up till this time his reading had been almost all of it of one kind. His father's library, although once he came on the little duodecimo volumes of *The Tatler* in it, hidden among folios, and felt as if he had come on buried treasure, could little satisfy his curiosity regarding life. He would wander about it restlessly, pulling out this tome and that, seeking something to satisfy his hungry mind, but finding little, among the commentaries and treatises on theology and tomes of ecclesiastical history of which for the most part it consisted. Sometimes he would give up the search and content himself with looking, baffled, at the names on the outside of the volumes, baffled even by these—so remote did they seem from all he wished to know. In this austere library Foxe's *Book of Martyrs* and Neal's *History of the Puritans* and Calamy's *Account* of the Two Thou-sand Ejected Ministers ranked almost as light literature. These his father gave him to read, and he knew them well. Every page of *The Pilgrim's Progress* he knew too, every line of the prints that decorated the volume. Nor did he read these Puritan classics without interest and profit, and there can be no doubt that they made a lasting im-pression on his mind.

But the literature of flesh and blood was still to seek.

What had fed his mind and nurtured his imagination up to this time more than anything was Bible story itself. There can be no question as to the strength with which this took hold of him, shaping both the direction of his sympathies and of his imagination. After-wards he spoke of the stories of the Old Testament as being incompar-able in their "power of exciting awe and admiration, or of rivetting sympathy." The story of Joseph and his Brethren, of Rachel and Laban, of Ruth and Boaz, of the deliverance of the Jews out of Egypt, or the account of their captivity and return from Babylon, the descrip-tions in the Book of Job—all these touched him deeply. And perhaps more than all these, the story of Jacob's Dream! His memories of this afterwards made Rembrandt's picture intensely moving to him. The sight of the Man lying on the ground like a bundle of old clothes while his dreams opened up a way from earth to Heaven, affected him as if some one had thrust a hand into his bosom and turned his heart right over.

Mingled with all these stories in after years was of course the thought of all he most loved—the play of expression on his father's face as he read, the tones of his father's voice, the presence of those who were dear to him all gathered together in a little room: and these things deepened the tenderness he felt towards them. When he looked at West's "Christ Rejected," and remembered from his childhood the tones of the voice reading "Woman, behold thy son," he turned away from the mechanically executed canvas as an offence against his own "old recollections and yearnings of tenderness." But even at the time he first heard "the Orphic hymns of David, the prophetic denunciations of Isaiah, the gorgeous visions of Ezekiel"—these things fell on a soul made of very "penetrable stuff."

We have dwelt on the interpenetration of his mind by this material, because we believe it was all-important in moulding him. Hebrew literature, before he had outgrown his childhood, had already become to him "A power like one of Nature's." He had learned from it the love of that which is high. This was the grand compensation of his rearing. But for the rest, his reading was on the whole arid. He had read little, he tells us, before 1792, except the Bible, ecclesiastical history, and the Puritan classics we have mentioned. As yet he had only made acquaintance with English literature through text-books.

But here again he was in one respect very fortunate. His principal guide was Enfield's *Speaker*. This delightful book had emanated from the famed Warrington Academy, and the William Enfield who had compiled it had certainly known how to choose and to arrange selections from literature so as to nourish the mind, so as to form the foundations of a taste in literature, so as to whet the appetite for further reading and even so as to encourage the beginnings of the critical faculty. From this book he gained some acquaintance with the work of Milton and Dryden, with the periodical literature of the eighteenth century and the verse of most of the eighteenth-century poets, and with the drama of the age immediately preceding his own. Above all, he gained some acquaintance with Shakespeare, who is so well represented that the book lays the foundations of a knowledge of what is best in his work.

This is no small body of material to be included in one book; and it is so presented as to lead the mind to the discovery of the unity of literature and experience. There is no rigid division between ancient and modern. Thus the section called Orations and Harangues opens with a couple of speeches from Livy that might interest a boy, that of Junius Brutus over the body of Lucretia and that of Hannibal to his soldiers; it includes from Sallust the fiery speech of Caius Marius to the Romans, on their hesitating to appoint him general in the expedition against Jugurtha merely on account of his extraction; two speeches from Quintus Curtius, and one from Tacitus. These lead up to speeches of modern times, including one of Walpole's—bearing on questions of the day; and the section closes with three well-chosen speeches from Shakespeare, the speech of Brutus on the death of

Cæsar, that of Gloucester to the nobles, and that of Henry V to his soldiers. We can imagine the boy many times during his schooldays, when much that he had to do made him impatient or bored, turning over the pages of his "Enfield" and browsing on what he found there, delighting in much of it. It was there that he first came upon Mrs. Barbauld's poetry, with the pleasurable sense of coming upon an old friend when he discovered among the names of the English poets that of the one who had been his first preceptress, and Mrs. Barbauld's poetry pleased him no less than her books for children had done. For some time, he tells us, he was divided in allegiance between her *Ode to Spring* and Collins's *Ode to Evening*.

He loved to declaim some of the speeches he found in Enfield. We can imagine the sympathy with which he would repeat the words of Caius Marius: "What if I can show no statues of my family! I can show the standards, the armour, and the trappings, which I myself have taken from the vanquished; I can show the scars of those wounds, which I have received by facing the enemies of my country. *These* are my statues." He tells us that his declamation of young Norval's speech from Home's *Douglas* gave great satisfaction both to himself and to others. Ever afterwards he had an affection for this play, which he pronounced "a green spot in the desert of eighteenth-century tragedy."

William Enfield knew how to teach, and his book, unlike most books of excerpts, nourished instead of teasing the mind, and tended to lay the foundations not only of knowledge but of character, while no one who had been reared on it could be in much danger of acquiring a false taste in literature. Yet in its nature it was but fragmentary. It gave but the crumbs of literature. The best thing it could do for its readers was to make them long for the whole loaf, and this was exactly what it had been devised to do. For this the boy began to long, and into it he began to cut, as he tells us, in his fourteenth year.

He seems to have read only two completed novels or romances up to this time Fenelon's *Télémaque*, in a translation on which he had come during his visit to Liverpool, and which he persuaded his sister to read on his return, and Mrs. Radcliffe's *Romance of the Forest*, which, insipid though it be, had enchanted him with what he calls its wild sweetness. But in 1792 Cooke's Select Edition of the British Novels began to appear. The first of these which began to arrive in sixpenny numbers at the parsonage in Wem was *Tom Jones*. At once his mind seized on it like a starved thing, feeling that it gave him food of a different relish from any he had tasted before. It "smacked of the world" in which he wanted to live. It was "sweet in the mouth" and yet "not bitter in the belly." This, then, of all books, was the first, as he tells us, that "broke the spell." *Joseph Andrews*, with its ravishing illustration of Fanny, never afterwards to be forgotten by him, he read soon after this, and in due course the works of Smollett and Sterne, but *Tom Jones* was always to be for him the work that "broke the spell." This was the first corrective to his brooding over books that looked only heavenwards. He felt almost, in coming to it, as if a burden had dropped from his back. More than this, he felt as if it were now "perpetual gala-day" with him, while he could feast on its instalments. He was able at last, with the help of the little dusty duodecimos that arrived once a fortnight, "to get a peep at the raree-show of the world." It is at mankind that he now gazes, although as yet only through the glass of fiction, staring fixedly "as we do at wild beasts in a menagerie, through the bars of the cages—or at curiosities in a museum, that we must not touch." But he realises that at last it is mankind he is seeing, that he is looking at creatures who are travelling on the road he is presently to take himself. In a year's time he will be setting out upon the road. Then he will no longer see as through a glass. He will continue to see; he may perhaps also contrive to touch.

5

It was in this year, too, he tells us, that he made his first conscious effort at thought. It would seem that this may be dated in the spring of this year, and that he was prompted towards it by his old friends the Test and the Corporation Acts. In May, 1792, the Unitarians made yet another of their many attempts towards having these Acts repealed. The Unitarian Society petitioned the House of Commons, and their petition was supported by Fox, much as an earlier attempt of the same kind had been supported by Chatham. Burke, in his speech against Fox's motion for leave to bring in a Bill for repeal and alteration, made a bitter attack on the Unitarian leaders, especially on Dr. Priestley and Dr. Kippis. As to the main body of the Unitarians themselves, he drew a distinction between them and the older religious sects. His finding was that while the older sects had more or less justified their existence, the Unitarians brought not "airs from heaven" into the life of the community but rather "blasts from hell."

Such accusations had their echoes in the Unitarian congregation at Wem, so that coming out of meeting one day William heard a discussion between his father and an old lady of the congregation "respecting the repeal of the Corporation and Test Acts, and the limits of religious toleration." This—and possibly the challenge thrown out to the Unitarians by Burke's insults—set him thinking on the nature of government, and during the remainder of the year, indeed for several years to come, he was constantly trying to reason out for himself a "system of political rights and general jurisprudence." He was, we know, a child on whom the thought of the past wrought powerfully.

In his study of history he had always been conscious of the age-long fight between Liberty and Oppression. Ever since he could remember he had heard of Habeas Corpus, "the trial by jury, Magna Charta, the Bill of Rights, of the Bastille in France, and the Inquisition in Spain and the Man in the Iron Mask." These things had made an indelible impression on his mind of the extent to which human institutions influenced for good or evil the liberties and happiness of nations. Also he lived in a district in which there was much to touch his mind to thoughts of the past. Both what he saw and what he heard made it living to him. The sound of village bells seemed to him to link the workaday life of the present with that of the past, for it was "the poor man's only music."[37] The curfew seemed to him to tell the tale of the generations that are lost. The castle bell, on the other hand, "with its brazen throat and iron tongue," spoke to him of "the conqueror's iron rule and peasant's lamp extinguished," and filled his mind with a touch of fear and wonder. Now his thoughts swung between the past and the present, no less filled with fear and wonder, trying to frame some such conception of government as would not be oppressive to his conception of the Liberty that must be conceded to man. To reconcile the idea or conception of Liberty with some conception of government was now his main problem. He wrestled to define for himself the limits of "rights" and "laws," finding a means of reconciling the two conceptions by coming to the conclusion that a man's "right" is that which seems good to a man himself, but that "law" is that which determines the bounds of "rights" in relation to the collective good of the inhabitants of a country. That some form of government was necessary to determine the bounds of "rights" and "laws"—if there were not in store for man a worse tyranny than that of absolutism, the tyranny of anarchy—the news coming in from France from day to day was sufficient to teach him. Dr. Price had cried, "Peace, and there *will* be Peace," but Dr. Price was dead, and in the autumn of that year, even as the rustling leaves of the dwarf oaks at Wem were turning red, the streams in the passes of the Argonne were turning red too; nay!—the streets of Paris itself were turning red, and the warmest apologists of the Revolution were aghast at the consequence of the sudden unleashing of human passions.

It is not without interest that even as he was in the obscure travail of his first original train of thought, of which the events of the time would ultimately help to deliver him, others too, like himself, born to mould the thoughts and express the infinitude of the passions of man, each according to his capacity, were also being caught in the train of events and being moulded by them. Young William Wordsworth has now reached Paris. He seems to hear coming up to him from the streets that had so recently been drenched with red spray a voice crying, "Sleep no more," and the corrosive sublimate of Fear touches his genius, ever afterwards to condition its workings. Johann Wolfgang von Goethe, caught in the retreat northwards from Verdun, sees one of the horses of an ammunition-wagon fall down; sees the other horses cut loose and the press of the retreat passing over the one that is fallen even as it struggles to rise, sees how its legs, under the wheels, go crashing and shuddering. "Die and become!" Alas! What can become of a poor overladen horse crushed under the wheels in that desperate press? Something not unconnected with the rights and destinies both of man and beast! Something that will yet quicken many a new birth—a jet of pity quivering along the nerves of a great poet!

6

According to his own testimony, then, the year 1792 was a year of primary importance in William's development. He began to make his way into the main stream of literature, and he began to think. There is as yet no suggestion that this development brought trouble of mind with it, although we can readily believe that William, disappearing for hours to read, or sitting dreaming of what he himself would one day write, or "still as any stone," as was his way when wrapped in a coil of thought, must have seemed very different to those around him from the merry, ever-companionable little being William had been in his childhood. Indeed the growing boy, withdrawn into his own mind, realising for the first time what a kingdom he had in it, was without doubt very different from the child who had shared his every mood and thought with those around him. He did all things with intensity, and in his absorption in his new interests he may have seemed self-centred, slack, and sullen.

In the following year, however, in the course of 1793, influences both from without and from within began to play upon him, which to a certain extent *forced* his development, and which began to condition and to disrupt his relationship both with the outside world and with the little home circle in which his affections were centred. The force from without which conditioned a new and painful phase of his development was the drawing to a climax of the suspicion, coldness and hostility with which the rulers of the country had from the beginning viewed the Revolution in France, culminating, on February 11th, 1793, in a Declaration of War. There are several elements to be distinguished in the first reaction of the Unitarian brotherhood—in the midst of which he was growing up and forming his opinions and sympathies—to this Declaration. There was mingled disappointment and shame that the English Government, in declaring war against a country struggling desperately for civil Liberty, should seek to extinguish the light England herself had kindled in the night of absolutism in Europe, and that its power should be exerted to the uttermost towards loading with opprobrium every sentiment and maxim on which her own Liberty rested. There was scorn for the rulers of a country calling itself free and professing to prize Liberty, who could look on coldly at the difficult birth of Liberty in a neighbouring country, who were ready to assist, yet in the same ice-cold way, in poisoning it when it had been born, but who flamed into heat and found that they were touched to the soul when there came the matter of the opening up of the Scheldt. It was felt as a stain that by an illiberal, mean and envious foreign policy the hope of lasting and universal good to mankind should not only be prejudiced and jeopardised, but deliberately assailed with intent to destroy. The opening of the Scheldt was looked upon as a mere pretext for [38] drawing Holland into the war: the real attack was on the assertion of the liberties of Peoples. There was anger at the vicious cruelty with which the Government prosecuted many of those opposed to its policy. This was shared by all of liberal sympathies, among them William Wordsworth, who until a short time previously had been by no means politically minded, but who now found himself in protest against the injustices which were being perpetrated in the name of justice:

> "Our Shepherds . . . at that time
> Thirsted to make the guardian crook of Law
> A tool of Murder; . . .
> . . . in their weapons and their warfare base
> As vermin working out of reach, they leagu'd
> Their strength perfidiously, to undermine
> Justice, and make an end of Liberty."

There was grief in the sense that the Revolution itself was being goaded into a fearful madness. If the boy William Hazlitt had had his first glimpse of "the great Devil" in the burning of Priestley's house, it must now have seemed to him as if "the great Devil," crested and Horror-plumed, with his dread accompaniments of Fire, Famine and Slaughter—was now openly beginning his reign upon earth, and inaugurating it by the unleashing of all the passions associated with war, and the turning of the promised good into evil.

But the most enduring distress of all, to those who sympathised with the struggle of France for Liberty, was that the Declaration of War so confused the issues at stake as to give the friends of Liberty a specious appearance of being the enemies of their country. Many could not bear the odium this brought upon them, and fell off from the side that had suddenly become unpopular. This was the first defection from the ranks of liberalism, which the succeeding years were to winnow out with ever-increasing rigour. Others still held to their hopes and their convictions, but in doing so suffered a fearful conflict of sympathies. Among these we must once more mention William Wordsworth. He grieved for the fair stained plumage; but he pitied yet more the dying bird. Walking along the Loire he had chanced

> "One day to meet a hunger-bitten Girl
> Who crept along, fitting her languid gait
> Unto a Heifer's motion, by a cord
> Tied to her arm, and picking thus from the lane
> Its sustenance, while the girl with her two hands
> Was busy knitting, in a heartless mood
> Of solitude. . . ."

And she had become for him the symbol of the scarecrow misery of the France without hope for the People that was being swept away and replaced by a France that at least had hope before its eyes. He held to his faith and his conviction, yet he was almost wrenched asunder by the conflict between this universal human sympathy and his deep inalterable love for his own country, whether it were in the right or in the wrong. For all forward-looking minds the year was one of difficulty and wrenched sympathies. The holding fast to principle meant actual suffering, and steadfastness in suffering, for the two noblest impulses in man's nature—love of country and love of kind, or sympathy for the needs and aspirations of his fellow-man— had been set at variance with each other by the mere act of the Declaration of War, through the rousing of national feeling against the French. Through an unscrupulous prostitution of names and things it had been made to appear to the unthinking many as if this were the old national quarrel with France, needing to be fought out once more ere Europe could have peace, instead of being, as it actually seemed to most forward-looking minds, nothing less than a declaration of war on "the great cause of mankind."

For the Unitarians, as a whole, the difficulty was far deeper. They, being already separated from their fellow-men by their religious convictions, were inured to misrepresentation, not only the mis-representation of the ignorant and unthinking, but to deliberate mis-representation by first-rate minds. Burke, in his speech of May 11th, 1792, had prejudiced opinion against them by misrepresenting them as having "a zeal for propagating" their opinions by force, and as holding principles violently and fanatically pursued and "taught to their children, who are sworn at the altar like Hannibal." As to the falseness of this, we have the unconscious witnessing of their children. William

Hazlitt's early letters show that he had already learned to detest the arbitrament of force. The child's unpremeditated utterances do but reflect the temper of those around him. Priestley, in 1791, had refused to let his friends defend his house, because he did not believe in the use of force.

This, however, had not prevented him from being nicknamed Gunpowder Joe, nor had the consistent hatred to violence shown by the Unitarians as a whole prevented Burke from injuring them in May, 1792, both by misrepresentation and by rhetoric based on the taking for granted of this misrepresentation as truth and designed to make them seem loathsome. In November of the same year they were pelted with doggerel, echoing in its crude way such misrepresentation, and denigrating Priestley by linking him with Paine.

After the Declaration of War they all came in for a double share of misrepresentation, suspicion and abuse. For one thing, although the calumny of wishing to propagate their opinions by force was so often raised against them, they were known to hate war. Their own utterances showed them to be inveterately opposed to it. They were strangers to Burke's acceptance of and even admiration of "the mode of civilised war which, more than anything else, has distinguished the Christian World."[39] In season and out of season their leaders had declared that war was only justifiable as the last resort of self-defence. For another—as a body they were known to have been in sympathy with the aspirations of France. It is not too much to say that the Declaration of War placed them at the mercy of their enemies. Any one who wished to injure them could bring trouble upon them by accusing them of being haters of their country, and this was the calumny of all calumnies that was hardest to bear. Spies of debased character were accepted as witnesses against them. Several of their ministers were prosecuted. The Rev. J. Jebb, of St. John's College, Cambridge, was tried for sedition. More famed was the trial of the Rev. W. Frend, formerly Fellow of Jesus College. The enthusiastic hand-clapping, whenever a point was made in his favour, of a youth whose thick open mouth contrasted in an extraordinary way with his god-like brow and with the glorious expression of his eyes, helped him not a whit. An obscure undergraduate like Samuel Taylor Coleridge might approve of him, but the authorities would have none of him. He was expelled from the University on May 30th. The Rev. T. Fyshe Palmer, the Unitarian minister of Dundee, was sentenced to transportation for seven years, of which sentence he died, his offence having been that he had corrected the proof of a handbill by a member of The Society of the Friends of Liberty at Dundee. For many other Unitarian ministers the Declaration of War meant that they were suddenly committed to walk in darkened ways. The times were hard, and such minorities bore the brunt of popular passion. Robert Aspland expressed only the sense of oppression felt by many when he said that Truth itself had become seditious.

These things had repercussions on the personality of the youth growing up, amid this welter of opinions, in a Unitarian presbytery at Wem. It was not in his nature to deny a principle in which he believed, because the upholding of it brought him into constant difficulty and conflict. Yet the difficulty of the conflict must have intensified in him about this time both his passionate hatred of injustice and that passionate sympathy with the forlorn hope which to some extent had always been his, and which never deserted him.

Thus elements from without, and entirely beyond his control, were disrupting, just as he was about to make his entry into the outside world, the harmony of his relationship with the majority of his fellow-countrymen, were breeding in him the consciousness that he was on the rebel side. Yet these elements had no power to touch the core of his life, to injure his relationship with those most dear to him, with whom he had to be fully in sympathy else must he endure the burden of an almost insupportable desolation of heart.

But now, just about the same time, there came the strain of the development of forces within himself, which he was equally powerless to control, affecting little his relationship to the outside world, but affecting very deeply his relationship with those nearest to him and most dear. Whither are these to lead him? How are they going to affect his moorings? He has begun to read, and he has begun to think. What is going to happen to one bred in rules of conduct so rigid and circumscribed, bred in a circle of ideas limited though profound, when he begins to apply his power of thought to what he reads? He recognised afterwards that the moment in which he had begun consciously to think had been for him the moment of Fate, that it had determined the course of all his future life, not so much because of the train of thought it had started, as because in that moment he had first given rein to that "original bias or craving to be satisfied of the reason of things" which afterwards dominated him and drove him relentlessly on his stormy, questing way. About the same time as he was reading *Tom Jones* he was dipping into deistical literature. Burke had inquired scornfully in his *Reflections:* "Who, born within the last forty years, has read one word of . . . Chubb?" William Hazlitt as yet had never read Burke, but he was just getting ready to read Chubb,[40] and to read him with extreme intellectual relish, whetting his mind on what he read. What if, in the course of his reading, whether of Chubb or of some account of Newtonian philosophy or of the philosophy of his day, towards which his mind is now driving him, he find a new train of thought awakening in him, and discover that in no way can his newly awakened power of reasoning "reconcile the faith delivered to the saints with the subtleties and intricacies of metaphysics!" One thing we know from himself, that the moment, when it came, was exceeding bitter, and the blow staggering, that ever afterwards he regarded as the beginning of sorrow the coming of "whatever sets or leaves the dogmas of religion at variance with the dictates of the heart."

He may have attempted to drop the matter out of his mind for the moment. Indeed, it is likely that he did so, seeing that he made no alteration in the plans that had been arranged for him, of going to London in the autumn to study with a view to entering the ministry. Yet he could not altogether dismiss it, for if his training had taught him anything, it had taught him that he must never give the lie to his own soul. There is no getting away from it—a cloud has appeared upon the horizon of his life: as yet it may be of small dimensions, no bigger than his own hand, but who can tell to what dimensions it may grow, until presently it may hang over his whole life, trembling and obscure? He says nothing of what is troubling him, for he feels his thoughts to be a kind of treachery towards his father: he gets ready to proceed dutifully to Hackney College. Yet, silent though he be, his acts begin to speak for themselves. They puzzle his mother and sister, bring to his father a deeper hurt. He behaves at times with a curious inconsiderateness, even with a suggestion of churlishness. He is no longer the child whose idea of an agreeable Sunday it had been to go twice to chapel and hear two good sermons, who had been accustomed to repeat the text afterwards and give an intelligent account of what had been said, who had seemed indeed, in the turn of his speech and the direction of his thought, the very pattern of a Dissenting minister in embryo. Sometimes on a Sunday he is not to be seen at all. In the morning his place in the chapel is vacant; in the afternoon his father looks round for him. There is still no sign of his William. The minister goes on with the service, is perhaps a trifle heavier in manner than had been his wont, perhaps pulls out his watch once or twice involuntarily, and glances at it with lack-lustre eye.

If in addition to these things we consider that the boy had been bred in the presbytery at Wem almost as if he were spirit alone, that his spirit had been disciplined and watched over, whereas little care had been taken for his developing body and its impulses and urgings, beyond the attention given to its simple daily needs; that it was being borne in upon him that he was spirit and body too, that indeed sometimes the body took the lead; that he was beginning to be conscious of a deep division in his nature, of a tendency to react from extreme refinement of feeling to extreme grossness of desire; if we remember, too, that in him "the nerve of sensibility is strung up almost to the point of pain"—we may begin to realise how it was that while to those around him he seemed remote, difficult, and sullen, to himself in the obscure distress or disturbance of nerves that sent him scudding through the fields on moonlight nights like a wild creature trying to out-distance its own heartbeats, he seemed, altered as he was, to have become—O grief and shame!—little better than a dumb and brutish changeling!

Part Two

THE WRITER'S PREPARATION

There is a method of trying periods on the ear, or weighing them with the scales of the breath, without any articulate sound. Authors, as they write, may be said "to hear a sound so fine, there's nothing lives 'twixt it and silence."

HAZLITT.

Chapter One

STUDENT DAYS AT HACKNEY (1793-1795)

"Another interesting acquaintance . . . was William Hazlitt, a man who has left a deservedly high reputation as a critic, but who at the time I first knew him was struggling against a great difficulty of expression. . . . He was the younger brother of John Hazlitt the miniature painter. His first design was to be a dissenting minister, and for that purpose he went to the Unitarian New College, Hackney, and he was one of the first students who left that College an avowed infidel. . . . The moment I saw him I saw that he was an extraordinary man."

HENRY CRABB ROBINSON.

I

WE HAVE seen that while the child William Hazlitt was enjoying the Montpelier Tea-Gardens in September, 1787, a group of his father's friends had just succeeded in establishing a College at Hackney. Institutions devoted to providing education for the sons of Dissenters, excluded from the universities on account of their religious scruples, had on the whole a difficult and precarious life. The famous Warrington Academy, from which Enfield had sent out his *Speaker* and which Mrs. Barbauld had celebrated in verse, had at last been dissolved, partly, it would seem, because of the usual financial difficulties in institutions kept up chiefly by fluctuating voluntary subscriptions, partly because the experiment of collegiate residence had in the end presented insuperable problems of discipline: the Divinity students had not, as it had been hoped, proved able "to leaven the mass"[41] of the lay students, as the numbers increased.

The New College at Hackney was one of the institutions which were raised, as it were, on the ruins of this justly famed institution, and which shared in the treasure salved from it. Students were admitted at the age of fifteen. It was almost inevitable that when William Hazlitt had reached that age this college should claim him. Not only had his father's old friends laboured to bring it into being; not only was his father in perfect sympathy with its aims and aspirations—but many friends throughout the country were in one way or another connected with it. Mr. Yates of Liverpool was on the committee; the Rev. William Shepherd had received some of his training there; Mr. Rowe of Shrewsbury was one of the subscribers. It was open to students of all denominations, but it had been brought into being by the efforts of the leading Unitarian ministers, and Unitarians had almost a family interest in it.

In the autumn of 1793 it was entering on the sixth year of its existence; William Hazlitt had had his fifteenth birthday in the spring of the year; the time has now come for the college, symbolic of all that his father's generation had found good, and the youth, who has yet to find out for himself what seems good to him, to make acquaintance with each other, get on with each other, if they can; or if not, prove each other's mettle, and part. We know little as to the financial arrangements which made it possible for him to go there. The fees were £60 per annum. It is quite impossible that Mr. Hazlitt should have paid this sum, which was almost double his annual income. There were—we know—reduced fees for students who intended to proceed to the Divinity course. Even so, it is difficult to see how Mr. Hazlitt could have met them. It is more likely that his own services to the Unitarian cause and his friendship with Dr. Kippis enabled him to have his son placed on the foundation. One thing we know, that William received an annual grant, and that it was increased during the time he was at Hackney. At any rate, some arrangement was made which put it in his power to go.

Thus at the end of September, 1793, he takes the road from Wem to Shrewsbury, as full of hopes and fears as ever a youth was, when about to make his entry into the wide world. From Shrewsbury—the mail coach to Piccadilly! And the new life has begun.

2

Before we follow him into this new life, we might pause to consider what the college had become, by the time it received him, for brief as his stay at it was, there can be no doubt at all that it influenced him, perhaps more than he realised. It may justly claim the distinction of having had some share in the forming of an intrepid spirit.

From the beginning it had been open to lay students, to whom it offered a three-year course, as well as to Divinity students, to whom a five-year course was offered. In its first days it was very unpretentious. The opening lectures had been given, in October, 1786, to a little group of six students, in a room in Dr. Williams's library, the use of which had been granted by the trustees. There Dr. Price, Dr. Kippis, and Dr. Abraham Rees had lectured at such times as they could spare from their congregational labours. In 1787 the large house at Hackney, standing "in about 18 acres of land," had been secured,[42] and the New College, as it was called, when it opened there at the end of September, had consisted of fourteen students. It was expected that the numbers would very soon increase, and as most of the rooms in the house would then be required as lecture rooms and public rooms, the committee, undeterred by the difficulties of discipline that had arisen at Warrington through having the students in residence all together in one large home, set about the immediate erection of a new residential wing, to be composed of thirty studies and bedrooms.

There were at the time of the opening of the college at Hackney six tutors, including Dr. Price, Dr. Kippis, and Dr. Abraham Rees, who was to be the resident tutor, and to reside in a house contiguous to the college. Mr. Kiddle, the assistant resident tutor lived in the college, and his wife looked after "the family."

The college was intended, as Dr. Price put it, "for the education of youth in general at that period of approach to mature life when they are most liable to seduction, and most in danger of taking the wrong turn."[43] Its teaching was designed "to promote such a spirit of inquiry and candour, as shall form worthy citizens for the state, and useful ministers for the church."[43] The training of the students for citizenship was always emphasised, and it was comprehensive. Dr. Priestley adjured those who were members of the teaching staff not to let the students forget their responsibilities towards the world at large. It is well—he says—that the students should be trained to be conscientious private citizens; but it is still more important that they should be taught to remember that they are also "members of the larger society of mankind" and ought therefore to care for "whatever respects general liberty and general happiness." For such training, he stated in April, 1791,[44] the times were propitious: "Another and most important circumstance which calls us to attend to the proper education of our youth, is the new light which is now . . . bursting out in favour of the civil *rights of men*, and the great objects and uses of *civil government*. While so favourable a wind is abroad, let every young mind expand itself, catch the rising gale, and partake of the glorious enthusiasm. . . . Let the liberal youth be every where encouraged to study the nature of government. . . ."

The college was thus far more liberal in tone than the universities. It is not too much to say that it was daring in its experimentalism. The three things which it most strove to inculcate were—independence of thought, the love of Truth for its own sake, and intellectual courage. "Youth," said Priestley, "should be so trained up as, without fear, to look for every species of ill-usage in a good cause."

The New College in Hackney was, in fact, an experiment in freedom. How it would have fared in ordinary times we know not, but in less than a couple of years after it started the entire order of existing things was affected by the outbreak of the Revolution in France, and it is certain that in the fiery political atmosphere of the following years, the independence of thought commended to the students and the encouragement given to them to care for "whatever respects general truth, general liberty, and general happiness," inevitably brought certain perils in its train, and occasioned a good deal of criticism both of the staff and of the students, who were so far from being backward in taking an interest in the politics of the day that they erred rather in excess of zeal, and perhaps may have surprised and disturbed even their liberal-minded mentors by the *gusto* they displayed. It was said that a handbill which had emanated from the students of the college and which had been circulated in Birmingham in July of 1791 had been one of the things which had inflamed the mob and had contributed to the excitement which had led to the burning of Dr. Priestley's house. At the beginning of the following session the students forwarded an address of sympathy to Dr. Priestley. In the course of it some eighteen or nineteen of them invited Tom Paine to sup with them, and "had the most glorious republican party that the walls of the College ever contained." Paine, before he left, promised to call on them "whenever he came to Hackney." Such exhibitions of enthusiasm during such a time could not but add to the difficulties usually encountered by Dissenting colleges in their struggle for existence, for they laid the college open not only to honest criticism, of which it had its share, but to calumny and to the attacks of prejudice.

It seems, too, that here, as in Warrington, the system of collegiate residence gradually gave rise to problems of discipline within the college itself. Charges of indiscipline were frequently levelled against the institution by its many hostile critics. These no doubt were due largely to prejudice; but these were not the only charges. We begin to hear of the misgivings of friends also. Gilbert Wakefield complained of the interruption to the work of the students and the constant "dissipation of ideas and unsettlement of mind" caused by the way in which they yielded themselves to the excitements of the day. Among these he mentions the trial of Warren Hastings. By June, 1791, he had become a bitter critic of the college, and at length he resigned his connection with it, feeling, as he said, that he had "no alternative but to escape from a crazy and sinking vessel." The Rev. Thomas Belsham, who was the assistant resident tutor during the years Hazlitt was there, a man not at all violent of temperament, as was Wakefield, strikes a note less of such indignation as Wakefield's than of bewilderment and even dismay. What he felt most keenly was the corrosive action of contemporary influences on faith. "When a number of young men live together in the same house, there will always be some irregular and even immoral," he wrote. "But this is not the only ground of complaint—there is an unaccountable tendency in the young men, in this part of the world, to infidelity, and the studious and virtuous part of our family have very generally given up Christianity. This is an evil to which no remedy can be applied. Actions may be restrained, but thoughts must be left free."

At the time he wrote this letter, he too had "determined to relinquish" his connection with the college.

Although no doubt complaints like those of Burke that the college was "an arsenal" for the fabrication of revolutionary weapons and a breeding place for revolutionary ideas, "a volcano of sedition," "a nursery of riot" even "a slaughter-house of Christianity" are the mere ebullitions of enmity, we cannot but feel, when we consider some of the complaints made by its friends, that the New College at Hackney, by the time William Hazlitt entered it, was not quite answering the purpose for which it had been founded, and that the students, who were gradually getting out of hand, were tending to distort the purpose for which it had been founded. In ordinary times the insistence on independence of thought and on the application of thought to world affairs might have done nothing but good. But the times, so far from being ordinary, were a powerful forcing-ground for opinion. Even during these stormy times, in which truth, if it were not utterly suppressed, ran the risk of being pushed to the point of distortion, if the teaching staff had been larger, if it had consisted of younger men, or if it had consisted of men peculiarly suited for the training of youth, even if Dr. Price, who had expressly disclaimed any republican tendencies, had still been alive to guide its destinies—perhaps all might have been well. As it was, it is difficult to avoid the conclusion that by the autumn of 1793, the students needed the rein rather than the spur, that they were too full of crude life for those set in authority over them, that they were inclined to intervene mischievously in matters in which as yet they had no power to intervene usefully, and that the tolerant idealism and generous liberalism of the founders were being abused rather than used, to an extent that imperilled the usefulness and came near to endangering the existence of the college. Southey wrote of it in 1817: "It is well known that the Socinian Academy at Hackney was given up, notwithstanding the high character and learning of some of its conductors, because almost all the students pushed the principles in which they were educated farther than their tutors. The dry-rot was in the foundation and the walls, as well as in the beams and rafters, and the unfortunate pupils came away believers in blind necessity and gross materialism—and in nothing else."[45] This, of course, like Burke's onslaught, is the work of a professed enemy, pressing home an attack on Unitarians in general and on Hazlitt in particular. It exaggerates the drawbacks of the institution, and gives a distorted impression of their effects on the students, but yet we think it may be taken as truth that "the students pushed the principles in which they were educated farther than their tutors."

This, then, was the institution in which William Hazlitt was educated from his fifteenth to his seventeenth year. While he was quick to reject the red-hot element in the sympathies of his fellow-students, and the enthusiasms that were merely bred of the hour and that would pass with the hour, the independence of thought that was encouraged conformed to and confirmed the habit of mind he had already formed while puzzling things out for himself in the solitude of Wem. The college at Hackney undoubtedly had its share in his "inveteracy." Something of a bear-garden it was, but this at least can be said for it: it was successful in its attempts to foster the fine rare flower of mental courage.

3

Of these things the student from the country beginning his life in the college tells us nothing in the first letters he sent home. He does, indeed, reply somewhat dryly to his father's admonition to him to acquire politeness: ". . . this is not the best place possible for acquiring it." He goes on to explain that he does not intend this as a criticism, yet his explanation leaves the impression that as a school of manners it was sui generis: "I do not say at all that the fellows who are here do not know how to behave extremely well; but the behaviour which suits a set of young fellows, or boys, does not suit any other society." His letters of this time are very inexpressive. The opening one, indeed, of October 6th, contains an attempt, awkward enough, yet very touching, for he hardly expects it to be understood, at an explanation of what had made him seem so "difficult" to those around him in the last months he had spent at Wem: "With respect to my past behaviour, I have often said, and now I assure you, that it did not proceed from any real disaffection; but merely from the nervous disorders to which, you well know, I was so much subject. This was really the case; however improbable it may appear." But for the most part his letters have reverted to childishness, in that they are a mere huddle of facts. They show none of the eager flow of thought and confidence that had marked the letters written during the visit to Liverpool. Either the habit of unbosoming himself to his father has been broken, or the new life pouring in upon him has left his powers of expression completely outstripped. Possibly both these difficulties made it difficult for him to write freely. But for the saving grace of a momentary quickening here and there, they might be described as rather inhuman letters. They require to be interpreted in the light of his reminiscences, if they are going to enable us to realise what was happening to him.

Even as the child whom his American playmates had called "Billy" had been outstripped by the boy "William," "William" has now become "Hazlitt" to his companions, "young Hazlitt" to his father's friends: his tutors address him as "Mr. Hazlitt." He is beginning to be treated as a man, but truth to tell, never as a child had he been as bewildered as now, just when he is expected to have put away all childish things. The impact of London upon him has proved confusing rather than stimulating. Among the crowds, through which he slips like a shadow, he is conscious of a feeling of vacuity, perplexity, even of insignificance and littleness, as if each person he meets to whom he is unknown is a blow to his personal identity. As he scans the procession of unknown faces, each one of which is like a teasing unknown riddle to him, he feels almost wearied, as one might be who was compelled to read through the first leaf of all the volumes in a great library.

It is hardly surprising that within the college all around him should seem strange, uncertain, even adverse: "a hubbub of confused noises, a chaos of shifting objects." He feels, within its walls, as if severed from his real world. He is very homesick. Faithful Joe Swanwick has come up to the college with him, does not like to be separated from him, clamours to be allowed to take the same classes as William Hazlitt. This does not prevent William Hazlitt from being so homesick that his ears strain at night for the sound of the letter-bell, to him like a reassuring music, strengthening him, reminding him with a sudden sense of comfort that he still has links connecting him with the outside universe, bringing before his eyes visions of the blue line of the hills of home. The postman's knock fills his heart with hope and longing. If there is no letter at the expected time, "what a pang is there!" The sight of the mail-coaches as he sees them pouring through the streets, although the splendour of it never fails to thrill him, quickens the longing in him. When he catches a glimpse of the Shrewsbury mail especially, his link with home, he finds his eyes filling with sudden tears. He is puzzled by himself. He seems to be outgrowing his own identity, even as he had outgrown his last year's clothes. A set of divers objects, of the existence of which he had not a suspicion, engages his whole attention. He has glimpses of shapes and colours of all varieties, and of gorgeous tints, interrupting his conception of what he had been, so that his continuity of consciousness crumbles and falls in pieces. His perceptions have the brightness and yet the indistinctness of a trance. The way before him seems strange and obscure. Above all, he is conscious of transition in his blood and soul. His feelings are chaotic, confused. They seem strangers to each other, with nothing to harmonise them, strange intruders even to himself. He wants to set his feet firmly on the ground again; but life no longer seems to hang together. It winds along towards the infinite obscure future, straggling, disjointed. He has to spell each day out to himself, as if he were learning a lesson for the first time. Every advance he makes is slow and doubtful. Even of himself he is not sure, for he seems to himself to be many beings in one—and he never knows which of them is to be uppermost.

Of one thing alone he is sure, that he wants to express the chaotic struggling of thought and feeling within himself and thus bring some order out of it. This is now the master impulse within him. Yet he is still all but dumb.

In the course of that year William Wordsworth had begun his career as a poet.[46] He too is having a struggle. His verse is not in the least expressive of the movement of his mind, and although friends discern the breath of genius ruffling its trim mediocrity, he himself is chiefly conscious that there is a long struggle before him, before he can express even dimly what he wants to say. An artillery-major under General Carteaux in Provence has his pen in hand too. No dimness here! He is afterwards to seem to William Hazlitt the sword-arm of the Revolution. At the moment, the pen with which he analyses its genius and predicts its inevitable course is clear as the sword he wields, fine-edged as his own mind, which already cuts through unrealities and discerns that relying upon words is vanity, that the man who would make himself the master of the times and avoid being the plaything or the victim of the wild genius of the times must examine actions, not words.[47] Edmund Burke, grown old and angry, is writing too, and writing as usual like a man to whom blindness in one respect has given profounder vision in another. At the moment he is pouring forth anathema[48] on friend and foe alike. He sees no genius in the times at all, only a raucous devil-worship, but he sees clearly enough with vain anger that the Coalition against France, stronger in brawn than in brain, is injuring the cause for which it is fighting. While the young poets of the day, the friends of the People, the liberal-minded statesmen, and all who had hoped for the birth of a better world, are lamenting that the menace of the allied forces is goading the Revolution into madness, he, who would only wish to see it foam itself out in madness and shame, realises that the Coalition is welding what he would fain regard as a "revolutionary faction" into a People; that it is calling forth from the revolutionists a terrible and formidable nervous energy which has endless powers of resistance; that—even to the counter-revolutionaries in France—the force of "English, Spaniards, Neapolitans, Sardinians, Austrians, Hungarians, Sclavonians, Croatians" advancing upon France must seem less like an advance of friends coming to their assistance than like the gathering together of all the hereditary foes of a distracted country about "to be fought for as a carrion carcass and picked to the bone by all the crows and vultures of the sky."

William Hazlitt as yet does not know any of these. He knows only that he wants to write. He has indeed written "some things," but has finished nothing. How can he finish anything when even to himself he seems to cast the slough of his existence daily! Yet there is great nervous strength in him. He is determined to prove himself. He hopes; and he perseveres.

4

The first clear glimpse we get of our future Essayist during his college days is in connection with his refusal to write an essay. We realise from his account of the incident how difficult, in his obstinate uncurbed individualism, he must have been to deal with in a community of students. Yet he could have done no other than he did, for his temperament made it impossible for him to tread the beaten way in matters of thought, or to consume gratefully such thistles as chanced to be flung to him by way of intellectual provender. Had his integrity been less unflawed, he would have been much easier to handle.

It was his absorption in his own writing that brought about the conflict. Young Mr. Corrie, his classical tutor, was accustomed to suggest "themes" on which the students were required to exercise their powers of thought and writing. Possibly the exercise was profitable enough to most of the students, but to one who might have said like an earlier youthful rebel against intellectual constriction:

"I have some naked thoughts that rove about[49]
And loudly knock to have their passage out,"

and whose mind was at the time drooping with the pressure of its own thought, it seemed almost an insult that he should be required to turn aside from his chosen way and spend his time in writing mechanical exercises on subjects on which his mind was not functioning or which were alien to his temperament—his "genius," as he was wont to call it, using the word in this restricted sense. He might as well have been asked to amuse himself with a top. A student with more of the instinct of self-protectiveness and less mental courage might have strapped together a set of mechanical phrases that would have received their due meed of mechanical criticism, and might thus easily have avoided friction. William Hazlitt, who had never written for the sake of writing, to whom already writing was the difficult garnering of truth attained through hard thinking, found it impossible to do this.

Accordingly, at the end of the week, when Mr. Corrie summons him to read his theme, we see him very ill at ease—for he has nothing to show—and uncommonly sulky-looking. He cannot express what he feels about the futility of mechanical exercises in writing, so he looks at the floor and says only that he has not written an essay. Mʳ. Corrie's manner is sharp as he answers:

"You should have a very good reason indeed, sir, for neglecting it."

"Why, really, sir, I could not write it."

"Did you never write anything in your life?"

"Yes, sir, I have written some things."

"Very well, then, go along and write your theme immediately."

Being dismissed thus peremptorily, he sits for an hour looking at his paper, jotting down a word or two on it now and again; but by this time he is really incapable of writing, and this forcing of his mind and mood, to which he is unaccustomed, has brought on some signs of nervous distress. When Mr. Corrie's bell summons him at the end of the hour, for a lecture, he is more sullen than ever, and his eyes look swollen. At the end of the lecture, Mr. Corrie, who is puzzled by him but who has thought the matter out in the meantime and who realises from his pupil's distressed look that this is not an ordinary case of impertinence or disobedience, that young Hazlitt is labouring under some pressure of feeling and evidently feeling himself badly used, calls him back, and asks him again, quite gently this time, whether it is possible that he has never written anything in his life. He replies again that he has written "several things." Mr. Corrie, still speaking gently, asks if he may be allowed to see any of these compositions, whereupon "Mr. Hazlitt" goes with alacrity to his papers, and returns with part of an Essay on Laws he had written. The tears are in his eyes as he hands it over to be read. Mr. Corrie looks over it, asks a few questions, is struck by the intelligence of the way in which he is answered, and says finally: "I wish you'd write some more such things as this."

"Why, sir! I intended to write several things which I have planned, but that I could not write any of them in a week, or two or three weeks."

"What did you intend to write?"

He replies that first of all he intended to enlarge and improve upon the Essay on Laws.

"Ay!" says Mr. Corrie. "I wish you would."

"I will do it then, sir."

Mr. Corrie, perhaps realising now that the grey eyes which so seldom look into his directly are very shy, rather than sullen, says kindly: "Do so, and take your own time now; I shall not ask you for it; only write it as soon as you can, for I shall often be thinking of it, and very desirous of seeing it."

This contest, and the issue of it, are worth recording, because they determined his development while at college. He attends to the routine work satisfactorily enough, but all his thoughts are on his writing. No sooner has he expanded the Essay on Laws, than it appears that this essay is only a fragment of a larger essay, on The Political State of Man. He works at this theme, and places in Corrie's hands the introduction to it, whereupon he is told to proceed with the essay itself. At length he has completed the first half of it.

But now his father, hearing constantly of this writing progressing from week to week, begins to feel that things are not going quite as he would wish, that his son is exhausting himself over work of a kind which after all he has not been sent to Hackney to do, and begins to try to persuade him to discontinue work on this interminable essay. He is not reassured when William replies that so far is his writing from exhausting him or making him gloomy and low-spirited that he is never so perfectly happy as when he is engaged on it. He feels it to be of vital importance to his own development, and acts accordingly.

Mr. Hazlitt at length begins to think he had better come up to town himself to see what William is doing. William thinks only of the joy of the prospect, wishes that his mother and sister could come too.

He writes more of Corrie than of his other tutors, because Corrie took an interest in his personality and in his writing, but it is of Dr. Rees that he writes with most affection. Dr. Rees, ever since the college had been opened, had lived in the house contiguous to it, and had acted as resident tutor. He is now the only member of the original band of tutors left. Gentle Kiddle and Mrs. Kiddle who looked after "the family" have gone long since; Dr. Kippis, who travels about the country a good deal, no longer has time to give his lectures on Belles Lettres; Gilbert Wakefield has passed through it like a bird of storm; a year after his departure stormier Priestley has come, to read lectures on History; others have come and gone who are but names to us. But Dr. Rees remains through all brunts and changes. He has now become part of the college, and the kindliness of his personality makes him much loved. So kindly is he, that unlike any of his colleagues, he has even a gracious word to say for universities that exclude Nonconformists. The students call him affectionately "Dominie." "I like Dominie," [50] William writes home to his father, "and his lectures very much." "Dominie" lectures to him on Mathematics, and under Dominie's tuition he passes the Ass's Bridge "very safely and solitarily," he tells his father. In his next letter he has to answer his father's inquiry as to what the Ass's Bridge is: "By the by, the Ass's Bridge is the tenth proposition of the geometry."

Of Belsham, the assistant resident tutor, who lived in the college with the students and who lectured to them on Hebrew, he says little, although he brackets Belsham's lectures along with "Dominie's" as being interesting: "I like Hebrew very well, the mathematics very much. They are very much suited to my genius." He says little also of Priestley, although he observed him closely. Corrie was quick to see the possibilities of the obstinate student from Wem, and to humour his idiosyncrasy, but there is nothing to show that Priestley ever noticed specially the erstwhile defender whose shy grey eyes so seldom met his—although now and again they cast upon his an upward glance, fleeting yet searching—but whose pen was afterwards to estimate his personality so clearly and accurately. Hard-driven Priestley has doubtless more to do at this period of his vexed life than to concentrate on his students, no matter how full of promise they may be. He has cares and preoccupations enough at the moment—especially those connected with his projected emigration to America.

In one respect, Mr. Hazlitt was quite right. His William is working far too hard, is indeed, although he does not realise it himself at the time, injuring himself "irreparably" by over-study. His day begins at seven in the morning, and goes on, with little relaxation except an hour and a half for walking, until eleven o'clock at night. It is difficult to see, from the time-table he outlines for his father, when he takes time to eat and drink. He attended in the course of his first year lectures on Greek Grammar, Greek and Latin Literature and Antiquities, Hebrew, History, Geography, Logic, Mathematics and Shorthand. The preparation for these lectures takes up a fair amount of his time. In addition there is his writing; and he spends the last hour and a half of the day, from half-past nine until eleven, which is supposed to be his bedtime, reading David Hartley. Possibly he prolongs his reading much later into the night. He reads with extreme interest; yet without much satisfaction, for he feels always as if Hartley is eluding some essential problem. His reading leaves him with a heightened perception of the value of the classics, "surviving all the shocks of accident and fluctuations of opinion," and with a grateful sense of their enduring quality, proving to him that there is something "really great and excellent in the world." He feels already, dimly, that their beauty is the corrective to the impression left on him by such reasoning as Hartley's, tending to falsify and belittle the nature of the soul of man.

5

When his father, towards the close of 1793, had tried to dissuade him from continuing to work upon his essay, William had defended the value and urged the necessity of the work he was doing, in terms

which show that he was engaged on no less a task than trying to work
out for himself a reasoned political creed. While many of the students
around him were far more advanced in opinion than he was himself,
their zeal was often less the effect of any conviction profoundly
engraven upon their minds than of "the wild and irregular enthusiasm
of youth." Without knowing it, they were merely worshipping the
echo of the times, and being without reasoned conviction they were
apt to be driven this way or that by every wind that blew upon their
lives. Hazlitt already wanted more than this.[51] He was already
temperamentally averse to drifting with the stream, to sailing before
the breeze. Being "nothing if not critical," he may have felt dimly
that the cant of democracy was already in the air, and that he wanted
to separate it from the reality, for he cared as little for the cant of
democracy as for the cant of aristocracy. He would not let himself
be carried away into any avowal of republican sympathies, like many
of those around him; yet his belief was that the best government of
the People was by the People and for the People, and he wished to
express for himself and to test the train of reasoning that had led
to this belief, so that he might be able to justify his faith both to
himself and to others, and so that he might have a creed to which he
could adhere through all vicissitudes, although he did not exclude
the possibility that he might have to revise or modify it in such ways
as might seem to him necessary and reasonable in the light of what he
read or of what he experienced in later years. While a young Breton
emigré named François René Chateaubriand, whom he might have
brushed against in the street any day he went to visit his brother in
Long Acre, was at work in semi-starvation in a poor room in Holborn
on an attempt to clarify his feeling towards the Revolution, and
floundering in the meantime between the new ideas and the old,
William Hazlitt, although ten years his junior, was writing to his
father in the following direct and purposeful strain: "My chief reason
for wishing to continue my observations is, that by having a particular
system of politics, I shall be better able to judge of the truth or falsehood of any principle which I hear or read, and of the justice or the
contrary of any political transactions. Moreover, by comparing my
own system with those of others, and with particular facts, I shall have
it in my power to correct and improve it continually. But I can have
neither of those advantages unless I have some standards by which to
judge of, and of which to judge by, any ideas or proceedings I may
meet with."

The events of 1794 cannot but have whetted his interest in the
political state of man, and intensified his sense of the value of the work
on which he was engaged, its necessity, at least for himself, if he were
to keep himself from being swept off his feet in the political passion of
the moment; for one thing after another happened in the course of

the year, which created excitement enough throughout the country, but which touched very closely and intimately indeed the life of Hackney College and the lives of those associated with it. First of all there was the agitation connected with the sentence that had been passed on Thomas Fyshe Palmer. The legality of the atrocious sentence passed on him had been called in question, and both his case and that of Muir came before the House of Commons on March 10th. Fox made a noble appeal, not for mercy, but for justice. Pitt, on the other hand, in what has been called "perhaps the worst speech of his whole career," [52] denied that there had been any miscarriage of justice, condoned any irregularities that had characterised the trials, and defended even the packing of the jury in Muir's trial, which had been presided over by Braxfield the notorious. The sentences were upheld and both Palmer and Muir were transported.

In the impression made on him by this speech may perhaps be found the origin of the dislike, bordering on contempt, which Hazlitt afterwards showed consistently towards Pitt, and of the bitterness which he afterwards compressed into the sentence: "I would avoid the arm of power, as I would escape from the fangs of a wild beast."

Earlier in the year Priestley had come to the conclusion that the only course left to him was to emigrate. On April 7th he embarked at Gravesend, and the college and its students, who had presented to him "an affectionate Address" before his departure, saw him no more. Nor, indeed, did England see him any more. He may have realised by this time that it was not only in England that the friends of Liberty, in these times of "dereliction and dismay," fared badly. Even in liberated France some of them are falling on evil days. Tom Paine no longer visits Hackney College to have rollicking "republican" suppers with the students. He eats "republican" suppers indeed, but in the Luxembourg now, where he lies with plenty of time to reflect on the No-Rights of Man under a Rights-of-Man *régime*. He will be lucky, in these whirling days, if he escape having his republican head whirled off—like many another—to glut the appetite of a republic that has begun to crave the blood of her own children.

Priestley had not been gone a month before the arm of power reached out again and touched the life of one closely connected with the college. This was the Rev. Jeremiah Joyce, who since he had completed his course at the college, had been acting as tutor to the sons of Lord Stanhope. He had become a member both of the London Corresponding Society and of the Society for Promoting Constitutional Information. On May 4th he was arrested at Lord Stanhope's house at Chevening, Kent, on the charge of "treasonable practices." On May 19th he was committed to the Tower. Among others who came to London to see him was Mr. Shepherd of Gateacre, who was untiring in his efforts to be of assistance. Mr. Shepherd during his stay in

London paid a visit to the college, dined there—no doubt renewed his acquaintance with young William Hazlitt, now altered almost out of recognition.

Joyce was charged along with other members of the Corresponding Society and the Society for Promoting Constitutional Information more distinguished than he, the chief of them being Thomas Hardy, Horne Tooke, Thelwall and Holcroft. When the trials came on in October the excitement in London, where troops had to be called out to keep the crowds around the Old Bailey under control, and throughout the country, reached fever height. The morning after Hardy's acquittal we get a glimpse of a young man—on whom we are accustomed to look as a model of sobriety—running through the streets of Colchester at six in the morning with a newspaper in his hand, knocking on his friends' doors and crying out "Not Guilty! Not Guilty!" The young man sending this excited cry through the mists of a November morn is Henry Crabb Robinson, afterwards to be well known to us.

We can guess that the excitement in Hackney College was even more intense, and that it reached its climax when Joyce among others was acquitted and discharged, like Holcroft, without trial, it being, of course, inevitable from the moment Hardy and Horne Tooke were acquitted, that the lesser men should be released.

Such things provide plenty of food for meditation to a thoughtful youth nearing his seventeenth birthday, who for over two years has been striving to give expression, soundness, and cohesion to his political creed.

Nor were other intellectual stimulants lacking during this year. One night in November Samuel Taylor Coleridge, whom last we saw as a threadbare open-mouthed undergraduate at William Frend's trial, clapping his hands for joy when a point was scored in Frend's favour, picked up in a friend's room at Cambridge after supper a translation of *Die Räuber*, sat down at twelve o'clock to read it, found himself trembling "like an aspen leaf," shaken perhaps by some obscure premonition of his own fate, as he considered "this picture of a great misguided soul, endowed with every gift of excellence, yet lost in spite of all its gifts,"[53] because the deep taint of vices had been allowed "with slow perdition"[54] to murder the whole man, and at one in the morning wrote to his friend Robert Southey: "My God, Southey, who is this Schiller, this convulser of the heart?"

The translation of *The Robbers* reaches the college at Hackney, is passed round there, is read by ardent spirits. William Hazlitt too reads it—it is the first tragedy he has ever read[55]—and he feels the reading of it to be a profound experience, comparable in its effect on him to the first seeing of Mrs. Siddons. He is startled and half-stunned; yet he is sensible of a strong aspiration and a deep impulse towards good arising in him. Ever afterwards he associated the effect produced by the reading of it with that produced by the acting of Mrs. Siddons: " We do not read the tragedy of *The Robbers* twice; if we have seen Mrs. Siddons in Lady Macbeth once, it is enough. The impression is stamped there for ever."

6

Belsham grieved because many of the students under his care had "given up Christianity." We take this opportunity of saying that William Hazlitt was never among these. We note the same tendency to judge for himself, and the same refusal to let himself be swept off his feet by the moods of those around him, the fashion of the moment, or the cant of the hour, in his attitude to religious as well as to political discussion. While experiencing some intellectual difficulties as to the faith in which he had been bred, now as always his attitude towards it was both tender and reverent. He detested the cant of scepticism, and anything in the nature of irreverence was both offensive and wounding to him. In one of his reminiscences of this year he touches on the tone of some of the conversation to which he listened and on the way in which it affected him: "I remember being present in a large party composed of men, women and children, in which two persons of remarkable candour and ingenuity were labouring (as hard as if they had been paid for it) to prove that all prayer was a mode of dictating to the Almighty, and an arrogant assumption of superiority. A gentleman present, said, with great simplicity and *naïveté*, that there was one prayer which did not strike him as coming exactly under this description, and being asked what that was, made answer . . . "*Lord, be merciful to me a sinner!*" This appeal by no means settled the sceptical dogmatism of the two disputants, and soon after the proposer of the objection went away; on which one of them observed with great marks of satisfaction and triumph—'I am afraid we have shocked that gentleman's prejudices.' This did not appear to me at that time quite the thing, and this happened in the year 1794."[56]

In 1795 we find him deeply absorbed in the effort to distinguish between what was true and what was false in the system of metaphysics for which most of those around him were enthusiasts, and here, too, we find that his pursuit of truth drives him into taking up an independent position. This undeviating search for truth, pursued with all the intensity of his rapidly developing consciousness, presently leads him into deep waters. Among his tutors, two at least, Belsham and Priestley, were enthusiastic admirers of English experientialist and empirical philosophy. Both of them had eulogised in public "that philosophy which the sagacity of Locke first recovered from darkness and barbarism, which the comprehensive genius of Hartley has exhibited in open day; and which the ingenious labours of succeeding philosophers of the greatest name have placed within the reach of ordinary capacities." Belsham defined this as "the philosophy of mind."[57]

The student under their care could not accept this enthusiasm unreservedly. We have seen that in the winter of 1793 Hazlitt had fallen into the habit of reading Hartley before bedtime; and that he was not finding the reading wholly satisfactory. More and more he found that it teased rather than satisfied his mind. Sometimes he felt oppressed by the way in which Hartley always reasoned from the concrete object, never from the abstract or essential properties of things. This made him feel rather as he imagined a creature must feel when shut up in wood, wedged in and enclosed by matter, from which no escape seemed possible. And he had more and more, in spite of Belsham's praise of Hartley as being the philosopher of the mind, the sense that Hartley was failing to get at the nature of the mind itself, was doing little more than presenting a dissected map of the brain, as if, having failed to get at the mind, he were satisfying himself with "vicariously torturing and defacing its nearest representative in matter." As for the soul—all Hartley seemed to him to do was to beg the nature of it by proving it to his own satisfaction to be something like a white curd, and then on the assumption that this white curd was the human soul, to lay claim to giving some account of the human soul through the analysis of this pseudo-Psyche of his own invention. This analysis of a pseudo-Psyche seemed to him to have so little relation to the nature and operations of the Psyche itself that it aroused infinite dissatisfaction in him.

He had not as yet the reasoning power that would enable him to challenge the interpretation of mind given by the empiricists, that it is itself with all its operations nothing but matter and motion; no one had ever told him as yet that to the axiom *nihil in intellectu quod non prius in sensu,* Leibnitz had added the "sublime" restriction, *nisi intellectus ipse*; but the feeling that Hartley was evading rather than explaining the nature of consciousness and his desire to get at the root of the matter drove him further afield among such books of philosophy as were to be found in the college library. He now plunged into the study of metaphysics with such ardour "as to make a toil of a pleasure," for the subject had taken hold of him, and he being nothing if not passionate, it was his way to pursue a conflict, even a conflict with an idea, *à l'outrance.* The dry and powerful work of Hobbes was not yet accessible to him, and from Locke, as from Hartley, he derived little satisfaction. Proceeding to the French philosophers, he found that these pushed the line of Hartley's thought still further. Hartley had in the end seen the impossibility of identifying matter and motion with the nature of thought, and, being himself greater than his own system, he had been content to leave his system imperfect. But his followers "soon had all its deficiencies supplied, and its doubts cleared up, to the entire satisfaction of all the dull, the superficial, and the ignorant." As he ranged through these—through Helvétius, Condillac, Mirabaud, Baron d'Holbach, La Rochefoucault, Condorcet and others, his mind began to settle on one idea, which he found meeting him everywhere in the work of the English and French metaphysicians of the past two-centuries, explicit in some, merely implicit in others, but present everywhere, so much so that it seemed to him to be the cornerstone of their philosophy. This was the doctrine "that Man is a purely sensual and selfish animal, governed solely by a regard either to his immediate gratification or future interest." He had of course been nurtured in faith in the gradual improvement and ultimate perfectibility of Man. The quality of the idealism bred in him can best be estimated from the measure in which this metaphysical doctrine of the innate and necessary selfishness of the human mind shocked and distressed him. It seemed to him to turn the idea of virtue into a fable, and thus to negative all hope of man's progress. Seeing that already he always argued from first principles, he felt that if it could not be disproved it annulled the value of all human effort, for it had that in it, which if not combated, would inevitably paralyse the will and seal the spring of human action. At times the burden of his vexed thought seemed to him to weigh down his body like a porter's burden.

From the dejection to which it reduced him, he at last roused himself, resolved at least to combat this doctrine with all his might, for he felt not only that it was hateful, but that it was false. His mind constantly hovered about it, watching for a point at which it could be attacked, hawk-like "returning in endless circles with suspended wings," yet unable to find the point at which to strike. It is one thing to disbelieve and repudiate; it is another to be able to disprove. But he knows that he will have no peace until he has done battle on this foe.

In the meantime, he dwells in his thoughts on such spiritual correctives as he knows. As yet he does not know the true corrective, a glance at the paintings of Raphael or Correggio. Twenty-seven years afterwards, when art seemed to him the best witness to the divine element in the mixed nature of Man, he recommended these to his son: "The best antidote I can recommend to you hereafter against the disheartening effect of such writings as those of Rochefoucault, Mandeville and others, is to look at the pictures of Raphael and Correggio."

Surely this tender attempt, made many years afterwards, at shielding his son from the poison of rank or cynical thought, is the most trustworthy witness as to the extent to which he felt the trouble of this idea had sunk into his soul.

Does it seem strange that he should care so much? Is the account he gives of his suffering credible? To us it seems not only perfectly credible, but inevitable, he being what he was. But lest there be any to whom such distress seems merely fantastic, we would remind the reader that his suffering was not unique. There was at least one other of his contemporaries who suffered in much the same way. The struggle William Wordsworth went through in that year was similar in kind, although it was the teaching of William Godwin that had come near to paralysing the springs of feeling and action in William Wordsworth. Such as these, men cast in an unusual mould, were as sensitive to ideas as those cast in a more ordinary mould are to actual physical blows. Any shade of falsity was like a merciless goad to their minds. Untruth or insincerity pierced more keenly than a spear. We have their own record that it was so. They have told us all about their struggle except that which "lies far hidden from the reach of words."

In such reading, writing, and speculation, added voluntarily to the ordinary routine of work in the college, our young William of the restless *hunting* mind might have worn himself out, were it not that fortunately for him, during the two years he was at Hackney, the week-end usually brought with it change and distraction. John Hazlitt was now married and living in Long Acre; often he came out to Hackney on the Saturday or Sunday and at least once a fortnight William went to his brother's home. His account of the discussion on prayer, the tone of which jarred on his ears in the year 1794, suggests that during these visits he began to touch the fringes of the world in which Godwin and Holcroft moved, and to receive its stimulus, while yet he viewed it critically. He may have met at his brother's house some of the painters of the day also. Apart from these visits, he found his chief relaxation in the theatre. He could only afford to go once or twice a year, but he lived in retrospect so richly in what he had seen that this delight became an integral part of his life. Indeed, Mrs. Siddons contributed so greatly to his development that she stands in the front rank of those who helped to make him a writer. Her influence on him was no less profound than that of Burke, Rousseau, or Coleridge, and it was earlier. It was from her that his genius received its first profound excitation, for it was she who first made him realise the nature of his underconscious mind. To the retired and lonely student, weeping unnoticed in the gallery, it seemed as if the lightning of her eye, flashing right through his soul, startled out of its depths his inmost thoughts, as if her voice, circling through his labouring breast, roused deep and scarce-known feelings from a long slumber. So deeply could she arouse in him a capacity for emotion of which he had been quite unconscious, that for weeks after seeing her in her greatest parts, it would seem to him that she had robbed him of his ordinary identity, or transported him into a mode of being hitherto unknown to him. At such times, while he felt not unlike one who had been staggered by a blow, he seemed to those around him stunned and torpid. Yet his life had received quickening from her, and also, in the release of feeling he experienced through her, it had received healing. She loosened the constriction about his heart and the tension that locked his nerves at a time when such loosening was of all things the most necessary to him.

From others he derived sheer amusement, from King, "whose acting left a taste on the palate, sharp and sweet like a quince:" it was ever a delight to him to watch King in Sir Anthony Absolute or Sir Peter Teazle. No less a favourite was Jack Bannister, as Lenitive in *The Prize*, coming "out of his shell like the aurelia out of the grub" when the beau becomes superimposed on the apothecary, and "shining like a gilded pill." But next to Mrs. Siddons he loved Mrs. Jordan, for she too gave him something of which his life at that time stood in need, the rich golden sunshine of her personality. There was some comfort even in looking at her person, "which was large, soft, and generous as her soul." Her voice gladdened him like wine; to hear her jolly laugh was to drink nectar; her singing was "the very twang of Cupid's bow." She seemed to exude enjoyment of life. There was something about her that defied care. Here was "Cleopatra turned into an oyster-wench, without knowing that she was Cleopatra or caring that she was an oyster-wench. An oyster-wench, such as she was, would have been equal to a Cleopatra; and an Antony would not have deserted her for the empire of the world."

She made him feel, as he watched her, once more as he had felt when a child, that his cup was filled to the brim with pleasure. He could forget every care—except one.

As for that one—it now met him at every turn. The cloud, at first no bigger than his own hand, which had first appeared on the horizon three years before, now seemed at times to cover the whole sky. Somehow or other he had drifted into a false position, both with regard to his father and with regard to the college. He realises fully now that he cannot accept his father's faith except with such reservations as would make it dishonest for him to follow his father into the Unitarian ministry. It is not that he is an atheist. He believes in God, and—as we have said—he feels the utmost tenderness towards and reverence for Christianity; never does he hear it scoffed at or spoken lightly of without wincing; nor is any attack on religion itself a passport to his favour. Any note of irreverence, flippancy, or even hardness introduced into an argument on religion is hateful to him, for both his temperament and his training have made religion sacred in his eyes. Yet he has found no way of reconciling his faith with his reason. And his increasing nonconformity of mind and temper, which makes of him an ultra nonconformist within the ranks of what we might call orthodox nonconformity itself, which will one day make of him a man apart even among his own folk and among those whose political faith is in most respects like his own—makes it impossible for him to accept anything on trust. He is nonconformist in another degree even than those around him. Here is the one who pushes nonconformity, in every reaction towards life, *à l'outrance*, so that it threatens to disrupt Nonconformity itself, who feels its value as an attitude of mind, who tends to identify it with integrity, believing that it requires some fortitude to oppose one's opinion to that of all the world, none at all to agree with it. Here, in fact, is the first great and original writer since Bunyan to be bred of the struggle of English Nonconformity, of its tradition, and of its thorny "genius."

Even apart from his difficulties with regard to the *minutiæ* of faith and his deep temperamental aversion to identifying himself with any creed, he has other misgivings. For one thing, he does not now feel himself suited to be a minister. He knows that such a life as his father's, which he sometimes feels to be lived "'twixt the sleep and wake," would be impossible for him. All his interests are turned away from it; his instincts shrink from it; and the youth and energy in him repudiate it as being not life but rather a waking dream, even although a dream "of infinity and eternity, of death, the resurrection, and a judgment to come." He feels that it would be a poor thing to barter away for any dream the sharpened realities of sense and reason.

Also, he may have felt intuitively that for one of his temperament the restrictions of clerical life would be ruinous, driving him either towards excess or towards hypocrisy.

It seems likely that he came to an understanding with his father on this point at the close of his second year at Hackney, for he was withdrawn from the college in the course of the summer of 1795. As to his not returning there during the year 1795-1796, and finishing his course as a lay student, we can only conjecture that it was impossible for Mr. Hazlitt to keep him there any longer, when the special grants and terms available only for Divinity students could be his no more.

We know that it was an enduring regret to him to have to frustrate in this way his father's dearest desire, but he could not gratify it without giving the lie to his own soul, and that he could not do. As to what Mr. Hazlitt and his friends felt about the matter, the letter written to Mr. Hazlitt by kind Dr. Kippis on August 14th indicates sufficiently:

"DEAR SIR,—I should have written to you much sooner, but have met with various hindrances, and, particularly, have been upon a long tour to South Wales. Now I do sit down to write, what can I say to you? I can only say that I sincerely sympathise with you in your affliction. I deeply feel for your distress and disappointment, and wish that I could impart to you any sufficient thoughts or words of consolation. At any rate, you have the consciousness of your own integrity to support you. You have done everything in your power to make your son a wise and useful man, and may we not hope that he will be a wise and useful man in some other sphere of life? What the other sphere will be I cannot point out, nor is it probable that I can be of service to him in any line from that for which he was originally intended.

"It grieved me that he could not have a ten pounds which I had procured for him; but the donations are appropriated, by will, to students for the ministry and designing to continue such. . . .

"I am, dear Sir,

"Your very affectionate friend and servant,

"AND. KIPPIS."

7

So William of Wem is not to be allowed his "bounty" of £10. No matter! Before he leaves the college he has already won for himself a proud consolation which will support him through that, and through much heavier losses. What his other sphere is to be Dr. Kippis cannot point out. This too matters the less, because he himself knows that he has received election to his other sphere. His sphere has made choice of him, not he of it, and therefore his confidence is the greater. In other words, before he had left the college he had experienced the moment which had called upon him to consecrate himself to the pursuit and the interpretation of Truth. There is no predicting the way in which such moments come. The moment of consecration had come to William Wordsworth some years before, in

". . . all the sweetness of a common dawn,
       Dews, vapours, and the melody of birds,
       And Labourers going forth into the fields."

The moment came to William Hazlitt within the four walls of his study, when poring over Baron d'Holbach's *Systéme de la Nature*. For months he had been patiently soliciting his mind, in the endeavour to find some flaw in the doctrine of man's innate selfishness. For months, as we have seen, his thoughts had hovered over this doctrine, "hawk-like, in endless circles, with suspended wings." Now they dart "right forward in one level line upon their prey." In one moment all is clear to him. At last he sees where to strike at the coil that has come near to strangling the life of his spirit and his hopes for the progress of Man. He has received his "call"—will lose no time in answering it.

Three times in his after life he tried to express something of what this moment in his life meant to him. All these passages are memorable. The first is content to describe the moment itself:

"There are moments in the life of a solitary thinker which are to him what the evening of some great victory is to the conqueror and hero—milder triumphs long remembered with truer and deeper delight. And though the shouts of the multitudes do not hail his success, though gay trophies, though the sounds of music, the glittering of armour, and the neighing of steeds do not mingle with his joy, yet shall he not want monuments and witnesses of his glory, the deep forest, the willowy brook, the gathering clouds of winter, or the silent gloom of his own chamber, 'faithful remembrancers of his high endeavour, and his glad success,' that as time passes by him with unreturning wing, still awaken the consciousness of a spirit patient, indefatigable in the search of truth, and a hope of surviving in the thoughts and minds of men."[58]

In the second passage it is on the divine sense of release experienced by him that he dwells:

"Oh! how little do they know, who have never done anything but repeat after others by rote, the pangs, the labour, the yearnings and misgivings of mind it costs, to get the germ of an original idea—to dig it out of the hidden recesses of thought and nature, and bring it half-ashamed, struggling, and deformed into the day—to give words and intelligible symbols to that which was never imagined or expressed before! It is as if the dumb should speak for the first time, or as if things should stammer out their own meaning, through the imperfect organs of mere sense."[59]

In the third passage he emphasises his sense of consecration:

"I owed something to truth, for she had done something for me. Early in life I had made (what I thought) a metaphysical discovery; and after that, it was too late to think of retracting. My pride forbad it: my understanding revolted at it. I could not do better than go on as I had before. I too, worshipped at no unhallowed shrine, and served in no mean presence. I had laid my hand on the ark, and could not turn back."[60]

Life had quickened for him during his last year at Hackney, but it had also thickened. Now it has lightened again. Once more, we make use of his own words:

"From that time I felt a certain weight and tightness about my heart taken off, and cheerful and confident thoughts springing up in the place of anxious fears and sad forebodings. The plant I had sown and watered with my tears, grew under my eye; and the air about it was wholesome and pleasant. For this cause it is, that I have gone on little discomposed by other things, by good or adverse fortune, by good or ill report, more hurt by public disappointments than my own. . . ." [61]

His fortune was indeed to be adverse, for he has been chosen to go against ills, and he was to find that "*Tu ne cede malis*" [62] is a hard word of command. To some of those around him his conduct appeared perverse. He appeared to be going against Fortune, to be flying in the face of Fortune. He was very lonely. With many, as he said afterwards rather bitterly, not only at that time, but for some years to come, he "passed for an idiot;" even those near to him could not give him much sympathy; the best they could offer him was a patient tolerance. He was to find it exhausting to be always striving against the stream. But the joy within him "dallied with distress." The consolation that had come to him was all-sufficient. If he had to do without the approbation of others, to live day by day without encouragement and support, he knew that he was obeying the law of his own nature. He had, in fact, come to the stage of development which comes to every great and original writer at one point of his life or another. His genius had received the impulse which had made "the unrestrained development of its own powers its ruling passion." As for the risks he took, already he knew that "one must risk something in order to do anything."

Chapter Two

TOWARDS COLERIDGE (1795-1798)

"His manners are to 99 in 100 singularly repulsive—:
brow-hanging, shoe-contemplative, *strange*."

COLERIDGE.

I

THE NEW COLLEGE at Hackney, although it was all that a small band
of devoted men working under difficulties in times unpropitious to
such an institution could make it, might have been better in many
respects. We have noted the suggestions in contemporary criticism
that it was in some ways crude and undisciplined. Yet it would have
been difficult, in the England of that time, to have found any institution in which Hazlitt could have thriven better. His gains from it were
great. Apart from such benefit as he derived from the curriculum,
probably the least of the benefits he received from the college, he had
there at his disposal for the first time in his life a library which at
least was well stored in those branches of literature in which he most
wanted to read. He came into immediate contact, in a far greater
degree than he would have done in either of the universities, with
tutors who were all of them, if not men of genius, at least men of
mark. Dr. Rees, Corrie, Priestley, Belsham, the lover of truth, with
his characteristic admonition, "Buy the *truth*, and think no price too
dear for the purchase," were all of them no mean men. Above all, the
freedom of thought encouraged, if it endangered the safety of the
college, was the best thing in the world for a mind like his. All he
needed was to be left free to develop without too much interference
from those in authority over him, and this freedom he enjoyed. In
after years, when the sense of the constricting tendency of authority
lay heavy upon his spirit, he glanced back at these opening years in
words which throw a light on all that their freedom meant to him:
"A rose was then doubly sweet, the notes of a thrush went to the
heart, there was ' a witchery in the soft blue sky ' because we could feel
and enjoy such things by the privilege of our human nature, ' not by
the sufferance of supernal power.'"[63] The special bent of his genius
was confirmed there; the interests which nourished its roots were
strengthened.

There were of course losses too. Afterwards he felt that his
education had been too sectarian: "It was my misfortune (perhaps)
to be bred among Dissenters, who look with too jaundiced an eye at

85

others, and set too high a value on their own peculiar pretensions. From being proscribed themselves, they learn to proscribe others, and come in the end to reduce all integrity of principle and soundness of opinion within the pale of their own little communion."[64] The misfortune was perhaps less than he imagined. At any rate, rough as the college was in some ways, wild as some of the students were, it is clear, from the way in which he reacted against the element of cynicism with regard to the bases of human action upon which he came in his metaphysical studies, that from life itself his idealism took no wound while he was there. *That* too, as the wound seemed to him to be all the bitterer and the shock all the more overwhelming when it came, he may have felt as a misfortune. We cannot feel it to be so. His idiosyncrasy had time to grow, unassailed until the time came when it was strong enough to survive and even to digest any assault upon it. As for the narrowness, if his education had begun and ended in the college it would have been a disadvantage, but the teaching he received at the college represented only the first stage of the training of his early manhood; it represented a stage necessary for him, but no sooner had he outgrown it than he was passed on, as soon as he was fit to learn from them, to other agencies and Masters. It should not be forgotten, either, that even while he was at the college he had, as a powerful corrective to any narrowing tendency, the influence of his brief contacts with the life of London itself.

The roots of his genius were undoubtedly established while he was at Hackney. Although we say this, we would emphasise once more that, while the two years he spent there were years of natural development for him and years that strengthened his roots, the deeper training he would need if his genius were ever to put forth a single flower was all to come. The roots are sound and firm; they are hidden, as they should be, in the earth; but as yet there is nothing to show that they are there; as yet they have not put forth a single shoot; the stem and the branches, the leaf and the flower and the fruit are all to come, and they will not come until master gardeners have turned over the soil.

All he has done as yet is to pass through the first stage of his initiation into the movement of life and thought. In the three years that follow his withdrawal from the college he enters upon the second stage. For a short time he is to be his own tutor; but he has trusted himself to his Fate, or as he himself would put it, he has trusted himself to the impulse of his own mind. It will not betray him. This solitary effort, grinding as it is, is also necessary to his development, but as soon as he has disciplined himself so as to profit by the ministry of Master-teachers, the Powers that preside over the destinies of such spirits will show that they have by no means forgotten his needs.

2

He spent most of his time during the remainder of 1795 and during 1796 under his father's roof or his brother's. Of his life at Wem we need say little at the moment, for it went on much the same as in former years, although it was somewhat shadowed perhaps by his father's disappointment in him and by anxiety over the future, and on the other hand, invigorated by his own obstinate faith that he had something to say and by the hope that he might yet prove himself to be a writer. His life in London, however, took a new turn. When we consider that he was at the time obscure and without prospects, we feel that he was singularly fortunate in the way in which he came at once into contact with some of the original writers and thinkers of the day, and with their friends. This no doubt was chiefly due to his acquaintance with Godwin, and his acquaintance with Godwin was due to the friendship there had been between his mother's family and the Godwin family for three generations. Mrs. Hazlitt's grandfather had come from Hull to Wisbeach along with Godwin's grandfather; her father had been friendly with Godwin's father, who had been a dissenting minister at Wisbeach, which he had quitted in 1758; she herself, until her twelfth year, had been the playmate of the Godwin children. It was natural that Godwin, then in the height of his fame, should show some courtesy towards her son, especially towards a son who, although he could not as yet define his ambition with any precision, was certainly tending towards Literature.

Towards Godwin himself Hazlitt had less sympathy than might have been expected, considering the nature of his interests. He had read *Political Justice*, but he had by no means been swept off his feet by it like so many of his contemporaries, because he had discovered some flaws in the reasoning of the apostle of reason, because he found that it did not discriminate too clearly between right and wrong, and because it seemed to him to be spun out of the author's brain rather than evolved from a consideration of nature and the needs of human nature. Nor was he greatly attracted by Godwin himself, who was rather cold in manner, and who as a talker was disappointing. All the vitality of the man seemed to be reserved for his writing. One of the most human things about him was his love of the theatre. When he spoke of seeing *Venice Preserved* in a country town when he was only nine years old, and of the unforgettable impression it had left upon him, he became human and likeable. Hazlitt could fully sympathise with such memories as these. The theatre was still his chief recreation, and he felt very conscious of its human value. It seemed to him a place in which all sorts of people whose lives would otherwise never have met, could rally round the standard of their common humanity. To him at the time it was of special service, in drawing away from his mind the dissatisfaction and *ennui* that sometimes plagued him and the depression that threatened to overwhelm him when he felt how little his own efforts and pursuits mattered to the majority of those around him.

Although he was never in complete sympathy with Godwin, the acquaintance was of service to him in that it led to meetings with others who were of interest to him. By the autumn of 1796 he had met Mary Wollstonecraft, whose easy playful manner in dealing with Godwin's objections to some opinion she advanced he much admired. He met also angry Holcroft, who blocked him at every point in an argument by such questions as "What do you mean by a sensation, sir?" or "What do you mean by an idea?" Arguing with Holcroft was prickly work. Best of all, he made the acquaintance of Godwin's admired friend, the Rev. Joseph Fawcett, poet and preacher, formerly Unitarian minister at Walthamstow and Sunday evening lecturer at the Meeting-House in Old Jewry, where his preaching had attracted large audiences, including Mrs. Siddons in the height of her fame and William Wordsworth while he was yet obscure. He was one of those who had hoped most from the Revolution in France, who had grieved when it had been tortured into excess, who had sorrowed over the outbreak of war with a people striving for their liberties. This capacity of his for feeling public calamities as men of a narrower and more selfish disposition only feel their own personal sorrows, even if it had been the only generous thing in his character, would have won Hazlitt's respect and affection; but the old man and the young had also many other sympathies in common. Fawcett was now only an occasional visitor in town, for shortly after the Declaration of War he had retired from the ministry and gone to live at Edgegrove in Hertfordshire; but sufficient sympathy had sprung up between the older man, gifted, charming and eloquent, and the young man, gifted indeed, but so shy as to be almost repellent in his manners, and at times tongue-tied in a degree almost painful, to lead to visits to the Hertfordshire home. Hazlitt regarded this friendship as a most precious possession. He wrote afterwards of Fawcett: "He was almost the first literary acquaintance I ever made, and I think the most candid and un-sophisticated." At the time, the harmonious friendship with a man older than himself was of inestimable benefit to him. Fawcett had read much, had enjoyed much, and had the gift of communicating his pleasure to others and of stimulating them to read what he had enjoyed. The two friends discussed literature together to their hearts' content. Sometimes Fawcett, who read excellently, and who had an especial enthusiasm for the poetry of Milton, would read aloud in his "fine, deep, mellow-toned voice," the voice that had drawn great audiences to the Meeting-House in Old Jewry, from *Paradise Lost* or

Comus. These readings from the Poet of Poets Hazlitt found "a feast to the ear and to the soul."

3

But none of these contacts with such men of letters as he met in town helped him in any way to achieve the task which he had set before him and which held possession of his thoughts during this time both by night and by day. Fawcett, who had an affection for him, would no doubt have helped him if he could, but how help one who, despite his efforts to overcome his inexpressiveness, could hardly make himself intelligible when he began to converse on the subject that dominated his thoughts! Before he had left college Hazlitt had known the travail of an original idea. The essential history of the years that follow is the history of the second travail that came to him, the travail of the original writer, inevitably following upon the travail of the original thinker, and no less sore. In his later writing we find the record of this travail. He had found that there is no means of constraining Truth, but that it sometimes reveals itself to those who long and patiently solicit it:

"It comes when least expected, like a thief in the night; it is given to our vows and prayers, to our thoughts ever intent on the unperverted impressions of things. . . . All great truths . . . are owing, not to system, but to accident; the condition of all discovery is to be involuntary . . . the phenomena are infinite, obscure, and intricately woven together, so that it is only by being always alive to their tacit and varying influences, that we can hope to seize on the power that guides and binds them together, by seeing it manifested in some strong aspect or more remarkable instance of the kind. . . .

"But by turning over a subject long and late, these prizes in the wheel turn up oftener; and our incessant vigilance and search, do not go unrewarded."[65]

To despair because "these prizes in the wheel" are slow in coming is a lack of fortitude:

"There is no reason to despair because the required solution does not come in a day; it is well if it comes, ' with healing on its wings ' at the end of years.

". . . the better grounded our hopes are, the more deep and unwearied our aspirations, the less we shall be disposed to anticipate the lucky minute—with the greater fortitude, and mixture of pride and humility, shall we gird ourselves up to our allotted task."[66]

Now as he struggles for expression of the truth he has discovered, he knows that it is with the Word in which truth is expressed, as it is with Truth itself. The Word too cannot be constrained; and it comes only by patient soliciting of the mind. The counterfeit words, or the words that just fall short of inevitability, will come in plenty; but the one word needful "does not come at the moment we want it, but of its own accord afterwards, from the effort we have previously made." When it comes, like Truth, it is unmistakable: "We know when we have got the right word." When a word that is not fully expressive is used, it is an offence against the writer's vocation: "if we take up a wrong word it is wilfully, and because we prefer sloth to sterling pains, the evasion of a difficulty to triumph over it."

While Napoleon Buonaparte is engaged on the conquest of Italy, the young Englishman who was to discern his special greatness and to become his biographer is thus busy with his own necessary preliminary task, the conquest of the Word. All that he wrote of the writer's struggle in later years is coloured by the memory of this first long struggle of his; and always, he insists on patience and watchfulness as the foundations of all true writing:

"The author owes a debt to truth and nature which he cannot satisfy at sight, but he has pawned his head on redeeming it. . . .

"He may turn a period in his head fifty different ways, so that it comes out smooth and round at last. He may have caught a glimpse of a simile, and it may have vanished again: let him be on the watch for it, as the idle boy watches for the lurking-place of the adder. We can wait. . . .

"There is some word, some phrase, some idiom that expresses a particular idea better than any other, but he cannot for the life of him recollect it: let him wait till he does. Is it strange that among twenty thousand words in the English language, the one of all others that he most needs should have escaped him? There are more things in nature than there are words in the English language, and he must not expect to lay rash hands on them all at once."[67]

Of his difficulty in completing his first essay on Political Rights he wrote towards the close of his life: "If from these briars I have since plucked roses, what labour has it not cost me?"

The difficulty, not of completing, but of bringing into being in any shape of form, of the essay On the Disinterestedness of the Human Mind, which lay within his brain, was even greater. The subject in itself was daunting; and he could not find the words in which to clothe his thought. The marvel is that he did not lose heart altogether and turn to lighter work. But that was not his way. That would have been evading a difficulty over which he was resolved to triumph. Perhaps he was sustained by some dim feeling that he was of those who until they can do all, can do nothing—by the hope that one day he might do all.

All we know is that he did not relinquish the struggle.

He does not give up hope, yet the late autumn of 1796 finds him discouraged. On Sunday, October 23rd of that year,[68] he writes from London to his father, who although loving can never give him anything like full comprehension of the nature of his struggle. There is an unusual note of yearning in this letter:

"My dear Father, I write, not so much because I have anything particular to communicate, as because I know that you, and my mother, and Peggy will be glad to hear from me. I know well the pleasure with which you will recognise the characters of my hand, characters calling back to the mind with strong impression the idea of the person by whom they were traced, and in vivid and thick succession, all the ready associations clinging to that idea, and impatience with which you will receive any news which I can give you of myself. I know these things: and I feel them. Amidst that repeated disappointment, and that long dejection, which have served to overcast and to throw into deep obscurity some of the best years of my life, years which the idle and illusive dreams of boyish expectation had presented glittering and gay, and prosperous, decked out in all the fairness and all the brightness of colouring, and crowded with fantastic forms of numerous hues of ever-varying pleasure,—amidst much dissatisfaction and much sorrow, the reflection that there are one or two persons in the world who are [not] quite indifferent to me, not altogether unanxious for my welfare, is that which is, perhaps, the most ' soothing to my wounded spirit.'"

On the following day he gives an account of the essay itself:

"As to my essay, it goes on, or rather it moves backwards and forwards; however, it does not stand still. I have been chiefly employed hitherto in rendering my knowledge of my subject as clear and intimate as I could, and in the arrangement of my plan. I have done little else. I have proceeded some way in a delineation of the system, which founds the propriety of virtue on its coincidence with the pursuit of private interest, and of the imperfections of its scheme. I have written in all about half a dozen pages of shorthand, and have composed one or two good passages, together with a number of scraps and fragments, some to make their appearance at the head of my essay, some to be affixed to the tail, some to be inserted in the middle, and some not at all. I know not whether I can augur certainly of ultimate success. I write more easily than I did. I hope for good. I have ventured to look at high things. I have toiled long and painfully to attain to some stand of eminence. It were hard to be thrown back from the mid-way of the steep to the lowest humiliation."

It is evident that although he has not given up hope, he thinks that the struggle has been hard enough. Yet he has already done more than he knows. He has not yet written much, but his search for truth of thought and truth of word have enabled him to lay the foundations of enduring writing. According to the definition he was later to give of a "true author" as distinguished from a mechanical or commercial writer, he was already, although he seemed frustrated in many ways, a true author:

"Till they can do justice to the feeling they have, they can do nothing. For they look into their own minds, not in the faces of a gaping multitude. What they would say (if they could) does not lie at the orifices of the mouth ready for delivery, but is wrapped in the folds of the heart and registered in the chambers of the brain. In the sacred cause of truth that stirs them, they would put their whole strength, their whole being into requisition. . . .
"Such a person then sees farther and feels deeper than most others. . . . Nature is his mistress, truth his idol. The contemplation of a pure idea is the ruling passion of his breast. . . . What will tell, what will produce an effect, he cares little about, and therefore he produces the greatest. The *personal* is to him an impertinence, so he conceals himself, and writes. Solitude ' becomes his glittering bride, and airy thoughts his children.' Such a one is a true author."[69]

But he has yet a long hard road to travel before he can deliver himself of the "airy thoughts his children." Fortunately, the sympathies, even the dyspathies, that will aid his search and act as solvents to his thought, all unknown to him, are at last about to cross his path. Help such as he could never have dreamed of, such as he could never have consciously sought out for himself, is coming to him, first of all from books, and then from his fellow-man.

4

In 1796 Edmund Burke, now grown old, angry, and sad, is once more attacking[70] "the revolution harpies of France, sprung from night and hell," who "flutter over our heads, and souse down upon our tables, and leave nothing unrent, unrifled, unravaged, or unpolluted with the slime of their filthy offal." As for the consequences of the Revolution: "They shake public security; they menace private enjoyment. They dwarf the growth of the young; they break the quiet of the old." Hazlitt, whose life, far from being dwarfed by the progress of the Revolution, had waxed with it, and would come near in the future to waning with it, comes upon an extract from this *Letter*, the passage which he was ever to consider the finest passage of Burke's prose, that in which the British monarchy is compared to "the proud Keep of Windsor." He notes it one day in the *St. James's Chronicle*, admires it, presently gets hold of the *Letter* in its entirety, is struck dumb with admiration, lays it down, takes it up again in despair to wring from it the secret of its power, again admires, begins to study the texture of the words through which the swell of indignation, sorrow, scorn and irony in the author's soul has been expressed, realises the extent to which literary allusion can be made to play on the strings of feeling, laughs over and exults in the stately play of Miltonic reminiscence.

Here was a writer who also had had to struggle for expression, not for lack of ideas, but because he too had had ideas to which no words fully did justice. Yet the result of the struggle had been that in the end his words were "the most like things" that could be conceived. It was an unqualified triumph, such a triumph on the part of the Master as to leave the rapt pupil flushed and breathless. From this moment all other writers of English prose seemed to Hazlitt completely outclassed. Johnson seems in comparison like one walking on stilts; Junius, whom he had greatly admired, seems now suddenly to shrink up "into little antithetic points and well-trimmed sentences." Burke alone is the man; so he reads and rereads Burke, with almost trembling awe and admiration, learning ever more and more of the secret of this powerful prose, relishing ever more and more the severity it retains even when it is most rhetorical. At length he rises renewed. Now he is learning. If as yet he has not learned to *do*, he has at least learned what will *not do*, knows that he will never rest until he has taught himself to *do*, somewhat after his Master's fashion, yet in his own fashion too. In the irony of fate the cloak of the old man eloquent is about to be claimed by the young man "dumb and a changeling" to whom he seems "the great apostate from liberty and betrayer of his species"—and whom he would, if he could, have crushed out of life as he would have crushed the young of the adder. To him it has been given to make of his words fire in the mouth of his foe. Yet in one thing he was fortunate: the young adversary, so whole-hearted in his admiration of the old man's "eloquence of despair," so whole-hearted in his detestation of what he considered the taint in the old man's thought, was, by reason of the power and passion in him, by reason of the courage too, worthy of any gift he might inherit. He too might have said: "'*Nitor in adversum*' is the motto for a man like me." And foe though he be, he pays fitting tribute to the grand adversary whose pen has taught him something of his own strength and cunning. Nay! because the words placed in his mouth are true fire, there is no knowing when, even in later days, he will suddenly flame out in praise of "the great apostate" whose work he both deplored and adored: "If there are greater prose-writers than Burke, they either lie out of my course of study, or are beyond my sphere of comprehension. I am too old to be a convert to a new mythology of genius. The niches are occupied, the tables are full. If such is still my admiration of this man's misapplied powers, what must it have been at a time when I myself was in vain trying, year after year, to write a single Essay, nay, a single page or sentence; when I regarded the wonders of his pen with the longing eyes of one who was dumb and a changeling; and when, to be able to convey the slightest conception of my meaning to others in words, was the height of an almost hopeless ambition! But I never measured others' excellences by my own defects; though a sense of my own incapacity, and of the steep, impassable ascent from me to them, made me regard them with greater awe and fondness."[71]

Other help comes too. One day he picks up on a stall some of Rousseau's pieces "in a coarse leathern cover," goes home and begins to read them. This too is for him a day of spiritual emancipation. From Rousseau he learns presently to understand somewhat of the movement of his own under-consciousness.

In the meantime, Samuel Taylor Coleridge, him whom we last saw thrusting the noble and puissant locks back from his pale brow and trembling like an aspen leaf as he burned the midnight oil in Cambridge over Schiller's *Robbers*, has himself become a poet. His friend Charles Lamb writes to him of his poems on November 4th, 1796: "I love them, as I love the Confessions of Rousseau. . . ."[72] Before the year is out, Coleridge appears as a poet-prophet. Already, in February, 1795, he had lectured at Bristol on the war as an evil of incalculable magnitude, and had proved to his own satisfaction "its total causelessness."[73] His *Ode to the Departing Year*, published on the last day of December, 1796, after drawing a gentle picture of the beauty and the peace of England, rebukes "the thankless Island" because, though within her own borders she has peace, though her own "herds and cornfields" are secure, though her valleys are fair and unsullied as the bowers of Eden, she has chosen to partake of the evil thing,

"And join'd the wild yelling of Famine and Blood!"

throughout Europe, so that the nations curse her in her island security and immunity. Her downfall is predicted, for one day this curse must reach her and smite upon her security.

His passionate sonnet in praise of *The Robbers* has been published

COLERIDGE IN 1795
By kind permission of the National Portrait Gallery

in the course of the year. Barely another year shall have passed before William Hazlitt too will be carrying Coleridge's Poems in his pocket, will be able to say: "I love them as I love the Confessions of Rousseau," will be thinking, in a transport of admiration, that the author of the sonnet on *The Robbers* is as sure of a place among the Immortals as Schiller himself.

Before this can come to pass Samuel Taylor Coleridge will have moved to a cottage in Nether Stowey, in Somerset; William Words-worth will have moved to the mansion-house of Alfoxden, just three miles away from him; also Samuel Taylor Coleridge will have visited Wem, a little place hitherto unknown to him, by way of Shrewsbury; and William Hazlitt will have been at Wem at the time of his coming. And why do they all do as they will do, this little group of men whose lives are destined to be inextricably woven together? They will each of them no doubt have an excellent reason for their movements. The youngest of them all will say that he moves from Wem to London and from London to Wem because he wants to collect material for his writing and then to have peace to write, and that he oscillates between London and Wem because, until he has mastered his theme and has made himself independent by his writing, he must live under his brother's roof or his father's; a second of them will say that he had moved from his native regions in the North to Racedown, some forty miles from Nether Stowey, because he had been offered a house there rent-free, and that he moved afterwards from Racedown to Alfoxden because there he could secure a good house at a nominal rent and also be near to Coleridge, who had visited him one day at Racedown and had loved him instantly; a third of them will say that he had left Nether Stowey to journey to Shrewsbury because he had lacked the two great necessaries of life, Bread and Cheese, and had thought that possibly the Unitarian congregation at Shrewsbury might have provided him with them.

But perhaps this third of them will have moments when the whole movement of life may seem different to him, when it may seem to him that he does not move at all, but *is moved*:

> "But why drives on that ship so fast,
> Without or wave or wind?"

> "The air is cut away before
> And closes from behind."

5

In later years Hazlitt wrote of 1797 and 1798 as being the happiest years of his life. Is this inconsistent with the yearning and wistfulness of the letter he wrote in the autumn of 1796, with his account of his struggle as a writer, with the description he gave also, in later years, of the state of frustration, almost of prostration, in which the beginning of 1798 found him? Not in the least! If he had been charged with inconsistency in the testimony he gave at various times as to the state of his mind in these years, he would have been ready with his answer: "Truth is not one, but many; and an observation may be true in itself that contradicts another equally true, according to the point of view from which we contemplate the subject."

At times, when he thought of these years of struggle and obscurity, the element of suffering that there had been in them was uppermost in his mind. But it had been largely his inexpressiveness, his fear lest he might never be able to express the movement of his thought, that had made him unhappy. In later years, when he had achieved expression, and this fear had been lifted from him, when he was in the height of his fame, it may well have seemed to him that the lonely youth, who plodded on with his task, writing "a page or two perhaps in half a year," caring not in the least for the approbation of the world, but resolutely bent on attaining truth and integrity of expression, was more in the scale of Nature than the successful journalist, compelled to write so as to please both Public and Editor, and living in a great measure on the fruits of what he had thought, read and experienced during the early austere days; and that the integrity of the struggle during the early years had in itself been sufficient happiness and consolation.

Or the thought of the "full brimming cup of thoughtless freedom" which he had then quaffed may have seemed to him, in retrospect, sufficiently delightful to compensate him for any of the drawbacks of his life at that time:

"I cared for nothing; I wanted nothing. I took my time to consider whatever occurred to me, and was in no hurry to give a sophistical answer to a question—there was no printer's devil waiting for me. . . . If I was not a great author, I could read with ever fresh delight, 'never ending, still beginning,' and had no occasion to write a criticism when I was done. . . . I had no relations to the state, no duty to perform, no ties to bind me to others: I had neither friend nor mistress, wife or child. I lived in a world of contemplation, and not of action. This sort of dreaming existence is the best."[74]

Apart from such fluctuations of feeling, the truth is—he was so constituted that it was of the nature of his unhappiness to have an element of happiness in it and of his happiness to have in it an inseparable element of suffering. There was sometimes a very narrow margin between the state of being which he knew as bliss and the state of being which he knew as suffering, and very often the two states were fused in poignancy. On the whole it would be truer to say of him that he lived poignantly than to say that he lived either happily or unhappily.

The "Friends" of such are "exultations, agonies."

From his reminiscences we gather that he paid the first of the two visits he made during his early manhood to his mother's people at Peterborough, in the course of the autumn and winter of 1797, walking most of the way. There was considerable sympathy of temperament— he tells us—between him and his "old hair-brained uncle," Mr. Loftus, whose taste in pictures was like his own, and his cousin, Tom Loftus, who shared some of his literary enthusiasms. He tends in his reminiscences to fuse or run together his memories of these two visits. We can distinguish, however, as belonging to the first—the joy he felt in the road; the exhilaration of his blood as the wintry sun smote it while he listened to the ploughman driving his team afield or watched the lark mounting in the sky; his glorious sense of freedom; the delight he took in being his own master in the inn at night and setting off again the next morning on a fresh stretch of road, thinking his own long thoughts. In a few words he describes himself as he seemed to himself at the time: "I could at this time do nothing. I could not write a line—I could not draw a stroke. ' I was brutish.' . . . In words, in looks, in deeds, I was no better than a changeling."

But that is not all. There is the other side of the picture. If he has no utterance, he has yet for compensation the swift exhilarating movement of blood and thought: "I had at this time, simple as I seemed, many resources. I could in some sort ' play at bowls with the sun and moon; ' or at any rate, there was no question in metaphysics that I could not bandy to and fro, as one might play at cup-and-ball, for twenty, thirty, forty miles of the Great North Road, and at it again the next day, as fresh as ever. . . . I had my sports and my recreations too. . . ."[75]

His mind at this time was like a greyhound, ever coursing, and the object of its pursuit was always some abstraction or other. In pure, clear prose, sparkling as cold rill water, he refers to the combination of ordinary circumstances which suggested to him a train of thought leading to a refutation of Hartley's doctrine of vibrations. This we quote in illustration of the way in which his mind provided him with entertainment:

"If from the top of a long cold barren hill I hear the distant whistle of a thrush which seems to come up from some warm woody shelter beyond the edge of the hill, this sound, coming faint over the rocks with a mingled feeling of strangeness and joy, the idea of the place about me, and the imaginary one beyond will all be combined together in such a manner in my mind as to become inseparable. Now the doctrine of vibration appears to exclude the possibility of the union of all these into one *associated* idea. . . ."[76]

Similarly, when resting after his day's walking, at the inn at Witham Common, between North and South Witham in Lincolnshire, he noticed or experienced something from which he felt able to deduce the proof of what he had long felt to be true, that likeness was not mere association of ideas. Such was his delight over this train of reasoning that ever afterwards he numbered this inn among those inns, in the regions he traversed when visiting his mother's home country, that for one reason or another were memorable to him. Another such was the inn at St. Neot's, in Huntingdonshire, where some years afterwards he first met with Gribelin's engravings of the cartoons of Raphael.

If he were at times oppressed in spirit during these years, he was also at times gifted with a curious and very beautiful translucency of feeling. He chose to diet himself mainly on metaphysics, yet he was even more a poet at heart than a metaphysician, although as yet—O cruellest of Nature's jokes!—a poet without words.

6

But despite his *sports and his recreations*, his occasional bliss and his moments of felicity, he is now almost at the lowest point of the wheel on which he has been revolving ever since he left his happy childhood behind him in 1790. By the beginning of 1798 the constant sense of frustration is beginning to sap his hope and energy. He feels as if he could do no more. To repeat his own idiom, he is "dumb, inarticulate, helpless, like a worm by the way-side, crushed, bleeding, lifeless." He cannot help himself further, and it seems as if nobody can ever help him. He has reached the end of one stage of his journey, and it looks to him as if he has journeyed thus far only to come out on nothingness. It seems as if for him help there is none.

But help there is, and near him. The Powers that preside over the destinies of such spirits have not forgotten him. This time it is the human aid which we have already foretold for him, that they are granting to his sighs and prayers. They are sending to him the one man on earth whose mission it is to liberate all such spirits. This one has only to knock on the tree, and lo!—the obstinate trunk is riven, and the imprisoned spirit, so long crying within the wood, is no longer "cabined, cribbed, confined," but free to set a girdle round the universe.

7

By the beginning of 1798 Hazlitt had heard of Samuel Taylor Coleridge. Perhaps mention had been made of his name by Godwin and his friends, or possibly Coleridge's fame had already reached Unitarian circles in Shrewsbury and Wem. All who spoke of this young poet-preacher were agreed on one point, that as a conversationalist he was incomparable. Mr. Hazlitt regarded a poet at the best of times as "a kind of nondescript," and although by this time he had grown resigned to the knowledge Dr. Kippis had thrust upon him, that "all the vacancies go to the younger men," he may have heard without enthusiasm that this bustling young poet was being named as a likely successor to Mr. Rowe of Shrewsbury. On the other hand, his son is keenly interested in the prospect of having such a neighbour. He is so much interested that having heard Coleridge is scheduled to preach his trial sermon on the morning of Sunday, January 14th, he gets up before daybreak and walks the ten cold, raw, comfortless miles into Shrewsbury to hear him. He arrives a little late, just as the congregation is singing the hundredth psalm. Little as he knows it, while the voices of the congregation rise and fall in the well-known cadences, his soul is suspended between two states of being, for the moment the psalm is over and the preacher rises, dark and scarred of face, with a touch of prophetic wildness about him suggesting at once the idea of Saint John, of "one crying in the wilderness," the voice of this extraordinary being, floating—it seems—not only through the chapel but throughout the universe as it utters the words: "And he went up into the mountain to pray, HIMSELF, ALONE," overwhelms his imagination and his heart. The moment he meets the fine frenzy in the eyes that look out from under masses of rough, pendulous, raven-black hair, he knows that a shaft of light has pierced into the most secret recesses of his soul. His whole subconscious nature storms towards it. His spirit rushes forth to meet the god. The next moment he is faint and spent as after a crisis; his body feels a mere husk or empty shell; his face is pale as alabaster; he looks half dead. He is either lost—if to have had his soul merged for a moment in another soul is to be lost—or he is found.

How should it be otherwise with him! Here before him is the sublimation of all that heredity and temperament and training have made most dear to him—the heroic look with the suggestion of something suffering and marred in it; the heroic text, with its suggestion of limitless loneliness; the heroic words of the commentary, which to one listener at least seems such as might shake the pillared rottenness of the world; the voice that is not only music but poetry and perfume and passion and the reverberation of all heroic thought. When he sets out on his long walk home, all on which he looks seems the same. The wan sun is still labouring through the clouds, obscured by thick mists; the red leaves of the oak trees rustling in the wind still make an accompaniment to the sound of his footsteps; the cold dank drops of dew still hang half melted on the beard of the thistle; the Welsh hills are still in their place, and he still keeps watching their blue tops through the wintry branches. But the passionate creature William Hazlitt is not the same. He feels, as always, after a deep emotional experience, half stunned, yet with a sense that the momentary torpor is the prelude to new life. He feels at the same moment as if he is half asleep, and as if he is just awakening from deep sleep. He feels as one who has experienced the mystery of elemental forces, as we may conceive the rude clay to feel when the shaft of lightning has visited it; as we may conceive the subterranean spring to feel when the diviner's rod, but for whose pointing it will never know the blessed light of the sun, has first swayed towards it. He feels! . . . But who shall say what he feels! "What a fine instrument the human heart is! Who shall touch it? Who shall fathom it? Who shall sound it from its lowest note to the top of its compass? Who shall put his hand in among the strings, and explain their wayward music?"

8

His experience had been complete in itself, but the diviner of genius has not yet done with him. Coleridge has signified his intention of coming out to Wem to pay his respects to Mr. Hazlitt. William awaits this visit in longing mingled with a touch of dread, for he fears that Coleridge may have heard in Shrewsbury reports to his prejudice— of his obstinate withdrawal from the ministry; "of his repudiation of Christianity;" of his failure, despite his father's efforts to make a good and useful man of him, to do anything to justify his existence; of his selfishness in remaining at home to be a burden on parents certainly not burdened with riches. He is not kept long in suspense, for on the Tuesday morning he hears from his room the stir of Coleridge's arrival. Despite his longing, he lingers until summoned to meet the visitor, goes downstairs at last, still half hoping, half fearing,—to be reassured by a very gracious reception. He sees, to his surprise, that Coleridge in social converse looks very different from the Coleridge of whom he had had a moment's vision in the dim light of

THE UNITARIAN CHAPEL AT SHREWSBURY

the chapel. Either his imagination had played tricks with him or the obscurity of the lighting had then transformed the face. There is no longer any suggestion of prophetic wildness about it; it is not scarred —he had thought it marked by the smallpox—and in the sunlight the complexion is seen to be clear; there is even a slight suggestion of the bloom of early youth on the skin. The chin is round and good-humoured; the nose is insignificant; the lips are thick, even gross: they are often open, and then they reveal bad teeth. All the beauty is in the upper part of the face. This is as he remembers it; the rough black hair falls over the brow; the grey eyes, not remarkable in any way in shape or colour, have still, as he turns them this way or that, the suggestion of "a fine frenzy" in them; the forehead is altogether glorious, broad and high, and "light as if built of ivory."

As for the voice, it now seems to rustle round the wainscoting in silken sounds. It has the room almost to itself. Mr. Hazlitt, it is true, puts in a word now and again, but William, on whom the familiar curse of dumbness has alighted, sits perfectly silent, now and again stealing a look at their guest; but for the most part his eyes are directed towards the floor. He seems inert, but every word that is said by Coleridge slides into his soul. Coleridge is more used than most men to having people sitting silent in his presence, nor is he inclined to think the worse of any one for being a good listener, but after a couple of hours he possibly begins to feel that there is something uncouth and forbidding in this younker's complete passivity. At length, however, the conversation turns on Burke, and then, lo and behold! the "bashful younker" comes suddenly and startlingly to life, expresses with energy and force his admiration of Burke, and concludes by saying authoritatively that the speaking of such a writer as Burke with contempt has always seemed to him the true criterion of a *vulgar* democratical mind. Coleridge sees at once that whatever young Hazlitt is, he is no fool, but one who has thoughts of his own which he can express in a way of his own, "well-feathered" thoughts, indeed, which he is capable when he likes of sending straight forward towards the mark "with a twang of the bow-string." He agrees with the observation and commends it. Mr. Hazlitt, with a characteristic gesture, pushes back his spectacles on his forehead, and William realises suddenly how much his father, who has never had such a feast of conversation in his life before, is beginning to enjoy himself. They are now all of them at ease. When Mrs. Hazlitt summons them to dinner, they carry on a conversation that has become general and animated. The visitor diffuses a sense of happiness and enjoyment that falls like blessing on them all. Even the simple food seems blest by his presence. William thinks that the leg of Welsh mutton and the turnips of which they partake have the finest flavour in the world.

His spirits are dashed the next morning when he comes down to breakfast, for the first thing he hears is that Coleridge is not going to be their neighbour after all, as his friend Wedgwood has offered him an annuity which will enable him to devote all his time to Literature. The letter is lying on the table; Coleridge seems to have made up his mind to accept it, in the act of tying on one of his shoes. William feels as if his god has been suddenly whisked off to the Delectable Mountains, to which he himself can in no wise find the way. However, he revives when Coleridge, who has divined the morbid sadness in him as well as the genius, and who, being at that time a healer of souls no less than a diviner of genius, is touched by it, perhaps intrigued by it also, asks for pen and ink, writes his address on a card, and gives him an invitation to visit his home in Nether Stowey in a few weeks' time. This seems to him such a miracle of good fortune that he can only stammer out his acceptance and thanks.

Shortly afterwards he sets out to accompany Coleridge part of the way back to Shrewsbury. Their talk is now of metaphysics. They discuss Hume, Berkeley and Butler. Coleridge speaks very highly of Butler's sermons. Hazlitt has not yet read them, but gathering from Coleridge's conversation that they uphold the dignity and disinterestedness of the human mind, he is beguiled into speaking of his own slow-moving essay, and of the train of reasoning whereby he hopes to destroy root and branch the doctrine of the natural selfishness of the mind of Man. He fails to make himself understood. Indeed, Coleridge thinks him strangely confused and dark in his argument.

They part at the sixth milestone. Although neither of them as yet knows it, this is to be their real parting. They will have further meetings, and further contacts, valuable ones too, but Coleridge's essential work for Hazlitt has already been done. The spiritual mating is already over. Its fruits will one day show. But the moment of severance from the deep close union has already come, and neither of them knows it. The forces that have brought them together for the momentary intense contact, needful at least to one of them, are already gathering to rive them apart.

Is this fantastic? Nay, nay, 'tis *true!—but yet the pity of it, Iago! O Iago, the pity of it, Iago!*

They part at the sixth milestone.

Chapter Three

TOWARDS COLERIDGE AND WORDSWORTH (1798)

> "I recollect saying to my sister about this time:[77] 'Whom do you suppose I hold to be the cleverest person I know?' 'Capel Lofft perhaps?' 'No.' 'Mrs. Clarkson?' 'Oh no!' 'Miss Maling?' 'No.' 'I give it up.' 'William Hazlitt.' 'Oh, you are joking. Why, we all take him to be a fool.'"
>
> HENRY CRABB ROBINSON.

I

AFTER parting from Coleridge, Hazlitt, who realised that he had once more failed to make himself intelligible in speech, returned home fired with the determination to make himself intelligible on paper. No longer does he feel himself a worm by the wayside; or at least, he now knows that the worm has wings. At Coleridge's touch, he knows that the worm has wings.

He gets fresh paper and new pens. He is going to start anew on his essay On the Disinterestedness of the Human Mind. His thoughts gallop. But as soon as he looks at the virgin sheet before him, he is assailed by his old impotence. His words come meagre, and dry as the remainder biscuit. He is painfully conscious of their poverty. For a time he agonises. At last he flings his pen aside in despair, and lays his head on the paper.

Coleridge, remembering his laboured, almost grotesque effort to deliver himself of an idea, might well say of him: "he delivers himself of all his conceptions with a Forceps;" but even this was overstatement. At this time he has no forceps, nor can he deliver himself of anything at all on that day, the 17th of January, 1798, except of the tears of utter despondency he left on his blank unfinished paper.

For yet a little while longer the worm must continue to lie by the wayside. As yet the wings cannot be unfurled. One day they will be strong enough for a flight. But as yet they cannot be unfurled. They are the tenderest pinions that ever were seen—the meagrest wings. They are indeed barely discernible to the eye, discernible at times, even to himself, only through the growing-pains about their roots.

He lays the essay aside for the one and twentieth time, and resumes the ordinary tenor of his life, walking, thinking, studying. Despite his admiration of Coleridge, he was far too critical to accept all Coleridge had said until he had subjected it to analysis. It seemed to him that Coleridge had done but scant justice to Hume, whose *Treatise on*

Human Nature[78] he himself greatly admired. He continued to relish "this metaphysical choke-pear," and also to read Berkeley, to whose *Essay on Vision*[79] Coleridge had done ample justice. He extended his acquaintance with the English novelists and dipped into some of the dramatists, feeling that when it came to estimating the literature of flesh and blood exhibited through manners his judgment was not far out—although Coleridge had made him conscious that there were regions of literature of which he knew next to nothing, and especially that he knew little of the special pleasure poetry can give. He slaked, as he could, his thirst of German sentiment, for Coleridge's sonnet on Schiller had revived his delight in it, and he longed for it "as the hart that panteth for the water-springs." Rousseau, whom he had been reading throughout the previous year, he continued to read steadily. He had long before digested *Du Contrat Social*. He read *Émile* without being conscious of being much influenced by it, for it was too much in accord with the natural tendency of his own mind to bring him any fresh development. Such development, however, he gained from *La Nouvelle Héloïse*, which he absorbed as new-turned soil absorbs the dew. It moved him so much that at times he found himself shedding tears over it

> "as fast as the Arabian trees
> Their medicinal gums."

Over certain parts he cried his eyes out. There were passages which were to him like delicious banquets to which he would repair again and again. He read with such intensity of feeling that the places in which he sat or lay as he read became blended with the reading itself and remained stamped on his mind as if they had been connected with some primary emotional experience. He tells us that he read the first part of *The New Eloise* one clear day in a field in which the young green blades of corn as they glittered in the sun were now and again stirred by a fitful breeze. What he saw seemed to him part of the book, and the book seemed to him part of what he saw. The style itself seemed like drops of morning dew before the sun had scorched them. His thoughts, taking their tone both from what he read and from the sights and sounds around him, were pure and free. "I never felt what Shakespeare calls my 'glassy essence' so much as then," he wrote of this experience more than twenty-five years afterwards. In it he had tasted happiness.

But much as he loved *The New Eloise* with its occasional felicities and conscious as he was of the expansion of mind and the extension of feeling it had brought to him, the *Confessions* meant much more to him. It was not merely, nor chiefly, because of its beauties that the *Confessions* moved him. Its value was to him of a deeper, more intimate

kind. He loved it as he might have loved someone who had helped
him to understand and to reconcile the obscure and conflicting impulses
of his own body and soul. In it he discerned an earlier traveller on the
road he had taken himself, on the road he was yet to take—a traveller
who had left a true record of all that had befallen him on the road.
Far more to him than the beauty of any special passage or any felicity
of style was his consciousness of the man who was revealed throughout
the book, and his own deep sympathy with the man. There was much
in the *Confessions* that he would understand fully only in later years,
when he had himself gone a little further in the journey of his life;
there were some things that the puritanism in him would never
stomach; but there was already much that he understood, much with
which he sympathised, much also that illuminated such experience
as had already come to him. There was nothing in Rousseau's account
of the various planes of experience on which his life had moved during
adolescence that he could not understand. The conjunction of extreme
refinement and innocence of feeling with animal impulse, even with
the indecorous and fantastic expression of animal impulse, was
perfectly intelligible to him, and the truth of the portraiture brought
him solace: here was one who was also "brutish," yet as far removed
as it is possible for man, born of the flesh as well as of the spirit, to
be from being a brute! His own excessive sensibility enabled him to
understand every *nuance* of the sensibility delineated by Rousseau, to
understand also the vivisection to which it was sometimes subjected.
Rousseau's wistful realisation that too much loving does not cause the
lover to prosper already found an echo in his own experience, and the
account of the early love that failed to come to fruition because it was,
as it were, petrified by its own exquisiteness, enchanted him by its
truth, its delicacy, and its subtlety of perception.

Already he understood, too, most of what related to the slow dawn
of Rousseau's genius—the anxious doubts and misgivings, the intense
aspiration after good, the continuous intensity of feeling and capacity
for "relishing all more sharply than others," the pains taken in silence
and obscurity, the terrible patience of the man *constrained* to write.

Nor, deep as was his personal debt to Rousseau, was his gratitude
merely personal. He was passionately grateful also for the service
Rousseau had done to humanity. As he put it, in later years: "It was
Rousseau who brought the feeling of irreconcileable enmity to rank and
privileges, *above humanity*, home to the bosom of every man,—identified
it with all the pride of intellect, and with the deepest yearnings of the
human heart. He was the founder of Jacobinism, which disclaims the
division of the species into two classes, the one the property of the
other. It was of the disciples of *his* school, where principle is converted
into passion, that Mr. Burke said, and said truly—' Once a Jacobin,
always a Jacobin.'"

This intensity of sympathy not only with the genius but with the doctrine of Rousseau explains Hazlitt's absorption in Rousseau's work throughout 1797 and 1798, and the development that came to his own genius through this sympathy: Rousseau no less than Burke at this time helped to make him a writer. Even if he had not had Burke to teach him the craft of writing and the nature of the inheritance of English prose, even if he had not had Rousseau to help him to grope his way towards knowledge of the foundations of human nature, he would have been a writer, for he would have found his way out to literature even as a river finds its way out to the sea; but his debt to these was so great that the writing would not have been Hazlitt's writing as we now have it.

Yet the help coming to him from these would in itself not have been sufficient at this time to save him from the extremity of his despair. Although the experience of Rousseau fitted as closely to his own sense of truth as the glove fits the hand, although he felt at times as sure of what had passed through Rousseau's mind as he did of what was passing through his own, although Rousseau, helping to liberate his under-conscious nature, even as the acting of Mrs. Siddons had done, loosened the constriction that locked his nerves, he would have fared badly, with a great weight of thought and feeling pressing on him like a burden, or perhaps rather, fermenting dangerously within his bosom and turning to poison, had not the one human contact which could help him most come to him at the moment when he most needed it, at the moment when his life was in most danger of becoming obscure and cramped, even of falling into distortion. Coleridge had come just in time.

Not realising that the full perfection of this contact is past, Hazlitt looks upon it as something which is going to be renewed constantly, and through which his life is going to be lightened and quickened. Now as he reads, his pleasure is doubled, for he knows that when the spring comes in he will have some one to whom he can impart all he thinks and feels, some one who at a time when he "passed for an idiot" had recognised in him at once a living, suffering human being with some kind of gift, as yet unexpressed, that patience and effort might help him one day to impart to others and to share with them. He is filled all the time, even as he spends his days in reading and meditation, with a longing for Coleridge that is half pleasurable, half painful. As the days draw on towards March he has only one thought: he is to visit Coleridge in the spring. He wakes in the morning with this prospect in his mind. He sleeps with it at night. Because of it he welcomes the morning and the evening star. Because of it the sight of the first brave flower that pushes its head through the hard soil is reassurance to him; the unfurling of the first tender leaf is a delight; the coming of the first mild day is inspiration. His is a lover's calendar.

He is still dumb, brutish, half a changeling, but all will yet be well with him. He is to hear again the necromantic voice; he is to drink again of necromantic words.

He is *to visit Coleridge in the spring!*

2

In Hazlitt's letter to his father of October 23rd, 1796, among the familiar names of those to whom he was accustomed to send his greetings in every letter, such as Kynaston and Joe Swanwick, there appears the name of a new friend John Wicksteed.[80] During the three weeks in which Coleridge had been at Shrewsbury John Wicksteed had been one of his admirers. In the beginning of March he wrote to Coleridge about a little trail of trouble and gossip left behind in the Unitarian congregation at Shrewsbury, caused by some indiscreet remarks of the kind which so often got Coleridge into difficulty. Coleridge's reply is the usual mixture of explanation, self-exculpation, and very disarming apology for any indiscretion he might have uttered. At the end of the letter is a postscript: "On looking for your address I perceive it is Wem. I have therefore opened my letter to beg that you will tell young Mr. Hazlitt that I remember him with the respect due to his talent, and that the wish which I expressed of seeing him at Stowey still lives within me." [81]

This message, with its gracious assurance of welcome, coming to "young Mr. Hazlitt" at a time when Coleridge was never out of his thoughts, probably accounts for the lightening of his spirits in the days that followed, preceding his departure for Nether Stowey. If there was any time in his life in which he was completely happy, it was this.

He did not, after all, visit Coleridge in the spring, for when he proposed a time for his visit, Coleridge wrote asking him to postpone it until the summer, but assuring him of a very warm welcome if he could come then. The reply was such as to increase rather than damp his ardour.

3

On his twentieth birthday, April 10th, 1798, he set out to walk to the Vale of Llangollen. He looked upon this walk as an initiation into the joy he expected to have in sharing the beauty of Devon and Somerset with Coleridge. An initiation it was, but it also became an experience by itself, perhaps the most flawless experience of unsullied joy that life was to yield to him. Europe at the time was heaving like a sea, and the fear of invasion hung heavy over England, for young Buonaparte, whose spectacular successes in Italy had already made him dreaded by the enemies of his country, had returned to France, and his eye was directed towards England. To Hazlitt even such things as the appointment of Buonaparte to the command of a force prepared for invasion were at the moment infinitely remote. The nature of the joy and expectancy within himself, of the stimulus that had just come to his mind and the stimulus he expected to receive, excluded the possibility of either anxiety or fear. He felt light as air. His body was so far from being that day "the rude prison-house" of his soul that it was but the willing "vehicle and instrument" of a soul saturated with its own content. It might almost be said of him that *his body thought.*

Coleridge still walked by his side, the most perfect of invisible companions, sensitive to his thought and mood as the strings of the Æolian harp are to the wind, and altogether "pliant to his soul's bidding." With this invisible companion he walked in the new world which the gentle ministry of his companion had opened to him. There was a sound in his ears, a sound that Coleridge had made him hear for the first time: it was the voice of Fancy. There was a light before his eyes, a light which Coleridge had made him see for the first time: it was the light of Poetry. Until his meeting with Coleridge he had fed his mind chiefly on gnarled roots of political theory and the thistles of metaphysics. Coleridge, the first great poet he had met, and one who answered so well to the inspired name, had led him towards Helicon. This day he felt as if he were receiving baptism in its waters.

When he turned off into the road to Llangollen between Chirk and Wrexham he was meditating some of the lines in Coleridge's Ode to the Departing Year:

> "Not yet enslaved, not wholly vile,
> O Albion! O my mother Isle!
> Thy valleys, fair as Eden's bowers,
> Glitter green with sunny showers;"

when all at once he came upon the valley and its amphitheatre of barren hills, and heard the crying of the sheep pasturing on the greener slopes, Coleridge was still his commentary; when he walked along the high road commanding the valley, it was with Coleridge's phrases that he continued to clothe his thoughts. The river Dee babbled over its stony bed. He stopped to note a delicate ash-tree, just budding, which dipped the tender green of its branches in the waters of the river, as if to refresh their beauty. Measureless content was in his heart. And more beautiful to him even than the valley he had come to see, sweeter than the busy music of the river, were the words coursing through his mind, all of them for him symbolised by the personality of Coleridge—Liberty, Genius, Love, Virtue.

The evening was as perfect in its way as the day had been. No bread and cheese for supper for him on this day of days!—but a chicken and a bottle of wine at the inn, after the day's walking. Over his sherry he pulled out of his pocket *The New Eloise*, and read the letter in which "St. Preux describes his feelings as he first caught a glimpse from the heights of the Jura of the Pays de Vaud." This favourite passage was the *bonne bouche* he had reserved to complete the felicity of the evening.

We do not know how long he remained at Llangollen, but it was sufficiently long for him to feel that the vale had been for him "the cradle of a new existence," and to think of its river as of the river of Paradise.

> "There are in our existence spots of time
> Which with distinct pre-eminence retain
> A vivifying Virtue, whence . . . our minds
> Are nourished and invisibly repair'd."

We have dwelt on this day and its translucent experience, because it was for Hazlitt one of these "spots of time." It was one of those moments of his existence which he gathered up afterwards "like drops of honey-dew to distil a precious liquor from them." It was a day that stood apart from other days in its perfected happiness at the only time in his life when his soul seemed to him to have emerged from its loneliness, its infinite longings satisfied, when he had at least the illusion that his heart had found a heart to speak to, that among men he had found his fellow. He may return to the Vale of Llangollen in after years, but he will never see it "glitter green with sunny showers," as he saw it that day. Nor will he return to it with the *Ode to the Departing Year* in his heart and on his lips. He will never again have the vision of that day, with the words Liberty, Genius, Love, Virtue written across it in rainbow hues. He will never again see it as "the cradle of a new existence"; for the state of mind which had made all these things possible—the sharing of his thought with an inspired companion walking invisible by his side, the merging of his being in another being—can never come to him again. Even as he gazes on the vision, its hues are fading.

4

To explain why we say this, we must leave him for a moment and turn to the one who had inspired the vision. Coleridge during this greeny-glittering April of 1798 is also caught into experience that is no less translucent in quality although different in its origin; for it is immediately conditioned by the political ferment of the hour. He too is being born again. The cradle of his new existence is a quiet coombe in the Quantocks. Musing in this coombe, one day when the oppression of the fear of invasion lay over the country, he thinks of the mood in which, less than five years before, he had composed the *Ode to the Departing Year*, and of the almost exultant way in which he had prophesied that one day blood-soaked Europe would avenge itself on the country which, while sending war abroad, ever continued to preserve the blessing of peace within her own borders. Now that the moment has come when the prophecy looks as if it may come true, he sickens at the thought of it. As he drinks in the delicate loveliness around him he is appalled at the thought that the pollution of war may come to it. If there must be wars, let them not be waged in the English countryside. His cry is now:

> "Spare us yet awhile!
> Father and God! O spare us yet awhile!"

Once he had blamed his countrymen for going forth against the French. His cry is now:

> "Sons, brothers, husbands, all
> Who ever gazed with fondness on the forms
> Which grew up with you round the same fire-side,
> And all who ever heard the sabbath bells
> Without the infidel's scorn, make yourselves pure!
> Stand forth! be men! repel an impious foe,
> .   .   .   .
> Render them back upon the insulted ocean,
> And let them toss as idly on its waves
> As the vile sea-weed, which some mountain-blast
> Swept from our shores!"

He is no less oppressed by a sense of his country's guilty responsibility than he had been three years before, but now he no longer feels towards it as a prophet, thundering out denunciation of it. Now he takes his place along with his countrymen, acknowledging, with low anguished crying, the burden of guilt common to them and to him:

> "We have offended, Oh! my Countrymen!
> We have offended very grievously,
> And been most tyrannous."

Now he knows only that every fibre in him clings to his country, that every nerve in him thrills to her need, that every drop of blood in him is ready to be spilt in protecting her from "the evil thing." He has been called the enemy of his country. It is false. He takes his stand with her. In her hour of peril he knows that he is bone of her bone, flesh of her flesh. He pours all the love of which her danger has at last made him conscious into a verse invocation of which the theme is:

> "There lives nor form nor feeling in my soul
> Unborrowed from my country!"

Even as Hazlitt is wandering in Wales, making of the *Ode to the Departing Year* his Bible, its author, shaken by these musings, is casting the slough of the former existence in which he had conceived the poem, is repudiating the point of view from which it was written, is discovering himself anew, not primarily as a friend of Man or as a friend of Liberty, but as a Lover first and foremost of England, finding all that he loves most, enclosed within the limits of his native shores. On April 20th, ten days after Hazlitt's twentieth birthday, he co-ordinates these musings under the title of *Fears in Solitude*. Four days earlier, he had published in *The Morning Post* a block of strong-wrought, angry verse entitled *The Recantation*, in which, moved by the French invasion of Switzerland, he had stormed out his repudiation of all his previously expressed sympathy with France, and implored the forgiveness of Freedom for his blindness in having once mistaken her enemies for her champions. But the deeper, fuller recantation, expressing a profounder movement of the spirit, is to be found in *Fears in Solitude*, flung forth, not from an impulse of anger, but from a rediscovery of love for his country and a genuine rediscovery of his own personality. From the moment he sees his country endangered his primary love is the filial love for her:[82] the Delilahs of his imagination are all banished. And for him at the moment his country is symbolised by the peace of the Quantocks, their coombes and their green sheep-tracks and their tinkling sheep-bells; by the church-tower of Nether Stowey; by the roof of his own cottage, sheltering his child and his child's mother; and by the other lowly roofs that cluster around it. He has discovered that he is primarily an Englishman. Beneath that name alone, nourished by its strength, and if need be gladly accepting its limitations, he will seek his office upon earth, will love God and serve his fellow-man.

His youthful politics had been red-hot, but they had been largely conditioned by the fashion of the hour. Temperamentally, he inclined to go with the stream. Perhaps even in his newly discovered love of country, genuine though it was, and incomparably sweet in his expression of it, he was to some extent influenced by the fashion of the hour, for talk of invasion had made patriotism the cry of the day. He was Conformist rather than Nonconformist in temper, although he had for a time dallied with Nonconformity, and had, because of his own personal genius, attracted towards him in that brief dalliance the one in whom was expressed the genius or soul of Nonconformity.

In the meantime the one whose impulse was always to go against the stream and to turn his back on the cry of the hour, still held fast throughout all brunts and despite all fluctuations of events or of public opinion, to the scale of values he had already reasoned out for himself, and this, although he too loved his country, carried him far beyond that which he himself afterwards called "*exclusive* patriotism." It was his life's charge to be "true to glory, true to country" but first and foremost to be "true to a cause far above both these names," the cause of Liberty on earth, ensuring the emancipation of the spirit of Man in all nations, tribes and kindreds, from the age-long oppression under which it had been bowed. Liberty, Genius, Love, Virtue are all written in rainbow hues across his vision of a regenerated world, but the first of these, and the one inscribed in the most sanguine hue, is Liberty.

Now it was not only in his attitude to France that Coleridge was altering at this time. The reversal of his attitude towards France involved him gradually in an upheaval of thought far more profound, leading gradually towards an alteration in his attitude towards the aspiration of Liberty on earth. The beginning of this alteration, which in the end disrupted the whole man, can be discerned amid his out-pourings of patriotism. In his disgust with the transmutation of French aspiration towards Liberty into French aggression against Liberty he has begun to doubt the possibility of the preservation of Liberty itself in any government framed by Man, and is beginning to place his hope, his confidence and his joy not in the perfecting of human institutions, but in other things. He is beginning to feel that all governments to a certain extent mangle Liberty, and that this is unavoidable because the corruption of governments is only the visible sign of the corruption lurking in the governed. It is not excised by change of government, seeing that the nature of man himself does not change. A change of government was beginning to seem to him merely like a change of coat. He was beginning to feel that the ideal of Liberty may be worshipped in the winds and ocean waves, in the clouds,

"Whose pathless march no mortal may controul,"

but not in any government of Man's devising.

We say that this marks a profound change in the man, for to say this of Coleridge is to say that he is already on the threshold of despair. Once he had been "hopeless concerning no one."[83] He had regarded any evil in man as the effect of environment. Now he is altering rapidly. It is hardly an exaggeration to say that the bright soft glow of his newly dis:overed patriotism masks the inception of a dull leaden despair, which never ceases from now onwards to operate as a corrosive sublimate upon his genius, even as the corrosive sublimate of fear had already begun to operate on Wordsworth's. His mind comes back again and again to that one black plague-spot, destructive of hope and best forgotten in opium dreams, that the corruptibility in man is not confined to any one grade in society, but is indivisible; it is to be discerned not only in those who govern, but in those who are governed; not only in those who shear, but in those who are shorn; not only in those who eat, but in those who are eaten. It is of the nature of man.

In consequence, he is beginning to refuse what he now tends to regard as a vain battle. In a little time he may without injustice be numbered among those fallen off

> "To selfishness, disguis'd in gentle names
> Of peace, and quiet, and domestic love."

How then, between the passionate spirits of Hazlitt and Coleridge, each of them possessed with its own "frenzy," can the pleasure henceforth ever be pure![84] Are there not in it already "the hidden stings"!

5

Just about four months after Hazlitt had started out on a dark January morning when even the thistles looked as if the cold had pierced their stubborn stalks, to walk the road from Wem to Shrewsbury to hear Coleridge preach, he started out with tireless feet and unworn eager heart upon the road from Wem to Shrewsbury, on a morning in the second half of May. He thinks of Coleridge as he passes each of the six milestones, as he passes Harmer Hill, the pines on which —he would have sworn—had stooped their heads to listen when Coleridge had gone by, as he passes the rows of sturdy oak trees, now no longer rusty-red or sere but in the freshest moment of their expanding greenery. All his thought is of Coleridge, for the road from Wem to Shrewsbury, which has so often led him outwards towards some new experience, is now the first stage of his journey towards the Delectable Mountains. The diviner of genius who at the beginning of the year had been reft away from his reluctant eyes to these pleasant places, has at last beckoned to him to come.

His heart was as light as his foot as he traversed the country towards the south-west, from Shrewsbury to Worcester, through Upton, where he thought of Tom Jones and the adventure of the muff, to Tewkesbury, then on to Gloucester and Bristol, the beginning of the country around which Coleridge had woven a circle. From day to day again he quaffed "the full brimming cup of thoughtless freedom" and met other travellers who quaffed it as thoughtlessly as he did himself. By the banks of the Severn he exchanged greetings one fine morning with a strolling player whose shining face seemed to shoot back the sun's broad rays. Play-bills streaming from his pockets, in his hand a music-score which he sang out blithe and clear, "carolling to the echo of the bubbling stream," this carefree wanderer passed on his way "brisk as a bird, gay as a mote, swift as an arrow from a twanging bow, heart-whole." Hazlitt felt as if in meeting him he had met in the environment natural to such gay creatures one of those friends of his childhood who had glittered "along the street . . . like mealy coated butterflies or insects flitting in the sun." Such meetings sent him on his way with an acceleration of the pulse of joy.

He passed through the country in the morning sunshine, and felt the sparkle of it reflected in his own pleasurable thoughts; but even the dusk was brighter to him than the noonday sun in days when he had been less happy. To sit by a well-side in the heat and cool himself and satisfy his thirst was good, or to sit in the sunshine when he felt inclined; but when the rain came down continuously, as it sometimes did for a whole day in the south-west, he felt that the summer showers dropped with blessing on his head, and that even as they drenched his body, they were sweet to him, for they but made him more conscious of himself and of the happiness in store for him. In the morning he set out when he pleased; he walked as he pleased, rested or lounged when he pleased; stopped and refreshed himself with a glass of sparkling ale when he felt thirsty, and went on again till evening, when he took his ease at an inn. He went early to bed when he pleased, or he sat up half the night reading, as he did at the inn at Tewkesbury, where he came upon a copy of *Paul and Virginia* which he started to read and wanted to finish before he left. Thus sometimes hurrying, sometimes sauntering, sometimes loitering in pleasant places in wood or dale or by the banks of the streams, he covered the distance between Shropshire and Somerset in about a week's time. He had made such good speed that he arrived at Bridgwater two days earlier than the time arranged, and spent a couple of days in lounging and sauntering and reading *Camilla*. On the third day he walked over to Coleridge's cottage in Nether Stowey.[85]

6

Coleridge had just returned from a few days' expedition to Cheddar, for which he had set out on Wednesday, May 23rd,[86] with Wordsworth and his sister. For him, May had been a troubled month. He had been greatly grieved by the deaths of three of his friends, two of whom belonged to his immediate circle. In the beginning of the month the daughter of his friend, old Dr. Toulmin, the Unitarian minister of Taunton, had put an end to her life in a moment of melancholy madness. Coleridge felt deeply for the old minister. "These griefs cut cruelly into the hearts of old men,"[87] he wrote to his friend Mr. Estlin, the Unitarian minister of Bristol. To his brother George he wrote: "it is plain that it has cut deep into his heart."[88] He gave to the bereaved father the fullness and sweetness of that sympathy which at this time of his life he knew so well how to give, and at the same time he took a practical burden off the old man's shoulders by going to Taunton to preach for him on the Sundays. Even on Sunday, May 13th, when his wife's labour was approaching, he walked into Taunton to preach all the Sunday services for Dr. Toulmin. In the evening he walked home, to find his cottage in all the bustle attending the birth of Berkeley.

Tom Poole's brother Richard was very ill that same Sunday. In the course of the week he died, and Coleridge, who if he did not spare his friends certainly did not spare himself when he could serve them, did all he could to comfort both Poole and his old mother in their bereavement.

His letters show how these things pressed upon him. "I have had lately some sorrows that have cut more deeply into my heart than they ought to have done,"[89] he wrote in one of them. Another contains a confession of nervous strain: "So many unpleasant and shocking circumstances have happened to me in my immediate knowledge within the last fortnight, that I am in a nervous state, and the most trifling thing makes me weep."[90]

Among the "unpleasant" circumstances were the constant practical reminders he was receiving at this time of the estrangement and hostility of three of those whom he had numbered among his best friends. He had sent to *The Monthly Magazine*, in November, 1797, three mock sonnets ridiculing his own youthful style, and that of Charles Lamb and Charles Lloyd, whose verse had appeared with his own in the second edition of his *Poems*. As he had not spared himself, he had not realised that his fun might hurt the friends whose foibles he ridiculed along with his own, but both Lamb and Lloyd were angry, and Southey conceived himself to be injured also. This storm would have blown over quickly, perhaps, were it not that Coleridge had also exposed himself to criticism by his habit of unguarded speech, a frailty of his fraught with more danger to himself than he realised. We have seen that even at Shrewsbury his unguarded speech had made trouble. It was with reference to a scene originating in this that John Wicksteed had written to him in March. In that same month, he had evidence of the way in which his own careless words were estranging his friends. Charles Lloyd, who had lived under his roof the previous year and had expressed the most extravagant love and admiration for him, wrote to Cottle, his publisher, informing him that he did not wish his poems to be reprinted along with Coleridge's in their third edition. In April his novel *Edmund Oliver*, containing what if it had been better executed would have been a caricature of Coleridge, was published. Worse still, by repeating careless words Coleridge might have used at his own fireside, Lloyd had estranged Southey and Lamb from their old friend. Coleridge wrote affectionately to Lamb, insisting that both he and Lloyd, in a painful reaction from their former excess of admiration, were making him the victim of their moods: "Both you and Lloyd became acquainted with me when your minds were far from being in a composed or natural state, and you clothed my image with a suit of notions and feelings which could belong to nothing human. You are restored to comparative sanity, and are merely wondering what is become of the Coleridge with whom you were so passionately in love."[91]

To this Lamb replied with an extraordinarily wounding list of questions, which reached Coleridge in May, and which might be called spiteful, were it not that the bitterness of the disillusionment they convey is tragic. It is not too much to say that Coleridge felt his integrity challenged by these. Lloyd had already thrown out dark hints as to his bodily vices, for Edmund Oliver's Journal had contained the words: "if at any time thought-troubled, I have swallowed some spirits, or had recourse to my laudanum."

The double attack, denying him all soundness of soul as well as of body, stimulated Coleridge at last into action. Hearing towards the end of May that Lloyd was in the district, he determined to seek him out and reason with him, to knock some sense into him if possible, and also, if possible, to bring him back to Nether Stowey. In this resolution he was supported by Wordsworth, and it was with this end in view that along with Wordsworth and his sister, he had set out for Cheddar on Wednesday, May 23rd.

Their quest was unsuccessful. While they were on the road they heard that Lloyd had set out for Birmingham. Coleridge, bound by his engagement with Hazlitt, returned home along with Dorothy Wordsworth after they had all visited the Cheddar caves together. Wordsworth, determined to find out for himself what Lloyd had been doing or was doing, and wishing to see his friends the Pinneys as he found himself so near their home, went on by himself to Bristol.

7

It was just at this moment, when Coleridge was feeling done to death by Lloyd's insinuations as to his physical vices and Lamb's challenge as to his spiritual integrity, when his self-love was bleeding from the deepest injury it had ever received, when he was so nervous that the most trifling thing was apt to make him weep, that the lonely student of Wem, whose conversation had struck him as having in it something original, whose brow had seemed to him "the most metaphysical" he had ever seen, and whose morbid sadness had touched and interested him, appeared at his cottage door. The gods were kind to Hazlitt in this, for he could not have presented himself at a time more favourable to the growth of his intimacy with Coleridge. His visit brought with it more reassurance and even comfort to his troubled host than he would ever know. His very presence in Nether Stowey was a living proof to Coleridge of his own limitless ability to attract. Even if old friends dropped away in savage disillusionment, he need never be lonely ; new ones, equally passionate, would come forward immediately in their stead. Coleridge still felt that "Lamb and Lloyd & Co." were making him suffer less because he was to blame than because they were on the rebound from their own excess of admiration, and he still felt the danger of such worship; but he would not have been man if at that moment it had been unwelcome to him to be sought out by a new friend inclined to clothe his image "with a suit of notions and feelings which could belong to nothing human," or to be made to realise afresh that he was still, in spite of the flaying to which he had been subjected, the Coleridge with whom every now and again some admirer fell "passionately in love." He could have wished that his new admirer's manners were less "shoe-contemplative" and "*strange*," but in Hazlitt's joy at seeing him again, in Hazlitt's sense of privilege at being admitted to his poor home, in Hazlitt's devotion, obvious although controlled, there was the perfect balm for his wounded self-esteem.

There was another and a deeper reason why Hazlitt's presence at this moment was welcome to him and of service to him. Coleridge was not only the diviner of genius; he was the diviner of genius *par excellence*. It was this which inspired the passionate gratitude of Wordsworth's apostrophe:

"O most loving Soul!
Placed on this earth to love and understand,
And from thy presence shed the light of love,
Shall I be mute ere thou be spoken of?"

He was as sensitive to genius as is the divining-rod to the presence of water, even if deep concealed. Indeed, at no time did he feel so strongly a sense of power as when he sensed the presence of genius concealed, undivined of any save himself; at no time did he feel the sense of fulfilment more completely than when he both discerned and evoked it. Or he was like a potter whose sense of power was greatest when he dealt with the clay in the rough,.when he could mould it with his hands and fashion out of it that the possibility of which no eye had visioned but his own, when he could feel almost as if he were breathing into the rude clay the breath of his own nostrils. He felt as the spirits of other men quickened under his ministry somewhat as if he were their creator. This, the moment when the genius of another was identified with his own power to evoke it, was the moment when his sympathy with it was most profound. Afterwards, when it had kindled and had attracted the admiration of others, when it was well able to shift for itself, he was apt to repudiate what he had helped to quicken and to mould, to throw aside carelessly what was in a measure his handiwork, even to treat it with contumely, as if he begrudged the pains he had spent on it and considered himself impoverished by the help he had given.

But the opening phase of such a relationship was always exquisite to him, and his relationship with Hazlitt was altogether of this kind. He had given the invitation at Wem on an impulse of kindness, but what had conditioned the impulse was that the young awkward Hazlitt had made, all unwittingly, an unusually deep appeal to his sense of power. The labouring mind, oppressed by an obscure mass of thought, the uncouth evidences of conflict and self-conflict in word and temper and look, the desperate and thwarted attempts at self-expression, had all called out to the creative instinct in him. It would have been natural to him at any time to take one so gifted, yet so helpless, as helpless as the young Jean-Jacques himself! under his fostering care; but in view of the moment at which Hazlitt had arrived, it was inevitable that he should do so, for in the exercise of his tutelary gifts on one so burdened yet so full of promise and so passionately loving, he could forget the ingratitude of those earlier friends who had become rebel to his teaching, thrown off his yoke, and strangered themselves by their insults. In any circumstances Hazlitt would have been sure of a gracious welcome from Coleridge, who was gracious both by nature and by habit, but coming at a moment when his presence brought with it not only healing and balm but positive stimulus, he found Coleridge brimming over with welcome and prepared to give him of his very best.

The best gift of all, in Coleridge's scheme of values at this time, was an introduction to the poetry of "the giant Wordsworth, God love him!"—so no sooner had Hazlitt made the acquaintance of pretty, friendly Mrs. Coleridge and the two babies, fascinating elf-like Hartley, not yet two years old, and the recently born Berkeley, than he found himself hurried over to Alfoxden. The Poet had not yet returned from Bristol, but his sister, who seemed only to live in her attachment to her brother and his friend, welcomed them and gave them a simple meal. When they had finished eating, Coleridge asked her if they might have a look at William's poems, and she immediately placed before them the loose sheets on which were transcribed the poems which her brother called "Lyrical Ballads."

8

Coleridge had been impatient for Hazlitt to see some of Wordsworth's poetry, but apart from this, it was small wonder that he had hurried his friend over to Alfoxden. In its spaciousness, its air of settled comfort, and its quiet it formed a great contrast to his own cottage standing in the village street, with its low poor rooms, its steep and crazy staircase, and its stir of woman life and infant life. It would have been difficult to find a pleasanter place anywhere. The house was set on the lowest reach of the Quantocks. Its front windows looked on to the slopes of a park covered with bracken and trees at which the deer would nibble in hard weather; one of the side-windows looked towards the sea. The approach to it was through a lovely wood in which a waterfall made music, and from which glimpses of the sea and the Welsh hills might be had. Hazlitt slept that night in an old room with blue hangings and walls covered with family portraits of the time of George I and George II. The windows of his bedroom looked on to the rustling, bracken-covered, tree-studded slopes. At that time of his life he was accustomed to "sleep o' nights"—but had he lain awake he might have heard many a sound of wild life during the night-hours. The first sound that fell on his ears at break of day as he lay between sleeping and waking, with indistinct but glorious shapes of happiness passing through his mind and a sense that, happy though he was, something better was yet to come, was the loud belling of the stag from the slopes in front of his windows.

As soon as breakfast was over he strolled out into the park with Coleridge, who had Wordsworth's poems in his hand. They seated themselves on the trunk of an old ash tree that lay on the ground and Coleridge read aloud some of the poems, his voice gradually falling into a chant as the poetry took hold of him. At first Hazlitt listened with the ear of faith rather than of understanding. In the Ballad of Betty Foy he felt touches of truth and nature, but as yet he did not realise what an extension of the domain of poetry the poem represented to Coleridge, although he was ready to accept his friend's estimate of its value. It was different when he listened to *The Thorn*, *The Mad Mother*, and *The Complaint of a poor Indian Woman.*[92] Then the poetry itself instantly convinced him of its quality. Not only was he affected by its power and pathos, but he heard in it a note that he had never heard in poetry before. He realised why Coleridge found it so exciting. It made him, too, feel as if he were on the brink of a new discovery, and the quality that he felt in it made him think somehow of the earth and of the tang of soil that has been freshly turned over. When he spoke of this, Coleridge said with some regret that the only criticism he had to make of some of his friend's poetry was that it was too much of the earth, that his genius sprang out of the ground like a flower, instead of descending to him through the air, that it was earth-born rather than heaven-sent. This, however, he added, applied only to the poetry in familiar subjects, or to some of the descriptive pieces: the philosophical poetry far transcended any such objection.

They spent the day at Alfoxden. In the cool of the evening they walked back to Nether Stowey, through echoing groves and by stream and waterfall gleaming in the summer moonlight. Hazlitt had fallen into the habit of walking alone, and ordinarily he much preferred to be alone with his thoughts when in the country. He did not need companionship at such times, and he found that human companionship flawed the perfection of the companionship he got from Nature. But he could not feel like this about a companion who was himself like the incarnation of the *genius* of the place, who "talked far above singing," whose speech seemed to waken the thoughts that lay "slumbering on golden ridges in the evening clouds," and whose words intoxicated him with what may be called "a fine madness:"

> "If steady moods of thoughtfulness, matur'd
> To inspiration, sort with such a name;
> If prophecy be madness; if things view'd
> By Poets in old time, and higher up
> By the first men, earth's first inhabitants,
> May in these tutor'd days no more be seen
> With undisorder'd sight."

9

In the course of the following evening the Poet arrived at Coleridge's cottage. Had Hazlitt only known it, he was now meeting the one man of his time whose struggle for expression had been as difficult, obscure, intense, prolonged and patient as his own. He thought that Wordsworth in some ways answered to Coleridge's description of him, and that yet at first sight he did not answer to any preconceived idea of a poet any one could have formed. Indeed he looked definitely what might be called prosaic. Whereas the light in Coleridge's eyes immediately suggested the thought that here was a poet, Wordsworth, rolling in from the wayside, gaunt and dusty, carelessly, even quaintly dressed in striped pantaloons and a brown fustian jacket, matter-of-fact in his manner and speaking with a Northern burr, suggested rather a countryman than a poet, although a countryman with a touch of Don Quixote about him. Saying that unlike Southey he knew a good thing when he saw it, he instantly began to make havoc of the half of a Cheshire cheese on the table. As he ate he talked very naturally and freely, in a deep voice that now and again when he raised it had light clear tones in it. His conversation was simple and unaffected. Now and again it had a touch of hard Northern idiom or colloquialism, as when, *à propos* of the duel which Tierney had just fought with Pitt on Putney Heath, he took them by surprise with the roughness of his exclamation: "I wish Tierney had shot out Pitt's tongue and put an end to his *gift of the gab*."

But when supper was over he lounged across to the window, and looking out of it, exclaimed: "How beautifully the sun sets on that yellow bank!" It was then that Hazlitt, noticing the fixture of regard, the fires, half burning, half smouldering, that came into the eyes as they watched the sunset stream upon the objects facing them, first saw him as a poet. The words, and the manner in which they were uttered, made an ineffaceable impression on him. He thought: "With what eyes these poets see nature!" Wordsworth looked at the moment as if he saw something more in objects than their outward appearance, or as if he looked through the outer husk of things to something which had suddenly transformed him from a simple-mannered countryman into a being who was either mad or inspired. Thus might the eyes of Ezekiel or Isaiah have looked.

Afterwards, as Coleridge talked, Hazlitt had leisure to study Wordsworth's face, to note the high narrow forehead, the Roman nose, the cheeks somewhat furrowed by feeling, the severe worn pressure of thought about the temples, the drooping weight of thought that sometimes settled on it. It was a face that in repose was stately, almost solemn, yet now and again there were movements about the mouth that belied the suggestion of solemnity, for they might have been indicative of suppressed laughter, and his smile had a peculiar sweetness. Coleridge's speech, no matter what he touched on, was, as always, like the music of the spheres; Wordsworth's, in comparison, was lowest plainsong, and often he fell into silence. He made no effort at all to attract attention. But once or twice, when poetry was mentioned, he spoke like a man inspired, and then the look that accompanied the words was far above eloquence.

10

The following day they walked over to Alfoxden again and the Poet read *Peter Bell* to them in the open air. Hazlitt was not sure what he felt about it; Wordsworth's voice, like Coleridge's, fell into a chant when he read poetry, and he thought that this method of recitation might be giving the words a quality which they did not in themselves possess. But whatever he felt about the poem, he was conscious of a stirring of sympathy when he saw how much it meant to its author: Wordsworth's face, as he read, "was as a book where men might read strange matters."

In the evening the Poet and his sister accompanied them part of the way home. The nightingale was singing, and Coleridge, who walked with Miss Wordsworth, tried to teach her to distinguish between the notes. He did not succeed in making himself quite intelligible to her. Neither did Hazlitt, who was with the Poet, make himself intelligible when he spoke of metaphysics.

This day was the prelude to many such. Coleridge's cottage was noisy and narrow, but the Quantocks were near, and Alfoxden was on the Quantocks. They spent much of their time in walking, or in lying in the groves of Alfoxden or among the hills, conversing. They do not seem to have talked much of politics. This may have been because their talk took the form of discussion, and Hazlitt may have taken it for granted, from the nature of the sermon he had heard Coleridge preach, that their views were in the main in sympathy with his own. On the other hand Coleridge and Wordsworth, whose sympathies with France had also been alienated by the invasion of Switzerland, being conscious that they were now in a moment of transition, may not have been at all eager to define their position with one who was so passionately in sympathy with the views they were just beginning to discard. Thus "the hidden stings" do not as yet "stimulate to hurt."

On books they talked much, whetting one another's wits in argument. Hazlitt found that some of his favourites in English literature were by no means Coleridge's favourites, and that Coleridge's criticism, while profound when it was based on sympathy, became unfair or even perverse when the basis of sympathy was lacking. Listening to Coleridge, he came to the conclusion that fine taste consists in sympathy, not in antipathy. Wordsworth was so much absorbed in his own poetry that he was less given to discussing the merits or demerits of individual poets than Coleridge was, and also his range was narrower; but when he sympathised, it was profoundly, and then his judgments were always excellent. Hazlitt and he joined hands in their admiration of Milton's poetry. When Wordsworth said one day that he could read the lines:

"Nor appear'd
Less then Arch Angel ruind, and th' excess
Of Glory obscur'd:"

till he felt a certain faintness come over his mind from a sense of their beauty and grandeur, Hazlitt saw no extravagance in the statement but only truth of feeling carried to its utmost extent.

Coleridge, being a critic by temperament, could not help exercising his mind on anything that came his way. Wordsworth, on the other hand, being primarily a creator, tended to exert his mind in criticism only when forced to do so by the needs of his art. His criticism was altogether practical in tendency. If he spoke a great deal about poetry it was because his mind was pondering the foundations of the structure he hoped to rear. At such times as he discussed the nature and the medium of poetry Hazlitt listened intently, conscious that new vision was being vouchsafed to him. Coleridge had given him his first initiation into the nature of poetry; in the Vale of Llangollen he had felt as if he were receiving his poetic baptism. Now he was beginning to walk in strength and faith according to his new creed. Day by day as he listened to the talk of these two poets, so closely united in sympathy yet so unlike each other in many respects, his mind opened and expanded as a plant opens and expands under the contrary influences of rain and sun. He was learning from the only two men in England who could have taught him the lesson, that poetry was not, as his earlier training had inclined him to consider it, the mere decorative border of literature, nor yet an ingenious arrangement, devised to give pleasure to the eye and ear, of words, rhymes and rhythms. It was, on the contrary, something that was co-extensive with life. It was the finer breath of all knowledge; it was the quintessence of all experience; it was the fiery particle within the bosom without which man's life were as poor as a beast's. The more he listened the more he wanted to hear. For their talk, so different from any he had heard before, he thirsted "as one bit by a dipsas." Gradually he learned to see with these men's eyes, and it was like seeing the old earth rolled away and a new earth and a new heaven revealed.

There was one other subject of which he could never tire, the joy Wordsworth had sensed in France when he had passed through it in the autumn of 1790: the dances garlanded with flowers which he had witnessed under the night-sky and the songs he had heard sung, the rejoicing of those who had grown tired of being treated as Nature's bastards and had asserted their rights as Nature's sons, and the quickening of the pulse of hope which had made it sufficient bliss to be alive when France had called to all her children to partake of equal blessings under her laughing skies.

If Wordsworth told him also of the uneasiness hanging over Paris

two years later, of the voice which he had heard in his dreams crying
"Sleep no more"—it made less impression on him than the tale of dance
and song.

II

At Nether Stowey they were constantly in the company of Tom
Poole the tanner, a friend no less dear to Coleridge than Wordsworth
himself. It was to be near Poole that Coleridge had first come to
Nether Stowey, and his cottage lay in the shadow of Poole's house much
as his life at this time rested under the sheltering tree of Poole's
friendship. A gate led from Coleridge's garden into Poole's, and
Coleridge when not at home or at Alfoxden was usually to be found
in the great windy kitchen of Poole's house, or sitting in an arbour
under his elm trees. When at Nether Stowey Hazlitt and he spent many
of the afternoons in this arbour, chatting and sipping their *flip* while
the bees hummed around them in the garden. Sometimes others,
"attracted to Coleridge's discourse as flies are to honey, or bees in
swarming-time to the sound of a brass pan," joined the party. Chief
of these was John Chester of Nether Stowey, whose felicity was complete when he could be in Coleridge's company and listen to his words.
Chester, who was short of stature and bowlegged and who had a drag
in his walk, had difficulty when out of doors in keeping up with
Coleridge; but so determined was he to lose no word which might
fall from his idol's lips, that he would break into a trot by his side
rather than fall out of hearing. Hazlitt, watching this performance,
thought Chester looked like a running footman by a state coach.
Comic though the sight was, it was also half pathetic, yet Hazlitt
sometimes thought that John Chester was at such moments the
happiest man among them all, happy as a dog is happy when in the
company of a beloved master.

When during the third week of Hazlitt's visit Coleridge and he
decided to make a three days' expedition down the Bristol Channel to
Lynton, Chester was their companion, dressed for the walk in a brown
cloth coat, boots and corduroy breeches, and equipped with a hazel
staff to assist his dragging foot in a walk that was nearer forty than
thirty miles. They marched by Watchet, past Dunster, looking,
between hill and sea, clear, pure and embrowned, like something seen
in an ideal landscape, through Minehead and Porlock, and so on to
Lynton. Their walk was very varied in character. For miles and miles
their path lay over brown heaths overlooking the channel, with the
Welsh hills beyond; now and again they descended into little valleys
near the sea; the ascent from these often led them up conical hills—
they would follow a winding path through a coppice only to come out

at last on a barren top "like a monk's shaven crown." The coming on of evening brought a touch of added picturesqueness. At sunset-time Hazlitt pointed out to Coleridge the bare masts of a vessel on the very edge of the horizon and within the disc of the setting sun, like his own spectral ship in *The Ancient Mariner*. Now and again a smuggler's face scowled up at them in the dusk from one or another of the valleys close to the seashore. At length darkness closed in on them, broken only by the cottage lights gleaming here and there. It was almost midnight before they reached the house in which they had hoped to find lodging for the night. At length, however, they succeeded in knocking the people up, and persuading them to cook an excellent supper of bacon and eggs. Coleridge was so far from being exhausted by the day's walk that when a few rumblings of thunder were heard he wanted to rush off at once to the Valley of Rocks to witness the play of the elements.

The next day they breakfasted on tea and toast, new-laid eggs and honey in its comb, taken from the hives within their sight and tasting of the thyme of which the garden was full. An old copy of *The Seasons* lay on the window-seat of the old-fashioned parlour in which they ate, and Coleridge, on seeing the little worn book, exclaimed: "That is true fame." Afterwards they lazed by the sea. A fisherman whom they met told Coleridge the story of the death by drowning of a boy the day before, and of how they had tried to save him at the risk of their own lives. "We have a *nature* towards one another," he said. Coleridge asked Hazlitt if that were not a fine natural illustration of the theory of the Disinterestedness of the Human Mind, of which he talked so much. Hazlitt, noticing a mark on the sand like the shape of a man's foot, broached to Coleridge the train of reasoning he had followed in the inn at Witham Common, from which he considered himself to have proved that likeness was not mere association of ideas. John Chester, although he had no idea what they were talking about, listened intently, and appeared to be greatly surprised that any one could suggest a new train of thought to Coleridge. In such talk and idling the day passed.

When they returned to Nether Stowey on the third day they were able to get some impression of those parts of the district which the coming on of night had hidden from them two days before. The smoke of many morning fires was now curling up in valleys where previously they had seen nothing but a few lights gleaming through the darkness.

12

On the Sunday following this walk Hazlitt left for home. He felt that his debt to Coleridge far transcended anything he could ever do in acknowledgment of it, but for Mrs. Coleridge he was planning a delightful gift, a miniature of her husband, to be executed by his brother the miniaturist as soon as Coleridge could give the necessary sittings.[93] Coleridge accompanied him on the first stage of his journey. He was preaching that day again for Dr. Toulmin at Taunton, but in the evening Hazlitt and he met at Bridgwater, and the next day they walked the thirty odd miles to Bristol together. Their talk was still of Poetry. As they rested by the side of a well Coleridge repeated a few lines from his tragedy *Remorse*.

The next time Hazlitt heard these lines it was on the boards of Drury Lane.

He had not gone to hear Coleridge preach at Taunton. This may seem surprising until we remember the jealous care with which he guarded his paramount impressions. He had not desired to see Mrs. Siddons twice as Lady Macbeth. He had not desired to read *The Robbers* a second time. How then should he wish to hear Coleridge preach once more! Such memories were not lightly to be disturbed. Nor were such experiences as these to be tarnished by handling, or dulled by repetition, or endangered by exposure to the common light of day.[94]

He told his father that he expected to arrive at Wem the following Saturday or Sunday. We may permit our eyes to linger upon him once more as he draws towards his childhood's home, for now again, having reached the end of a stage of development, he is about to undergo another of his Protean changes. At the moment he is still recognisable from the miniature taken of him as a boy in his teens. The lines of the face have been still further sharpened and refined, but wistfulness has now become the most marked characteristic of the expression. This wistfulness is perhaps enhanced by the pallor of the skin, thrown into relief by the black hair. Delicate as the face is, it has plenty of strength, shown especially in the lines of the finely modelled chin; yet the strength may not be of the kind that can protect the extreme sensitiveness. Here is one who has provided with all care for the intellectual being in himself, who has forged keen intellectual weapons and wrought fine intellectual armour, but who has taken no care to guard the sensitive being. Yet he needs to guard it more than most men, for he feels all things more sharply than others, and this, although he lacks neither spirit nor courage, makes him pitifully vulnerable.

Even his knowledge is one-sided. If he knows much of which most men know little or nothing, he is still in a state of dreaming ignorance as to much which all men realise. In particular, he lives as regards

HAZLITT AS A YOUNG MAN

Woman almost entirely in an ideal world. It would be untrue to assert or even to suggest that he had experienced in his twenty years of life none of those sensations which Wordsworth would describe as "slight shocks of young love-liking," but his life on the whole had progressed in such a way that women and girls had played comparatively little part in it. He knew few women intimately, apart from his mother and sister. During his childhood he had shared largely in his father's interests, which were those of an ageing man. During the years at college he had been more or less cut off from feminine society. In the following years his intellectual preoccupation had been so intense as to occupy most of his time and thoughts, and the Daimon of writing is one that tends to cast out all others. Just at the age when adolescent feeling might have been expected to come to a climax and to begin to operate on his life, his passion for Coleridge had swept him out of the normal course of emotional development.

Yet he has his ideal of Woman. This is a compound of the pleasant qualities of character of his mother and sister, the only two women who loved him, and of the physical and spiritual graces of his favourite women in fiction, all blended into one. His ideal woman is gentle; loving rather than sensual; selfless to the degree of appearing only to exist in her attachment to those she loves. Hers is the face "pale as the primrose;" the low voice that is noticed, as a violet is noticed, only because of its beauty; the loveliness that flaunts itself so little as to pass unobserved until all in a moment it is found to have taken possession of the heart through the perfection of its delicacy; the unobtrusive grace of a wild flower. Above all things else, this ideal of his has grace. She is among women what the primrose and the wild anemone and the violet are among flowers. She is Julia; she is Viola; she is Clarissa; she is Desdemona; perhaps more than any of these, she is faithful Imogen.

This ideal of his has little relation to his bodily desires, or indeed to anything connected with flesh and blood. She is rather a shadowy Grace, haunting his thoughts and his rare dreams. Although he is both passionate and sensual his thoughts of Woman are as yet dissociated from the physical desire that hangs about him, as it seems to him, like a clog thwarting and interrupting the essential movement of his life. Certainly he never thinks of her as the means of slaking this desire. He has hardly a thought about her that is not connected with, even saturated with sentiment.

In the presence of this shadowy Grace he is always recalled to quietness and content, but in the world of flesh and blood he is ill at ease with women. His torturing shyness prevents him from making any real contact with such women and girls as he meets. Even in the company of men, although now and again he can throw it off, it is so marked as to give him an appearance of eccentricity. In the company of women it makes him appear half an idiot. A poor shepherd lad, hardly knowing how to spell his name, is likely to make a more thriving wooer than the one who had cried his eyes out over the refinements of sentiment of *The New Eloise*.

Now his years of solitary study are over. He of the wistful countenance is going to be torn from his dream and flung forth into "the dangerous world"—dangerous at least to all such as he—to fend for himself in body and soul as best he may. How is such an one as he has become going to accomplish the transition from the ideal world to the actual? Is he not likely, as he stumbles along in the semi-twilight of his idealisms, to prove a temptation and a challenge to every ditch-bramble to lie in wait for him and shoot forth branches that mangle the bosom like spiteful tongues? Will not "mandrake and toadstool and dock and darnel" pour their poison into the air as he passes? Will not every creeping thing erect its head to strike and to hiss?

William of Wem! a poison-thorny way lies before thee!

Part Three

THE PLEASURE OF PAINTING

Portrait-painting is the biography of the pencil, and he who gives most of the peculiarities and details, with most of the general character,—that is, of keeping, is the best biographer and the best portrait-painter.

HAZLITT.

Chapter One

LEARNING TO PAINT (1798-1801)

"Like other gross sensualists, he had a horror of the society of ladies, especially of smart and handsome and modest young women."

HENRY CRABB ROBINSON.

1

WE HAVE tried to indicate the nature of the forces from within and the forces from without working upon Hazlitt between 1790 and 1798, so that the happy child gradually developed into the thought-oppressed, silent, constricted youth to whom Coleridge brought some measure of deliverance. We have now to record a second apparent transmutation of personality. We say "apparent" because the nature of the man remained unchanged throughout, although it was so complex that as this, that, or the other element in it was stirred into primary activity, to the casual observer it appeared to have changed completely.

That the years we are going to consider produced a change in outward seeming there can be no question. The Hazlitt who appeared in Keswick in the summer of 1803 and in whom Coleridge was not slow to discern a tendency towards sexual promiscuity might seem to bear little relationship to the Hazlitt who had come to Nether Stowey in the summer of 1798, knowing nothing of Woman.

Moreover, this seeming alteration of character was not the only alteration. There had been also a re-orientation of interests. When Hazlitt had come to Nether Stowey he had been obsessed by metaphysics to the point of torment. When he reappeared at Keswick he was obsessed to the point of torment by pictures, and not only by pictures, but by all the technical processes of painting. He was like a man with a new Love. He talked, thought and dreamed of pictures, both those he had seen, and those which thus far, although he saw them no less clearly, had existence only in his mind's eye.

129

Our task is now to relate the course of this "apparent" two-fold alteration, which we believe rather to be the inevitable continuation of all that had gone before, or the inevitable development of all that had gone before, under the influence of an entirely new set of circumstances.

2

This new set of circumstances came into being in the most ordinary way, and out of the most practical reasons. It was becoming imperative for Hazlitt by the summer of 1798 to learn how to make a living. Also it was beginning to seem to those who cared for him that he would never make a living by his pen. He is beginning to seem something of a problem to his people, for he has now two false starts to his discredit. He had drifted into preparation for the ministry and had withdrawn on finding that he had no vocation for it. He had been allowed three years in which to make progress with the work to which he felt he had been called, and although it is easy enough now for the onlooker to see that in these years he did much towards laying down the foundations of his life-work, both to his friends looking on and to himself at the time, it seemed as if he had done little. Yet he had no definite impulse towards any other calling. Therefore it may have seemed, both to his people and to himself, that his best chance lay in trying to prepare himself for making a living in much the same way as his brother had succeeded in making one. John could help him in his training, could perhaps help him in gaining clients after he had learned to paint. These seem to have been the motives which launched him forth into the study of painting, rather than any definite inclination of his own. It is true that as a child he had taken it for granted that he would do as his brother had done, that sometimes he had amused himself by drawing, and had told his brother about his drawings, but all that is long past. He knows little about pictures: indeed now and again he looks at them speculatively, wondering whether any one could possibly feel the same stimulus in painting them, the same excitement, anguish and uneasy delight as that which he himself had felt in writing.

Yet he goes to London to learn painting with a view to making a living as a painter of portraits. His means are straitened. He is apparently going to let himself be driven by the necessities of the moment into repeating the mistake he has already made, of drifting into preparation for a profession towards which he felt no special inclination and for which as yet he has shown no aptitude. He is drifting: but this matters the less because, as we have seen, his sphere has already made choice of him.

3

We find him then, in the autumn of 1798, beginning his life again as a student in London, but this time as a student of art. This beginning, simple and practical as had been its origin, is going to prove infinitely complex in its effects on his life and personality. That he should have made it was, of course, a confession of failure in the main purpose of his life, an admission of his consciousness that the training of his schooldays and college days, the training he had received from books, and the enlightenment he had received from two great poets, had left him dumb and inexpressive. What he did not know was that it was all that was needed to make all this earlier preparation fruitful to him. It was necessary for him that there should be set at work upon his spirit the corrosion of a phase of life utterly different from any he had hitherto experienced, and the discipline of learning a new art, before he could realise his aspirations in the art that was to be his own. The progress from the metaphysicians to the poets has to be completed by progress from the poets to the painters, for whom the poets, all unknowing what they did, have prepared him, especially by progress to intercourse with the master-spirits among the painters. Under their domination he must now remain for a time, not indeed to master their art, for that is not necessary, but to enter into it in the measure which is necessary for him before he can master his own.

4

The immediate effect of this plunge into a new world was not the quickening of his artistic sensibility but the subjection of his personality to forces which hitherto had not touched his life at all. If his education had been too sectarian, here at last is the corrective so powerful that for a time it may seem doubtful whether it is not going to unmake rather than to remake him. He has now been dropped into a world in which all the values in which he had been bred are, if not actually reversed, very much altered. If he had been inclined to think the sect in which he had been bred the salt of the earth, he had now come upon the complete antidote for any such spiritual pride or intellectual coxcombry. He is in a world in which "Rational Christianity" is little regarded, in which indeed the pursuit of any of the forms of religion is little considered. Disputes as to the interpretation of the texts of Scripture have little relevance here, or even discussion as to the bases of politics, thought and faith. Conduct is not made the criterion of value, nor is the formation of character a main preoccupation of this world. Right and wrong would at times appear to be shadowy words in it, names rather than realities. Little is heard of integrity of living. Yet this world has its religion too. In it integrity of art is what matters most, appears at times to be all that matters.

Apart from Benjamin West, the aged President of the Academy, whom Hazlitt, at least, considered "a man of no mark or likelihood," this world is dominated by three men, each of them absorbed in art, each of them subtle in distinguishing and interpreting human nature, each of them a remarkable conversationalist—Opie, Fuseli, and James Northcote. With Opie, Hazlitt had no acquaintance. The other two he knew, and he found each of them a species by himself. Each of them was extraordinarily disconcerting. Fuseli, who was then just three years short of his sixtieth birthday, was a little man with a lion face that readily became distorted with passion and a tongue that in its power to annihilate matched the expression of his face. His manners, too, like Opie's, were intimidating. At times he was foul-mouthed: always he was reckless and extravagant of speech. Erratic and eccentric, gesticulatory to the point of uncouthness, provocative, sceptical as to the value of all things except art and literature, exceedingly vain, while to poor or timid minds he was actually ruinous, he yet had much to give to youth if it were keen-witted, for he had imagination, devotion, and a touch of genius, even if it were not specifically the genius of the painter. Although he had devoted his life to painting, he was more than half a poet, and the spark of fire from heaven, which resided in him somewhere, sometimes alighted on and devastated not only the pretensions of others but his own pretensions, posturings, and posings. If he could flash a word like a searchlight through the soul of a fool, he could also turn round on his own folly and expose it in the searchlight of his own self-vision. He had a most disconcerting way of altering all in a moment from the vain and mannered artist claiming admiration in his vain dogmatic way for his posing and his blunders and ready to lap up any flattery, into the genuine man of vision who saw through himself and everybody else. He would stand at his easel in his studio in Wardour Street, clad in an old flannel dressing-gown, enjoying the picturesqueness of his appearance and performance, painting with his left hand, peering with his near-sighted eyes at the canvas on to which he would perhaps put a hideous touch of Prussian blue where he was endeavouring to indicate the gradations of flesh tints, would cover up this blunder with a dab of red to deaden it, and would claim admiration for the blunder, exclaiming challengingly to the tyro watching him: "By Gode, dat's a fine purple: it's vary like Correggio, by Gode!" but the next moment as likely as not he would whip round with a quotation from Homer, Virgil, Ovid, Dante or Tasso that annihilated all such affectation, and as if he were conscious of the "vigorous impotence" of his own achievement, would follow it up desperately with: "Paint *dat*, by Gode!"

When he touched on the great masters there could be no question of his power. He spoke with a tongue of fire.

Northcote,[95] some five years younger than Fuseli, was considered hardly less formidable, although the fear he aroused was awakened by means more subtle. He too was both eccentric and disconcerting in his ways. Now he would speak in silver tones that matched the silver in his hair; now he would break disconcertingly into the broadest Devon dialect. His speech could be most venomous when its tones were very fine and gentle, and he could say the grossest things so that they sounded the very essence of refinement. He seemed to have few human feelings. Those who knew him best would as soon have thought of going to a flint as of going to him in time of trouble. He was of life, but detached from it. Hazlitt, who feared neither of these men, for it was only with mediocrity that he was at a loss, speedily fell into some measure of companionship with Northcote, and into a relationship of what might be called impersonal friendship, in which he found a keen delight. He was seldom happier than when in Northcote's dirty painting-room in 39 Argyle Street, watching the painter at work, wandering round the studio looking at pictures that had been painted before he was born, listening to reminiscences of Sir Joshua or Burke or Goldsmith, whetting his wits in endless discussion and argument, delighting in the numberless stories that were poured out, not consecutively, as if conversation consisted in the stringing together of one story after another, but always with a view to illustrating some aspect of character or some point in argument. Where others feared, he relished the streaks of caustic comment with which the anecdotes were interspersed. Listening to such talk was like eating anchovy sandwiches, and he never tired of the fare.

Northcote was almost always engaged on something connected with his art, but there was no saying where he might be found or what he might be doing. Like Fuseli he was a little man, and sometimes his diminutive form would be perched on the top of a ladder, finishing a sky or painting the top of a palm tree in one of his pictures; sometimes he might be squatted on the floor, like a child at play, amusing himself by turning over a set of old prints. When he stood brush in hand before his easel, with his ancient blue-striped dressing-gown wrapped well round his emaciated figure, he looked not unlike a wizard or necromancer. In after years he seemed to Hazlitt like a history-piece or like someone who had wrought his way through to immortality, while yet existing in time: "His body is a shadow; he himself is a pure spirit. There is a kind of immortality about this sort of visionary existence that dallies with Fate, and baffles the grim monster, Death." By that time age had crowned his picturesqueness, but even in the early days of the tenuous, highly specialised friendship between the two men, Northcote, abstracted into his art, made a strong appeal both to Hazlitt's historical sense and to his imagination.

From such as these, Hazlitt learned to readjust and to extend his values. It would be difficult to imagine any one more unlike anything he had ever been taught to consider admirable than Northcote, whose heart and whose hand were both closed, who dropped out of his scheme of existence the very idea of the duty of practical benevolence as something which had nothing to do with his purpose in life, who did not even invite to eat at his table those with whom he shared his thoughts, whose sole hospitality was that of his silver-tongued, yet often malicious conversation. But he recognised that there was good in the man who would speak of Titian's pictures with tears in his eyes, and whose face, always fine and expressive, as he spoke of the painter he worshipped, seemed itself to take on some of the character of a painting by Titian.

Contact with such personalities brought to him an extension of experience, but his development was still more deeply affected by the crude unfashioned life of the school of art, by the heightening of sensual perception involved in his training as an artist, and by the conditions under which he worked, than it was even by these leading painters, each of whom was already enclosed as in cast iron in a personality conditioned primarily by a passion for art. The life that was still in the making and that was open to the play of all the forces that mould human nature influenced his own more than the life set in a mould that could henceforth never be altered.

Hazlitt nowhere states[96] that he studied at the Royal Academy School, but all that he says of his training seems to imply it. At any rate, it proves that he studied at a school of art. Here he learned to draw the human figure from living models. He who had been crying his eyes out at the beginning of the year over the refinements of sentiment of *The New Eloise*, but who had been almost too shy to look a living woman in the face, is now required to study and refine upon the body of Woman as an object of art. The effect of the shock of this experience wore off quickly. The stillness, the artificial light, the concentration of all around him, the publicity of the work, the difficulty of the task of reproducing even in some slight degree the wonder of the human form, the checks administered to sexual feeling by the pangs of mortified aspiration and endeavour, all these combined to invest the task with an atmosphere of impersonality. The work became exactly like that of copying from a statue; the artist's pencil acted as "a non-conductor to desire," the despair of rivalling in art what was seen in nature and the anxiety to copy the object exactly, deadened the likelihood of any personal reaction. The only moment that continued to trouble him was the moment when the posing was over, and when the model seemed almost like a statue coming to life again. In that moment indeed the eyes might grow hot and the blood begin to beat hard; but it was quickly over.

If, however, he became quickly inured to the work, so that the moments of excitement accompanying it were few and transitory, there was one circumstance accompanying it which was not transitory in its effects upon his life: the women who posed thus in the schools of art in England at that time were prostitutes. Hazlitt had not been in and out of London for five years without being aware of the tide of prostitution that poured through its streets. Nor was he insensible to the horror and the pity of it. It was afterwards objected to him that in his sexual relationships he recognised "no game laws." How should he, when to him as to Shelley, whose liveliest moods could always be overshadowed in a moment by the thought of prostitution, no human being was "game," when like Leigh Hunt, he was human enough to realise that "the seventy thousand prostitutes alone in the streets of London . . . most probably experience more bitterness of heart every day of their lives than is caused by any campaign, however wild!"

Now this tide is, as it were, brought within doors for him by the circumstances of his new profession. The year which has brought his first acquaintance with poets has also brought his first acquaintance with prostitutes, in a manner peculiarly distressing to any one in whom the fine edge of sensibility had not been blunted, and in whom compassion had not been dulled. Even prostitution has the reverse side of the shield, and it was the reverse side with which he first became acquainted. The women who posed for the students were all past their prime—Hazlitt himself referred to them as "battered" prostitutes—all very nearly past the hope of any further barter in the beaten way of sex, all driven by need to work they loathed, for they felt as a last humiliation the indignity of exposing their bodies to the passionless gaze of youths for the moment intent only upon their art, regarding and pointing out defects or beauties of figure precisely as if discussing clay or marble, looking them over with an eye to art just as the anatomist examines the human figure with a view to science. Humiliation in the ordinary course of human nature they had known, but here they felt as if they were being exposed to humiliation of a kind that went contrary to the ordinary course of human nature, so that the experience wrought on them with extreme bitterness: indeed, if there had been "crime" in their lives, the ingenuity of the spirits ironic could not have devised "punishment" so searching in the kind of suffering it inflicted. These women, declining in market value day by day, had reached the stage in their descent, when unable any longer to earn their bread by the degradation of the body alone, they had to earn it through subjecting themselves to a vivisection of the very instincts of womanhood too. Northcote, who was fine in grain, realised something of what was passing through their minds. If most of the painters, however, who hired them ever considered the matter at all, it was chiefly to regret that English art was hampered by having to deal with such poor worn-out material as this, that even Sir Joshua had only been able to get a "battered courtesan" to sit for his Iphigenia, while Canova, more fortunate in the conditions in which he worked, could get fresh and innocent girls to pose for him; but the women, posing in the artificial light of this artificial world, from which passion was supposed to be excluded, did yet passion with the sufferings of the damned. Some of them, unable to endure the exposure of their ininability any longer to earn a living in the legitimate way of their trade, came masked. So deep was their sense of humiliation that it was for them a triumph if, when the posing was over, certain of the students watched for them, followed them, and entered into connections with them.

The young raw students were variously affected by their reactions to this traffic in ageing and embittered womanhood. Some of those who, thinking that "profligacy was a part of genius," gained their first knowledge of Woman from these spirits unfortunate, found the experience blistering: not a few were ruined both in body and in spirit by the connection, ruined too, not only as men, but as artists. Others, absorbed in their work and insensitive to all that did not further it, were lucky enough to remain unaffected. Yet others were affected, but not in the immediate, grosser way. As to its effect on Hazlitt, we can only judge of it partly by what we can gather from his writing, partly by what we can discern of his nature. It is clear that, having been up to this time, in his home life, in his college life, and through his absorption in writing, exceptionally sheltered from the experience of the grosser forms of evil, on being brought up against the physical basis of passion in this way and the knowledge of its ugly ramifications, consequences and implications, he received a shock sufficiently painful to haunt his memory, and of a kind which made him resolute afterwards to shield his son from any similar experience. He had regarded his study of metaphysics as the study of one branch of the tree of the knowledge of good and evil, yet he now found that it helped him little in the shock of immediate experience. Indeed it seemed to him that sudden initiation into the knowledge of the world and its baser traffickings bore the more heavily on a mind that had been refined by and abstracted into long thought. Afterwards he wrote: "it must be owned that the practical knowledge of vice and misery makes a stronger impression on the mind, when it has imbibed a habit of abstract reasoning. Evil thus becomes embodied in a general principle, and shews its harpy form in all things. It is a fatal, inevitable necessity hanging over us. It follows us wherever we go: if we fly to the uttermost parts of the earth, it is there: whether we turn to the right or the left, we cannot escape from it. This, it is true, is the disease of philosophy; but it is one to which it is liable in minds of a certain cast, after the first order of expectation has been disabused by experience, and the finer feelings have received an irrecoverable shock from the jarring of the world."[97]

The simple reaction to shock of this kind would of course be an intensification of the Puritanism in which he had been bred: but Hazlitt, although Puritanism was the foundation of his character, was never simple in his reactions to experience. We have here no evidence to guide us as to his actions, but we can take into account not only the testimony as to what he was in 1798 and as to what he had become a few years later, but what we know of his nature, especially of his reaction to shock of any kind. Indeed, we can no longer postpone the attempt, difficult though it may be, and obscure though it may seem, at giving some account of an element in his nature which contributed largely to making his life what it became: for to those who close their eyes to this element, Hazlitt's life can never be either credible or intelligible. This element, when considered in a rough-and-ready way, may be named perversity, if attraction towards that which is most feared or hated or dreaded may be called perversity. Hazlitt himself did not define it as perversity, but as being temporarily subjected to the power of fascination. He was of those who when under powerful feeling of any kind, even if it were not pleasurable but painful, not desired nor desirable, but loathsome, are dominated by an intense and irresistible impulse, overpowering any other consideration, of carrying the feeling to its crisis. He could well understand how a girl, terrified at being shut in a room with a dead body, could end, under the intense and irresistible impulse of carrying her terror to its height, by embracing the corpse in a transport of fear and loathing. He could understand the fascination which makes it dangerous for many to stand on the edge of a precipice, because they are overcome by the longing to take the leap which they most dread.[98] He could even understand the confession of an acquaintance who told him that once when looking into a cauldron of boiling lead he had felt an almost overpowering impulse to hurl himself headlong into it. He could understand that there were some, to whom the sudden, ghastly appearance of a gibbet "rearing its spectral form in some solitary place at nightfall, by a woodside, or barren heath," and the sight of "the wretched scarecrow figure dangling upon it, black and wasted, parched in the sun, drenched in all the dews of Heaven that fall cool and silent on it," instead of serving as a deterrent to crime, might serve as the shock that precipitated them into daring their fear and tempting the same fate. He could understand how there are some to whom the fears of their prison-house have become so necessary that even when the doors are opened they dread to walk out, as they might dread walking

into total vacuity. He could understand how a man, not entirely
devoid of reason, when under the power of fascination of this kind and
a mere "fear of the event," could bind himself for life to a woman
he did not love; and equally how a man, under the influence of this
same fatal fascination, could turn and injure one whom he did most
truly love. There was no one of these "toys of desperation" the
mechanism of which he did not understand. He knew every implication, physical as well as spiritual, of the lines:

> "Never so sure our rapture to create
> As when it touch'd the brink of all we hate."[99]

To him, as to all such souls, pity is due! for to say all this is but to
say that the gods have dowered him with a two-edged knife over which
he has little control, and with which he will inevitably one day deal
himself wounds more cruel than either friend or foe will deal him.
Wordsworth afterwards called him "as perverse as Lord Byron himself,"[100] but the comparison is misleading. The only true fellow and
companion of Hazlitt among the men of his generation in this respect,
in its suffering, in its idiosyncrasy, its genuineness and its painful
distinction, was Beckford, who was cast in somewhat the same mould.
Byron, although he had a perverse streak in him somewhere, was
by comparison a posturer, merely engaged for the most part, when
he appeared to be perverse, in an attempt at an extension of his personality that would impress his immediate world. The true perverse,
being involuntary in character, when it takes possession of a man,
leaves no room for any touch of the coxcomb or any of the impulses
of coxcombry.

With this note on the nature of the reaction to shock, illustrated
many times in Hazlitt's life, of one whose impulses were thus conditioned by his nerves, noting too that when we see him in London
some years afterwards he certainly had a number of "*protegées*" among
the women of the town, we may leave for the moment our consideration of the elements affecting his development as a moral being
during his training as an art student, and pass on to our next theme—
the absorption in painting into which he fell presently and the development which came to him as an intellectual being through that absorption.

5

The immediate circumstance which led to this absorption was the
opening of an exhibition of Italian pictures, most of which had come
from the Orleans collection in Paris, in Pall Mall in December, 1798.

It is not too much to say that but for this exhibition Hazlitt might never have become a painter at heart. He would have learned doubtless the technique of painting, studying in a patient uninspired way, working as one who expected to earn a living as a portrait-painter; but it would have been mechanical learning. Nothing in his actual training or in the work of the living painters he had met had inspired in him the passionate love of art he was now to show. Even more strange to reflect upon, as we consider the many "chances," if such they may be called, of which Hazlitt's life was compact, than the sudden conflagration of mind brought about by these pictures, is the fact that had the exhibition come a year earlier in his experience it might have meant little to him, for he would have looked at it with unseeing eyes. Up to the time of his meeting with Coleridge he would have been as blind to its revelation as until that time he had been blind to the revelation of poetry, for although Coleridge knew nothing of pictures, it was Coleridge who, in making him understand the nature of poetry, had also placed in his hand the key to the meaning of art. When there came to him, shortly after Coleridge had made him understand the nature of the labour on which the creative mind is engaged, the opportunity of seeing the best pictures, he saw, because his eyes had been prepared to see, that the greatest painters, although using another medium, were also engaged in expressing in their own fashion what he had learned from Coleridge to recognise as poetry. This is the meaning of the transcendent excitement that took hold of him when he viewed the work of the old Italian Masters. He saw that they too were giving expression to "the fiery particle within the bosom." They too were looking on the world around them, as Wordsworth had looked on the sunshine setting upon a yellow bank, with eyes that burned, and each man was seeing, not something which was nonexistent in Nature, but something which existed yet which other men's vision failed to observe, and which had to be revealed by art ere it could be realised. All eyes looked upon it, but all eyes did not see. In being made to see what these men had seen, he felt as if he had been dowered with a new sense; and he realised that the secret of the greatest painting, as of the greatest poetry, was not mechanical excellence, although that too was necessary, but vision. Each great painter, even as each great poet, *saw* something, either in Nature or in human nature, that others did not see, selected it, and gave his life to revealing it. Even as the poet *sang* "of things invisible to mortal sight," the painter *made visible* on his canvas that which, though existent in the infinite mystery of Nature and of human nature, had as yet been "invisible to mortal sight." This was high art; the rest was mechanical. The substance of poetry was also the substance of painting. Fuseli, with his "Paint *dat*, by Gode!" had hit the mark. If the poet, repeating the miracle in Virgil, made the bark of the tree

to open its lips and discourse, the painter revealed the bark itself so
that what he showed was more than speech. He talked by natural
signs, and expressed his thoughts by objects; or rather, objects, as he
rendered them, were identical with the thoughts he wished to reveal.
Things, colours, lines, took the place of speech. Hieroglyphics were
substituted for words. The language was different, but what was said
in it had the same meaning.

This special vision or poetry of envisagement was to be found pre-
eminently in the infinite gradations of colour in Titian's landscapes,
in Guido's expression of the feminine character "in its fragile, lovely
essence," in Raphael's "speaking faces" and the hands "we always wish
to touch."

The first spiritual awakening had come to Hazlitt from the great
English actress of his time; the second from the greatest English poet
of his time. The third came from another country and from the
Masters of the past. In giving an impression of what it meant to him
he fell once more into the idiom he always used to express transcendent emotional experience. Now once again he was startled as if
from sleep, yet stunned with the premonition of new life to come,
as the Masters of Italian art called to him:

"My initiation in the mysteries of art was at the Orleans Gallery:
it was there I formed my taste, such as it is. . . . I was staggered when
I saw the works there collected, and looked at them with wondering
and with longing eyes. A mist passed away from my sight; the scales
fell off." [101]

The scales fell off! That, in some respect or other, was indeed the
sum total of each awakening. In this third awakening the falling off
of the scales was the herald of hope. Self-expression in some form or
another was necessary to him, but all his life he had thought only of
achieving it in words. Yet such was the tenuity to which his ideas had
been drawn, so deeply had he been plunged into the void of abstraction,
that he had thought without words or images at all, and the gulf
between thought and expression had begun to seem impassable. Now
he saw that he had been wrong in thinking there was nothing in the
world but books. It has suddenly burst in upon him that there is at
least one other mode of self-expression. For all he knows there may be
many others, but his immediate ambition is to attempt self-expression
in the new mode which he has discovered, and which has had such
marvels to offer him. He is determined to achieve in painting the
expressiveness which has been denied him in writing. Although he
does not know it, he will never be a great painter, even if by sheer force
of will he will make himself a competent one; yet will his effort not
have been vain. The day will come when he will have learned to unite

his tenuity of thought with the power to translate the colour and form and the natural symbolism of painting into words, and in that day he will write as no one had ever written before him and as no one has ever written after him, for his writing will be the thoughts of a metaphysician expressed by one who is a painter at heart and who has learned to express the essentials of painting in words. That day is not now very far distant. In one of the last acknowledgments he made to Coleridge, he wrote: "Till I began to paint, or till I became acquainted with the author of *The Ancient Mariner*, I could neither write nor speak." He did well to link these two experiences together, for the one of them, flowing directly from the other, was for him the origin of all good.

6

From this time he lived in a world of pictures. The Orleans exhibition was on view until July, 1799, and most of his leisure was now spent there. He tells us something of what it meant to him: "Old Time had unlocked his treasures, and Fame stood Portress at the door. We had all heard of the names of Titian, Raphael, Guido, Domenichino, the Carracci—but to see them face to face, to be in the same room with their deathless productions, was . . . almost like an effect of necromancy."[102] Some of the pictures haunted him. He could gaze at them by the hour together, thrilling to their beauty till his eyes filled with tears. One of these was Lodovico Carracci's "Susannah and the Elders." He never tired of the wonder of the expression the painter had succeeded in depicting on the face of the lovely Jewess, the mingling of terror and shame that yet left the "unconquerable sweetness" untouched, as Susannah, still beauteous in her fear, cowered down in the unguarded spot in which she had been surprised, her arms crossed, the whole figure "shrinking into itself with bewitching grace and modesty." He looked up day after day at the "Danäe" of Annibale Carracci, which happened to be hung very high, at the fine expectancy of the upturned face, at the figure "desirable, ample, worthy of a god," at the golden shower and at the landscape, which one might fancy shuddering and cold. He never ceased to marvel at the painting of the flesh in the huge "Raising of Lazarus" by Sebastiano del Piombo. It seemed dingy, already tainted, ready "to crumble at the touch," at the moment of liberation from its dread confinement. The delineation of the "Death of Adonis," by Luca Cambiaso, had on the other hand a faded loveliness. This was life expiring, yet still life, and lovely as a dying sunset. If these meant so much to him, what shall we say of the endless delight he took in the Titians! Now he could understand how Northcote, caustic and sparing of commendation though he was, could speak of Titian's art with tears in his eyes. He thought the "Diana and Callisto" had only one fellow in the world, and that was the "Diana and Actæon." In the "Diana and Callisto" the rich and serene harmonies, the landscape, the water so translucent that the snowy feet of the naked nymphs are reflected in it, the colours of the sky, dazzling, profuse, gorgeous, yet "blended, softened, woven together into a woof like that of Iris," the tints of flesh colour "as if you saw the blood circling beneath the pearly skin," the combination of prodigality and discipline displayed everywhere, gave him, all of them, inconceivable pleasure. In the "Diana and Actæon" it was the way in which Titian combined with the greatest prodigality of genius "the greatest severity and discipline of art" that specially compelled his admiration. Everything in this picture led the eye to the goddess, her faced edged with anger and scorn, her figure no less indignant and queenlike. The way in which the figure of Diana while it keeps its god-like separateness is yet made integral with the details of the picture, seemed to him a miracle of art. Many years afterwards he wrote of it: "Every colour is melted, *impasted* into every other, with fine keeping and bold diversity."[103] Again, he felt as if he would never forget the energy of the landscape in "The Punishment of Actæon," the sense of life conveyed by it, the "prodigious gusto."

These, which seemed to him, all of them, miracles of conception and execution, gave him more delight than the "Venus Anadyomene," lovely as he thought the single, exquisitely turned figure, the attitude, the gesture of the hands holding up the dripping hair, and the painting of the background. It had all beauty yet it did not satisfy his imagination. It showed a very lovely woman; but was it Venus, or Venus rising from the sea?[104]

Hazlitt now sought out good pictures wherever they were to be found. He was often drawn to the rooms, also in Pall Mall, of Noel Joseph Desenfans, picture-dealer and collector. There he had the opportunity of getting to know the pictures which were being collected with a view to forming the nucleus of a Polish National Gallery. Here he learned that the vision which made man only a little lower than the angels was not confined to the great Italian Masters. The Orleans collection was deficient in Dutch and Flemish pictures, but in the Desenfans collection this vision could be discerned in the extreme purity and silvery clearness of Vandyke, in the movement of some of the pictures of Rubens, in the soft transparent distances of Aelbert Cuyp's landscapes, in the peace of Van Goyen's canals and yellow-tufted banks, in the gorgeous obscurity of Rembrandt. Each Master had his own vision and his own gift. The painter who held him most deeply in thrall at this time was Rembrandt, and the painting which called most deeply to his spirit was "Jacob's Dream."

The contrasts in this picture, in which Rembrandt's art of contrast is itself sublimated, the dream landscape, the hills that look like the hills we see in sleep, the parched and stunted bushes in the corner, the scarecrow figure of the man flung down beside them like a bundle of old clothes, drowned in exhaustion, sleeping as if the breath were out of his body, all of them illuminated by the bright vision, equally dream-like, "the dazzling flights of angels' wings like steps of golden light, emanations of flame or spirit hovering between earth and sky," the shapes that were not human nor even angelical, but precisely such as we see hovering in dreams, bird-like, beaked, "white-vested, treading on clouds," ascending and descending "through the realms of endless light that loses itself in endless space," transported him out of himself. The spiritual contrast too, between the pity aroused by the earth-bound, travel-stained, travel-wearied body of Man, coated with the dust to which it is soon to return, and the solemn awe awakened by the vision of infinite light and life, was as great as the contrast between the obscurity in which Jacob lay and the gorgeous brightness of the angelic hosts. As he looked at it he felt that there would never be another such painting; that there would never be another painter whose imagination would grapple with the subject in this way, so as to make poetic imagination identical with the objects it represented; that there would never be another brush that could make darkness visible and paint what is "dark with excess of light," as Rembrandt had done; that never on canvas could there be anything painted that would realise in the same way the limitation of actuality and the infinity of dream.

He was intolerant of any criticism of the combination of powers displayed in this picture. If any one were imperceptive of its solemn awe, insensitive to its poetry, derogatory in speaking of the "realistic" treatment of Jacob or inclined to regard the "tatterdemalion" figure as a blot in the glory, in his thoughts he would rank them among the mechanics of painting, like West, rather than among the artists. If there were any discussion on the matter, he would rouse himself to prove that the leaden clay-weary figure with its mute questioning: "What are we but a bundle of clay resting upon the earth, and ready to crumble again into dust and ashes!" while yet it was shown to be of the nature of immortality in so far as through the medium of the clay-weary flesh the loftiest vision of the soul could be realised, was one of the things that showed Rembrandt to be a true poet in his painting, and his "Jacob's Ladder" to be at once the most romantic and the most poetical of all his paintings. He would contend, even when he gave offence in doing so, that those who could not see the perfected glory of Rembrandt's vision of man's physical and spiritual nature had not the root of the matter in them: they had neither learned anything of the true language of poetry nor of the true spirit of painting, let them be as skilled as they might in the practice of its mechanical part.

Having once realised the nature of the greatest works of art, instead of becoming exclusive in his taste and wishing to limit himself to the greatest work, he found himself becoming nothing if not catholic in his sympathies. He realised that in the realm of art there were many mansions, and he wished to explore them all. Even in the Desenfans collection he found many chambers of delight. The pictures here were exhibited in various small rooms. One of these was devoted to the work of the Poussins, and in this room he spent many a happy hour. He found that which he had come to look upon as Poetry in some of Nicolas Poussin's landscapes, found it, too, in some of Poussin's studies of childhood, perhaps especially in the comical gusto of the infant Bacchus drinking from a bowl held for him by a faun.[105] This was not perhaps poetry of the highest order, but poetry it was.

Although Hazlitt would always rate first among the painters those who could paint soul, he came to delight also in those who, if they did not paint soul, could at least, like Murillo, catch the glancing joy and sparkle of life, and at length he learned to appreciate, too, the work of those whose excellence is not poetical at all, for it embodies no vision peculiar to the artist, but consists chiefly in portraying with skill what all eyes can see. He could relish pictures of still life. He could relish too pictures of low life. Nothing that was honestly attempted seemed to him "common or unclean."

The only work his new-found catholicity of taste rejected was the work in which sex or any other of the toys of Time was allowed to impinge on an art that is purified both from the toys of Time and the toys of sense. This he could neither stomach nor tolerate. He hated what Van der Werff had made of "The Judgment of Paris," a parade of naked women; he hated Van der Werff's paltry Venuses; and he hated Poelenburgh's preoccupation with the Nymph and Satyr theme. The preoccupation with this theme offended him hardly less than the suggestion of grossness conveyed through the ignoble "finicalness" of the execution.

For the rest, he was indebted to his awakening to art not only because of the delight he was receiving from it but because through it he renewed his faith in man. He had reason to bless the names of the great painters if only because he found something in their pictures that lifted him above the toys of Time. "Battles, sieges, speeches in Parliament, seemed mere idle noise and fury, 'signifying nothing,' compared with these mighty works and dreaded names" that spoke to him "in the eternal silence of thought." He had found something that raised him

"Above all pain, all passion, and all pride,"

something that carried him "out of the magic circle of self-love" and

even purified him from the memory of its exorcisms, that armoured
him against the accidents of circumstances, that made him feel as
if nothing mean or little or ignoble could ever disturb him again.

He was of those who perish if they have nothing in which they can
believe. The best thing Art did for him, perhaps, was that it drew for
the time being the sting of evil out of the life surrounding him. It
led him into a world where "the harpy form" could no longer pursue.

7

Hazlitt's story at this time is essentially the story of his awakening
to art. Nothing else in his life during these years was comparable
to this in its effect on him. But his other interests had not died,
although for the moment they were overshadowed by his absorption
in painting, and now and again we catch glimpses of him in places to
which they have conducted him. He still delighted in the theatre and
in Mrs. Siddons's interpretation of tragic character. His heart still went
out to the poets. He was still athirst of the immortality of the written
word. When watching the melting of a thousand hearts at Belvidera's
sorrows, the tears shed by young and old over her fate, he found it in
his heart sometimes to wish that he could have lived like Otway, could
even have died like him, if his existence could thus have lived on in the
brain and throbbed in the bosoms of countless multitudes, his thoughts
thus have been breathed day by day by others like common air, in spite
of the distance of place and the lapse of time.

In February, 1799, we see him beginning to attend the course of
lectures which James Mackintosh, who in 1790 had crossed swords with
Burke, is delivering at Lincoln's Inn Hall. The author of *Vindiciae
Gallicae* has now taken the other side of the road, converted, it is said,
by one moment of personal contact with Burke. His lectures left no
doubt as to the thoroughness of his recantation of his youthful heresies.
Categorically and with gusto he stated his purpose in delivering them:
"It is my intention to profess publicly and unequivocally that I abhor,
abjure and for ever renounce the French Revolution, with its sanguin-
ary history, its abominable principles, and for ever execrable leaders."
The lectures made some stir, for they were well delivered; they were
dazzlingly illustrated; and they were charged with that authority
which Milton had declared to be "the life-blood of teaching." One of
John Hazlitt's friends, a young man called John Stoddart, who had been
one of the noisiest of revolutionaries a few years before, now garnered
carefully the pearls which fell from the lecturer's mouth. So much
impressed was he by Mackintosh's words that he collected them
diligently in notebooks and used them as his stock-in-trade of wisdom
in after years. The Rev. Joseph Fawcett, on the other hand, listened in

vain for any trace of original thought, and came away disappointed that one reputed to be a man of genius could speak at such length and say so little that was of any value. Hazlitt, although he had been fore-warned by Coleridge that Mackintosh had not a spark of genius, found the lectures disappointing. Apart from his dislike of their political trend, he felt that when they touched on philosophy they were so derivative as to come near to plagiarism, sometimes to plagiarism of what was in itself quite worthless. The air of authority with which they were delivered while impressive to those who did not reason closely, was only an irritant to a mind that was accustomed to pursue an idea into the last recesses of its origin. But it was characteristic of Hazlitt that what he disliked most about them was the air of light-hearted personal triumph with which Mackintosh drove home the failure of the great effort which humanity had made ten years before towards the liberation of the mind and soul of man. Even if the French Revolution had failed, and Hazlitt did not as yet agree that it had, it seemed to him that the failure of Man, having crawled forth on his hands and knees from the dark cave of oppression, to rid himself immediately of his cave-distortion and to draw himself erect and to create a world that should be as free from new injustices and oppres-sions as from the old crippling superstitions, shibboleths and shams, might well be a matter for sorrow rather than for rejoicing to any one in whose heart the love of humanity prevailed over petty and temporal prejudices. This lack of human feeling coupled to a subordination of universal hope for Man to personal or party triumph was in Hazlitt's eyes the gravest fault the lectures showed, and the only thing which in after years, when the echo of the lectures had long since died away, seemed to him still worth a sigh: "If all that body of opinions and principles of which the orator read his recantation was unfounded, and there was an end of all those views and hopes that pointed to future improvement, it was not a matter of triumph or exultation to the lecturer or anybody else, to the young or the old, the wise or the foolish; on the contrary, it was a subject of regret, of slow, reluctant, painful admission—

        ' Of lamentation loud heard through the rueful air.'" [106]

In the course of the summer he accompanied his brother to Bury St. Edmunds. John Hazlitt had patrons there among the prominent Nonconformists of the town, which was a centre of political as well as of religious Nonconformity. His miniatures of Samuel Robinson, his wife, his brothers John and Nathan, and his pretty niece Miss Kitchener, had appeared at the Exhibition of 1798 at Somerset House. [107] He may have taken William with him to the town, in the summer of 1799, with a view to helping him to make connections that might be of professional value to him in the future. During this visit Hazlitt made the acquaintance of Thomas Robinson the tanner and his brothers Hab and Henry, him whom we last saw running through the streets of Colchester in the darkness of a November morning in 1794, knocking on people's doors, with the news of the acquittal of Thomas Hardy. Henry Robinson had also attended Mackintosh's lectures, and as he was beginning to be alienated from his first sympathies with the French Revolution, he had been much pleased with them, Mackintosh not seeming to him to have gone "an inch beyond pure Whiggism." In spite of this, his sympathies were still sufficiently liberal to give promise of the possibility of some measure of friendship with Hazlitt, whose power of mind he at once descried. Another circumstance that might seem to give promise of friendship was that, having been released from the drudgery of a law-office through having been left a small legacy, he was now "tending towards literature," wondering how he might make an entry into it, and eager to cultivate the acquaintance of those who were connected with it. He would have given his eyes to know Godwin, and he may have felt that Hazlitt, who was acquainted not only with Godwin but with Holcroft, and who was on very friendly terms with two of the poets of the day, might be helpful to him in making such contacts as he desired.

Most of those in the Bury circle had trade or business or agricultural interests. They were plain business or farming people who yet did not let the preoccupations of their work exclude them from the world of thought. The bond that united them was chiefly composed of political or religious sympathy. Most of them were hard-working, high-thinking, plain-living but yet prosperous people. One of the acquaintances to whom Henry Robinson introduced Hazlitt was Anthony Robinson, a sugar refiner who was also a philanthropist. With him Hazlitt remained on affectionate terms for many years. Other members of note in the Bury group were Capel Lofft, constitutional lawyer and politician, and Thomas Clarkson, farmer, author and philanthropist, whose life was consecrated to his effort to procure the abolition of the slave trade. Clarkson had almost worn himself out in these labours, but the dignity and courage of his effort had graven themselves on his features. He looked what he was, "a true apostle of human redemption," and Hazlitt honoured him as such, with all his heart.

Apart from the interest of these contacts, the visit to Bury deserves recording because from it we get a direct impression of the difficulty Hazlitt now experienced in his social contacts with women and girls. We have noted the suggestion in his letters written from Liverpool in 1790, that he felt difficulty in these. The difficulty is now more marked. Poor, carelessly dressed, shy, oppressed by a weight of thought and feeling which he could not express, conscious of some value in himself, which he knew was buried far beneath the surface, conscious perhaps also that the things he valued most were unfitting him for easy social intercourse, he was always at his worst with women, and he was painfully conscious of this. Therefore he dreaded being in their company. With men, especially with men who shared his interests, he could now more than hold his own; but with women, especially those women who were protected from the buffetings of the world, who were preoccupied with the trivial doings of their own circle of friends, and regardless of all the things he valued most, he was tongue-tied and dumb as one who knew not the language in which they conversed. He knew the language of passion, but that availed him little in the social gatherings of this small circle. He was like one who had gold coin in his pocket, but it was the gold coin of a far country, and here it could not be changed, so that for lack of immediate small coin he appeared a beggar. The prettiest girl in every party was the Miss Kitchener who was the niece of his brother's chief patron, the daughter of a prosperous tea-dealer in Abbey Gate Street, and the betrothed of Hab Robinson. From Henry Robinson we get a glimpse of Hazlitt, daunted by her remarkable prettiness, awkward in her presence, silent, tortured by shyness. Miss Kitchener, who would never know anything of the world of thought and feeling in which he moved, but who, being young and pretty and admired and loved, ruled like a queen in her own comfortable circle of friends, tormented him unmercifully. According to Henry Robinson, she "drove him mad" by teasing him. There was no one to say to her, as Charles Lamb had said to Coleridge, regarding Charles Lloyd: "I tell you that his is not a mind with which you should play tricks." Nor would she have understood the caution if it had been addressed to her. She could not play on the fine instrument that had come in her way; yet she could fret it, and contribute her mite towards the spoiling of it. We can understand how the teasing words, that meant nothing to her, dropped one by one like grains of gunpowder into the heart of the man all at sea in his relationships with women—and remained there. It was no doubt some such youthful experience that was in his mind when he wrote to his son: "make up your mind to this, that if a woman does not like you of her own accord, that is, from voluntary impressions, nothing you can say or do or suffer for her sake will make her, but will set her the more against you. . . . Your pain is her triumph, the more she feels you in her power, the worse she will treat you."[108]

He is so vulnerable that other careless hands, the hands of those who, like the admirable Mrs. Thomas Robinson, "take him for a fool," will not be able to resist the temptation of adding other grains of combustible material to those that have already accumulated. Can we not now foresee the intolerable moment when a hand yet cruder, the hand of some nameless village jilt whose prettiness has attracted him for a moment, will find no better sport than to fling a lighted match on the growing pile, so that the man will be blown sky high, others too, along with him, in the endless train of great consequences brought about by causes trivial in themselves, and ending only when the puppets are put away and the play is played out!

8

From his own reminiscences, our sole trustworthy authority, we can gather a general idea of Hazlitt's progress from the moment of his awakening to art to the moment when, trembling betwixt hope and fear but conscious of the mind-sympathy that linked him to the greatest among the painters, he dared to whisper to himself the hope that one day he might be able to say, as Correggio had done when gazing on the work of Raphael: "I also am a painter."

First of all there was a period of unremitting, almost frenzied study, during which his progress was extraordinarily rapid, perhaps too rapid. It might have been better for him afterwards had he worked with more deliberation, with more hesitancy and attention to detail. This was followed by a period in which he copied pictures. Sometimes he was bored by this work; at other times, when he copied work with which he was in sympathy, he was absorbed in it. From his references to the kind of work he copied and the little room in which he painted, we surmise that he may have been given the opportunity of doing this copying at the Desenfans collection; and that he may have worked in one of the many small rooms in which the pictures collected by Desenfans were exhibited.[109] He copied some of Sir Joshua's work, but "without passion." A certain sober admiration was all he could ever give to it, for it was lacking in the vision and the touch of poetry that meant more to him than anything. On the other hand, he liked copying Van Goyen's peaceful work. As he sat, trying to reproduce the details of one of Van Goyen's pictures, the yellow-tufted banks, the gliding sail, the windmill and "the poor, low, clay-built cottage" beside the water, the hours were apt to seem to him like minutes. Labouring to reproduce the tremulous undulating reflection of the cottage in the water, he would realise only when the light began to fade and he had to shift his picture so as to catch the dim gleam from the fire, that the short winter day was over. He came to have a great affection for Van Goyen's canals "modestly pencilled, truly felt," for the yellow-tawny colour in the meads and the grey shades that could convey exactly the feeling "of a mild day towards the end of winter, in a humid, marshy country." This was work that had the perfection of quiet grace.

His absorption in Rembrandt, when he copied, was even greater, but his feeling was altogether different. It was one of impassioned aspiration. As he brooded over the half-finished copy of one of Rembrandt's heads he was sometimes not far from feeling that if the Prince of Darkness had appeared and offered to sell him the secret of the great Master of light and shade, he would have sold his soul as readily as Dr. Faustus had sold his and would have counted himself fortunate in the bargain.

We get a curious glimpse of him at one of *his sports and his recreations* during this period of strenuous aspiration, curious, and yet entirely characteristic, for he always delighted in rigorous exercise of the body and in perfection of any kind. He had seen Richer the rope-dancer at Sadler's Wells, and the extraordinary skill, exquisite ease and unaffected natural grace of Richer's performance had stimulated him as perfection never failed to do, and yet filled him with a despairing sense of the slowness and incertitude of progress in intellectual or artistic achievement, even if the last ounce of effort were put into the work, compared with the certainty of achieving skill and precision in any kind of mechanical work, if similar pains were taken. Behold him, then! turning from his copying of Sir Joshua to imitation of Richer's feats, and drawing after him in his desperate attempts at learning to dance upon a tightrope the first of his literary disciples, a fourteen-year-old poet called Sheridan Knowles,[110] who had become his devoted admirer.

How long these attempts were continued we do not know, but as for dancing upon a tightrope of one kind or another! some there are who would say that all his life he never did anything else.

9

If the period of study and the period of copying had been strenuous, it was followed by labours of a far more exacting kind, the first endeavours at painting. Now Hazlitt's progress has brought him back once more to the old familiar ordeal, not to be shirked by any one taking the first step into any kind of art. He had known the ordeal of the thinker. He had known the ordeal of the writer. He must now return to the familiar battle-ground. The thing to be created is different, but the nature of the ordeal of creation is the same. He is to find that it is with painting even as with thinking or with writing; the familiar pangs, the labours, the misgivings of the mind are all to be endured once more, ere the vision of the mind can see the light of day, ere the symbol of what has been seen can be made intelligible. No matter how he may change his course he will always be brought back to this ordeal, for there is something in him which goads him towards giving it expression, until at last he will no longer merely suffer, but bring forth.

Once more, then, we see him travelling over the ground that had become familiar to him, that is becoming familiar to us, in all its delights and its pains, in its occasional despair and its constantly renewed hope of one day doing something immortal and finding in that achievement "ample amends for pining solitude, want, and neglect." It is again for him a time of "conscious yearning after excellence." His struggle makes him sensitive to the experience of those who have preceded him. Sometimes he ponders the lives of artists, broods over their early struggles, and feels, in his sympathy, that these early rude attempts may be of more value in the sight of God and Nature than the perfected work more easily done. Sometimes he broods over the processes of creation, wonders whether the great artists were conscious of the magnitude of what they were doing. Rembrandt, for example, when he painted the figure of Jacob thrown on the ground or when the white-vested, beaked figures beckoned to him, was he conscious of the miracle of his vision, of the long deathless gust of fame that would follow in the train of his work, or did he just paint what came to him, thinking of nothing but the effect of the moment, his artistic purpose unflawed by any thought of self whatever, or any self-consciousness about his art? On the whole he thought it must be so, that the artist must have been altogether so possessed by his subject that no thought of self could enter his mind at all. Sometimes he thinks of the artists who had endured the creative ordeal to the utmost and who yet had failed, who had struggled to burst through the fetters that had bound them and to shake off the discouragement that had oppressed them, and yet "whose longing aspirations after truth and good" had been "palsied by the refusal of the hand" to execute them. A thing that never failed to pierce his heart was to see as he passed the doors of the brokers' shops the poor, battered, hawked-about pictures that had just failed to capture the quality that would win for them some kind of immortality, exposed for sale with the morning sun flaring full upon their forlornness. Sometimes, the sight of this would paralyse effort and put him out of spirits for the rest of the day. Might this be the ending of long aspiration? If so, was not effort vanity? On the other hand, he had only to see a fine picture for the hope in him to mount high again, even as it had mounted high in Correggio's heart when, looking at Raphael's pictures, he had felt that there was a kindred spirit in his own breast.

He would then return to his work with redoubled ardour. At the worst, he could only suffer; at the best, he would achieve; and if he failed, even to fail in an attempt so glorious, was no mean thing.

He tells us that among his first attempts at a picture was that made of his father towards the end of 1801; that this had been preceded by an attempt he had made at painting the head of an old woman after the manner of Rembrandt; and that this head had been immediately inspired by "a fine old head" by Rembrandt which he had gone to Burleigh to revisit when spending some time with his mother's people at Peterborough. We gather from what he says that his visit to Peterborough was made in the opening months of the year, before the rigour of winter had broken. All these things point towards the early months of 1801 as the time in which he entered upon the pains and the "uneasy rapture" of creation, and in which once more he experienced the startled joy of the mind when it thinks it has struck out of the formless void of thought and feeling something new that may last for ever.

The "fine old head" at Burleigh, which he found just as he had remembered it, "an exact and wonderful facsimile of nature," sent him on to Peterborough "dreaming of deathless works and deathless names," and feeling that if he could produce a head at all like it, it would be "glory and felicity and health and fame" enough for one lifetime. His model for the picture inspired by it was an old cottager whom he tried to paint with the upper part of her face shaded by her bonnet, and in painting whose face he tried to give such strong contrasts of light and shade as those which had delighted him in Rembrandt.[111] He was a most unwearied painter, and his patience was equalled by that of his model, who gave him endless sittings. Rembrandt had taught him the beauty that there can be in an old face, and he laboured indefatigably to catch the expression and to reproduce the fine network of lines that experience had graven. At first the work went swimmingly. He was amazed at the rapidity with which he had struck out the general semblance. It looked to him as if his task would quickly be completed. But when it came to refining upon the first rude outline, there seemed to be an infinity of detail to be mastered before he could reproduce anything like the lines which nature had drawn, endless corrections of the proportions to be made, endless softening of the gradations. The work absorbed him so much that he could hardly bear to leave it. When the twilight closed in on him he would still be gazing at what he had done, musing over it, wondering what he should retouch the following day. In the course of the evening he would set the picture on the ground, and gaze at it again with swimming eyes, new hope rising in him as he thought he saw how he could complete it. But gradually he came to realise the immense difference between a portrait that bears some resemblance to the original, and a portrait which reproduces nature and yet is identical with the painter's vision of nature. The passion for perfection left him no rest, and as he could not succeed in completing it to his satisfaction by the time the sittings were over, this, like so much other work that he had attempted, was left unfinished.

Yet he did not cease to cherish it, and the thought of it. No artist had ever painted the beauty of woman with more passion than he had expended on the delineation of an old woman's face.

Has he not altered somewhat since his last visit to Peterborough? He could not now say of himself that he could not draw a stroke. The way he has travelled has been obscure and hard, but he has been climbing towards the light. If he is still inexpressive in speech, he has learned another language, the language of signs. He has not yet found complete utterance in it, but he has still the hope that one day he may be able to express himself fully through it. He has now the painter's eye, and the painter's soul is ever with him. His mind is full of all he has most admired. Now he remembers Titian's gradations of colour; now the free movement of Rubens; now he thinks of Rembrandt's landscapes, as real as if they had been "dug out of Nature." In the meantime, Nature herself is before him. There is the field opposite his window. How to render the green dewy moisture in the tone, or the fresh marshes stretching out in endless perspective, or the movement of the fieldfares "gambolling in the air and sporting in the sun and racing before the clouds"?

It seems as if life will be all too short for the endeavour.

There is a great outward change; yet in some ways he has not changed since his childhood. There is still the same sensibility, the same habit of reverie. He makes once more a pilgrimage to the town in which his mother had been born, visits "the poor farmhouse" in which she had been brought up, leans, with sweet relentings of feelings and intertwinings of thought of his mother's youth and his own boyhood, upon the gate "where . . . she used to stand when a child of ten years old and look at the setting sun."

10

It seems to have been either on his way to Peterborough or on his return from it at the time of this visit that he saw Gribelin's engravings of the Cartoons of Raphael in the parlour of the little inn at St. Neot's. That was a moment not to be forgotten, for it marked for him the beginning of a life-long passion for the artist he knew he could never rival. At times he had hopes that he might do something like Rembrandt, or like Titian, but never in all his life, except perhaps for one wild moment of transport and delight, had he any hope that he could ever do anything like Raphael. Here was something not only beyond the compass of his pencil but beyond the range of his imagination too. Yet not beyond the compass of his spirit! Into the soul of the work he entered at once. Here were the heroic figures with the worship of which his childhood had been sanctified, "godlike spirits and lofty shapes" that descended and walked visible the earth, but "as if their

thoughts still lifted them above the skies." Here was the figure of
Saint Paul, "pointing with noble fervour to ' temples not made with
hands';" here was "the finer one of Christ in the boat," whose whole
figure seemed "sustained with meekness and love;" here again was
Christ surrounded by the disciples "like a flock of sheep listening to the
music of some divine Shepherd." He gazed at these figures with
mingled hope and fear, feeling, much as he had felt when he first read
Schiller, a strong aspiration after and a deep impulse towards good
welling up within him.

II

At the close of the year he was back at Wem, and in the best of
spirits. The opening of Peace negotiations had lifted a shadow from
his spirit, as it had from the spirits of all those who had been opposed
to war with France from the beginning. His own private affairs, no
less than public affairs, were now going to his satisfaction. He was
engaged in painting his father, and the attempt absorbed him. This
portrait, like the one he had attempted of the old cottager, was in the
manner of Rembrandt, with strong contrasts of light and shade.
It was painted with a broad light crossing the face, one side of which
was in shadow, and it represented Mr. Hazlitt in a characteristic
attitude, with his spectacles on, looking down at a book he was reading.
The work was one that gave infinite satisfaction both to the father and
to the son. They had ceased to have entire sympathy of thought with
each other, even to share their thoughts unreservedly with each other:
but the love between them was deep, and in this occupation it found a
mute expression that suited them both perfectly. They had found a
mode of companionship that was all the more satisfying, because it
was companionship without words. Also William's employment was
reassuring to Mr. Hazlitt. His son was not going to be a fine preacher,
as he had hoped, but at least he was not going to prove a nondescript.
If the picture he was painting were hung in the Academy, as they both
hoped it would be, he might be considered as making his way in a new
profession. As for William, when he achieved, after much mixing and
preparation of colours, the effect he had intended, when he had
managed to imitate the roughness of the skin, to give the effect of
"the blood circulating under the shadows of one side of the face," to
get "the clear pearly tone of a vein," he felt as if his fortune were made.
This was the time when every now and again he felt as if the day were
drawing near when he would be able to say: "I also am a painter."
What with the hope that was sustaining him, his love of the work, his
love of the old father who had kept himself "unspotted from the
world" through all the vicissitudes of a hard life, and whose personality

THE REVEREND WILLIAM HAZLITT

he was trying to express with all the skill of his hand and brain, as he worked in the place which had been the centre of his childhood's happiness, with the gleams of sunshine coming in through the chapel windows, and the thin shrewish warbling of the robin-redbreast coming in just as it had sounded in the first garden of his innocence, he came nearer to recapturing the unsullied happiness of his childhood than he did at any other period of his life. He was having, if not as yet his Indian summer, what we might call his Indian childhood. And to the father, watching his son's intentness on the work, the care with which he mixed his colours, the sense of responsibility, of importance and self-importance too, he felt in adjusting the smallest details; the way in which he would set his portrait on a chair when painting-time was over and ponder it, throughout the long evenings; the way in which, sometimes last thing at night, before getting into bed, he would come downstairs to have a last look at it; the way in which his first thought, on getting up, was to see how this same portrait looked in the morning light—may it not have seemed almost as if the William had been restored to him who had once watered the rows of cabbage-plants or peas with such assiduity in the evening and had gone out first thing the next day to see how they had looked in the morning light, who had delighted in pleasing all those around him, and who had had no other thought or care in the world than to con his little task and be happy!

Chapter Two

THE LOUVRE (1802-1803)

"He spent the winter in Paris, working in the Louvre from ten in the morning until four in the afternoon, suffering much from cold and other deprivations. But he cared little for these things while he had those noble specimens of genius before his eyes."

MARGARET HAZLITT.

I

IN MAY, 1802, greatly to his surprise, Coleridge, who although he had given a few sittings to John Hazlitt at the close of 1801 had not by any means considered the sittings at an end, learned from the newspapers that there was a picture of him in the Exhibition at Somerset House. Being quite in the dark about the matter, he conjectured that this must be the miniature [112] which William Hazlitt had promised to Mrs. Coleridge but had not given her because the sittings had not been completed. "Mine is not a picturesque face," he added characteristically when telling Tom Poole of this. [113]

William Hazlitt had in the meantime sent his portrait of his father to the Exhibition, "with a beating heart"—he tells us—and had the satisfaction of hearing that his work, as well as his brother's, had been accepted for the Exhibition of 1802. He might now fairly consider himself as having won his credentials as an artist. We know little of his movements in the opening months of the year except that he followed the portrait up to town. He was still in London in the middle of May, for we read of his having an evening at the theatre on Wednesday, May 19th, in the course of which he had the delight of seeing no fewer than four of his favourite players. Mrs. Siddons took the part of Hermione in *The Winter's Tale*, acting "with true monumental dignity and noble passion;" Jack Bannister, who had so often amused him as Lenitive, "fluttering like a piece of gold-leaf, gaudy as a butterfly, loud as a grasshopper, full of life and laughter and joy," took the part of Autolycus, and "roared as loud for pity as a sturdy beggar could do who felt none of the pain he counterfeited." In the Afterpiece of *The Wedding Day*, King, whose acting of Sir Peter Teazle had so often left a sharp-sweet taste on his palate, played along with Mrs. Jordan herself. As might be expected, "Nothing could go off with more *éclat*." This was one of the last opportunities admirers of King had of seeing him, for he took leave of the stage on the following Monday.

156

In the meantime, Hazlitt was turning over a dazzling project in his mind. The conclusion in March of the long-debated Treaty of Amiens opened the door to Paris, and the English, who had been debarred from it for ten years, "flocked over in crowds to it." It was, especially, a kind of Mecca to painters, for whom, thanks to Buonaparte, it shortened the road to Italy. In March, 1797, Buonaparte had said to his soldiers: "You have enriched the Museum at Paris with three hundred masterpieces of the arts of ancient and modern Italy which it required thirty centuries to produce." By March, 1802, there was hardly a first-rate picture to be met with on the Continent that had not found its way to the Louvre.

Here was an unrivalled opportunity of seeing collected all together most of the great pictures of the world. Hazlitt pored over a Catalogue of the Louvre which a friend had lent him, until he knew it almost by heart, and felt as if already he could visualise some of the pictures. The colours with which the painter had adorned the hair of the woman who—whether she be proved to be Laura de' Dianti or Isabella Boschetti or any other "not impossible she"—will continue to be known by right prescriptive as Titian's Mistress, were not more golden than those which played on his imagination and tantalised his fancy ere he had seen the picture. He read over and over again the descriptions of the portraits of "A Young Nobleman with a Glove" and "A Companion to it," until he had invested the thought of these pictures with all he could conceive of grace and dignity. He thought of the "Transfiguration" with awe, and was already "overshadowed with the spirit of the artist." He noted the name of the "Ippolito de' Medici," which Opie had pronounced the finest portrait in the world, and the name seemed like a sharp relish in his mouth.

But all this brooding over the Catalogue was far from satisfying him. He was consumed with the longing to go on a pilgrimage to this shrine of art, which, it must be remembered, represented also for him the triumph of the natural energy of unassisted man against the hereditary oppressors of mankind. That the triumphs of human genius assembled in the Louvre might be considered "as trophies of human liberty" was for him the chief justification for their severance from the places which had given them birth: but it was an all-sufficient justification. The thought of Liberty no less than the thought of Art fed the flame of his longing.

His desires all turned towards Paris. The difficulty was to find the means for a sojourn there. The way in which he solved this problem is our chief clue to his doings during the greater part of 1802. He felt by this time that he had made "some progress in painting," and he set about making use of this progress to provide him with the means of making further progress in his art. Thus he sought work among those with whom he had some acquaintance or connection. It was natural that this search should lead him towards Liverpool. Twelve years before, when as a child he had been there, his father had wished to make through his acquaintances there some connection for his brother John. "You will give my respects to Mr. Yates. I wish that he, amongst his friends, could procure for your brother engagements for about a score of pictures at Liverpool this summer," he had written on July 31st, 1790. Mr. Yates and Mr. Shepherd of Gateacre may have done what they could for Hazlitt at this time among the wealthy Unitarians of the town. At any rate, he was successful in obtaining at Liverpool work that would both take him to Paris and go far towards defraying his expenses while he was there. Before the autumn he had obtained a commission for copies of five[114] of the pictures of the old Masters at the Louvre. These were to decorate the "parlour" of the Mr. Railton of Liverpool who was one of his brother's patrons, and of whose beautiful daughter John Hazlitt made a very beautiful miniature on ivory. As he seems to have copied in all eleven pictures, he may have visited other places also in his quest for work, and may have had other commissions too. We know of at least one. Shortly before his departure for France he found Northcote one day poring over a print of the "Ippolito de' Medici" that was lying on the floor of his studio, and full of admiration for it as being, if not, as Opie claimed, the finest portrait in the world, yet one of the finest, by reason of the perfection of *keeping* shown in every detail of it. He was instant in offering to make a copy of it, and the offer was gladly accepted.

By copying of this kind, he intended, living with extreme frugality, to pay his way while in Paris. He had hopes, too, that in addition to the money he received for copying he might earn a little more by having prints taken and sold in London of some of the pictures he meant to copy. With these expectations and these hopes he set out for Paris in October, 1802. He had letters of introduction both from Holcroft and from Freebairn. Slender as his resources were, he was full of confidence. Possibly his people saw his prospects in a less sanguine hue. That his mother had some anxious thoughts about him we gather from a word or two in his first letter to his father from Paris: "I hope my mother is quite easy as I hope to do very well."

2

When Wordsworth had landed in Calais on August 1st, 1802, he had expressed in a sonnet which he had composed on that day,[115] the contrast he had sensed in the mood of the people from the mood they had shown when he had first landed at Calais in the autumn of 1790. Then:

"A homeless sound of joy was in the Sky;
The antiquated Earth, as one might say,
Beat like the heart of Man:"

now, he had heard but two greetings, reminding him of these times:
"Good morrow, Citizen!" and they had been hollow as if a dead man
had uttered them.

Perhaps his interpretation of the feeling of the people was coloured
by his mood; for most of the English who visited France in this year
were amazed by its air of prosperity, and some of them seemed almost
scandalised by it. Perhaps too, in his increasing Anti-Gallicanism, his
interpretation was coloured by his desire to see some alteration in the
spirit of the French. Certainly Hazlitt, when he landed in Calais in
October of the year, received a very different impression. The Calais
he saw when first he set foot upon "the laughing shores of France," far
from seeming Wordsworth's Calais of melancholy greetings, seemed
peopled "with novelty and delight." The busy hum of the place and its
stir of life were "like oil and wine" poured into his ears. As the sun
went down he listened to a mariners' hymn sung from the top of an old
crazy vessel in the harbour, and instead of feeling the sound an alien
one he felt as if he were breathing the air of humanity in general.
Ever afterwards Calais was for him a place associated with joy, and one
which he would go out of his way to revisit.

He remained long enough in it to get an impression of the town
itself, and to hear some interesting talk of the First Consul. The town
he found a poor enough place, but the remains of its fortifications,
although the hand of time was heavy on them, seemed to him beautiful.
There were several "ranges of ramparts, and ditches one with another,
' wall within wall, mural protection intricate,'" but the walls were
decayed and dark, and the ditches were now filled with reeds and long
grass.

The talk of Buonaparte arose from his falling into conversation
with a middle-aged Englishman named Lovelace. Just as the literary
association of the name had flashed across his mind his companion
told him that a nephew of his, a young English officer also named
Lovelace, had been presented at Buonaparte's levée, shortly after the
Peace of Amiens had been concluded, and that instead of the stereotyped "Where have you served, Sir?" the First Consul had remarked,
quick as lightning: "I perceive your name, Sir, is the same as that of
the hero of Richardson's romance."

Hazlitt, who never could hear enough about Buonaparte, thought
on hearing this: "Here was a Consul!" The story confirmed the belief
which was growing in him, that Buonaparte, although a soldier by
profession, was far more than a professional soldier.

Calais was only the point from which most people started out for

Paris, which had become the hub of the universe. In this respect things were even as Wordsworth, who had not moved one inch towards it, had described them, rather bitterly, in August:

> "Lords, Lawyers, Statesmen, Squires of low degree,
> Men known, and men unknown, Sick, Lame and Blind
> Post forward all, like Creatures of one kind,
> With first-fruit offerings crowd to bend the knee
> In France, before the new-born Majesty!"

The one among the "men unknown," forming part of this motley crew, whose fortunes we have chosen to follow, had come to France without a companion. This mattered little to him as he set forth for Paris, for he knew that he would have companionship and communion enough with those whom he held to be the greatest, once he reached the Louvre, which for him was the heart of Paris; nor did he care very much that his tongue seemed to cleave to the roof of his mouth when he tried to use his awkward French, for in that affliction too he had the same consolation: "I was at no loss for language, for that of all the great schools of painting was open to me."

In one respect he differs from those who "Post forward all, like Creatures of one kind," and this is as it should be, for he is a creature of another kind. He elected to do most of the journey on foot, partly no doubt because it was urgently necessary for him to travel as frugally as might be, partly because he wished to see the country more thoroughly than he could have seen it when "posting," partly because he was never happier than when walking. He may also have had in mind Wordsworth's reminiscences of the tour he had made in 1790, and descriptions of the laughing country through which Robert Jones and he had walked. But Wordsworth and his friend had chosen their route with a view to beauty. The country through which Hazlitt passed had long barren and miserable stretches. As he had not known pre-Revolution France, he was not troubled as were Frenchmen returning to their country at that time by the marks of a reversed order of things—the decayed castles, the broken statues of the saints, the absence of crosses in the churchyards and of bells in the churches; but as he walked day by day he saw well enough that in the country at least poverty was far from having been abolished by the Revolution; the peasants who went about their work in clogs and the women toiling in the fields still earned their scanty bread with hard and unremitting labour. In most of the towns also there were great numbers of beggars. It was not until he drew towards Paris that the appearance of the country satisfied his eye. The vineyards then looked delightful, richer than anything to be seen in agricultural England at that time of the year, especially those that were covered with the red vines. Afterwards, it was the beauty of these vineyards that he remembered rather than the poverty he had witnessed. In later years, recalling the confidence of his mood as he walked, he wrote: "I walked over vine-covered hills and gay joyous regions of France, erect and satisfied; for the image of man was not cast down and chained to the foot of arbitrary thrones."

But the first letter he sent to his father from Paris dwells on the poverty.

He reached Paris on October 15th and found a room in the Hôtel Coq Heron, Rue Coq Heron, near the Palais-Royal. His first impressions were not agreeable. He felt, as Holcroft had done in 1783, that the French capital had not come up to his expectations. Many of the streets seemed narrow, almost more like tall and dirty ill-smelling alleys full of slaughter-houses and barbers' shops than like the streets of a great city; their narrowness was accentuated by the piles of wood, greenstalls and wheelbarrows placed at the doors; and their disagreeableness was increased by the throwing of the contents of innumerable "cuvettes" out of the windows of a dozen stories. The shops, with greasy holes for windows, were mean, and many of the buildings were unfinished. After London it seemed fetid, uncared-for, and confined. Then to pedestrians especially it was "a beast of a city," for there was no footpath as in London, so that the foot-passenger had to walk along the middle of the streets with a dirty gutter running through them, and frequently had to fight his way through coaches, wagons and hand-carts trundled along by large mastiff dogs. This was uncomfortable enough, but reckless driving added a touch of danger to the discomfort. Hackney-coaches and cabriolets seemed to take a delight in hunting down pedestrians. He had either to keep looking around to see whether they were coming or suffer a dislocation of his nervous system, when they came right up against him unexpectedly with, as it seemed to him, a sudden perverse acceleration of speed and perhaps a liberal spraying of mud. If in the distress of the shock he again relaxed his vigilance, the whole business would be repeated the next moment. To any one used to the comparative safety of the streets of London, walking in Paris meant a series of nervous jars. The only place of peace or safety seemed to him at first his room in the hotel, but it was dull and cold. The Parisians themselves seemed to him to have developed nerves of cat-gut. He did not wonder that the sensitive Jean-Jacques had said that all the time he was in Paris he was doing nothing but trying to get out of it.

In after years nothing would persuade him that the light trip of the Parisian woman, to which he would never concede any true grace, was not merely the effect of the awkward construction of the streets, and of the "round, flat, slippery stones," over which the foot-passenger had to walk hurriedly as over a succession of stepping-stones.

3

The next day the moment he had got his *card of security* from the police-officer he went to the Louvre, and then he had to admit that along the riverside Paris had splendour enough to show, more splendour, indeed, than was to be found in any part of London. He was kept waiting for a long time in the Gallery in which modern paintings were exhibited, and this threw him into a fever of impatience, for looking through the door, as one in Purgatory might gaze towards Paradise, he could just catch a glimpse of the pictures he had come thus far to see—"from Poussin's noble mellow-looking landscapes to where Rubens hung out his gaudy banner, and down the glimmering vista to the rich jewels of Titian and the Italian school." He had not been more impatient when waiting for the curtain to draw up at his first play. At last someone took pity on him and told him that a bribe to the door-keepers would work miracles. Glad of this hint, he did what was expected of him, and at last passed through, to march "through a quarter of a mile of the proudest efforts of the mind of man, a whole creation of genius, a universe of art." As always, when undergoing new and transcendent experience, he felt half stupefied. He saw nearly one side of a large room covered by Paul Veronese's "Marriage of Cana."[116] It seemed to him as if that side of the room were thrown open so that he looked out "at the open sky, at buildings, marble pillars, galleries with people in them, emperors, female slaves, Turks, negroes, musicians . . . tables loaded with viands, goblets and dogs under them." Overwhelmed though he was, his senses were yet alert, as he took in the details of the picture and its variety of texture. He noticed that the pillars were of stone, the floor was of marble, the tables were of wood, the dresses were of stuffs, the sky was air, the flesh was flesh. It seemed "as if the very dogs under the table might get up and bark, or that at the sound of a trumpet the whole assembly might rise and disperse in different directions, in an instant." What now of Rubens's gaudy banner! Two pictures of Rubens hung by the side of this immense canvas, and in comparison they looked nothing. Their texture seemed of wool or satin or cotton, it did not matter much which; what mattered was that there was no differentiation: it was all alike, whereas in the picture of "The Supper at Cana of Galilee" every object seemed actually to have its own characteristic texture. In this immense and highly finished piece of workmanship there was only one flaw, but it was a considerable one: it was not of execution, but of feeling. The picture itself was almost a miracle, but no one would have divined from the faces of the spectators in the picture that a miracle was going on before their eyes.

"The soul of faith" was lacking.

He "ran the gauntlet of all the schools from the bottom to the top" that day, and in the end he secured admission to an inner room where some of the greatest works were being repaired. It was in this inner room that he saw for the first time in his life the two pictures which ever afterwards he considered the finest in the world—Raphael's "Transfiguration" and Titian's "Saint Peter Martyr." Our "man unknown" has won through on the second day of his visit to Paris to drawing sufficiently near to pictures which are as the sacred mysteries of the religion of art, to lay his hands upon them, for they stood on the floor, along with Domenichino's "St. Jerome." It seemed to him, who would gladly have bent the knee to them, that these great pictures were stooping to him to that he might receive all they had to give, somewhat as camels stoop "to unlade their riches"!

There was one other picture in this inner room, however, which did not stoop to unlade its riches, and which had no appearance of condescending to any worshipper, or indeed of making any concession whatsoever to any one at all, whether friend or foe. It stood on an easel with its back to the spectator, but as Hazlitt passed it and turned round to look at it, he was transfixed. The keen glance of the man with a boar-spear in his hand who looked out at him from the canvas struck him like a blow from the boar-spear itself. It made no attempt to intimidate. It had "no frown, no startling gesticulation, no affected penetration." It was quiet and simple. Yet its effect was withering. So much a thing of life, or rather of supernatural force and grandeur did this creature of the piercing look and the disdainful eye seem that it was the gaze of the living man that flickered and turned away. But if the gaze of the man quailed, the gaze of the painter returned to the picture fascinated, to note the amazing consistency of form and expression through which the extraordinary effect was produced. All the lines of the face, the eyebrows, the nose, the corners of the mouth, the contour, "presented the same sharp angles, the same acute, edgy, formidable, contracted expression." This was the portrait of Ippolito de' Medici which he had offered to copy for Northcote. At the moment he felt as if it would hardly be safe to be left in the same room with it, so relentless was the idea it conveyed of superiority, so daunting was the impression it made. This was a face which one would be as wary of rousing into anger or hostility as one would be "of setting in motion some complicated and dangerous machinery."

4

He returned to his hotel, after this first visit, determined to include among the pictures he copied for Mr. Railton two landscapes. One of these was very likely that "most divine landscape" by Rubens, which in his letter to his father of November 23rd he says he will copy "if Railton chooses." This "divine landscape" was probably the one with a rainbow, then occupying a recess half-way down the Louvre, and filling it with rich and dazzling colouring, of which he always wished to possess a copy of his own. In this picture "shepherds are reposing with their flocks under the shelter of a breezy grove, the distances are of air, and the whole landscape seems just washed with the shower that has passed off."

Before he could begin on the work, he had to go through the preliminaries to obtaining permission to copy such pictures as he pleased. This he did with the help of J. F. L. Mérimée,[117] the painter, to whom he had had letters of introduction, and who proved of infinite service to him not only in greater ways but in lesser, such as helping him to buy paints, canvases and such other things as his work made necessary to him. Up to this time he had not seen most of the portraits by Titian, as they had been put aside for copyists. The moment he saw them, his plans changed, for he fell in love immediately with the two companion portraits over the description of which in the Catalogue of the Louvre he had pored so often; or rather, he fell in love with the one and in awe with the other. The first of these was a very beautiful portrait of a young Neapolitan nobleman, dark of complexion, dressed in black, holding a glove in his gloved left hand, and looking, it would seem, forward, beyond this world. The total effect was one of extraordinary grace and distinction. The portrait seemed to him to convey the most exquisite idea possible of sentiment, and its harmony of expression to constitute as great a charm as its deep rich colouring. Indeed, the expression was all in all. The look on the face seemed one that could never pass away. It appeared inalterable as the deep sentiment which had given birth to it. It was the perfection of art; it was also the perfection of nature.

It had its own consistency, but in its consistency of harmony it presented the greatest possible contrast to the sharp angles of the impressive portrait he had already seen.

Its companion was also a portrait of a man dressed in black,[118] but older, graver, alert, perhaps a trifle minatory. It showed the face of one who, if he had suffered, could guard his secret well. The attitude caught the eye; the right hand was pressed to the side, and it looked as if it had just been placed there; so keen and so steadfast was the glance of the cool grave eyes that it staggered the spectator. One felt, despite the stillness of the figure, that there was a tongue in that steady eye, a brain at work behind the forehead half concealed by the heavy straight-cut hair. It was so living that it seemed like "the eye of the collection." It seemed to be looking at the other portraits, to be looking at the spectators too, and estimating them, coolly, while it kept them at a distance by its impenetrable dignity and impregnable reserve. If it was the eye of the collection, it might almost be said to be the soul also for it was the most living illustration possible of the lines:

> "For who would lose,
> Though full of pain, this intellectual being,
> Those thoughts that wander through Eternity,"

Often as Hazlitt had let his thoughts rest on these portraits, all that he had dreamed of their possible grace and dignity fell short of the reality.

From this time Titian took the foremost place in his thoughts. Heads like Titian's, rather than contrasts of light and shade in the manner of Rembrandt, were the height of his ambition. Titian expressions, Titian complexions, Titian dresses held his imagination. Before the end of the week he had selected the pictures he most wished to copy, the three Titians which had captured his imagination, the man with the boar-spear for Northcote, the other two for Railton's "parlour." His choice was conditioned by the fascination which these two portraits had for him. He could think of nothing he would desire for himself more than to have them hanging in his room with him for company. Of all other portraits, seeing them day by day, he might tire, but of these—never! This being so, he thought he served his patron well in providing him with copies of them. He may have been right in this, but in the end he decided to copy the "Ippolito de' Medici" also for Railton. It did not seem to strike him that this intimidating portrait, while it was eminently suitable for Northcote's studio, was as a "parlour" piece almost as incongruous as an eagle in a toy-shop.

The other pictures he meant to copy were—"A Portrait of an English Lady," by Vandyke, which had charmed him by its air of breeding and innocence, and its suggestion of a delicacy so sensitive as to start "even at the shadow of evil," the portrait of the "Cardinal Bentivoglio," which he regarded as "one of Vandyke's happiest and most spiritual heads," and "the fine stern globular head" of Leo X, by Raphael, which might have been inspired by the lines:

> "deep on his Front engraven
> Deliberation sat and publick care."

The landscapes he now held in reserve as alternatives. They were to be copied only if he found it impossible to get permission to copy some of the pictures of his choice. He held also in reserve "Titian's Mistress" and the "Head of a Sibyl" by Guercino.

But new enthusiasms took hold of him week by week. Although he worked like a man possessed, he copied only three of the pictures on which his choice had at first settled, and these were all Titians. The

"Ippolito de' Medici" he copied twice; and he finished his copies of "The Man with the Glove" and "Titian's Mistress." Why he did not copy "The Man in Black," which affected him so profoundly and of which he thought with such yearning afterwards, we do not know. It was certainly not because of any waning of interest. It may have been for lack of ability to do it justice. As to the Vandykes, we know what happened. He was successful in obtaining permission to copy the "Cardinal Bentivoglio," yet he left the work untouched, because having begun with Titian—the copy of "The Man with the Glove" was the first he attempted—he could not get over the feeling that there was, comparatively, a want of life and interest in Vandyke's portraits. This shows us the extent to which he was fascinated by Titian, for his love of Vandyke was real, and he always desired to have a copy of the "Portrait of an English Lady."

Afterwards, with his pen, he paid exquisite tribute to "its dove-like innocence of look."

5

We see him now, settling in to the work he had planned. He did everything with such involuntary nervous energy that he attracted more attention than he desired. His transports of feeling could not pass unnoticed. He always worked with fluctuations of mood, and these he could not altogether disguise even when his work had to be done in public. When alone, he was capable of slashing his canvas into ribbons when he felt it was betraying him. He is unlikely to have given way to his temperament to such an extent in the Louvre, but still, the agitation in which he worked made him noticeable. The painters around him might have been excused if they thought of him sometimes: "He hath a demon." At first they were inclined to ridicule both his passion and his aspirations, but when they saw how quickly his work progressed—even if he went at it like a lunatic—they changed their tune. It was but a step from his room to the Louvre, and on each of the best working-days of the week, Monday, Tuesday, Wednesday and Thursday, he was at his painting by half-past nine or ten o'clock. He generally remained there until half-past three or four, when the building was closed for the day. On Friday the Galleries were given over to the cleaners, and this made work difficult. Saturdays and Sundays were usually visiting days.

When at home he painted also, being usually at work on a portrait of himself, painted, as he told his father, "in the same view as that of Hippolito de' Medici, by Titian." At other times he made duplicates of some of his copies.

If the French painters and artists who were his companions in copying may have thought of him: "He hath a demon," he, for his part, most certainly thought of some of them that they went about their work as if they had not enough blood in them "to clog the foot of a flea." He found it impossible to understand how they found it worth while to pursue their art at all, so tepid they seemed about it. Their one virtue in his eyes was that they certainly had patience enough. There was one young artist who was making a chalk-drawing of a small "Virgin and Child" by Leonardo. He worked as if he had all eternity before him in which to complete his task. He would sit with his legs balanced across a railing when engaged on this work; yet all the time he would be talking to those about him, consulting their opinion at to his progress, which to the onlooker seemed almost imperceptible; now and again he would call a halt and go to the fire to warm his hands; or he would make a circuit of the room, chatting to those who were still engaged in copying, making always the same remark on the pictures, praising Titian "*pour les coloris*," Raphael "*pour l'expression*," Poussin "*pour la composition*," as if he were making these observations for the first time, then returning complacently to his work, to "perfectionate" it. Eleven weeks had passed before he had "perfectionated" his drawing. He was engaged on this one slight piece of work almost all the time Hazlitt was at the Louvre. Hazlitt, although he marvelled that any one who could only go at such a snail's pace could find it worth while to persevere, yet recognised it as a merit that this artist kept on with his immediate task, meagre though it was, instead of flying "to fifty things one after the other," as he himself was always doing, tempted by the richness of the treasure displayed before him, and tantalised by the shortness of the time allotted to him. He felt that there was something admirable in such continuity of purpose, even if it were not accompanied by any great effort or deep interest.

Even more foreign to his temperament were the ways of another artist. This was a student who, like himself, was copying "Titian's Mistress." He went at the work as if he were engaged on a piece of embroidery. First of all he pencilled out his canvas into squares. After this he began to work, not on the face or hair, but on the first square in the right-hand corner of the picture, containing, as it happened, a piece of an old table on which a bottle or some jar of ointment was standing. All seemed alike to him in interest—the table or the clear transparent freshness of the face, or the neck that was "like a broad crystal mirror," or the great rope of hair "like meshes of beaten gold," or the ardent dark face of the lover looking over the cool rounded snowy shoulder of the woman. He completed his picture by proceeding mechanically from square to square, until at last the canvas was duly covered. Hazlitt, always obsessed by his eagerness to reach perfection at a single bound, found this cold-blooded mathematical expansion achieved systematically day by day and the entire insensitiveness to "the poetry of the picture" which the lethargic progress revealed—an amazing, almost an unnatural phenomenon. He could not understand this painting "*par métier*," he who did not know how to paint except "*par passion*," who could have said as truly as Jean-Jacques himself: "Je savais que tout mon talent ne venait que d'une certaine chaleur d'âme sur les matières que j'avais à traiter."[119]

6

As for him, while he got through an amazing amount of work, it was certainly not in a mechanical nor even in a methodical way. We have already admitted that he was given to flying off "to fifty things one after the other." There was no saying what he might or might not do, for week by week his imagination was captured by some new beauty. Before the end of October he noticed a picture much less famed than those which until then had held his attention, but which seemed to him, once he noticed it, "the sweetest in the place." Both the sentiment of the picture, which was inspired by the dying Clorinda's "Friend, thou hast won!" and the execution captivated him. Possibly its literary connection also influenced him in his liking for it. It certainly did not lessen his sympathy towards the theme that it was taken from the Canto in *Jerusalem Delivered* in which Tasso describes Tancred's luckless love.

He copied out for his father the entire description of this picture from the Catalogue, as if it "relished" in his mouth: "842, by Ludovic Lana, born at Modena in 1597, died in 1646. ' The Death of Clorinda.' Clorinda, having been mortally wounded in battle by Tancred, is seen lying at the foot of a tree, her bosom bare, discovering the place where she was wounded. On the point of expiring she desires to receive the baptismal sacrament; and while Tancred administers it to her with the water he has brought in his helmet from a neighbouring spring, she holds out her hand to him in token of forgiveness, and breathes her last." He decided that the picture would look every bit as well on the walls of Mr. Railton's "parlour" as on the walls of the Louvre, and on November 1st he started to copy it. By November 14th he had decided to copy also "A Head of Christ crowned with Thorns," by Guido, and "Three Heads" which had taken his fancy. By the end of November he added "A Holy Family" by, Raphael, and two figures from the allegorical portrait of the Marchioness of Guasto, which he found "transparent with tenderness and beauty." On December 9th, after completing his copy of "The Death of Clorinda," he took a small canvas and began making a sketch of a head in one of the large historical pictures which reminded him of his father's. This he completed in a couple of hours. "It is a side face, a good deal like yours," he wrote to his father on

December 10th, "which was the reason of my doing it so rapidly." "This same sketch is certainly a very singular thing," he added, "as I do not believe there are ten people in the world who could do it the same way." He made up his mind to make sketches from a composition by Rubens, in the intervals of his regular work, in the same rapid manner. By January 7th he was at work on a copy of a part of the "Transfiguration."

Thus for four months of intense and absorbing happiness he painted and studied, or strolled about the Louvre, pondering or admiring this or that, until stopped in his labours towards four o'clock by the unwelcome warning cry that it was time to close the building. Then he would reluctantly put his work away, would cast a parting glance of pleasure at Ruysdael's sparkling woods and waterfalls as the last shafts of light gleamed on them through the high casement, and a few minutes afterwards would be back in his room. He felt in these days as if he were not only feasting his eyes on the pictures, but feasting his mind also on the thoughts of the great painters. He felt this especially with regard to Raphael. "I am as sure," he wrote afterwards, "if it is not presumption to say so, of what passed through Raphael's mind as of what passes through my own."

For the statuary he cared much less than for the painting. Statuary had never affected him as painting did, but apart from this, some of the famed pieces of antiquity left him unmoved. The "Apollo Belvidere" he thought positively bad. It seemed to him "a theatrical coxcomb and ill-made." As to the "Venus de' Medici" he hesitated. Thomson's description of it as "the statue that enchants the world" had played tricks with his imagination, as with the imagination of all men. Yet when he looked at it, he knew that he was not enchanted by it. He was very hesitant in forming any opinion that should go against the verdict of all the world, yet although he admired its softness, sweetness and timid grace, he was never much moved by it. It seemed to him "a little too much like an exquisite marble doll." He felt it to be "a very beautiful toy, but not the Goddess of Love, or even of Beauty." This was not the statue Pygmalion fell in love with, "nor did any man ever wish or fancy his mistress to be like it." In a word, it seemed to him that there was "something beyond it, both in imagination and in nature." Its final place in his affections may be estimated from the following confession, which represents his matured feeling as to it: "I would go a pilgrimage to see the St. Peter Martyr, or the Jacob's Dream by Rembrandt, or Raphael's Cartoons, or some of Claude's landscapes;—but I would not go out of my way to see the Apollo, or the Venus, or the Laocoon." [120]

7

His friend M. Mérimée came to his room one day, and had a look at his pictures, the "Head of an old Woman" and another picture which he had brought from home,[121] and professed to like them very much, contrary to the French style though they were. Hazlitt himself had no mean opinion of them. He thought that if his pictures were not in the French style, they might be said to be very much in the style of the Flemish and Italian painters, which was far better. "I like them better, instead of worse, from comparing them with the pictures that are here," he wrote to his father. He had no ambition whatsoever to paint "in the French style." Even Guerin's "Phaedra and Hippolytus," which he heard prodigiously praised during his stay in Paris, seemed to him, although he thought the Hippolytus in the picture very beautiful, to have a mannerism that denoted premature perfection, and that gave little promise of progression in power. The Exhibition of that year on the whole gave him little pleasure. Having said one day that he thought a landscape in it too clear, he found himself challenged by M. Mérimée's astonished exclamation: "I should have thought that to be impossible." He struggled to explain that what he meant was "that the parts of the several objects were made out with too nearly equal distinctions all over the picture; that the leaves of the trees in shadow were as distinct as those in light, the branches of the trees at a distance as plain as those near; that the perspective arose only from the diminution of objects, and there was no interposition of air." He added, although this was perhaps touching on metaphysical nicety, that "one could not see the leaves of a tree a mile off."

He thought that he had explained himself intelligibly, but the reasoning of a metaphysician who was trying to express himself through painting was too much for M. Mérimée, who merely shook his head in reply, and the subject was dropped.

It seemed that he was still doomed to be unintelligible in words. All the more reason for him, then, to get on with the language of signs.

Perhaps he had seemed captious to the French artist, for there were other things also, in the Exhibition, to which he took exception. It seemed to him to have been invaded by the "toys of Time." He found it stuffed with allegorical cars of Victory and triumphal arches of Peace, which if as fine as the rainbow seemed likely to prove as evanescent. These had little to do with art, although they served their purpose, in that they certainly bruited the glory of the hero of the hour, the man singled out by Providence for the accomplishment of its great designs, as he whom we last saw as a starving emigré in a garret in Holborn, François René Chateaubriand, is just about to proclaim Buonaparte to be.[122]

Chateaubriand is no longer an exile, nor is he starving. He too is in Paris, has thrown in his fortunes with the new order of things, has learned to flatter Power, has even won his own measure of fame. He is less likely now to rub shoulders with than to splash with the mud flung in the precarious streets of Paris by his coach, the *gauche* young Englishman who has not yet learned to flatter Power, who will never learn to flatter Power, and who afterwards, comparing his ways towards Buonaparte in this year of triumph and his ways towards Buonaparte brought very low by the turning of Fortune's wheel, will look *through* him and name him, for all that he is beyond doubt of the true aristocracy of words: "*Chateaubriand—the Quack.*"

8

Paris was during these days "on tiptoe" to make its thousands of English visitors "eat, drink, and look pleased." Hospitality was given, even to excess; and the women had never been more "prodigal of their fascinations." Hazlitt thought they greatly excelled his own country-women in the art of conversation. In England conversation with women was made insipid by the touch of "gallantry" which was thought necessary to it. It was thought ill-bred to give a woman the worst of an argument. Here the women asked no quarter. Nor did they need it, for they were "mistresses of the intellectual foils." They were conversant with ideas; and they talked, without affectation, to exchange ideas. Indeed, the interchange of ideas was considered "as one great charm in society between men and women," and the thirst of knowledge was not banished "by a grosser passion." These women would converse on all topics, and they were subtle reasoners. Logic, with them, was "more in requisition than gallantry." Nevertheless, they were "full of mischief into the bargain."

He noticed with surprise how fond of reading the French were, and that the habit of reading was by no means confined to the leisured classes. They read while they were doing all sorts of things, and in all kinds of conditions. Again and again he would see an apple-girl, sitting at her stall with her feet over a stove in the coldest weather, or protected from the rain by an umbrella over her head, deep in Racine or Voltaire; or a *grisette* at the back of some dingy little shop reading one of Marmontel's tales "with all the absorption and delicate interest of a heroine of romance." It struck him that a barrow-woman in London reading Shakespeare or Fielding in the intervals of custom would be regarded as a phenomenon. But the French, men and women alike, seemed to him to read incessantly. They read in garrets and cellars; they read out of doors when pushed out of their fetid homes by the want of air; they read in the midst of incredible clamour. They seemed to him to have the knack of shutting out actuality and of sinking themselves into the ideal world at will.

He came to the conclusion that they were a people very susceptible to ideas. Voltaire, Rousseau, and Racine were perpetually in their hands. Their minds were as wax in the hands of some half-dozen master-spirits. Curiously enough, just a little before these thoughts were passing through his mind, Wordsworth, inspired by his visit to France in August, had written the sonnet in which, determined now to take a dark view of France and all her affairs, he had accused her of having:

"No master spirit, no determined road;
But equally a want of Books and Men."

To Hazlitt it seemed that easy access to books was one of the main attractions of Paris. The bookstalls were everywhere, and their heaped-up, mealy-coloured covers always attracted him. Not only was their appearance delightful. They offered the choice of a library to the student inexpensively, for they contained "neatly-bound, cheap and portable editions of all their standard authors."

He found time to read some of "their standard authors" with a tutor who was passionately devoted to Racine, and who would exclaim, every now and again, at the best passages: "What have you got in Shakespeare equal to this?" But Hazlitt, who had brought his Shakespeare with him, could always fortify himself against such probings by opening it at *Antony and Cleopatra*, Act 4, and reading aloud to himself:

"Sometime we see a cloud that's dragonish;
A vapour sometime like a bear or lion,
A tower'd citadel, a pendent rock,
A forked mountain, or blue promontory
With trees upon't, that nod unto the world
And mock our eyes with air."

Then he would look around him with exulting eyes, and cry aloud: "Our Shakespeare was also a poet." At such times he would feel that the cloudy side of the Channel was also the poetical one, and rejoice that he belonged to it.

9

As to his sports and his recreations—we do not know whether, like Wordsworth just ten years before, he

"coasted round and round the line
Of Tavern, Brothel, Gaming-house, and Shop;"

or whether he tasted any of the pleasures of the Palais-Royal. If he had, what would it have been to him, for "where would he find the rocks of Meillerie in the precincts of the Palais-Royal?" or "on what lips would Julia's kisses grow?" He certainly could not have done much more than "coast round" any pleasure that cost money. He seems even to have left the theatre unvisited.[123] This may have been from sheer lack of time. Yet he found time for one or two simple pleasures which cost nothing and which were of the kind that pleased him most. He was fortunate in this, that during the months he spent in Paris he could indulge in his favourite recreation of walking. In the streets of course he did not walk much for pleasure, for he never got used to their nervous racking, and natural ease in walking seemed to him all but impossible on their irregular slippery stones. But luckily, Paris, although its structure seemed to him rather like that of an immense suburb than like that of a city, differed from London in this, that it had no actual suburbs. In London it had been his whim to have recourse to the vigorous gymnastic of rope-walking to keep himself exercised. Here he had no need of any such expedient. He was in the country as soon as he had passed the "fairy" barrier de Neuilly, for thus it always seemed to him when he viewed it through the archway of the Tuileries, at the end of the Champs Elysées, diminished by perspective and "exquisitely light and magical," like "a thing of air." If it seemed to him as if woven out of the fabric of a vision, the long tall avenue of trees leading to it had for him a quality hardly less visionary, for it put him so much in mind of the prints of pictures of foreign countries at which he had gazed as a child, that it became itself to him like something recalled from memories of his childhood, or like part of a dream, or like something in *The Pilgrim's Progress.* Passing through the barrier was like passing from one world into another, for not a hundred yards beyond it he was wont to come upon "an old shepherd tending his flock, with his dog and his crook and sheep-skin cloak," just as if he had been a hundred miles away from any city and looking as if he might have been in existence when

"Smooth life had Flock and Shepherd in old time,
Long Springs and tepid Winters on the Banks
Of delicate Galesus;"

he loved the quick transition from the feverish heartless bustle of the capital and all its abrupt nerve-tormenting noises and shocks and jars, to the suggestion of the continuance of this "smooth life."
Not the least of the attractions of this road for him was that it led

to the Bois de Boulogne, through which he was given to wandering, dreaming of hope and good. Of course he always saw it in its winter trim, but he enjoyed its many intersecting greensward paths, and shady alleys that ran for miles in opposite directions and "terminated in a point of inconceivable brightness," and he often pleased himself with thinking that when the air was perfumed with primroses and hyacinths and the many paths were enamelled with wild flowers, this favourite wood of his would look and smell and be exactly like an English wood in spring.

He often walked also in the Gardens of the Tuileries; and they too, like the Bois de Boulogne, carried his thoughts homewards. If ever he were homesick, he had only to pass into them to be recalled to quietness by their familiar sights and scents and sounds. The trees, the grass, the wet leaves rustling in the walks, would seem to him as much English, as much the trees and grass he had always looked upon, as the sun shining over his head was the sun on which he had looked in England.

10

Towards the end of his sojourn in Paris he began to receive many compliments upon his work. At the beginning, when he would have been the better of a word of encouragement, he had had to run the gauntlet of criticism, even had had to pursue his course in spite of derision. Now that the rapidity of his work made him independent of encouragement, praise began to rain in upon him. Some of the French painters praised his copy of "The Death of Clorinda," and began to find something to commend in his style of work. The day on which he had been making a rapid sketch of the head he had thought like his father's, an Englishman had come up to him and complimented him, in French, on his work, and upon his replying in English, had said to him: "Upon my word, Sir, you get on with great spirit and boldness; you do us great credit, I am sure." Another day he was asked whether he taught painting in oil. He replied with characteristic honesty and lack of assumption that he was more in need of teaching himself, that rapid sketching was what he did best of all, that his first outlines were good, but that afterwards, the more he worked at his pictures, the worse he made them. This was the truth. Although he realised it, he did not as yet realise that it pointed to a fatal flaw in his art. He still believed in the merit of his work, for it had character; he still believed that one day he would triumph as a painter. But his training as a painter had been far too rapid, and now the hastiness with which he had learned his art was beginning to reveal itself in his incapacity to finish any picture to his satisfaction. By the time he had completed his copying of the old Masters in the Louvre, he had reached the limit of his powers. Afterwards he realised this. At the time he still hoped, although puzzled by his inability to bring anything to perfection.

While yet a boy at school, he had learned from his "Enfield":

> "Learn to speak slow, all other graces[124]
> Will follow in their proper places."

He adapted this precept in after years so as to make it applicable to writing:

> "Learn to *write* slow; all other graces
> Will follow in their proper places."

But no one had ever said to him: "Learn to paint slow." Indeed, all the practical circumstances of his life had combined to make him feel the urgency of learning to paint quickly. His own headlong enthusiasm had also forced his progress; and now, the graces were refusing to follow his precipitate brush.

As for writing, he was learning that slowly enough, but he was learning; and nothing was surer, unlikely as this may have seemed to him at the moment, than that the graces would one day follow in the wake of his slow reluctant pen.

Towards the beginning of February, 1803, he left Paris and started his journey homewards. By that time, in addition to the copies the completion of which we have mentioned,[125] he had finished much of the work referred to in his letters to his father, such as his copy of two of the figures in the allegorical portrait of the Marchioness of Guasto and of "Raphael's Holy Family", and his sketches of four of the figures in the "Transfiguration."[126] He had also copied "The Deluge," by Nicolas Poussin. Of this intention there is no hint in his letters; but then the last letter we possess of his Paris days is a mere note written on January 7th, 1803. The picture was one for which he had the greatest admiration. It seemed to him to be "the poetry of painting." He may well have made it the subject of his labours during the three remaining weeks of his stay. In addition he may have brought away with him some other oddments. This would seem to be suggested by his reference, in 1819, to those "loose draughts and fragments" which he had brought with him from the Louvre, and which he had been forced to part with, during the intervening years, one by one, "like drops of life-blood," for "hard money."

He is now almost twenty-five years of age, and his education, as the word is commonly understood, is at last completed. It has been a remarkable one. If genius, as Wordsworth would have it, thrives on alternate "rest and excitation," perhaps it is also nourished by contrast.

Certain it is, that if some hand had determined to "compose" his life after the pattern of a picture by Rembrandt, it could not have been more in the manner of a study of contrasted light and shade. The country and the town, the chapel and the theatre, the Unitarian College and the School of Art, the oak-panelled parlour at Wem and the print-strewn floor of Northcote's studio, the Hebrew prophets and "the gospel according to Jean-Jacques," desolate Cape Cod and the swarming Palais-Royal—have all had their share in the making of him. Divines to whom a poet is "a sort of nondescript," and great poets who see life as co-extensive with poetry, metaphysicians who tend to be impatient with words, as too gross for the conveyance of their thoughts, and painters to whom words are the mere ghosts of the living forms and symbols whereby they work their wonders—have played on him in quick succession. He has felt for the troubles of his age; he has held converse with the past, and tried to receive its inheritance. The living are dear to him; but the dead are to him "a religion, or they are nothing."

The New England and the Old, the Present and the Past, politics, theology, metaphysics, poetry, painting—have all done for him all they can.

What then is there left for him to learn? May he not now say to the Powers and Destinies that preside over such spirits: "Am I not now to be allowed to take mine ease?"

Not yet—we fear. He is but at the beginning of the lesson. Now has come the time for him to be delivered over, as all such must be delivered over one day or other, ere they can fulfil the will of Life towards them, to initiation in the penal-flamy discipline of "that domain which we call the Passions."

Chapter Three

THE PORTRAIT-PAINTER (1803-1805)

"W. Hazlitt is in Town. I took him to see a very pretty girl
professedly, where there were two young girls—the very head
and sum of the Girlery was two young girls—they neither
laughed nor sneered nor giggled nor whispered—but they were
young girls—and he sat and frowned blacker and blacker,
indignant that there should be such a thing as Youth and Beauty,
till he tore me away before supper in perfect misery and owned
he could not bear young girls. They drove him mad. So I took
him home to my old Nurse, where he recover'd perfect tranquillity.
Independent of this, and as I am not a young girl myself, he is
a great acquisition to us."

CHARLES LAMB *to* WORDSWORTH.

I

PARIS had welcomed its English visitors with open arms in the autumn
of 1802, but even before Hazlitt left it in February, the growing
volume of abuse of Buonaparte in the English newspapers, the lengths
to which the caricaturing of "the Corsican" were carried, the bitter
attacks made on Charles Fox for accepting courtesy from the First
Consul during his visit to Paris, and the refusal to fulfil the terms of
the Treaty of Amiens, were already pointing towards a renewal of
hostilities. As early as February Buonaparte had had a conversation
with Lord Whitworth, the English Ambassador in Paris, in which
he had expressed the various causes of his dissatisfaction with the
English Government. On March 8th a speech from the Throne, which
recommended to the British Parliament the seconding of the Government in completing all measures of defence on the grounds of preparations of considerable magnitude which were said to be being made in
France and Holland, increased his dissatisfaction. English visitors who
read the signs of the times and who did not linger too long in Paris
were wiser than those who did, for when, prior to the actual Declaration of War, French shipping had been seized in English ports, Buonaparte retaliated by detaining all the English resident in France at the
time.

It is not possible to understand Hazlitt's mood at this time, the
modification that many of his personal relationships underwent, and
the personal crisis that came to him in this year, without reference to the

177

racking political tension of 1803, and the torturing cross-currents in
which he found himself again caught, after a brief emergence from
them during the Peace. In the course of this year the suffering of those
who had steadfastly opposed the war with France since its commencement ten years before, and who still continued to oppose it, came to its
height. In these ten years many of those who in 1793 had remained
firm in their opposition to the war, on conscientious grounds, although
their firmness had cost them misgivings and wrenching of sympathies,
had gradually fallen away. Many causes had contributed to this, the
chief being gradual alienation of sympathy from France, culminating
in an actual revulsion of feeling against the French Government after
the invasion of Switzerland in 1798. Nevertheless, the withdrawal of
their sympathy from France by no means meant that they desired the
continuance of the war or were eager to further its prosecution. When
in 1800 the Government had rejected the peace overtures made by
Buonaparte immediately after his assumption of the First Consulship,
both Coleridge and Wordsworth had censured the peremptory rejection,
not because they were at that time in sympathy with France, but
because they saw little to be gained through the continuation of
hostilities, and much to be jeopardised. Thus they, and many others
who felt like them, had rejoiced at the conclusion of the Peace of
Amiens.

But with the renewal of war agitation in the latter half of 1802
and at the beginning of 1803, they changed their ground entirely.
They held that the old war against which they had once been in
protest, the war on nascent democracy, had been concluded and dropped,
and that the war for which the Government papers were now clamouring was a new war aimed solely at checking French aggression, and
more especially, French designs on the Mediterranean. Not only
those who, like Coleridge and Wordsworth, had become genuinely
Anti-Gallican, but all who had become heartily tired of going against
the stream of public opinion, could now join in this cry without
exposing themselves to the charge of inconsistency, and justify the
reversal or modification of their attitude on the score of patriotism.
The charge of aggression raised against the French seemed to them to
alter the character of the war. The conflict was not now one of
doctrines, but of rival nations, the chief immediate issue being sea
power, and the control of the Mediterranean.

Thus in the war-agitation aroused by the cry of aggression, what
had been felt originally to be the grand issue, the fate of democracy in
Europe, was gradually pushed well into the background. It was
remembered only by a small, dwindling, and very unpopular minority.
To this minority Hazlitt continued to adhere—throughout all brunts.
He looked on the country as being divided into four parties—the High
Tory party, determined, open and declared aggressors all of them, who

still held to the contention of Burke that no peace should be concluded with a regicide republic which should never have been called into existence and which was to be pursued to extermination or unconditional surrender; the party led by Pitt and Addington, which did not differ much from the High Tory party in its aims, but which found it politic to dissimulate, and therefore was intent on diverting the appearance of aggression from itself to the French and on concealing the intention, from which it yet never wavered, of bringing about the restoration of the Bourbons; the third party, consisting of the body of the nation, duped by the second party into believing that peace had been concluded in 1802 in the spirit of peace, and that if it had been broken, it was because the spirit of the French had made its preservation impossible; and the fourth party, consisting of the minority to which he himself belonged. This was at the moment so reduced that it could hardly be said to be a party. To it adhered those who still believed that the war was essentially not a war of nations at all, but the war of democracy against the autocracies of Europe, although the main issue was now being masked by the plea of the necessity of checking French maritime aggression; who felt it to be a tragedy that at last it had been given the appearance of a war of nations; and who grieved because under the banners of nationalism the Peoples of Europe, who should have been united in a common cause, were being led forth to slay each other and to be slain.

Hazlitt, like others of this protesting minority, regarded the Treaty of Amiens not as a genuine attempt at establishing peace, but as a stratagem,[127] which had enabled a Government that had never for a moment intended to conserve peace, to renew the war on fresh grounds that obscured the real issues and therefore flung the whole weight of practical opinion in England for the first time since the opening of the war into the war scale, and a stratagem so successful that "many of the new converts who had hurled up the red-cap of liberty with most violence in the air, and whose suffrages it was an object to gain, were now foremost in raising the war-whoop and in cheering the combatants." He regarded the war as having been engineered by the deliberate inflammation of feeling through misrepresentation and calumny: "it was of little consequence by what means the popular mind on this side the channel was gangrened and inflamed. It was immaterial what ingredients were poured into the boiling cauldron of national hate, or employed to make the charm of loyalty ' thick and slab.' Whatever swelled the war-whoop or cut off the chance of reconciliation pleased." He felt sure that the purpose of the Government, concealed though it was, was inalterable, and that it was none other than the restoration of the rejected tyranny in France as the symbol of the victory of the old order of things. Liberated France, instead of being left to work out her destinies under her new rulers, was to have her strength once more stifled by "the coils of the Bourbon belly." It seemed to him, looking on at the preparations towards the consummation of this, as if he were watching the unwinding of a monstrous frustration and a monstrous tragedy; that Europe was going to be bedewed with blood to bring about an issue which every freeborn spirit must regret, the rout of the forces of democracy in uttermost confusion, and the bringing back of a second night of slavery that would prove longer than the first. For him, the war was still what it had been for Coleridge in 1800, a war without hope. If the French were victors, his country would be humiliated; if the French were losers, the Cause which was even more to him than country would perish, and this he regarded as fatal to the progress of humanity. Nothing was surer than that in the war itself, the innocent, the humble and the unprotected in all countries would be the chief sufferers. There would be a long agony, with little or no good to be reaped from it anywhere. He looked upon the Declaration of War as an unqualified calamity, and on those who had brought it about as the enemies of the happiness and the progress of man. Hazlitt is always needed to make Hazlitt credible, and never more so than in any account of the vehement anger which assailed him upon the renewal of the war in 1803 and inevitably made him fall foul of those of his fellow-countrymen whose opinions differed from his at this time. His own words, written not in the heat of the moment, but years afterwards, can alone bring home to us the passionate concern for the fate of mankind which consumed him:

"Great Britain declared war against France the 18th of May, 1803. Period ever fatal and memorable—the commencement of another Iliad of woes not to be forgotten while the world shall last! The former war had failed, and the object of this was to make another desperate attempt to put down, by force of arms and at every risk, the example of a revolution which had overturned a hateful but long-established tyranny, and had hitherto been successful over every attempt to crush it by external or internal means. The other causes assigned at different periods and according to the emergency were masks to cover this, which was the true, the constant, the sole-moving one in all circumstances and in all fortunes; through good report and evil report, in victory or defeat, in the abyss of despair or the plenitude of success, in every stage and phasis of its commencement, progress, or double termination. . . . Whether that object was just or not, is a different question; and there may be two opinions upon the subject, that of the free or the slave."[128]

Should anything further be needed to illumine for us the hot rebel heart of him, we may turn to some words which Coleridge jotted down in one of his notebooks in the course of this year:

"Hazlitt, to the feelings of anger and hatred, phosphorus—it is but to open the cork and it flames!"

2

We see him then, after the brief sunshine of the Paris days, thrust back once more to the rough and shadowed side of the road. He has been accused of choosing the shadows, but the truth is, that in view of the opinions—all of them grounded on principles which he had threshed out for himself—which he held consistently and inalterably from his boyhood to the day of his death, the renewal of the war inevitably threw him back once more among the shadows. His could be no other than a lonely, shadowed, uphill way.

But his strong political sympathies and dyspathies did not as yet condition his entire life. He set about earning his living by painting immediately after his return, and this brought a variety of experiences in its train. His son says that he "made a kind of professional tour through some of the Midland counties, and at Liverpool, Manchester and several other places, was successful in obtaining sitters." We get from his own expressive pen many glimpses of his way of living, his enjoyments, his encounters with people, and the shifts to which he was sometimes put as he painted, read, or copied. In Liverpool he painted what his son thought an excellent portrait of the Rev. William Shepherd. Possibly it was the connection with Mr. Shepherd and Mr. Yates that brought him into touch with William Roscoe, the well-known Whig banker and philanthropist, who makes his appearance everywhere in the literature of these times, from *The March to Moscow* to *Mary Barton*, and of some of whose political opinions he has left a record. The living he made was necessarily desultory and precarious, for it depended partly on the gift of conciliating and pleasing such wealthy patrons, and in this gift he was conspicuously lacking. At times he was almost penniless. Once, while in Manchester, he lived on coffee for a fortnight. He was at the time engaged in copying a half-length portrait of a Manchester manufacturer, and for this work he was to receive five guineas when it was completed. He says that sustaining himself on coffee was an experiment, but we note that the experiment came to an abrupt end as soon as he received his five guineas: "I rather slurred over the coat, which was of reddish brown, ' of formal cut,' to receive my five guineas, with which I went to market myself, and dined on sausages and potatoes, and while they were getting ready, and I could hear them hissing in the pan, read a volume of *Gil Blas*, containing the account of the fair Aurora!" He tells us that not Apicius himself ever understood the meaning of the word luxury better than he did at that moment.

Coleridge had written in July of the preceding year:

"There was a time when, though my path was rough,
This joy within me dallied with distress,
And all misfortunes were but as the stuff
Whence Fancy made me dreams of happiness."

He had felt as he wrote the lines that he had left this resilience of spirit behind him. But as yet it was Hazlitt's, in spite of all the difficulties and uncertainties he encountered. An occasional touch of hunger made his food all the sweeter when he could afford to eat; precariousness as yet but served to whet the edge of his pleasures when they came; the summer rain still seemed to him to have blessing in it. He was intensely alive. "The two great springs of Life, Hope and Fear," at least left him not a moment to be dull.

If *Gil Blas* made an agreeable accompaniment to his sausages, another book which he read in Manchester became the companion of his dreams. This was Mrs. Inchbald's *A Simple Story.* As was usual with him when he read a book with delight, all the circumstances connected with the reading remained vividly in his memory. "I recollect walking out to escape from one of the tenderest parts," he wrote in after years, "in order to return to it again with double relish. An old crazy hand-organ was playing "Robin Adair," a summer-shower dropped manna on my head, and slaked my feverish thirst of happiness." He is said to have assumed by this time the trappings of misanthropy. We would say, judging from such confessions, that such trappings of misanthropy as he assumed were but a protective covering for sensitiveness. The one who felt with such poignancy for Dorriforth and Miss Milner is not very far removed from the one who had cried his eyes out over *The New Eloise.*

Manchester seems to have been his headquarters, but he passed from place to place according to the likelihood of his obtaining work. It is thus that, later in the summer, he comes to Keswick and Grasmere.

3

There is no evidence to show that he had met Coleridge and Wordsworth in the years that had passed since 1798, although there are indications that he had not lost contact with them during these years. We hear little, from himself, of his visits to Keswick and Grasmere in 1803, although they determined largely his character and development. Possibly the humiliation which scored his life so deeply at the close of his second visit that it may be said to have come nigh to cutting him in two, made him reluctant to dwell much in retrospect on these months.

It is in one of Coleridge's letters that we first hear of him, and not with reference to his painting but to his literary plans. Hazlitt had at this time to do anything he could for a living. If he could not secure sitters for portraits, he was ready to do copying of pictures, not now of the old Masters, but of any the copying of which would put a few guineas into his pocket. If he could not bring to a conclusion his essay On the Disinterestedness of the Human Mind, on which he had long laboured, or any other essay in which he had sought to express the train of moral and political speculation on which he was perpetually engaged, he would be glad in the meantime to do any hackwork that would bring in a few pounds. One such project was an abridgment of Abraham Tucker's *Light of Nature Pursued*. We find Coleridge writing to Godwin on June 4th, telling him of this project, asking him to bring the proposal to the notice of any publisher of his acquaintance, Longman and Rees excepted,[129] and saying that he himself would prefix to the abridgment an essay containing the whole substance of the first volume of Hartley.

The first reference to Hazlitt as being at Keswick is contained in one of Coleridge's letters to Southey, written on August 1st: "Young Hazlitt has taken masterly portraits of me and Wordsworth, very much in the manner of Titian's portraits."[130] From this it might seem that Hazlitt had been in the district some time, but we must remember his way of working, the extreme rapidity and ease with which he was wont to throw out the first outlines of a picture, the pain, difficulty, and slowness with which he perfected the work.

4

Sir George and Lady Beaumont visited Keswick at the beginning of August. It is in connection with their visit that we get our next glimpse—an oddly characteristic one it is!—of Hazlitt, rebel, uncompromising, and implacable. The Beaumonts lodged next door to Coleridge, and at first Sir George, who was of the High Tory party, seems to have regretted finding himself in such close proximity to one whose earlier writings had been most distasteful to him. This feeling was soon converted into enthusiastic friendship, for Coleridge's political sympathies had altered to such an extent that there was now little risk of his offending Tory susceptibilities, and his personality completely captivated both Sir George and the sensitive, enthusiastic Lady Beaumont, whose nature he plumbed at the first sight of her. "You may wind her up with *any* music, but *music* it must be, of some sort or other," he wrote to Wordsworth. He ate with them; "wound"

Lady Beaumont up with such music of Wordsworth that if Wordsworth had entered when his praises were being sung she would have been ready to fall in homage at his feet; walked with them, and rode with them. "I was on horse just now with Sir G. and Lady B.—when Lord Lowther came riding up to us—so of course all dismounted—and he is now with his Jockey Phiz in with Sir G." Coleridge in fact was at his happiest and best, charming and being charmed. Hazlitt was probably at his prickliest and worst in such circumstances and in such company. Be this as it may, the electricity in him gathered and produced a dinner-table storm in the course of this visit, which deprived him of a patron who might have been very valuable to him. Afterwards he blamed Coleridge for provoking him beyond endurance on the occasion. It needs but little imagination to picture the scene: Coleridge, glowing and magnetic, making such music as he knew would please; Sir George gratified, fascinated and soothed by the silken sounds that rustled through the room; the third member of the party, pale, silent, negative, almost forgotten by the other two, until all in a flash, when Coleridge began, as it seemed to him, a canting attack on Junius, the pale and silent one was metamorphosed into a human thunderbolt that launched itself at Coleridge and shattered the summer day of his eloquence.

The next day Coleridge came to Hazlitt with an interlined copy of Junius, full of marginal notes, and said to him: "I am come to show you how foolish it is for persons who respect each other to dispute warmly, for after all they will probably think the same," and he demonstrated, with the help of the marginal notes, that he himself really agreed with all that Hazlitt had said. This was handsome; yet the gracious gesture did not mean that Coleridge's mind had freed itself from irritation. The "hidden stings," it would seem, are now no longer hidden. It cannot have been pleasant to him that a man who five years before had listened to him with something like reverential awe should have come near to putting him on the defensive as to his integrity.

Hazlitt's anger was no doubt quickly over. Of him in these days when the power in him was in conflict with the sensitiveness it might well have been said:

> "And thus awhile the fit will work on him;
> Anon, as patient as the female dove,
> When that her golden couplets are disclosed,
> His silence will sit drooping."

Yet the incident left its mark on him also. In his mind there was dawning the suspicion that Coleridge was inclined to "trim" in his opinions so as to suit his company.

As for Sir George, the mischief was done. He had commissioned Hazlitt to paint a portrait of Coleridge for him, but this, his first commission, was also his last. He was not the man to tolerate in any one dependent on his favour such transitions of mood. He could not have been more startled if an inoffensive-looking twig had suddenly uncoiled itself adder-like and stung him. He was so much offended both at Hazlitt's onslaught on Coleridge and at his determined defence of Junius that he never spoke to him again. Such an exhibition of temperament from the peripatetic painter he had invited to his dinner-table was neither to be forgotten nor forgiven.

5

At this time Hazlitt, although engaged in painting both Coleridge and Hartley, does not seem to have been staying under Coleridge's roof. He may have spent a few days at Keswick as Coleridge's guest at the beginning of his stay, but possibly he found it more convenient, there as elsewhere, to take lodgings about which he could scatter the impedimenta of his art, and from which he could sally forth, as the mood took him, to do sketching in the district. His life was such that it was better for him to be free to come and go as he liked.

Immediately after the dinner-table scene, he put himself beyond the temptation of outraging High Tory susceptibilities or marring the music that played on them, by going over to Grasmere to paint. His departure was evidently a surprise to Coleridge, who wrote to Wordsworth: "You would be as astonished at Hazlitt's coming, as I at his going."[131] This cannot have been his first visit to Grasmere as he had already painted a side-portrait of Wordsworth, and he never could paint except when he had the sitter before him. If he had expected to continue work on the details of this portrait, he must have been disappointed, as it had just been sent by the carrier to Keswick, where it was commented on and criticised freely. Mrs. Wilkinson of Ormathwaite, herself an artist's wife, swore it made Wordsworth look twenty years too old. The children, Hartley and Derwent, recognised it at once, but Hartley said: "it is very like, but Wordsworth is far handsomer." Mary Stamper, Mrs. Coleridge's maid and nursemaid, was very much of the same opinion: "it is very *leek*, but it is not canny enough," indicating at the same time that even so she did not consider Wordsworth specially "canny" by adding: "though Mr. Wordsworth is not a *canny* man, to be sure." "You and I, dear William, pass for an ugly pair with the lower orders,"[132] Coleridge wrote, half ruefully, half banteringly, when reporting this. His own objection to the portrait was that he thought Hazlitt had yielded to the temptation to make a fine picture rather than a faithful portrait: "every single person without exception cries out: 'What a likeness! but the face is too long!' You have a round face!—Hazlitt knows this: but he will not alter it. Why? because the Likeness is with him a secondary consideration—he wants it to be a fine Picture."[133]

Nevertheless, we have no doubt that the portrait was "very *leek.*" Perhaps some of Hazlitt's portraits would have pleased more if they had been less "*leek.*"

After his departure from Keswick, Hazlitt drops out of Coleridge's letters, and Wordsworth's to Coleridge of this date have not been preserved, so that we have no very clear impression of his relationship with Dorothy Wordsworth,[133 (b)] with whom he continued the acquaintance begun at Alfoxden, or with Mrs. Wordsworth, whom he met this year for the first time. The only member of the Grasmere household, apart from the poet, to whom he refers is old Molly Fisher, of whom he speaks, as did most people of this humble and faithful retainer of the Wordsworths, with a touch of affectionate amusement. What made his meeting with her memorable to him was what seemed to him the "worse than Gothic ignorance" in which she had lived, for in Old Molly, who yet had her own knowledge and her own wisdom, he came perhaps on the only woman in England who ten years after the outbreak of the French Revolution had never heard of it!

If we get no intimate glimpse of Hazlitt in Wordsworth's home circle, we yet see him very clearly, sketching around Nab Scar and in the district, having a word or two with the countryfolk who passed him as he was painting, wandering about by himself at night, perhaps running, amid the disturbing beauty of the hills, "like any wild thing," as once he had scudded along the moonlit fields at Wem. Certainly he provoked some unflattering comments among the country-people by what they regarded as his oddities in this respect, and doubtless he was not more discreet than any other man of his years would have been, whose nerves were on' the stretch and whose heart was "heaving with its load of bliss" on summer nights among the hills. We see him, in calmer moments, sailing with the Poet on Grasmere Lake, asking him if the idea of the Poems on the naming of Places had not been borrowed from the local inscriptions of the same kind in *Paul and Virginia*, and talking to him about his poetry. It is clear that he was privileged to see the manuscript of the "Poem to Coleridge," and a rough draft of what became Book I of *The Excursion*, some lines[134] of which took a firm hold of his memory and cast their reflections into his early prose. Another passage which captured his imagination and his memory was the glorious commentary on the so-called madness of the Poet, which afterwards formed part of the Third Book of *The Prelude*.[135] A third was the Poet's apocalyptic Dream or Vision of frail man endeavouring to secure the permanence of the treasures of his intellectual being in the midst of the destruction of his physical being and of his immediate physical universe.[136]

But what made the most profound impression of all on him was listening to some lines—from one of Wordsworth's manuscripts—which he remembered afterwards as being "put into the mouth of a person smit with remorse for some rash crime:"[137]

> "Action is transitory—a step, a blow,
> The motion of a muscle—this way or that—
> 'Tis done; and in the after-vacancy
> We wonder at ourselves like men betray'd;
> Suffering is permanent, obscure and dark
> And shares the nature of infinity."

We wonder at ourselves like men betray'd! In these words was sounded for Hazlitt the *Leit-motif* of the broken music that was to come.

6

Wordsworth and Dorothy left Grasmere for Keswick on Sunday, August 14th, and on the 15th they set out with Coleridge for a tour in Scotland. There is no evidence as to what Hazlitt did during the remainder of the summer. He was not given to letter-writing, and all that Coleridge in the late autumn could say as to his movements was that he supposed Hazlitt had gone back to his Manchester headquarters. He was not at Greta Hall when Southey arrived on September 7th. Nor was he there when Coleridge, who had parted from the Wordsworths early in the course of the tour, returned to Keswick on September 15th, after various fantastic wanderings in Scotland; but one of the first things Coleridge did on his return was to write a character sketch of him for Tom Wedgwood, which shows clearly enough that in the course of the summer he had become something less than Hazlitt's friend. Wedgwood, who was planning a tour abroad for the sake of his health, had long hoped to have Coleridge as his companion, but Coleridge, who knew himself to be so much under the dominion of opium that it was impossible for him to bear the strain of guarding his painful and shameful secret when living at close quarters with any friend, had given it as his opinion that he was not well enough to travel with another invalid. It seems that Richard Sharp, who had met Hazlitt at Grasmere and had liked him, had suggested that he might prove a suitable companion, whereupon Wedgwood had written to Coleridge for his opinion. This would have been a great opportunity for Hazlitt to see something of the world. Indeed it would have been a great opportunity for any man of genius whose circumstances were narrow and cramped, and who was hampered in the effort to develop his genius by the necessity of earning his daily bread. It would certainly have given Hazlitt the opportunity of correcting any asperities that had been fostered by a narrow upbringing, and to develop, unfettered for a time by anxiety as to ways and means, perhaps to mellow in the sunshine of a little immediate prosperity. Yet Coleridge, who had been quite ready to help Hazlitt to find a publisher who would commission him to abridge Abraham Tucker's *Light of Nature Pursued*, who had been delighted to give his blessing to this grinding piece of hackwork, negatived in no uncertain way the proposal which came to him from the man who by providing him with his own daily bread had given his genius the opportunity of soaring to its highest flights, of setting another and a younger man of genius free from the necessity of hack-work for a time. On the point at issue he wrote: "To be your companion he is, in my opinion, utterly unfit." As for Sharp's liking, he brushed it aside: "Sharp seemed to like him; but Sharp saw him only for half an hour, and that walking." A hint of the irritation caused by memories of the Beaumont dinner seems to linger in the emphasis Coleridge laid on the strangeness and repulsiveness of Hazlitt's manners. As to his character, after allowing him to be "a thinking, observant, original man," and admitting him to be "kindly-natured," and "very fond of, attentive to, and patient with children," he prefaced some further praise of Hazlitt with censure of a kind that would quite disqualify him for the proposed companionship: "he is jealous, gloomy, and of an irritable Pride—and addicted to women, as objects of sexual Indulgence."[138]

To Hazlitt's painting alone he gave almost unqualified praise, adding: "If you could recommend him as a Portrait-painter, I should be glad."

The upshot of it all is, Hazlitt is fitted to earn a "*Sabine* subsistence"[139] by abridging Tucker or wandering round the country as a portrait-painter, but he is not to be permitted to have a season of ease or even luxury as Wedgwood's companion.

We cannot doubt that there is much truth in the portrait. Coleridge touched not only on what was worst in Hazlitt, but on what was best. The best thing of all in Hazlitt was his love of that which is high, and his whole-hearted worship of the great men who had been. Coleridge made ample acknowledgment of this, as well as of his power of mind and occasional felicities of speech. When he touched on what was worst in Hazlitt, he wrote in all good faith. Hazlitt at the time was vexed and unsure of himself in his relations with women, and to any one not understanding the difficulty he was having in realising himself as a man, he may well have seemed merely "addicted to women as objects of sexual Indulgence." He may have disguised his sensitiveness and self-mistrust under bravado, and thus, in his talk, may have offended against Coleridge's religion of love.

The portrait has too much truth in it to be rated as caricature. Yet it certainly does not flatter. If Coleridge did not use false measure, he used Polonius-measure, which from one man of genius to another is perhaps shabbier. We cannot say that he did not use Hazlitt "after his desert," for Hazlitt played the fool at times, but he would have done better, considering his own frailties and Hazlitt's need of a helping hand, if he had remembered Hamlet's generous rebuke: ' "God's bodikins, man, much better! Use every man after his desert, and who should 'scape whipping? Use them after your own honour and dignity." And we say, that if any one had used Coleridge "after his desert" at this time, which fortunately no one did, and had forwarded to Wedgwood a character-sketch of him, drawn with the same lack of kindness, the same hard edge, the same inclusion of the best traits, while yet the worst had been heavily underlined, it would have sunk him. Hazlitt's ship was not sunk, but for years it was to labour in shallows and miseries, and never in all his life henceforth, even on his death-bed, was he to know respite from financial anxiety and literary labour.

Coleridge might well have left Hazlitt to the mercies or unmercies of "Heaven's scourge-stick." Nothing can be surer than that these will not fail to visit him.

7

At the end of October, Hazlitt, knowing nothing of the fortune which might have come his way and of which he had been pronounced unworthy, returned to Keswick to work on the portrait of Coleridge for Sir George Beaumont. He was at work also, in the course of the autumn, on a second portrait of Wordsworth.[140] Coleridge still had the appearance of friendship towards him, but the part he had played cannot but have made him conscious that dislike and impatience towards Hazlitt were growing in him, and, if he had only admitted it, a certain grudgingness. He was at the stage he usually reached with his one-time adorers, of half grudging them the breath that was in them as soon as it had become apparent to all men that it was not drawn from his own nostrils; and he would like Hazlitt none the better from the consciousness that he had acted a dog-in-the-manger part towards him. But even if there had not been this slackening of sympathy, the circumstances of the moment would have made perfect harmony between these two men impossible, for Hazlitt returned to Keswick at the most excitable moment of that year of crisis. By this time Buonaparte's "knock at the door of all England" had startled the whole country into violent activity, and his threat of carrying terror into the streets of London had whipped the blood of the nation to fever heat. Hazlitt has left his own description of the stir of preparation which was visible everywhere:

"Not a fishing-boat but seemed to have new life put into it, and to prepare for the conflict. Upwards of five hundred ships of war, of various descriptions and sizes, scoured the ocean in different directions. English squadrons blockaded every port in the Channel or Mediterranean; and our cruisers were either seen scudding over the waters, like seagulls dallying with their native element and hovering near their prey, or stood in and insulted the enemy on his own shores, cutting out his vessels or dismantling their forts. By land, the hubbub and consternation was not less. Britain armed from one end to the other to repel the threatened invasion. An army of volunteers sprang up like grasshoppers. Every hill had its horseman: every bush or brake its sharpshooter. The preparations were not the least active at the greatest distance from the scene of danger. Petitions were put into our liturgy to deliver us from an insolent and merciless foe who ' was about to swallow us up quick;' nor was there a church door in the remotest corner of Great Britain on which was not posted a call on high and low, rich and poor, to bestir themselves in the common defence, proceeding from Mr. Cobbett's powerful pen, which roused the hopes and fears of the meanest rustic into a flame of martial enthusiasm."[141]

Wordsworth poured out sonnet after sonnet of martial ardour in the course of October. In one of these he anticipated the sweetness of victory. In another he exhorted the Men of Kent, the "Vanguard of Liberty," to do great deeds:

> "No parleying now! In Britain is one breath;
> We are all with you now from Shore to Shore:—
> Ye Men of Kent, 'tis Victory or Death!"

Not content with placing his pen at the service of his country, he became one of the army of volunteers that had sprung up "like grasshoppers." While the poet Leigh Hunt, as yet unknown to him, was "playing at soldiers in Piccadilly," half shamefaced at wearing the trappings of war without incurring any of the risk, for he was of those who had not the least belief that Buonaparte would come, Wordsworth, along with the Grasmere volunteers, was marching two or three times a week in his red coat to be drilled at Ambleside, and was inclined to censure all those in the district who were not doing likewise, and to hound them on into taking their share of the responsibility of defence. He felt that while at Grasmere they had turned out "almost to a man," at Keswick they were "sadly remiss in putting themselves to trouble in defence of the country." Coleridge was not drilling, but he was quite unshaken by these censures. Indeed he felt himself in this hour of trial to be the man of the moment. He could not have been prouder if he had won the war solely by his own efforts than he, who had once described himself as "a child of peace," was of having "swell'd the war-whoop" and helped to bring on the renewal of war by his diatribes in the *Morning Post*. Especially he took credit to himself for the *Letters* to Fox of November 4th and November 9th, 1802, published in the *Morning Post* while Fox was being much criticised for having visited Paris, and accusing him of feeling and thinking "like a Frenchman," and of having made "a free-will offering of prostration" to the enemy. He had been filled with pride when Fox had said that the *Morning Post* had been responsible for the renewal of the war, even to the extent of saying that he would be proud to have the charge inscribed on his tomb. In his heart he believed that he had done more to foster a spirit of war-rancour simply by nicknaming Buonaparte "the Corsican" than all the state-papers and documents on the subject had done.

To Hazlitt this boast, like the accusation hurled at Charles Fox of thinking and feeling "like a Frenchman," seemed typical of all that he hated in the way the renewal of the war had been brought about. When he thought of Buonaparte's head and of "the fine iron binding" about his face, it seemed to him a shabby thing to attempt to dim his natural glory, just because he was not of noble birth, by labelling him "the upstart Corsican" or "the grateful *élève* of the Dictator Barras." If ever a man was a natural king, it was Buonaparte. Hazlitt thought the nickname Coleridge had invented did little credit either to its inventor or to those who could thus let themselves be prejudiced by a name. In 1795 Coleridge had written: "farther than names the vulgar inquire not." All his efforts had been directed against this foible, and he had sought to educate men out of it. How had he altered! Now he was preening himself upon having played successfully upon this once scorned tendency. When Hazlitt looked at him, he could not help comparing him with the man who even five years before had cried out in self-searching and contrition:

> "We have offended, Oh! my countrymen!
> We have offended very grievously
> And been most tyrannous,"

and who had felt so sensitively for all human beings caught in the blind tides of war.

There were here opposing points of view that could not be reconciled. Coleridge seemed to Hazlitt one of the bigots of war, and Hazlitt seemed to Coleridge one of "the bigots of the Revolution." Perhaps it should be emphasised here that the issue on which Hazlitt and Coleridge were at variance was not the necessity of defending the country—that necessity was taken for granted by both of them—but the conduct of affairs which had brought the country to the necessity of such defence.. Hazlitt held that it was not the danger of invasion which had produced the taking up of arms, but "the determination to take up arms" which had produced the danger of invasion, that "the threatened invasion was not the cause of the war, but the direct consequence of it."[142] But while he blamed the Government and the ministerial press, he never forgot that the Government was neither the country nor the People. He was as ready as Fox himself to defend the country in the hour of danger: there could be only one opinion on the necessity of defence in such a moment, and he promised Buonaparte a sharp welcome if ever he landed in England. Nor was this merely the heat of the moment. There is still vibration in the words he wrote towards the end of his life in describing the crisis of this year:

"Neither can I think so poorly of my countrymen . . . as to suppose that even if Buonaparte had made good his landing, it would have been all over with us. He might have levelled London with the dust, but he must have covered the country with heaps and *tumuli* of the slain, before the mixed breed of Norman and Saxon blood would have submitted to a second Norman conquest. Whatever may be my opinion of the wisdom of the people, or the honesty of the rulers, I never denied their courage or obstinacy. They do not give in to a conflict sooner for having provoked it. They would not receive a foreign invasion as a visit of courtesy; nor submit to be conquered like a nation of women, hardly complaining of the rudeness. . . ."[143]

But while he felt all this, he never ceased to regret a renewal of the war into which it seemed to him that Buonaparte had been forced, and to regard it as the crown of all the calamities in which the country had been involved by the narrow and selfish policy which the government had pursued ever since hostilities with France had broken out in 1793. Where others felt only the *élan* of patriotic endeavour and even the anticipatory joy of battle, he could only feel the tragedy of this game of cross-purposes played by men and nations, and the piteous futility of the vast human agony which he foresaw.

There is one last point on which we should touch in giving an account of the political passion by which Hazlitt was swayed at this time. It may be asked how, in the conflict of sympathies which racked him, he reconciled the readiness to defend his country at this moment with his principles and his scale of values: "true to honour, to country, and to that Cause which is dearer than both." Was he, to some extent, despite himself, carried away by the feeling of the moment? No! That would have been entirely natural, but it would not have been Hazlitt. If, like Rousseau, he felt all things more keenly than others, he also reasoned all things out for himself more keenly than others, and if we seek for the train of reasoning which determined his attitude

to public affairs we shall always find it. Thus far we have attempted
to explain his feeling by reference to his attitude to the Government
of his own country. We can only explain this last issue by reference to
his attitude to Buonaparte. His attitude towards his own country was
not simple. Neither was his attitude towards Buonaparte. He realised
that Buonaparte had two aspects, and that he was being gradually led
or forced in one of these aspects into some measure of betrayal towards
the Cause of which he had originally been the champion and the main
prop, of which he still, despite the alteration in himself, was the best
hope. The Buonaparte who said frankly, "I am for the white man
against the black, because I am white," and "I am for the French
because I am French," and "if it had been necessary to let all Italy perish
or sacrifice two of my army, I would have let all Italy perish, because
before all things I am of my army and for my army," who was ready
to crush any other people for the benefit of France, was betraying the
Cause of Man in the interests of Country and enunciating a patriotism
that was pernicious because "exclusive" and therefore to be opposed.
Hazlitt's attitude to this "exclusive" patriotism can best be defined by
his own words:

"True patriotism warrants no conclusion contrary to liberty or
humanity. . . . France, Engand is a mere name, a geographical or
political denomination, to which we are bound only by moral and
rational ties, *as a part of the great society of mankind*, whose welfare,
whose liberty, whose existence we are sworn to defend against the
unjust aggressions or encroachments of every other part, *but not to
sacrifice the whole to it*. Why should Buonaparte put the question of
sacrificing the lives of two of his soldiers, or letting all Italy perish?"[144]

It will be evident that in his conception of national and international values he was far ahead of his day. The society of mankind,
including blacks and whites and men of all tribes and nations, meant
far more to him than any one of its parts, whether English or French
or any other. But any part, if attacked by any other part, had the right
to defend itself, without offence against the society of mankind as a
whole. In the crisis of 1803, England, one part of the great society of
mankind, was defending herself against the threat of another part
of the great society of mankind, and therefore every English life should
be at her service.

In other words, while Hazlitt was determined not to give up to any
nation, even his own, what was "meant for mankind" and what therefore was sacred to mankind, he saw no reason to give up his own
nation to any other nation that, like England herself, was only part
of the great society of mankind. Buonaparte, in projecting an invasion
of England, was so far from thinking of the rights of the society of
mankind that he was merely indulging the will to crush an enemy and
endeavouring to make good his threat of carrying terror into the

streets of London. In so far as he too yielded to patriotism of the "exclusive and destructive kind," Hazlitt was his opponent. His feeling with regard to any man's duty at such a crisis is summed up in the words:

"When a nation is threatened with the loss of its independence, and with having an obnoxious yoke imposed on it by foreigners, whoever sets up for being more than a soldier in his country's cause, is less than a citizen . . . and makes his love of liberty a stalking-horse to hide his fear, his vanity, or his leaning to the enemy."

As to the second aspect of Buonaparte! In so far as he was the man of the People, given power by the People, confessing that he owed all to the People, and the man strong enough to become the symbol of the rights of the People to choose their own ruler, against those who said they had no rights, Hazlitt loved him almost on the other side idolatry. In the Buonaparte who opposed to hereditary power over the People power that had been chosen by the will of the People, he ever continued to see the best hope of the Cause of the Peoples of the earth.

8

We must not forget that this sharp division of opinion over main political issues conditioned the undercurrent of friction, even over lesser issues, between Coleridge and Hazlitt during the autumn of 1803. That there was this friction, even when matters were discussed that might surely have admitted of cool argument, Coleridge's note-books sufficiently show. They show, too, that he had met his match in argument, had met one who would not let himself be washed away by a flood of rhetoric, but who held tenaciously to the point at issue until it had been proved or disproved—and that he resented this. We come with amazement on an entry made in a note-book on October 26th, in which, when giving an account of "a most unpleasant dispute with Wordsworth and Hazlitt" he accuses them both of speaking irreverently and malignantly against the Divine Wisdom. Such irreverence would be quite out of character in Hazlitt, who was always upset and offended by irreverence of any kind, and in Wordsworth also. Presently we gather that the discussion was less on the "Divine Wisdom" than on Paleyism. What is most clear about this argument is that Coleridge has been greatly irritated by Hazlitt. His comment is: "Hazlitt, how easily raised to rage and hatred self-projected! but who shall find the force that can drag him up out of the depth into one expression of kindness, into the showing of one gleam of the light of love on his countenance."

He may have had some reason to complain, for Hazlitt detested Paley, regarding him as a "shuffling Divine . . . who . . . employed

the whole of his life, and his moderate second-hand abilities, in tamper-
ing with religion, morality and conscience—in crawling between
heaven and earth, and trying to cajole both," and regarding even the
celebrated *Moral Philosophy*[145] as nothing but "a very elaborate and
consolatory elucidation of the text, *that men should not quarrel with their
bread and butter*," and an attempt, not to show what was right, but
"to palliate and find out plausible excuses for what is wrong." In
attacking Paley, he may have been venting, to some extent, the irritation he was beginning to feel also with Coleridge's growing tendency
to compromise or even to moral casuistry. Coleridge, in addition to
confiding his displeasure to his Diary, seems to have reproached him
personally for his angry intolerance. We find Hazlitt, in later years,
touching on these complaints and, as was his way, admitting error
quite simply and frankly, when he was conscious of it. He was at least
a very straight fighter, and his vehemence in argument was unstained
by personal rancour or malice. His apology for his inveteracy throws
a great deal of light on his character:

"I have often been reproached for considering things only in their
abstract principles, and with heat and ill-temper, for getting into a
passion about what no ways concerned me. If any one wishes to see me
quite calm, they may cheat me in a bargain or tread upon my toes;
but a truth repelled, a sophism repeated, totally disconcerts me, and
I lose all patience. I am not, in the ordinary acceptation of the term,
a good-natured man; that is, many things annoy me besides what
interferes with my own ease and interest. I hate a lie; a piece of
injustice wounds me to the quick, though nothing but the report of it
reach me. Therefore I have made many enemies and few friends;
for the public know nothing of well-wishers, and keep a wary eye on
those that would reform them. Coleridge used to complain of my
irascibility in this respect, and not without reason."[146]

The day after the dispute about Paley all was serene after the storm.
Coleridge sat for his portrait, listened to Southey's account of the
"Institution of the Jesuits," made out satisfactorily to his own mind
the origin of evil, on which we gather a discussion was in progress,
and—he says—forced Hazlitt to agree to his statement of the metaphysical argument.

In these ways, in sketching, in painting the poets and Hartley, and
in talk with Wordsworth, Coleridge and Southey, Hazlitt spent the
time until the beginning of December. In the children at Keswick at
least he had friends. Of these "lile Hartley" was by far the most
absorbing and touching. His father, who sometimes felt his heart
move within him when listening to the talk of this beloved child,
might well call him "*piscis rarissima*." Hartley had always been a
fascinating child. At six years of age he was a child to enchant a metaphysician who was also a painter. Child though he was, he was

extraordinarily like Hazlitt himself in this, that things made no impression on him until they had been transmuted into thoughts or feelings. As to his thoughts, they might well confound a metaphysician who was also a painter.

The fat and beautiful Derwent had none of this subtlety of mind, but he was an affectionate little fellow with winning ways of his own. The "Coleridgiella," as Coleridge sometimes called his daughter Sara, was frail and quiet.

9

We come now to a consideration of the circumstances which led to Hazlitt's forced departure from the Lake district in December, and these, like most of the things conditioning his life and his human relationships at the moment, we hold to be closely connected with the war fever of the hour. If the glimpses we get of him in discussion with Coleridge, who had once sympathised with his views, and who might be expected to have some understanding of the cross-currents in which he was caught, are stormy enough, we may take it that his relationships with various other people in a district fiery with war enthusiasm and red with volunteers cannot have been very harmonious. At a time when even the greatly loved Charles Fox could be to some extent discredited by the accusation, "Your language—your sentiments were felt as Gallican," and accused of having "publickly expatriated himself" because he had taken the opportunity of going to Paris to examine some historical manuscripts during the Peace; at a time when the stranger in a district was suspect, Coleridge himself, during his tour in Scotland, having been taken for a spy on one occasion and promptly clapped into custody, Hazlitt, glorying in his memories of a visit to Paris in which he had been completely happy; warming up to impassioned enthusiasm when he spoke of the treasures in the Louvre; seeing in Buonaparte not the bloodthirsty monster of English caricature but the slight figure in blue he had glimpsed in the Paris streets, completely unassuming in dress and demeanour, yet haloed by the glory of high endeavour and great achievement; declaiming against the renewal of war against France as an outrage against humanity— cannot very well have passed unnoticed or escaped the charge of being Gallican in language or sentiments. We know that he prided himself on mental courage and that he would have regarded it as an act of cowardice to keep silent in any company where he felt that prejudice was being mistaken for truth and that under the mask of patriotism unleashed malignant passions were being indulged. Yet during this time of war-excitation he could not chat to a countryman without hearing talk of "the Corsican usurper;" he could hardly enter an inn for a glass of ale without leaving behind him a muttering that this wandering painter who had been about the place off and on ever since he had come back from Paris was half a Frenchman at heart, very likely little better than a spy; in every social gathering he heard his opinions challenged and had to keep silent or take the consequences of going against the feeling of the company. Everything was calculated to draw suspicion towards the moody saturnine painter who made himself the apologist of Buonaparte, and to attract the nervous tension of the moment towards him. The man crying:

"Ye Men of Kent, 'tis Victory or Death!"

gathered into his words the genuine sympathies and the noblest feelings of the moment. The man belabouring in the Government press "the Corsican upstart," pandered to the passions of the moment. The man insisting that the hurling at all those who disapproved of the renewal of the war the accusation that they wished the French to come and put every one in England to the sword, was the effect, not of the high-souled energy that supports a just cause, but of the hysteria of fear; protesting that it was the blind folly of the Government that had forced the war and exposed the country to the danger of invasion; declaring that Buonaparte could only be considered an upstart by those who did not believe in the right of a People to honour a chief Man when a chief Man appeared among them, and that natural aristocracy was of more value than hereditary mediocrity or imbecility, marshalled the passions of the moment against him. Though he spoke with the tongues of men or of angels he was hated. Southey said in 1817 of the Jacobinical play he had composed in 1794 that it had been written "when those who were known to entertain such opinions were exposed to personal danger from the populace." The risk of personal danger from the populace to any one expressing in the autumn of 1803 opinions that could be construed as favourable to France would have been far greater than it would have been nine or ten years earlier, when there had been no question of any invasion of England by France. The incident which in the beginning of December drove Hazlitt from the district and the consequences of which "' like a wounded snake dragged their slow length ' through the rest of his life," was in part conditioned by his own temperament, especially by the difficulty he was finding at the time in his relationships with women, but we are convinced that it was in part also the mere explosion of popular prejudice or even fury. It came with a breath-taking and apparently fantastic suddenness, but the materials for it may have been long preparing. It was the kind of thing that could only have happened to one who had gone very much against the tide, and against whom there were already the mutterings of the popular hue and cry. When the will to destroy is there, the victim has only to do something to draw attention to himself, has only to give some pretext for the hunt, and the whole pack will be after him. Oftener than not, it is a very innocent being who gives the pretext. The crafty and the guilty spend too much time on the gentle art of self-preservation to be caught in this way.

10

In attempting to get at the truth of this incident we have to remember:

1. That we have no account of it from any one who was an eye-witness of it or a spectator of it.

2. That we have no account of it dating from the time it happened.

3. That such accounts of it as we have are based on country gossip that had gradually grown into a Legend; for the hunting out of the district of a wandering painter who was Gallican in his sympathies was not a sport that could be enjoyed every day in the Lake district.

4. That such accounts of it as we have, although based on country gossip, do not reach us as mere country gossip. They consist of country gossip as detailed:

(a) By former friends of Hazlitt who had become his bitter enemies, and who in circulating this gossip were endeavouring to injure and discredit him socially and personally.

(b) By political enemies who were using it as propaganda against Hazlitt in the days when he was regarded as the fighting-man, the Courage, and the Nerve of the Opposition press. At the time they were using this story against him, they were also pelting him with accusations that were not only untrue, but of a kind that was the exact opposite to the truth. They were accusing him, these men who had never known the travail of an original idea and who were therefore incapable of recognising anything that was not derivative, of being devoid of any original gift; they were accusing him, these clumsy maulers and misusers of words, of being unable to write English; they were accusing him, these men who seemed to draw most of their inspiration from "the slopped table of a tavern parlour," of being an habitual drunkard and of bearing the visible marks of dissipation in a face that was covered with carbuncles. His writings alone give the lie to the first two charges. Nothing more need be said of them. As to the third, at the time these charges were being made, Hazlitt was conspicuous among the men in whose company he was usually to be found, because he was the only one of them who never touched a drop of alcohol. As to the fourth charge, or taunt, Hazlitt had only to enter a room to disprove it, for his skin was always as clear and pale as marble. The calumny was not silenced by this. Far from it! It did its low and lying work, and that was all that was necessary. For every one who could see that Hazlitt's fine brow was clear and pale, there would be thousands who would never see him, and with whom his writing would be discredited because his personality would be associated with the nickname "pimpled Hazlitt," blared at him with monotony of spite from various lungs of lead and throats of brass.

The only evidence against Hazlitt, then, that of personal enemies endeavouring to injure him and of political enemies endeavouring to break his career and destroy his means of livelihood, is, to say the least of it, suspect. To repeat it without investigation is not to repeat truth, but to perpetuate gossip swollen with the passing of time into Legend, wrought by ingenious malice into fantastic distortions, and sedulously circulated with intent to slay. Such gossip has little need to be assisted in perpetuating itself, for it has a vile immortality of its own. Once it has come into being, no word of protest will keep it from continuing to crawl. This snake can only be "scotch'd." It can never be killed. Yet shall it not continue to "raise its fork'd crest into the empyrean" and deploy itself in the light of the sun unchallenged!

We do not propose, at this point in our story, to lay before the reader the hostile charges. These will be given in their place, when we deal with the years in which they were circulated. Their presentation is not relevant to an account of what actually happened to Hazlitt in 1803. At that time he was obscure; he was not worth calumniating or slaying; and, as we said, no record from this year survives as to what happened. The years in which the various charges made against him were circulated were the years 1814 to 1818. Our immediate attempt is going to be to reconstruct what happened to him at the end of 1803. In putting together our account of what we believe to be the truth, we have considered carefully what was said in after years about Hazlitt by his enemies, and while rejecting what we believe to be calumny, we have accepted what we believe to be the basis of truth on which the distortions of calumny were reared. Also, in attempting to sift the true from the false, we have to some extent relied on those oblique references which Hazlitt himself made to the incident.

Hazlitt is always the truest recorder of his own life. If he errs, it is on the side of severity towards himself. He is as little inclined as was Rousseau to conceal or to excuse his faults of character, while except for one or two virtues, such as mental courage and intellectual integrity, to which he always lays claim boldly, he leaves us to discover his excellences for ourselves. With regard to the incident which drove him from the lakes, however, he leaves us almost entirely in the dark. Yet we are not left wholly in the dark. There are two indirect references. One of these occurs in the essay on the *Character of the Country People*, with reference to the prejudice of countryfolk against any one who differs, even in the matter of dress, let alone opinion, from their own standards:

"Any one dressed in a plain broad-cloth coat is in their eyes a sophisticated character. . . . A smock-frock, and shoes with hob-nails in them, are an indispensable part of country etiquette, and they pelt any one, who is presumptuous enough to depart from this appropriate costume.   This . . . is the meaning of the phrase in Shakespear, ' pelting villages,' he having been once set upon in this manner by ' a crew of patches, rude mechanicals ' who disliked him for the fantastic strangeness of his appearance."

The other occurs in the essay *On the Disadvantages of Intellectual Superiority*, written at Renton in 1822, when Hazlitt was a man of forty-four, and when the bitterness of a late, deep, and hopeless passion for a young girl was intertwined for the moment with recollection of the bitterness that had become mingled with memory of an early light love for a girl at Keswick:

"If the mistress smiles at their *ideal* advances, the maid will laugh outright; she will throw water over you, get her little sister to listen, send her sweetheart to ask what you mean, will set the village or the house upon your back; it will be a farce, a comedy, a standing jest for a year, and then the murder will out."

We think these few words, written not with direct reference to the Keswick affair, but oozing out unconsciously from the depths of accumulated bitterness in the mind of a man who felt that he had always been unlucky in love, and always more sinned against than sinning, are the most reliable clue to what happened. Considering this plaint in connection with what we take to be the grain of truth in the calumnies circulated about him between 1814 and 1818, we gather that the truth as to this incident was as follows: that Hazlitt believed himself to be having a pretty little pastoral *amourette* at Keswick, flattering to his self-love, and just of the kind to perfect for him the delight he took in sketching in that beautiful district; that the girl, quite incapable of understanding the nature of the eccentric painter who had been attracted by her prettiness, and used perhaps to the robuster wooing of shepherds and farm-hands, found his refinements of sentiment tedious, perhaps despised him in her heart for his "ideal advances," or indeed, as we know other women to have done, "took him for a fool;" that as he had made himself unpopular in the district, she thought it sport to betray or expose him to the derision of those who were only waiting for an opportunity to hurt one who most emphatically was not a bird of their feather; that he, on understanding what was happening, turned upon her in the hysteria of rage and that the sudden transformation of one who had seemed gentle and "ideal" in his advances into one who appeared all in a moment nothing less than diabolical in malignity, startled her, in her turn, into the hysteria of fear; that this drew her friends down on him in a pack so that he was manhandled by them and narrowly escaped ducking; that he appeared at Greta Hall dishevelled and distressed, believing that the pack was still after him; that he was helped by Coleridge, set out over the hills for Grasmere, arrived at Dove Cottage towards midnight and was taken in by Wordsworth, who lent him money enough to continue his journey the next day.

To reconstruct this incident in detail is not possible. If our reconstruction of its *character* be true, it will be seen afterwards that the reports circulated in later years as to its *character* by his enemies were not only lacking in truth but, like most of the calumnies circulated about him at the same time—that he was illiterate, that he was lacking in originality, that he could not write English, that he was a drunkard, that he was carbuncled—of a nature as opposite as possible to the truth.

As for the girl's terror, no physical violence need have been offered her to account for that. Without being in the least timid, she might well have been appalled by the display on Hazlitt's face of the anger and accumulated sense of bitterness that must almost have burst his heart at the moment. We know from his own confession that he was capable of the hysteria of rage; but it is also well attested that even when he was moved to ordinary anger his appearance was terrifying. More than one of his acquaintances felt that in the startling way in which his face, noble in expression when in repose, altered under the operation of passion so as to assume the very distortion of anger or suffering, he resembled no one so much as Edmund Kean in moments of climax or transport upon the stage. One of his friends compared his face at such moments to Kean's when acting Sir Giles Overreach cornered by his enemies, and we know that the sight of that was sufficient not only to make women faint but to convulse Byron, and to overwhelm Hazlitt himself. We have no doubt at all that in the hysteria of rage he must have looked appalling. Leigh Hunt in after years noted the cuts and furrows which temper ploughed in his face. Southey said of him: "Mr. Hazlitt recognised his own features and expression in one of Michael Angelo's devils." And have we not seen that a master of words had already recorded the startling effect of this swift leaping into passion:

"Hazlitt, to the feelings of anger and hatred, phosphorus—it is but to open the cork and it flames!"

II

He returned to Wem, probably by way of Manchester and Liverpool. His departure had been so precipitate that he had left undone much that he meant to have done.

He had not begun a proposed portrait of Southey; he had left the second portrait of Wordsworth unfinished,[147] also he had not completed the portrait of Hartley to his satisfaction. The three poets, although they would not have been human if they had not been somewhat irritated with him for having got himself into such a troublesome scrape, behaved admirably to him, one and all of them. Perhaps they had not forgotten that five years before, when their opinions had been much the same as Hazlitt's, they could do nothing right in the eyes of some of their country neighbours. Southey, writing to Richard Duppa on December 14th, pronounced Hazlitt "a man of real genius." Coleridge, who had often told him that he had "guts in his brains," advised him to set about putting his metaphysics on paper, and told him that if he could only do so he might "laugh at all the tittle-tattle" about him. Wordsworth did him very practical service. Coleridge, who was getting ready to set out for Malta, left Keswick himself on December 20th, before he had had time or energy to attend to the forwarding of the things which Hazlitt had had to leave behind at his rooms—his pictures, his supply of paints, and his personal belongings. Hazlitt wrote to Wordsworth about them in February,[148] and about the portrait of Hartley, which he wished to have by him for alteration. Wordsworth, although reluctant to send the portrait of Hartley, which, he said, they all valued as it was, because of "the life and character about it," promised to "take particular pains" to hunt after the other things that had been left behind in Keswick, the first time he was able to go there. In a pleasant letter written on March 5th, 1804, he expressed sympathy over the death of "poor Fawcett," the friend of Hazlitt's youth, gave an account of the progress of the "Poem to Coleridge," described a delightful piece of mountain brook scenery which he wished Hazlitt could see, and mentioned that he had passed the day before under Nab Scar, where Hazlitt had been sketching in the summer, and had thought that it looked "infinitely finer" in its winter trim. He sent remembrance from all at Dove Cottage, and signed himself "very affectionately yours, W. Wordsworth."

The letter contains no reference to Hazlitt's humiliation except the words: "No body durst venture to seize your clothes or box." Its tone gave promise of continued friendship.

In the meantime Hazlitt, as if determined to prove to himself that he was neither "the baby of a girl" nor the man who could be broken by the malice of a few rustics, set to work in good earnest upon his metaphysics. Possibly his work drew him back to London, for he was there before April 9th, when Coleridge sailed for Malta. At Godwin's he met Coleridge again and made the acquaintance of Charles Lamb, who took his fancy in the course of a fierce discussion between Holcroft and Coleridge as to which was the better, *man as he was*, or *man as he is to be*, by stammering out: "Give me man as he is *not* to be." His liking

CHARLES LAMB
By kind permission of the National Portrait Gallery

was returned. Soon Lamb was sitting to him for his portrait, and the friendship between the two men grew apace.

At Christmas-time he was back at Wem, and at work on a portrait of his father.[149] In the course of the year he had at last finished his essay On the Disinterestedness of the Human Mind. In the following year he found a publisher for it, under the title *Essay on the Principles of Human Action*, in Joseph Johnson; and his "Portrait of a Gentleman," which was possibly his portrait of Lamb, was hung at the Exhibition. These things may have made him feel that he was at last beginning to do what he had long wanted to do in writing, and that he was on the way to doing what he wanted to do in painting. In the autumn of 1805 he returned to Wem and was again happily engaged in painting his father. The news of Trafalgar came while he was there, the relief and joy it brought being dimmed only by sorrow over the death of Nelson. "Wasn't you sorry for Lord Nelson?" Lamb wrote to him. "I have followed him in fancy ever since I saw him walking in Pall Mall . . . looking just as a hero should look; and I have been very much cut about it indeed. He was the only pretence of a Great Man we had. Nobody is left of any name at all."

Once more the stubborn courage and vigilance of the sailor, the true "wooden walls of old England," had saved English soil. The army that had sprung up "like grasshoppers" had had nothing to do. It had had all "the trappings, the boastings, and the triumphs of war" without any of "the tragic accompaniments."

But if Hazlitt rejoiced over Trafalgar, he rejoiced hardly less over the defeat of the Russians at Austerlitz, when the news came in mid-December. How should it not be so, when for years the hope that makes the music of the Marseillaise had pounded in his blood and nerves! The war waged in Europe was ever primarily for him the war between the new-born Democracy and the ancient despotisms that had tried to strangle it in its cradle, and he rejoiced with all his heart that the myriads marshalled by Czarist Russia had been overcome by the soldiers whom the struggles of the French Republic had bred. The day lingered long in his memory as one in which the world had seemed to him bright with hope for the poor man. There was still the prospect that Government of the People by the People for the People might yet be the lot of the Peoples of the earth. The evening star setting over a poor man's cottage late that winter afternoon seemed to him to shine with special promise.

This hope coincided with some measure of personal hope, for it chanced also that he had finished his portrait of his father on that day, and that looking at it, he had found it good.

Has he then passed through his first valley of humiliation unscathed? By no means! although he may have drawn from it the

temporary stimulus of desperation! The effects of the valley of
humiliation are infinite in variety. There are some, glad souls "without reproach or blot" who can pass through it and remember of it
only that it has its own peace. As a rule, the worst of its terrors have
not touched them. There are others who bear to their dying day the
marks of that one night's journey. Hazlitt was of these. We know of
what happened in his mind not from any word of his, but from the
effect he produced on others who did not in the least understand the
source of his trouble, when the memory of his humiliation came upon
him. Charles Lamb, taking him some time afterwards to see some
pretty girls, saw to his stupefaction that "W. H.", as he was beginning
to call his friend, went black in the face with self-conflict. Lamb,
whose friendship was of the quality that accepted the whimsies of
friends, accepted this as a peculiarity quite new in his experience, but
not necessarily unamiable, and therefore to be humoured; but he told
Wordsworth of it as a joke against Hazlitt, for a good-looking man of
twenty-eight who professed to hate girls seemed to him a quaint
performance on the part of Nature. For Hazlitt the matter was no
joke. The truth was, he did not hate, as he said, but believed himself to
be hated. The sound of girls' voices was to him as a danger-signal.
For years to come the laughter of girls was to smite on his ears much
as the laughter of the hyena smites on the ears of the man lying
wounded in the desert. He was now in the first stages of the terrible
fixed idea, which crippled his life to such an extent, that no young,
unspoiled, attractive and delightful woman could look on him without
repulsion. One of his pseudo-friends called this a monomania, and
hardly exaggerated in doing so. The girl at Keswick had played with
phosphorus and it had flamed at her. She had had a bad fright. Beyond
that we do not know how it fared with her. But we know that she
left the fine instrument which she could fret but on which she could
in no wise play, and which other fingers had fretted before her, this
time with some of its sensitive strings broken.

We wonder at ourselves like men betrayed. Could he but have come
upon Rosalind instead of Phebe under the shadow of Skiddaw, how
different might things have been for him! It was not to be! Phebe
has marred him. What hope is there now for one who is so sensitive
and who has been thus injured to form the human relationship with
a woman, of which he is sorely in need? It may be thought that the
best hope for him would lie in encountering a woman who would treat
him with long and patient kindness. Nay! there is no hope for him
here. She would have come too late, for the worst thing his experience
has done for him is that it has made it all but impossible for him to
trust in a woman's kindness. If he is attracted to a woman, while he
can suffer indifference or even impatience with resignation, as if it
were no more than he expected, at the first sign of favour or kindness—

and these were often accorded to him—he is off like a wild creature who has heard the rattle of a trap from the jaws of which he had once writhed himself free. In woman's kindness he now sees nothing but a cruel snare, or a mask which conceals the desire to triumph in his pain. Already in his heart he is repudiating it. *"Beautiful mask, I know thee!"*

What then can be left for him but some relationship in which lack of trust is taken for granted, some kind of commerce in sex—whether it be in wedlock or out of wedlock makes little difference to the quality of it—in which, if there can be no question of fulfilment, at least there can be no dangerous masking of ugly realities?

He was all his life a man who tended to get entangled with any bramble that lay in his vicinity, and instead of disentangling himself carefully or if that were not possible cutting himself loose from it, to show more valour than discretion in the onslaughts he made on it. Voltaire himself was not more distinguished in this species of wounding and altogether unprofitable conflict, more indefatigable in attacking the nuisance "with potent steel implements, wood-axes, war-axes, brandishing and hewing," till at last he had "stirred up a whole wilderness of bramble-bush," and made himself "bramble-chips all over." In dealing with the ditch-bramble that had lain in wait for him at Keswick, however, Hazlitt had done for the one and only time in his life the one and only thing to do when caught by a bramble of this kind: he had cut himself loose immediately. Yet this had not availed him, for the bramble that had caught at him there was of a peculiarly virulent kind. A rare bramble this—more like a poison-tree! He had cut himself loose, yet not before it had flayed off the bloom of his youth. Worse still, a poison-thorn from it had lodged itself in the nerve of his manhood. All in a moment, with the rapidity of sudden death, the spirits sinister and ironic had accomplished their jest on his life. From the poison-thorn that had entered into him he is never more to be free.

Yet the beauty he desires is that of Woman. Perhaps *in the city of seventy thousand whores* he may find at least something of what he desires.

Part Four

TENDING TOWARDS LITERATURE

An author's appearance or his actions may not square with his theories or his descriptions, but his mind is seen in his writings, as his face is in the glass.

HAZLITT.

Chapter One

EARLY WRITINGS ON LIBERTY (1805-1807)

"Determine as wisely as you can in regard to Hazlitt; and, if your determination is to have him, Heaven send you many happy years together. If I am not mistaken, I have concluded letters on the Corydon Courtship with this same wish. I hope it is not ominous of change; for if I were sure you would not be quite starved to death, nor beaten to a mummy, I should like to see Hazlitt and you come together, if (as Charles observes) it were only for the joke sake."

MARY LAMB *to* SARAH STODDART.

I

BRYAN WALLER PROCTER, who loved both Hazlitt and Lamb, thought that the greatest gain the year 1804 had brought to Lamb was the friendship of Hazlitt. "The intimacy of that extraordinary man, William Hazlitt, was the great gain of Lamb at this period of his life," he wrote in the Memoir of his friend which he published in 1866. If the friendship was a boon to Lamb, to Hazlitt it was one of the greatest blessings conceivable. Lamb's "attic story" at the top of "four pair of stairs" in 16 Mitre Court Buildings, with its high small-paned casement windows looking down on the river and out towards the Surrey hills, its prints, and the long plain bookcase completely filled with old books which looked as if they were in disorder although the owner could lay his hand in a moment on any one of his "ragged veterans," became for him the heart of London. For the first time of his life he found himself in sympathetic contact, on equal terms, with a man whose genius matched his own. Coleridge had aroused something like idolatry in him; Wordsworth had compelled his admiration. Both these men, his seniors not only in years but in experience, had taken his homage for granted. The moment he ceased to yield it they would feel that he had transgressed against his natural relationship towards them. Lamb's relationship with them was somewhat of the same kind. But Lamb and Hazlitt had for each other from the beginning the easy unstrained affection of brothers. They talked to each other, criticised each other, jested with each other, as man to man. Procter's account of the gradations in Lamb's manner towards Wordsworth, Coleridge and Hazlitt is revealing as to the nature of the friendship and mind-partnership existing between Hazlitt and Lamb. He says that to Wordsworth Lamb was "almost respectful in manner;" to Coleridge, although he idolised his genius, he behaved sometimes rather like one *privileged* by this known idolatry to play the fool a little; with Hazlitt "he talked as though they met the subject in discussion on equal terms."

Hazlitt in this atmosphere of easy friendship seemed to slough yet another existence. Although now and again he may still *shy* at something or somebody unexpectedly and give an astonishing exhibition of nerves, although now and again he may fall into desperate dejection of mood, he can no longer be described as "brow-hanging, shoe-contemplative, *strange*." He becomes sociable. His shouts of laughter astonish as often as his moodiness. The Lambs and their friends find him the best company in the world. Talfourd realised afterwards that the secret of the alteration that came to Hazlitt through his intercourse with the Lambs was the sympathy they both showed towards him, Mary no less than Charles: "It was . . . by the fireside of the Lambs, that his tongue was gradually loosened, and his passionate thoughts found appropriate words. There, his struggles to express the fine conceptions with which his mind was filled, were encouraged by entire sympathy; there he began to stammer out his just and original conceptions of Chaucer and Spencer, and other English poets and prose-writers, more talked of, though not better known to their countrymen; there he was thoroughly understood, and dexterously cheered, by Miss Lamb, whose nice discernment of his first efforts in conversation were dwelt upon by him with affectionate gratitude, even when most out of humour with the world."

None of his letters to Lamb at this time are extant, but the letters sent to him at Wem from 16 Mitre Court between the autumn of 1805 and the summer of 1806, when he returned to town, are eloquent as to the quality of the friendship. Lamb, who valued peace and quietude of mind above all things, did not encourage political discussion among his friends. This, although it deepened the peace which Hazlitt found in this friendship, cut at one of his main interests. Had it been any other man who debarred discussion of this kind, he might have felt conscious of a certain flatness or staleness in the relationship, but Lamb's letters show that the mind-sympathy between these two men was of such a kind that no exclusion of any one topic of discussion affected it. The thought and fancy of each of them played on an infinite variety of things, and in the free interchange of ideas and play of comment there was the perfection of quiet companionship.

In his letter of November 10th Lamb wrote: "Luck to Ned Search and the new art of colouring." This gives us our clue as to what Hazlitt was doing at Wem at the close of 1805, apart from painting his father and studying the art of colouring. Having at last brought his slender close-knit essay On the Disinterestedness of the Human Mind to the light of day, he had embarked on the second of those labours which occupied him between 1804 and 1808, the years in which he was engaged in his initial up-hill struggle for existence as an author. This was the long-talked-of abridgment of Tucker's *Light of Nature Pursued*, abbreviated by Lamb into Ned Search, because the book had appeared originally under the pseudonym Edward Search. The last of its seven volumes had appeared in the year of Hazlitt's birth; he had long known the book and admired both it and the character of the author; he had long' regretted that its discursiveness and desultoriness had obscured its value, and that certain sections of it, which he thought valuable correctives to the material philosophy of the day, should be so little known. It was with a view to clearing away the load of unnecessary matter, so that the value and distinction of the thought might be apparent to all, that he undertook the abridgment, on which he bestowed infinite pains, in the effort to reject all that was redundant and wearisome, while yet preserving everything that was best. Probably he had left town and settled down at Wem for the winter, so that he might get on with the work in peace.

He seems also to have had some thoughts about this time of planning a Life of his friend Joseph Fawcett.

By the beginning of 1806 he had reduced the first two volumes of Tucker to about a third of their bulk and forwarded them to Joseph Johnson, as a specimen of the scope and nature of the work. Then came a struggle to get Johnson to look at what he had done. The reception of the essay On the Disinterestedness of the Human Mind had not been such as to encourage its publisher to believe that there might be any profit in the author's work, and Johnson was very slow to commit himself, even although Godwin exerted himself in Hazlitt's favour. Lamb's next letter, of January 15th, 1806, is primarily a bulletin about the fortunes of the "Search": "Godwin went to Johnson yesterday about your business. Johnson would not come down, or give any answer, but has promised to open the manuscript, and to give you an answer in one month. Godwin will go punctually again (Wednesday is Johnson's open day) yesterday four weeks next: i.e. in one lunar month from this time. Till when Johnson positively declines giving any answer." In this there was little encouragement. On the chances of a Life of Fawcett, however, Lamb was cheerful. He evidently thought of it as a book hastily strapped together to make a little money, and gave some practical advice as to a possible publisher for such a book. Hazlitt never wrote this Life. It would be characteristic of him that he found it quite impossible to strap together a Life of his friend in this way. Fawcett had won his love, and could only be dealt with as those were dealt with who had won his love or captured his imagination, in words few and brief, but quite unforgettable, written when some spring of memory or feeling had been touched.

In this letter of January 15th Lamb complained of being distracted by visitors and visitings: "I never have an hour for my head to work its own workings: which you know is as necessary to the human system as sleep." Despite this grumble, he had one visitor staying with them at the time whom he mentioned to Hazlitt with special liking. This was a sister of the John Stoddart who had taken notes so diligently at Mackintosh's lectures in 1799: "As for news—we have Miss Stoddart in our house, she has been with us a fortnight and will stay a week or so longer. She is one of the few people who are not in the way when they are with you."

In the idiom of Charles Lamb, this was praise indeed!

In five weeks time Lamb wrote again, only to report that Hazlitt's manuscript had not yet been considered. All he could say by way of consolation was that he would certainly "goad" Godwin into calling on Johnson at the end of another month, if necessary. He added: "Pray write to us—This is no Letter, but I supposed you grew anxious about Johnson."

That Lamb, who of all men was the most sensitively averse to asking a favour, should have undertaken to "goad" Godwin or anybody else on Hazlitt's behalf was indeed a very strong proof of the strength of his attachment. When he wrote again, in the beginning of March, he did not forget to add a postscript about the languishing *Tucker*: "Johnson shall not be forgotten at the month's end."

This is the last we hear of the care and thought Lamb gave to the "Search." By June Hazlitt had returned to town. Mary Lamb wrote of him to the Miss Stoddart whom her brother had praised so highly: "William Hazlitt, the brother of him you know, is in town. I believe you have heard us say we like him? He came in good time, for the loss of Manning made Charles very dull, and he likes Hazlitt better than anybody, except Manning."

In the idiom of Mary Lamb, this was praise indeed!

2

Hazlitt had not yet heard from Johnson one way or the other. Henceforth the loathsome task of "goading" must be undertaken by himself, and for such a task he was almost as unfitted as Lamb. The uncertainty as to the fate of his work may have depressed him, for the one or two references we have to him indicate that he was out of spirits, and far less effective in cheering Charles Lamb than Mary had hoped he would be. The first glimpse we have of him this summer in Lamb's company in June is during that unlucky visit to the "Girlery," in which he gave such an astonishing exhibition of temperament, if not of temper. We see him next, on Friday, July 4th, accompanying Lamb to Sadler's Wells, while Mary amused herself as she awaited their return by reading one of his manuscripts. Both he and Lamb returned to Mitre Court Buildings after their evening's entertainment, in such miserable spirits, "so dismal and dreary dull," as Mary put it, that she felt quite out of patience with them, and gave them both "a good scolding—*quite a setting to rights*." She does not say how Hazlitt reacted to this, but she felt that it had done Charles some good, for he brightened up immediately, and continued to be "very chearful" during the remainder of the week-end. Although she had been out of patience with Hazlitt's moodiness, Mary did not forget to invite him to dinner on the following Sunday. She only wished Miss Stoddart could have joined the party. But Miss Stoddart was now in Wiltshire. When in the midst of her preparations on the Sunday morning Mary found time to dash off an appetising little note to her: "I am cooking a shoulder of Lamb (Hazlitt dines with us); it will be ready at two o'clock, if you can pop in and eat a bite with us."

3

Both Charles and Mary had more reason at the moment to be cheerful than had Hazlitt. Their literary ventures were going very well; Charles's farce, *Mr. H——*, had been accepted; they were looking forward to seeing it produced at Drury Lane about Christmas-time; and Mary had already got the length of hoping that Miss Stoddart could accompany them to its first night. As for Hazlitt, he had not Lamb's light touch, and there seemed little ahead of him but undefined and on the whole thankless drudgery of one kind or another. Yet he had completed one piece of writing since the beginning of the year which was so far from being hack-work that it contained the quintessence of his political thought. He had brought the manuscript to town with him, and he meant to publish it, even if he had to pay for the printing himself, for his pamphlet dealt with affairs of the moment, and no time was to be lost if it was to have its share in influencing public opinion.

While Pitt had remained in power there had been no hope for any change of policy on the part of the Government, but after his death on January 23rd the assumption of office by Fox seemed to offer some gleam of hope that there might be some modification of policy which would lead to a respite from war, perhaps even to the negotiation of peace with honour. Hazlitt's pamphlet, which he called *Free Thoughts on Public Affairs*, was written during this brief gleam of hope. It had reference both to the home and the foreign policy of the Government. While it was a review of the means whereby the country had been plunged into a renewal of the war in 1803, and a plea for a reconsideration of foreign policy if Europe were not be to kept for ever "bathed in a fountain of blood in vain," it was yet more a plea, made at this turn of the tide, for the preservation of civil Liberty, which during Pitt's administration had been grievously whittled away and tampered with, and a defence of the kind of patriotism that does not exclude watchfulness over the activities of the Government, of which indeed watchfulness is one of the main elements, vigilance as well as courage being required of a nation if Liberty within its borders is to be preserved in times when war emergency could be made the justification of almost any infringement of private liberties. It is the intensity of this, his first sustained appeal for Liberty at home, that gives his pamphlet its enduring value, rather than the survey of British policy abroad.

This is the first piece of work published by Hazlitt which is fully characteristic of him. Almost overnight, it would seem, he has come into his strength and attained the fullness of his powers. At the close of the pamphlet, in which he contends that a commercial spirit in a nation is a very weak as well as a very dangerous substitute for the love of Liberty, he attempts to define the nature of that civic courage, no less necessary to a nation's greatness than the courage of a soldier, through which alone the liberties of a nation can be preserved and conserved:

"The courage of the soldier and the citizen are essentially different. The one is momentary and involuntary; the other permanent and voluntary. It is one thing to do all in your power to repel danger when it is unavoidable, and another to expose yourself to it when you may avoid going into it. Fear, or rashness or necessity may be supposed to kindle all the fury of battle: but principle alone can make us willing to return to the charge after defeat. It is for this *reaction* that we ought chiefly to be prepared. For this nothing can prepare us but a true love of our country, not taken up as a fashion, but felt as a duty; a spirit of resistance not measured by our convenience, but by the strength of our attachment and the real value of the object; but steady enthusiasm;

but a determination never to submit while hope or life remained, and an indifference to every thing else but that one great object."[150]

This is no youthful outpouring, but a considered statement of the creed from which Hazlitt never wavered, made in the grand style, and in its spirit in direct inheritance from Milton. All that had gone to the moulding of him is expressed in it; and the manner of the expression shows him to have entered on his inheritance as a writer. Passionate though it is, it is balanced and controlled; rhetorical though it can be at times, as when he contrasts the value of the commercial spirit in a nation with the value of the spirit of Liberty, and tells those whose care is only for gain and who engage in war solely to defend or to increase their wealth, that Liberty "is in their eyes a coarse homely figure, but for the jewels that sparkle on her hair and the rings on her fingers,"[151] both rhetoric and feeling are rigorously adjusted to the exposition of the theme; powerful though it is, it is very finely tempered.

If Hazlitt has entered into his inheritance as a writer, he has entered upon his inheritance as a preacher too. He had refused to enter a Unitarian pulpit. Yet he could escape his inheritance as a preacher as little as he could escape his inheritance as a writer, because he was at heart a preacher. It has taken him a long time to reach the pulpit from which he can deliver himself of the burden of his appeal; he has reached it by devious ways; nay! in the end he has had to *make* it for himself. Now at last he enters it, and his first appeal to such of his fellow-countrymen as have the *soul* to hear, like his last, is a recall to principles rather than interest in the conduct of public affairs, and to Liberty as the source of all national strength and good. Had not the "gigantic strength and towering greatness" of France herself in recent years arisen solely from "her convulsive struggles . . . in the cause of that Liberty which had been denied her!" The doctrine of his appeal is the duty of "an inviolable resolution and integrity in the defence of those rights which are the common privilege of humanity." Other things may be allowed to depend on calculation or prudence. But the defence of Liberty, which includes the defence of Virtue and Truth, is "a stern command of duty that admits neither of compromise nor delay."

4

During Coleridge's absence from Keswick the portrait of him by Hazlitt had given little comfort or pleasure to his friends. It was felt to be a very good likeness, yet Dorothy Wordsworth came to feel that she never looked at it without foreboding. There was something so heart-rendingly sad in it that she shrank from the sight of it. It made her think "of Coleridge dying, and not merely dying, but dying of sorrow."

What Hazlitt had seen in Coleridge to make him perpetuate such a look upon his canvas who shall say! but who, remembering Coleridge's heavy brooding in 1803, his night-cries of anguish, his preoccupation with the terrible fantasies that tortured him,

> "Rage, sensual passion, mad'ning Brawl
> And shame and terror over all!"

shall say that Hazlitt painted a look that was not sometimes to be discerned on Coleridge's face, although in the ordinary intercourse of life it was mercifully hidden from his friends! When Coleridge suddenly reappeared in London on August 17th, 1806, this look of fixed inward anguish had driven out all other expression. To his friends it seemed that they were looking on a leaden mask rather than on the face they had known. Knowing himself to be terribly altered, knowing himself to have no soundness within himself, knowing himself unfit to take up once more the battle for existence, he shrank from almost all men. The thought of meeting the living friends who were most dear to him filled him with almost as much sadness as the thought of the friends who had died while he had been away. In this plight, penniless, travel-worn, cowering over his own spiritual bankruptcy, he sought out first of all among his friends the two who were the least critical, the simplest in their kindness, the readiest to accept him as he was and to love him despite anything he was or might become— Charles and Mary Lamb.

Hazlitt, who by this time was a privileged person at 16 Mitre Court Buildings, must have seen a good deal of Coleridge between the time when he threw himself on the Lambs' hospitality and the time of his departure for the North towards the end of October; but unlike some of Coleridge's friends, he has said nothing indicative of what he felt as to the alteration in him at this time. The two reminiscences he has left of Coleridge at the time of his return from Malta deal rather with what had long been familiar to him. If Coleridge, swollen beyond all recognition with fat, with the eyes that held "a fine frenzy" in them sunken in the flesh of the face and dulled with misery, with the face that had been changeable as the sea settling into a terrible mask-like immobility, seemed a stranger to all who had known him some years before, no sooner had he opened his lips than he recovered his personal identity—and all men thought of was that there was but one Coleridge. The silken sounds issued as before, albeit any one watching his face closely when he was talking might have thought his lips moved mechanically.

There is evidence to show that Coleridge and Hazlitt when they met during this autumn of 1806 stimulated each other, argued with each other, irritated each other to some extent, and that at times the phosphorus flamed; but there is no evidence as to any deep contact. Nor is there any evidence that Coleridge gave Hazlitt any help in his precarious literary ventures. The "Tucker" was still "hulling on the flood," but there is nothing to show that Coleridge now cared whether it reached port or not, or that he had any recollection of his promise to write a Preface for it. This is not surprising. He was so locked in his own misery that he had become all but impervious to the feelings of others, while the sense that he had frustrated his own powers was beginning to make him look askance at the achievements of others.

He still talked of what he would do. Among other things he proposed to write a study of Fox, who had died on September 13th, having seen before he died the last gleam of hope for peace extingnished. The rot of hatred had gone too far by this time to be stopped by mediation. A peace negotiated with honour had become an impossibility, for Napoleon had now come to feel that the only safety for France and for his own *régime* lay in continued conquest. In Europe the conflict had now shifted to Prussia, to culminate in the heavy Prussian defeats at Jena and Auerstädt, and the entry of Napoleon into Berlin.

It was Hazlitt, not Coleridge, who wrote the character-sketch of Fox in the course of the autumn, and it can have been little to Coleridge's liking. But already, by the publication of *Free Thought on Public Affairs*, Hazlitt had made open profession of a political faith directly opposed to that professed by the man whom the world still regarded as his friend. Indeed, one word in it, the censure of those who "blow the blast of war for a livelihood in journals and pamphlets," may have seemed to Coleridge, seeing that he had boasted openly of his share in bringing about the renewal of war in 1803, to have been aimed directly at himself, and may thus have sown the first seeds of active personal enmity. It is about this time, shortly after Hazlitt's public profession of his political principles, that the attitude of Coleridge towards Hazlitt began to alter in the direction of hostility.

One thing more we note: if the word written by Hazlitt had galled Coleridge, a word withheld by Coleridge at this time starved some of the scanty hope left in Hazlitt. With infinite toil, and with constant thought of Coleridge, he had, as we have seen, during Coleridge's absence, completed the essay on The Disinterestedness of the Human Mind, which Coleridge had told him to write. He alone knew what the accomplishment of this had cost him. He felt that it was not derivative, that in it he had expressed the original bent of his own mind. He felt that it deserved recognition. But it had fallen stillborn from the press.[152] For a time he had almost despaired of himself as a writer. Yet he had retained the hope that he would feel he had made contact with another mind, as soon as Coleridge had seen it.

A copy had been forwarded to Grasmere for Coleridge. The only spark of encouragement that had come to him out of this had been from Southey, who although not a metaphysician had read it and praised very generously one isolated outburst of reminiscence into which the essay had digressed, had recognised the quality of the prose in this outburst, and had pronounced it to be something between the manner of Milton's prose and Jeremy Taylor's. The book had never reached Coleridge. Yet it was to have been expected that Coleridge, upon his return, might have taken some notice of it and of its publication. Even if sympathy were not given, any kind of discussion would have been better than silence, although anything that might have been said would have been hard-earned. But nothing at all was said. The hope in Hazlitt gradually died. It seemed almost to him as if he had accomplished what he had first proposed to Coleridge too late, and to little purpose. Nothing was left to him but to withdraw into that desperate patience which never quite deserted him, even amidst what seemed to others like his most desperate impatience. He was determined at all events to follow out the impulse of his own mind.

5

In the beginning of December, 1806, a flutter of hope, anticipation and excitement went through the circle of Lamb's friends, because the long-talked-of farce, *Mr. H——*, was at last to be produced. On the morning of December 10th it seemed to some of them as if the town were filled with the rumour of the play. "Bright shone the morning on the play-bills that announced thy appearance, and the streets were filled with the buzz of persons asking one another if they would go and see *Mr. H——*, and answering that they would certainly:" Hazlitt wrote of that day in retrospect. Lamb and his brother between them knew so many people who had been asking each other that question in the course of the day that in the evening there was quite a regiment of their friends in Drury Lane, ready to assist the fortunes of the play. Miss Stoddart was not there, for although Mary would have liked her to be present with them, Charles, uncertain as to how the piece would fare, had not told her the date; but Hazlitt and Henry Robinson, who had recently been introduced to the Lambs, sat with Charles and Mary in the front row of the pit. Nothing could have gone better than the Prologue, which was received with shouts of laughter from the house. By the time it had worked its way along to the final quip, the applause was thunderous and prolonged; there were calls of *encore*, and Lamb, who seemed quite to have forgotten his parental relationship to the lines, was roaring with laughter along with all the others; perhaps, too, he was hugging himself in anticipation of the one or two jests at his friends' expense and his own, which he had slipped neatly into the dialogue. But alas! when the farce itself came to be performed, it was soon found that a quip which might serve as the basis of a very amusing Prologue, became tedious in the course of even a short play. Once the first dreaded hiss had broken the silence there was no checking the storm of disappointment that broke forth. Lamb's nonsense was not the audience's idea of nonsense, and his friends could not prevail against the disapproval of the house, which was indeed so infectious that Lamb himself, just as he had been one of the most uproarious of the laughers, now literally let off steam by hissing as loudly as anybody there.

Inevitably, the one who felt such a disappointment most sharply of all was the one in whom the nerve of sensibility was always "strung to the point of pain." While the humour and sweetness in Lamb helped him to get over the disappointment quickly, the recollection of Lamb roaring with laughter, of Lamb the next moment hissing gamely along with the public, was long poignant to Hazlitt. Night after night it troubled him in his dreams. He would hear again "the full diapason of applause at the end of the Prologue;" or he would dream that little alterations had been made which had made all the difference in the world to the piece, that it had been revived at some minor or provincial theatre with great success, or even that it was considered *it might do at the other house.* When this had gone on for about a month, he saw that he was wearing himself out merely because that was possible to the imagination which was impossible in fact, and then, because the strength in him balanced the sensibility, he set himself to put a brake on his imagination. As soon as he found himself beginning to wish that things had turned out otherwise, he checked himself sharply. Yet the regret that Charles had not had his fun with *Mr. H—— * never quite passed.

6

About this time he moved into rooms at 34 Southampton Buildings. His only "true and constant companions" were now his few books and the pictures to which his heart clung and from which he refused to be separated—one or two copies and sketches reminding him of the golden absorption of the days in the Louvre, his "Head of an old Woman," although day by day the colours of it were fading, and a picture of his own on which he was working, the one to which he referred as his "great picture," and which may have been the "Jacob's Dream" on which he worked for years. But he was not likely now to suffer from solitude, for he had a number of friends within easy visiting distance.

His brother at 109 Great Russell Street was within a few minutes' walk. So were the Lambs, who were always glad to see him. In fact, although Charles, whose leisure for his own pursuits was very scanty and therefore very precious, sometimes grumbled a good deal at his "nocturnal alias knock-eternal visitors," both Mary and he always welcomed Hazlitt's coming as a godsend. Joseph Hume lived farther away, but Hazlitt occasionally journeyed to Bayswater to find him, or to Pimlico to attend Captain Burney's whist parties. Sometimes he breakfasted with Henry Robinson, who by this time had made himself acquainted with all the members of his family, having paid his respects to Mr. and Mrs. Hazlitt at Wem, and having liked them exceedingly. Also there were the Wednesday evenings. Lamb, perhaps with a view to keeping the other evenings of the week free from interruptions, had just started these "Wednesdays" which were to mean so much to this little circle of friends. At these cribbage or whist was the order of the evening. The cards were laid out on a mahogany table which usually had a snuff-box on the corner of it. A cold supper to which the guests could help themselves when they pleased was always placed ready on a sideboard. When the game was over, punch or brandy and water became the order of the night, and usually talk, which more often than not was light, but sometimes, we are told, "there was a flight of high and earnest talk that took one half-way to the stars." Sometimes it might chance that the whole evening was passed "with cards, and nothing but cards." At these meetings many friendships were formed, for Lamb, coming forward "with his grave sweet smile of welcome" and his cheery "Well, boys, how are you? What's the news with you?"[153] seemed to gather his Wednesday-men into an atmosphere of good-fellowship which brought out all that was best in each of them. At his "What will you take?" which usually followed his first greeting, they all felt happy and at home, and it was easy for spirits that were at all congenial to discover each other. It was difficult for any one whom Lamb numbered among his friends to lack companionship. There was not a spark of jealousy or exclusiveness in his nature. Nothing delighted him more than to see his friends liked and respected by his friends.

In these days the men who gathered around his fireside were not famous: Godwin and Holcroft were the only two of them who could be described as having achieved fame. Some of them afterwards became famous, but at Lamb's evenings there never was any first nor last. Not even Coleridge, although he drove Holcroft out on one occasion, was allowed to drown the voices of the other guests. The mahogany table, no matter what its shape, was plainly discerned of all to be a true round table. Among those who gathered round it most frequently in the days when the institution was young were Captain Burney and his son Martin, the argumentative John Rickman, Secretary to the

Speaker, Ned Phillips his clerk, of whom Hazlitt said "a better fellow never breathed," Joseph Hume, as fond of a joke as Phillips himself, the amiable, unworldly, and absent-minded George Dyer, James White, Lamb's schoolfellow, the quiet Mrs. Reynolds, who had once taught Lamb and who liked to come and listen to an argument, and W. H. himself.

7

Hazlitt was welcome also about this time at the houses of some friends older than himself—perhaps we should rather call them patrons—with whom his relations, although pleasant, were more formal in character. Chief of these were Horne Tooke and the Richard Sharp who had met him in Grasmere in 1803, and who, perhaps because he delighted in metaphysical discussion, being indeed known because of his prowess in this field as "Conversation" Sharp, had liked him and relished his talk.

He regarded Horne Tooke, who was seventy years of age at this time, as "the finished gentleman of the last age," and had a boundless admiration for him in his private character, although he had little regard for him as a political leader. He felt that it was a sight to see Horne Tooke sitting like a king at the head of his own table and laying down the law. It was an education to see him manipulating the motley crew of guests he attracted to his Sunday evenings at Wimbledon, now stimulating, now repressing, now encouraging, now outrageously provocative, and then perhaps turning with gracious, almost caressing courtesy and solicitude, to some "old friend and veteran politician sitting at his elbow" and talking of old times, of Wilkes and Liberty, till the conversation seemed "mellowing like the wine with the smack of age."

It is as likely to have been at Horne Tooke's as at Godwin's that Hazlitt made the acquaintance of Curran of the flashing eye, the musical speech, the passionate heart, and the tongue both witty and terrible. He had one thing at least in common with the famed Irish orator, a passion for Mrs. Siddons. Curran told him that when he had been a young man studying law at the Temple, his chief delight had been to see Mrs. Siddons in her great parts. In his vivid way he added that all he had lacked on such occasions was a couple of *pails* on either side of him for his tears.

Richard Sharp also was often present at the Sunday parties at Wimbledon, and he may have renewed his acquaintance with Hazlitt there, but as he had just entered Parliament as a follower of Fox, it is more likely that the publication of *Free Thoughts on Public Affairs* specially brought its author under his notice. As Hazlitt speaks of him as a "patron," it is not unlikely that Sharp may have given a helping hand to one who gave promise of being a powerful political writer, and who had already proved himself a metaphysician. He was much younger than Horne Tooke, yet he too seemed a link with the last generation. To look round his room, hung with portraits of the famed men he had known, Johnson, Burke and Reynolds, was to feel in living contact at once with painting, history and literature. Hazlitt, who visited him many times at his home near Boxhill, never ceased to think of him with affection and admiration, and to regard the evenings spent at Boxhill, where he was encouraged to talk his best, and as he says, "paid to shine," as among the happiest he had known. In later days, when he was given to numbering and recalling one by one the happiest times in his life, he did not forget to mention the evenings at Boxhill, "before Buonaparte was yet beaten," the "deep-empurpled woods," and the hospitable board at which wit, beauty and friendship had presided.

At Wimbledon he looked on the wine when it was red, and at Boxhill he drank of a vintage which seemed to him "of attic taste," but in his rooms in Southampton Buildings his living was hard and bare. As he cooked his own meals his fare is likely to have been Spartan. Sometimes his father sent him a little store of good things from the country, a piece of Welsh mutton or pickled pork, a couple of fowls or tongues. He usually shared such windfalls with the Lambs, whose supper, although always substantial and good when they expected friends, was apt to be on the spare side when they were alone, and who heartily relished good food, Charles especially. A couple of fowls or a piece of pork made a nice addition to their larder. Hazlitt managed to cook to his own satisfaction the share of his dainties he reserved for himself. Mr. Hazlitt had the satisfaction of hearing how good one of these dinners had tasted to his William after he had come in from a long walk: "I have just finished the cheeks which I had dressed last Friday for my dinner after I had taken a walk round Hampstead and Highgate. I never made a better dinner in my life."[154]

He spent the Christmas of 1806 in London, not without thoughts of the two previous years when he had been busy about a portrait of his father at Christmas-time. "*Tempus praeterlabitur*"[155] is his comment, when reminding his father of this. On Christmas Day he had dinner at Hume's; on New Year's Day he supped at Godwin's. He was also at Holcroft's one evening. He makes no special mention of any festivity at the Lambs' during this Christmas season. Perhaps this is because Charles was taking advantage of his few days' holiday to get on with his *Dramatic Specimens*, and both Mary and he were hard at work.

8

Hazlitt himself had almost brought his immediate literary labours to a conclusion by the end of the year. Johnson had kept him waiting to hear about the "Tucker" until the autumn, when he had made up his mind at last that the abridgment might find readers. Not only was the work now completed; the Preface which Coleridge had pledged himself to write had been done by Hazlitt himself, and by the beginning of January it was in print. Of this its author speaks very modestly: "It is very long, and for what I know very tiresome." This is far from doing justice to the work. Long it is, but not tiresome. It is exactly what such a piece of work should be, excellently adjusted towards throwing light on the nature of the book it introduces; and it does exactly what such a piece of work should do: it interests the reader immediately in the thought and the personality of Tucker. Also, like everything Hazlitt now writes, it is Literature.

The other piece of work on which he had been engaged was a compilation. In settling upon it he showed once more the faculty he had shown in his endeavours to popularise Tucker—a sense of what might be at once a serviceable piece of work on the part of the compiler and one calculated to interest a fairly wide section of the reading public. His choice of it was determined by the interest he had taken in political theory as long as he could remember, even as his choice of Tucker had been conditioned by his interest in Ethics and Metaphysics. Sometimes he had wished, when hearing the orators of other times praised, to see what figures they cut beside the orators of his own day, with whose speeches he was well acquainted; when hearing the praises of Chatham sung, he would have liked to be able to compare Chatham's speeches with Burke's, or when hearing Walpole commended, to be able to compare him in point of dexterity and plausibility with Pitt. It struck him that many readers of the speeches of the day might have the same curiosity, that he could gratify it by rescuing from "the musty records of Parliament" such speeches as seemed to him most deserving of being rescued from the oblivion in which they were buried, from the seventeenth century onwards, and that the work would be more interesting and intelligible if he added notes on the speakers. Most of these are brief. One of the very briefest is the cryptic one with which a speech of Horne Tooke's is introduced: "I shall only say of the following speech that it is worthy of the celebrated man by whom it was delivered." Yet brief though they are, many of them, like many of Johnson's brief *Lives* of the Poets, are singularly interesting, and for the reason that Johnson's were, that the author has a feeling for humanity. If at times "the scorn of fools" which they exhibit makes them pungent reading, the keen relish of personality prevents even these abbreviated biographies from becoming mechanical. But the glory of the compilation is the group of full-length comparative studies of Burke, Fox, Pitt and Chatham. Of these the one which shows most power of mind and the most profound understanding of the subject is the "Character" of Burke. Hazlitt's perception of the mixed or divided nature of man made him realise the extent to which Burke's conception of a mixed form of government corresponded to the complex actualities of human nature; as for the element of "prejudice" admitted in Burke's conception of government, he realised it had to some extent its justification in instinct; Burke's realisation of links, at once more subtle, more delicate, and more powerful than community of material interest, which held society together, seemed to him also to be grounded on knowledge of the nature of man:

"The simple clue to all his reasonings on politics is, I think, as follows. He did not agree with some writers, that that mode of government is necessarily the best which is the cheapest. He saw in the constitution of society other principles at work, and other capacities of fulfilling the desires, and perfecting the nature of man, besides those of securing the equal enjoyment of the means of animal life, and doing this at as little expense as possible. He thought that the wants and happiness of men were not to be provided for, as we provide for those of a herd of cattle, merely by attending to their physical necessities. He thought more nobly of his fellows. He knew that man had affections and passions and powers of imagination, as well as hunger and thirst and the sense of heat and cold."[156]

But it is an injustice to Hazlitt to quote isolated passages from this close-knit, powerful piece of writing. He said himself that the only way to do Burke justice was to quote all of him. Certainly the only way to do justice to Hazlitt's interpretation of Burke is to quote all of it, and as this is impossible we must content ourselves with saying that "the legislative wisdom, piercing sagacity, and rich, impetuous, high-wrought imagination of Burke"—find all of them magnificent exposition in Hazlitt's character-sketch. We would add, however, a reminder as to the generousness with which, at this time of his life, Hazlitt treated this great adversary. In illustration of this, it is only necessary to glance at his comment on the reactions of Burke and Fox to the French Revolution. He responded to the personality of Fox (indeed his character-sketch of Fox has a note of personal affection absent from any of the others), and the personality of Burke was alien to his sympathies; he felt that the consequences of Burke's writing on the French Revolution "as instruments of political power" had been almost fatal to the well-being of mankind, while Fox had been from the beginning its warm apologist; yet he did not hesitate to describe Burke as "a profound commentator on that apocalyptical chapter in the history of human nature," and to say that to him Fox had never seemed such. They had both of them "tried their strength in the Ulysses' bow of politicians, the French Revolution," and they had both been foiled, but "Burke was to Fox what the geometrician is to the mechanic."

Yet if the truth in him compelled him to concede to the one whom he regarded as having been the enemy of mankind in its hour of crisis, that vision which he denied to the one who had wished to be the friend of mankind, the truth in him enabled him also to do ample justice to the statesmanship, the humanity, and the passionate oratory of Fox, which is again enacted in his words, so vivid are they:

"Every thing showed the agitation of his mind. His tongue faltered, his voice became almost suffocated, and his face was bathed in tears. He was lost in the magnitude of his subject. He reeled and staggered under the load of feeling which oppressed him. He rolled like the sea beaten by a tempest. Whoever, having the feelings of a man, compared him at these times with his boasted rival, his stiff, straight, upright figure, his gradual contortions, turning round as if moved by a pivot, his solemn pauses, his deep tones, ' whose sound reverbed their own hollowness,' must needs have said, This is a man; that is an automaton."[157]

The conclusion of this paragraph gives the temper of his estimate of Pitt, who seemed to him, as to Coleridge, Wordsworth and Landor, a clever mediocrity. His conviction of Pitt's mediocrity is again summarised in a few words in the midst of the character-sketch of Walpole:

"Nothing ever assumed a new snape in passing through his mind: he recalled his ideas as they were originally impressed, and they neither received nor ever threw a sparkling light on any subject with which he connected them, either by felicity of combination, or ingenuity of argument. They were of that loose, general, unconnected kind, as just to fill the places they were brought out to occupy in the rank and file of an oration, and then returned mechanically back to their several stations, to be ready to appear again whenever they were called for."

It is evident that in considering these three contemporary statesmen Hazlitt is constantly comparing them with the one great statesman of the preceding age. He was in some measure satisfied with his work. Although at first he had felt some doubts as to whether he had done justice to Burke, he felt in the end that these three sketches at any rate expressed settled opinions which he was not likely to change,[158] and feelings long matured; that he had dealt justly with the men he had estimated; and that he had succeeded in steering clear of his own strong prejudices. As to the value of the character-sketch, however, of the great man with whom he compared them and by whose standards he measured them—that William Pitt, Earl of Chatham, who had poured forth his life in one last effort of passionate oratory a few days after William Hazlitt had struggled into the world—his opinion fluctuated. At first he had thought it better than the sketch of Burke; but afterwards he felt that it had perhaps been written too much in the heat of the first impression made on him by reading Chatham's speeches, and that therefore it suffered from not having been matured in his mind as the other sketches had been. We do not think it equal to the Burke, yet it *moves* more, because in it we hear once more Hazlitt's utterance of his worship of Liberty, as it was before the hatred of persecution and the bitterness of political strife had charged it with their discords. Here is no "harsh croaking voice." Hazlitt had music in his heart in these days and his words sing:

"Lord Chatham's genius burnt brightest at the last. The spark of liberty, which had lain concealed and dormant, buried under the dirt and rubbish of state intrigue and vulgar faction, now met with congenial matter, and kindled up ' a flame of sacred vehemence·' in his breast. It burst forth with a fury and a splendour that might have awed the world, and made kings tremble. He spoke as a man should speak, because he felt as a man should feel, in such circumstances. He came forward as the advocate of liberty, as the defender of the rights of his fellow-citizens, as the enemy of tyranny, as the friend of his country, and of mankind. He did not stand up to make a vain display of his talents, but to discharge a duty, to maintain that cause which lay nearest to his heart, to preserve the ark of the British constitution from every sacrilegious touch, as the high-priest of his calling, with a pious zeal. The feelings and the rights of Englishmen were enshrined in his heart; and with their united force braced every nerve, possessed every faculty, and communicated warmth and vital energy to every part of his being. The whole man moved with this impulse. He felt the cause of liberty as his own. He resented every injury done to her as an injury to himself, and every attempt to defend it as an insult to his understanding. He did not stay to dispute about words, about nice distinctions, about trifling forms. He laughed at the little attempts of little retailers of logic to entangle him in senseless argument. He did not come there as to a debating club, or law court, to start questions and hunt them down; to wind and unwind the web of sophistry; to pick out the threads, and untie every knot with scrupulous exactness; to bandy logic with every pretender to a paradox; to examine, to sift evidence; to dissect a doubt and halve a scruple; to weigh folly and knavery in scales together, and see on which side the balance preponderated; to prove that liberty, truth, virtue, and justice were good things, or that slavery and corruption were bad things. He did not try to prove those truths which did not require any proof, but to make others feel them with the same force that he did; and to tear off the flimsy disguises with which the sycophants of power attempted to cover them. . . . There is nothing new or curious or profound in

Lord Chatham's speeches. All is obvious or common; there is nothing but what we already know, or might have found out for ourselves. We see nothing but the familiar every-day face of nature. We are always in broad daylight. But there is the same difference between our own conception of things and his representation of them, as there is between the same objects seen on a dull cloudy day, or in the blaze of sunshine. His common sense has the effect of inspiration. He electrifies his hearers, not by the novelty of his ideas, but by their force and intensity. He has the same ideas as other men, but he has them in a thousand times greater clearness and strength and vividness. Perhaps there is no man so poorly furnished with thoughts and feelings but that if he could recollect all that he knew, and had all his ideas at perfect command, he would be able to confound the puny arts of the most dexterous sophist that pretended to make a dupe of his understanding. But in the mind of Chatham, the great substantial truths of common sense, the leading maxims of the Constitution, the real interests and general feelings of mankind, were in a manner embodied. He comprehended the whole of his subject at a single glance—every thing was firmly rivetted to its place; there was no feebleness, no forgetfulness, no pause, no distraction; the ardour of his mind overcame every obstacle, and he crushed the objections of his adversaries as we crush an insect under our feet."[159]

The compilation was published under the title *The Eloquence of the British Senate*. Hazlitt felt that in completing it he had reached the end of a stage of development. He had also the feeling that the writing he had done was more than task-work, or hack-work, that it was indeed of a quality that made it incongruous in a compilation of this kind. Especially he felt this of the "Characters," of which he wrote to his father: "These four, viz. Burke, Chatham, Fox, Pitt, with Sir R. Walpole's will be the chief articles of the work, and if I am not mistaken, confounded good ones. I am only afraid they will be too good, that is, that they will contain more good things than are exactly proper for the occasion."[160] This confession shows that he now knew himself to be a writer. He knew also—although he had no small opinion of the portrait of his father he had completed in 1805—that his writing had developed more in the past three years than his painting had done. Yet he still hoped for his painting, and his mind was much occupied by it. To his father, still the faithful confidant of his aspirations, he confessed this hope: "I have done what I wanted in writing, and I hope I may in painting."[161]

9

From this confession we might have expected to find him giving his pen a rest, returning to the country, and devoting himself to his picture. But hardly had he put the finishing touches to the great series of "Characters" than he found himself beginning on a fresh literary labour. This, a piece of stormy controversial writing against a book which he regarded as an attack upon the liberties of the poor, occupied him throughout the spring and early summer of 1807—while the war agony, against which his spirit was also continuously in protest, rolled on abroad, now in Poland, and the Russians showed that they were only to be beaten by being "hewn in pieces like logs," so that the ground between the French and the Russian lines became "not merely strewed, but literally choked up, with the bodies of the dead and wounded," and Dantzig after a long siege was taken by the French, and the Battle of Friedland was won by Napoleon after overwhelming efforts, until at last, in July, the Treaty of Tilsit brought respite once more.

The object of Hazlitt's attack was Malthus's *Essay on Population*. The immediate stimulus was Samuel Whitbread's introduction of a Poor Law Bill in the House of Commons on February 19th, 1807. Hazlitt was jealous for the poor, vigilant over their interests. He had no great belief that Whitbread had any real understanding of their situation, notwithstanding the evidences this "fighter of hopeless battles" had given of sympathy with the distresses of the poor. He felt that their best advocate would be someone who had entered into their lives: "The ' champion ' should be the child of poverty. The author of our religion, when he came to save the world, took our nature upon him, and became as one of us: it is not likely that any one should ever prove the *saviour* of the poor, who has not common feelings with them and who does not know their weaknesses and wants."[162] But what compelled him to take action was less lack of faith in Whitbread than fear lest the proposed modifications of the Poor Law might be discussed and perhaps carried through in the spirit of the recommendations made by Malthus, or, to use his own caustic phrase, that "the parent discovery" might "overlay the ricketty offspring." Malthus's *Letter to Samuel Whitbread* appeared in the course of 1807. Nor was the figure of Malthus about the House of Commons with his Essay in his hand, "lobbying" members while the Bill was under discussion, reassuring to one whose sympathies were with the poor.

When the Rev. T. R. Malthus had first published his *Essay on Population* in 1798, he had attacked Godwin's conception of the possibility that a perfected human society might come into being if man grew up among perfected human institutions, by the assertion that "the principle of population" made the existence of such a perfected state impossible, for the checks provided by Nature herself upon the growth of population in excess of the means of subsistence in the world were Vice and Misery. Were these checks removed in a perfected state, the population would rapidly increase beyond the means of subsistence, because whereas "population, when unchecked, increases in a geometrical ratio, subsistence only increases in an arithmetical ratio;" the struggle for life would thus be sharper than ever; in the course of it Vice and Misery would inevitably reappear and begin their necessary scavenging upon the *surplus* population, and the end of the state that had tried to improve upon Nature would be far worse than the beginning.

Malthus, who regarded his argument as "conclusive against the perfectibility of the mass of mankind," had exposed himself to the charge of presenting the vices and follies of human nature, with their by-products of War, Famine and Disease, as "benevolent *remedies* by which nature has enabled human beings to correct the disorders that would arise from the redundance of population which the unrestrained operation of her laws would create," almost of giving his approbation to the vices and follies of human nature, with their by-products of War, Famine and Pestilence, as being nature's salutary checks on worse evils; he had exposed himself also to the charge of inculcating a doctrine of despair. As Hazlitt himself puts it: "It is plain either that existence is upon the whole a blessing and that the means of existence are on that account desirable; that consequently an increased population is doubly a blessing, and an increase in the means of existence doubly desirable; or else life is to be an evil, and in this case it would be well if all the inhabitants of the earth were to die of some easy death to-morrow." Even if euthanasia were rejected, as the logical sequence of such teaching, moral apathy equivalent to death-in-life must follow upon the acceptance of it:

"The pilot might let go the helm, and leave the vessel to drift helplessly before the stream. When we are convinced that the degree of human virtue and happiness can no more be influenced by human wisdom than the ebbing and flowing of the tide, it must be idle to give ourselves any more concern about them."[163]

Malthus's doctrine that the substitution of benevolence for self-love as "the moving principle of society" would be disastrous, and that to self-love "we are indebted for all the noblest exertions of human genius, all the finer and more delicate emotions of the soul, for everything, in fact, that distinguishes the civilised from the savage state,' seemed also to Hazlitt, who had been engaged in attacking this claim for over ten years, a doctrine of despair.

In its first form the Essay, even if distasteful to Hazlitt and those who thought like him and who yearned to see "some prospect of lasting good to mankind," remained a speculation advanced in reply to a speculation. Nor could the tone of it with regard to "the common people of England" be called offensive. The Essay shows little or no class rancour. Although it insists that the relief of poverty is "beyond human ingenuity," what is said of the poor is incidental to the main speculation. It views with more equanimity than becomes a man the fate of "the unhappy persons who, in the great lottery of life, have drawn a blank;" yet as long as it remained a speculation advanced in reply to a speculation, a speculation, moreover, in the truth of which Hazlitt had no belief, and the morbid nature of which, it seemed to him, might readily be discerned by all, he did not feel any compulsion put upon him to reply to it. In the second edition of the Essay, however, published in 1803, and in each of the editions following upon it—there was one in 1806 and another in 1807, for the book fell in with the prejudices of the times—Malthus, who was anxious to escape from the charge of inhumanity or callousness, assumed the tone of monitor towards "the lower classes of society," as he now calls "the common people of England." In this character he added to the lists of deterrents upon dangerous excess of population the exercise of "moral restraint" by the poor. Thus he embarked on the task of making applicable to the population begotten in civilised society, and especially to the surplus or "redundant" population, as he called those who lived on the edge of poverty in his own country, the theory he had deduced from observation of the operation of Nature in the raw. In advocating the discontinuance of Poor Law Relief, for there would be no greater cruelty to the poor man than to allow him to repose on the hope that if he begot children whom his income would not support the state would stand between him and starvation, he urged that when the poor man contemplated marriage, he should be publicly warned by the clergyman of his parish of the duty to refrain from begetting children whom his wages could not support, adding:

"After the public notice . . . had been given, and the system of poor-laws had ceased with regard to the living generation, if any man chose to marry, without a prospect of being able to support a family, he should have the most perfect liberty to do so. . . . When nature will govern and punish for us, it is a very miserable ambition to wish to snatch the rod from her hand and draw upon ourselves the odium of executioner. To the punishment therefore of nature he should be left, the punishment of want. He has erred in the face of a most precise warning, and can have no just reason to complain of any person but himself when he feels the consequences of his error. All parish assistance should be denied him; and he should be left to the uncertain support of private charity. He should be taught to know that the laws of nature, which are the laws of God, had doomed him and his family to starve[164] for disobeying their repeated admonitions, and that he had no claim of *right* on society for the support of the smallest portion of food, beyond that which his labour would fairly purchase."

Although marriage must not be made too easy, and the poor man, once married, is to be browbeaten, bullied, discouraged and cowed into "moral restraint," Malthus is thrown into as great a panic by Condorcet's advocacy of birth-control as by any encouragement given to marriage among the poor; for as the latter might lead to the production of more workers than were necessary to the country, the former might lead to the production of fewer. Any "artificial and unnatural modes of checking population" would remove "a necessary stimulus to industry."[165] The poor would have their natural tendency to indolence greatly increased if they had it in their own power—by any means except that of moral restraint—to limit the number of their children; and the population would not reach its "natural and proper extent."

In his own idiom, Nature must still continue to "govern and punish." The poor, least of all, must be permitted to "snatch the rod from her hand," and to make themselves in any way her master. If they cannot exercise the moral restraint to the practice of which they have been exhorted, they are to be left to the great checks on their redundance Nature had supplied—War, Famine, and Pestilence.

The tone of the second edition of the Essay, and of each of the editions which followed it, is odious, while the Essay itself, instead of confining itself to the speculative, has become practical in its intention. Whereas the first edition had been a courteous retort to Godwin's theory of the perfectibility of Man, the later editions seem hardly less than an attack on such liberties as the poor in the England of Malthus's day still continued to enjoy, made by one who resolutely turned a blind eye on the extent to which they were already the victims of the social system of the day. The severity falls most heavily of all on the most helpless of all, even among the very poor: "With regard to illegitimate children . . . they should not be allowed to have any parish assistance, . . ." Hazlitt was not tilting at windmills, but endeavouring, in attacking the spirit of Malthus, to combat what he sensed as a real danger to the poor. In the later editions of the *Essay on Population* we have, if ever it is to be found in a book, "a vulgar selfishness, consolidated into principle, like marsh water that has become sordid ice." Or, as Hazlitt himself put it, with biting contempt, this is such writing as Blifil might have given to the world, had he turned author.

It was not, then, his objection to the original speculation, but his fear lest legislation should be influenced by the popularity the later editions of the Essay had won with all who were averse to relieving distress and inclined to regard the poor as implements of labour, that brought Hazlitt at last into action, that led also to his first venture in journalism, for he opened his attack with three long and searching letters contributed to Cobbett's *Political Register* between March and May of the year. Afterwards, when he prepared his material for book form, under the title of *A Reply to the Essay on Population*, he added two more Letters, and a long commentary in which he could express himself at more length than in the form he had first chosen. It is chiefly the second edition, so much more repellent in its tone than the first, that he attacks. Malthus making use of his "principle" of population to confute Godwin's theories as to the perfectibility of Man was one thing; Malthus making use of his "principle" to "shut up the work-house, to *snub* the poor, to stint them in their wages, to deny them any relief from the Parish, to preach lectures to them on the new-invented crime of matrimony,"[166] as well as on the old sin of fornication, so that the poor man should "neither be supposed to keep his wife, nor his girl;"[167] Malthus demonstrating the application of his "principle" to the distresses of the time and getting the ear of the framers of the country's laws—was quite another. Hazlitt felt too that the trans-ference of the issue from the speculative to the practical was the end towards which Malthus had all the time been striving—for the "principle" would not have been worth a farthing to him without the application—and that he aimed with cruel gusto at enforcing the application with the knife:

"He will hear of no short-cuts or obvious expedients for bettering the condition of the poor. All his benefits are extracted by the Cæsarean operation."[168]

With Malthus's theories as such we have no concern. Nor, at the present time, when the doctrines of Malthus have almost become matter of legend, is there any need to follow Hazlitt in his exposure of his antagonist's plagiarisms, illogicalities, "snivelling inter-polations," tergervisations, false assumptions, pusillanimous self-contradictions so great as to involve a retractation of first premises, shiftings of ground on the score of expediency, treacherous half-truths, so much more difficult to expose than downright falsehoods, poverty of mind, poverty of spirit, and poverty of practical resource— nor to follow the steps by which he reaches his conclusion, that Malthus's book is "a nullity in the science of political philosophy." Suffice it to say that on this his first entry into controversy he showed himself no less terrible in attack than in later years when his opponents had long since learned to their cost that, being roused, he could mingle gall and copperas with his ink. We should be the poorer, however, in understanding of his character, did we not fully realise the principal cause of his anger. To him it seemed that the popularisation of Malthus's theories might lead to an assault on Liberty in one of its forms, and it is again as the defender of Liberty that he takes the field, in opposition to a theory which was in danger of being converted into one of the instruments of power that was corrupt, or at least suspect. Already he had pled the necessity of civil Liberty to the well-being of the country; through his sketch of Chatham he had saluted the principle of Liberty itself; this time he comes forward in defence of the Liberty of the poorest sons of the soil, which he thinks may well be hacked-at and whittled away by any legislation ushered in under the shadow of Malthus. He pled for the liberties of those who were not sufficiently articulate to make any effective assertion of, or any effective protest against the diminution of their rights; and surely, the history of Enclosure in that century shows that the poor sorely needed such a pleader. His attitude, and the intensity of feeling which conditioned it, will best be understood from his own words:

"Mr. Malthus's reputation may, I fear, prove fatal to the poor of this country. His name hangs suspended over their heads, *in terrorem*, like some baleful meteor. It is the shield behind which the archers may take their stand, and gall them at their leisure. He has set them up as a defenceless mark, on which friends and foes may execute their malice, or their wantonness, as they think proper. He has fairly hunted them down, he has driven them into his toils, he has thrown his net over them, and they remain as a prey to the first invader, either to be sacrificed without mercy at the shrine of cold unfeeling avarice, or to linger out a miserable existence under the hands of ingenious and scientific tormentors. . . . I confess I do feel some degree of disgust and indignation rising within me, when I see a man of Mr. Malthus's character and calling standing forward as the accuser of those ' who have none to help them,' as the high-priest of ' pride and covetousness,' forming selfishness into a regular code, with its codicils, institutes, and glosses annexed, trying to muffle up the hand of charity in the fetters of the law, to suppress ' the compunctious visitings of nature,' to make men ashamed of compassion and good nature as folly and weakness, ' laying the flattering unction ' of religion to the conscience of the riotous and luxurious liver, and ' grinding the faces of the poor ' with texts of scripture. . . .

"While the prejudice infused into the public mind by this gentle-man's writings subsists in its full force, I am almost convinced that any serious attempts at bettering the condition of the poor will be ineffectual. . . . But, it seems, that whether practicable, or no, Mr. Whitbread must bring in a Poor Bill. The effect of it appears to me to be putting the poor into the wardship of the rich, to be doing away the little remains of independence we have left, and making them once more what they were formerly, the vassals of a wealthy aristocracy."[169]

Youth is as a rule generous. But such rallying, in a moment of need, to the cause of the forlorn was characteristic of Hazlitt all his life. It is perhaps most marked of all in his later years, and never more so than when his day was far spent.

In the year in which Malthus had published the first edition of the *Essay on Population*, Wordsworth had been trying to ascertain how far "the language of conversation in the middle and lower classes of society" was "adapted to the purpose of poetic pleasure," and had been finding in the joys and sorrows of the poor that which he conceived to be Poetry. While Malthus had been expressing in the Preface to his Essay—written in June, 1798—his sense of the "dark tints" and the "melancholy hue" of human life, the *Lyrical Ballads* had been receiving the finishing touches.

In the course of the spring and summer of 1807, while Cobbett was calling *rogue* and *scoundrel* at every second word, and Hazlitt, with finer weapons that yet, we would swear, twinkle sardonically every now and again as he trains them on his adversary, was slashing into ribbons Malthus's claims to be regarded as a thinker, Wordsworth had made his second plea for the poor, in his own fashion, the quiet way of sympathy. His *Poems*, in two volumes, had been published early in the year. These contained *The Leech Gatherer*, the sonnet:

> "Though narrow be that Old Man's cares, and near,
>   The poor Old Man is greater than he seems:
>   For he hath waking empire, wide as dreams;
>   An ample sovereignty of eye and ear."

and the exquisite warning to the covetous to respect the sacredness of the poor man's few possessions:

> "Think what the home would be if it were thine,
>   Even thine, though few thy wants!—Roof, window, door,
>   The very flowers are sacred to the Poor.
>   The roses to the porch which they entwine:"

Any one of these poems, in thought and utterance ranging from the simple to the apocalyptic, had that in it which would overthrow the spirit of Malthus. But such words have to bide their time. They can work upon the mind of man only by leavening it. At the moment of conflict they are almost unheard in the clashing of the strife, and even if heard they are not understood. Yet in the end they become "A Power like one of Nature's." Their operation, if slow as that of the mills of God, is also as sure.

10

Hazlitt's weapons certainly twinkled not only sardonically but wickedly when he attacked Malthus's conception of "the passion between the sexes," yet in the midst[170] of this attack he fell into a vein of reminiscence, in the course of which he allowed a confession to escape him which is our chief clue to his love life—which he lived on a different plane of feeling from that of his sex life—up to his twenty-ninth year:

"I never fell in love but once; and then it was with a girl who always wore her handkerchief pinned tight round her neck, with a fair face, gentle eyes, a soft smile, and cool auburn locks. I mention this, because it may in some measure account for my temperate, tractable notions of this passion, compared with Mr. Malthus's. It was not a raging heat, a fever in the veins: but it was like a vision, a dream, like thoughts of childhood, an everlasting hope, a distant joy, a heaven, a world that might be. The dream is still left, and sometimes comes confusedly over me in solitude and silence, and mingles with the softness of the sky, and veils my eyes from mortal grossness."

The delicate word-portrait looks out upon us, incongruously enough, from among all "the paper pellets of the brain," with which the place of controversy is strewn.

The next thing we have to record of W.H. is that by the late autumn of the year he finds himself regarded as the lover of a woman who was in all respects the exact opposite of the original of the exquisite portrait limned on his imagination. This was the Miss Stoddart whom the idiom of Charles Lamb had commended to him, and to whom he had been commended in the idiom of Mary Lamb.

"Dear H., thou art certainly a pretty fellow. I wonder what makes thee such a favourite among the ladies!"[171]

Chapter Two

TOWARDS WINTERSLOW (1807-1808)

". . . the Defunct was naturally of a discoursible and communicative temper, though of a gloomy and close aspect, *as born under Saturn*. . . ."

CHARLES LAMB.

I

SOME attempts have been made to identify the original of Hazlitt's pen-portrait of the only love of his youth. It has been suggested that there had been an attachment between Hazlitt and Miss Railton, the beautiful daughter of one of his Liverpool patrons, and that disparity of fortune had prevented it from coming to fruition; but there is no documentary evidence to support this suggestion. It has also been suggested that the original of the portrait may have been the Sally Shepherd with whom we know Hazlitt to have been violently in love at one period of his life. This we regard as impossible. Such evidence as we have—and it is very meagre—indicates that the passion for Sally Shepherd was of a much later date. Also the few words relating to it show it to have been entirely different in character from the love felt by Hazlitt for the original of the portrait. It was described as "a frenzy," whereas the portrait makes its appearance in *A Reply to Malthus* precisely for the purpose of confuting Malthus's conception of love, or what Hazlitt took it to be, with a description of a love in which "frenzy" had no share whatsoever, and in which gentleness had much.

There are, however, a few words scattered here and there throughout Hazlitt's writing, hints kept studiously vague, but which yet to some extent substantiate the suggestion of the portrait, and which seem to indicate that Hazlitt had loved, possibly during the early painting days, before the Keswick episode had injured him, a girl whom fortune had placed quite out of his reach, but who seemed to him to express the feminine character entirely in what he called "its fragile lovely essence;" that the love, of which fulfilment was denied him in actuality, settled itself in his imagination, thereby securing some degree of permanence, for whereas what had to do with the senses was quickly effaced for Hazlitt by the recurrence of similar experience, that which affected his imagination never passed out of his life; and that this love gave him understanding of a region of feeling of which it is sometimes taken for granted he knew nothing, and had its share in making him what he became as a writer and in conditioning his development as a man.

One of these is the passage which connects his reading of *A Simple Story* with Manchester. In it he makes credible the reality of this plane of feeling, amid all the other planes of feeling more easily realisable, upon which the complex being William Hazlitt lived during this or that period of his life:

"Mrs. Inchbald was always a great favourite with me. There is the true soul of woman breathing from what she writes, as much as if you heard her voice. It is as if Venus had written books. I first read her *Simple Story* (of all places in the world) at M—— No matter where it was, for it transported me out of myself. . . . Her heroine, Miss Milner, was at my side. That dream has since been verified:— how like it was to the reality! In truth, the reality itself was but a dream."[172]

Elsewhere he numbers Miss Milner among "the brides of the fancy, such as ' youthful poets dream of when they love.'"[173]

The next two suggestions are contained in references to the shadowy Miss Walton, for whom Harley, the Man of Feeling, cherished a love that was hopeless because his fortunes did not permit him to pay court to an " heiress of £4,000 a year." Hazlitt writes:

"of the Man of Feeling I would speak with grateful recollections: . . . and that lone figure of Miss Walton in it, that floats in the horizon, dim and ethereal, the day-dream of her lover's youthful fancy—better, far better than all the realities of life!"[174] and again:

"I have a sneaking fondness for Mackenzie's *Julia de Roubigné*—for the deserted mansion and straggling gilliflowers on the mouldering garden-wall; and still more for his *Man of Feeling*; not that it is better, nor so good; but at the time I read it, I sometimes thought of the heroine, Miss Walton, and of Miss —— together, and ' that ligament, fine as it was, was never broken! '"[175]

Now Henry Mackenzie's description of Miss Walton is delicately drawn:

"Her complexion was mellowed into a paleness, which certainly took from her beauty; but agreed, at least Harley used to say so, with the pensive softness of her mind. Her eyes were of that gentle hazel colour which is rather mild than piercing; and, except when they were lighted up by good humour, which was frequently the case, were supposed by the fine gentlemen to want fire. Her air and manner were elegant in the highest degree, and were as sure of commanding respect, as their mistress was far from demanding it. Her voice was inexpressibly soft; it was, according to that incomparable simile of Otway's:

> "'. . . like the shepherd's pipe upon the mountains,
> When all his little flock's at feed before him.'"

This was a description to take Hazlitt's taste "supremely." Beauty of the unassuming kind in women, no less than in flowers, charmed him most. "The phrase ' violets dim,' to those who have never seen the object . . . seems to convey a slur rather than a compliment, dimness being no beauty in itself; . . . but to those who have seen, and been as it were enamoured . . . what other word is there that so well recalls its deep purple glow, its retired modesty, its sullen, conscious beauty?"—he writes in one of his latest essays when defending the little flower over which he had so often hung, "looking at it again and again (as misers contemplate their gold—as fine ladies hang over their jewels)." Much in the same way, when defending beauty of the timid kind in women, he wrote: "If delicacy, beauty, and grace are insipidity, I, too, profess myself an idolizer of insipidity." As we have seen, no face pleased him more than the face "pale as the primrose;" no eyes stirred him more than those "cast half down, the eye-lashes, like strokes of a pencil" over the white of the skin: the lowered lids, that had a melting, half-sleepy look, affecting him like the languid perfume of half-concealed flowers, held his senses—as it were—"enamoured" of their gentleness and delicacy. He felt that there was something in this description that made him connect it with his thoughts of the girl to whom he refers as Miss —— There is also much in it to remind us of his description of the girl he had loved—the same gentleness, the same suggestion of the grace which meant far more to him than beauty itself. We are not here dealing with certainties, but with hints and tenuous clues to feeling; but we suggest that there is here an indication that the unknown Miss —— shadowy as Miss Walton herself, may be identical with the unknown original of the pen-portrait.

One last word from Hazlitt—it is the last also in respect of date—and we have done. In the essay *On Personal Identity* he makes a confession which certainly suggests that he had been "baulked of" the goddess of his idolatry, or at least that but for disparity of rank or fortune he might have found happiness in marriage:

> "Had I been a lord, I should have married Miss —— and my life would not have been one long-drawn sigh, made up of sweet and bitter regret."

These passages, it seems to us, should be well pondered by any one endeavouring to understand the experiences that built up Hazlitt's personality, and the love that in the end overwhelmed him. Perhaps it matters comparatively little to our understanding of him who Miss —— was, or even whether the original of the pen-portrait was identical with Miss —— We think it likely that she was, but on such an identification it is not possible to be positive, nor do we wish to labour the point. On the other hand, it matters a good deal in any attempt to understand Hazlitt, that full cognizance should be taken of the indications given as to his experience of what is called "ideal" love—both by the portrait and by such passages in his writing as seem by their tone and sentiment to connect themselves with it. Otherwise we shall be in danger of failing to realise the suggestion given by these indications that Hazlitt, whom so many of his contemporaries described as "a gross sensualist," but who to himself seemed rather a frustrated idealist, had indeed known the kind of love which is primarily "ideal" or spiritual, that the memory of it remained with him as something by which to test the value and quality of other loves, and that at times, the love which existed primarily in the imagination seemed to him the sweetest of all.

As to the way in which such experience influenced his writing, deepening it, exalting it, refining it, and extending both its sympathies and its range—this can readily be demonstrated if we turn to his review of Sismondi's *Literature of the South*, and its defence of Petrarchan love:

"Mr. Sismondi wishes the connexion between Petrarch and Laura had been more intimate, and his passion accompanied with more interesting circumstances. The whole is in better keeping as it is. The love of a man like Petrarch would have been less in character if it had been less ideal. For the purposes of inspiration, a single interview was quite sufficient. The smile which sank into his heart the first time he ever beheld her played round her lips ever after; the look with which her eyes first met his, never passed away. The image of his mistress still haunted his mind, and was recalled by every object in nature. Even death could not dissolve the fine illusion: for that which exists in the imagination is alone imperishable. As our feelings become more ideal, the impression of the moment indeed becomes less violent; but the effect is more general and permanent. The blow is felt only by reflection; it is the rebound that is fatal. We are not here standing up for this kind of Platonic attachment; but only endeavouring to explain the way in which the passions very commonly operate in minds accustomed to draw their strongest interests from constant contemplation."[176]

This appeared in the February of 1815, at a time when Hazlitt was drinking hard and living hard, and when scandal was catching up with his name. Both friend and foe might justly have said to him that his actions did not square with his theories, and he might as justly have replied that even if they did not, his mind might be seen in his writings, as the face is seen in the glass. The words in which he described Petrarch's love bear the unmistakable imprint of integrity. No one, who had not experienced it, could have made thus credible the kind of love they describe.

Few of his contemporaries could have done so. Wordsworth had his own knowledge of idealisms, could sympathise with some which to the onlooker seemed hardly to come short of mania:

> "And I have scarcely pitied him; have felt
> A reverence for a Being thus employed;
> And thought that in the blind and awful lair
> Of such a madness, reason did lie couch'd."

But of the ideal love Hazlitt described he knew nothing. Such an interpretation of it as Hazlitt had given would have been beyond his range, for Coleridge spoke the truth when he said that Wordsworth's conception of sexual love did not go beyond the idea of tenderness that was mingled with lust. Coleridge himself could have given an interpretation of it—as what could he not have given!—yet he would have lacked the background of sensual knowledge which in Hazlitt throws the ideal knowledge into relief and makes it poignant. "Even death could not dissolve the fine illusion: for that which exists in the imagination is alone imperishable." Such writing as this is not of immaculate conception. Nor is it virgin gold. It is all the purer for that—gold *tried in the fire*!

2

No woman was less likely either to inspire or to desire an ideal passion than Miss Stoddart. We see her, from the time of her life in which our acquaintance with her begins, the year 1803, to 1807, the year in which Hazlitt's acquaintance with her began, chiefly through the eyes of her brother, Dr. John Stoddart, and of Mary Lamb. Her brother, who just at this time had been appointed King's Advocate at Malta, was formal, conventional, and precise. He looked but coldly on a sister who had all the faults most displeasing to a man of his temperament, for he found her manners hoydenish; he considered her lacking in good taste and discretion; and he deplored the buoyancy in her which kept her always on the alert for excitement, amusement and interest. The strong life in her ruffled him and filled him with a sense of responsibility. He wished to see it controlled, or at least regulated by decorum. It was because he hoped that Mary Lamb would make a gentlewoman of her that he encouraged her intimacy with the Lambs.

He probably did her less than justice, her temperament being the exact opposite to his own. On the other hand, we see her chiefly through the eyes of Mary Lamb, who was a very faithful correspondent of hers, and these were the most indulgent eyes in the world. Yet it is clear that Mary found certain things in Miss Stoddart's standards and outlook alien to her own way of looking at things. Little inclined as she was to interfere, she found herself every now and again compelled to express her difference of feeling as to these, although she was half inclined, at the same time, to reproach herself for seeming to assume the attitude of critic and mentor towards a friend who was the best company in the world, whose sense of life and cheerfulness attracted her, and of whom both Charles and she were genuinely fond. Throughout the correspondence she writes much as an elder sister might, although Miss Stoddart, at the time the correspondence opens, was not in her first youth, being indeed, although ten years younger than Mary herself, about the same age as Charles, and about three years older than Hazlitt. Although she now and again came to town to stay with the Lambs, she spent most of her time very quietly with her old parents. Her father, a retired naval officer, was settled in Salisbury.

The first of Mary Lamb's letters to her friend was written in September, 1803. In the course of that summer Lieutenant Stoddart had died, and his daughter, who had now a small income of her own, of about £80[177] a year, instead of continuing to live with her mother, with whom she was not greatly in sympathy, and towards whom Mary Lamb thought she behaved with a certain lack of sensibility, decided to accompany her brother to Malta. Although with him also she was little in sympathy, she thought that in Malta she would have a pleasanter life than at home, and one that would open out more promising prospects to her. Her brother had just married Isabella Moncrieff, the daughter of Sir Henry Moncrieff, a Scottish baronet who was also a clergyman, and she felt that she was more likely to make a "rich" marriage under his auspices than she was if she remained with her mother in Salisbury, or buried alive at Winterslow, a little village some seven miles north-east of it, where her father had left her some property. By the autumn she was preparing to set out for Malta, and in consequence of this she had driven what Mary Lamb thought a hard bargain with her lover of the moment, of whom we know nothing except that he was named William and that partridge-shooting drew him to Wiltshire in the autumn. The bargain seems to have been that she was to consider herself free to marry if she could make a good match, but that if she returned un-

married she would be ready to listen to a renewal of her lover's proposals. Mary Lamb in her letter touches on these things, rather
regretfully, yet accepting in her friend even what she cannot understand: "When you leave your mother and say, you shall feel no
remorse, and when you make a *jewish* bargain with your *Lover*, all this
gives me no offence, because it is your nature, and your temper, and
I do not expect or want you to be otherwise than you are. I love you
for the good that is in you, and look for no change."[178] She confesses,
however, that in one respect she would like to see an alteration: "*But,
certainly, you ought to struggle with the evil that does most easily
beset you—a total want of politeness in behaviour, I would say modesty
of behaviour, but that I should not convey to you my idea of the word
modesty; for I certainly do not mean that you want real modesty.*"[179]
She also finds that secrecy, even in the midst of what looks like entire
frankness and openness, is one of Miss Stoddart's great failings towards
her own people.

She gives her blessing to the Malta plan, but she is evidently
perplexed by the relationships in which a personality so different from
her own is involved. Thus, although she writes in the earlier part of
the letter: "as I said before, as I cannot enter into your feelings and
views of things, *your ways being not my ways*, why should I tell you what
I would do in your situation? So, child, take thine own ways, and
God prosper thee in them!" she concludes with a curious postcript
which shows that in her heart she hopes the Malta plans will not
succeed, and that her friend will come home unmarried and resume
her relationship with "William": "God bless you, and grant you may
preserve your integrity, and remain unmarried and penniless, and
make William a good and a happy wife."[180]

Miss Stoddart set sail then for Malta early in 1804, to make her
fortune, with a light heart, a trunkful of finery, and a string of pearls.
Before Coleridge had set out for Malta she was sending to Mitre Court
news of her dancing partners and gaieties: "You tell me of your gay,
splendid doings," wrote Mary Lamb in a letter in which she commended Coleridge to her friend's special care: "tell me likewise, what
manner of a home-life you lead. Is a quiet evening in a Maltese
drawing-room as pleasant as those we have passed in Mitre Court and
Bell Yard?"[181] She added: "Rickman wants to know if you are going
to be married yet. Satisfy him in that little particular when you
write." Presently there came news of a disappointment. One of Miss
Stoddart's lovers had failed to come to terms with her, because he too
wanted to marry money, and a wife who could only bring him an
income of £80 a year was little to his purpose. Mary did her best to
sympathise, but for the life of her could not take a disappointment of
this kind very much to heart. There followed for Miss Stoddart a
misadventure much more serious, a disagreeable scrape of some

kind in which she was involved by a lover who was afterwards denounced by Mary Lamb as "a vile wretch," and by whose conduct she felt herself to have been injured. Although she may not seem to have been made of very penetrable stuff, this affair caused her a good deal of distress, and probably had its share in making the life of the garrison town, which had at first appeared so brisk and gay to her, begin to seem brittle and mechanical. Before the summer of 1805 she had decided to return to England.

By the end of the year or the beginning of 1806 she was receiving matrimonial overtures from a new lover. When she paid a long visit to the Lambs in the January and February of 1806, these proposals were at a standstill, because she had felt it necessary to tell her lover about the affair in Malta. After her return to Winterslow, towards the end of February, Mary wrote to her telling her how highly Charles approved her candour in having done so;[182] at the same time, she urged the necessity of formal conduct in the future.

No sooner had this lover, Mr. White, disappeared from the scene, than he was succeeded by one whose name rubs shoulders with that of William Hazlitt in the letter Mary wrote to her early in June. After touching on their liking for William Hazlitt, Mary issued a kind of *questionnaire* as to this lover: "What is Mr. Turner? And what is likely to come of him? and how do you like him? and what do you intend to do about it? I almost wish you to remain single till your Mother dies, and then come and live with us; and we would either get you a husband, or teach you to live comfortably without."[183] Mr. Turner was succeeded by the young farmer to whom Mary refers as Corydon, and whose courtship proceeded so rapidly that in the course of the summer Dr. Stoddart was informed of it. In October Mary received a letter from him containing what she thought a very curious request, that she should go to Salisbury and inspect his prospective brother-in-law, as he trusted her judgment and felt sure his sister would be guided by it. This proposal she declined with spirit. "A pretty sort of an office truly," she wrote to Miss Stoddart. "You have gone too far in this affair for any interference to be at all desirable, and if you had not, I really do not know what my wishes would be. When you bring Mr. Dowling at Christmas I suppose it will be quite time enough for me to sit in judgment upon him."[184]

She had shown a great deal of sympathy, a great deal of interest, and a great deal of patience in listening to Miss Stoddart's accounts of all these love-affairs, but she seems to have felt a touch of desperateness or at least impatience about this engagement, for there follows a very strange blessing upon it

"If you fancy a very young man, and he likes an elderly gentlewoman; if he likes a learned and accomplished lady, and you like a not very learned youth, who may need a little polishing, which probably he will never acquire; it is all very well, and God bless you both together and may you both be very long in the same mind."[184]

Miss Stoddart did not come to town with Mr. Dowling at Christmas. She had, it seems, been mistaken in his intentions. The next letter we possess from Mary Lamb to Sarah Stoddart is dated just a little over a year later. It is the letter in which we find the no less strange provisional blessing on an engagement which seems about to be concluded with William Hazlitt.[185]

3

Miss Stoddart's "comical love affair" with William Hazlitt, as Mary Lamb called it, must have shot up almost as suddenly as her love affair with "Corydon" the previous year. Although Dr. Stoddart had now returned from Malta and taken a house in London, the wooing was done not under his roof but under the Lambs', and the Lambs were not likely to have been able to receive visitors until September, for Mary had had a severe attack of illness in the June of 1807. We may expect her to have been settled at home again by September, but not earlier than that. We know that Miss Stoddart left town not later than the middle of November, and that by that time she had certainly come to an understanding with Hazlitt, although she was not as yet formally engaged to him—so that her intimacy with him must have developed between the latter part of September or the early days of October, and November.

It is still from Mary Lamb, and not from either of the principals in the affair, that we hear of its progress. Towards the beginning of December she wrote to Miss Stoddart,[186] who had evidently been complaining that Hazlitt had been remiss about writing, explaining that she had just seen Hazlitt and that an "Effusion" of his had just been dispatched; but what she says of Hazlitt seems to indicate some degree of nonchalance on his part, even of carelessness as to whether he pleased or displeased. He was certainly the less eager of the two.

Mary made a request in this letter, which surely she could not have made unless she had in her heart a low opinion of Miss Stoddart's delicacy, here unconsciously revealed: "I learn from the Lover that he has not been so remiss in his duty as you supposed. His Effusion, and your complaints of his inconstancy, crossed each other on the road. He tells me his was a very strange letter, and that probably it has affronted you. That it was a strange letter, I can readily believe; but that you were affronted by a strange letter is not so easy for me to conceive, that not being your way of taking things. But however it be, let some answer come, either to him, or else to me, showing cause why you do not answer him. And pray, by all means, preserve the said letter, that I may one day have the pleasure of seeing how Mr. Hazlitt treats of love."[187]

Mary might have seen this "Effusion" without being any the wiser as to how "Mr. Hazlitt" treated of love—although all the world might one day satisfy its curiosity on that point—but her words, and the curious words of quasi-congratulation at the close of the letter with the suggestion that Charles felt it would be worth while to see these two friends of his come together "for the joke sake," indicate something of what the Lambs felt about the matter. They were pleased to see two friends of theirs, who had met in their home and who had been predisposed in favour of each other by their recommendations, make a match of it, but knowing what Hazlitt was like, and knowing all about Miss Stoddart's foibles—about which, we may be sure, they would tell no tales out of school—they were more than a little nervous; they were also very curious as to the character of Hazlitt's love, for Lamb had seen Hazlitt, ever since the visit to the "Girlery," in the light of the Woman-hater. Also the whole affair had for them, despite the danger they felt might be in it, something of the character of comedy. Not only did they see the Woman-hater "hoist," as it seemed to them, but it must have seemed to them also an exquisite comedy-ending to Miss Stoddart's matrimonial ventures that their friend, who had shown herself not a little mercenary in her attitude to marriage, should be willing to join hands and fortunes with one of the poorest men in all England. She had undertaken a long and what was at the time a dangerous voyage, with the undisguised intention of securing for herself a rich husband, and here, at the end of it all, she was marrying a man she had met at their own fireside, and one who was, as Lamb put it to Manning, so much poorer than herself that he had no "settlement" except what he could claim "from the parish." They watched the affair with an amused joy that yet had in it some touches of fear, and until the marriage ceremony was actually over they were in some uncertainty and tension over it.

Mary may have breathed more freely when by the middle of December her friend's engagement was at last a settled matter. On December 21st she wrote to Miss Stoddart, who certainly by this time was not taking the matter lightly, who seems indeed to have shown with regard to it a seriousness unusual in her: "I most heartily congratulate you on having so well got over your first difficulties; and now that it is quite settled, let us have no more fears. I now mean not only to hope and wish, but to persuade myself, that you will be very happy together.

"Endeavour to keep your mind as easy as you can. You ought to begin the world with a good stock of health and spirits; it is quite as necessary as ready money at first setting out."[188]

She set herself to pilot Miss Stoddart safely through such difficulties
as indiscretion might cause. She forbade her to come up to town
without first consulting Dr. Stoddart; and she said also that it would
never do for Hazlitt to go to Winterslow, where Miss Stoddart was now
living in one of the cottages left her by her father. One curious little
difficulty had arisen already. Dr. Stoddart had not been told of his
sister's engagement. Mary felt that he ought to be told of it at once—
otherwise he might take offence over the matter—and she felt also that
Hazlitt was the one who ought to approach him on the subject: but
Hazlitt proved averse to taking the initiative in this. Mary therefore
urged Miss Stoddart to impress on him the importance of his doing so:
"If you chuse that I should tell him, I will; but I think it would come
better from you. If you can persuade Hazlitt to mention it, that would
be still better; for I know your brother would be unwilling to give
credit to you, because you deceived yourself in regard to Corydon.
Hazlitt, I know, is shy of speaking first; but I think it of such great
importance to you to have your brother friendly in the business, that,
if you can overcome his reluctance, it would be a great point gained."[189]

4

We have now touched sufficiently on the light in which this
engagement was seen by the onlookers. What now of the principals
in the affair, and the impulses that moved them? Charles Lamb
came in the end to the conclusion that there was "love o' both sides."
If we believed this, we should have no more to say on the subject. But
we cannot believe it, for it does not accord with the evidence we have
either before or immediately following the engagement; and it is of
some importance to the understanding of Hazlitt's life from this time
onwards that we should make some attempt at understanding what
happened to him in the autumn of 1807, obscure though we feel the
matter to be.

Unlikely though it may seem, considering the brisk "wooing
weather" of the course Miss Stoddart had steered in the four years
preceding her engagement to Hazlitt, we think that what Lamb said
may have been true in so far as it applied to her. She cared so much
about money that it is difficult to understand why she should have
sought to wed with a by-no-means ardent Hazlitt, had she not fallen
in love with him. It must be remembered that she usually saw him
by the Lambs' fireside, and that his best was a very impressive best.
Surely she must have loved him, seeing that no woman, thinking
primarily of money, or security, or of prospects, would have married
William Hazlitt, no woman even thinking primarily of ease and a
quiet life—for she must have realised that she was marrying a man

reckoned by all who knew him to be exceptionally "difficult." In his blood-relationships alone he was steady, dependable, inalterably attached. In all others the wind was not more incalculable.

That Hazlitt did not love Miss Stoddart we feel quite sure. As to the way in which he was more or less captured by her, although not captivated by her, like much else that was true to fact in Hazlitt's experience, it may well seem fantastic. This, however, makes it none the less characteristic of him.

It will be remembered that the hideous termination of his *amourette* at Keswick had left him to some extent injured, and that although constantly attracted by women, he was inclined to be so distrustful that it was almost impossible for him to enter into any human relationship in which he could find satisfaction, with any woman who aroused sexual feeling in him. The only women with whom he was at ease were those whom he considered, as he considered Mary Lamb, in the light of a friendship that had no element of sexual feeling in it at all. In his relationship with these he had no fear of springing once more upon himself the trap he feared. Now before he had met Miss Stoddart, he had always thought of her in connection with Mary Lamb. She was Mary's best friend, and therefore, even though he would not have thought of her as "an elderly gentlewoman," as Mary once called her in a moment of imperfect sympathy, he would never have thought of her as a girl. She would have seemed to him definitely a woman of the decade preceding his own, for although she was only three years his senior, in 1807 there was a greater difference in apparent age between a man of twenty-nine and a woman of thirty-two than there is now. The man was still reckoned young; he had all his life before him: the woman had reached the age at which she was regarded as no longer very likely to marry. Hazlitt, therefore, while of course prepossessed in her favour by what the Lambs had said about her, would have formed in his mind rather an impression of a pleasant companionable woman who, as Charles had said to him, "was not in the way" when she was with one, than of a woman who might in any way disturb or attract or excite him. That is to say, he would have been off his guard.

Nor, when he met her, would he have seen anything to put him on his guard. There was little in her appearance or manner to allure him, little that had any special appeal for him. He was charmed by grace; she was so brusque in her movements that she was inclined to knock against things and hurt herself. He worshipped harmony of manner; her manner, while it was open and entirely free from embarrassment or affectation, was so abrupt as to seem at times almost rude. He admired fragility of appearance; she was inclined to be florid. She was not even distinctively feminine in appearance, for she wore her hair cropped. On the other hand she was, as the Lambs had said, very

good company; she was merry of word and look; she obviously
enjoyed her life; and when she ate mutton chops and drank up her
porter at the Lambs' table with obvious relish, or perched her feet
comfortably on the fender at night, sipped her brandy and water, three
parts brandy, and gossiped about Coleridge, Malta, her brother or her
own concerns, while Charles smoked and joked and Mary listened
indulgently, taking now and again a pinch of snuff, it was possible to
be as much at ease in Mitre Court as if only Charles and Mary were
present, or as if she had been a man. Most certainly she was "not in the
way."

Nor did Hazlitt find her a difficult guest when he himself entertained her to a meal. His pleasantest memories of her were connected
with eating and drinking. In the only so-called "love" letter of his to
her which has survived, he wrote: "I think I won your good liking
myself by giving you an entertainment of sausages when I had no
money to buy them with. Nay now, never deny it!"

It is ever Nature's way to diversify the traps whereby she compels
her children to her will. The man who has learned to avoid one kind
of snare may be caught by another kind, just because he is so intent on
avoiding the first that he has no thought of danger when he is near the
second. Hazlitt, who had become so wary in guarding himself against
one form of wounding, who certainly would have sought not to let
himself be ensnared or hurt by a woman who moved or attracted him
specially by her youth or grace, now came within the reach of a woman
against whom he put up no defences, just because he was not moved by
her, but who, having long wished to be married, now wished to be
married to *him*. Seeing much of her at the Lambs' fireside, presently he
found himself regarded by her as a lover, regarded also, perhaps before
he realised it, as her lover by other members of the circle of Lamb's
friends; and made, as he thought, the best of the matter in acquiescing
in the engagement which Miss Stoddart so obviously desired. The
warning of intuition was never quite silent, but it was low; and it was
all but drowned in the noise and chatter, the laughter and the chaffing
amid which his intimacy with Miss Stoddart was more or less rushed.
Afterwards he knew he should have regarded it. The warning he gave
to his son in after years shows this: "If you ever marry, I would wish
you to marry the woman you like. Do not be guided by the recommendation of friends. Nothing will atone for or overcome an original
distaste. It will only increase from intimacy."[190] Some hint as to the
complexity of the factors that conditioned the position in which he
found himself may also be contained in the words: "How few out of
the infinite number of those that marry and are given in marriage, wed
with those they would prefer to all the world; nay, how far the
greater proportion are joined together by the mere motives of convenience, accident, recommendation of friends, or not infrequently

by the very fear of the event, by repugnance and a sort of fatal fascination."[191]

Possibly all of these, convenience, accident, recommendation of friends, on the influence of which he touches more than once when he writes of marriage, and, he being what he was, "the very fear of the event," and "repugnance and a sort of fatal fascination"—combined to influence him.

However that may be, he was unfortunate in his choice. Miss Stoddart had some good qualities; but if she had every good quality under the sun, which she had not, she could not have satisfied the heart-hunger in Hazlitt unless she had had both sensitiveness and sensibility; in the first of these qualities she was notably lacking; of the second she had none at all. It would have been difficult to have found a woman who had less. Therefore it was not in the nature of things that Hazlitt and she, even if they lived together, would grow into each other, or take root in each other's lives. Fourteen years afterwards, when he flung out an utterly desperate word about her, the only word we know him to have uttered in criticism of her, it was because in a moment when he was in a frenzy of tortured nerves she pressed unendurably upon his sensibility. But when he met her in the autumn of 1807, she pressed upon his sensibility less than a younger woman would have done, because she moved him less. She was not a girl, and because W.H. was W.H. and no other HE—that, we believe, was what conditioned this very curious union. He was to a great extent the victim of his own morbid fear of the qualities in Woman which attracted him most. Of the two, the lady had the more reason to be satisfied with the precipitate engagement. She might have said as truthfully as Lamb: "as I am not a young girl myself, he is a great acquisition."

5

By the end of the year Hazlitt had said nothing to Dr. Stoddart of the engagement. He did not much care for Stoddart, and he had reason to think that Stoddart did not care for him. Also, he knew that the first thing Stoddart would talk about would be marriage settlements, and this, for a man who had nothing to live on except the money he earned now and again by portrait-painting or the publication of books of a kind little likely to be popular, would be not a little humiliating. But apart from this distaste to approaching Stoddart, he had fallen ill before December the 21st, the date on which Mary Lamb had tried to get Miss Stoddart to urge him to take up the matter. The illness was one of those low nervous disorders into which Hazlitt fell two or three times in his life, usually after periods of crisis, illnesses arising as much from spiritual as from physical causes, and characterised by such an ebbing of vitality and "almost inconceivable dejection" that they seemed to come near to making a ghost of him. Day by day he sat in his room at 34 Southampton Buildings looking into the fire; if he turned over his manuscripts it was with a very listless hand, and usually before he had added a line to them he went to sleep over them. Now and again he crawled about the room like a cripple, or went to examine his picture, to which he had not the heart or energy to add a stroke. During the Christmas season of 1807, when all his friends were gathering together at their various homes, he was to be found in none of his usual haunts. It was with the good-natured intention of rousing him from his languor and apathy that Lamb, just when the Christmas season had passed without bringing any one a glimpse of W. H., concocted an elaborate and fantastic joke, in carrying out the various stages of which he was ably seconded by Joseph Hume, designed to give him a hint that it was time he returned to the haunts of men and to lure him back to them. The joke might not have been to every man's taste, and it may be thought a joke not peculiarly cheering to one who felt himself to be becoming half a ghost, but Lamb's friends understood his ways, and Hazlitt entered into it with as much spirit as he could summon. It opened with an announcement sent on December 29th to Joseph Hume of Hazlitt's death:

"I suppose you know not what has happen'd to our poor friend Hazlitt. If not, take it as I read it in *The Morning Post* or *Fashionable World* of this morning:—

"' Last night Mr. H. a portrait-painter in Southampton Buildings, Holborn, put an end to his existence by cutting his throat in a shocking manner. It is supposed that he must have committed his purpose with a pallet-knife, as the edges of the cicatrice or wound were found besmeared with a yellow consistence, but the knife could not be found. The reasons of this rash act are not assigned; an unfortunate passion has been mentioned; but nothing certain is known. The deceased was subject to hypochondria, low spirits, but he had lately seemed better, having paid more than usual attention to his dress and person. Besides being a painter, he had written some pretty things in prose and verse.'"

Hume replied to this in a letter which he described as written in the "swelling sorrow" of his heart, and the documents were forwarded to 34 Southampton Buildings so that Hazlitt's contribution might be added to them. That the joke did not serve its immediate purpose of drawing Hazlitt forth we know from Hume's letter to him of January 13th:

"For God's sake come down here, and convince those silly fellows
. . . that talk about your death, that you are alive.
           "Yours until death,
                                    "JOSEPH HUME."

But it drew from Hazlitt on January 10th that amazing piece of
self-portraiture[192] which brings him nearer to us than anything he
wrote up to his thirtieth year, and which in turn drew from Lamb,
who affected to treat it as a forgery or a ghostly communication, the
inimitable thumb-nail sketch of "the Defunct" as being "of a gloomy
and close aspect, *as born under Saturn.*"[193] This self-portrait brings
Hazlitt nearer to us, indeed, than any of his later self-portraits do,
for they were dashed down in the middle of work intended for the
public eye, while this was written for intimate friends who understood
his "humour." Even after we have made all allowances for the spirit
of the jest, the tone of raillery in which it was written and the vein of
continuous irony in which it was conceived, we feel that what is breath-
taking about the portrait is the fidelity of it. It is humorous, but the
humour is of quite a different quality from that of Lamb's or Hume's
contributions. It is sad as Swift's. In this exquisitely entertaining
piece of work, if anywhere, is the justification of the curious reference
Coleridge made after Hazlitt's death to the "misanthropic sadness"
of his early years, a reference which seems to suggest that Coleridge
found something morbid in it, and that the basis of it might be some
physical morbidity. This strange piece of self-portraiture is harrowing
in no less a degree than it is amusing. It is entitled: "The humble
petition and remonstrance of William Hazlitt, now residing at No. 34,
Southampton Buildings, in the parish of St. Ann's, Holborn, showing
that he is not dead." In a note he explains the reason why, having been
described as "a portrait-painter," he has left a blank line after his name:

"A blank is here left which the modesty of the writer would not
permit him to fill up. Perhaps he belonged to the class of *non-descripts*
rather than any other. The opinion of the world was divided: some
persons being inclined to regard him as a gentleman, and others
looking upon him as a low fellow. It is hard to say whether he ought
to be considered as an author, or a pourtrait-painter. It is certain that
he never painted any pictures but those of persons he hired to sit for
him, and though he wrote a number of books, it does not appear that
they were ever read by any body."

Is not this the very humour of Swift! Were ever "the accepted
hells" more quietly intimated!
    The "petition" aims at proving that the petitioner is not dead, by
"setting forth his manner of life," under several headings:

"And, first, that he, the said W. Hazlitt, has regularly for the last month rang the bell at eleven at night, which was considered as a sign for the girl to warm his bed, and this being done, he has gone to bed, and slept soundly for the next twelve or fourteen hours."

"Secondly, that every day about twelve or 1 o'clock he has got up, put on his clothes, drank his tea, and eat two plate-fulls of buttered toast, of which he had taken care to have the hard edges pared off as hurtful to the mouth and gums, and that he has then sat for some hours with his eyes stedfastly fixed upon the fire, like a person in a state of deep thought, but doing nothing."

"Thirdly, that not a day has passed in which he has not eat and drank like other people. For instance, he has swallowed eight dozen of pills, nine boluses, and as many purgative draughts of a most unsavoury quality. What he has fed on with the most relish has been a mess of chicken-broth, and he has sent out once or twice for almonds and raisins. His general diet is soup-meagre with bread and milk for supper. That it is true that the petitioner has abstained both from gross feeding and from all kinds of intoxicating liquors; a circumstance, as he conceives, so far from denoting a natural decay and loss of his faculties, that on the contrary it shows more wisdom than he was always possessed of."

"Fourthly, that in regard to decency he has been known to walk out at least once a week to get himself shaved."

"Fifthly, that growing tired of his sedentary posture, he has occasionally got up from his chair and walked across the room (not as an *automaton* or a dead man pulled with wires might be supposed to do, but with . . . . an inequality in his gait, resembling a limp). At one time he turned the front of his great picture to the light, but finding the subject painful to him, he presently turned it to the wall again. Also, that he has attempted to read some of his own works, but has fallen asleep over them."

"Sixthly, that the said W.H. has, it being Christmas time, received several invitations to entertainments and parties of pleasure, which he politely declined; but that on occasions he has generally about the hour of four in the afternoon been tormented with the apparition of a fat goose or a sirloin of beef."

"Seventhly, that in compliment to the season, and to show a fellow-feeling with his absent guests, he has ordered a wine-glass and a decanter of water to be set upon the table, and has drank off a glass or two, making a show as if it were port or sherry, but that he desisted from this practice after a few trials, not finding it answer."

Among other activities which he cites as evidence of continued life are that he had been known to borrow money within the past three weeks, that he had held more than one argument which nobody could understand but himself, and that he had made several good resolutions which were to be put into practice as soon as he had recovered from his illness: "as namely, to live better than he had lately ,done, not to refuse an invitation to a haunch of venison, nor to decline drinking to a lady's health, to pay a greater attention to cleanliness, and to leave off wenching, as injurious both to the health and morals."

His "Lastly" scores beautifully off Hume: "Lastly, as there are some appearances against him, and he is aware that almost everything goes by appearances, in case it should be determined that he is a dead man and that he must be buried against his will, he submits to this decision, but with two provisos, first, that he shall be allowed to appear as chief mourner at his own funeral, secondly that he shall have leave to appoint Joseph Hume, Esq., of the Victualling Office his executor and administrator of his effects, as a man of prudence and discretion, well-looked on in the world, and the only person he knows, who will not be witty on the occasion!"

There follows a list of his "effects and valuables," chiefly pictures and copies of pictures which "should be principally appropriated to pay his apothecary's and washerwomen's bills."

Here we see Hazlitt in the process of transition from the energy of his youth into the initial stages of that alteration which gradually resulted in his becoming in later years the man we can discern *through* the distortions of P. G. Patmore's portraiture of him. The late rising, the tea-drinking, the apparent complete inertia of the hours spent in meditation, the languid walk, the wistfulness of the abstinence from wine, the suggestion of the habit of abstraction carried to such a point that it seemed at times to cancel out physical life—all are here, but as yet connected only with a passing bout of illness, which for the moment had made the threads that bound him to existence seem finespun and rare.

The "petition" not only conveys to the reader the languid pulsation of Hazlitt's life at the moment. It gives more than one hint as to the light in which he regarded his engagement. His "Eighthly" adduces his recent amorous exertions as proof of continued life:

"Eighthly, be it known that the person, concerning whom such idle reports are prevalent, has actually within the given time written a number of love letters, and that a man must be dead indeed, if he is not alive when engaged in that agreeable employment. And lest it should be suggested that these epistles resemble Mrs. Rowe's *Letters from the Dead to the Living*, being just such vapid, lifeless compositions, it may be proper to state, by way of counteracting any such calumny, that they are full of nothing but ingenious conceits and *double entendres*, without a single *grave* remark from beginning to end. Farther that they had some life in them, he is assured by the quickness of the answers, which he received with that sort of pleasing titillation and gentle palpitation common to flesh and blood, reading them with alternate smiles and sighs, and once letting fall a tear at a description given by the lady of the ruinous state of a cottage or tenement, which he hopes one day to call his own."

He adds: "That as it is possible he may not after all be able to defeat the arts of his calumniators, who may persuade the young lady before alluded to that the petitioner is a dead man, not able to go through the ordinary functions of life, that he has therefore formed divers plans for his future maintenance and creditable appearance in the world, as writing a tragedy, setting up as a quack doctor, or entering into holy orders."

The "petition" closes with a postscript on his engagement:

"Whereas it is scandalously and falsely asserted in a written paper circulated at the expense of the above-named W.H. that he has been heard to spout amourous verses, and sing licentious ditties and burthens of old songs with his latest breath, a number of penny ballads and verses being also strewed about his room in an indecent manner, he begs leave to state that the only song he has once thought of of late is the Cuckoo song, but that this has run a good deal in his head, and that he has often broken out into the following verse:

' Mocks married men from tree to tree.'

Also once, upon receiving some expressions of tender concern and anxious inquiries into the cause of his illness from a person that shall be nameless, he sung in a faint manner the following parody on two lines in the *Beggar's Opera*:

' For on the pill that cures my dear
    Depends poor Polly's life! '"

To us it seems, even allowing for the jest which called forth these allusions, that there is something *falsetto* about them, as coming from Hazlitt, and that the impression they give is of a relationship that is spongy and unsound. "*Double entendres* from a man in love!" Joseph Hume exclaimed with mock-piety in his commentary on the "petition." "Too absurd, too absurd!" This at any rate was perfectly true in its application to Hazlitt. He was the last man on earth to make *double entendres* when he loved, and he could torture himself almost to death, and make a monstrous pother for others, if he thought that there was the least suspicion of a *double entendre* about any of the utterances of the woman he loved. No matter what he might do, in the last recesses

of his mind, of his thought, and of his feeling, he was inalterably a
Puritan, even a Puritan of the bitter kind. The flippant reference to his
love-letters is only one more piece of evidence tending to show that at
the moment of framing the "petition" he was as far from being in love
as he had ever been in his life.

He was ill, however, tired, in a reaction of utter lassitude from the
strain of the continuous labours on which he had been engaged from
the opening of 1804 to the summer of 1807, in a reaction of lassitude
also after the strain of the brisk comedy-courtship in which he had been
engaged, or to which he had been exposed.

A couple of days after concocting his "petition" he wrote to Miss
Stoddart, and his letter, were it not that it contains one or two business
suggestions and that it tends to stray off into an essay on Boccaccio's
heroes, might serve as an illustration of what he had said of his love-
letters, that they were full of nothing "but ingenious conceits and
double entendres." "What is become of you?" he writes. "Are you
married, hearing that I was dead (for so it has been reported)? Or are
you gone into a nunnery? Or are you fallen in love with some of the
amorous heroes of Boccaccio?"[194]

Here he plays on the theme of Boccaccio's heroes, and on the
jealousy he would feel of them, did he not know "that a living dog is
better than a dead lion."

Two days later he continues the letter, thanking her for a book
of extracts she had sent him:

"The book is come. When I saw it I thought that you had sent it
back in a *huff*, tired out by my sauciness and *coldness*, and delays, and
were going to keep an account of dimities and sayes, or to salt pork and
chronicle small beer as the dutiful wife of some fresh-looking rural
swain; so that you cannot think how surprised and pleased I was to
find them all done.

"I liked your note as well or better than the extracts; it is just such
a note as a nice rogue as you ought to write after the *provocation* you
had received. I would not give a pin for a girl whose ' cheeks never
tingle ' nor for myself if I could not make them tingle sometimes.
Now, though I am always writing to you about ' lips and noses ' and
such sort of stuff, yet as I sit by my fire-side (which I do generally
eight or ten hours a day) I oftener think of you in a serious sober light.
For indeed, I never love you half so well as when I think of sitting
down with you to dinner on a boiled scrag-end of mutton, and hot
potatoes. You please my fancy more then than when I think of you in
—no, you would never forgive me if I were to finish the sentence.

"Now I think of it, what do you mean to be dressed in when we are
married? But it does not much matter! I wish you would let your hair
grow; though perhaps nothing will be better than ' the same air and

look with which at first my heart was took.' But now to business. I mean soon to call on your brother, *in form*, namely, as soon as I get quite well, which I hope to do in about another *fortnight*, and then I hope you will come up by the coach as fast as the horses can carry you, for I long mightily to be in your ladyship's presence—to vindicate my character."[195]

The sprightliness of this letter seems to us to ripple over an under-current of that perfunctoriness or *coldness* of which—as we saw—Miss Stoddart had complained in the earlier days of the relationship. He appears to know that he has laid himself open to the charge of careless-ness and to be prepared to repudiate it, yet without any of the energy in such a matter which was characteristic of him when he was in earnest.

It is curious, too, to find him introducing, we might almost say dragging, into this letter a reference to a former "flame" of his, almost as if he wished his bride-to-be to have no illusions as to his constancy, or as if he wished to dispel any suggestion that he was to be regarded as a "one-woman" man:

"Talking of departed loves, I met my old flame[196] the other day in the street. I did dream of her *one* night since and only one. Every other night I have had the same dream I have had for two months past. Now if you are at all reasonable, this will satisfy you."

The tone of this is utterly in contrast to the tone of any of his genuine love-letters, which have at the core of their abandonment a wild self-abasement.

6

The nicest thing in all this elaborate epistle is the simplest thing in it, the word on which it closes: "Goodbye, little dear!" When a month all but a few days since the Tuesday in January on which he had begun it, had passed in lingering illness, he left town suddenly, on the afternoon of Saturday, February 6th. The Lambs, knowing that he was still ill, took it for granted that he had gone to Wem to get some of the care he needed.

A few days after his departure Mary Lamb had a letter from Miss Stoddart, enclosing a drawing of the cottage in which she lived at Winterslow. Thinking that Hazlitt would like to have it, she sent it off at once to Wem. In the meantime, she busied herself with trying to smooth the way of the engaged couple with Dr. Stoddart, who had at length been told of the match, and who, although not actually enthusiastic, seemed quite friendly towards it. Mary had been wishing to invite Sarah to town, but she thought it wise to consult Dr. Stoddart first of all about this, and on doing so she had found that he felt it would have "a very strange appearance" if his sister stayed at any house but his own in the months preceding her marriage; he could not ask her to stay at his own until nearly the end of April, as he had visitors until then, but after that time he would be free to receive her. He also expressed his desire that if his sister were to be married it should be "*from his house*" and "*with all proper decorums.*".

On February 12th Mary wrote to Miss Stoddart at length about this, explaining that she was ready to invite her if there were no other way of arranging a meeting with Hazlitt, but that it seemed a pity to offend Dr. Stoddart, for all the difference a few weeks would make. On the other hand, if Sarah were determined to be married in London before the date on which her brother could receive her into his house, the Lambs were quite ready to invite her, even at the risk of offending Dr. Stoddart. Mary had thought the matter over carefully and she felt that while she was very reluctant to incur any unnecessary hostility, she was ready enough to bear the brunt of any friction arising out of such action as might be necessary to her friend's happiness. As she put it in her letter: "Let there be a clear necessity shewn, and we will quarrel with any body's brother."[197]

Some days afterwards there came to the Lambs a letter from old Mr. Hazlitt, who was agitated because the letter and enclosure from Mitre Court had duly reached them, but of William, or of any intention on his part of arriving there, nothing had been heard. Naturally he wanted such news as they could give him of his son.

Charles set out to get such information as he could. On inquiring at 34 Southampton Buildings he found that directions had been given for Hazlitt's shirts to be forwarded to Winterslow, and that Hazlitt himself was not expected to return until the beginning of March. It was then on the eighty-mile journey to Winterslow that he had set out, ill though he had been, on the afternoon of the 4th. The drawing of Middleton Cottage had been his. He had hoaxed them nicely. Even as Mary had been writing, conveying Dr. Stoddart's feelings as to the necessity of preserving "all proper decorums," and preparing the way for a marriage that would have the full approval of the bride's brother, the two indecorous ones had been enjoying together the joke they had pulled off at the expense of their patient mentor, who after that was more inclined to leave them—as she said somewhat dryly—to their "own inventions."

It was not Hazlitt's way to abuse Mary Lamb's considerateness, but it was the merry Sarah's way to be involved not infrequently in petty friction, and sometimes, because of the odd combination of lack of discretion and lack of candour in her nature, to be the occasion of

HAZLITT AT THE TIME OF HIS FIRST MARRIAGE

friction between others: so perhaps we may take it that this time the woman tempted him.

That they had some rubs with Dr. Stoddart afterwards which must have been somewhat galling to Hazlitt we gather from Lamb's letter of the 26th to Manning: "A treaty of marriage is on foot between William Hazlitt and Miss Stoddart. Something about settlements only retards it."

The remainder of the chronicle of the from-day-to-day doings of this little group of friends and acquaintances whose lives were in one way or another interlinked during the spring of 1808 may be given in one breath:

That S.T.C. having come to town in January and gone to roost, bemused and unhappy, in rooms over the *Courier* Office, had begun a course of lectures and had broken down miserably in the second of these, delivered on the day before W.H. left town; that W.W. came to town at the end of the month to save S.T.C. from despair, but found, to his chagrin, that S.T.C. was too much occupied with affairs to have leisure to receive him except during the evenings; that W.H. returned from Winterslow; that Miss Stoddart followed him long before the time indicated by her brother as decorous, and that "Hazlitt and his beloved," as W.W. called them, became the chief glories of the "Wednesday evenings," while S.T.C. in the meantime hurt the Lambs by never coming; that W.W. came one night in March, but was glacial, thawed, however, sufficiently in the course of the evening to read the beginning of *The White Doe*, and draw W.H.'s attention to a passage which "*ought*" to interest him "as a Painter;" that Miss Stoddart worked a beautiful border for Mary Lamb, which Mary insisted on giving to Peggy Hazlitt, because, as she said: "Her brother William is her great favourite, and she would be proud to receive his bride's last work;" that Manning sent Mary a beautiful piece of Chinese silk, of "a dead-whiteish-bloom colour," which he wished her to wear at Hazlitt's wedding; that on the first day of May, 1808—it was the day on which a Spanish peasant struck down and killed a French soldier in the streets of Madrid, thus ushering in the war in Spain—William Hazlitt and Sarah Stoddart entered into the bonds of holy matrimony, all difficulties about marriage settlements having been at last negotiated, at St Andrew's Church, Holborn, where they were married by special licence; that Mary Lamb was the bridesmaid, and that Charles was at the wedding but behaved without "proper decorums," yet atoned for this, at least in the eyes of posterity, by leaving an apology[198] for his conduct on which the imagination can play as it listeth:

"I was at Hazlitt's marriage, and had like to have been turned out several times, during the ceremony. Any thing awful makes me laugh!"

Chapter Three

WINTERSLOW (1808-1811)

"You cannot think how very much we miss you and H. of a Wednesday evening. All the glory of the night, I may say, is at an end. Phillips makes his jokes, and there is no one to applaud him; Rickman argues, and there is no one to oppose him.

"The worst miss of all to me is, that when we are in the dismals, there is now no hope of relief from any quarter whatsoever. Hazlitt was most brilliant, most ornamental, as a Wednesday-man; but he was a more useful one on common days, when he dropt in after a quarrel or a fit of the glooms."

MARY LAMB *to* SARAH HAZLITT.

I

DURING the years of the Spanish war, while Wordsworth, from amid all the things which were the sources of his strength,

"dark wood and rocky cave
And hollow vale which foaming torrents fill
With omnipresent murmur as they rave
Down their steep beds, that never shall be still:"

pondered "the hopes and fears of suffering Spain," Hazlitt watched the developments in the new theatre of war from a solitude no less deep. Directly after his marriage he made his home in Winterslow. He tells us that he has no idea at the time he settled in Winterslow of ever becoming "a voluminous writer." This must mean that he still hoped to earn his bread mainly by painting. He took commissions for portraits when he could get them; he spent much of his time in sketching; he continued work on his "great picture." Yet it is in connection with a new literary project that we see him most clearly. His confidence was unshaken that his mind contained a portion of truth which would not let him rest until he had imparted it to the world. Part of this truth was concerned with metaphysics; and it was on metaphysics that his mind was most steadily at work during the months following upon his marriage. He was meditating a work on English philosophy through which he felt that he could enlighten and clarify the thought of his time, and in which he could to some extent fulfil himself. This work, which was to be far more ambitious than anything he had as yet attempted, he planned and pondered, and by the end of the year he had come to a conclusion as to the form it was to take. He was confident of his power to write it. His only fear was that it might be difficult to get a publisher for a philosophical work of the proportions he envisaged.

He had many sources of simple happiness during these early months at Winterslow. First of all he had again a home. Of Hazlitt, during great stretches of his life, it might be said, "He seldom had any home," and this explains much about him. So little did he ever complain of the material conditions of his life—for his treasure was in the things of the spirit and almost all his repining was over spiritual disappointment of one kind or another—that it is not generally realised how hard the years had been for him since he had set out to earn his living. There had been the months of poor, hard, bare living in Paris; the equally precarious days of portrait-painting that had followed, during which he had passed to one set of lodgings after another; the attempt to make a living in London by portrait-painting and by executing heavy, ill-paid, almost thankless literary tasks of one kind or another, which had culminated in a lingering illness or breakdown of the vital forces, at the end of 1807 and the beginning of 1808. These days had their ups as well as their downs, but they certainly had many downs.

It is not easy to see how he found the wherewithal to set up a home. One of Mary Lamb's letters suggests that his family may have helped. She wrote to Miss Stoddart on December 21st, 1807: "Hazlitt's brother is mightily pleased with the match; but he says you must have furniture, and be clear in the world at first setting out, or you will always be behindhand. He also said he would give you what furniture he could spare." Hazlitt himself, on January 12th, 1808, wrote lightheartedly enough to "his beloved" as to ways and means: "I think you had better sell the small house, I mean that at £4.10, and I will borrow £100. So that we shall set off merrily in spite of all the prudence of Edinburgh."[199] Apart from these hints, there is nothing to indicate how he managed. Possibly he added very little to the few things that must have been in the cottage when Miss Stoddart had lived in it by herself. We know that the furnishing was very bare. But in Winterslow a home he had, and a home that he loved. He had a roof of his own over his head and a roof that was none the less dear to him because it was a cottage-roof; and this home of his was within reach of much that he loved not only in nature but in art. Wilton House, just over three miles from Salisbury, and Longford Castle, which contained two fine Claudes, the "Morning" and "Evening" of the Roman Empire, and a Magdalen by Guido, with streaming hair and streaming eyes looking upwards—were then open to the public. Stourhead was less than twenty-six miles from Salisbury. Fonthill Abbey, although then sealed against the curiosity of visitors, was within walking distance. Stonehenge, the "huge, dumb heap," as he called it, which meant more to him than perhaps any of these, was also near. This was exactly as he would have wished things to be. "I should always choose to live within reach of a fine prospect, rather than to see one from my windows," he confessed in after years. "A number of romantic, distant objects staring in upon one (uncalled for) tantalise the imagination and tempt the truant feet; whereas, at home, I wish to feel satisfied where I am, and sheltered from the world."[200]

When he returned from expeditions to these places, or from the many shorter ones he made, to the place where he felt "sheltered from the world," he found within its low and narrow walls much of what he loved most also—the paraphernalia of his painting, of which Charles Lamb made such fun, sometimes such gruesome fun, scattered about his small room, the picture on which he was immediately engaged, his few books, and some fine prints from Claude, on "the fleecy flocks, the bending trees, the winding streams, the nodding temples, the air-wove hills" of which he could dwell for ever, trying "to translate them" into the lovely, living hues of the originals. There was one, of the Arch of Constantine, which day after day he could contemplate with delight by the hour together. Of it he wrote in after years: "It was the most graceful, the most perfect of all Claude's compositions. . . . Never was there scene so fair, 'so absolute, that in itself sumn'd all delight.'"[201] On this print he was wont to gaze literally like one enamoured, for he kept imagining in the meantime the colouring of the original—the trees of vernal green, the sky like that of a mild dawn or softened evening.[202]

His felicity was complete when he was able to add to these prints a set of the Cartoons of Raphael. Then indeed he had "Infinite riches in a little room."

The second source of his joy was the country itself. In its air he could recover his strength; in its peace his thoughts could mature; in its beauty his eyes found delight that renewed itself day by day with the rising and the setting sun. Winterslow and its peace was after all the best gift his marriage brought him. He came to love it almost as he had loved Wem, and to associate with certain places, even as he had done in Wem, moments in which he had felt intensely. Places, like facts, for him still continued to have meaning only when they became transmuted into thought or feeling. There was one spot which he never passed without thinking of *The Flower and the Leaf*, which he had first read there, and of the pleasure he had got from the poem and the way in which the thought of the young beauty, shrouded in her bower and listening with ever-fresh delight to the repeated song of the nightingale close by her, had charmed him; there was another which he associated with the cry of hounds, ever since he had one day seen "the fatal group" issuing from the wood, as the "mastiffs gaunt and grim" had issued in the tale of Theodore and Honoria; there was a third which always brought back to his memory the day on which he had come upon a wood-pigeon dabbled in its own blood, lying at the foot of a tree, and had pitied it as "it left its little life in air." There were many other places thus charactered for him by the memory of feeling. One of these was a low sheltered valley on Salisbury Plain. Strolling one day along the margin of a stream, skirted with willows and plashy sedges, in this remote recess he was startled when, all of a sudden, the sound of an organ fell on his ear, accompanied by the sweet singing of village maids and children. It came from a little parish church near, but as tall elms and quivering alders had hidden this completely from his sight, at the moment it seemed to him as if the earth itself had broken into song. The sound rose like an exhalation and filled the valley like a mist. He felt as if the dew from a thousand pastures were gathered into its softness; as if the silence of a thousand years spoke in it.

These low valleys on Salisbury Plain seemed to him hardly less suggestive of other days and of other life than Stonehenge itself lifting up its pale head above its barren bosom.

Then at Winterslow also he had perfect conditions for his work. He looked on the country around him with a painter's eye, selected what he pleased, and painted what he pleased, working according to his own mood. From morning to night he could be completely happy in work of this kind, when the inspiration moved him. He was, if anything, even more fortunate in the conditions of his intellectual work. For him, as for Rousseau, time for that long and patient soliciting of the mind in which alone his work could reach fruition was absolutely necessary to his well-being. In town he did not stint himself of this. When he sat for hours, with an appearance of curious inertia, looking into the fire, he was engaged on this patient and prolonged communion with his mind. But like Rousseau, he felt that his mind was never so much alive as in the country. He was never more conscious of its infinite movement than he was when among the woods or fields. He spent many an hour of intellectual no less than physical gymnastic when walking. But sometimes he was most busy when most idle, lying so still that he might have been a log flung under one of the great trees in the woods of Tudorleigh, or motionless on Salisbury Plain, apparently engaged in endless contemplation of the sheep nibbling at the short sweet grass.

The work itself also was of all work that which was most congenial to him.

His satisfaction in his life had little to do with his intercourse with the country-people around him. He, who never had had any illusions as to the character of country-people, felt the inhabitants of the cottages around his own in Winterslow to be very much like those of any other English village he had known. They read little, yet they were always employed in "hearing or telling some new thing." Their books were the lives of their neighbours. He said of them that the draw-well was the source from which they pumped up idle rumours, and the blacksmith's shop the place at which they forged the proofs. Scandal, gossip, and local rumour meant far more to them than any of the doings of the outside world. Having no need of books, they tended to despise them, and to regard the writer who had come to be a settler on their soil almost as a cumberer of the ground. He seems to have sensed in them some vague hostility towards himself. "The people here cannot tell how an author gets his living or passes his time," he wrote of them in one of his essays, "and they would fain hunt him out of the place as they do a strange dog, or as they formerly did a conjurer or witch." Perhaps the best suggestion as to his relationship with his cottage neighbours is that given in some lines usually attributed to Mary Lamb, although Charles may have had a hand in them too:

> "There lives at Winterslow a man of such
> Rare talents and deep learning, that by much
> Too wise he's counted by his country neighbours;
> And all his learned literary labours
> Occasion give for many a wild surmise.
> Even his person in their rustic eyes
> Has somewhat strange in it, his sallow looks
> His deep o'erhanging brows when o'er his books
> (Which written are in characters unknown)
> He pores whole hours with a most solemn frown."

They may not have been hostile to him, as he thought, but most certainly they felt, as the Keswick rustics had done, that he was not a bird of their feather. In their own way they were pronouncing him, as Coleridge in earlier days had pronounced him, "brow-hanging, shoe-contemplative," and above all, what is most offensive of all to people whose minds run in a rut—"*strange.*"

Yet we get glimpses of him holding converse with them, sympathising with the hardships of their lot, understanding the tedium or the anxieties which occasioned some of their vices, and being helpful or neighbourly when the opportunity to be so offered itself.

We have said that Winterslow was the best gift Hazlitt's wife brought to him, yet it is to be noted that in all the many glimpses he gives of himself in its loved places we never see him companioned by her. This must have been because, as she had never touched his imagination, he could not share with her the secret of the sources of the life he drew from it, her exclusion from it being on his part at this time not voluntary, but a matter over which he had no control. It is not clear to us how much he discerned of her nature in these early days beyond those things which were obvious to everybody, that she was vivacious and pleasure-loving, that she had plenty of animal spirits, that she added lustre to a social evening and was a pleasant and reliable person to have at a card-party, that she was unaffected and hospitable, and that there was no malice in her; but his marriage, in its early days, seems to have been happy enough, and to have included in it companionship of a kind, even if it were companionship on a different plane from that on which he lived his essential life. Possibly he realised even before his marriage that it would be thus. At any rate, he had given Miss Stoddart fair warning at the beginning of 1808 as to the things he expected most to enjoy in her company. But there were so many things, not touching the essentials of his nature, yet necessary to his daily life, and pleasant enough, in which she could share—bed and board among them—that she may not have realised how much there was in his life which she did not, and could not share; while he, for his part, may have found sitting down to dinner with her "on a boiled scrag-end of mutton and hot potatoes," with perhaps a few mushrooms fresh-gathered from the fields thrown into the dish, just as pleasant as he had told her before their marriage he anticipated it would be.

Yet there was one "hidden sting." We have said that Hazlitt, although his actions by no means squared with his theories, was puritanical to the core. His bond with Puritanism was as strong as if it had been formed "of all the cables of the British navy," for it was a triple-woven bond, the strands of which were those of inheritance, of temperament, and of training. This Puritanism sometimes showed itself in his dealings with men. Although he was himself "no flincher" in words, there was no saying when he would turn upon in anger or away in disgust from any one who seemed to him guilty of actual grossness or foulness in thought or speech. Joseph Hume, who was at times not "nice" enough in his choice of words to please this fastidious companion of his, bantered him occasionally upon the contracted brow and scornful movements of the mouth with which he at times rebuked any conversation "that might not altogether square with his most squeamish and maidenly delicacy."[203] Despite all the fluctuations of passion, Hazlitt's estimates of the women he valued were conditioned by this Puritanism. The inherited Puritanism in him was so deep that it was all but impossible for him to make any allowance for any deviation—on the part of a woman who shared his life—from the strictest lines of conventional morality, or even from the forms of virtue. This being so, it remained with him as a rankling, deep-lying grievance, tending to erupt in moments of crisis, that his wife had not been a virgin at the time of her marriage to him. This affected him less in the early days of their marriage than afterwards, for his temperament being what it was, this was the kind of sore that gradually worked its way inwards. Its presence explains to some extent his ways towards his wife in the later years of their marriage, the licence he allowed himself throughout their married life, his lack of tenderness, and his final dealings with her.

How little chance the first Sarah in his life had of making headway against his feeling in such a matter may be gathered from his own bitter words:

"to find that a woman whom we loved has forfeited her character, is the same thing as to learn that she is dead!"[204]

2

If Hazlitt sometimes sensed in the minds of the country-folk around him, who earned their bread by the sweat of their brow, some dim grudge against him, amounting to a feeling that a man "*ought*" not to live by pen and ink, he was yet resolute in his will to earn some, at least, of his bread by the sweat of his brain. He had a roof over his head, and his wife's small income would keep them from starving, but it was urgently necessary for him to earn all he could both by writing and by painting, if they were going to live in any real sense of the word as distinguished from merely keeping themselves alive. His sense of urgency must have been stimulated by the birth of his first child, a boy who like his father and his father's father was named William, on January 15th, 1809. About this time we find him endeavouring to make arrangements that would ensure the publication of the book on metaphysics he had planned. He had decided to cast what he meant to say into the mould of a History of Modern English Philosophy, in which he meant to give an account of English philosophy from the time of Bacon onwards; to comment on and expose some of the falsities of the materialistic philosophy of his own day, based, as it seemed to him, on a misapplication of Bacon's appeal to experience and on "a wrong interpretation of the word experience;" and "to lay the foundation of a system more conformable to reason and experience, and in its practical results, at least, approaching nearer to the common sense of mankind," than the one which had been generally accepted throughout the past century. Knowing that his work would run contrary to the trend of accepted opinion, or, as he put it, "to the fashionable paradoxes" of the moment, he felt that it would have little chance of making its way unless he could rely on some initial support for his venture. Therefore he composed a Prospectus of the proposed History, and had it printed for him. By the middle of February he was engaged in forwarding it to such as he thought might be interested in such a project and likely to subscribe to it, along with a letter in which he solicited support for the work. The project was very near his heart, and the book was of the kind he would most enjoy writing, if only he could secure such patronage as might make it reasonable to proceed with a task that would be long and laborious, and possibly costly in some of the research involved. His eagerness is shown in the letter he enclosed along with the Prospectus to Mr. Windham, whom at the time he considered the ablest speaker in the House of Commons, Sheridan alone excepted:

"Sir,—I take the liberty to offer to your notice the enclosed Prospectus. I have no other excuse to make for the intrusion than that I believe the design of the work is such as may meet with your approbation—and the natural wish of every one that what has employed many years of his life and many anxious thoughts may not be entirely lost."

The list of Contents in the Prospectus is followed by the essay called Plan of the Work. In this fine clear stretch of prose Hazlitt shows the keen interest in what would to-day be called Psychology (although in his day it was included in the name Metaphysics) with which his later essays are saturated, and which constitutes one of their chief preservatives and one of the chief sources of their power to interest.

Shortly after the Prospectus had been printed he went up to town. As it is almost always in pursuit of one or another of his plans that we find him in London during the years in which his home was at Winterslow, it is reasonable to assume that his visit was made with the object of pushing the fortunes of his book. His exposition of what he had meant to do in his History of English Philosophy might have been expected to win subscribers for the work. Not only was it Literature: it was obviously the work of a man who both possessed his subject and was possessed by it. Horne Tooke, Godwin, and still more, his "Patron," Richard Sharp,[205] might have been expected to lend powerful support to such a project. Yet we do not know of a single subscriber whom he gained; and we do know that he did not meet with sufficient encouragement to justify him in proceeding with a work of such scope. Hazlitt, while at the height of his powers, was yet obscure. In later years, when what he regarded as ephemeral work had brought him fame, he had neither the time nor the energy for the prosecution of a task like this, requiring a long-sustained effort of mind, if the book were to be as he wished it to be. Thus passed his chance of writing for what he, like Coleridge, regarded as The Permanent. If he had had even a small regular income—as Wordsworth, Coleridge and Southey all had—there is no saying what he might have done. But all his life he was bare to the wind.

All that we know of him during this visit to town is that he was labouring under some nervous stress. The hatefulness, to him, of having to solicit subscribers, and the ill success of his effort, may have accounted for this. Afterwards he excused himself for not having called on Henry Robinson on the score of the nervous tension he had felt while in town after coming up to it from the country: "my being in the Country makes me more nervous than I generally am." But apart from his own disappointment, there were other things that might press on him. The Lambs were about to leave their "dear, old, dirty chambers" at Mitre Court, and both they and their Mitre-Courtiers were feeling in a certain measure "unsettled and unhomed" over this. Holcroft—no longer angry Holcroft, but pathetic Holcroft, begging the doctor to keep him alive but six months longer, so that he could complete some record of his strange hard life—was dying. On his deathbed he was dictating, a single word at a time, those Memoirs which by sheer force of will he succeeded in bringing up to his fifteenth year, and the simple and noble prose of which wrung from Byron one of his rare genuine words: "Holcroft's Memoirs are valuable as showing strength of endurance in the man, which is worth more than all the talent in the world." On Thursday, March 23rd, he died.

Shortly afterwards Hazlitt was recalled home to Winterslow by the illness of his child.

About the time of his going, the Lambs moved into his old lodgings at 34 Southampton Buildings, where they were to remain until their new rooms at No. 4 Inner Temple Lane were ready for them. They were both in miserable spirits. A letter which Mary wrote to young Louisa Martin on Wednesday, March 29th, and in which she mentioned Hazlitt's departure, is a tissue of melancholy news. When Charles took up the pen, his depression showed not in any confession of sadness, such as Mary had made, but in that curious forcing of humour almost to the point of heartlessness, or what might have seemed like heartlessness to one who did not know him, which was the protective armour he occasionally assumed against the assaults of melancholy. His master-piece in this vein is his embroidery of Mary's reference to the illness of the Hazlitt baby:

"Hazlitt's child died of swallowing a bag of white paint, which the poor little innocent thing mistook for sugar candy. It told its mother just two hours before that it did not like sugar candy, and so it came out, which was not before suspected. When it was opened several other things were found in it, particularly a small hearth brush, two golden pippins and a letter which I had written Hazlitt from Bath."

3

As Hazlitt was not allowed to get on with the work for which he offered himself, there was nothing left to him but to get on with the work which offered itself to him. He now threw all his energy into two tasks, both of them undertaken under Godwin's auspices. One of these was the preparation of *A New and Improved Grammar of the English Tongue*, which Godwin was to publish; the other was the completion of the records of Holcroft's life, based on materials placed in his hands by Mrs. Holcroft, and planned on lines agreed on in discussion with Godwin, who was at this time on very affectionate terms with him, who showed the greatest respect for his powers of mind, and who, although one of the least demonstrative of men, referred to him in the course of this year as "one of my inward friends."

In this work the second summer at Winterslow passed away. It was overshadowed for the Hazlitts by the illness of their child, and his death, on July 5th. To Hazlitt, who was very tender towards his children, the loss of his first-born was an enduring grief. They grieved too for the Lambs. Mary had hardly crossed the threshold of her new home in Inner Temple Lane before she was laid low by a severe attack of her malady. Charles, who spent a very desolate and lonely summer, was hardly less to be pitied.

But the autumn made them all some amends. In October Charles had a month's holiday, and Mary and he, along with Ned Phillips of "Wednesday" fame, came to Winterslow to spend it with the Hazlitts. Phillips slept and breakfasted at the "Hut," as the primitive little inn at Winterslow was called. The Lambs were under the Hazlitts' roof. Everything about the visit was perfect. The summer had been wet throughout, but October was brilliant and fine; the autumn flowers and the woods looked their best in the sunshine; and—although Lamb tells us that on one occasion Phillips sat at cards from sunrise to sunset, when the gorgeous colours of a never-to-be-forgotten sky over Salisbury Plain at last lured him from the table—for the most part they were all out of doors during the long succession of bright days, in the woods or walking on the plain or visiting the many interesting places in the neighbourhood. Their walks varied in length from eight to twenty miles a day. Charles was happy because he could see that Mary was recovering her strength, and could feel that she was getting her serenity back and even beginning to enjoy her life again: at any rate, she had well outdistanced the heavy shadows of the summer. Mary liked the long expeditions none the less because she grumbled a little sometimes as she followed Mrs. Hazlitt's brisk energetic footsteps or gasped a little as they went uphill. The evenings, in which they sat down to a substantial meat supper for which the day's walking had given them all good appetites, were no less pleasant. After supper they gathered round the fire, and talked or played cards—not without a quarrel or two—or roasted the nuts they had picked up during the day.

There was not one of them who was not the better of this memorable month. Charles, who had found the summer shattering, expressed what Mary and he felt about it when he wrote to Coleridge after his return to London: "The country has made us whole." Mrs. Godwin got the first benefit of his improved spirits. He told her that Hazlitt had found a well in his garden, which, water being scarce in that district, would bring him in two hundred a year, whereupon she came running round to Mary in great haste to ask if it were true! Mary wrote to her hostess: "The dear, quiet, lazy, delicious month we spent with you is remembered by me with such regret, that I feel quite discontent and Winterslow-sick. I assure you, I never passed such a pleasant time in the country in my life, both in the house and out of it." She tells of some of the things they did to remind them of their holiday: "We have got some salt butter to make our toast seem like yours, and we have tried to eat meat suppers, but that would not do, for we left our appetites behind us: and the dry loaf, which offended you, now comes in at night unaccompanied." But the excellent meat suppers have made an impression on Mary, for she goes on to say: "Jane and I have agreed to boil a round of beef for your suppers, when you come to town again."

Charles and she felt that the holiday was indeed over, when they went to Pimlico on the first Friday in November, and roasted the last of the Winterslow nuts at the Captain's. But when Lamb wrote to Manning, two months later, he thought it worth while to pass on the best of his holiday puns: "A constable in Salisbury Cathedral was telling me that eight people dined at the top of the spire of the cathedral, upon which I remarked, that they must be very sharp-set."

In the course of December, it looked as if Hazlitt might make an entry into journalism. This was owing to the help of Henry Robinson, whose influence, on Hazlitt's affairs, we may perhaps discern earlier in the course of the year.[205 (b)] Henry Robinson had been invited by Samuel Tipper, the publisher of *The London Review*, to collaborate in the production of this Quarterly, under Cumberland. He took the opportunity of speaking to Cumberland of Hazlitt's talents, and suggested that this new ally should be invited to join them. Hazlitt was delighted with the proposal, although in accepting it he showed a touch of diffidence. "I am obliged to you for thinking of me as a coadjutor in the Review," he wrote in the beginning of December,[206] "and am willing to try what I can do in the way you proposed to the Editor. I am only afraid I shall disgrace your recommendation and shew that you have more good nature than discretion in your opinions of your friends."

His Grammar, which had been finished in the course of the summer, had just been published,[207] and he was now longing very much to be finished with the "Holcroft" also. "I am tired to death of the work, having been at it unceasingly the last fortnight," he confessed to Henry Robinson, when accepting the offer of work on *The London Review*. He seems to have driven himself into completing it by the end of the year.[208]

4

Thus the year 1810 opened for him with bright prospects, but when he went up to town with the manuscript of the "Holcroft," all ready—as he thought—for the press, a squall blew up in a most unexpected quarter, which blew him right out of his course. Godwin had approved the manuscript, but an Appendix, consisting of a Diary which Hazlitt wished to include in the book, had—most unfortunately —not been forwarded to him along with it.[209] When at length the Appendix reached him, he flew into a furious rage, and wrote a letter of expostulation to poor Mrs. Holcroft which frightened her almost out of her wits, dependent as she then was to a great extent on the favour of her husband's friends. After insisting that the publication of the Diary was a violation of the terms agreed on with Hazlitt, which had stipulated that the book should consist of a Life and a selection of letters, he continued: "Many parts are actionable. . . . By what I here write, therefore, I beg leave to enter my protest on the subject, and so to discharge my conscience. I will be no part or party to such a publication."[210]

Some words in this letter indicate that the violence of Godwin's outburst was occasioned by wounded vanity. If he were angry at what others had been reported as saying, he was still more angry that he himself had not been given a speaking part at all: "For myself, I can fairly say that if I had known that every time I dined with or called upon Mr. Holcroft, I was to be recorded in a quarto book, well printed, and with an ornamental frontispiece, in the ridiculous way of coming in to go out again fifty times, I would not on that penalty have called upon or dined with him at all."[211] The violence of his resentment settled the immediate fate of the book. Mrs. Holcroft was full of fears. She hardly knew what might or might not bring down vengeance on her head. Two months later Mary Lamb described her as still running about "from Nicholson[212] to Tuthil, and from Tuthil to Godwin, and from Godwin to Tuthil, and from Tuthil to Godwin, and from Godwin to Tuthil, and from Tuthil to Nicholson, to consult on the publication, or no publication, of the life of that good man her husband,"[213] till every one grew sick of the matter, and the Life strapped together with such haste in Winterslow came to be known in London as "the Life Everlasting."

In the meantime Hazlitt had returned to Winterslow, on Saturday, February 25th. Both the hopes he had carried to town with him in January had been crushed, for *The London Review* gave up the ghost just as he had seemed likely to obtain work upon its staff. His hopes with regard to this obscure periodical may not have been very high, but the rejection of his book, on the score of editorial indiscretion, and at the instigation of Godwin, who thus far had been a very good friend to him and had held golden opinions of his judgment, must have been a grievous rebuff. To some extent, Godwin's explosion must have been bewildering to him. He had no wish to offend Godwin, and he would have realised at once that Godwin would have been offended if any story had been included in the book that placed him at a disadvantage—but he could not have conceived that Godwin would have been so indignant merely because Holcroft had not judged his conversation worth recording. For the rest, he had no reason to be surprised. Although he had not at this time the very nice sense he afterwards developed as to what was actionable and what was not, he knew perfectly well that the Diary contained some high explosive,[214] and that there was risk in publishing some portions of it, but characteristically, he thought the risk worth taking because of the interest of the material. He had anticipated that its publication might have led him into "scrapes" of various kinds.

The jettisoning of the book as a consequence of his daring was, however, a heavier penalty than he had ever anticipated. Nor was there any reason why the book should have been jettisoned—for the offending material could easily have been excised—except that Godwin's irritable vanity had now made him altogether hostile, and therefore very difficult about the matter.

Unfruitful and troublesome as his journey to London had been, Hazlitt was still full of fight and full of resource. The withdrawal of Godwin's hand was a blow, but his chief hope had always lain, not in what others might do for him, but in the powers of his own mind. All he doubted was his power to make his wares a marketable commodity. On Sunday, February 26th, the day after his return to Winterslow, he wrote to Henry Robinson: "I have in short many plans and projects in my head, but I am afraid none of them good ones." One thing which suggested itself to him was that he might make a little money by translating for Samuel Tipper, as Henry Robinson formerly had done. He thought a translation of *Les Martyrs*, which had been published in the course of 1809, might find a ready sale. He was ready to attempt this at any remuneration he could get for it, "2½ guineas, 2 or 1½ per sheet."

Another project which he mentioned was the conversion of the material he had gathered for his *History of English Philosophy* into a volume of essays. What he says of this suggests that he was beginning to realise wherein his strength as a writer lay, rather in exposition and argument than in narrative.

March was a month in which the Hazlitts struggled through domestic difficulties. In the beginning of the month[215] Mrs. Hazlitt miscarried of her second child. After her convalescence she thought of having a month's holiday with the Lambs. Mary was eager to welcome her and to cheer her. Her only regret was that the weekly "Wednesdays" had now become fortnightly "Wednesdays." "I shall be very much joyed to see you," she wrote, ". . . and I have been setting my wits to work to think how to make you as comfortable as the nature of our inhospitable habits will admit. . . . The alternating Wednesdays will chop off one day in the week from your jolly days, and I do not know how I shall make it up to you; but I will contrive the best I can."[216]

One of the letters Hazlitt wrote to his wife during her visit to the Lambs gives us a clearer picture of him as he was during the years in Winterslow when his ship was still "hulling on the flood" than any other evidence as to him which has been preserved. If it does not contain, like his "petition," a complete self-portrait, it gives at least an excellent sketch of him as he was in his thirty-second year. The blithe Horace Twiss had discerned, God knows how! through the passionate pity and invective of the *Reply to Malthus*, that the anonymous author was "a pert, brisk young gentleman enough." Through this letter of April, 1810, we discern rather a man who in single-mindedness and aspiration is very much like the child who had made himself ill by his application to Latin grammar, and who, when the armour in which he now confronts the world is laid aside, has still a good deal of the child in him. Hazlitt's reminiscences of his Winterslow days tell us a great deal about him, but through them it is chiefly the spiritual being we discern. In this letter we see him as he lived his day-to-day life in the cottage in 1810, while his wife was away, at work in his small room and happy in it; surrounded by his prints and delighting in the company of his complete set of the Cartoons: "Here I sit with my doxies surrounded," as he puts it with luxurious satisfaction; fending for himself and getting his simple supper; taking stock in his intervals of leisure of the new neighbour who had arrived the day after his wife had left, and whose passing made a spot of colour in the village: "I have heard nothing of her but that her name is Armstead, nor seen anything of her till yesterday and the day before, on one of which she passed our house in a blue pelisse, and the other in a scarlet one. She is a strapper, I assure you;" lending coals to a couple of cottagers near him, and "delicate" about having them returned, because he thought they might be needed: "Little Robert and his wife still continue in the house. They returned the coals but I sent them back thinking they would be badly off, perhaps. But yesterday they walked out together, he smart as a buck, and she skipping and light as a doe." For the rest, his letter is all of prints and pictures and painting. At the end of February he had written to Henry Robinson: "One more push I must make, and then I hope to be afloat, at least for a good while to come." What this "push" was we do not know, but as the letter was all of literary projects we take it that it must have been one of these. Possibly there came a reaction shortly afterwards against the literary hack-work he was doing and contemplating doing, following on two years of strenuous and, on the whole, unsuccessful literary work, for now his thoughts seem to be altogether absorbed by painting. He thanks his wife for a couple of parcels of prints she has sent him, perhaps those completing his set of the Cartoons. He comments on a Catalogue of a sale of pictures she had forwarded, and asks: "Did Lamb go to the sale, and what is his report of the pictures?" but his longing to see them is qualified by the satisfaction he feels in his own completed Raphaels; he says that he has just taken out his little copy of a Rembrandt to have a look at it, and has been so much pleased with it that he has had half a mind to send it up to town to see whether it would fetch a few guineas, but that he has given up the idea, being "not at present in the humour to incur any certain expense for an uncertain profit." For the rest, from dawn to dusk he is at work on his picture of Jacob's Dream. The upping stone on the down has given him an idea as to the ladder. Only—his imagination has not yet been able to conceive the procession of angels. It is clear that, because the subject is still genuinely possessing him, he still has hope in the work and joy in the endeavour: "With respect to my painting, I go on something like Satan, through moist and dry, sometimes glazing and sometimes scumbling, as it happens, now on the wrong side of the canvas and now on the right, but still persuading myself that I have at last found out the true secret of Titian's golden hue and the oleaginous touches of Claude Lorraine. I have got in a pretty good background, and a *conception* of the ladder which I learned from the upping stone on the down, only making the stone into gold, and a few other improvements. I have no doubt there was such another on the field of Luz, and that an upping stone is the genuine Jacob's Ladder. But where are the angels to come from? That's another question, which I am not yet able to solve." In the few words in which he speaks of himself and his wife there is no indication at all of passionate feeling, but there is every indication all the same that in this second year of their marriage there was a true union between them, on the plane of their day-to-day life, sympathy, and the honest kind sharing of fortune: "My dear Sarah, I am too tired and too dull to be witty, and therefore I will not attempt it. I did not see the superscription of the wrapping paper till the morning, for which I thank you as much as for the prints. You are a good girl and I must be a good boy. I have not been very good lately. . . . It is supper time, my dear, and I have been painting all day, and all day yesterday, and all the day before, and am very, very tired, and so I hope you will let me leave off here, and bid you good night."[217]

We could wish that Hazlitt had left more of such easy fireside letters. His small beer is as pleasant as Cowper's.

In a postcript he wrote: "Before you come away, get Lamb to fix the date of coming down here." The date was not fixed while Mrs. Hazlitt was in town, but shortly after her return Mary Lamb wrote to her,[218] to tell her that Charles and she were planning to come about the beginning of July, possibly with Phillips again, and that young Martin Burney, who had been ill, wanted to come along with them. This letter is notable because it throws light on the sympathy and loving-kindness that there was between the Lambs and the Hazlitts at this time, on Mary Lamb's understanding of Hazlitt too, far exceeding his wife's. It was of the nature of her friendship with Hazlitt that she knew what would hurt him, and that she sought, then and afterwards, to shield him from it. Knowing that Hazlitt must be straitened for money this year owing to the jettisoning of his book on Holcroft, and knowing that the resources of his home were slight and bare, she set herself to plan, almost as if she were herself his helpmate in life, so that this invasion of his small domain by four people, most of them staying for a month, should not be burdensome to him. Martin's father had agreed to give him £5 for his travelling expenses and his bed and breakfasts at the Hut, and Mary thought that they might arrange things so that some of this might go to swell Mrs. Hazlitt's housekeeping funds:

"Martin says, if you can borrow a blanket or two, he can sleep on the floor, without either bed or mattress, which would save his expences at the Hut; for if Phillips breakfasts there, he must do so too, which would swallow up all his money. And he and I have calculated that, if he has no Inn expences, he may as well spare that money to give you for a part of his roast beef."

All the same, Mary had no intention that Martin, who was still "very weak and pale" after his illness, should sleep on the floor, for later on in the letter she slips in, inobtrusively, her own suggestions as to Martin's sleeping-quarters: "I tell you what Martin and I have planned, that, if you happen to be empty pursed at this time, you may think it as well to make him up a bed in the best kitchen."

Charles and she are also to contribute to the housekeeping fund, but Hazlitt is not to be told about this: "We can spare you also just five pounds. You are not to say this to Hazlitt, lest his delicacy be alarmed."

The Lambs came by the night-coach towards the beginning of July. Our impressions of this visit are not as clear as of the first, for they are gained chiefly from a word or two thrown out about it some years afterwards by Hazlitt himself.[219] From these reminiscences we catch a glimpse of him going for walks with Charles and Mary in the evening coolness, or of the whole party strolling through the fields and gathering the mushrooms that sprang up at their feet, to throw into the pot simmering on the fire for supper, while at least one member of it watched the Claude Lorraine colouring of the sky, as the azure gradually melted into purple and gold.[220] During the visit Lamb wrote a letter to Basil Montagu which suggests that he was by no means in such spirits as he had been while at Winterslow the previous autumn. He was tired, and the night journey had left him headachy; he may have been oppressed by an undercurrent of anxiety about Mary, who was, indeed, drawing towards another illness. But also, during this visit, he seems to have been acutely affected by his consciousness of the distress in the district. There was a lull in the war, yet it was but an ominous lull. Napoleon had once more forced Austria to her knees; his marriage with the Archduchess Marie Louise in March seemed to have set the seal on his triumph. Holland had just been annexed to France. During the pause of apprehension in the rest of Europe all eyes were turned to Spain, but as yet little progress seemed to have been made. In the meantime, the country was cracking under financial strain and the sense of insecurity. While at Winterslow, Lamb had the opportunity of seeing at far more close quarters than he would have seen them in London, the effect of these things on the fortunes of those whom the war had reduced from comfort to poverty.

Possibly Hazlitt was thinking of Lamb's lack of spirits during these days, rather than of the earlier visit during which Lamb had made at least one memorable sally, when he wrote afterwards: "Lamb once came down into the country to see us. . . . The country people thought him an oddity, and did not understand his jokes. It would be strange if they had: for he did not make any while he staid. But when we crossed the country to Oxford, then he spoke a little."[221]

They "rode in triumph in Johnny Tremain's cross-country caravan through Newbury,"[222] and entered Oxford, Lamb clad in a pair of breeches "of a lively Lincoln-green" which had been forced on him by the pragmatical tailor of Pitton, near Winterslow, instead of the snuff-coloured garments in which he delighted, and which it was his custom to wear—but at the moment, in the zest of the expedition, "fearing no colours." This was on July 31st. Hazlitt conducted his parting guests around Oxford and Blenheim, and enjoyed his showmanship. "I once took a party to Oxford with no mean *éclat*," he wrote more than ten years afterwards, "showed them the seat of the Muses at a distance,

' With glistering spires and pinnacles adorn'd '—

descanted on the learned air that breathes from the grassy quadrangles and stone walls of halls and colleges—was at home in the Bodleian; and at Blenheim quite superseded the powdered Cicerone that attended us, and that pointed in vain with his wand to commonplace beauties in matchless pictures."[223]

The reason that we hear little about this visit from the Lambs themselves is that the illness which had been dogging Mary caught up with her on the Monday after their return to town, and that Charles, instead of forcing his spirits as he sometimes did at such times, fell into the quietness of something very near despair, for this was the second time a bad illness had overtaken her after a return from their yearly holiday. "Our pleasant excursion has ended sadly for one of us," he wrote to Hazlitt. "You will guess I mean my sister. . . . I think I shall be mad if I take any more journeys with two experiences against it. . . . I have lost all wish for sights. God bless you. I shall be glad to see you in London."

Hazlitt's next visit to London was made in the autumn. He arrived about September the 18th, just as Mary was recovering from her summer's illness, and he left on October 19th, on a day on which Charles was almost distracted, because it seemed as if Mary, who had been wearied by too many visitors, were about to be plunged into another. It is in connection with painting that we see him during this visit. It seems to have been during it that he began work on, or at least entered into arrangements for painting, a portrait of Mr. Clarkson which he completed in the earlier half of 1811.[224] This must have been a task in which he took pleasure, for if there was any human being for whom he felt unqualified affection and respect it was Mr. Clarkson. Not only did he feel that there was something in Mr. Clarkson's appearance which reminded him of more than one of the Apostles in the Cartoons of Raphael, but that there was something in his character which entitled him to be added to the Twelve.

His portrait was thought a very good one—it was almost the only one of his which gave universal pleasure[225]—but he did not think it good enough for Mr. Clarkson. He wrote of it afterwards to Thomas Robinson: "I am glad to hear that Mr. Clarkson's picture is thought like, and only wish it were what it should be."

In the meantime, a review of the *Reply to Malthus* had appeared in the *Edinburgh*. Hazlitt objected to this review, not because it castigated him, nor even because his book had been made a pretext by the reviewer for "a formal eulogy" on Malthus, but because it was disingenuous, in so far as it sought to commend Malthus to the many who would never have anything but a hearsay knowledge of him, by deliberately masking all the repellent features of his work.[226] He forwarded a reply in a Letter to *The Political Register* in which, characteristically, his aim was not to defend his own work, but once more to unmask the "vulgar selfishness consolidated into principle, like marsh water that has become sordid ice," so that it should be visible everywhere and at least known for the hateful thing it was.

His Letter appeared in *The Political Register* of Saturday, November 24th. Lamb, pleased that Cobbett had printed it so quickly, forwarded it to Winterslow on the day on which it appeared. On the Wednesday following he wrote to return thanks for an addition to their larder which had just arrived from Winterslow: "We have received your Pig and return you thanks, it will be drest in due form with appropriate sauce this day." Most of his letter deals with his anxiety over Mary's health: "Her indisposition has been ever since that night you left town, the night Miss W. came;[227] her coming, and that damn'd infernal bitch Mrs. Godwin coming and staying so late that night, so overset her that she lay broad awake all that night, and it was by a miracle that she escaped a very bad illness which I thoroughly expected." Mary had not been ill enough to make it necessary for her to leave home, but if she had been even a shade worse it would not have been possible to have let her remain at home. She was on a very careful diet, and she never went out; not even to the Captain's did she venture to go. Wednesday shone no more to her now. It was like dying by inches rather than living. Charles, who was beginning to feel desperate about her, had made up his mind to protect her from being led by her willing and eager hospitality into any repetition of the experience of October 19th. He had decided that she must never have any friend staying with her overnight, no matter how intimate. Even Sarah Stoddart was to be no exception to the rule: "I have made up my mind that she shall never have any one in the house again with her, and that no one shall sleep with her not even for a night, for it is a very serious thing to be always living with a kind of fever upon her, and therefore I am sure you will take it in good part if I say that if Mrs. Hazlitt comes to town at any time, however glad we shall be to see her in the daytime, I cannot ask her to spend a night under our roof. Some decision we must come to, for the harassing fever that we have been in, owing to Miss Wordswˢ coming, is not to be borne, and I had rather be dead than so alive."[228]

Later in the evening, after sampling the Wiltshire fare, Lamb, now in more cheerful mood, opened his letter to say how much he had enjoyed it: "the Pig upon proof hath turned out as good as I predicted. My fauces yet retain the sweet porcine odor." He added a word of brief, but all-sufficient praise for the Letter to Cobbett.

Well might he do so. By way of making short work of the agreeable mask with which the "Edinburgh" reviewer had provided Malthus, Hazlitt had concluded his Letter with a series of eighteen questions, each of them swift and decisive as the thrust of a rapier. The concluding ones reveal once more the fiery spark of sympathy for the inarticulate poor which lay at the core of him and which had set him ablaze three years before:

"13. Whether the principle of moral restraint, formerly recognised in Mr. Malthus's latter writings, and in reality turning all his paradoxes into mere impertinence, does not remain a dead letter, which he never calls into action, except for the single purpose of torturing the poor under pretence of reforming their morals?

"14. Whether the avowed basis of the author's system on the poor-laws, is not the following:—that by the laws of God and nature, the rich have a right to starve the poor whenever they (the poor) cannot maintain themselves?

"17. Whether Mr. Malthus has not been too much disposed to consider the rich as a sort of Gods upon earth, who were merely employed in distributing the goods of nature and fortune among the poor, and who themselves neither ate nor drank, ' neither married nor were given in marriage,' and consequently were altogether unconcerned in the limited extent of the means' of subsistence, and the unlimited increase of population?

"18. Lastly, whether the whole of the reverend author's management of the principle of population, and of the necessity of moral restraint, does not seem to have been copied from the prudent Friar's advice in Chaucer?[229]

> "' Beth war therfor with lordes how ye pleye.
> Singeth *Placebo*, and I shal, if I can,
> But-if it be un-to a povre man.
> To a povre man men sholde hise vyces telle,
> But nat to a lord, thogh he sholde go to helle.'"

To us, as to Lamb, this seems "complete."

5

In 1811 Hazlitt was much in London. This, as it chanced, was the year in which Henry Robinson began to keep a Diary. Now this diligent "snapper-up of unconsidered trifles" being—although on the whole a good man and a kind—entirely lacking in the sensibility without which any measure of sympathy with Hazlitt could not be established, understood nothing of him, except what all might see, that although brilliant he was finding uncommon difficulty in making for himself a place in the universe. Yet because he kept a record of what he saw and heard, or rather, of what he believed himself to have heard, his Diary, from February to April of this year, gives us some understanding of the originality and penetration of Hazlitt's talk; it throws some dim light on the gradual transmutation of Hazlitt's early love for Coleridge into the curious complex loving hatred or hating love of the later years; and it gives a hint, too, as to the crisis in Hazlitt's life in the spring of 1811, which led to his finally putting aside the hope of ever becoming a great painter, and to his devoting himself exclusively from that time onwards to Literature.

As to the first of these—as we read the Diary we can listen already to Hazlitt talking much as he talked in later years in many an essay. On March 29th, Henry Robinson made notes of a discussion on abstract ideas between Coleridge and Hazlitt, to which he had listened in Hazlitt's rooms, in which Hazlitt repeated practically what he had written in the essay in which he had explained the scope of his projected *History of English Philosophy*, but with one addition which shows how carefully his structure of thought was based upon experience. He had insisted in his essay on the impossibility of having an exact knowledge of all the infinite number of parts of any given object, prior to having a general idea of the object. From the report given by the Diary of his conversation we learn that it was the experience of the painter which had taught him the impossibility of this, the trained eye ministering to the trained mind: "Hazlitt said that he had learned from painting, that it was difficult to form an idea of an individual object—that we first have only a *general idea*; that is, a vague, broken, imperfect recollection of the individual object." Here we catch a glimpse of that constant testing of theory by actuality which purged his thought of all waste matter or pretentiousness, enforced integrity upon it, and made his quiet conversation at times so impressive. Many are the witnesses that Hazlitt never talked loosely or rhetorically or for show, as Coleridge sometimes did, but that he talked only to insist upon the truth, even in small matters, where the truth could be put to the proof. Conversation for him, when it was serious, was but a hunting down of the truth in company.

More interesting than this, for it is all-illuminating as to Hazlitt, is the passage in which a conversation with Hazlitt on Blake is recorded. Henry Robinson had showed Blake's engravings for Young's *Night Thoughts* to Hazlitt, who had seen "no merit in them as designs," and had said so. Then he had read aloud some of Blake's poems. The Diary continues:

"He was much struck with them and expressed himself with his usual strength and singularity. 'They are beautiful . . . and only too deep for the vulgar. He has no sense of the ludicrous, and, as to a God, a worm crawling in a privy is as worthy an object as any other, all being to him indifferent. So to Blake the Chimney Sweeper, etc. He is ruined by vain struggles to get rid of what presses on his brain—he attempts impossibles.'"[230]

We think that in reporting this, the Diarist's memory played a trick with him, so that, much as a humorless person can ruin a joke by altering the word on which it turns, he flaws, in this jerky account of the conversation, the sensitiveness of what Hazlitt said. Seeing that at a time when Blake passed for a madman, even among his fellow-poets, Hazlitt saw that he was "a profound mystic," he is not likely to have used the word "ruined." What he meant is more accurately expressed by the words he used afterwards, when he numbered Blake among those "whose ideas are like a stormy night, with the clouds driven rapidly across, and the blue sky and stars gleaming between." That is not expressive of ruin, although it is expressive of turmoil. But, even allowing for such inexactitude as might be introduced into the utterance of a poetical mind when reported by a matter-of-fact mind, this, as an immediate response to the quality of Blake's poetry, shows an altogether extraordinary power of penetration by sympathy. Hazlitt had been brought up on the eighteenth-century poets, and he loved them, but his response to the voice that sang of a region of experience from which most of them were excluded, is as instant as it is complete. This is criticism by flashlight. No one could have been more swift. No one could have revealed more—or said more.

He had taken his old lodgings at 34 Southampton Buildings for the time he was in London. Consequently he was seeing a good deal of Coleridge, who although he lived with his friends the Morgans at Hammersmith, had taken a room at 32 Southampton Buildings, it being convenient for his work that he should have a *pied-à-terre* in town. The entry in the Diary for March 4th hints at the element of pain which had intruded itself into the relationship with Coleridge by this time, and which was to increase until it had obscured everything but the original spark of love, which was in its nature quite indestructible: "after dinner . . . I took tea with W. Hazlitt and had two hours' pleasant chat with him. Hazlitt spoke of Coleridge with the feelings of an injured man."[231] The Diary goes on to relate the story of the Beaumont dinner. Coleridge's conduct on this occasion had been irritating to Hazlitt, just as Hazlitt's had been irritating to Coleridge, but this would not account for the undertone of wounded feeling conveyed by Hazlitt's way of speaking of Coleridge. We are left to conjecture, from our knowledge of Coleridge's ways to Hazlitt from 1806 onwards, as to what could have occasioned it. Hazlitt, we know, had greatly disliked such political writing as Coleridge had done during these years. He had disliked Coleridge's attempts to defend the seizure of the Danish fleet at Copenhagen in the summer of 1807, and the expedition to Walcheren in which seven thousand men had lost their lives in 1809. Above all, he had disliked what he described as "the undertone of casuistry" and "the unlimited philosophical scepticism" of "an elaborate article on tyrannicide" which had appeared in *The*

Friend on February 8th, 1810, at a time, shortly before the marriage of Napoleon to Marie Louise, when the assassination of Napoleon had been "a common topic of conversation, and a sort of *forlorn hope* in certain circles." But we cannot conceive that the antipathy he felt towards the tone of Coleridge's comments on the events of the day could have left him, at this time, with any sense of having been personally injured by Coleridge. It is more likely that Hazlitt, seeing a great deal both of Coleridge and Lamb, had become conscious of Coleridge's growing jealousy of his intimacy with Lamb and persistent attempts to exclude him from it. Or he may have been given some hint that Coleridge, who had apparently ignored the essay On the Disinterestedness of the Human Mind, after his return from Malta in 1806, had yet been prejudicing opinion against its author by claiming as his own all that was of any value in it. Hazlitt certainly knew of this some years afterwards. If some hint as to the matter had been given him at this time, he was justified in regarding himself as injured by Coleridge, for if any of his books was completely his own, it was this.

The entry in the Diary which throws light on the pain Hazlitt felt over his failure as a painter is dated April 15th:

"Godwin related me an anecdote concerning Hazlitt. The painting he had made of . . . a handsome young man had been sent home with an abusive letter by the mother. Poor Hazlitt left town in great agony. He has not sent my brother's picture, and I fear he does not mean to let it go out of his hands; perhaps he has already destroyed it. . . . I saw also Mr. Howel's portrait. It is a good caricature likeness, but a coarse painting."[232]

We turn from the glimpse given here of Hazlitt fleeing from town "in great agony" with one hope, at least, put away from him for ever, a day or so after his thirty-third birthday, to the hopes which had sustained him when he had come to town in February. The chief of these was that he might be able to arrange for the delivery of a course of lectures on philosophy, which would provide him with the greater part of a year's income. He had little confidence in his gifts of oratory, but he believed in the value of the work he had done on English philosophy, and just as he had thought of shaping the material for his History into essays the preceding year, he was now thinking of turning it into lectures. He received sufficient encouragement for this project to justify him in hoping that the lectures might be delivered in the autumn. In the meantime, he would seem to have paid his way while in town chiefly by painting. We know only of the sitters mentioned by the Diarist—Thomas Robinson, the Mr. Howel whom Henry Robinson had introduced to him but whose portrait he pronounced a coarse daub, and the young man whose portrait seemed to his mother an outrage on his beauty; but there may have been others. He was, nevertheless, very poor, and before he left he was ready to execute almost any task that offered itself to him. One such was the revision of a manuscript, for which he was to receive £10.

I go on something like Satan. The time was to come when to friend and foe alike these would seem the perfect words to denote the manner of his progress through life. At the moment we see him rather as one still desperately patient in his desperate impatience, driven forward despite all rebuffs by the consciousness of his own power, always "tending towards" Literature, and with his eyes as steadily fixed upon his goal as if he had said to himself: "Other brunts I also look for; but this I have resolved on, to run when I can, to go when I cannot run, and to creep when I cannot go."

But of brunts for the moment he has had sufficient. Let us hope that after shaking the dust of the town from his feet, in his home at least he still felt himself "sheltered from the world."

6

It is not easy to estimate the pang Hazlitt felt on returning to Winterslow in that sweet season of the year when the woods were covered with primroses and hyacinths for miles together and everything in nature smote upon the painter's eye and tempted the painter's brush—with the hope in him broken that his canvas would ever capture the secret of all this beauty; would ever convey the charm of his favourite walk through the woods "closed in on each side by copsewood" and the pin-point of light that terminated it; would ever reveal the soft hues of the low green sward on which he loved to tread. The days for him were past when, if he had nothing else to claim his time, he could sit all day at his easel, completely happy, until night at last found him very tired, but still completely happy. A woman's churlish word had robbed him of a world of delight. He had turned his back on her, just as he had turned his back on Godwin's cold tittle-tattle and Henry Robinson's cold pity and the cold surmise in the eyes of those speculating on the issue of his life-effort—but nothing could give him back the world of his delight, for although this word of brutal criticism had been the immediate cause of his losing hope that he would ever become the painter he wished to be, and of his flinging down his pencil in despair, there can be little doubt that it was not the deepest cause. It must have acted on some doubts on his own part, by which it had been preceded, some sense of incapacity to reproduce the image of beauty stamped upon his mind, some hardly acknowledged sense of coming short—or its effect would not have been so shattering. He had turned away in his youth from the copying of pictures, at which he was reckoned excellent, feeling that there was a lack of courage in imitating the art of other men, and wishing "to trace the living forms of nature" as his own eye saw them. Now he realised that despite all his effort he was among those who lacked "an eye quick enough, a hand steady enough, and colours bright enough" to achieve the kind of painting at which he aimed. His delight in the hope of achievement had been great. We have his word for it that in proportion to "the pleasure and the confidence produced by consummate skill" in painting "so is the pain and the desponding effect of total failure." A paragraph from one of his essays is probably an exact reflection of what he suffered at this time:

"When for the fair face of nature, we see only an ugly blot arising from our best endeavours, then the nerves slacken, the tears fill the eyes, and the painter turns away from his art, as the lover from a mistress that scorns him. Alas! how many such have

> ' Begun in gladness
> Whereof has come in the end despondency and madness '—

not for the want of will to proceed (ah! no) but for lack of power."[233]

He had indeed taken the portrait of Thomas Robinson on which he had been engaged since February back to Winterslow with him, and it had to be finished, because it had been paid for in advance and he could not refund the money; yet he could not get on with it. He who had once worked with such energy because his nerves had been strung with hope, now found that his hand could do little because the work now went against his nerves. When Thomas Robinson wrote to him about it in midsummer he could only answer apologetically that he hoped to finish it before returning to town in the autumn. His letter, written on July 10th, shows the extent to which he had lost confidence in himself: "I have the picture with me, and brought it down with a full intention to set about improving it immediately. I have however put it off from day to day and week to week first from an unfortunate habit that what I ought to do, I seldom do, and secondly from a fear of doing away what likeness there is without mending the picture." He adds: "I will however do what I can to it before I come to town in October, and will then leave it with your brother. Till then I do not forget that I am your debtor."

There was another whose debtor he was since he had left town and whom he could not satisfy even with a painting done by forced labour, whose claims he had also to postpone until October. A letter to Thomas Hardy, who was a bootmaker as well as a political reformer,

shows how bare of profit his work done during the spring had left him.
It might serve as an illuminating footnote to what he wrote afterwards in the essay *On the Want of Money*: "Another of the greatest
miseries of the want of money is the tap of a dun at your door . . .
to have no way left to escape contempt, but by incurring pity." To
Hardy he wrote: "I was obliged to leave London without discharging
my promise, the reason of which was that I was myself disappointed in
not receiving £20 which was owing to me. . . . I am at present
actually without money in the house. If you can defer it till October,
when I shall be in London to deliver some lectures, by which I shall
pick up some money, I shall esteem it a favour, and shall be glad to
pay you the interest from the time I was in London last."[234]

Mary Lamb had written to Miss Stoddart in the summer of 1804:
"I shall yet live to see you a poor, but happy English wife." The first
part of her prediction had certainly come true, so true that Hazlitt
may have smiled somewhat wryly when after the birth of his second
son, whom he also named William, on September 26th of this year,
the felicitations he received from Lamb took the following form:

" Delighted Fancy already sees him some future rich alderman or
opulent merchant; painting perhaps a little in his leisure hours for
amusement like the late H. Bunbury Esq.

"Pray are the Winterslow Estates entailed? I am afraid lest the
young dog when he grows up should cut down the woods, and leave
no groves for widows to take their lonesome solace in. The Wem
Estate of course can only devolve on him, in case of your brother
leaving no male issue."

A few words which follow are eloquent as to Lamb's affection for
his brilliant, struggling, troubled and sometimes troublesome friend:

"Well, my blessing and heaven's be upon him, and make him like
his father, with something a better temper and a smoother head of
hair, and then all the men and women must love him."

Although painting had failed him, metaphysics still remained to
him both as a solace and a pleasure. The six[235] lectures he had ready
by the autumn show that at least he was not idle during the summer.
In October he went to town not to deliver the lectures but to conclude
his arrangements for giving them. His stay there affords us a curious
and illuminating glimpse of the jealousy with which Coleridge viewed
his intimacy with Lamb. When Mary Lamb had been seized with
illness in the March of this year, it had seemed to Hazlitt, to Henry
Robinson, and to others, that one of the contributory causes of her
illness was the presence of Coleridge in town and the way in which,

being at the time unhappy because he had estranged himself from the Wordsworths, he had pressed on her sympathy. Lamb, whose measures of defence for Mary were growing more and more decisive, had since that time insisted that he should not be visited until after eight o'clock at night. Coleridge, breaking through this law, had one day in October come to dine and had brought his friend Morgan with him, with the result that Lamb had had to talk to him on the matter and that Lamb's friends had tried to impress on him the necessity of considering the difficulties of Lamb's life. In a letter to Rickman we find Coleridge excusing himself in his usual very disarming fashion, but presently digressing from his apology and almost forgetting the offence which had occasioned it, in launching an attack on Hazlitt, whose ways towards Mary were marked by the utmost understanding and consideration, who because he felt for her sensitiveness as delicately as she did for his never preyed on her vitality, and who suffered, even as Charles did, when he saw her at the mercy of one who either could not or would not consider her. After interpolating a word of approval of Lamb's firmness he continues: "permit me to say to you in confidence that as long as Hazlitt remains in town I dare not expect any amendment in Lamb's health, unless luckily H. should grow moody and take offence at being desired not to come till 8 o'clock. It is seldom indeed, that I am with Lamb more than once in the week—and yet I see what harm has been done even by me—what then if Hazlitt—as probably he will—is with him 5 evenings in the Seven?"[236]

As Hazlitt, by his own confession, was held "in durance vile" all the time he was in town by "one of the greatest miseries of human life . . . a pair of tight boots," which, he said, made it impossible to move a step without "being put in pain and out of humour"[237]—we may take it that Coleridge's solicitude for the Lambs was unnecessary.

While in town he succeeded in getting some thirty subscribers to take tickets for his lectures, at two guineas each. After his return to Winterslow, he wrote to Henry Robinson, asking him to assist, if he could, by gaining one or two more.

By the end of November he was in London again, and settling himself in rooms for the winter. A few words that had been jotted down in Henry Robinson's Diary in the middle of the month seem to suggest that Hazlitt, in his visits to town, had been giving rein to his temperament or at least that he was not living too wisely about this time: "Chatted a little with Charles Lamb, who expressed himself morally concerning both Hazlitt and Coleridge and their habits." As the censure of Hazlitt is coupled with censure of Coleridge, we may be sure that this touch of disapproval meant no diminution of friendship on Lamb's part. Even if he had criticised either of these himself, he would not readily have endured criticism of either of them from others.

Far more serious than Lamb's criticism of Hazlitt's ways was

Wordsworth's growing disapproval of those opinions of which Hazlitt
made religion. The sonnet with which he closed a series in which he
had commented on the struggle against Napoleon contained a direct
rebuke of these in the solemn warning it gave:

> "That an *accursed* thing it is to gaze
> On prosperous Tyrants with a dazzled eye."

So little do men see into each other's hearts that he was beginning
to regard Hazlitt—who ever kindled to the forlorn cause, who all
his life battled against wind and tide, who never had a more impassioned sense of Napoleon's greatness than in the days which succeeded Waterloo, whose fortunes and interests were ever sacrificed to
the cause of Liberty—as one who was allowing himself to be hypnotised
by the immediate glitter of successful tyranny. Hazlitt was now not
far from being regarded by him as one of the foremost of the class
"whose besotted admiration of the intoxicated despot"[238] seemed to
him "the most melancholy evidence of degradation in British feeling
and intellect."[238(b)] Southey shortly after this time declared it to be a
source of chagrin and humiliation to him that Spain, which two
centuries before had produced half a dozen men resolute enough,
although in a mistaken cause, to slay the Prince of Orange at the cost
of their own lives, had not in the course of the war "found one to aim
a dagger at the heart of Buonaparte."[239] Wordsworth was far more in
sympathy with this point of view than he was with Hazlitt's premonition that the defeat of the armies of France would mean the
triumph of reaction and even Tyranny in every country of Europe.

But the most serious antagonism of all—for Hazlitt—was that
which was daily increasing between his spirit and Coleridge's. Wordsworth's utterance during these years was noble, no matter how short-
sighted his political vision might seem to those on the other side of the
question, but Coleridge's diatribes against Napoleon in the course of
this summer had degenerated into "a vile jelly." His constant casu-
istical disquisitions on tyrannicide, his insistence that any one who
referred to Napoleon except in the language of abuse was lacking in
patriotism, his outrageous insinuation of illegitimacy levelled at the
Emperor of the French, and the paltriness of some of his gibes, as when
after the terrible battle of Albuera he taunted Napoleon with indifference to the fate of men and nations because the Emperor continued
to find time to look in on his son's nursery—bore all of them the marks
of a Government tool. Indeed, this last gibe, accompanied as it is with
the suggestion, one might almost say the unctuous hope, that the baby
King of Rome might prove an idiot, shares with the harping on Fox's
"having prostrated his grey hairs at the feet of the usurper in 1802"
the dishonour of representing the nadir of Coleridge's political journal-

ism.[240] When protest was made in Parliament against the indiscriminate abuse of Napoleon in certain papers and the encouragement given to the idea of assassination, he professed himself appalled by this outrage on his patriotism: "Neither the battles of Austerlitz, nor Jena, nor Wagram, filled us with such fears of approaching subjugation and slavery. . . . We conceived we felt the chains of Buonaparte crawling around our limbs, the halters of the Mamelukes at our throats." He appeared to think that any mud thrown at Napoleon sanctified the hands that had thrown it; that in calling Napoleon "a wretch whose every measure has betrayed a wish to rebarbarise Europe," "the Gallic Gog and Magog of our day," "the Tyrant," "the Usurper," "the Monster," and of course "the Corsican Upstart," he was giving his countrymen an example in the exercise of "deliberate valour," and that by his outpourings of abuse he was doing more to win the war than those who were opposing the French arms with their flesh and blood. Even his close friends could not regard the performance with admiration. Hazlitt watched it with deepening scorn and bitterness, for he could not bring himself to believe that this quaking huddle of invective had even the excuse of sincerity. Coleridge seemed to him to be "mangling his own soul with a prostituted . . . pen."

7

In his Diary under the date December 7th, Henry Robinson wrote: "A call on William Hazlitt to pay him subscription money for his lectures—I found him alone and gloomy." With his usual serviceableness, he had induced his friend John Collier and Mrs. Clarkson's brother, John Buck, to take tickets for the lectures, and he was now able to pay six guineas into Hazlitt's hands. Yet he still felt doubtful as to the speedy maturing of the scheme. He wrote to his brother Thomas on December 15th: "When the lectures will be delivered I cannot tell. He means to deliver them as he does to deliver your picture, and will probably do both sooner or later. But we must bide his time."

His doubts were not justified. Hazlitt had in the meantime—apparently on his brother-in-law's advice—proposed his course of ten lectures to the Committee of the Russell Institution, and on December 19th his proposal was accepted. The lectures were advertised to begin on Tuesday, January 14th, 1812.

Many years afterwards he was to write: "There are a million of people in this single metropolis, each one of whom would willingly stand on the pedestal which you occupy. . . . Beware how you climb the slippery ascent; do not neglect your footing when you are there."

At the moment, it contents him that after four years of never-ceasing effort, he has at last gained his first slight footing.

Part Five

THE POLITICAL ARENA

*Mankind are a herd of knaves and fools. It is necessary to join the crowd,
or get out of their way, in order not to be trampled to death by them.*

HAZLITT.

Chapter One

TOWARDS WATERLOO (1812-1815)

"As for Hazlitt, it is not to be believed how the destruction of
Napoleon affected him; he seemed prostrated in mind and body,
he walked about, unwashed, unshaved, hardly sober by day, and
always intoxicated by night, literally, without exaggeration, for
weeks; until at length, wakening as it were from a stupor, he at
once left off all intoxicating liquors, and never touched them
after."

BENJAMIN HAYDON.

I

IT WAS about this time that Charles Lamb's fancy began to play with
Henry Crabb Robinson's name, so that Henry Robinson emerges
presently from the "deal of" Robinsons who swarmed in Bury, thick
as rats in Hamelin town, and becomes known in the circle of his
London friends as Crabb the Only, "Crabius," "the Crab," or even
"Crabby," as Mary Lamb, in her pleasant kindness, sometimes called
him. "Crab might have answered by this time: his juices take a long
time in supplying, but they'll run out at last,—I know they will—
pure golden pippin," Lamb wrote in one of his letters to Coleridge.
In the same letter he reports the rumour that "the Crab is on the eve
of setting out for France." In another letter to Coleridge he confirms
this: "Crabius is gone to Paris. I prophesy he and the Parisians will
part with mutual contempt. His head has a twist Allemagne, like
thine, dear mystic."

In January, 1812, Crabius has a busy time of it, for he is Facing-
both-Ways. Coleridge's lectures, delivered on Mondays and Thursdays
at the Philosophical Society's rooms in Fleet Street, are not yet finished,
and William Hazlitt has begun his at the Russell Institution, Great
Coram Street, Brunswick Square. The Crab is an acquisitive Crab, so
he must not miss what he can acquire from either of these. each of

whom he has recognised as being among the outstanding personalities of the time, although of neither does he approve unreservedly. He spends a good deal of his time backwards and forwards between Fleet Street and Great Coram Street, is, indeed, a peripatetic Crab, who manages to be present at the lectures even if now and again he finds himself "forcing his attention," or perhaps even dozing a little. A most valuable indefatigable Crab, rescuing from the sea of oblivion much that would otherwise never have reached the shore!

Hazlitt's troubles began with his first lecture, delivered on Tuesday, January 14th, at eight o'clock. This was almost a complete fiasco. The story of his *début* as a lecturer is a tragi-comedy. He had spoken of himself as lecturing "in spite of the muse that presides over eloquence," but he could hardly have anticipated the plight in which he found himself, during that unfortunate opening lecture, owing to his utter inexperience and his inability to adapt himself to the needs of the moment or of his audience. He had come fortified with an excellent lecture on Hobbes, but unluckily it was one that would have taken almost three hours to deliver, while on his arrival he was informed by the Secretary that his lecture must finish within one hour. Here was a perplexity. There was only one thing to do in such a situation—to put his manuscript aside and speak to his audience; but nervousness disqualified him for this. He could not, on the spur of the moment, cut out any part of his close-knit, closely-reasoned lecture for fear of making it unintelligible; nor could he leave the lecture unfinished, for the same reason. Being not of the "strapped-together" kind, but organic, it was not readily adaptable. A less finished piece of work could have been operated on far more easily. In this predicament, Hazlitt resorted to reading his lecture at breakneck speed, apparently with but one idea in his head, of getting the material in it hurled at his audience within the space of one hour. A lecture on any subject delivered under such conditions, without any kind of contact between the lecturer and the audience, would have been a penance to listen to; but a lecture on material as intractable as that which he had chosen to expound, material which could only be made intelligible by slow and careful exposition, and each point in which required plenty of time to sink into the minds of the listeners if they were not going to become clouded and wearied—when delivered with such reckless and merciless haste, was stupefying in its effect. Crabius, while realising that the matter was good, could hardly force himself to listen. It is he who has preserved for us his impression of the lecturer, too nervous to bestow a single glance on his audience; of the eyes fixed on the paper all the time as intently as if their preservation depended on their never being raised from it; of the low monotonous voice, of the extreme rapidity of articulation. He came away feeling that Hazlitt's lectures would be more than flesh and blood could bear, unless the lecturer altered his manner. There was another critic in the room too—one at whose mercy Hazlitt hated to be—his brother-in-law. Dr. Stoddart, who had admired the micaceous lectures of James Mackintosh so much in 1799 when Hazlitt had found them flimsy things, felt of Hazlitt's first performance as a lecturer, "This will never do," and wrote to say so. Hazlitt was hurt and irritated by his brother-in-law's letter of advice. He had to bear the brunt of other commentary too. If Stoddart had irritated him, Crabius, meeting him at Lamb's "Wednesday" the following evening, applied the unguent of a tiresome kindness that almost inflamed the irritation into a sore. He went up to Hazlitt to express the "compassion" he had felt for him the previous evening, on beholding him "so oppressed in delivering the lecture." Mary Lamb saw this with dismay, and as soon as she could told him that he had done the wrong thing, whereupon good Crabb completed his act of mercy by writing to Hazlitt that he had meant not to hurt but to help by what he had said.

Other friends dealt with Hazlitt with more understanding than his brother-in-law and Crabius had done. Both Hazlitt and Lamb at this time were seeing a good deal of Basil Montagu. The following Monday they were both at Montagu's house in Bedford Square, and Hazlitt was persuaded to read his lecture to a group of friends there; but he was now nervous enough to shy at his own shadow. Half-way through he broke off abruptly, and nothing would persuade him to continue. Yet the attempt to adjust his difficult material so as to hold the interest of a few friends may have helped him in the effort he had to make to adjust his material so as to hold the attention of a public audience, and the evening may have helped him and restored his confidence somewhat, for Mrs. Montagu, like Mary Lamb, understood him and knew how to draw the best out of him.

At all events, whether from such readings or no, he learned very quickly to adjust himself to an audience. His second lecture, on Locke, delivered the day after he had read part of his first at the Montagus', was a great improvement on the first. It was read in a strong voice and with an air of confidence which Crabius regarded as bordering on arrogance, but which pleased the audience, for it was several times interrupted by bursts of applause. He had meant to treat of Locke in one lecture also, but having profited by the misery of his first performance he divided his material into three sections, of which he delivered the first only in his second lecture. This made it impossible for him to keep to his syllabus. He had meant to give his third lecture on Berkeley, but the third and the fourth were also on Locke. In the fifth and sixth, in which he lectured on the Disinterestedness of the Human Mind and Self-Love, he retrod most of the ground he had covered in his early essay on the subject. The seventh was on Hartley. The eighth, which was pronounced "interesting and animated," was on Helvétius. This was delivered on March 3rd. The weekly lectures were exhausting him, and after delivering the eighth Hazlitt postponed his remaining lectures until the end of the month. Crabius prophesies woe at this stage. "I fear his debts oppress him, so that he cannot proceed," he wrote in his Diary on March 10th. But Hazlitt, after a few weeks' respite, finished his course, although now with intervals of a fortnight between the lectures. On March 31st, he spoke on Free-Will and Necessity. This was followed on April 14th by a brilliant lecture on Horne Tooke. The concluding lecture was delivered on April 28th. In it he touched on the uses of metaphysics. If his lectures had begun inhumanly, they closed on a quaint and human note, for he ended by confiding to his audience a story that often ran in his mind in these days—the legend of the Brahmin who was turned into a monkey and who continued to spend such time as was not occupied in eating coconuts in the study of metaphysics. His audience must surely have warmed to him when he took leave of them with the words: "I too, should be very well contented to pass my life like the monkey, did I but know how to provide myself with a substitute for coconuts."

The preparation of these lectures, the adaptation of them to the audience, and the forcing of his nerves necessitated by their delivery, between the middle of January and the end of April, were considerable drains on the strength of a man of his temperament. It may have been this which led him into the way of drinking too much at this time; or it may have been that the pressure of poverty and insecurity, which had seemed to him redoubled ever since he had become the father of a child he loved passionately, may have made him sometimes betray the day because it was necessary for him to forget the morrow; or it may have been that he was constantly in the company of men who drank more than was good for them. Lamb, although he did not drink very much, frequently got drunk; John Hazlitt had for years been a very hard drinker. Crabius reported of Hazlitt, whom he had met at dinner at Thelwall's on February 27th, that he had said little and drunk little, "and therefore behaved inoffensively," as if the reverse of this were now his custom.

Lamb's circle of intimates at this time had one new recruit. This was none other than that James Henry Leigh Hunt, of whom we caught a glimpse in 1803, playing at soldiers in Piccadilly and being rather shamefaced over his cheaply-won military glory. Leigh Hunt had known Lamb by sight since his childhood, for when a schoolboy at Christ's Hospital he had often seen Lamb revisiting his old haunts, and had noted with a kind of dawning affection the fine intelligent face that now, although it was a little careworn, he found still finer. His invitation to his fellow-Hospitaller to contribute to *The Reflector*, a quarterly which he edited in 1810 and 1811, had led to personal acquaintance with Lamb and then to friendship. This eventually led

to acquaintance with Hazlitt also. What he remembered most vividly
in after years about his first meeting with Hazlitt was the way in
which a mass of fine dark curls had poured about Hazlitt's ears and
framed his very finely-chiselled features the moment he had taken his
hat off.

As for Hazlitt, he who had never done anything all his life but
encounter one difficulty after another, who when he was entering on
his thirty-fourth year was still struggling to make his entry into
journalism, saw before him a man six years younger than himself, on
whom the gods seemed already to have showered all their gifts, and
who in most ways seemed the exact antithesis of himself. Leigh Hunt
in his twenty-eighth year was handsome in a foreign or gipsy-like
way, with his bushy black hair, olive skin and dark eyes, extraordinarily
facile and charming in his manners, full of fun, and so able that he had
won wide recognition as a poet, as an essayist, as a critic of distinction
and distinctiveness, his dramatic criticism having had from the outset
what Hazlitt afterwards called "the true pine-apple flavour," and as
one of the most gifted journalists of the day, for under his Editorship
The Examiner had become a real force in the life of the country. Not
unlike a colt in these days was young mettlesome Leigh Hunt. But
the bit is just about to come. Twice he had come near to being prosecuted by the Government, but the danger had passed by, and now he
laughs at it. "No one can accuse me of not writing a libel," he
declared, rather vaingloriously, at Lamb's in the spring of the year.
"Everything is a libel, as the law is now declared." On the very
next day, it is St. Patrick's Day of 1812, the guests at an Irish banquet
refuse to drink the health of the Prince Regent. *The Morning Post*
publishes a eulogy in verse, assuring the Prince Regent of perpetuity
of remembrance along with all "Monarchs of Immortal Fame," and
apostrophising him as Adonis, and our young coltish Hunt *shies* at
the word, and draws the eyes of the whole country upon his prancings
and curvetings.

Such is the chain of events. And yes! The bit is about to come.
The bit is undoubtedly due to come.

2

The lectures safely shipped over, Hazlitt, who for some months
past had been feeling himself "too much i' the sun," retired to that
"vacant interlunar cave" from which so often he defied the curiosity
of his fellow-mortals. Good Crabb, whose curiosity was not of the
easily-defied kind, visited him once or twice, and affords us brief
glimpses of him. One bad debt, not easily redeemed, Hazlitt had
hanging over him in these days. He still owed Thomas Robinson

his portrait, and the completing of this teasing piece of work went badly against the grain with him. In June he was still struggling with it.

Although he had renounced painting, his devotion to pictures was unaltered, and he was still always to be found where they were to be found. We may take it that he visited the Exhibition in May, not only for that reason, but for another also which was even more personal. In that year among the portraits exhibited by his brother was the last portrait of old Mr. Hazlitt—who was now about to retire from his long ministry—painted by either of his sons.

In these summer days of 1812 the world of Hazlitt's youth by a gradual process of corrosion was ceasing to be. One tie after another was slipping from him. Everywhere there were signs of the passing of time. Two things especially drove home the sense of change. The home of his childhood at Wem was just about to be broken up; and the great actress who had first quickened his imagination in his youth was just about to take her farewell of the stage. She was playing that summer, but she was not what she had been. At last time was laying its hands upon her, and withering her long and magnificent flowering. On June 29th she took her leave of the stage in Lady Macbeth. Whether Hazlitt went to see her in her farewell performance we do not know. It would have been more his way to have left undisturbed a memory that could never be surpassed. Knowing him, we know that he would not have let that 29th of June pass by unmarked, but we have no glimpse of him on that day. We catch a glimpse of him at his easel, however, on the following day, from a remark in the Crab's Diary, which is both cryptic and vigorous: "At chambers in the fore-noon till half-past two, when I called at William Hazlitt's, who was operating on Thomas." The entry on July 1st leaves the impression that such "operating" as Hazlitt was doing on the portrait was not making a thoroughly bad business very much better: "A call . . . on William Hazlitt, who at last did make a finish of Thomas's picture, which is now more tolerable than before, though it still has some of the fierceness of the Saracen."

If in this summer of 1812 the things which in his private life had meant most to Hazlitt in his youth were passing, there began at the same moment the uncoiling of that tentacle of the long war which was in the end to lead to the strangling of the public hope in which he had been nurtured. Napoleon had begun that hunting of the Russian Bear which lured him into becoming the prey of a monster far more terrible. On June 24th, the Grand Army had crossed the Niemen, and from Russian soil there was heard arising to heaven the invocation of Liberty; and that cry, strange-sounding from that soil, yet wild-instinctive, was no less provocative of the extremity of man's endeavour than it had proved on other soils, although the liberty for which the people beyond the Niemen fought was—as it seemed to Hazlitt—merely "the liberty . . . of being sold like cattle in the market-place," although their only country was "the estate on which they were live-stock," although their only title to "a reversion in the skies" was their being deprived on earth of everything that makes a man a man, although their only conception of justice bound them at the whim of their leaders to give their lives for any injustice these leaders might decree. In July and August the long columns of the Army which called this kind of Liberty no liberty at all, which had come into being in championship of another kind of Liberty, wound its way in the drowsing heat of the Russian summer towards Moscow, with the Russian Army retreating before them. On September 14th, Napoleon looked down on "the golden city," the half-barbaric jewel that clasped Europe and Asia, now "glittering with a thousand colours in the sun"—with no premonition of the Monster even at that moment cellared and couchant, but soon to be liberated and rampant, and licking towards him with billion tongues. Towards the end of November, just as the Grand Army, an army of spectres now, covered with sores and rags, poor winter-broken husks of men, driven by their Fate, were nearing the Berezina, and attempting the perilous crossing of the river which lay between them and some measure of safety, the news of their first disasters began to reach England. While Napoleon gives orders for the building of new bridges, while the sappers work up to their necks in the water until the ice strikes at their hearts and they fall, to be immediately replaced by others, coffee-house politicians canvass their fate, debate whether Napoleon will be able to save any part of his army, discuss the measure of his guilt. Some hold that he has added to his crimes by ordering the execution of those who, so the report went, had been left behind to fire Moscow. Godwin defends the action. Coleridge thinks it is of no special significance in the struggle one way or other. What seems to him of the very greatest significance, however, is that faith in St. Nicholas had kept at bay in Russia the fear, amounting in the rest of Europe to a superstition, of the Destinies of Napoleon the Great: the Russian campaign—he held— had been won and lost largely in the realm of the imagination, for the physical forces of the Imperial despot had been baffled chiefly because the Russians, unlike other nations, had made themselves inaccessible to his imaginary forces. Crabius says that the great enemy of mankind has always been odious to him less because of specific acts of cruelty than because of his tyrannical laws. Many believe that Napoleon's star has begun to wane; others that the hour of retribution has come for him. Some hold that "the Corsican" never had any special great- ness, assert, like Wordsworth, that he is not only the worst of men, but "of Men the meanest too." Southey has visions of the Cossacks in the streets of Paris. Charles Lamb and his barber still agree cheerfully that the Emperor of the French is after all a fine fellow, let people say what they will. Hazlitt glares fell on those who choose this moment to discover that Napoleon is nothing but a charlatan; tells those who speak of retribution that the men who had fallen in the attack on the Russian despotism had glory and liberty for their bed-fellows, and that the hag Despotism was still the hag Despotism, even when she flaunted herself over Moscow *dressed in a robe of flame-coloured taffeta.*

Hazlitt's private fortunes by this time have taken a turn for the better. By the beginning of the autumn they had been somewhat desperate. Crabius had been beginning to fuss over them rather than to do anything effective towards helping them, and Hazlitt had been in danger of being hurt and humiliated both by him and by Stoddart, when the Lambs had suddenly taken a hand in the game, and thus set one of the greatest of English writers on the path from which he never looked back. Mrs. John Dyer Collier, whose husband worked for *The Morning Chronicle,* had happened to mention one day at the end of September to Mary Lamb that the Editor was in need of an additional reporter, whose work would be chiefly to report parliamentary debates for the paper. Charles, knowing that Hazlitt by this time was "at his wits' end" for a livelihood, had gone at once to ask him whether he would undertake this kind of work, had found that he would be only too glad to get it, and had written at once to Collier, asking him to recommend Hazlitt to James Perry, the Editor: "He is . . . I should think, specially qualified for such an employment, from his singular facility in retaining all conversations at which he has ever been present. I think you may recommend him with confidence. I am sure I shall *myself* be obliged to you for your exertions, having a great regard for him." Once Collier had persuaded the Editor to consider Hazlitt, it must have been obvious to Perry that he would not readily get any one better qualified to work for *The Morning Chronicle,* which at this time was distinguished for its excellence in reporting the proceedings of Parliament. The work Hazlitt had already published, especially *The Eloquence of the British Senate,* gave instant proof of his political sympathies and of his capacities, while he had work as yet unpublished, the *Life* of Holcroft, who had been Perry's friend, also showing him to be conversant with the politics of the day. It would certainly have been no disadvantage to the new reporter's chances that at Hackney College he had studied not only Greek, Latin and Hebrew, but short-hand. By the end of the week he had been enlisted among Perry's men. Years afterwards, in one of those passages which flash a sudden brief shaft of light on the struggles of his early days, he wrote: "To be in want of money . . . is to be a law-stationer, or a scrivener, or scavenger, or newspaper reporter." But at the moment the four guineas a week which rewarded his labours seemed to him "riches

fineless." Lamb's fortnightly "Wednesdays" in the course of this year
had become fortnightly "Thursdays." We get a glimpse from Crabius
of our "newspaper reporter," not at all dissatisfied with his lot, at the
last "Thursday" of the year, the day before Christmas:

"Called late on Charles Lamb. The party there. Hazlitt I was
gratified by finding in high spirits; he finds his engagement with
Perry as Parliamentary reporter very easy, and the four guineas per
week keep his head above water. He seems quite happy."

But Hazlitt had not yet redeemed his debt to the Robinsons. The
portrait of Thomas Robinson, although the Crab had thought it
finished on the first day of July, had not satisfied its painter, and it
had never been forwarded. The Crab, finding Hazlitt in a care-free
mood, thought this a propitious moment for reminding him of his
obligation. He concluded the entry in his Diary about it with the
words: "I believe I shall get it."

3

Shortly after securing work on *The Morning Chronicle* Hazlitt rented
No. 19 York Street, Wesminster, from Jeremy Bentham, and brought
his wife and child up to town. The house was small, awkward in
construction, and difficult to manage. Hazlitt had made choice of it
less because it was comfortable than because it was near his work.
Possibly what determined his choice more than anything was that
it had once been tenanted by Milton, and was thus, for him, classic
ground. The door from the street led immediately into a room "with
very red brick floor and upright posts, that one rubbed one's shoulders
against,"[241] at the other end of which was a door which opened on to
another step from the ground, opposite a narrow, ladder-like staircase,
leading to a dark landing-place. An old large room, wainscoted and
square, which opened off this landing was the living-room of the
family. The awkward ground-floor room served merely as entrance.
The wide windows of the upper room looked on to a small garden or
yard at the back of the house, and two fine old cotton-trees which
might have been growing there in Milton's time. Hazlitt, finding in
the district a tradition that "one Mr. Milford, a celebrated poet,"
had formerly lived in the house, had a stone, overarched by the
beautiful old trees, placed in the wall at the end of his domain and
inscribed with the words: "Sacred to Milton, Prince of Poets." Often
he saw Bentham, whose garden adjoined his own, pausing as he took
a turn round it with one of his many visitors, to look at this stone with
lack-lustre eye—for the old philosopher had not himself very much

feeling for such things—and point it out, perhaps, to some expatriated patriot or transatlantic visitor.

Hazlitt's satisfaction in this stone may have made up to him for many inconveniences in his new home. We have at least four impressions of his household and its ways, which leave on the mind some impression of lack of comfort. One is given by Benjamin Haydon, whom Hazlitt had met at Northcote's studio in the course of 1812. He had said à few civil words to Haydon on his "Macbeth," and as Haydon was both passionately devoted to his art and passionately desirous of appreciation of his aims—these words led to a friendship which was enduring, although there was always some imperfection of sympathy between the two men. Haydon sometimes thought that Hazlitt was grudging towards him, owing to his having been himself disappointed in his aspirations as an artist. Hazlitt, on the other hand, was not only perfectly genuine in regarding his friend's work as falling short of the first order of merit, but was more than inclined to believe, as their acquaintance developed, that Haydon served a very flourishing Egoism rather than a genuine Daimon. Notwithstanding this, they saw a good deal of each other in the years following their meeting. Hazlitt got to know Haydon's gifted friend David Wilkie. Haydon, who made the acquaintance about this time of Leigh Hunt and Lamb, has left an impression of their meetings in the words: "Hazlitt's croaking, Leigh Hunt's wit, and Lamb's quaint incomprehensibilities, made up rare scenes. Lamb uttered his quaintness in snatches, like the fool in Lear, and with equal beauty; and Wilkie would chime in with his ' dear, dear! '"

Haydon, who always held that one of the most beautiful things in Hazlitt's character was his tenderness towards his child, relates in his Autobiography how Hazlitt, in the impulsive and informal way in which he issued invitations, asked him one day if he would come along to a christening dinner. He accepted the invitation, but at four o'clock, when he arrived, Hazlitt was not there; and Mrs. Hazlitt, who received him, seemed in anything but hospitable trim; she was not well, and at the moment of his arrival was sitting over the fire in a bedgown. No signs of preparations for guests were visible. Haydon thereupon went out to seek his host, and met Hazlitt coming home in a rage because he had not been able to get a clergyman. Back to York Street the two men returned, Hazlitt damning the Church and parsons under his breath. Still there were no signs of preparations, but presently all sorts of odd and clever people began to drop in, among them Charles and Mary Lamb. At last a maid entered, who set the table carelessly and roughly, and served the dinner. Haydon's irritation by this time extended to the joint itself, which he describes as being "a great bit of beef with a bone like a battering-ram toppling on all its corners," to the potatoes, "old, waxy and yellow," and to the child, who "kept

HAZLITT'S HOME
NO. 19 YORK STREET , WESTMINSTER

squalling to put his fingers in the gravy." Hazlitt and Lamb set cheerfully about doing the hospitalities, but Haydon felt that even Hazlitt's talk and Lamb's wit could not atone for the carelessness of the board; that even dining in a room in which Milton had meditated was not compensation enough for the penalty of being treated to such unappetising fare; and that even the indisposition of his hostess was not sufficient excuse for the neglect and indifference to comfort shown in the entertainment.

An account by P. G. Patmore, which describes Hazlitt's house as it was some years later, in the beginning of 1818, leaves us again with the impression that it must have been unusually comfortless and bare. It would seem that Mrs. Hazlitt had not been able, in the years that had passed since she had settled in 19 York Street, to turn it into a home. Patmore says that the door was opened by a "sufficiently neat-handed maid," but that the ground-floor room into which it led was so bare that he might have thought he was entering an uninhabited house; that the ladder-like staircase was quite bare; that the dark landing on to which it led was bare; that the great windows of the living-room were curtainless, and that the whole of the wall about the chimney-piece, right up to the ceiling, was covered with scribblings.[242] He says that although it was winter, there was no fire in the fireplace, and that although the hour was two in the afternoon, a table with breakfast things upon it stood close to the empty grate. Hazlitt was still at the table. Mrs. Hazlitt was sitting on a sofa, which along with three chairs completed the furnishing of the room.

Haydon may have written with prejudice or with "the malice of a friend," and Patmore is always inclined to exaggerate Hazlitt's peculiarities and to distort and shabby all that related to him—we note for example that Hazlitt's "beautiful old cotton-trees" become "some dingy trees" in his account. The two remaining descriptions, however, are by genuine friends. William Bewick, one of Haydon's pupils and an enthusiastic admirer of Hazlitt, had the same impression of lack of comfort when he visited Hazlitt's London home, and Procter, who yielded to no man in his admiration of Hazlitt, tells of a meal at 19 York Street, in 1819, which struck him as being spare. Hazlitt, who—it may be remembered—liked to share with his friends such windfalls as came to him from the country, asked him in to dinner one day to share a couple of Dorking fowls which had been sent up to town for him. "I went," says Procter, "expecting the usual sort of dinner, but it was limited only to the fowls and bread. He drank nothing but water, and there was nothing but water to drink. He offered to send for some porter for me but I . . . declined and escaped soon after dinner to a coffee-house, where I strengthened myself with some glasses of wine."

Procter certainly gives the impression that one of Hazlitt's feasts was something from which men who cared much for eating and drinking were glad to escape, but he is careful to add what he considers the reason for the meagreness for Hazlitt's table:.

"Do I mention this spare entertainment as a charge against Hazlitt? Oh no, I do not; on the contrary, I am sure that the matter had never entered his mind. He drank water only, and lived plainly, and not unreasonably assumed that what sufficed for him was sufficient for others. He had nothing that was parsimonious or mean in his character, and I believe that he never thought of eating or drinking except when hunger or thirst reminded him of these events."

This we believe to be the truth. Even when Hazlitt was a boy, he noticed little what he ate or drank, if the conversation of the houses to which he was invited proved interesting to him. Nevertheless the impression left on the mind by all these accounts touching on 19 York Street, is that this "classic ground" and abode of the Muses was a place of habitation not nearly as cheery, nor as happy, as the cottage in Winterslow had been during the first few years of Hazlitt's married life. All that we hear of the cottage leaves the impression that it was a home, and that those who visited it thoroughly enjoyed their entertainment and their fare. All that we hear of 19 York Street leaves the impression that it was a place where a man and a woman lived together, but which neither the man nor the woman had contrived to turn into a home. The suggestion of even loyal Procter's words is that the meal in which he shared was "not the usual sort of dinner." Yet surely, with a couple of fowls as the basis of the repast, something attractive might have been managed by any one who cared to take the trouble to prepare it. Mrs. Hazlitt apparently, although she for her part was anything but indifferent to good food, did not. Nor, although 19 York Street may have been a difficult house to make comfortable, does she seem to have made the best of her London home.

The paper on which Hazlitt had found work was the leading Whig daily. Its Editor, although utterly lacking in literary discrimination, had at one time or another enlisted the services of many distinguished contributors. A self-made man, he was both energetic and amiable. He was at once cordial and yet somewhat grating in manner. The worst that could be said of him was that he had a touch of vanity, that he sometimes pretended to taste in matters of which he knew little, that he was rather too complaisant towards men of rank, and that he was too much inclined to court their company; but Hazlitt would have been tolerant towards faults far greater than these, because Perry, during all his long tenure of the office of Editor of *The Morning Chronicle*, had been remarkably honest and consistent in his politics, and had adhered steadily to principle. He liked Perry, and even after the coolness which led to his discontinuing his work for the *Chronicle*, spoke of him without the least touch of malice.

We have heard from Crabius that he found the work easy. The reporters worked in shifts. Each one listened to the debates for an hour at a time, after which he left to transcribe his notes for the Press, while his place in the Press gallery was taken by a colleague. The only one of these colleagues of whom Hazlitt has left any distinct impression is his Irish friend, spirited Peter Finnerty, who had just returned to work after an eighteen months' term of imprisonment for having charged Castlereagh with cruelty in Ireland.˙ After a time, the chief drawback of the work to Hazlitt was that he found it tedious. He wrote of it afterwards: "the House of Commons, it might be said, hates anything but a commonplace!" Day in day out he had to listen to the same things repeated over and over again. This to a man of his temperament was galling. The friend who wrote on him after his death, in *The New Monthly*, says that once, at least, he yielded to the temptation to cut his work: "upon one occasion, to the great annoyance of some of his colleagues, he preferred his wine with a few friends, to taking his share in reporting an important discussion in the House of Commons."[243] It is not unlikely that he did this on more than one occasion. But for the most part, the reporter could do nothing but endure these speeches. The essayist afterwards spoke his mind about them. The conventionality, the conservatism, and the complete domination by the herd-instinct of the House of Commons in 1813— were the three things about it that made the most lasting impression on him.

We cannot altogether regret his boredom, for out of it sprang the first exquisite trifle produced by his pen. While Coleridge spoke of his "well-headed and well-feathered thoughts" sent "straight forwards to the mark with a Twang of the Bow-string," Talfourd wrote of his "minikin arrows" and "exquisite banter." Both were right. The "minikin arrow" was as characteristic of Hazlitt in some moods as the more powerful one sent straight forward with a twang of the bow-string was of others. Talfourd's dainty phrase describes perfectly his first journalistic venture, a light commentary on the speech delivered on Indian affairs by Lord Wellesley on April 9th, 1813. This speech had been looked forward to with keen anticipation. Crabius says that it had "brought a great number of members of the House of Commons behind the Throne." He had gone himself to hear it, but had been disappointed by it. "After listening for an hour and a half," he wrote in his Diary that night, "my patience was exhausted, and I came home." Hazlitt, who could not leave at will, had also grown very tired of the orator "soaring into mediocrity with adventurous enthusiasm, harrowed by some plain matter-of-fact, writhing with agony under a truism, and launching a common-place with the fury of a thunderbolt," and took his revenge in a commentary which has as its text: "And such other gambol faculties he hath as

shew a weak mind and an able body." This, the earliest of his many
"Trifles Light as Air," is all but flawless. It appeared by some odd
chance in *The Courier*, on April 13th. Perry noted the work of the man
who was at the time his Parliamentary drudge, was entertained by it,
and had it inserted into the *Chronicle* on the 14th.

No further work from the reporter's pen graced the regular columns
of the paper until September. In that month Hazlitt contributed two
long letters, challenging some remarks on English comedy made by
William Mudford, at that time the dramatic critic of the *Chronicle*,
and formulating a theory as to the nature of comedy, which he had
adumbrated six years before in *A Reply to Malthus*. These were at once
recognised as masterly by all who were interested in the subject, and
presently they led to his appointment as dramatic critic. He was
now in the first joy of what he afterwards called "a honeymoon of
authorship." This joy is reflected in his opening articles, the first of
them on the appearance of young Catherine Stephens as Mandane in
the English opera *Artaxerxes*, the second on her appearance as Polly in
The Beggar's Opera. We know at least one reader who on opening his
Chronicle on Saturday, October 23rd, realised that a new writer had
appeared, and one whose work looked almost incongruous among the
more or less stereotyped articles that surrounded it. Thomas Noon
Talfourd, a struggling student who had come to London in February
to read law, and who lived on the next staircase to Lamb, thought the
short notice of *The Beggar's Opera* a perfect piece of work. Some years
after Hazlitt's death, recalling that moment of amazement and delight,
he wrote: "What a surprise it was to read it for the first time, amidst
the tempered patriotism and measured praise of Mr. Perry's columns!"

Thus the first service he did for the stage was to claim recognition
for a delightful young English singer who was not at the time getting
her due—it seemed to him—because she was not Italianate. His next
service, in the beginning of 1814, was of greater weight and of other
metal. To him it was now given to fight the battles of a genius as
struggling and eccentric as his own. Never in all his life henceforth,
because of the sympathy that subsisted between it and his own, and
also because of the way in which his life was linked to it, did he fail to
rally to it in its moment of need, or to turn with lion ramp upon its
imitators, its disparagers, and its persecutors.

4

It is now the evening of January 26th, 1814. Edmund Kean is
trudging to Drury Lane through the snow. The pang of the future is
as yet undreamed-of, but the pang of the present is more than enough.
His thin dark face, were it not for the flicker of life in the eyes, might be

the death-mask of suffering. The hour towards which his life has long
striven—nay rather, long passioned!—is now upon him, for to-night,
after many lets and hindrances, he is at last to make his appearance on
the boards of Drury Lane. Yet no excitement upholds him. Rather, he
feels that he has suddenly become deficient even in common vitality
and energy. He fears that his heart and his voice may fail him. He is
wrapt in gloomy thought as in a mantle. What is there that he does not
fear! The miseries of the past four months, the wretched death of
Howard, his first-born child and his darling, the uncertainties and
anxieties he has endured since his arrival in town, the disparagement
of his fellow-actors, the shabby, slipshod rehearsal of the morning,
during which Raymond, the manager, had said to him: "This will
never do, Mr. Kean,"—these, added to semi-starvation, although they
have not broken his spirit, have yet brought him very low. As he
walks, he wishes but one thing more than any other—that he were
dead.

Courage! little Jupiter *tonans*! Your divinity will flow back into you
the moment it is needed. You too shall launch your thunderbolt.
You shall have all the triumph of which your soul can conceive.
To-night you quiver as you pass the steps of the theatre; in a little
time, if that can make you forget the wounds your pride has taken,
you shall force your horse to mount them, with none to baulk your
wild whim. To-night, Drury Lane, although there is in it one kindred
spirit that will warm to the power and passion in yours, is half hushed
and cold; before a month is out the crowds will be pulsating before
the theatre by noon, and the pit will echo at night to tumultuous
shouting that will be hushed in the silence of breathless expectancy
the moment you make your entry. To-night you walk through the
snow, and as the slush slips over your poor hard shoes, you carry your
silken stockings in the pocket of your shabby coat; by the time the
spring flowers have come, if that can make you forget the delicate
child you lost in your poverty, you shall see your little Charles, whom
you carried along the bare autumn hedgerows on your back, at play in
the shelter of your home—with the yellow leprosy of gold trickling
through his baby fingers.

5

Kean was a man unknown, and the next day, his first appearance
on the London stage was unnoticed by various papers, including *The
Times*, which regarded only established reputations as worth their
notice. But Hazlitt's article in the *Chronicle* beat with a powerful
personal dynamo which immediately fixed the attention of the town

on the new aspirant to fame. Hazlitt afterwards denied that he had "written up" Kean:[244] In a sense this was true. His criticism was never rhapsody. From the beginning he held Kean's genius in the severest keeping. Just because of the completeness of his response to it he never trifled with it, pandered to it, nor even flattered it. In his notice on Kean's first performance of Shylock he admitted that he had seen many an actor who had conveyed more profoundly the idea of a man who had become warped by brooding over one idea; realising at once that Kean was not merely a genius·but an actor who had subdued his genius to the resources of his art, or as he put it in a later article, that Kean's acting was "not in the least of the unpremeditated, *improvisatore* kind," but throughout "elaborate and systematic," he touched on what was already one of Kean's mannerisms, the length of some of the pauses, and he hinted to him the danger of relying too much for the conveyance of feeling on. expression, which could not be seen clearly from all parts of the great London theatres. But with all this, he conveyed such an impression of power that he brought the town to Drury Lane. After that all who thrilled to the miracle of genius could judge for themselves. Kean no longer needed an advocate with them. Byron became the mouthpiece of such as these when he exclaimed: "By God, he is a Soul!" But during this first season, Hazlitt's assertions that, magnificent as was the work Kean had done, his power had never as yet been fully unleashed, kept on the tiptoe of expectation all who were inclined to hold, like Perry, that Kean's genius was of the "freak" variety, and that the brilliance of his acting was only a flash in the pan, while it daunted all·those who were ready to say, like Crabius, that Kean, because he was a little man and because his voice was hoarse, would "never be qualified for heroic parts;" and swept into an enthusiasm that was largely imitative of his own, the great multitude of people who have no opinion of their own but always follow any lead that is energetically given. Nothing sweeps people off their feet like genuine passion, and Hazlitt's articles on Kean's performances were unique in theatrical criticism by virtue of their passion. This is not surprising. Not only did he find in Kean the one thing needful, the fire from Heaven which would have made nothing of physical disadvantages a hundred times greater than Kean's, but he, who had brooded over Shakespeare's plays until they had become part of his blood and spirit, who had pondered interminably each *nuance* of character, whose mind was not only attuned to the beauties which all could see, but had lingered over the *minutiae* of each play—found in Kean someone who had also lingered not only over the general interpretation of character but over the *minutiae*, and who, moreover, had the gift of making what he felt not only visible but pictorial.

But if the intellect was stimulated to the highest degree of excitement by Kean's performances, the eye was stimulated no less. From the

beginning Kean satisfied the artist as well as the thinker in Hazlitt. He
did something to the imagination which caused the eye to see the play
as "a succession of striking pictures." Kean as Shylock, leaning on
his staff, and beginning to tell "with the garrulous ease of old age,"
the tale of Jacob and his flock; Kean as Richard leaning against the
side of the stage before coming forward in the courtship scene with
Lady Anne; Kean as Hamlet coming back after he had gone to the
extremity of the stage, as if caught by a pang of tenderness, to press
his lips to Ophelia's hand—these things left impressions on the mind
which made Hazlitt say that Kean bade fair to supply the town with
the best Shakespeare Gallery it had ever had. Of the first of these
he felt that it carried the spectator back to the olden time; of the
second he said all when he said: "It would have done for Titian to
paint;" of the third he said: "It had an electrical effect on the house.
It was the finest commentary that ever was made on Shakespeare."
There was one other moment in Kean's playing during this first
season the impression of which remained before Hazlitt's eyes like that
of a vivid picture. This was the moment in which Richard, after being
disarmed, stands as if petrified, with his empty hands outstretched
"in motionless despair—or as if there were some preternatural power
in the mere manifestation of his will." Of this gesture Hazlitt wrote:
"He fought like one drunk with wounds: and the attitude in which he
stands with his hands stretched out, after his sword is taken from him,
had a preternatural and terrific grandeur, as if his will could not be
disarmed, and the very phantoms of his despair had a withering
power."

The appeal to the intellect and the appeal to the imagination of the
artist made by Kean were completed for Hazlitt by the sympathy
between the sheer power and daring in the younger man and the as yet
still unused power and daring in himself. As to the nature of this
bond, when he said of Kean: "In one who *dares* so much, there is
indeed little to blame"—he said all.

In this first season, Kean played Shylock, Richard and Hamlet, in
January, February and March, to packed houses in which the enthusiasm bordered on hysteria, and Hazlitt, who watched over the unfolding of his genius with the anxious care with which a father might
have watched over the unfolding of a son's—there was always something tutelary in his attitude to Kean—still held that the little man
with the "great soul" had not yet reached his high-water mark, that
there were deep reserves of power in him as yet not called into play.
Not until he had seen Kean's greatest performance as Othello did he
feel that these deep reserves of power had proved themselves, and that
Kean had done that which placed him far beyond the touch of Time.

Hazlitt's articles on Kean not only swept an actor of genius from
obscurity into fame; they brought some measure of reputation to

himself. As his dramatic criticism had caused some stir, it was inevitable that he should make his appearance in other sections of the
paper also. "Something I did, took, and I was called upon to do a
number of things all at once. I was in the middle of the stream, and
must sink or swim," he said afterwards to Northcote, when explaining
the way in which he had been launched into journalism. From the
beginning, his articles on drama had made it evident that he was even
more gifted as a literary critic than as a dramatic one. Any time
the play was of interest, he tended to say more of the play than of the
actors. He did this sometimes even when he was interested in the
actors: thus it was as throwing new light on the genius of Gay that
the account of .The Beggar's Opera had delighted young Talfourd,
rather than because of what it had said of the charm of Miss Stephens's
singing. When the actors were only moderately interesting, he
tended still more to give the greater share of his comment to the play.
In his account of Antony and Cleopatra, on November 16th, the actors
are all huddled together in a short paragraph at the end of the article,
which is concerned chiefly with expressing dissatisfaction with the
stage version of the play, in which scenes from Dryden's All for Love
had been grafted on to Shakespeare's tragedy. Hazlitt as a literary
critic never surpassed either in discrimination or in power of phrasing
what he said here as to the folly of mixing the gold of Shakespeare with
"the heavy tinsel" of Dryden. The comparison of Shakespeare and
Dryden which follows shows that a literary critic of the first rank had
arrived.

Nothing could be more natural than that presently he should
launch into reviewing of the more elaborate kind. Before he ceased
to work for the Chronicle he had contributed to its columns a number
of articles of literary criticism.

Inevitable as it was that Hazlitt should pass from dramatic criticism
to pure literary criticism, it was still more inevitable, in the days that
followed Leipzig, that he should pass from dramatic to political criticism, his gift in which, like his gift in literary criticism, had also been
hinted at in his articles on drama. Everything at the moment tended
to project him towards such work. The victory of the Russian and
Prussian armies at Leipzig had been followed by rejoicing on the part
of most of his old friends. Wordsworth had celebrated it in a sonnet
praising the fortitude which the King had displayed during the long
struggle. Crabius in the winter of the year was showing this sonnet
everywhere. Southey, who had just been made Poet Laureate, published
the Carmen Triumphale, the first four stanzas of which made their
appearance also in The Courier. Hazlitt, on the other hand, felt "crushed
like the worm and writhing beneath the load." But even if he felt
crushed, he was a dangerous man to meet these days for a loudly-
jubilating Crabius, who reports of one of these encounters: "Returned

to Lamb's. Hazlitt was there, and overbearing and rude. Disputed
with him on politics. He mixes passion and ill-humour and personal
feelings in his judgments on public events more than any man I know,
and this infinitely detracts from the value of his opinions, which,
possessing as he does rare talents, would otherwise be very valuable.
He always vindicates Buonaparte."

He always vindicates Buonaparte! Yes! and even if he be writhing
beneath the load he still has skill and strength to carry on notable
guerilla warfare on Buonaparte's enemies through whatever piece of
work he happens to be doing. In his review of the *Carmen Triumphale*
he gibes savagely at Southey for pouring mechanical abuse on Buonaparte: "We confess, we wish to see Mr. Southey, like Virgil, in his
Georgics, scatter his dung with a grace," and three days after the solemn
strains of the *Carmen Triumphale* had been reproduced in *The Courier*, he
retorts on them with exquisite banter. But flouting retort of this kind
could in no way discharge the burden of sorrow and anger which
pressed upon the heart of one who regarded the issue which had been
decided at Leipzig as "whether the princes of Europe should be put in
a situation to dictate laws and a government to France." It was this
burden of sorrow and anger which pressed him, in the development of
events following upon the battle, into taking his stand as the principal
adversary of all those who followed the Prime Minister's announcement
that terms of peace would be proposed "consistent with the honour,
rights and interest of France," by setting up the cry, "no peace with
Buonaparte," among them Southey, whose Ode,

> "Who counsels peace at this momentous hour,
>   When God hath given deliverance to the oppress'd,
>   And to the injured power?"

made its appearance both in *The Courier* and *The Times*. It was in answer
to the challenge of this, uttered in all sincerity by Southey, but echoed
by a hundred venal tongues, and with determination to do mortal
combat on the spirit out of which it issued, the spirit which, as he
conceived, had turned Europe into "a fountain of blood," and might
yet keep it in a welter of blood in the centuries to come, that Hazlitt
launched his denunciation of all "those harpies of the press, whose
business it is to scare away the approach of peace by their obscene and
dissonant noises, and to tear asunder the olive-branch, whenever it is
held out to us, with their well-practised beaks"—and thus, in his
thirty-fifth year, entered the arena which he was only to quit with his
closing breath.

Among these "harpies" he numbers the "hired scribbler" sitting
"secure and self-satisfied" at his desk, sending thousands of his fellow-
countrymen to death "with a venomed word, or a lie that looks like

truth," and quite content to scribble on, regardless of the enmity he has inflamed and the suffering he has set in motion; the scribes of *The Times*, *The Courier*, *The Sun*, *The Star* and *The Morning Post*; all who "in blowing the blast of war for a livelihood" serve their own interests at the cost of the weal of mankind, and pass this self-service off as patriotism; and lastly, what he calls "The Political Automaton." The most biting of his attacks is couched in the form of a character-sketch of The Political Automaton, "the thing . . . hired to soothe or inflame the public mind, as occasion requires."

His bitterest and most scornful attacks during these days are on his brother-in-law, Dr. Stoddart, who had now become acting Editor of *The Times*, and whose endless outpourings of abuse upon Napoleon had by this time earned him the nickname of Dr. Slop in the opposite camp; but his most sustained attacks, and those which drew from him the clearest statement as to the principles which determined his attitude to the struggles of the day, were on the letters which Edward Sterling, under the pseudonym of Vetus, contributed to *The Times* from his home in "somniferous green Llanblethlian" in the vale of Glamorgan, between November, 1813, and January, 1814. Vetus was generally known as "the Thunderer" of *The Times* newspaper. Carlyle said of his *Letters*: "The tone, whenever one glances into this extinct cockpit, is trenchant and emphatic." We do not wish to recall the extinct cockpit. Nor would we pause to record, were there only this to record, that Hazlitt met the fury of Vetus with equal fury, nor even that "the Thunderer" fared somewhat badly at the hands of this challenger. We pause to consider the replies to Vetus, not because they are of controversial interest, but precisely because, glittering though they be, they cannot be dismissed as mere controversial fireworks. They coruscate, it is true, but they are at the same time charged with meaning and with warning. They are the first of Hazlitt's writings which can be regarded as "prophetic"[245] in character. They are "prophetic" in their denunciation of that which being wrong in the relations between men and nations, must lead inevitably, sooner or later, to the "fountain of blood;" they are "prophetic" in their pleading for a new relationship between nations, the possibility of the establishment of which had been envisaged by very few of his contemporaries; and they are "prophetic" because in all that he says on this new relationship Hazlitt has succeeded in expressing his deepest intuitions, as these have been evoked by the experience of having passed through an apocalyptical chapter of human history. They are of the *nature* of Burke's writings on the French Revolution, different in their creed though they be, and they are the only political writings of the period that in quality in any way resemble these. Hazlitt writes as a metaphysician: all he says, apart from the mere fireworks of controversy, is occasioned not by accidental happenings or temporary occurrences, but is referable to principles, themselves referable to reason, or to intuition, by which we mean "reason working on a deeper level," and it is deduced primarily from that study of what in his day would be called the "underconscious" nature of Man, which was his chief preoccupation during his lifetime, as the fruits of this study form the substance of his writing.

All the attitudes of mind which Hazlitt denounced in these days were the objects of his denunciation because they were provocative of war, and because it seemed to him that they must inevitably lead to another general European catastrophe, as soon as the war-spent nations recovered their strength, for the maintenance of general peace depended more on the spirit in which international relations were conceived than on anything else. Thus the first object of his denunciation is the spirit of implacability of which Vetus and all such writers as Vetus, make a virtue:

"We will also venture to lay down a mixim, which is—That from the moment that one party declares and acts upon the avowed principle that peace can never be made with an enemy, it renders war on the part of that enemy a matter of necessary self-defence, and holds out a plea for every excess of ambition or revenge. If we are to limit our hostility to others only with their destruction, we impose the adoption of the same principle on them as their only means of safety. There is no alternative."[246]

The second object of his denunciation is the spirit of acquisitiveness of which Vetus and all such writers as he make a virtue, the constant iteration of

> "the simple Plan
> That they should take who have the power
> And they should keep who can."

Vetus had written: "I have stated . . . as the only legitimate basis of a treaty, if not on the part of the continental allies, at least for England herself, that she should conquer all she can, and keep all she conquers." Hazlitt pronounced this to be less the basis of a lasting peace than the breeding-ground of a new war, "for the very ground of war is a peace whose conditions are thought to bear hard on one of the parties," and denounced the spirit in which such a basis of a peace-Treaty was proposed, as tending to close up in perpetuity the avenues by which European peace might be attained, and thus to shut the gates of mercy on mankind. He condemned such a proposal as bred not out of courage, but out of Fear—the perpetual irritant of all the passions provocative of war:

"Instead of a proud repose in our own strength and courage, these writers only feel secure in the destruction of an enemy."[247]

The third object of his denunciation is that distortion of patriotism in which love of country becomes narrowed down to suspicion of the well-being of any nation save one's own. In this• connection he denounced the assumption underlying all Vetus's writings on foreign affairs, that "every addition to the general stock of liberty or happiness" in other countries must be "so much taken from his own," and that "hatred, suspicion and contempt·for other nations are the first and last principles of the love which a patriot bears to his country." This leads him into an analysis of the kind of patriotism to be discerned in any of Vetus's recommendations as to British policy in Europe, which seems to him "inconsistent with the common privileges of humanity," and which, if it were held up as an ideal in each country of Europe, would inevitably end in the cancellation of European civilisation. To this kind of patriotism he gives the name "exclusive patriotism," and proceeds to define it as follows:

"We mean by it . . . not that patriotism which implies a preference of the rights and welfare of our own country, but that which professes to annihilate and proscribe the rights of others—not that patriotism which supposes us to be the creatures of circumstances, habit and affection, but that which deprives us of the character of reasonable beings—which fantastically makes our interests or prejudices the sole measure of right or wrong to other nations, and constitutes us sole arbiters of the empire of the world—in short, which under the affectation of an overweening anxiety for the welfare of our own country, *excludes* even the shadow of a pretension to commonsense, justice and humanity."247(b)

He accuses Vetus of having advocated a species of patriotism that would warp an instinct which should be a blessing to mankind into a curse that eats from generation to generation into the life of mankind, and terminates in mutual destructiveness on the part of neighbouring nations; and repudiates this advocacy as likely to lead to a second catastrophe which might mean the submergence of Europe under the ruins of the civilised world:

"We shall not learn of him, for his 'yoke is not easy, nor his burden light.' . . . Vetus mistakes the nature of patriotism altogether. *He would transform that principle which was intended for the tutelary genius of nations, into the destroying demon of the world.* . . . In his whole system, there is not room for 'so small a drop of pity as a wren's eye.' His patriotism is the worm that dies not; a viper gnawing at the heart."248

Talfourd said of Hazlitt: "he never wrote willingly, except on what was great in itself." This, like most of what Talfourd said of

Hazlitt, is very true, but we venture to add to it, that often, when forced to write on what was temporary or of the moment, he related it to what was great in itself, or made it the basis of discussion of what was great in itself. His political writing, although done for the leading Whig daily, is never classifiable as mere party journalism. Thus from an examination of the tendency of Vetus's conception of what British policy in Europe should be, he passed on to an examination of the nature of true patriotism, which led to his endeavour, in these times when nothing but Anti-Gallican fury was sacred, to remind his country-men that all patriotism "not founded on, nor consistent with truth, justice and humanity, is a painted sepulchre, fair without, but full of ravening and all uncleanness within."[249] Love of country was for him identified with love of peace, of social happiness, of independence, above all of Liberty.

Even as he pled against the adoption of "exclusive patriotism" by his own *or any other nation*, as certain in the long run to bring about a general conflagration and general ruin, he pled in the same way against the adoption of an "exclusive" conception of Liberty, which was the logical sequence of the adoption of an "exclusive" conception of patriotism. He enforced his protest against this "exclusive" con-ception of Liberty by immediate reference to the proposed restoration by Austria, Prussia and Russia of the Bourbons to the French nation:

"let them not, in the name of honour, or of manhood, receive the royal boon of Liberty at the point of the bayonet."[250]

It is this theme which called forth from his pen the noblest piece of writing which the trouble and confusion of the time had as yet wrung from him:

"We shall not hail such a catastrophe, nor such a triumph. For out of the desolation would arise a poisoned stench that would choak almost the breath of life, and one low, creeping fog of universal despotism, that would confound the Eastern and the Western world together *in darkness that might be felt*. We do not wish for this final consummation, because we do not wish the pulse of liberty to be quite destroyed, or that the mass of our common nature should become a lifeless corpse, unable to rouse itself against never-ending wrongs, or that the last spark of generous enthusiasm should be extinguished in that moral atheism, which defaces and mangles the image of God in man. We do not wish that liberty should ever have a deer's heart given her, to live in constant fear of the fatal, inevitable, venal pack behind her; but that she may still have the heart of a lioness, whose mighty roar keeps the hunters at bay, and whose whelps revenge their parent's death!"[251]

The last of Hazlitt's articles to appear before the abdication of Napoleon was published just seven days before the armies of "those systematic lovers of justice," the countries that had followed up the storming of Ismail and Warsaw by a second partitioning of Poland, in the opening years of the war with France, made their entry into Paris. This article is a passionate plea for the sacredness of art, evoked by an article which had appeared in *The Times*, hailing the possibility of the sacking of the Louvre by the Cossacks. Hazlitt's reply is a cry that the "Transfiguration," the "St. Mark," the two paintings of St. Jerome, the "Marriage at Cana," the "Deluge," the "St. Peter Martyr" and "all the glories of the antique world," should be placed by man far above the fluctuations of human passion or the mutterings of the fury of political or even national quarrels. The anger in which he wrote as he envisaged the possibility of the destruction of the Temple of Art and the shrine of his youthful worship, whipped his words into a white-heat. It was for him as if the Ark of the Covenant were in danger of being desecrated by barbarian hands:

". . . once destroy the great monuments of art, and they cannot be replaced. Those mighty geniuses, who have left their works behind them as an inheritance to mankind, live but once to do honour to themselves and their nature. 'But once put out their light, and there is no Promethean heat that can their light relumine.'"[252]

Crabius reported in his Diary on April 10th, 1814, the full confirmation of the various rumours that had been reaching London as to the abdication of Buonaparte. Thus the long war, which Hazlitt had regarded from the beginning, not as a national quarrel but as a war over a question of political principle, which had been forced on Europe by France's rejection of the Bourbon dynasty—whether the peoples of Europe existed for their governments or whether the governments existed for the peoples—came to an apparent conclusion. Compared to the principle at stake—the balance of power between governments and peoples—the question of the balance of power in Europe, which because of the unexpected strength of France had become intermingled with the original question, had always appeared to him temporary and insignificant. He had viewed the commencement of the war with disapproval; he had watched its progress, in the course of which the extreme wrong had seemed to him many times to have been made to appear the extreme right, with continuous pain; he viewed its apparent ending with something like despair. Apart from anything else, it seemed to him to outrage a people's rights, a people's dignity and a people's choice. He had no doubt, although despite their war-exhaustion he scorned the French for submitting to it, that it was hateful to the French nation as a whole, especially to the inarticulate peasantry, whose sons had fought under Napoleon's banners as they had never fought under the banner of any Bourbon king—no matter what it might be to the intriguing politicians in Paris, the Talleyrands and the Fouchés, and all the petty jobbers in their train, to the philosophers, and to the turncoat men of letters, like Chateaubriand *the Quack*.

Carlyle says that "the hearts of all English and European men awoke staggering as if from a nightmare suddenly removed, and ran hither and thither." Not all felt as if the nightmare were over: there were some who felt as if a chapter of human endeavour that might have created a new and a better world had ended in the re-establishment of a tyrannous old one. But that they ran hither and thither is certainly true, each man reacting to the events of the hour according to his kind. Byron, angry with Buonaparte for not having ended his career with a Byronic gesture, frothed over into doggerel:

> "'Tis done—but yesterday a King!
>   And armed with Kings to strive—
> And now thou art a nameless thing:
>   So abject—yet alive!"

Coleridge thought, like Fouché, that Bounaparte, if not closely watched, would be back with the next year's violets. Crabius went from man to man collecting Voices, came to the conclusion from what he heard that Poland would not regain her independence when the victorious Powers met at the conference-table, and put the matter out of his mind with the comfortable reflection that perhaps she would not have been able to make use of it if it had been restored to her. Vetus did the most surprising thing of all. With his wife and his two little boys, John and Anthony Sterling, aged five and seven respectively, he left "somniferous green Llanblethlian" to make his home in the country against which he had so long been thundering—was not, however, to find it "somniferous." Haydon also, who in his boyhood had led out his friends to the cornfields to cut off Frenchmen's heads, and had cried as each poppy-head was sliced from its stalk: "There goes a Frenchman, huzza!"—also went over to France and looked at it with eyes as wondering as if he had dropped from the moon: "Everything was new and fresh. We had thought of France from youth as forbidden ground, as the abode of our enemies. It was extraordinary. They absolutely had houses, churches, streets, fields and children." Another thing he learned from every soldier he met—was that Buonaparte had never been beaten. "Il était trahi; il était trahi"—was the cry of all; and the officers, when among themselves, instead of the national anthem sang a verse of their own beginning with the lines:

"Vive Buonaparte!
Vive ce grand conquérant!"

He arrived at Paris when "the ashes of Napoleon's last fire were hardly cool, the last candle by which he read was hardly extinguished, when the last book he had read was to be seen turned down where he had left it"—could in no wise get over the wonder of seeing the table this mysterious being had leaned upon and inked, "the chairs which he had sat upon and cut; the bell-ropes he had pulled." Napoleon's bedroom! To have been admitted to Apollyon's bedroom would hardly have seemed more out of the course of nature. He could scarcely give his attention to the pictures in the Louvre, because of the amazing sense of being in contact with History that possessed him; went, however, to Gérard's, and there again! Napoleon! or rather a head of Napoleon which made all the other heads in the room look like those of children, a head with eyes in it which once seen were not to be forgotten, even by one who had sliced off poppy-heads in his youth: "Gérard's horrid head of Napoleon has haunted me . . . that bloody glassy eye looked you through without mercy."

Haydon had left for France, flushed with pleasure and with hope, because of the recognition which his picture, "The Judgment of Solomon," had won. It had not been so much the congratulations of his fellow-artists, of Smirke, or of Flaxman, or Turner, that had filled him with triumph, but that Hazlitt, on seeing it, had extended "two cold fingers" to him, and said, "By God, Sir, it is a victory." Of Hazlitt in these days when all the world was in motion, we see little, because he held himself aloof from the rejoicings of his fellow-men. He mourned over the lives that had been thrown away merely, as it seemed to him, to teach the survivors the lesson that they were "born to bear *fardels*" for their masters.[253] The thought that the blood of almost six million men had been shed to bring about such an ending, still more the thought that his fellow-men could rejoice over what seemed to him a climax of futility, vanity and cruel imbecility, haunted him night and day. His withdrawal from the rejoicings of the moment was misinterpreted by his enemies, and by some of his friends too, who thought that, like Byron, he was "confounded by the conduct of Buonaparte,"[254] and that he was therefore "ashamed to show his face in public places." The worst thing we have to relate of him in this black mood is that one day he turned upon Charles Lamb, who although by no means a disparager of Buonaparte steadily refused to be drawn into the heat of politics either on the one side or on the other, and rent him. As Lamb put it to Wordsworth in August: "he blowed us up about six months ago, since when the union hath snapt."

Some time afterwards he vented the bitterness with which he

viewed the antics and gesticulations and runnings hither and thither of his fellow-mortals in the words:

". . . if instead of packing off Louis the Desired from Hartwell, we had sent over that idol of Eastern temples, the *Boa Constrictor* from Piccadilly, decorated with the symbols of the Universe and Ancient Wisdom, instead of Lilies and San Benitos, we can see no reason why John Bull and the French people might not have been equally satisfied: nor what should have hindered Mr. Southey from adapting one of Wesley's hymns to the occasion, or Mr. Wordsworth from mouthing out some deep no-meaning about "royal fortitude" and "time-hallowed laws," or Mr. Coleridge from proving that the Serpent was the more ancient and sacred symbol of the two."[255]

6

Talfourd wrote shortly after Hazlitt's death: "The events of Mr. Hazlitt's true life are not his engagement by the *Morning Chronicle* or the transfer of his services to the *Times*, or his introduction to the Edinburgh Review . . . but the progress and the development of his understanding as nurtured or swayed by his affections. ' His warfare was within.'" All this is true—yet it requires some qualification. It is certain that the truth of Hazlitt's life, as indeed of most lives, lies at a deeper level than that of fact, that the essentials of his life thus far were not so much events, as the struggle towards thought, in his adolescence, towards expression, in his early manhood, then towards assimilation of the new regions of thought and feeling opened out to him by Coleridge, towards perfection in painting following upon the meeting with Coleridge, and towards re-creating himself both as a writer and as a painter in the humiliation that followed upon the first sexual episode in his life of which there is any record. But yet throughout all these years, no matter how his other preoccupations fluctuated, his development was closely and constantly related to his hope for the liberty and the happiness and the progress of mankind; this hope reached its climax of intensity in the years in which he was making a beginning in political journalism; and his passings from one newspaper or periodical to another are therefore events of his "true life" in so far as they are symbols of the various crises through which he passed, and of the inveteracy of opinion which made it impossible for him to be in complete sympathy even with those who like himself were forward-looking in politics.

Thus shortly after the Abdication of Napoleon he severed his connection with the *Chronicle*, the chief reason being that the immediate turn events had taken in France had discredited him with Perry as a political commentator. The impassioned article on the

treasures of the Louvre which had appeared at the end of March
was the last political article he wrote for the *Chronicle*, was indeed the
last political article of any consequence by his pen to appear in any
paper for over half a year. He may be said to have been silenced for a
time even in the Liberal papers. He was not dismissed by Perry, but
ceased to call at the *Chronicle* Office because Perry's manner made it
clear to him that he was unwelcome. He had—it is true—many other
strings to his bow, and could have filled the columns of the *Chronicle*
easily without touching on politics at all, but Perry had little taste in
literature, art or drama. He had no idea of the quality of the work
Hazlitt was doing for him—although others were quick to note it—no
awareness of the extent to which everything Hazlitt touched turned to
literature in his hands. The chief sympathy between the two men was
that they were both of them men of indisputable political integrity.
When the strain of the critical times caused even this bond to snap, and
Hazlitt's Napoleonic sympathies, which were so intense that even
to his close friends they seemed sometimes to interfere "with his better
reason," [256] proved altogether too much for his Chief, there was little
to hold Hazlitt and Perry together, and there were many minor irritants[257] to fray their relationship.

The loss of his regular work, and of his four guineas a week, was
at the time a source of great regret to him. In the long run this
apparent misfortune proved no misfortune at all, for it sent him
forward towards Editors more qualified to understand and appreciate
his literary gift, his intellectual tact, his range of subjects and his
power in dealing with them, than was vain, honest, grating Perry,
of the cordial voice, the blunt mind and the harsh speech. We should
not forget to mention, however, that while he was working for the
Chronicle, he made his first appearance as an essayist. The first piece of
original work he contributed to its columns was an essay, slight, yet
at once exquisite and profound, on The Love of Life. This was to find
a noble companion and complement in the essay on The Fear of Death,
which his pen was to produce after eight years' further schooling in
"that domain which we call the Passions." Slight though the essay
on The Love of Life is, in it, for the first time, all the finer strings of a
very fine instrument are touched.

Before Hazlitt had quite severed his connection with the *Chronicle*,
he had made one contribution to *The Examiner*. This, the first piece of
writing contributed to the weekly with which his fortunes were
afterwards to be so closely associated, and which was to play so valuable
a part in developing his special gift, was an essay entitled *On
Posthumous Fame*. It was as an essayist that his new connection with
The Examiner tended, right from the outset, to develop him. There
was at the moment no opportunity for him to do such routine work for
Leigh Hunt as he had done for Perry. Hunt had been imprisoned in

the Surrey Gaol since March, 1813, but he continued to edit *The Examiner* throughout his imprisonment. The political commentary was in his own hands. He was quite well able also during his imprisonment to deal with the reviewing, while the only thing he could not do himself, the dramatic criticism, had already been undertaken by Thomas Barnes, and Hunt's brother Robert was installed as art critic. Thus Hazlitt, who had done political criticism, art criticism, dramatic criticism and reviewing for the *Chronicle*, either "dwindled into" or was "enlarged into"—according to the view we take of the matter—an essayist for *The Examiner*. Hunt, who was a charming essayist of the light kind, realised that in Hazlitt he had come upon a born essayist, whose work was entirely different in scope, in tone and in temper from his own. Before the end of the year he had proposed collaboration to him, in a series of essays to be contributed to *The Examiner* under the general title of *The Round Table*. There can be no doubt that this first year's work with Hunt tended to develop his characteristic gift, to enable him to realise the possibilities of the essay as a commentary on human nature, and to help him to perfect it as a medium of expression.

In the meantime, by the end of June he had begun to work for John Scott, who was the Editor of *The Champion*. Here he was able to undertake work of the routine kind. His work for Scott up to the end of this year consisted chiefly of art criticism and dramatic criticism. It might be said that the work he did for *The Examiner* developed his art, while the work he did for *The Champion* kept the wolf from his door.

The work he had done by the end of 1814 for these two distinguished periodicals, each of them edited by men of literary tact and discrimination, included three articles which are worth noting because of their bearing on his life. The first of these is his first contribution to *The Champion*, an essay on West's "Christ Rejected" which appeared in its columns on June 26th. Although the article was almost universally censured as being too severe an onslaught on the aged President of the Royal Academy, its distinction and power swept him into immediate fame as a critic of art.

The second of these is worth noting chiefly because of the light it throws on Hazlitt himself at the moment, and because it drew a trail of regrettable consequences across his life, for it won him the declared and not ineffectual enmity of Wordsworth. It is the article on *The Excursion* which he contributed in three sections to the columns of *The Examiner* between August and October, 1814. Some time afterwards Charles Lamb told Crabius that Hazlitt had wept over this review, and Crabius wrote in his Diary: "I do not believe that Hazlitt cried," which only goes to show how little he understood of the struggles of such a soul. We can only realise the incredible welter of feeling in which Hazlitt read this poem in 1814 by putting ourselves in his place for a moment. He read it when the cause in which he had hoped seemed to him to have failed utterly, when the light for him was wellnigh extinguished, and it brought his life tumbling down about him like a pack of cards. He had read parts of the poem in 1803, and they had made a deep impression on him; he may even have read some of it in manuscript in 1798, when he had not as yet realised that Wordsworth's political development was to take a course contrary to his own. He read it with memories of Wordsworth's conversation in these early days as to the hope and joy that had surged through France in the opening years of the Revolution. And now that the poem was completed, he found in it the friend of his youth looking forward with hope to the defeat of the forces of Liberalism, a defeat which, by the time the poem had been published, had been accomplished. He found also the friend of his youth turning into a kind of scarecrow figure of warning a still earlier and a very much dearer friend of his youth, one who had felt the troubles of the time more deeply than any private sorrows and who had died partly in consequence of his grief over the distortions and difficulties that had come to the Revolution, the Rev. Joseph Fawcett, Wordsworth's model for the Solitary. Fawcett had died as much of loss of hope as of anything else,[258] and Wordsworth had made of him a kind of example in a sermon.

Apart from that the poem in its delineation of the peasantry of the Lake district brought back to Hazlitt's memory the one thing in life he wished more than anything to forget—the treatment at their hands which had driven him from the Lakes in 1803.

If we remember these things, if we remember that the poem was almost a symbol to him of all the things in his life and in his human relationships the passing of which he most regretted, if we remember that it recalled to him also all he most wished to forget, if we remember that, appearing at the moment it did, it must have seemed to him almost like a monument erected to commemorate the triumph of the cause he despised over the cause in which he believed, we shall understand why it is that the surface of his review is churned up by feeling that otherwise would be unintelligible, and broken up by digressions —like that on the character of country people—which otherwise would seem fantastic. If ever a review was written in sorrow it was this one. Hazlitt never wrote more from his heart than when, after commenting on the hope Wordsworth had expressed for the triumph of the forces that had gathered against France, he raised his voice in lament over his own loss, in this moment of defeat, of the hope that his desires for the happiness and progress of mankind would be consummated:

"that season of hope is past; it is fled with the other dreams of our youth, which we cannot recall, but has left behind it traces, which are not to be effaced by birth-day odes, or the chaunting of *Te Deums* in all the churches of Christendom. To those hopes eternal regrets are due; to those who wilfully and maliciously blasted them, in the fear that they might be accomplished, we feel no less what we owe—hatred and scorn as lasting."[259]

The third article to comment on which we must pause is the essay on Iago which Hazlitt contributed to *The Examiner* on August 7th. It compels special notice not only because of the light it throws on Hazlitt's development as a man, or perhaps we should rather say, as a sexual being, but because in it, for once, he ran badly "out of the course"—as he used to say half jestingly when confessing the extent to which his intransigeance had been wont to tease Perry—in literary criticism, and this was afterwards used by his enemies against him, in a very wounding fashion, long after he had expiated the offence. This extraordinary essay developed out of his criticism of Kean. In May Kean had played Othello. He had followed this up by playing Iago, and his performance of the part had acted as an irritant on Hazlitt's mind. While the Othello, although the acting in Act three had been "a master-piece of profound pathos and exquisite conception," had been unequal, the Iago seemed to him the most faultless of all Kean's performances thus far: that is to say, it seemed to him the most consistent and entire piece of acting Kean had ever achieved. Yet he thought that the entire conception of the part was wrong. He returned to the subject in July, confessing the measure in which Kean's interpretation had amazed him, not exactly censuring Kean for its strangeness, for, as he said: "It was ever the trick of genius to be thus," but proceeding to a masterly analysis of Iago's character, by way of laying bare before Kean, to whose genius throughout this year he was ever tutelary, the intellectual bases of it. This profound piece of analysis reads much like a Letter of Advice from one man of genius to another. Every word in it is of permanent value, for every word is related to that metaphysician's conception of human nature from which all that is of most value in Hazlitt's work is flung. Had he stopped at this point he had done "nothing but well and fair." But in *The Examiner* a fortnight later, he reappeared with a conclusion to his essay, in which he went off at a most extraordinary tangent. Instead of pursuing further the tainted scent of his quarry, he suddenly stops and snuffs appreciatively where it is rankest, lingers over it, and finds that the scent is an honest scent after all. Iago's suggestion that Desdemona's love for her dark-skinned lord had arisen out of something like sexual perversity seems to him to probe the nature of woman's love to the quick. Iago's words: "If she had been bless'd she would never have loved the Moor," and his assertion that in her choice of such a husband

" . . . one may smell . . . a will most rank,
Foul dispositions, thoughts unnatural,"

seem to him "most learned and irrefragable." "For our part," he says, "we are a little of Iago's council in this matter; and all circumstances considered, and platonics out of the question, if we were to cast the complexion of Desdemona physiognomically, we should say that she had a very fair skin and very light auburn hair, inclining to yellow! We at the same time give her infinite credit for purity and delicacy of sentiment: but it so happens that purity and grossness sometimes

> ' nearly are allied,[260]
> And thin partitions do their bounds divide.' "

As if this were not enough, he added a long Footnote on the character of Desdemona, in which, with extreme bitterness, he ridiculed the idea that any woman could be moved by or respond to a man's spiritual nature. Leigh Hunt, in his "Note upon Note, or a word or two on the Passion of Love in answer to some observations in our last week's *Examiner*," which appeared on August 14th, registered his protest against Hazlitt's tendency to rail at woman's love as being mostly compounded of animal appetite. Crabius in his Diary registered his entire disapproval of all that Hazlitt had said both of love and of the character of Desdemona: "He has written in *The Examiner* a review of the character of Iago, very ably executed, and has added a gross attack on the pretensions to chastity in women: not even Desdemona escapes him." As for us, we agree for once whole-heartedly with Crabius. We have not a word to say in defence of Hazlitt's Footnote on Desdemona as a piece of literary criticism. It is clean "out of the course." Moreover, as Hazlitt said to Kean of some of the detail he had introduced in his Iago, like his triumphant pointing to the tragic loading of the bed, it "is not in the text" of Shakespeare: Desdemona's love was bred of mere admiration not untouched with pity. In another play in which he had a share, Shakespeare has given a study of a woman who was moved by a lust of the blood of the kind from which he expressly dissociates Desdemona.[261] If Perry had said of this Footnote what he was unjust enough to say of one of Hazlitt's political articles, "This is the most pimping thing I ever read," we should feel little disposed to quarrel with him. It is saved from ignobility only by the note of torment in it.

But if we have not a word to say in defence of it as a piece of literary criticism, we shall have somewhat to say of it as a human document, when we pass on from considering Hazlitt's career as a journalist at this time, to considering his development as a man. At the moment we can only pause to note the interest of the matter, not only as showing the way in which Hazlitt's private unhappiness at the moment distorted his criticism, but as showing the way in which the life of his work struck sparks out of others; and the way in which the obstinate mental courage in him, compelling him to say what he felt, whether it was of good report or evil report, inevitably involved him in controversy with those around him. Not only the Editor of the paper for which he wrote, but Thomas Barnes, the regular dramatic critic, challenged him on the issues arising out of this controversy. Barnes concluded his challenge with a palpable hit when he said that "W.H." in delineating Iago as a man actuated by the love of power, by the craving for excitement, and by the need to keep himself and others perpetually "in hot water," had perhaps some existing character before him, for at any rate his picture bore "a much stronger resemblance to Buonaparte than to Shakespeare's Ancient."

"W.H." had written little enough for the past six months on Buonaparte. On October 23rd, he made his appearance in *The Champion* with the sole political article—except one slight gird at Talleyrand's postponement of the abolition of the slave trade by France—which he had published since March. This is a commentary on an article on The Opening of the Congress, in *The Examiner* of October 16th, in which Leigh Hunt, who in the course of the year had been busy, as Hazlitt put it afterwards, in "strewing the path of the Allied Sovereigns with flowers," had expressed his aspirations as to the great things to be accomplished by the Congress of Vienna. Hazlitt was in complete sympathy with all these hopes and aspirations, but looking at the members of the Congress he saw little chance of their being realised. The rulers of Europe, when united against Buonaparte, had invoked the name of Liberty, and in that name they had conquered. Now that they were victors, they were likely to return to their old ways. The Golden Age was not likely to be ushered in with the restoration of the Bourbons. What hope could there be for the regeneration of Europe, from an opportunist like Bernadotte, a "royal marmoset" like Ferdinand of Spain, an inheritor of the tradition of Frederick the Great, like the King of Prussia, from the Emperor of Austria, from the King of France, from the Pope? Hazlitt answered the question in the following survey of their doings since Buonaparte had been overthrown:

"No one will in future look for ' the milk of human kindness ' in the Crown Prince of Sweden, who is a monarch of the new school; nor for examples of romantic generosity and gratitude in Ferdinand of Spain, who is one of the old. A jackall or baboon, dandled in the paws of a Royal Bengal tiger, may not be very formidable; but it would be idle to suppose, if they should providentially escape, that they would become tame, useful, domestic animals.

"The King of Prussia has recovered the sword of the Great Frederick, his humane, religious, moral and unambitious predecessor, only, as it appears, to unsheath it against the King of Saxony, his old companion in arms. The Emperor of Austria seems eager to snatch at the iron crown of Italy, which has just fallen from the brows of his son-in-law. The King of France . . . has improved his reflections during a twenty years' exile, into a humane and amiable sanction of the renewal of the Slave Trade. . . . His Holiness the Pope . . . employs his leisure hours in restoring the order of the Jesuits and persecuting the Free-masons. Ferdinand . . . shuts up the doors of the Cortes—and throws open those of the Inquisition. To us it is all natural, and in order. From this grand gaol-delivery of princes and potentates we could expect nothing else than a recurrence to their old habits and favourite principles."[262]

In this article Hazlitt also prophesied the impermanence of the settlement that had been effected for the French:

"They will not relish the Bourbons long, if they remain at peace; and if they go to war they will want a monarch who is a general."[263]

To us it is all natural and in order! Crabius, who met Hazlitt on February 5th of the following year, has left a summary of his conversation which—despite the curious shade of inaccuracy in the report—throws light on the mood in which these words were written and in which this article was conceived:

"I then went to Alsager's to dinner. The party consisted of Sergeant and Mrs. Rough, Ayrton, Martin Burney and William Hazlitt. Hazlitt, while he continued sober, was excellent company. . . . Afterwards, he became warm on politics, and declaimed against the friends of liberty for their apostacy. He attacked me, but was at the same time civil. He expressed his pleasure at the present conduct of the sovereigns of Europe as confirming his anticipation. The main difference in feeling between Hazlitt and us is that he maintains that there was at no time so great danger from the recent and unestablished tyranny of Buonaparte as from that of ancient governments."

That Hazlitt did not express pleasure at the immediate state of affairs we feel sure, for he felt none, but Crabius confirms the consistency of his claim to have seen in it the fulfilment of his anxious presentiment as to what would happen in Europe if the armies of France were overthrown.

7

Although Hazlitt was not given much opportunity of political
writing in these days, when his apprehension as to the intentions of
the old governments of Europe far surpassed those of all his friends, he
made himself many an opportunity of sending forth both "minikin
arrows" and some that were not "minikin," in the course of his other
writings. In January, 1815, when he reprinted in *The Examiner* his
essay On the Love of Life, he managed to slip in, in connection with
his theme, that "the strength of our attachment to life" is a "very
fallacious test" of happiness, a passionate vindication of Buonaparte's
greatness, against all those who thought the fallen Emperor a shabby
fellow, because he had not achieved the Byronic gesture:

"Many persons have wondered how Buonaparte was able to survive
the shock of that tremendous height of power from which he fell.
But it was that very height which still rivetted his backward gaze, and
made it impossible for him to take his eye from it, more than from a
hideous spectre. The sun of Austerlitz still rose upon his imagination,
and could not set. The huge fabric of glory which he had raised still
'mocked his eyes with air.' He who had felt his existence so keenly
could not consent to lose it!"[264]

On the first day of the following month, March 1st, 1815, "he who
had felt his existence so keenly" once more made all Europe conscious
of the intensity of that existence. The whole surface of existing things
was churned up as by a violent storm, for on that day Napoleon landed
with a small band of men at Fréjus, and in the days that followed made
his way through a country the peasants of which came to meet him
with flowers in their hands, the rhythm of the dance in their feet,
laughter on their lips and fragments of song pouring out of their
throats. Their greeting for him was:

> "Bon! Bon!
> Napoléon
> Va rentrer dans sa maison!"

while towards the King who had been set over them by Talleyrand and
the Allies their cry was:

> "Roule ta boule, roi cotillon,
> Rends ta couronne à Napoléon."

Violets seemed to spring up everywhere to deck his path and grace his

welcome home. There had not been such a general overflowing of
light-heartedness under the skies of France since the early days of the
Revolution. Everywhere the influence of the advancing presence was
felt. Men reacted to it in various ways, but no man remained unaffected by it. Louis, as if to prove that he was indeed "roi cotillon,"
hurried out of his palace like a servant caught disporting himself in
the house of his master, and over the frontier. The Comte D'Artois,
too, as was his wont, "disappeared in the storm." Chateaubriand
also, who had hailed the First Consul as the Instrument of Providence,
who had been the first to desert, to renounce and to denounce the
fallen Emperor, stayed not to dispute the issue, but crossed the frontier
along with many another Quackery. "The big European tide rushing
into all the smallest creeks" caught out great and small alike. It reached
our friend Vetus, "the Thunderer" of *The Times*, at the home he had
made for himself at Passy, and set him adrift or at least afloat again,
with but little thunder left in him for the moment, not before the two
little "Veterans," John and Anthony Sterling, who almost from their
birth had looked upon Napoleon as the great enemy of mankind, had
seen their schoolmates go wild with joy, and had heard them fill the
air with the shrill childish cry of *Vive l'Empereur*. It reached Vienna,
et voila le Congrès dissous. It swept into the *Examiner* Office in Maiden
Lane, *et voila la Table Ronde dissoûte*. It reached *The Champion*, and
sundered Hazlitt, who could not understand how "the friends of
liberty" could unite with the enemies of Buonaparte, after the
exhibition of a tyrannical and grasping spirit the Allies had given to
the world during their year of triumph, from his friend John Scott,
to whom the immediate duty seemed to be to make a last stand against
the menace of French power. Coleridge preened himself on the fulfilment of his prophecy. Hazlitt felt as if ice had melted about his heart.

We get one impression of him during the excitable days of April,
from Crabius, who encountered him again at Alsager's, on the 15th:

"I stayed till near two . . . and debated with Hazlitt, in which
. . . I was also not successful, as far as the talent of the disputants was
involved, though Hazlitt was wrong as well as offensive in almost all
he said. When pressed, he does not deny what is bad in the character
of Buonaparte. And yet he triumphs and rejoices in the late events.
Hazlitt and myself once felt alike in politics, and now our hopes and
fears are directly opposed. . . . Hazlitt is angry with the friends of
liberty for weakening their strength by going with the common foe
against Buonaparte, by which the old governors are so much assisted,
even in their attempts against the general liberty . . . his *hatred*,
and my *fears*, predominate and absorb all weaker impressions."[265]

As for Hazlitt's joy, brief-lived though it was, the memory of it had power to stir him to the day of his death. In his closing years, when he wrote of the "romantic walk"—as Leigh Hunt had called it—which Buonaparte took "from the sea-coast to his home in Paris,"[266] a note of exultancy once more leapt into his words:

"It was indeed a merry march, the march from Cannes. Those days were jocund and jubilant—full of heart's ease and of *allegresse*. Its footsteps had an audible echo through the earth. Laughed eyes, danced hearts, clapped hands at it. It ' loosened something at the chest; ' and men listened with delight and wonder . . . to the unbarring and unbolting of those doors of despotism which they thought had closed on them forever. All that was human rejoiced; the tyrant and the slave shrunk back aghast, as the clash of arms was drowned in the shout of the multitude."[267]

During May and the first weeks of June, the tension of breathless expectancy was felt in London. On June 22nd it broke at last. Haydon, returning late at night from John Scott's house in the Edgware Road to his rooms in Great Marlborough Street, had the first news of Waterloo from a Foreign Office Messenger, who was hurrying to Lord Harrowby's with tidings of the victory, and ran back to Scott's bursting with excitement and joy. Almost his first thought was: "*Now*, will the Imperial Guard say again to me, *Napoléon n'était jamais battu!*" All the next day he was nearly as drunk with excitement as his model, old satyr-like Corporal Sammons of the 2nd Life Guards, who had been through the Spanish campaign, had "popped his hand" into King Joseph's coaches at Vittoria and brought away "a silver pepper-box," and who, although he was perhaps more a danger to every pretty girl he met than he had ever been to the King's enemies, seemed, even in the midst of his joy, totally "astounded" that the last battle of the war should have been won without him. Crabius spent the day over the newspapers in the Surrey Institution, was dissatisfied, however, that the people as a whole, who had showed little enthusiasm for the renewal of the war, now showed few of the signs of rejoicing that might have been expected after such a victory. He found the illuminations at night but "dull," and he noted "scarcely any marks of public zeal or sympathy," in the parks or streets of London. John Scott rushed almost immediately over to Paris, and was in time to see the four bronze horses, the noblest of the spoils reft by Napoleon from Venice in his day of power, removed from the gates of the Tuileries and let down into a cart on the backs of English artillerymen, from one of whom, to mark the day, he bought the head of the pole of the triumphal car to which the brazen horses had been yoked, a gilt ram's horn, for eighteenpence. "I saw the Venetian horses go," he wrote, in the highest spirits, to Wilkie and Haydon, who realised with satisfaction that to the people of Paris there could hardly be "a more hideous mortification" than the lowering of these proud trophies. Charles Lamb, reacting differently to the triumph of the moment, said that he would not mind standing bareheaded at Buonaparte's table "to do him service in his fall,"[268] and there were apparently a fair number of his countrymen who felt likewise, for when the ship which had carried Buonaparte to England lay in Plymouth harbour, huge crowds gathered from all over the country and cheered—now that the terrible sword had been struck from the hands that had held all Europe at bay—for the little Emperor Nap who had held all from the People, as they had never gathered and cheered for the Autocrat of all the Russias and his Prussian friend, who was generally despised as "the worst whiner in Europe" in adversity, and one of the worst bullies in prosperity, although the one was the descendant of the Great Catherine and the other the successor of the Great Frederick. Napoleon "stood on the deck of the *Bellerophon*, like the King of the very world that had conquered him,"[269] and all England seemed to be posting towards Plymouth as all Europe had once posted towards Paris, in a delirium of curiosity, or as if irresistibly attracted by some strong animal magnetism. Haydon himself, a Plymouth man, was a second time nearly seduced from his art by the frenzy. It was all he could do not to throw his paint-brushes to the winds and go posting with the rest to Plymouth. His sister Harriet Haviland was scandalised at the way the people stood up in their boats and huzzaed. She told her brother that the loyalty of the people would be undermined if Buonaparte were kept longer off Plymouth, for all seemed fascinated by him. Nevertheless she, too, like all the world, rowed out to see what she could see, and was much disappointed at being kept at such a distance by the guard-boats that she could not distinguish his features. Mary Russell Mitford swore that had she been at Plymouth she would not have been baulked in that way. She wrote with much less than her wonted poise to her friend Sir William Elford, Plymouth's Recorder: "Goodness! if I were in your place I *would* see him. I would storm the *Bellerophon* rather than not get a sight of him, ay, and talk with him too."[270] But then Miss Mitford, although she would have said that she loathed romance and pathos, was undoubtedly, even as her friends said, "*folle de Napoléon*," and the presence of the fallen Emperor in English waters had for the moment inflamed her feeling to "a passion and a gallantry."

The slackness in the public rejoicings in the South could not be reproached to the North, or at least to the district in which the Poet lived. On August 21st, Wordsworth, looking "like a Spanish don" in a red cloak which he had borrowed for the occasion, his wife and sister, Southey with his wife and two of his children, Lord and Lady Sunderlin, James Boswell, the son of Johnson's adorer, who was staying with them at the time, "some adventurous Lakers," and "Messrs. Rag, Tag and Bobtail,"[271] all climbed to the top of Skiddaw to see the bonfire set ablaze, roasted beef there and boiled plum-puddings, sang *God Save the King* round the flaming tar-barrels, "drank a big wooden bowl of punch," and rolled great blazing balls of tow and turpentine down the steep side of the mountain.

In the meantime, in the course of the month of August, 1815, while the poets drink healths and make merry among their fair mountains that had never been cursed with the smell of gunpowder, nor ever looked down upon slaughter, Corporal Sammons, who was still very angry that Waterloo had been won without him, and who kept fighting it over and over again with those of his comrades who had been invalided home from the battlefield, brought a party of these wounded men, all of them powder-scorched, powder-scarred, and powder-marred, to Haydon's rooms, to tell the story of the battle and of their wounds and of their comrades' fate, to Haydon, John Scott and mild David Wilkie. They were all men of the 2nd Life Guards, and most of their stories were of their encounters with the Cuirassiers. Haydon had a personal as well as an historical interest in their tales, for some of his own models had been in the battle, and he wanted to know how they had fared. They were able to give him news in par-ticular of brave John Shaw, the Life Guardsman and famed pugilist, who had sat for him, and of Dakin, who had been his model for one of the sleeping grooms in his "Macbeth." He was much impressed by the simplicity with which these men spoke of what they had seen, suffered, or done. Now and again what they said touched a spring of feeling in him, much as certain kinds of poetry might have done. One of the men, the finest of all his models, a man called Hodgson, who stood six feet four inches and would have been the perfect model for Achilles, told with remorse of how in the heat of the battle he had refused mercy to a French officer, whose helmet, when it had fallen off in the en-counter, had disclosed a bald head with a few white hairs that showed him to be an old man. Hodgson had cleft him through the skull. Now that the battle was over, he could not get the thought of the white hairs out of his mind. The recollection—he told them—*pained* him often.

This was a battlefield on which extremes of age and youth had met. Hodgson had also experienced a pang when on charging up to the French baggage, he had seen Napoleon's latest recruits, little artillery driver-boys of sixteen, mere children, crying on their horses.

They said of the meeting of the Life-Guards and the Cuirassiers that day, that it was "like the ringing of ten thousand blacksmiths' anvils." Hodgson said also that he would never forget the shock of his first cut at a cuirass. He had thought it was silver lace, and it had nearly shivered the bone of his arm.

Everybody, including Southey, who wrote to his friend Grosvenor Bedford telling him to keep his ears open for any first-hand information he could get about Waterloo, was avid to collect all the anecdotes of the battle that could be heard. Hazlitt was always eager to listen to anything he could hear of Napoleon and Napoleon's wars. He had spent many an hour with Haydon's veterans talking over their campaigns with them, especially with Sammons, to whom he would talk endlessly about the Peninsular War and Napoleon, only to be told invariably at the end of the discussion by the Corporal, who "was proof" against all his arguments, that *the Duke was the better man.* He reckoned John Shaw a very gallant soldier, and afterwards said so in his *Life of Napoleon.*[272] It does not appear, however, that he was of this party: indeed, if he valued his life, he did well, in these days, to avoid gatherings of the men who had borne the brunt of Waterloo. We know little about him in the summer that followed it except that he wandered about the streets of London like a ghost among living men, and drank himself blind in the effort to forget what seemed to him the final passing of the hope of seeing "some prospect of good to mankind," such as that with which his life had begun. Mercurial Haydon, before the month of August was over, was already beginning to feel that "Waterloo was getting an old story," and was getting ready to leave History, in which he became absorbed spasmodically, for Painting, his permanent love. With Hazlitt it was far different. While most of his fellow-countrymen were rejoicing simply and whole-heartedly, no matter of what party they were, in a great national victory and the final crushing of the enemy, for the man whose mind forced him to make an abstract question of everything and to follow to its utmost conclusion a train of reasoning in which he could find no flaw or a metaphysical principle which he believed himself to have established, Waterloo, although it was a national victory, was also the symbol of the passing of hope for the progress of the cause of the Peoples of Europe from the world of his day—the final triumph of the spirit of autocracy over the spirit of democracy. He was as one staggered and stunned mentally and physically by this second shattering of hope. To all who met him his utter prostration of mind and body seemed a thing they could never have believed if they had not witnessed it. Who could measure the loneliness of his spirit in these days! He is neither of the one camp nor of the other, for he goes far beyond any of his friends in his anticipations of the reaction of tyranny in Europe, of which it seemed to him Waterloo was the herald—and most of his friends look askance at him and what they call his "croakings." No longer William of Wem is he, but rather William of No-Man's-Land, and from such glimpses of him as we get it would appear that he behaved very much as any other man might do who wandered for months companionless and unfriended in such a No-Man's-Land.

One alone in all England there was who perhaps suffered more in this hour—although for him it was an hour of complete triumph—than Hazlitt did in his hour of humiliation. The poets' bonfire on Skiddaw might "fairly put out the moon," as Southey claimed, but to this one the sun and the moon were alike dark. Hazlitt ever held that all that had been done by "the yearnings of the spirit and intellect of man," and that had promised "a proud opening to truth and good through the vista of future years," had been "undone by one man, with just glimmering of understanding enough to feel that he was a king, but not to comprehend that he could be the king of a free people!"[273] Yet it was not those who praised the King, nor those who flattered him, nor those who saluted his "royal fortitude," nor even those who loved him, who expressed most poignantly the King's Tragedy—but his companion in the loneliness of these days, this unrelenting William of No-Man's-Land, who held him primarily responsible for having checked and defeated the better mind of his generation, and especially for having brought into being and kept in motion by his obstinacy until no power on earth could stop it, the dread game of cross-purposes which had ended at last in the final agony of Waterloo, and who judged him accordingly:

"Persons who are fond of dwelling on the work of retribution, might perhaps trace its finger here. The Monarch survived the accomplishment of all his wishes, but without knowing that they had been accomplished. To those who long after passed that way, at whatever hour of the night, a light shone out from one of the towers of Windsor Castle—it was from the chamber of a King, old, blind, bereft of reason, ' with double darkness bound ' of body and mind; nor was that film ever removed, nor those eyes or that understanding restored to hail the sacred triumph of Kings over mankind; but the light streamed and streamed (indicating no dawn within) for long years after the celebration of that day which gladdened the hearts of Monarchs and of menial nations, and through that second night of slavery which succeeded—the work of a single breast, which it had dearly accomplished in darkness, in self-oblivion, and in more than kingly solitude!"

Chapter Two

THE AFTERMATH OF VICTORY (1815-1817)

"When I first met Hazlitt, in the year 1815, he was staggering under the blow of Waterloo. The reappearance of his imperial idol on the coast of France, and his triumphal march to Paris, like a fairy vision, had excited his admiration and sympathy to the utmost pitch; and though in many respects sturdily English in feeling, he could scarcely forgive the valour of the conquerors; and bitterly resented the captivity of the Emperor in St. Helena, which followed it, as if he had sustained a personal wrong. On this subject only, he was ' eaten up with passion; ' on all others he was the fairest, the most candid of reasoners. His countenance was then handsome, but marked by a painful expression."

THOMAS NOON TALFOURD.

I

NEITHER drink nor despair is a preservative of youth: the two when united are as corrosive as lightning. It was about this time that the first frosting of grey began to appear in Hazlitt's hair, and that the look of suffering, often noted on his face when in repose, began to leave its imprint on his features.

The origin of this look of suffering may of course be traced partly to the overthrow of his public hopes and to his estrangement from most of his fellow-men during a time of national rejoicing: he must have seemed in these days to others, even as he seemed to himself, a species by himself. But the overthrow of his public hopes, which all realised, was only part of his misery. He tells us that it coincided almost exactly with what at the time he regarded as the final overthrow of his private happiness, a misery as yet concealed from the world. Of the way in which his private happiness was blighted at this time he has left no direct record; but he lets fall in his writing now and again certain hints which seem to suggest that at this time he may have been staggering, not only under the blow of Waterloo, and under the sense of disappointment with his marriage, but under the blow of some disappointment in love. His wife's comparison of the passion which consumed him in 1822 to his former passion for "Sally Shepherd," seems to indicate that this earlier passion was one into which he fell in the course of his married life. We think it likely that it is to this period of his life this "frenzy," as Mrs. Hazlitt called it, should be referred, and that the effects of this united with the effects of the

326

overthrow of his public hopes to produce in him some such breakdown as he afterwards experienced in 1822 and 1823, after the unhappy ending of the chief passion of his life.

However this may be, there can be no doubt that some of the effects of a "frenzy" of this kind appear in his writing at this time, whenever it touches on the relationship between man and woman. It is clear that his sense that neither in wedlock nor without could he find any union which satisfied the spiritual being in him, has become a trouble corroding his whole inner life, its outward manifestation being the extraordinary bitterness with which he writes of Woman. Our first indication of what was happening to him at this period is given in a Letter on the Character of the Literary Man,[274] which he contributed in October, 1813, to *The Morning Chronicle*. In endeavouring to trace, in the course of this Letter, the difficulty experienced by the man-of-letters, or the man-of-letters of a certain temperament, in his relationships with women, he throws direct light on the origin of his own sense of frustration, on what he regards as the chief source of his own difficulties, and on the quality of the bitterness which has begun to consume him. It is clear that he feels his life has made shipwreck on the idealism of his youth. The effect of having lived in an ideal world —he holds—is to produce for the man-of-letters some degree of difficulty in all human relationships, but most especially in his relationships with women, for he cannot find in the real world anything to compare with what he has found or imagined in the ideal:

"Where, O where would he find the rocks of Meillerie . . . or on what lips would Julia's kisses grow? . . . . One trifling coquette only drives out another; but Raphael's Galatea kills the whole race of pertness and vulgarity at once."[275]

In this confession as to the disenchantment of the idealist by actual contact with women, although there is a good deal of sadness, there is as yet no anger. It closes almost on a note of resignation. But presently, in the writing of 1814 and 1815, there are definite indications of a violent reaction against an idealism which he has come to consider ruinous. Resignation has given way to anger with women for their incapacity to understand or to value and honour the spiritual or intellectual being in Man, and to a bitter railing, both against women for the measure in which they had betrayed his faith, and against his own idealism as the hidden reef on which his hope of human happiness had wrecked itself. In the Footnote on Desdemona which we gave up as indefensible in so far as it claimed to be literary criticism, this at last turns to fury:

"If Desdemona really 'saw her husband's visage in his mind,' or fell in love with the abstract idea of his ' virtues and his valiant parts,' she was the only woman on record, either before or since, who ever did so. . . . The idea that love has its source in moral or intellectual excellence, in good nature or good sense, or has any connection with sentiment or refinement of any kind, is one of those preposterous and wilful errors, which ought to be extirpated for the sake of those few persons who alone are likely to suffer by it, . . . who, treading securely the flowery path, marked out for them by poets and moralists, the licensed artificers of fraud and lies, are dashed to pieces down the precipice, and perish without help."[276]

In the violence of his reaction against his idealism he goes so far as to commend Iago's view of the matter:

"Iago is indeed a most learned and irrefragable doctor on the subject of love, which he defines to be ' merely a lust of the blood, and a permission of the will.'"[277]

Crabius thought that some of Hazlitt's writing about this time showed "a twist either about his heart or his head." Good unintricate Crabius! say rather—his life has here flung out what may yet prove to it a mortal coil!

2

The beginning of the Hundred Days and the sharp clash of opinions on the political situation between Hazlitt and John Scott led to the discontinuance of his work for *The Champion*. But the work he had done for it had already procured him one enviable distinction, that of being admitted to the ranks of the "Edinburgh" Reviewers. In February, 1815, he made his first appearance in the *Edinburgh* with a long article on Standard Novels and Romances. The contact thus established with Jeffrey, as well as the reputation as an art critic he had made for himself when writing for *The Champion*, may have led to his being invited presently by Macvey Napier, who was editing the Supplement to the new edition of the *Encyclopædia Britannica*, to contribute the article on The Fine Arts.

Also, shortly after discontinuing his work for *The Champion*, he took over the Theatre for *The Examiner*. On March 19th, just a fortnight after he had ceased to write for *The Champion*, the first article he wrote as regular dramatic critic for *The Examiner* made its appearance. After this date his contributions were regular. Thus he had not only the occasional, but highly lucrative work for the *Edinburgh* to occupy him, but steady work as dramatic critic and as essayist for

The Examiner, which was to absorb all his weekly journalism for the next two years.

In the meantime, he was still excluded from political commentary.

Nowhere in Hazlitt's writing can we see how deeply Waterloo and the aftermath of Waterloo affected him, as clearly as in the weekly dramatic commentary of this year. His criticism is so deeply scored with the troubles of the time that it might be said to be compact of jars. All the joy of the early work in the *Chronicle*, all the freshness is gone. Much of it is like a withering sleet. In the opening months of 1816, although he always reacted to the strong stimulus of Kean, and although Kean always had his due share from him of praise, criticism and advice, it is clear that he saw everything else with little interest or enjoyment. The note of fatigue, impatience, severity, disillusionment and sheer ill-temper persisted throughout the greater part of the year. In the autumn he began to toy with those great favourites of his, the Miss Dennetts, three lovely sisters, like "three red roses set on a stalk,"—as he said—whose dancing charmed him, and in the following months he carried on with this "little trinity of innocent delights" a dainty flirtation which restored some of the sparkle to his writing. When watching these "three kindred graces" dancing in their "trinal simplicities below," he could say, as he once said at Winterslow, when watching a lily expanding its petals after a summer shower: "my cloudy thoughts draw off." But they never drew off for long.· The storm of angry politics was in his blood. It may have been because he had no opportunity of finding an outlet for his feeling as to the events of the day, that the storm never went out of his blood. Certain it is that it was not until he returned to political journalism and was able to unpack his heart at will in stormy words, that the clouds cleared from his dramatic criticism. During the year in which he was excluded from political commentary, his pent-up sense of the trouble with which the country was heaving, made the whole business of the theatre, formerly such a delight to him, seem at times a hideous impertinence. Sometimes his sense of the trouble in the real world surged into his commentary on the ' make-believe ' world. Thus in a month of extreme distress in the country, remembering that all the starving people could get in reply to their indecorous crying for bread was the admonition on the part of authority, "Down, wantons, down!" conjoined to redoubled efforts to keep the distress out of sight, he opened one of his articles with the biting irony of the words: "We think the tragedy of *Jane Shore*, which is founded on the dreadful calamity of hunger, is hardly proper to be represented in these starving times; and it ought to be prohibited by the Lord Chamberlain, on a principle of decorum."

3

Towards the close of 1816 he was permitted by Leigh Hunt, who by this time was quite disillusioned as to the nature of the "settlement" which had been made in Europe, and who was therefore much less inclined to regard Hazlitt as merely a "gunpowder" man, to return to political journalism. Hunt, who had been so quick, after the first abdication of Napoleon, to chaunt the Descent of Liberty, looking around him in 1816, saw that the victory of the Czar, the King of Prussia and the Emperor of Austria in Europe, meant that the Peoples of Europe found themselves locked in far grimmer bands of servitude than they had known during the days of Napoleon's utmost power. The triumph, not of Liberty, but of a grey and ignoble and petty tyranny had come. Most of the liberal-minded felt as he did. Those among them who had been most sharply divided from Hazlitt before the triumph of the Allies, who had thought it a madness on his part to identify the triumph of the Allies with the setting-in of a tide of despotism throughout Europe and of oppression for the great bulk of the People of England herself, had now to realise that what they had hailed as the triumph of Liberty had been turned into what looked very much like the triumph of autocracy. Not only was there widespread dissatisfaction with the reaction towards autocracy throughout Europe. It was generally felt that during the long years of warfare civil Liberty, within England herself, had receded. The foreign foe had been beaten, but by many of the lovers of Liberty it was felt that the foe within the wooden walls of Old England was still more dangerous. Stendhal described the Government of England in these years as "*L'aristocratie masqueé par une charte*;" he felt that Liberty had been chased from England, and only chased from it, about this time.

Thus Hazlitt found himself no longer isolated, but one of a group of fighting-men who, if they helped to influence the new faint stirrings of Liberty in some of the countries of Europe, did even more, at a time when government through spies and *agents provocateurs* was "rapidly growing into a system," when the reports of such vile creatures as Castles and Oliver, human birds of carrion battening on the ruin of their fellow-men, were made the pretext for the suspension of Habeas Corpus, when the liberty of the press was assailed, when the masses of the workers of the country were all but enslaved—to preserve the liberties of their own countrymen. They drove the government spy overseas; they preserved the right of free speech; they pled the rights of human personality; they resisted tyranny howsoever, whensoever, and wheresoever, in the days in modern history when it was most necessary in England to build a wall of defence around the liberties of the subject, especially around the liberties of the poor man.

Our readers may perhaps be expecting us to add to this account of the ending of Hazlitt's long and painful period of isolation, that being no longer isolated, but working with a group of friends for a common cause, the rebirth of Liberty, not only in Europe but in his own country, and having a certain prestige among them because he alone had foreseen that a retrogression of Liberty in all the countries of Europe, including his own, would be the result of the destruction of the ideals of civil liberty that had interpenetrated the thoughts of France, had indeed regarded it as the inevitable consequence, because the logical one, of the sequence of events—he mellowed or softened in the companionship that had now come to him. We cannot report that this was so. He gave no quarter to those whom he regarded as oppressors of the People, because he felt that they wished to crush civil courage out of the hearts of the People, and to substitute for it the habit of mechanical docility. He would make no truce with those whose scheme of government included the coercion of men and women into working automata. To have made any such truce in the years that followed Waterloo would have seemed to him a treachery against that of which he made religion. He had never been saccharine. At this time, when he fought with all his might, in a country ruled, and ruled with a rod of iron, by an aristocracy, for progress towards democracy in the England of his day, the harsher discords came into his mind and speech. Even before he had begun his steady outpouring of political journalism, the play of forked lightning had begun, not only in his dramatic criticism, but in his essays and occasional work. It glittered dangerously now whenever he touched on Burke. We have tried to indicate our sense of the generousness with which Hazlitt, in 1807, laboured to convey some impression of the greatness of Burke. The intensification of bitterness which had come to him in the intervening years is illustrated by a Note on Burke which he added to one of the essays he contributed to *The Examiner* in the February of 1816:

"This man . . . who was a half poet and a half philosopher, has done more mischief than perhaps any other person in the world. His understanding was not competent to the discovery of any truth, but it was sufficient to palliate a lie; his reasons, of little weight in themselves, thrown into the scale of power, were dreadful. Without genius to adorn the beautiful, he had the art to throw a dazzling veil over the deformed and disgusting, and to strew the flowers of imagination over the rotten carcase of corruption, not to prevent, but to communicate the infection. His jealousy of Rousseau was one chief cause of his opposition to the French Revolution. The writings of the one had changed the institutions of a whole kingdom; while the speeches of the other, with the intrigues of the whole party, had changed nothing but the *turnspit of the King's kitchen*. . . . The genius of Rousseau had

!evelled the towers of the Bastile with the dust; our zealous reformist, who would rather be doing mischief than nothing, tried therefore to patch them up again, by calling that loathsome dungeon the King's Castle, and by fulsome adulations of the virtues of a Court strumpet." [278]

It will be seen how far behind this has left the magnanimity of the earlier study. Here, if anywhere, is to be found some justification of Gifford's description of Hazlitt as "a sour Jacobin."

The change of temper that had come over him between the years preceding Waterloo and the years following it may be illustrated no less completely from his own definition of the word "Jacobin" in the years following what he regarded as the final overthrow of the cause of Democracy in France. For Hazlitt, until political strife had embittered him, Jacobinism meant little more than sympathy for the poor, the desire that the poor man might live his life without the constant fear of extreme distress, that he should have rights human and political, that he should have liberty of thought, that he might, in short, not pass from the cradle to the grave having it dinned into his ears on all sides that the poor man's lot on earth at its best could and should be nothing but to work, eat, sleep and obey. In a letter which he had written in January, 1814, to the Editor of *The Morning Chronicle*, his definition of a Jacobin was conditioned purely by sympathy:

"He who has seen the evening star set over a poor man's cottage, or has connected the feeling of hope with the heart of man, and who, although he may have lost the feeling, has never ceased to reverence it—he, Sir, . . . is the *true Jacobin*."

In the years following Waterloo, now that he was fighting against those who gave no quarter to the Jacobin, and who tended to regard every poor man as a Jacobin, he gave a definition of the true Jacobin which is coloured not primarily by sympathy towards the poor man but by implacability towards the poor man's oppressor:

"To be a true Jacobin, a man must be a good hater. . . . The love of liberty consists in the hatred of tyrants. The true Jacobin hates the enemies of liberty as they hate liberty, with all his strength and with all his might, with all his heart and with all his soul. His memory is as long, and his will as strong as theirs, though his hands are shorter. He never forgets or forgives an injury done to the people, for tyrants never forget or forgive one done to themselves. . . . He makes neither peace nor truce with them. His hatred of wrong only ceases with the wrong. The sense of it, and of the bare-faced assumption of the right to inflict it, deprives him of his rest. It stagnates in his blood. It loads his heart with aspics' tongues, deadly to venal pens. It settles in his brain—it puts him beside himself."[279]

This we should say, in connection both with his anger and his bitterness, the things against which he fought were all evil. It was because of the tenacity of that fight, carried on in years when authority was independent of, if not entirely divorced from public opinion in England, that these evil things were driven from the kingdom before they had taken root in it. He fought for the People at a time when the People sorely needed such championship. He insisted both on the dignity and the responsibility of the People at a time when the tendency of the Government was to treat it like "the vassals of a wealthy aristocracy." Also, he fought a very straight and open fight. Coleridge spoke of the use of "poison gas."[280] If poison-gas were used, or any other kind of poison, it was not by Hazlitt. Procter said of him: "He did not carry poisoned arrows into civil conflict." This was true. He gave no quarter, but his arrows were never dipped in poison, although they were dipped both in anger and scorn. As to the passion of his political writing, while it may seem excessive to those who consider it merely as literature, if it be read in connection either with the Parliamentary debates of the period, on which it is largely a commentary, or in connection with the record of events from day to day in the newspapers of the period, there is nothing in it that is not intelligible; there is very little in it that, even at this distance of time, does not seem justified by its civic courage and vigilance in the attempt to preserve the liberties of the nation. To a political opponent who wished him better principles and a better temper, he replied: "I despair of either. For my temper is so bad as to be ruffled almost as much by the roasting of a Protestant as by the spoiling of my dinner: nor have I better hopes of mending my principles, for they have never changed hitherto." He might have added that the fight against parliamentary corruption, the fight against inertia with regard to the distress of the poor in years of unprecedented hardship, the fight against the gag and the scourge, the fight against the ill-treatment of political prisoners, the fight against the decimation of English villages by game-preserving landlords who showed an almost complete disregard of human suffering, the fight against the creation in the great towns of a helot class in what had hitherto been a free country—had little in it to sweeten any man's temper. Nor had loss of hope, and Hazlitt fought, believing that he fought on the losing side. "The chain in which they hung up the murdered corse of human Liberty is all that remains of it," he wrote in the summer of 1816, "and my Lord Shallow keeps the key of it!"[281]

4

Hazlitt's writing on foreign affairs at this time was directed chiefly against that reissue from the mint of Talleyrand's brain of the old doctrine of the Divine Right of Kings, "new-vamped up," as he put it, "under the style and title of Legitimacy."[282] This formula seemed to him the source of most of the corruptions of Power rampant in his day. As he cast his eyes over Europe, and saw what was being done to it by a doctrine which made it a matter of religion that the posterity of those who had formerly held sway in any country should be established in perpetuity in authority over the descendants of those over whom their fathers had ruled, that they should be maintained on their thrones by force even if their misgovernment should at length goad their subjects into attempting to bring about a change of government, and that those who rebelled against their "legitimate" rulers should be regarded as guilty of impiety and should be repressed without mercy by the armed forces, not only of their own rulers, but if necessary of all the rulers who had pledged themselves to support the principle of Legitimacy, it seemed to him the monstrous claim that threatened the liberty of the civilised world. He felt that it outraged the dignity of human personality, and also, that the elevation of an outworn Formula, which had long ago been rejected by the common sense of his own countrymen, into a principle, outraged the human understanding. Again and again he used the same phrase in connection with this sense of outrage, when he said that it haunted the understanding "like a frightful spectre." His abhorrence of the "principle" of Legitimacy was of triple ply. Not only as a man did he detest it, for it seemed to him to make of man something less than man, but as a metaphysician, whose preoccupation was with the bases of human nature, and as a political thinker, who had always endeavoured to look at actuality, and who knew that formulas should be made for the convenience of man and not man for the convenience of formulas. His attacks on it, throughout the whole body of his writing, are numberless, and numberless are the methods of his approach. He attacks it now with vigorous plain prose, now with intricate dazzling metaphor, now with irony, now with indecorous mockery, now with gravity, settled purpose and deadly quietude, now with what we can only call frantic gesticulations of disgust and repudiation. Perhaps the single passage which is most representative of his feeling is the one in his essay, *What is the People?* He himself regarded the passage as "the sum and substance" of all he had ever said on Legitimacy. Even as he said of *King Lear* that it was the best of Shakespeare's plays because it was the one in which he was most in earnest, we might say of this passage that it is the best of his expositions of the effects of "Legitimacy" because it is the one in which he is most in earnest, although there are many which are more violent, more bitter and more picturesque. It is a protest, at once powerful and sorrowful, against the outrage perpetrated on human nature by those who would dispose of it with a formula:

"What is the People?—And who are you that ask the question? One of the people. And yet you would be something! Then you would not have the People nothing. For what is the People? Millions of men, like you, with hearts beating in their bosoms, with thoughts stirring in their minds, with the blood circulating in their veins, with wants and appetites, and passions and anxious cares, and busy purposes and affections for others and a respect for themselves, and a desire of happiness, and a right to freedom, and a will to be free. And yet you would tear out this mighty heart of a nation, and lay it bare and bleeding at the foot of despotism: you would slay the mind of a country to fill up the void with the old, obscene, drivelling prejudices of superstition and tyranny: you would tread out the eye of Liberty (the light of nations) like ' a vile jelly,' that mankind may be led about darkling to its endless drudgery, like the Hebrew Samson (shorn of his strength and blind) by his insulting taskmasters."[282]

It slays the mind. This we take to be the core of Hazlitt's hatred of the Formula which had taken possession of Europe. Look where he might, he saw men's minds being slain and the life drained out of them by a vampire Formula. In Spain unrelenting cruelty was directed against any free exercise of the mind. On the frontiers of France an army of occupation lay within call, lest by any chance the people of France should rally a third time and drive out of the country the Formula which had been restored to them in the baggage-train of their enemies and placed on the throne to rule over them. In Germany obedience to the Formula was alone encouraged. "I require obedient subjects, not enlightened citizens," Francis I had said, and the Austrian empire was ruled on this principle. From Vienna the Formula was thrust upon Italy. It sucked the life out of Lombardy and Venetia. It reigned in the small Italian duchies and kingdoms which had been "settled" under the legitimate rulers, and to repress any stirrings of independence in which the armed force of Austria was always at hand. A "low creeping fog of servility," emanating from Vienna, seemed to be making its way all over Europe, affecting all countries, stretching from Russia and the borders of the East to the islands of the West. As Hazlitt looked upon this envelopment, it seemed to him that he saw, in every country in Europe, including his own, and in every sphere of life, in the encouragement given to all that is low, in the systematic discouragement, amounting to persecution, of all that is independent and high, the generous impulses in man denied, the

ignoble impulses sedulously cultivated, the slaying of thought and
the torturing of mind, the Master, Genius, pelted from its place by
low and servile hands, and the Lacquey, Mediocrity, set to reign in
its stead, placed in authority by those who genuinely preferred mediocrity to genius, knowing that nothing was to be feared from the
Lacquey whereas in a world erected on a Formula everything was to
be feared from the Master.

5

Even as the shadow of "Legitimacy" dogs all Hazlitt's writing on
foreign politics, so does the shadow of the agonising distress that held
the country in its grip in the years following the conclusion of the
war hang over all his writings on the course of politics at home.
Throughout these years Hazlitt, while he fought for the rights of the
People as a whole, actually made himself the voice of the poor, and the
special pleader for those who suffered under the indifference, or even
under the callousness, shading off readily into positive hostility, of
a Government in which they had no share.   His theme might be
said to be:

> "Take physic, pomp;
> Expose thyself to feel what wretches feel,
> That thou may'st shake the superflux to them
> And show the Heavens more just."

"What is it, then, that makes a great Prince?" he writes in his essay
on The Regal Character. "Not the understanding Purcell or Mozart,
but the having an ear open to the voice of truth and justice! Not a
taste in made-dishes, or French wines, or court-dresses, but a fellow-
feeling with the calamities of hunger, of cold, of disease and nakedness!
Not a knowledge of the elegances of fashionable life, but a heart that
feels for the millions of its fellow-beings in want of the common
necessities of life!"[283]

Two attitudes prevailed throughout the country, in the course of
1816, among those who were raised by their rank or by their wealth
above personal experience of "the calamities" of hunger and cold and
nakedness, as to the distress which was exenterating their fellow-men
less fortunately placed. There was the attitude, taken for the most part
by Authority, and by those who wished to bask in the sunshine of
authority, that the distress was only the necessary and inevitable
consequence of an abrupt transition from war to peace, that if not
tampered with, if kept well curbed by authority, and above all, if kept
concealed, it would pass, without any very grave danger to the nation,

but that if it were exposed and emphasised, it might end in Revolution. There was opposed to this the attitude of those who felt that while the extremity of the distress was partly conditioned by the transition from war to peace, the distress itself, which had long been patient, was due to causes of a deeper root, and had increased to such an extent that it was no longer tolerable; that apart from the offence against humanity involved in letting it perish unrelieved, there was grave danger to the nation in neglecting every possible means of alleviating it, for if it were pushed further along the road to desperation it might end in Revolution (although no classes of the community raised above the level of distress wished this, least of all those who pressed for constitutional reform) with the cry "Blood or Bread" gradually swelling into the cry "Blood and Bread," for the sufferings of the people were far greater than they had ever been before, even in the early years of the war, and would not endure careless or violent treatment; that something more might be done in the way of the pacification of Hunger in country districts than the hurried passing of an Act, in a year when Starvation walked abroad in the open light of day, sentencing the belly-pinched countryman caught poaching in a wood or park to seven years' transportation; that a reformed Parliament should be called into being to deal with the changing condition of the country and prevent the exploitation of the unrepresented classes by the represented; that there should be a redistribution of taxation so that public money should not be "wrung out of the bowels of the poor;" that every effort should be made by the present Government towards retrenchment in public expenditure; and that, in such starving times, the list of sinecure offices, some of them of enormous value, should be reconsidered, or even that sinecures, if not abolished, should be suspended until the country had made some recovery. Hazlitt, who held that where there was a disposition in Governments to lessen the sum of human misery there was the power, and that the spirit of humanity was the great thing lacking in the attitude of the rich of his day towards the poor, put the matter thus in an essay on The Distresses of the Country:

"We are not for equalising ranks or property. When all is right on board the vessel of the state, let every one be paid according to his particular claims. But when we are launched into the long-boat and going on the forlorn hope, the captain and passengers must abate some of their pretensions or expect to be thrown overboard."[284]

These, then, were the opposing views. The opposition of opinion was limited to the attitude taken to the distress. No one could deny the existence of the distress itself, which had its roots deep in the changing conditions of the time, both of the agricultural life of the country, in which the past century had seen a silent revolution, and of the industrial life, which was on the threshold of a revolution. In the agricultural districts, the distress which had threatened the cottagers and labourers ever since the enclosing of common land had begun, had reached a climax. The labourer was pressed between the upper and the nether millstone of the Farmer and the Parish. Ever since his strip of common land, the "anchorage" of the Commoners of England, had been taken from him by successive Acts of Parliament, gradually whittling away his immemorial rights or communal privileges, while his inarticulateness, illiteracy, poverty, and lack of representation in Parliament prevented him from making any effective protest, his life had been precarious, for to a labouring peasant the possession of a cow, a few fowls, a pig and a little piece of his own native soil for tillage or pasturage made all the difference between sufficiency and independence, and distress and pauperism. The loss of these few possessions had meant that he was entirely dependent on his daily wage. His first attempts, during the scarcity of 1795, at "combining" to secure a living wage had been suppressed. The policy of securing to him a minimum wage by Act of Parliament had also been defeated, and instead, as it was thought that if wages were increased during the period of war they would never be lowered afterwards, he was forced to accept a wage that was recognised as being lower than that necessary to support life during a period of war, on the understanding that this wage should be supplemented by the parish in which he lived. In other words, "the Poor Law which had once been the hospital became now the prison of the poor." The majority of them at the end of the war had neither any land—even their gardens had been taken from them— nor had they a living wage. The agrarian Revolution which had been going on quietly had deprived them of all but their lives. Their independence was gone. Their standard of living was reduced. Even when they were in employment, their life was one of continuous distress. In addition to this, many of them were now out of employment. In 1816, a bitter summer followed by a meagre harvest was the prelude to a winter unprecedented in its distress. By the end of the year wheat, which had been rising steadily, reached the famine price of 103s. The loss of their land, the fixing of their wages at less than the minimum required to support life, the failure to supplement the in- adequate wage adequately, scarcity, high prices, and the loss of hope consequent upon mental as well as physical distress, had brought those who were once known as the Commoners of England, who were now usually referred to as the Poor or the Lower Classes, to a degree of misery which seemed to leave them little to do but to despair and die, if they were not content to struggle along in a kind of half-life and in a state of semi-starvation.

Yet, desperate though their plight was, they were by no means the only, nor even the chief sufferers, in the years that followed the Peace. Every branch of the national life was affected. What might almost have been called the British monopoly of trade on the seas had ceased; ships stagnated in the harbours and seafaring men were thrown out of work. Both the export and the import trade were much decreased. The iron trade was almost at a standstill, and in consequence of this destitute miners from Staffordshire and Shropshire wandered about the countryside. There was no longer the market there had been on the Continent for British manufactures, and this, together with the increasing substitution of machinery for hand-labour, threw hundreds of thousands of workmen in the great manufacturing centres out of work. Birmingham was like a city in the power of a spectre; in Nottingham and Leicester the frame-work knitters "easily distinguished by their care-worn, anxious faces from other handcraftsmen," were starving; in Spitalfields alone there were forty thousand people out of employment; maimed and disbanded soldiers and maimed and disbanded sailors swelled the ranks of the unemployed, and many of them, drifting through the streets of London with the fear of becoming destitute eating out their hearts, wished that they had died in the smoke and excitement of battle instead of thus dying by inches day by day in the streets or on the roads of a country in which they had suddenly become the "surplus" population. In addition to all these things, while "the conditions created by Armageddon" which had brought an appearance of prosperity to the country had passed away, the conditions that had been fraught with distress for the poor were perpetuated, and the sufferings of poverty exacerbated, by the Corn Law of 1815. If the rulers of the country were, as the Government papers claimed, the Shepherds of the People, they were Shepherds to whom the feeding of their flocks no longer seemed a primary duty.

As always, even among the very distressed, the poverty bore hardest upon the weakest, the women and the children. These were the days when Shelley winced at the sight of the miserable children in the lace-manufacturing villages of Buckinghamshire; when the sound of the harlot's curse at the night-watchman in the streets of London, waiting to take his toll of the profits of her trade, tore at his spirit; when the words "Blood or Bread" scrawled on the dead wall where the Hampstead Road passed into the Tottenham Court Road, or similar ones staring at him from any

> "brick house or wall
> Fencing some lonely court,"

came between his eyes and the sun, when suddenly, walking in the Strand with Leigh Hunt, the distress and concern he felt overflowed in the words: "Look at all these worn and miserable faces that pass us, and tell me—Hunt—what is to be thought of the world they appear in!" These were the days when the Editor of *The Times* was publicly advised, if he wished to have his complacency enlightened, to spend an *al fresco* night at London Bridge, where his next neighbour could inform him how little England could afford either employment or charitable relief to hosts of men in their prime, able and willing to work. These were the days when Hazlitt, who needed no such advice, for he saw wretchedness enough both within the theatres, where needy Youth made the best bargain it could for its charms with greedy Age, and without the theatres, as he walked homewards towards Westminster at midnight or in the small hours of the morning after having written his account of the play, felt sometimes, at the sight of the beggars, and, worse still, the half-starved creatures ashamed to beg because unused to it, "crawling about the ground and getting into holes and corners to die, like flies blind, shrunk and feeble at the end of summer,"[285] as if the world were being reduced by degrees "to a spital or lazar-house, where the people waste away with want and disease, and are thankful if they are only suffered to crawl forgotten to their graves."[286] These were the days when the country poor, their "anchorage" of land having been reft from them, drifted, many of them, towards the town, seeking their fortune in London—only to be gathered in from the streets in bedraggled hordes, and committed to Bridewell as vagrants, until they could be sorted out and drafted back again to the parishes on which they were chargeable and to which their poverty had made them hateful. These were the days when Malthus's abstraction Misery took on flesh and blood and walked from corner to corner of the land, sometimes accompanied by its fellow-abstraction, Vice, but not as often as might have been expected, for Misery was for the most part patient, often anxious only, as Hazlitt said, to creep to the grave unnoticed. It met Shelley on Hampstead Heath, in the guise of a woman fallen in the snow, and was helped, supported and carried by Shelley, until the shelter of Leigh Hunt's house, never closed to Misery, was reached. But Misery seldom met with such knight-errantry or chivalry. As a rule where it fell it lay— by the hedgerows at night, or in the fields, or under archways; or sometimes it floated in rafts on the rivers; or it crawled into lime-kilns or lay on the top of brick-kilns, and seeking to know again what warmth was like, was burnt or suffocated or even "baked" to death by the fatal heat which had allured it. It surged round the Mansion House, in half-naked crowds, imploring admittance. It lay four in a bed in the workhouse, and counted itself fortunate to be thus har-boured. It was swept in batches like autumn leaves during the sharp autumn nights out of the alcoves of Blackfriars Bridge and London Bridge and Westminster Bridge, in which destitute sailors were wont to congregate, seeking rest—and gathered into the prisons to give an account of itself to Authority on the morrow. It looked out of the fixed leaden despair in the faces of the Spitalfields silk-weavers, watching their wives and children perishing day by day, or glared out of the eyes of the men who had deserted their families, because they could no longer endure the sight of their famishing children. It was made to know that in a world ruled by "the grim Idol" Power, there is nothing so much hated by Power in any form, as Misery in any form. It expressed itself throughout the year in sporadic rioting in many country districts. At the end of the year it stormed itself to a crisis in London after a meeting of the people held in Spa-Fields, and foamed itself away afterwards in an outburst of vain rioting, leaving behind it to fall into the hands of the authorities several pieces of human flotsam and jetsam, including a half-starved sailor named John Cashman, who had been impressed into the Navy, discharged from it, pensionless, as unfit for further service, at the age of twenty-eight, who had drifted towards Spa-Fields because every one was moving thitherwards, but as to what all the stir and tumult was about, having as little understanding as a child.

6

Hazlitt's political writing of 1817 is related chiefly either to events which were the consequence of or which were closely connected with the meeting of Spa-Fields. On February 28th, after determined opposition had been made to the measure, both within and without Parliament, the Habeas Corpus Act was suspended. On March 12th, John Cashman was hanged. He died, as he had lived, "perplexed i' the extreme." He had greatly feared being carted through the streets as a vagrant; now he was to be carted through them as a felon, for a gallows had been erected in Skinner Street, opposite the gunsmith's shop in which he had been seen with other rioters, and he was to be executed there. His chief regret was that he had not died in battle. As the prison bell tolled for the procession to start a few minutes before eight o'clock in the morning, he gave one last look at the walls of the last lodgement he had known on earth and said: "I have done nothing against my King and Country, but fought for them." The cart passed through streets filled with a multitude of people, from whom groans, tears, confused ejaculations of pity, and cries of "Murder! Murder!" burst forth at the sight of him, as the white-faced crowds surged behind barriers well guarded by the military. When he had mounted the scaffold, he said to the Ordinary of Newgate and the priest attempting to bring him "to a sense of his awful situation:" "Don't bother me—it's no use," and then: "I want no mercy but from God." When they put the cap over his eyes he said: "For God's sake, let me see to the

last! I want no cap!" He called to the executioner: "Come, Jack—
let go the jib-boom!" He was attempting a cheer when the plank fell
from under his feet.

Complacent Malthus wrote in 1798: "The histories of mankind
that we possess are histories only of the higher classes." But as for
Hazlitt, whose writing is the complete antidote for complacency, it is
of such things as Cashman's fate, typical in many things except its
unusually painful ending of the fate of many men of his time, and
illuminating as to the use and abuse of man by the social machine
of that harsh age, that he would say: "*These* are the materials of
History." His comment on the way in which the unrest of that troubled
year coiled itself around the throat of this poor victim, disguises
feeling under irony. Yet his words are not playthings:

"Governments . . . certainly '*grow milder*' as they grow older.
Our Government, the other day, instead of six hundred citizens, taken
at a venture from the wards of Cripplegate or Farringdon-without,
only suspended Cashman and the Habeas Corpus."[287]

In the course of the summer of 1817, four of the leaders of the Spa-
Fields meeting were tried in the Court of King's Bench on a charge of
High Treason. The opening trial began on June 9th. The chief witness
for the prosecution was a certain John Castles, who had wormed himself into the confidence of the accused men, and who had been closely
associated with them. On Thursday, June 12th, the Counsel for the
defence forced Castles to admit that he had twice been committed to
prison, the first time, three years before, on a charge of forgery,
when he had turned evidence against his companion, who had been
hanged on his testimony, a second time, for aiding the escape of a
French prisoner, when he had defended himself on the score that he had
not meant to aid the enemy of his country, but merely to relieve him
of his money and then betray him; that he had abandoned his wife;
and that he lived at the present moment with a certain "Mother Tims"
who "kept a lodging-house for females." That he was, in fact, what
others called him, the "bully" in a house of ill-fame, he denied. Popular
feeling was already running high against this witness, when there
appeared on Saturday, June 14th, in *The Leeds Mercury*, an exposure of
the activities in Yorkshire of the Government spy Oliver, who had
been engaged since the end of April in fomenting sedition in the
Midland counties, Lancashire and Yorkshire, pressing and almost
cajoling distressed and unhappy and confused men into the utterance
of or agreement with seditious sentiments, inveigling them into
attending meetings that could be classed as seditious, and arguing them
into acquiescence with arrangements for risings throughout the
country, while in the meantime he forwarded to the Government

information on which they might be prosecuted, and which might be used to justify the suspension of Habeas Corpus during a second period, when the original term of suspension expired on July 1st. The effect of this exposure, which left no doubt that Oliver had actually been creating disaffection and then earning his bread or earning blood-money by reporting it to the Home Office, on the fate of the Spa-Fields men, was immediate. At the beginning of the following week they were all discharged, amid great popular rejoicing.

Notwithstanding the effect of the disclosures as to the character and activities of Castles and Oliver, Habeas Corpus was again suspended at the end of June, for a further period of eight months, but an attack on the Government for the employment of such men as Castles and Oliver as part of the system by which the country was governed was vigorously pressed forward by the Opposition and by the Opposition press. Hazlitt assailed it with raillery hardly less bitter than that of inimitable Curran, who said of one of these hired incendiaries and informers that he had been "buried as a man and dug up as a witness." His article *On the Spy-System* assailed on June 30th the defence Castlereagh had made of his foul human tools:

"Lord Castlereagh, in the debate some evenings ago, appeared in a new character. . . . According to his Lordship's comprehensive and liberal views, the liberty and independence of nations are best supported abroad by the point of the bayonet; and morality, religion and social order are best defended at home by spies and informers. It is a pretty system, and worthy of itself from first to last. The Noble Lord in the blue ribbon took the character of Castles and Oliver under the protection of his blushing honours and elegant casuistry, and lamented that by the idle clamour raised against such characters, *Gentlemen* were deterred from entering into the honourable, useful and profitable profession of Government Spies. . . . One of these delicious *protégés* of ministerial gratitude, was, it seems, at one time a distributor of forged notes, and gained the reward offered by Act of Parliament, by hanging his accomplices. Could not his Lordship's nice notions of honour relax a little farther, and recommend the legal traffic in bank-notes and blood-money, as a new opening to honourable ambition and profitable industry? Castles's wife was also the keeper of a house of ill-fame. Could not his Lordship with the hand of a master, have drawn a veil of delicacy over this slight stain on his character, and redeemed a profession, not without high example to justify it, from the vulgar obloquy that attends it?"[288]

In a continuation of this article which appeared in the *Chronicle* on July 15th, he attacked the home policy of the Government, its

inertia in relieving distress, its zeal in persecuting it, and its opportun-
ism in making it the pretext for undermining the liberties of the
country. Four days later, in commenting on a terrible attack made on
Castlereagh by Brougham in the House of Commons on July 11th, he
gave a stinging summary of the abuses of a Government dominated
by Castlereagh's personality.

During this month Hazlitt was engaged also in pleading for the
humanitarian treatment of those who were being kept in prison
without having any charge brought against them, and without hope
of release, under the powers assumed by the Government on the
Suspension of Habeas Corpus. Among these was a certain Thomas
Evans, a bracemaker, a man who although he was of little note had
become an object of suspicion to the Government because he was
Librarian to the Spencean Society. Evans had been suddenly arrested
at his house in Newcastle Street, Strand, between eight and nine
o'clock on a Sunday morning in February, and had been imprisoned
ever since. Oppressed by the knowledge that his business was falling
to pieces, that his wife was nearing destitution, and that his family was
being reduced to beggary through the loss of their bread-winner, he
complained in a Petition which was brought to the notice of Parliament
on June 27th, of the condition in which he lay without hope of trial, as
being unnecessarily oppressive and injurious both to mind and body.
Castlereagh objected to having a Parliamentary inquiry into the circumstances of his confinement, on the ground that Parliament, if it
began this kind of thing, might be inundated with petitions. Hazlitt
attacked this position with that admirably controlled raillery which
tended to be the weapon selected by him when dealing with "my
Lord Shallow":

"Our readers will have seen that Lord Castlereagh disposed of the
motion relative to the treatment of poor Evans with that characteristic
coolness which sits so agreeably upon his Lordship. . . . How much
are the House obliged to him for abridging their labours, and lightening the weight of their duties, by taking their whole exercise and their
whole responsibility upon himself! He first vests in himself and his
colleagues the power of arbitrarily imprisoning the subject at will, on
the plea that any abuse of this power will be impossible, as it will be
instantly open to the cognisance and redress of Parliament, and then
he shuts the door in the face of all inquiry, and of all redress of abuses
in the exercise of this arbitrary power, on the plea, that as the House
cannot possibly inquire into all abuses that may possibly be committed,
or pretended, they must inquire into none. . . . In reading his Lordship's speeches, we are not to admire the ingenuity, or even the presence
of mind, with which he contrives to get rid of the objections of
humanity, of justice and reason, so much as the happy constitution of

temperament by which the petty distinctions of right and wrong are so frequently lost upon him."[289]

What is even more characteristic of Hazlitt than the irony, is the way in which, in his second article on The Treatment of State Prisoners, he reduces the matter, as he would say himself, to "an abstract metaphysical principle" which goes right to the source of all the suffering that is inflicted on the political prisoner by arbitrary power:

"It is the making light of the distresses and complaints of our victims, because we have them *in our power*, that is the principle of all cruelty and tyranny. Our pride takes a pleasure in the sufferings that our malice has inflicted; every aggravation of the case is a provocation to new injuries and insults; and their pretensions to mercy or justice become ridiculous in proportion to their helplessness of redress."[290(a)]

In his treatment of other themes arising out of the political controversies of the times we note also this reference to principle, as when he insists on the right of labourers to form "combinations" for the rise of wages, and when pleading for reform of the penal law. In pleading for this reform he wrote primarily as a metaphysician, concerned not only with the effect of excessive punishment on the victim of it, but on the society which inflicted it. More of the psychologist than of the humanitarian is revealed in what he says. Indeed, while denouncing some of the arguments against penal reform as "loathsome jargon," he was ready enough to admit that there was, too, "a cant of humanity" on the subject. It is only when he comes to deal with the undue harshness shown by the law towards offences against property which were the effect of the distresses of the time that he writes as a humanitarian. But "humanitarian" is a word that savours too much of the jargon he loathed. It would be truer to say that he wrote as if he felt that every poor man was his brother. In these days when George Cruikshank felt his heart turn to water within him as he saw the bodies of poor women dangling on the gibbet opposite Newgate, Hazlitt pled the constant corrosion of temptation on extreme poverty, and the strength of the resistance commonly opposed to it: "by far the greater part of them are continually holding out to the last extremity of despair, of sickness, and often of life itself, in struggling against these temptations."[290(b)]

We are apt to-day to forget the courage of much of this literature of attack, at a time when Habeas Corpus was suspended, and Southey, "with shrill eunuch's voice," as Hazlitt did not hesitate to call it, was crying out for "gagging Bills" and transportation by way of silencing the voices that dared to challenge Power. Brave flaming Cobbett had described the governing classes as offering to the English poor, who desired above all things to keep their independence, "a Basin of Carrion soup in the one hand and a Halter in the other." His vigorous word on this grim mingling of coercion and charity was in everybody's mouth. To Southey, Hazlitt's bitter controlled prose, although it appealed to readers very different in kind from those who took their opinions from *The Political Register*, seemed more dangerous than Cobbett's. Yet Cobbett, despairing of the fight against the injustices of the time, once the suspension of Habeas Corpus had been passed, had thought it prudent to put three thousand miles of water between himself and the hand of Power.

7

In stating the nature of the task he had undertaken Hazlitt wrote: "In the *servile war* which Mr. Southey tells us is approaching, the service we have proposed to ourselves is to neutralise the servile intellect of the country."[291] He could go into the battle, like Roland, "with face calm and smiling," when the battle was with "my Lord Shallow." It was otherwise when, in pursuit of his chosen task, he attacked the three poets who had been the friends of his youth, each and all of whom, during the first few years of distress which succeeded Waterloo, came forward with writings, each and all of which were insensible to the distresses of the country, and strong in their encouragement of merely repressive measures. This writing lacks the grace of the other, for it is ploughed up with feeling, and marred with self-conflict, while now and again its surface is churned into foam by the play of passion underneath. There is none of Hazlitt's writing which requires more to be considered closely in connection with the circumstances that occasioned it than this literature of attack. If it be viewed in isolation, much of it may seem to refute Procter's testimony as to Hazlitt: "He was never cruel." If it be viewed, however, in relation to the circumstances of the moment, and to the part played by the Poets with reference to these circumstances, there is very little of it that does not seem necessary, if Hazlitt were to fulfil his chosen task. At least it will be evident that most of the attacks are not personal ebullitions of spleen, but attacks which seemed to Hazlitt necessary if the weaker side, which to him was the sacred side, were to be protected against those who had come to be "ever strong upon the stronger side," which by this time he had come to regard as "the unclean side."

The most formal of his attacks was on Southey. Southey, who in 1794 had been a Jacobin of the red-hot kind of which Hazlitt had never approved—for he had sensed its violence to be the effect of that "cant of democracy" which he detested as much as he detested the "cant of aristocracy"—was now white-hot on the side of Power. Feeding his mind on rumours of unrest fostered by spies who found the propagation of such rumours a lucrative employment, and driven by that fear of a *bellum servile* or "insurrection of the Yahoos," as he put it, with which he wearied his contemporaries, he would have anticipated the repressive measures of a Government already deeply stained by its savage administration of justice, or rather of injustice, towards the poor—and would have instituted some, which even a Castlereagh-Sidmouth administration did not see fit to introduce. Hazlitt's attack on him opened in March, 1817, just after the publication of *Wat Tyler*—an early Jacobinical play by Robert Southey, the manuscript of which had fallen into the hands of the Poet Laureate's enemies—had thrown into sharp relief the contrast between the opinions of the youthful unfee'd Robert Southey, and the Robert Southey who had become one of the band of Gifford's "Gentlemen Pensioners." The play, which was "peppered like a turkey's gizzard," as even its author confessed, was certainly a *sauce piquante* to Southey's recent article on Parliamentary reform and recent writings on the distresses of the country. Southey was instant in dissociating himself from any of the opinions expressed in this early work of his, and on March 18th, he moved in the Court of Chancery for an injunction "to restrain Messrs. Sherwood, Neely and Jones," from printing and publishing the play.[291(b)] Hazlitt provides a scornful and passionate commentary on what he felt to be the servility towards the powerful and the insensibility towards the distressed classes revealed in Southey's words and actions:

"In courtly malice and servility Mr. Southey has outdone Herodias's daughter. He marches into Chancery, ' with his own head in a charger,' as an offering to Royal delicacy. He plucks out the heart of Liberty within him and mangles his own breast to stifle every sentiment left there: . . . Famine stares him in the face, and he looks upon her with lack-lustre eye. Despotism hovers over him, and he says, ' Come, let me clutch thee.' He drinks the cup of human misery, and thinks it is a cup of sack. He has no feeling left, but of ' tickling commodity;' no ears but for court whispers; no understanding but of his interest; no passion but his vanity."[292]

This attack was made with the practical purpose of preventing Southey "from injuring and insulting other people." It was felt that Southey's writings in the *Quarterly* might be dangerous, and that insistence on the character of *Wat Tyler* might prove the antidote to this danger, that "the healing might come from the same weapon that gave the wound." Nowhere does Hazlitt attack Wordsworth in this sustained manner. Every now and again, however, he lets fall a word or two about Wordsworth's utterances, showing how their tone was wounding his mind, as when he wrote:

"The object of poetry is to please: this art naturally gives pleasure, and excites admiration. Poets, therefore, cannot do well without sympathy and flattery. It is, accordingly, very much against the grain that they remain on the unpopular side of the question. They do not like to be shut out when laurels are to be given away at court—or places under government are to be disposed of, in romantic situations in the country. They are happy to be reconciled on the first opportunity to prince and people, and to exchange their principles for a pension."[293]

Coleridge, on the other hand, although he, too, was not attacked in any frontal way, like Southey, was constantly reviewed by Hazlitt in these years—we might almost say pursued—both in *The Examiner* and in the *Edinburgh*. There was some justification for this pursuit, for Coleridge had now taken to identifying Jacobinism publicly with everything he hated, and with everything of ill-report, as if he wanted to make the word synonymous with obloquy. In one of his public lectures he went so far as to give an interpretation of Caliban as the original of Jacobinism. Hazlitt seized on this almost gleefully: "Caliban is so far from being a prototype of modern Jacobinism, that he is strictly the legitimate sovereign of the isle, and Prospero and the rest are the usurpers who have ousted him from his hereditary jurisdiction by superiority of talent and knowledge. 'This island's mine by Sycorax my mother.'" Presently, as if ashamed of this easy sport, he gave it the check noble in the words: "Why does Mr. Coleridge provoke us to write as great nonsense as he talks?" Yet he was well justified in dealing with prejudice carried to this length, in saying dryly that no doubt there were many who would regard the sheep as being affected with Jacobinical principles when they made some noise at shearing-time, and as ultra-Jacobinical if they struggled a little when having their throats cut. In dealing with Coleridge's *Lay Sermon*, however, he dropped all raillery. At this, advertised as being on the distresses of the country, addressed "to the Higher Classes of Society," and published in the height of the most cruel distress, at the close of 1816, his soul well-nigh fainted within him. In the *Lay Sermon*, "in a diagonal side-long movement between truth and falsehood," Coleridge merely overlaid the distresses of the moment "with obscure noises," while he proved to his own satisfaction that the Bible was the authority for the Right Divine of Kings, and recommended it to statesmen as a manual of statecraft. Hazlitt felt with pain the entire divorce from reality of such writing: he was nauseated by the disingenuousness of it, and by the extraordinary way, too, in which it revealed Coleridge's growing power of voluntary self-delusion. "Compared with such powers of inconceivable mental refinement," he wrote, "hypocrisy is a great baby, a shallow dolt, a gross dunce, a clumsy devil!"[294] After he had reviewed it there came poignantly into his mind the memory of the sermon he had heard in Shrewsbury on a raw morning in January nineteen years before. That sermon, too, had been "upon peace and war; upon church and state." But then Coleridge had preached not upon the alliance of church and state, but on their separation—"on the spirit of the world and the spirit of Christianity, not as the same, but as opposed to one another."[295] The sincerity of the words had gone straight to his heart. Now—"of all the cants that ever were canted in this canting world," the turning of' the Scriptures into anti-Jacobin propaganda seemed to him the worst. It was fitting service done to the idol served by Castlereagh and Castles—each in his fashion. The Poets had all gone over to the unclean side. They had all ranged themselves with Power, let it do what it might. They too worshipped the grim Idol that the world adores, let them say what they might. Southey, no matter what flimsy disguise of benevolence he might from time to time think it expedient to assume towards the Poor, whose morals he would fain improve so much that they might learn to live without eating, *rhymed* up to it; and Wordsworth *mused* up to it; and Coleridge *canted* up to it. That was all the difference there was between the three. They had not set out in the beginning to serve it, but gradually, insidiously, they had been drawn towards it; and they had found out how pleasant were the rewards it offered to its votaries, and so at last had yielded themselves to it. With literary it was the same as with any other form of prostitution: it was always the first step that cost the most.[296] That once taken, they were bound to Power with cobweb fetters which none of them could throw off. It was because they were still half-conscious that they were in servitude, because they were half-conscious that they were denying the best in them, that they had become so extreme. The spectre of their former sympathies glared perpetually behind them, and if they turned round, would stare them in the face and cause the pen to drop from their nerveless hands. Therefore they could none of them dare to turn and look round. In a sense, they were all haunted men. The Formula, too, was sucking the manhood out of them all, and therefore the Poethood, seeing the Poet was but the sublimation of the Man, was making them but the husks of the men they had been. Coleridge did nothing. Southey's latest verse was "beneath contempt;" Wordsworth, cut off from what had been the sources of his strength, was becoming a poetaster, or even a kind of versified Wilberforce. Their muse was "on a peace-establishment." It had grown heavy and drowsy. Hazlitt's most explicit comment on the petrifaction that was coming to them all in this respect is given in the words:

"This we do know, and it is worth attending to; that all Mr. Southey has done best in poetry, he did before he changed his political creed; that *all* that Mr. Coleridge ever did in poetry, as *The Ancient Mariner*, *Christabel*, or *The Three Graves*, his Poems and his tragedy, he had written when, according to his own account, he must have been a very ignorant, idle, thoughtless person; that much the greater part of what Mr. Wordsworth has done best in poetry, was done about the same period; . . . All the authority that they have as poets and men of genius must be thrown into the scale of Revolution and Reform. Their Jacobin principles indeed gave rise to their Jacobin poetry. Since they gave up the first, their poetical powers have flagged, and been comparatively or wholly ' in a state of suspended animation.' . . . Poet-laureates are courtiers by profession; but we say that poets are naturally Jacobins. . . . The poets, we say then, *are with us while they are worth keeping*."[297]

As to their attitude to the People, there the alteration was tragic. In later years Hazlitt, feeling that they had deserted the People in the hour of extreme need, said that their hearts had failed them in the valley of the shadow. At the moment it seemed to him that Wordsworth offered them a stone when they were crying for bread; that Coleridge, "with inconceivable refinement of mind," delighted in proving that the serpent he offered them was the very fish mentioned in the gospel according to St. Luke; and that Southey, comfortably rewarded by the *Quarterly* at the rate of £100 per article for saying of them what was comfortable to the ears of Power, merely flung them the threat of a scorpion by way of silencing their crying.

If Hazlitt disliked the tone of the poets' utterances, he blamed them still more for their silences, or perhaps it would be truer to say that he was filled with a deeper despair by their silences—some of which seemed to him despicable. In touching on these, he differentiates in his manner towards the three objects of his attack. He usually, although not always, assailed "Robert Shallow," as he assailed "my Lord Shallow," with a touch of irony. Southey always seemed to him incapable of principle, because, disqualified, by incapacity to reason, from viewing any subject in its entirety. When Wordsworth fell short of his own honour and dignity, on the other hand, Hazlitt suffered, because of the respect he had for the Poet's genius, yet not in the deepest degree, for he had never loved Wordsworth. But when Coleridge fell short, Hazlitt's suffering had a touch of desperateness in it. Coleridge and he, because of the undying spark of love that there was in the heart of the one, and the undying need of that spark of love that there was in the heart of the other, were indissolubly bound to each other, no matter how they might hack at each other. They were like two men strapped to each other in a girdle-duel. They had once been so close to each other that the memory of the contact could never die. Each of them could never find peace without renewal of the "at-one-ment" that had once existed. The "at-one-ment" was no longer possible, but the link which remained from the time when it had been accomplished made the duel of loving-hate or hating-love—in which these two, strapped to each other, hacked each other well-nigh to death—all the more terrible. To look on at this performance is to watch tragedy so deep that we cease to think which was in the right and which was in the wrong, and think only of the pity of it all. In his attacks on Hazlitt Coleridge mangled his own soul. In his attacks on Coleridge Hazlitt mangled his own heart: we think it no exaggeration to say that some of them were written in tears and blood. Their invective is the invective sorrowful. When he associates Coleridge with the two other poets, in his attacks on their silences, a note of fearful passion comes into his words, that is lacking in the attacks he made singly or jointly on Southey and Wordsworth. It is evident that rage and grief overpower him. The most terrible of all these, and the most powerful, is the passage in which he turned and rent them all for their silences as to the horrors of the White Terror in France and the brutalities perpetrated upon the Protestants of Nîmes. But there were tears in his heart when he wrote of Coleridge: "His genius has angel's wings; but neither hands nor feet;" there were tears in his heart when he cried out that the poets were expiating "the follies of their youth by the heartless vices of approaching age;" and the passionate apologue with which, after the bitter winter of 1816, he ushered in the political writing of 1817 is suffused with this complex sorrow :

"And we saw three poets in a dream, walking up and down on the face of the earth, and holding in their hands a human heart, which, as they raised their eyes to heaven, they kissed and worshipped; and a mighty shout arose and shook the air, for the towers of the Bastile had fallen, and a nation had become, of slaves, freemen; and the three poets, as they heard the sound, leaped and shouted, and made merry, and their voice was choked with tears of joy, which they shed over the human heart, which they kissed and worshipped. And not long after we saw the same three poets, the one with a receipt-stamp in his hand, the other with a laurel on his head, and the third with a symbol which we could make nothing of, for it was neither literal nor allegorical, following in the train of the Pope and the Inquisition and the Bourbons and worshipping the mark of the Beast, with the emblem of the human heart thrown beneath their feet, which they trampled and spit upon!"[298]

8

It was not to be expected that Hazlitt's pursuit of "the servile intellect of the country" would go unrequited by "the Paymaster of the band of Gentlemen-Pensioners." Politics conditioned the reception of his first set of Essays, for when, in February, 1817, he published, under the title of *The Round Table*, the essays he had been contributing to *The Examiner* for over two years, with one or two other pieces of earlier prose which he wished to preserve, and a few of Leigh Hunt's essays— *Gifford was unmuzzled*. The review in the number of the *Quarterly* dated April, 1817, discerned in these two volumes nothing but "loathsome trash," a medley of "vulgar descriptions, silly paradoxes" and "misty" sophistries served up in "broken English," garnished with ill-humour, rancorous abuse, and leaving in their wake a track of "slime and filth."

In the meantime, although Hazlitt had been in very poor health during most of the winter of 1816-1817, and although the weekly journalism in which he was engaged was heavy enough, he had put together, under the stimulus of Kean's acting, a set of essays on the Characters of Shakespeare's Plays, which were published some months after the appearance of *The Round Table*. These were dedicated to Charles Lamb, "as a Mark of old Friendship and lasting Esteem." This Dedication was the climax to demonstrations of affection and regard for Lamb which Hazlitt had been giving ever since his entry into journalism.

The old friendship had proved itself. In the meantime, in these years, new friends and acquaintances were coming about Hazlitt, some of them attracted to him by his own growing fame, some of them brought into contact with him by his connection with Leigh Hunt, and his close friendship with Leigh Hunt's brother John. There is some evidence that Edmund Kean began to appear in the circles Hazlitt frequented, early in 1816, and also some evidence that Hazlitt had some personal acquaintance with Kean by this time, for one of Kean's letters, dated March 30th, 1816, contains an apology for failure to keep a dinner engagement. Our first evidence as to a meeting between Hazlitt and Shelley is dated February 9th, 1817. Mary Shelley, in her Journal, makes note of a discussion on Republicanism and monarchy which went on till three in the morning, and in which Hazlitt, although he never professed himself an advocate of republicanism, as contrasted with any other form of government in which the People were justly represented, united with Shelley in presenting the case for republicanism. Yet Hazlitt was never much in sympathy with Shelley. He was far more drawn towards young John Keats, all spirit and fire, although the fire was tempered with gentleness, whom he met in the beginning of 1817, who from the outset of their acquaintance felt both sympathy and admiration for him as a man, and whom we soon find both catching and copying his mannerisms. "It's the finest thing, by God— as Hazlitt would say," he wrote to John Hamilton Reynolds in March. Keats thought Hazlitt not unlike Edmund Kean, whom he too idolised. For Hazlitt as a writer he had an unbounded admiration. "How is Hazlitt?" he wrote to John Hamilton Reynolds in September. "We were reading his *Table* last night. I know he thinks himself not estimated by ten people in the world—I wish he knew he is." At times we find him exulting in the movement of Hazlitt's style, as when he describes one of Hazlitt's militant sentences as being "like a whale's back in a sea of prose."

In the latter half of 1817 Hazlitt made the acquaintance of Bryan Waller Procter, afterwards famous as "Barry Cornwall, the poet," who was to become a steadfast friend of his. In the previous year Procter had been reading with interest Hazlitt's essays in *The Examiner*. He had been told that their author was "fierce and anti-social," but he knew that there was more in the author of these essays than fierceness or unsociability, so when someone pointed out Hazlitt to him at an Exhibition he looked towards him "with curiosity and respect," and felt drawn towards "the earnest irritable face" with the curling black hair, lightly frosted with grey, combed backwards from it, and thought that Titian might have been pleased to paint such a face and head. When he met Hazlitt at Leigh Hunt's in the following year, he found him, among friends, unexpectedly quiet, grave, and unassuming, not at all over-eager to talk, seeming, indeed, always "to have reasoned with himself before he uttered a sentence." Before the evening was over he had realised that it was always Hazlitt who said the best thing on any subject that came under discussion, and that the eyes, although not remarkable in colour, and so shy that they seldom looked directly at any one, were very remarkable in their expression when anything was said that interested him. He felt too that it was nonsense to describe those reticent grey eyes as having sometimes "a sinister expression," although they certainly could fill with flame when the owner was indignant.

It is from Procter that we know Hazlitt had left off drinking by this time. His ill-health in the winter of 1816-1817 may have led to his doing this. In the beginning of 1816 he was still drinking heavily. It would seem that in the spring of the following year he was still drinking more than was good for him. Haydon, writing to Wordsworth in the middle of April, 1817, mentioned that he had met Hazlitt one night, "half-tipsy, and therefore more genial than usual." Hazlitt always held that there was only one way for any one who had been a hard drinker to master the craving for liquor—and that was, to give up stimulants altogether. He did not believe that for any one who had once yielded to excessive drinking there could be such a thing as moderate indulgence. By the latter part of 1817 he had given up drinking altogether. As his indulgence had formerly made him a marked man, so now did his abstinence make him a marked man in circles where almost every one drank a good deal. Now and again he would look wistfully at his friends' glasses: now and again he would savour the bouquet of good wine. But he never broke his rule.

This abstinence probably accounts for the difference between the impression we get of Hazlitt from Procter, grave and quiet, and such impressions of him and his "ferocious" ways as are up to this time frequent in the pages of Crabius, for if Hazlitt was inclined to be "more genial than usual" when half-tipsy, as Haydon has it, he was certainly inclined to be more "ferocious" than usual when "liquored every chink."

We say nothing of the suffering involved in this complete reversal of habit, for Hazlitt himself made no complaint of it, but the extreme quietude of his manner which may have been occasioned by it about this time is confirmed by another witness, with whom he became acquainted at the end of 1817, and with whom he was afterwards to have an intimacy that yet did not include real friendship. Towards the end of this year Hazlitt was just rising into fame. He was known as an essayist of distinction, as a dramatic critic of great authority, and as a powerful controversialist, not only in the field of politics but of art, for in the course of 1816, in addition to his political polemics, he had, in his articles on *The Catalogue Raisonné of the British Institution*, attacked the obscurantism and selfishness of the Royal Academy, and he had joined hands with Haydon in the battle to secure the Elgin Marbles for the nation. His reputation, too, as a critic of art was great. As we have seen, he had made it, in a day, with his article on West's "Christ Rejected," in *The Champion*. He consolidated it, in December of this year, with a magnificent commentary on the claim made by the President of the Royal Academy to have achieved the "terrible sublime" in his picture of "Death on the Pale Horse." These things led, at the close of the year, to negotiations with the Committee of the Surrey Institution for the delivery of a set of lectures. In the course of these negotiations he went out one day to the Institution, which was close to Blackfriars Bridge, to discuss some details in connection with the proposed course. It was on this luckless day, luckless at least for him, that he first came into contact with Peter George Patmore, who at that time was Secretary to the Institution.

The years that have passed since we last looked at him closely, the overthrow of his public and private hopes, the troubles of the time, his illness in the opening months of the year, the rigid discipline, both moral and physical, involved in the conquest of the habit of intemperance in the course of this year, or rather of the state of dreamy stupor it induced, to him its greatest attraction—have all worn him somewhat. Tenuous now he is, fine-drawn to excess! Patmore, who had heard rumours about his character and private life which had thrown him into a state of mingled repulsion and fascination at the thought of meeting him, but above all, of a curiosity even greater than that to which Procter had confessed, was amazed, on entering the committee-room into which Hazlitt had been shown, to see a man pale as a ghost, thin as a spectre, and silent as a shadow, whose eyes stared into vacancy, whose hands were folded in utter listlessness on his knees, whose whole attitude was "loose, unstrung, inanimate" as that of a being "whose life is leaving it from sheer emptiness and inanition . . . apparently with scarcely energy enough to grapple with an infant or face a shadow." But the silence must have been electric, the pallor incandescent, for presently he was aware that his own life had quickened suddenly; even the dark, impersonal committee-room took on character, now that it framed this "pale anatomy of a man." His imagination began to play tricks with him. It seemed to him that the little dark room became dungeon-like, that the eyes that never looked at him but continued to gaze into space were the eyes of a scourged and captive spirit, that in the face in which there was no animation, no fluctuation of feeling, no shadow of change, but only the fixed stare of a victim that had ceased to struggle against its state of suffering, he saw before him a face which recalled to him that of Sir Joshua's Ugolino. In this body through which no blood seemed to flow there was still a wildly beating heart. The showman began to awaken to the possibilities of this; the business sense took precedence of the imagination; with an instinct only comparable to that by which the hyena knows the lion on the broken meats left over by whose wars he is going to feed handsomely, without risk and without danger, Patmore discerned and selected his man.

9

There was nothing in any of the activities through which Hazlitt at the time was rising into fame to account for such mingled repulsion and fascination as Patmore felt. Yet the feeling was genuine enough, and also, it can be accounted for to some extent. Rumour had been very busy with Hazlitt's name during the years in which he had been winning a reputation for himself as a writer and critic. Even as he had been gaining fame for himself, notoriety had been gaining upon him, so that by the end of 1817 and the beginning of 1818 his notoriety marched apace with his fame. Procter had felt that he did not care to pin his faith on the word of others as to what Hazlitt was, and had waited until he met Hazlitt before estimating him. Patmore, who had not this independence of judgment, had taken, from various reports which had reached him, a very dark view of Hazlitt's character. "I remember the time," he wrote afterwards, "when no words could express the horror I felt at the (supposed) personal character of William Hazlitt or were deemed too strong to openly set forth those feelings. . . . From all that I had heard, both from his enemies (and even from his so-called friends) . . . I looked upon him personally, as little better than an incarnate fiend." He went on to explain that the "inexpressible horror and dread" which had caused him to observe Hazlitt so closely, which had aroused his extreme curiosity and which had impelled him to "anatomize" Hazlitt and attempt to discover what bred about his heart, had been awakened in him by the rumours that were gradually spreading through London at the time as to Hazlitt's moral obliquity: "my first impressions were derived not from my own observations, but from the report of those who ought to have known better, and who certainly would have known better, had not their personal feelings been enlisted into the cabal against him."

We can proceed no further with the story of Hazlitt's life without attempting to give some account of the nature of this rumour, and of the extent to which it affected Hazlitt's life. This is no easy matter, for rumour is of all things the most difficult to trace. Yet while the whisperings by obscure people in many obscure corners may and indeed must pass unrecorded, sufficient has remained of what was said and written of the matter by his famed contemporaries, or reported as to what they said, to give some indication as to the origin of the rumour, to give a very fair idea as to the way it circulated, and to give some impression of the way it was used to injure Hazlitt's life. It was not the fault of those who circulated it if the life Hazlitt had succeeded in building up for himself in London did not come tumbling down about his ears, if he himself did not become an outcast, or if he were not driven to despair.

There were two things which may have spread this rumour and caused it to assume proportions so fantastic as to cause men unknown to Hazlitt, like Patmore, to regard him long before they had come into personal contact with him as "a fiend incarnate." One of these was his position in the extreme van of liberalism, and the reckless daring he showed in the fight to win back for the country the liberties that had been surrendered by it during the long war or wrested from it during the aftermath of war. He was, in days when "the Cabal, the bustle, the significant hints, the confidential rumours" were at their height, a predestined target for those assailed by his stinging pen. He prized Liberty so much that he was inevitably an object of detestation to those who hated it. The second was the direct consequence of his own cloudy humours. During the angry, heartless, listless years that followed the failure of his public and his private hopes, in the semi-estrangement from his wife which preceded the separation from her and the breaking-up of his home in London, and in his reaction from the idealism on which he now believed he had wrecked his life, he had fallen into habits of careless living. But if political rancour on the part of his enemies and some measure of irregularity of life on Hazlitt's own part had their share in spreading the wild rumours regarding him, these things had nothing to do with the inception of the rumours. Many men of the day were the victims of political spite, or were no whit less irregular in their lives than was Hazlitt, while some were far more so, without being regarded "with inexpressible horror" or as monsters in the form of men or as fiend-like spirits walking the earth in the garb of flesh, by those who knew them only by reputation.

Our first piece of evidence points to Wordsworth as the one who brought to town not what he had understood to be the reason of Hazlitt's misadventure at Keswick in 1803, at the time of the misadventure and in the course of the year following it, when he was still on "very affectionate" terms with Hazlitt, but the gossip that had grown up about it in the intervening years. In December, 1814, shortly after Hazlitt had given proof, in his review of *The Excursion*, of his power to affect the fortunes of a book, while the invitation he had received to become an "Edinburgh" reviewer seemed to indicate that he was likely to become a power in criticism and a force in liberal journalism, Wordsworth, to whom Lamb had confessed some temporary irritation with Hazlitt, took the opportunity of trying to convert a passing coldness into a breach, by informing Lamb of the circumstances in which Hazlitt had taken his flight from the Lake district, eleven years before. This we gather from the tone of Lamb's reply, which, while it shields Hazlitt, touches perfection in the light yet decisive way in which it repels any suggestion that the accusation is to be considered seriously: "The ' scapes ' of the great god Pan who appeared among your mountains some dozen years since, and his narrow chance of being submerged by the swains, afforded me much pleasure. I can conceive the water nymphs pulling for him. He would have been another Hylas. W. Hylas."[299] That is all, wedged in among miscellaneous chat, yet saying more clearly than any serious vindication of Hazlitt could have done, that one friend's ear, at least, was closed against such rumour.

In the same letter Wordsworth had evidently inquired the name of the Editor to whom Hazlitt had transferred his services after breaking with the *Chronicle*, for Lamb's reply was: "One J. Scott, (I know no more) is edit: of *Champⁿ*."

Our second piece of evidence points also to Wordsworth. When in town in May and June of the following year, he saw a good deal of Haydon, and through Haydon, of John Scott. He informed Haydon also of Hazlitt's misadventure. Some words in Frederic Wordsworth

Haydon's Memoir of his father suggest that the story of the "emergency" from which the Poet had rescued Hazlitt afterwards became legend in the Haydon household. When touching on his father's repertoire of stories about Hazlitt, he added: "Wordsworth added to the stock by one (of Hazlitt's evening amusements at the lakes) which combined such an union of the fiendish, the ludicrous, and the sublime as not to be surpassed by any story ever told of Hazlitt."[300] Now Hazlitt's reputation was safe enough with Lamb. But to place such a story in Haydon's hands was to place Hazlitt's reputation in the hands of one who was not only notoriously capricious but also notoriously indiscreet.

Together on Sunday, June 11th, Haydon and John Scott took Wordsworth to call on Leigh Hunt. As Wordsworth's relations with Leigh Hunt or Leigh Hunt's with Wordsworth had up to this time been unfortunate, Haydon, like Crabius, may have been surprised at this gesture on Wordsworth's part, although in a vague kind of way, for his extreme egoism made him bat-eyed as to much that was going on around him. At any rate, the entry in his Diary seems to indicate that he felt such a move from Wordsworth required a note of explanation: "Hunt was very ill, or it would have been his place to have called on Wordsworth."

And certainly, it was rather Wordsworth's humour, when in town, to receive those who sought him out, than to seek out new acquaintances for himself.

Four days after this visit, Wordsworth gave an account of it to Crabius, whose report of the conversation shows that one of the subjects discussed with the Editor of *The Examiner* had been Hazlitt's gibe at the Poet for his sonnet on the "royal fortitude" and comparative glance at Milton's politics and at Wordsworth's, which had appeared in that Sunday's *Examiner*. Wordsworth told Crabius that Hunt had "disclaimed the article." Whether this disclaimer on the part of the Editor of *The Examiner* led to any further conversation about Hazlitt with his Editor we are not told, although it seems unlikely that Wordsworth would have let the matter drop until here, as elsewhere, he had defined his attitude towards Hazlitt in no uncertain terms. However this may be, it certainly led to further conversation about Hazlitt between Wordsworth and Crabius, in the course of which, for the third time, we find Wordsworth repeating to one of Hazlitt's friends—for at this time Crabius was regarded as one of his friends—the story of the misadventure in the Lake district. Good Crabius, ever avid of hearing something new, now heard such a piece of scandal about the viper whom he had been, if not harbouring in his honest bosom, at least tolerating within his just domain, as it would never have entered into his head to conceive. After reporting Hunt's disclaimer of Hazlitt's article, in his Diary, on June 15th, he added:

"This led to Wordsworth's mentioning the cause of his coolness towards Hazlitt. It appears that Hazlitt, when at Keswick, narrowly escaped being ducked by the populace, and probably sent to prison for some gross attacks on women. (He even whipped one woman, *more puerorum*, for not yielding to his wishes.) The populace were incensed against him and pursued him, but he escaped to Wordsworth, who took him into his house at midnight, gave him clothes and money (from three to four pounds)."

This, then, was the story which Lamb merely let slip off him as easily as a bird lets gutter-water run off its wings. This was the story which in the Haydon circle was regarded as combining "the fiendish, the ludicrous, and the sublime," in a manner "not to be surpassed by any story ever told of Hazlitt." This was the story in recording which Crabius had recourse to cipher and "the decent obscurity of a learned language," but which from this time onwards coiled itself around every thought he had of Hazlitt and strangled any feeling of kindness he had ever had towards him. This was the story which benumbed like a torpedo touch many another human relationship in which Hazlitt might have found life and warmth.

In justice to Wordsworth, it should be remembered that Crabius often reported conversations with gross inexactitude. We would fain believe that he did so in reporting this story, for it contains one statement which we know to be untrue. Wordsworth's letter to Hazlitt of March 5th, 1804,[301] proves conclusively that Wordsworth remained on very affectionate terms with Hazlitt after the incident which in later years was painted in such dark colours. There is no suggestion in it whatever that the scrape which drove Hazlitt from Keswick either was "the cause" of coolness between Wordsworth and Hazlitt, or was likely to become the cause of it.

Moreover, if Hazlitt's behaviour in 1803 had been understood to be of the kind described in this report, there can be no doubt that Wordsworth would have broken off relations with him there and then. It follows from his not having done so that what Wordsworth related to Crabius was not what was understood to be Hazlitt's behaviour in 1803, but such scandal as had attached itself, in a country district where, people having little new to talk of, scandal has a virulent life of its own —to such an incident as the hunting of a wandering Jacobin painter out of the district. It is evidently given in its most virulent form, for Wordsworth, at a moment when he was acutely irritated by one of Hazlitt's attacks on his inconsistency in politics, was relating it to Crabius with the intention of alienating him from Hazlitt, even as he had related it to Lamb with a similar intention, at a moment when he had been acutely irritated by Hazlitt's review of *The Excursion*.

Haydon was so capricious, irritable and indiscreet, that we cannot but regret that Wordsworth should have confided such a story to him. Yet Haydon was primarily interested in his art, and only interested in a secondary degree in the doings, scandalous or otherwise, of those around him. In making such a statement to Crabius, however, Wordsworth placed Hazlitt's painful vulnerability at the mercy of one whose vital and essential life consisted in hearing something new and in going from house to house reporting and discussing it. We cannot but believe that this did Hazlitt as much harm as even his worst enemy might desire. There can be little doubt that the consequences of it in Hazlitt's life were withering.

On two other occasions, previous to 1818, the year in which Hazlitt drove scandal-mongering at his expense at least underground, we come on traces of Wordsworth's endeavours to injure Hazlitt's reputation, and to cause him to be looked askance at within the circle of his London friends. On June 11th, 1816, he wrote to John Scott: "Haydon will tell you something about my quondam connection with Hazlitt, & how it was broken off. He is a man of low propensities, & of bad heart, I fear."[302] The second attack was made, almost a year later, once more to Haydon. On April 7th, 1817, Wordsworth wrote to Haydon: "The miscreant Hazlitt continues, I have heard, his abuse of Southey, Coleridge and myself in the *Examiner*.—I hope that you do not associate with the Fellow, he is not a proper person to be admitted into respectable society, being the most perverse and malevolent Creature that ill luck has ever thrown into my way. Avoid him—*hic niger est*—And this, I understand, is the general opinion wherever he is known, in London."[303]

As for this, we can only say that if it were not the general opinion, wherever Hazlitt was known in London, it was not for lack of effort on Wordsworth's own part. Crabius suggests that even Charles Lamb more or less "dropped" Hazlitt while Wordsworth was in town. After reporting in his Diary on June 15th, 1815, the version given to him by Wordsworth of the Keswick episode, he added:

"Since that time Wordsworth, though he never refused to meet Hazlitt when by accident they came together, did not choose that with his knowledge he should be invited. In consequence, Lamb never asked Hazlitt while Wordsworth was in town, which probably provoked Hazlitt, and which Lamb himself disapproved of. But Lamb, who needs very little indulgence for himself, is very indulgent towards others, and rather reproaches Wordsworth for being inveterate against Hazlitt."

This, although true in the indication it gives that Lamb's sympathy was with Hazlitt, is untrue in the impression it leaves that Lamb practically "gave up" Hazlitt when Wordsworth was in town. It would have been out of character for Lamb to do this, and it would have been out of character for Hazlitt to accept continuance of friendship on such terms. We need say little on this point, because the evidence is clear. One of Lamb's letters, written to Wordsworth during this visit,[304] shows not only that Lamb did not "give up" Hazlitt while Wordsworth was in town, but that he indicated, on the contrary, that Wordsworth, if he did not choose to come when Hazlitt was there, could stay away and take his chance of a meeting some other evening. The letter is altogether cool in tone.[305] Moreover, two days after Crabius had entered into his Diary the statement that Lamb never asked Hazlitt while Wordsworth was in town, he entered into it an account of a party at Lamb's. We note that Hazlitt was there, along with a great many other "interesting and amusing people," and that Wordsworth was not.

We emphasise this point, because Crabius here does less than justice to Lamb, and to that long-continuing loyalty on the part of Lamb to Hazlitt which, after many years of provocation on the part of all three of the Lake poets, exploded at last in 1823 in the public rebuke administered to Southey.

But Lamb was a man very much by himself. What Patmore says as to his own feeling with regard to Hazlitt before he had come into personal contact with him and as to the "bad eminence" to which Hazlitt's name had by this time been raised, seems to indicate that by the end of 1817 Hazlitt's reputation had received almost irreparable injury.

In considering the part played by Coleridge towards Hazlitt when applied to by Tom Wedgwood for his opinion of him, we said that Coleridge had given Hazlitt Polonius-measure. We feel that Wordsworth in these years gave Hazlitt less than Polonius-measure, which at least would have used every man according to his desert. He was causing Hazlitt to be judged in 1815, not even by the sins of his youth, but according to such scandal as had been begotten by the folly of his youth. It would have gone hard with Wordsworth in 1815 if any one had meted out the same measure to him. If any friend of his youth who had been with him in Orleans or Blois in 1792 had appeared in London in 1815 and made it his business to disseminate, not the facts of Wordsworth's relationship with Annette Vallon, but such gossip as might have grown up about it in the intervening years, it would have been ruinous to the reputation Wordsworth then enjoyed with Haydon and others as "a purified being," and might— most unjustly, of course—have earned him the least enviable of all reputations.

Coleridge in March, 1817, made some very strong protests against the practice of attacking any man for the indiscretions of his youth. Yet in these years he was no less persistent than Wordsworth in pressing home against Hazlitt charges based on the indiscretions of his youth. On September 25th, 1816, he wrote to Hugh J. Rose:

"Hazlitt possesses considerable Talent, but it is diseased by a morbid hatred of the Beautiful, and killed by an absence of Imagination, and alas! by a wicked Heart of embruted appetites. Poor wretch! he is a melancholy instance of the awful Truth—that man cannot be on a level with the Beasts—he must be above or below them."[306]

In June, 1817, labouring under the impression that Hazlitt had "cut up"[307] *Christabel* for Jeffrey, he wrote to Francis Wrangham:

"both my health and my circumstances have been such that my powers of volition, constitutionally weak, have sunk utterly under the weight of embarassments, disappointments and infamous calumny. For instance, the author of the Articles in the *Edinburgh Review* and the *Examiner* (W. Hazlitt) after efforts of friendship on my part which a brother could not have demanded—my House, Purse, Influence—and all this, tho' his manners were dreadfully repulsive to me, because I was persuaded that he was a man of great talents and utterly friendless —his very father and mother having despaired of him—after having baffled all these efforts at the very moment, when he had been put in the way of an honourable maintenance, by the most unmanly vices that almost threatened to communicate a portion of their infamy to my family and Southey's and Wordsworth's, in all of which he had been familiarised, and in mine and Southey's domesticated—after having been snatched from an infamous punishment by Southey and myself (there were not less than 2 or [308] men on horses in search of him)—after having given him all the money I had in the world, and the very shoes off my feet to enable him to escape over the mountains— and since that time never either of us injured him in the least degree— unless the quiet withdrawing from any further connection with him (and that without any ostentation, or any mark of shyness when we accidentally met him) not merely or chiefly on account of his Keswick conduct, but from the continued depravity of his life—but why need I say more? This man, Mr. Jeffrey has sought out, knowing all this, because the wretch is notorious for his avowed hatred to *me* and affected contempt of Southey.

"He has repeatedly boasted, that he wrote the very contrary of all he believed—because he was under heavy obligations, and therefore *hated* me."[309]

Truly the girdle-duel is a grievous thing. In this painful outpouring a grain of truth is monstrously overlaid by a superstructure of mere fantasy and self-deception. As Hazlitt's relations with Coleridge have already been recorded by us, we do not think it necessary to examine these claims in detail. The closing charge, however: "He has repeatedly boasted, that he wrote the very contrary of all he believed," calls for some comment. This, as said of Hazlitt, is monstrous. Hazlitt's integrity was his finest possession. It was shown no less consistently in his literary than in his political criticism. He never wrote a line in the *truth* of which he did not believe. The noblest praise given in that age to Burke, Scott, Wordsworth, and—above all—to Coleridge, was given to these four by the one who was their most implacable political adversary.

We have laid before the reader such evidences as time has left of the growth of that subterranean stream of scandal which left on those who did not know Hazlitt personally the impression shared by Patmore up to the time of his first meeting with Hazlitt, that the most redoubtable champion of the French Revolution in England at that time was in his private life a "fiend incarnate." There were many who knew nothing at all about him except that he was reported to be " the Devil and all." There were many who, knowing him but slightly, thought of him, like the poet Campbell, as " that devil Hazlitt." Now—because we wish to make clear work of this subject, so that we shall not have to return to it, we are going to anticipate somewhat our narrative of Hazlitt's doings in the following year, by relating how in the course of 1818 the subterranean stream at last forced its way into the open, and thus brought matters between Hazlitt and his calumniators to a climax. A few months after Coleridge's denunciation of Hazlitt to Francis Wrangham, *Blackwood's Magazine* opened its attack on what it called the Cockney School of Poetry, the principal object of attack being Leigh Hunt, and the principal charge brought against him being that of immorality. The first of these articles, which was signed Z, appeared in October, 1817; it was followed, intermittently, by other attacks, all of them harping on the theme of immorality, until the autumn of the following year. Leigh Hunt, although a sensitive man, was not very deeply affected by their brazen misrepresentation. His life was so entirely innocent that he could afford to let it run off him easily, once he had invited his accusers to come out into the open, in a challenge strong enough, as he said, " to rouse any decent animal from its hiding-place."[310] As the animal was very evidently not a decent animal, he was probably not very much surprised either that it refused to be roused from its hiding-place, or that it continued its attacks from the shelter of its obscurity—while to such calumny or gossip, arising out of the charges brought against him, as that his wife's sister was the mother of at least one of his children, he could reply cheerfully that he might as well be accused of using his grandmother's shin-bone for a switch, as of the incestuous connection imputed to him.[311] But Hazlitt, because of the circumstances of his life, was vulnerable, where his happy-natured innocent friend was not, and from the beginning of 1818 *Blackwood's* had the air of directing some kind of veiled threat

at him, almost as if it were conscious of being in possession of some
trump card which it intended to play when the moment was ripe for its
use. In March the vague threat of dealing with him according to his
deserts was exchanged for a gibe at "pimpled Hazlitt's coxcomb
lectures." That phrase is what Hazlitt himself might call a "thumper,"
for within four words, one of them containing his name, it managed
to pack a couple of lies, the one as to his appearance, the other as to his
disposition. Even Patmore was astounded that even *Blackwood's* could
refer to Hazlitt's pale face as "pimpled;"[312] and there was never the
least touch of the coxcomb about Hazlitt. His passage through life
would have been less lonely had he had just a touch of the coxcomb
about him; but no one, except *Blackwood's*, would ever have thought of
granting him any. The June number referred to him in doggerel
verse. In the July number he was gibed at as "Bill the painter" and
"the amiable Bill Hazlitt, him the immaculate." We are assured that
"the day is perhaps not far distant when the charlatan shall be stripped
to the naked skin." In the August number, at last, the murder is out.
The Blackwood men have had their cue from Gifford, who in the
meantime has flung out a gibe at "the purity" of Hazlitt's morals.
And what is the sweet morsel that rank-feeding "Z," or that portion
of the composite monster "Z" whom we discern to be none other than
"the slinking Leopard" of *Blackwood's*, our old Lake acquaintance,
John Wilson, has been relishing upon his palate all this time, to the
whetting of the curiosity of innumerable readers of *Blackwood's*. He
has an eye that sees not, a heart that feels not, but a rank scent and a
throat of brass, so that when the *bonne bouche* is at last fairly ejected, we
see without surprise that it is no sweet morsel at all, but stale

> "As the shrieve's crusts, and nasty as his fish-
> Scraps out of every dish
> Thrown forth, and raked into the common tub."

In the course of a long series of insulting questions, entitled *Hazlitt
Cross-Questioned*, raked together, we take it, by the "plouthering"
paws of the Leopard and saved from the invertebrateness that character-
ises most of his carrion rakings by the nicer manipulation of Lockhart,
who certainly has communicated to it some of the sting of the
"Scorpion" of *Blackwood's*, "that wild, black-bill Hazlitt" is interro-
gated as to whether he had not called Desdemona "a lewd woman"—
which he had not, although in insinuating that Desdemona was a
woman whose sexual sensibility had been heightened by the gross
physical disparity between herself and the Moor, he had said that
which merited rebuke—and as to whether he had not polluted the
pages of his *Reply to Malthus* (in which indeed we have admitted that
his rapier twinkles wickedly at times, although his cause is righteous)

with obscenities "hideous as those of Aretine, and dull as those of Cleland." But these questions are merely intended to whet the reader's appetite. The *piéce de resistance* of this banquet, the pungent morsel which has been carefully guarded all the summer, is the oft-turned-over piece of carrion talk which the Leopard had carried with him, as it were, like treasure-trove from lovely Grasmere to lovely Scotland. Here at last it is displayed for all the world to see. If Hazlitt had striven to overcome his early humiliation, henceforth he will never be allowed to forget it, for now all the world is made the spectator of that which took place many years before beneath the shadow of Skiddaw; and all the world's coarse thumb and finger may probe the hidden sore of his youth:

"Query 1.

"Mr. William Hazlitt, ex-painter, theatrical critic, review, essay, and lecture manufacturer, London, Did you, or did you not, in the course of your late Lectures on Poetry etc. infamously vituperate and sneer at the character of Mr. Wordsworth—I mean his personal character; his genius even you dare not deny?

"2. Is it, or is it not, true that you owe all your ideas about poetry or criticism to gross mis-conceptions of the meaning of his conversation; and that you once owed your personal safety, perhaps existence, to the humane and firm interference of that virtuous man, who rescued you from the hands of an indignant peasantry whose ideas of purity you, a cockney visitor, had dared to outrage?"

Hazlitt wrote *A Reply to " Z,"* which to us seems "complete," except that he turned away, as if sickening at it, from the brutal impertinence of Query 2, merely remarking: "I beg to be excused answering this question except as it relates to my supposed ingratitude." Hazlitt would answer Coleridge or Southey, would bestir himself to cross swords with his equals in personal duel, but from certain aspects of the mindless malevolence of the word-maulers of *Blackwood's* he seems to have turned away with something of the feeling: " *Ce ne sont pas des hommes, ce sont des choses: on ne s'explique pas avec des choses.*"[313] The *Reply to " Z,"* and the remaining queries of *Hazlitt Cross-Questioned*, will be dealt with presently. It is sufficient to say in the meantime that the *Reply* was not published.[314] In the course of the autumn, Hazlitt, who had probably known nothing of the nature of the rumour which pursued him until *Blackwood's* brazen blare, proclaiming it abroad, came upon him with a shock that both sickened and stunned him, determined to fight down publicly the accusations and innuendos which were damaging his life, instituted proceedings for libel. In this way he muzzled the Leopard, who usually proved, when counter-attacked, an animal nimble in retreat. Yet he could not repair the

damage the matter had done to him. He said of it afterwards that it
had nearly put him underground.

It was noticed by his friends in after years that there were three
subjects at the mention of which his face would darken with suffering.
One of these was the treatment meted out to Napoleon; the second was
"the passion of Love;" the third was Calumny.

What was most dangerous to him in his personal life, was the
tendency of such treatment to drive a man of his temperament into
playing with what he would call "the toys of desperation" and thus
into precipitating his life towards a crisis in which his conduct might
seem to justify the calumny that had provoked it. But worst of all for
him was the intensification which came to him with the levelling of
such a charge against him publicly, of the distrust with which he
approached Woman. In addition to the long-rankling and humiliating
secret consciousness, torturing both his idealism and his self-love, that
womanhood had offended against him in a way which would not have
been possible were he not "a species by himself," he had now the
distress of feeling that in the eyes of the world he was "in a manner
marked" as one who had offended against womanhood. This public
branding deepened to agony and inflamed to fever-heat the baseless
and fantastic fear which had long been present with him, that no
woman could look upon him without distaste. Careless and hostile
hands had gone a long way towards pushing this painful eccentricity
well on the way to monomania. Patmore said of it that in the end it
became "fraught with an almost painfully pathetic interest" that
had never "been equalled either in kind or degree, even in fictitious
narrative"—except perhaps in the fairy-tale of *Beauty and the Beast.*

Hazlitt could fight down open insult, but a story like this about a
man whom every circumstance of his life now made conspicuous,
once it had been freely circulated, could never cease to pass hither and
thither in the world of his day, driven like a dead leaf before the
strong winds of passion and prejudice. Nor did its life cease when his
own had ended. It reappeared in 1838 in Gillman's *Life of Coleridge,*
the element of ingratitude on which Wordsworth and Coleridge had
harped so much being here emphasised, although the benefactors
through whose exertions "his very life had been saved" are in this
version of the story Coleridge and Southey. It appeared in the sketch
of Hazlitt included in 1854 by Patmore in *My Friends and Acquaintances,*
garnished with the usual apparent defence masking concealed
depreciation:

"Many extravagant and ridiculous stories were related, or rather
whispered about vaguely, all of them discreditable to the personal
character of Hazlitt, as the *immediate* cause of his alienation from the
distinguished friends of his early life; and in the most discreditable

of them all there was, I have been led to believe, some truth. I allude to a story relating to Hazlitt's alleged treatment of some pretty village jilt, who, when he was on a visit to Wordsworth, had led him (Hazlitt) to believe that she was not insensible to his attentions: and then, having induced him to 'commit' himself to her in some ridiculous manner, turned round upon him and made him the laughing-stock of the village. There is, I believe, too much truth in the statement of his enemies, that the mingled disappointment and rage of Hazlitt on this occasion led him, during the madness of the moment (for it must have been nothing less) to acts which nothing but the supposition of insanity could account for, much less excuse. And his conduct on this occasion is understood to have been the immediate cause of that breach between him and his friends above-named (at least Wordsworth and Southey) which was never afterwards healed."

It is obvious that Patmore's report is based on the gossip of the day, not on any reference to the matter ever made by Hazlitt. In this gossip, however, in so far as he could test it by his own knowledge, Patmore distinguished two layers of untruth:

1. That this incident was the cause of the rupture of his friendship with the Lake Poets.

2. That Hazlitt's subsequent criticism of the Lake Poets was in any way connected with resentment towards them bred out of the incident.[315]

The story has continued to win acceptance up to the present day. It is still frequently related against Hazlitt:

1. Without any investigation as to its origin in a report given, years after the incident itself, with intent to injure Hazlitt's reputation, by one who had been at Grasmere at the time the incident took place at Keswick, and whose conduct at the time proves that this retrospective account of the incident was based not on personal knowledge of it nor on what was said of it at the time, but on what scandal made of it afterwards.

2. Without any consideration of the circumstances of the circulation and fanning of the report, by political enemies, at a time when political feeling was inflamed.

3. Without any investigation as to the extent to which this report was garbled by the one who recorded it.

4. Without due reflection as to its relevance to a man of Hazlitt's upbringing and character.

The evidence as to the episode is now all laid before the reader. We, for our part, have no hesitation in determining, through a comparison of all these accounts with the few hints as to the nature of the experience through which he passed, given by Hazlitt himself, and with what is known as to his attitude to women in his youth, the extent to which exaggeration and distortion appear in these reports. We have already given it as our opinion that the girl outraged both his sensitiveness and his self-love, and that in his anger he terrified her. That is the essential nature of the incident. As to whether he used violence towards her or no—who would venture to pronounce on that? Only two people could know that, Hazlitt and the girl herself. Hazlitt never spoke of the matter. As to what the girl said, or the measure of truth in what she said—again, who can report on that? She would have been most unlikely to have circulated such reports of her own humiliation as Wordsworth carried to Crabius—but no doubt local gossip circulated such embroideries on the incident, by way of accounting for her fear, or Wordsworth would not have reported them.

If there had been evidence of any kind against Hazlitt, it is unlikely that those who were out to slay him would have dropped their cause so hastily under the threat of a suit for libel. Again, if there were evidence against Hazlitt, it is unlikely that he would, in his father's lifetime, have brought a suit the course of which would have been an extreme distress to his parents, and in the prosecution of which he himself would have felt like a man whose nerves were being broken on the wheel. As it was, even the "whisk and wind" of this fell process, as he said, put him "nearly underground."

We have only one more word to say. Again and again, in matters relating to Hazlitt where full evidence is obtainable, we can prove that the report made of them by Crabius is twisted out of shape by inaccuracy, misunderstanding and prejudice. He understood nothing of Hazlitt; he never showed any sympathy towards him; he tended consistently to take the darkest view of his prospects, of his staying-power as a writer, of his character, and of any gossip about him. This tended occasionally, in any matter touching Hazlitt's sexual life, to lead to actual distortion. The accusation he reported, that Hazlitt had narrowly escaped being "sent to prison for some gross attacks on women," is a gross absurdity. Any such offences would have been impossible for a man of Hazlitt's temperament. Any kind or degree of forcing would have been alike offensive to his idealism and to his self-love. What was not given him freely would have been nothing to him. On this point, we require no further evidence than the tone which prevails through all his writing, in his many references to women and to what he calls "the sexual passion." Yet there is one piece of very cogent evidence. When in the grip of the most powerful passion of his life, he scorned to take what was not readily and lovingly yielded to him. He put it thus in the idiom of what some called his madness: "The gates of Paradise were once open to me, and I blushed to enter but with the golden keys of love."

Hazlitt, in his reaction against the natural and instinctive idealism he had come to regard as a barren folly, ruinous to his own self-fulfilment, went far astray in his relationships with women, and for this he endured what he sometimes felt to be the eternity of punishment in this life. We think he was overpunished, but we have no desire to extenuate what he did or to whitewash him in this respect or in any other. Our task is only to narrate the truth in so far as we can discern it. We can say, like his friend Stendhal: " *Je ne blâme, ni n'approuve, j'observe.*" He would have thanked no one for white-washing him. He never desired to extenuate or excuse that of which he did not approve in his own conduct. "You know I am not in the habit of defending what I do," he said on one occasion in reply to a reproach made to him. "I do not say all that I have done is right." He would have laughed at any one who thought of him, or indeed of any other man, as "a purified being."

But if we feel no desire, any more than he did himself, to prove that all he did was right, we yet have an extreme objection to seeing one whose vulnerability where women were concerned—a vulnerability which caused kite, crow and corbie, in addition to some who can in no wise be classed among such carrion fowl, to gather around him and peck his eyes out—arose primarily out of idealism, misrepresented by his enemies and by his pseudo-friends to such an extent that he is made to appear the exact opposite of what he was. According to his own theory of human nature, man was neither a god nor a brute. If Hazlitt was not a god, he was also, like Rousseau, as far removed from the brute as it is possible for man to be. We desire to make the line of demarcation here, which some have sought to obliterate, as broad and clear as possible.

As to the incident itself, we may now take our leave of it in the words in which he dismissed one of the charges made against Napoleon, which he held to be non-proven:

"dark hints were thrown out, and it became a painful mystery, over which imagination drew its worst colours, and malice and prejudice left no doubt of the truth."

We have seen how the showman, the anatomizer, and pseudo-friend reacted to the calumny that poisoned Hazlitt's life. We have seen also how lightly one true friend dismissed it from his thoughts. Talfourd, also a friend, castigated it, noting at the same time the corroding effects of slander on Hazlitt's life. He spoke of Hazlitt's will, as having been made "irritable and capricious by the most inexcusable mis-representation and abuse with which the virulence of party-spirit ever disgraced literary criticism," and went on to say: "His words were shamelessly garbled; his person and habits slandered; and volumes, any one page of which contained thought sufficient to supply a whole *Quarterly Review*, were dismissed with affected contempt, as the drivelling of an impudent pretender, whose judgement was to be estimated by an enthusiastic expression torn from its context, and of whose English style a decisive specimen was found in an error of the press."

Procter said simply with that quietude which is so impressive in his writing when he speaks of Hazlitt:

"He was crowned by defamation."

He may have been crowned, but oh! it was a cruel crown to place upon that dark and struggling brow, poison-thorny! We have said that he cut himself loose from the ditch-bramble that had caught at him in Keswick, yet not before a poison-thorn from it had lodged itself in the nerve of his manhood. But that was not sufficient. It was no ordinary bramble that had caught at him. So virulent a life has it that any fragment of it which drops to the earth has power to take root again and grow, to unite with other parts, and because it is watered with the hatred of mighty poets, to shoot up like Jack's beanstalk, to pursue the victim it has wounded yet not destroyed across space and time, to wind itself about his brow and put out the light of his eyes, to weave itself around him in poisoned Nessus-folds that eat through skin and flesh into the heart and goad it towards madness. Did not one who had sickened of watching human beings spend the brief time allotted to them on earth in the pastime of mangling one another's souls and lives once write in his bitterness: "Last week I saw a woman flayed, and you will hardly believe how much it altered her person for the worse!"[316] No doubt in the marts of the world it is more usual for a woman to be served thus: the sport may be the better, as a woman's skin is generally reckoned the finer. But we are assured that on those occasions where the process is applied to a man, although the sport may be somewhat less delicate, the results are yet not less positive.

Chapter Three

TOWARDS PETERLOO (1818-1820)

"Somebody once asked Hazlitt about his father. 'Say nothing about my father,' said Hazlitt. 'He was a good man. His son is a devil, and let him remain so.'"

BENJAMIN HAYDON.

I

ON the evening of Tuesday, January 13th, 1818, Hazlitt began at the Surrey Institution the course of lectures on English Poetry the details of which he had arranged with Patmore. During this year and the following one lecturing on English literature was to be his chief work and his principal means of livelihood.

His audience was composed of such heterogeneous elements that the most experienced lecturer in the world might have had difficulty in welding it into a unity. It consisted chiefly, says Talfourd, "of Dissenters, who agreed with him in his hatred of Lord Castlereagh, and his love of religious freedom, but who ' loved no plays; ' of Quakers, who approved him as the earnest opponent of slavery and capital punishment, but who ' heard no music; ' of citizens, devoted to the main chance, who had a hankering after ' the improvement of the mind ' but to whom his favourite doctrine of its natural disinterestedness was a riddle." Then there were a few enemies who came to sneer; a few pseudo-friends who came chiefly to carp; and a few friends, including some of the painters of the day, who thought Hazlitt's conversation incomparable, and who realised that to hear him talking at length on poetry would be a privilege. Mixed as his audience was, he succeeded in commanding its attention as if it were one man. Although he was "pallid as death"[317] at the opening of his first lecture, and so nervous that he came near to breaking down, he was now no longer the novice of 1812, who had thought that all a lecturer had to do was to pack on to paper all the hard thought that could be hurled at an audience within the compass of an hour's time. He had learned, in lecturing as in writing, how necessary it was to punctuate the thought with material that gave some relief from hard thinking; he had learned how to amuse; and he had learned how to adorn. His initial training had been austere. He had been taught to think honestly, not to garnish his thoughts. He had had it impressed upon him that "flowers of rhetoric in . . . serious discourses are like the blue and red

371

flowers in corn, pleasing to those who care only for amusement, but prejudicial to him who would reap the profit."318 But he had discovered for himself that serious discourses, like serious writing, tired the listener when ornament was too rigidly excluded. His early training would always keep him from tending too much towards the ornamental or the rhetorical; indeed to the end he half despised ornament in writing, for the dry movement of thought was what he respected more than anything. There would always be in what he said or thought the hard kernel of thought. But just because of this, he could afford to give his work the adornment the necessity of which he half regretted. He could let the blue and red flowers come up in the corn, without any risk to his harvest—and sometimes, to the delight of all onlookers, he now lets them run riot. His friends find great beauty in his style. Even his enemies admit its sparkle.

Apart from this, he had learned how to keep in contact with his audience. In saying this we do not mean to suggest that he always pleased. It would be truer to say that sometimes he commanded attention by displeasing. But at least—he was in touch with those to whom he spoke. He startled his hearers sometimes into sudden gushes of thought with his paradoxes; he roused them by flicking at their prejudices with his wit; he delighted in forcing a new angle of vision on an audience largely compounded of "Saints;" he curbed the storms he excited, by his satire; now and again, he carried his hearers away in sympathy by the sheer intensity of his feeling. Whatever might be said of his lectures, no one could describe them as having, like Orlando's horse, every imaginable excellence, and only one fault, that of being dead. They might or might not, according to the opinion of the listener, have every imaginable fault; but they had the one thing needful, in that they were alive, and in this they differed from many excellent lectures, listened to by audiences half 'twixt the sleep and wake, to which no fault at all is ever imputed, and which, by reason of the exceeding softness of their texture, present as few assailable points as a jellyfish. Hazlitt's lectures, because they were altogether living, bristled with points that invited, nay! compelled attack. Sometimes he aroused a storm of protest among those sections of the audience which had no special sympathy with him. But at least, his lectures were not lullabies. Crabius, who often felt sleepy at Coleridge's lectures, and who had sometimes found himself adoze when Coleridge had tended to prose, found himself one day in Hazlitt's lecture yielding to the indiscretion of hissing. That hiss tells us all as to the way in which Hazlitt stimulated his hearers so that their customary self-consciousness deserted them. One member of Hazlitt's audience found some of the scenes in his lectures indecorous, and wrote to *The Times* to complain about them: "I am in the habit of attending the lectures at the Surrey Institution, and on Tuesday last was present at one delivered by Mr. Hazlitt . . . in the course of which he made (as he not infrequently does) an unfortunate and irrelevant political allusion, which was instantly followed by rounds of applause from some, and hissing from other parts of the audience. . . . I am myself very little moved by party differences, and looked upon this scene with calm composure, and was not a little shocked at seeing so well dressed and (to my own knowledge) generally respectable an audience emulating the uproar of a one-shilling gallery—behaviour totally at variance with the dignity and decorum due to the place and occasion, and highly offensive to everyone who professes to be, with the writer, a friend to order." We get the impression that such scenes disconcerted Hazlitt little. William Bewick tells us how he dealt with them. When hissing broke out he would "calmly look towards the place whence the hissing came, turning back the leaf of his copy, and deliberately repeating the sentiments with greater energy and a voice more determined than before."[319] We have ample testimony as to the clash of will there sometimes was between him and his audience, no testimony that he ever failed to assert his right to freedom of speech. Not without recollection of Keats's feeling that he resembled in some respects Edmund Kean, we think that both Hazlitt's appeal as a lecturer and the antagonism he inspired may be explained through some words of his own, in which he explained, with more than his customary magnificence of phrasing, how it was that there were people who could honestly prefer the unruffled mediocrity of Young to the fire from heaven that showed itself in the eyes of Edmund Kean:

"It has been remarked, as a peculiarity in modern criticism, that the courtly and loyal make a point of crying up Mr. Young, as an actor, and equally running down Mr. Kean; and it has been conjectured in consequence that Mr. Kean was a *radical*. Truly, he is not a radical politician; but what is as bad, he is a radical actor. He savours too much of the reality. He is not a mock-tragedian, an automaton player —he is something besides his paraphernalia. He has ' that within which passes show.' . . . Mr. Kean has a heart in his bosom, beating with human passion . . . he is a living man, and not an artificial one. How should those who look to the surface, and never probe deeper, endure him? He is the antithesis of a court-actor. His *overt* manner must shock them, and be thought a breach of all decorum. They are in dread of his fiery humours, of coming near his Voltaic Battery—they chuse rather to be roused gently from their self-complacent apathy by the application of Metallic Tractors. They dare not trust their delicate nerves within the estuary of the passions, but would slumber out their torpid existence in a calm, a Dead Sea—the air of which extinguishes life and motion!"[320]

No one who preferred an automaton to a man, or a man of straw to one of flesh and blood, would care for Hazlitt's lectures. No one who went, like the correspondent of *The Times*, to have his mind gently improved, in the company of other "well-dressed" and "respectable" people, would relish very much the doctrine of the one who wrote in this year: "there is not any term that is oftener misapplied, or that is a stronger instance of the abuse of language, than this same word *respectable*. By a *respectable* man is generally meant a person there is no reason for respecting." No one whose conception of a faultless lecture was a nullity in criticism that presented no openings for challenge would ever find Hazlitt's way of sweeping his hearers into the mind of a great writer by a tidal wave of sympathy that for the moment robbed them of their own identity, other than a menace to their peace and an insult to their self-complacency. But all who loved books and good talk about books caught fire from him. The genuine writers of the day learned from him. The young painters listened to him as to an oracle. And four poets at least, Lamb and Procter and Leigh Hunt and Keats, delighted in the true pomegranate colour and texture of his criticism. Indeed Keats felt that "Hazlitt's depth of taste" was one of the three things which reconciled him to the age and civilisation in which he lived.

Impressions as to this first course of lectures on English literature have come down to us from many of his contemporaries. Talfourd tells us how he startled the audience at the first lecture, which was on the nature of poetry, by the "fine extravagance" of the words: "There can never be a Jacob's Dream. Since that time the heavens have gone farther off, and grown astronomical. They have become averse to the imagination." We could wish that someone had told us how his audience reacted to the even finer "extravagance" of the claims he made for the subject-matter of poetry:

"there is no thought or feeling that can have entered into the mind of man, which he would be eager to communicate to others, or which they would listen to with delight, that is not a fit subject for poetry. It is not a branch of authorship; it is ' the stuff of which our life is made.' The rest is ' mere oblivion,' a dead letter; for all that is worth remembering in life, is the poetry of it. Fear is poetry, hope is poetry, love is poetry, hatred is poetry; contempt, jealousy, remorse, admiration, wonder, pity, despair, or madness, are all poetry."

Crabius came away from the second lecture, which was on Chaucer and Spenser, feeling as if he had caught some of the perfume of poetry in it. Keats came hurrying up to the lecture-hall, an hour late, just as the audience was dispersing. He was met by Hazlitt, John Hunt and his son Henry, John Landseer, who two years before had himself been the lecturer at the Surrey Institution, his sons Thomas and Edwin, young William Bewick, to whom Hazlitt had presented a ticket for the course, Charles Wells, and others of Hazlitt's friends. From the way in which he says he was "pounced upon" by these, "aye and more," we gather that he ran the gauntlet for his lack of punctuality. To enthusiastic young William Bewick, who reported to his family that the lectures were considered the finest ever delivered, and who himself thought Hazlitt "the Shakespeare prose writer of our country," far transcending all others "in truth, style, and originality," Keats must have seemed careless of his opportunities. However, he was present at the third lecture, and after that he attended regularly. In this third lecture, on Shakespeare and Milton, Hazlitt paused for a moment to contrast with the liberal interpretation given to poetry by these, what he called "the devouring egotism" of the Lake poets, and he swept his audience into sympathy with him. At the close of the fourth lecture, on Dryden, some of the Restoration poets, and Pope, he gave what was perhaps his apology for such onslaughts, when after saying of Cowley that he was "a great man, not a great poet," he added: "I never wish to meddle with names that are sacred, except when they stand in the way of things that are more sacred." In his fifth lecture he delighted the "saintly" part of his audience by reading Cowper's parallel between the poor cottager, resting on her simple faith, and happy in it—and Voltaire. At the lines:

> "Just knows, and knows no more, her Bible true—
> A truth the brilliant Frenchman never knew:"

the "Saints" broke into a "joyous shout" which seemed to indicate that they were congratulating themselves because they were "so much wiser than the brilliant Frenchman." This was Talfourd's impression of their mood. Whether it were true or no, Hazlitt certainly applied the antidote to such a spirit in his following lecture, the sixth, in which he tried to do justice to the good that Voltaire had done: "He stole away its cloak from grave imposture. If he reduced other things below their true value, making them seem worthless and hollow, he did not degrade the pretensions of superstition and tyranny below their true value, by making them seem utterly worthless and hollow, as contemptible as they were odious. This was the service he rendered to truth and mankind." The greater part of the audience received this with but little relish, and Crabius associated himself with its displeasure: "He . . . even eulogised the modern infidel, so indiscreet and reckless is the man." Perhaps Hazlitt was somewhat indiscreet in his choice of some of the material on which he touched in this lecture. His graceful words on Prior, perfectly adjusted to the subject though they were, were but frigidly received. Crabius, who had been inclined, ever since Wordsworth had confided to him the story of the Keswick episode, to take a very dark view of all Hazlitt said and did, described them as "almost obscene." But the real battle of wills came over Gay. Perhaps the sour looks with which his graceful eulogy on the "laughing grace" of Prior's muse had been received had roused the demon of perversity in Hazlitt, for he proceeded to read out aloud almost thirty of Gay's ribald lines on the intolerable prosing of Blackmore, the poet who

> "Undid Creation at a jerk,
> And of Redemption made damn'd work.
> Then took his Muse at once, and dipt her
> Into the middle of the Scripture."—

regardless of the electricity which was gathering in the air. Crabius was one of those who were simmering indignantly at the quotation, but it is Talfourd who has left the most vivid impression of the battle of wills: "He went on doggedly to the end, and by his perseverance, baffled those who, if he had acknowledged himself wrong by stopping, would have visited him with an outburst of displeasure which he felt to be gathering." What vexed Hazlitt much more than the mutterings among the "congregation of Saints," as Crabius called them, was that at the close of this unlucky lecture he hurt Keats. It was Hazlitt's firm belief that no man who was conscious of great powers, and to whom the development of these powers had consequently become the ruling passion, could ever voluntarily put an end to his life. Therefore, hallowed by misfortune though Chatterton's name was, he could not believe in the accepted estimate of Chatterton's powers, and he concluded his lecture with a confession of this scepticism: "He did not show extraordinary powers of genius, but extraordinary precocity. Nor do I believe he would have written better, had he lived. He knew this himself, or he would have lived." It is not difficult to understand the chill these words must have struck on the ears of Keats, who even at that moment was haunted by the fear that he might die before he had gathered in his harvest. He had the matter out with Hazlitt after the lecture. Hazlitt's opinion, which was of long standing, remained unshaken. But he opened his next lecture with some words of gracious and gentle explanation which surely must have removed any element of wounding from what he had said, for the substance of them is that genius is ageless and dateless: "I am sorry that what I said in the conclusion of the last Lecture respecting Chatterton, should have given dissatisfaction to some persons, with whom I would willingly agree on all such matters. What I meant was less to call in question Chatterton's genius, than to object to the common mode of estimating its magnitude by its prematureness. The lists of fame are not filled with the dates of births or deaths; and the side-mark of the age at which they were done, wears out in works destined for immortality."

This lecture, the seventh, was on Burns, and here Hazlitt approached dangerous ground, for he could hardly touch on Burns without touching on Wordsworth's *Letter to a Friend of Robert Burns*, which, published just two years before, still rankled deeply with most of the admirers of Burns, to whom it seemed offensive in its egoism and damaging in its patronage. The words in which he dealt with "the formidable patronage of Mr. Wordsworth's pen" were so cutting that Crabius, who for some time had been simmering, at last boiled over: "Hazlitt was so contemptuous towards Wordsworth, speaking of his letter about Burns, that I lost my temper and hissed. . . . I was led to burst out into declamations against Hazlitt which I afterwards regretted, though I uttered nothing but the truth." What is most valuable in this lecture, and most characteristic of Hazlitt, is his insistence on the prerogative of genius, his claim, many times royally advanced in defence of the one great actor of the day, that "a man of genius is not a machine." He had made it applicable to Kean and Rousseau. Here it is made specially applicable to those of whom it can be said that the gods have made them poetical:

"poets are men of genius; . . . they live in a state of intellectual intoxication; . . . it is too much to expect them to be distinguished by peculiar *sang froid*, circumspection and sobriety. Poets are by nature men of stronger imagination and keener sensibilities than others; and it is a contradiction to suppose them at the same time governed only by the cool, dry, calculating dictates of reason and foresight."

Hazlitt's audience had been steadily increasing throughout the series of lectures. More and more listeners came to hear him, who were drawn merely by intellectual sympathy. At the last lecture, on The Living Poets, which was delivered on the first Tuesday of March, the Hall was "crowded to the very ceiling."

Some of this audience may have come in the hope of seeing sport, for the attack on Wordsworth's *Letter to a Friend of Robert Burns* had made some talk. Also Hazlitt was reported to have given Crabbe "an unmerciful licking," when he had touched on him in his fifth lecture. Possibly there were many who came to this last lecture in the expectation of seeing and hearing Hazlitt "break the staff," as Crabius put it, over the heads of the living poets; for to hear Hazlitt "breaking the staff" over anybody's head was an experience not lacking in exhilaration. As admiring Keats put it: "Hazlitt . . . is your only good damner, and if ever I am damn'd—damn me if I shouldn't like him to damn me." If Hazlitt's friends had expected fireworks, they did not get them, for Hazlitt let off only one rocket in the course of the lecture.[321] But they got something far more memorable, in the only lecture of the series which in its quality matched the incomparable first. It was Hazlitt's opinion that what was most necessary to a critic was courage—courage—and always courage! If there were few fireworks in the lecture, there was plenty of profound and searching criticism, which only a man of great courage would have ventured, for Hazlitt, refusing to palter with his subject, insisted on judging the work of his contemporaries by the standards he had applied to the work on which time had set its seal. Thus at almost every point in his lectures he must have made enemies, for the poets, no less than some of the painters of the day, were avid of being classed among the immortals, even during their lifetime. From Hazlitt they got their due, and no more. At the outset of the lecture, which beats throughout with the pulse of life, he warns his hearers that fame is "the recompense, not of the living, but of the dead;" he tells them that usually those who are most deserving of fame, are the least eager to forestall their immortality, or "mortgage it for a newspaper puff;" they can afford to wait, for "fame is not popularity, the shout of the multitude, the idle buzz of fashion, the venal puff, the soothing flattery of favour or of friendship; but it is the spirit of a man surviving himself in the minds and thoughts of other men, undying and imperishable." He began his commentary with a gracious salutation to the women writers among his contemporaries, including his favourite Mrs. Inchbald, Mrs. Barbauld, the first poetess with whom he had made acquaintance, Miss Baillie, who seemed to him to have "all the grace which women have in writing," and dwelling with special affection on the delicate beauty of the work of Mary Lamb. He trod very gently in this part of his lecture, yet even here he could not avoid ruffling the susceptibilities of the "Saints"—for there was one woman writer, much beloved of them, whom he liked as little as he did Wilberforce. Indeed this writer seemed to him to approximate to Wilberforce in the complacency with which she accepted tribulation as the natural lot of the poor in this life, while holding out to them the prospect of treasure in Heaven. Her he dismissed briefly in the words: "Mrs. Hannah More is another celebrated modern poetess, and I believe still living. She has written a great deal which I have never read,"—whereupon the rustle of disapproval among his hearers became vocal in a cry from one corner of the room: "More pity for you!"

From the women writers he passed on to some of the minor poets of the day, holding his criticism well under control, yet at every moment, leaving behind him as many men who had turned into stone against him as Deucalion and Pyrrha had left behind them stones which were to turn into men. He pronounced Samuel Rogers "a very ladylike poet." With him he bracketed Thomas Campbell. Campbell's venomous hatred of him dated from this moment. He gave the grace of Moore's poetry its due, but told him that he "ought not to have written *Lalla Rookh*, *even* for three thousand guineas." He rebuked Byron for his ignoble changes of attitude towards Napoleon, and when some members of the audience demonstrated against this, he re-read the passage "with slow emphasis." On Byron's poetry he spoke with extraordinary insight. He found its characteristics to be power and passion, and he discriminated with extreme nicety the nature both of the passion and the nature of the poetry: "It is not the passion of a mind struggling with misfortune, or the hopelessness of its desires, but of a mind preying upon itself, and disgusted with, or indifferent to all other things. . . . It is like a cancer, eating into the heart of poetry. But still there is power; and power rivets attention and forces admiration. ' He hath a demon; ' and that is the next thing to being full of the God."321(b) To Scott's poetry Hazlitt was just, praising it as having "all the good qualities which the world agrees to understand." From Scott he passed on to the Lake Poets. He read the whole of *Hartleap Well*, always a favourite of his, remarking that those who did not feel "the beauty and force of it," might save themselves "the trouble of inquiring farther." From this he launched into a clear-sighted exposition of the nature and origin of the work of the Lake Poets. The few words on Southey which followed were just. While calling him "the undertaker of epics," he praised some of the shorter poems, including *The Holly Tree*. All this time there must have been many in his audience who were wondering when he was going to come to Coleridge, and what he would say of Coleridge. As time drew on, there must have been more than one who wondered if Coleridge were being reserved for "an unmerciful licking," a crowning attack, brief and terrible, that would be the climax of the lecture—and when the lecture was obviously drawing towards its conclusion, whether it were possible that Coleridge was going to be attacked in the way of silence. But no! At last they heard him say: "It remains that I should say a few words of Mr. Coleridge." As he spoke, those who had any know-ledge of the two men must have understood why he had taken as the text of his lecture the lines:

"No more of talk where God or Angel guest
    With man, as with his friend, familiar us'd
    To sit indulgent."–

for there was no fight in his words, no anger, but only longing. They must have understood too the nature of the pulse of feeling that had been beating throughout the lecture, as he had spoken of the lesser men, for there was deep sadness in his words as he approached the one whose Genius, if it had neither hands nor feet, like that of men who adjusted themselves more easily to the world around them, yet had angels' wings, which theirs would never have. It was obvious that if Coleridge came last in the lecture, he was both the first and the last, the Alpha and Omega, the beginning and the end, in the lecturer's thoughts, as Hazlitt continued:

"and there is no one who has a better right to say what he thinks of him than I have. 'Is there here any dear friend of Cæsar? To him I say that Brutus's love to Cæsar was no less than his.' But no matter."

Having said a word or two on *The Ancient Mariner*, he quoted at length the passage on the poisoning that could come to deep friendship, which he ever regarded as the finest thing in *Christabel*. As he read the lines, it was evident that he saw them "through the fine medium of passion," and that the yearning they expressed was identical with his own. After an impatient word or two on Coleridge's early prose, the *Conciones ad Populum* and *The Watchman*, which he described as "dreary trash," he gave up any further critical consideration of Coleridge's work, and turned towards the man himself and towards what was always in his longing thoughts, the memory of the Jacob's Ladder, which this one man had had the power to create for all on whom the eyes filled with a "fine frenzy" had looked, for all who had come under the spell of the "strange power of speech"—the glory of it, and the evanescence:

"I may say of him here, that he is the only person I ever knew who answered to the idea of a man of genius. He is the only person from whom I ever learnt any thing. There is only one thing he could learn from me in return, but *that* he has not. He was the first poet I ever knew. His genius at that time had angelic wings, and fed on manna. He talked on for ever; and you wished him to talk on for ever. His thoughts did not seem to come with labour and effort; but as if borne on the gusts of genius, and as if the wings of his imagination lifted him off his feet. His voice rolled on the ear like the pealing organ, and its sound alone was the music of thought. His mind was clothed with wings; and raised on them, he lifted philosophy to heaven. In his descriptions, you then saw the progress of human happiness and liberty in bright and never-ending succession, like the steps of Jacob's ladder, with airy shapes ascending and descending, and with the voice of God at the top of the ladder. And shall I, who heard him then, listen to him now? Not I! . . . That spell is broke; that time is gone for ever; that voice is heard no more; but still the recollection comes rushing by with thoughts of long-past years, and rings in my ears with never-dying sound."

What a fine instrument the human heart is! Even in a girdle-duel, shall it not whisper the edge of the knife!

2

Just as Hazlitt's lectures were drawing to a close, in the first week of March, the famous electioneering contest in Westmorland was beginning, in which the Lowther monopoly of the representation of the county was challenged by Henry Brougham. When Lord Lonsdale's sons, Lord Lowther and Colonel Lowther, had been put forward as the two candidates for Westmorland it had been felt in many quarters that the county should not be completely represented in Parliament by the one family, and finally Henry Brougham had been nominated, chiefly with a view to contesting Colonel Lowther's seat. Thus the election was regarded as a trial of strength between the forces tending towards reaction and the forces tending towards reform, or between hereditary monopoly and the forces in favour of popular election. The issues being what they were, it was inevitable that Wordsworth and Hazlitt should be on opposite sides in this conflict, and that they should both be hotly engaged in it. Wordsworth's public exertions in the Lowther interest were common knowledge, and there were not lacking those who were accusing the Poet of rendering sycophantic service "to a borough-mongering earl," to one, moreover, to whom it was almost a work of supererogation to render such service, Lord Lonsdale being famed throughout the country for his resource in electioneering. It was the bitterness Hazlitt had felt over what seemed to him a prostitution of Wordsworth's powers which had conditioned what Crabius called the "contemptuous" tone of that reference to Wordsworth, in the lecture on Burns on February 24th, which had stung Crabius into hissing. The reference in his essay *On Respectable People*, which was written about this time, is still more "contemptuous" and cutting: "the only way for a poet now-a-days to emerge from the obscurity of poverty and genius, is to prostitute his pen, turn pimp to a borough-mongering lord, canvass for him at elections, and by this means aspire to some importance, and be admitted on the same respectable footing with him as his valet, his steward, or his practising attorney."

As Easter drew near, the excitement over the election was keen both in London, where the opposition press was busy with it, and in Westmorland, where Dorothy Wordsworth, who thought the opposition press brought out nothing worth reading, regretted that to all appearance the County had gone blue, because of the pusillanimity of the Lowther partisans about wearing their colours; "no lady would venture to appear in a yellow ribband in Kendal streets," she wrote, "though you cannot walk thirty yards without meeting a dirty lad or lass with a blue one! and the *ladies* of that party also have no fear of displaying their colour." At the same time she complained: "the misguided mob, including almost all of the lower classes who have no votes, cry aloud for Brougham." Although these things were to her matters of regret, her words make it clear that popular feeling was with Brougham.

Hazlitt, be it noted, was much more for "independence" than he was for Brougham, whose speeches, fluent though they were, always seemed to him "short of the mark." But he associated himself wholeheartedly with the *Examiner* campaign, because of the Cause. Here he looked to the principle at stake, rather than to the man.

For the rest, until the middle of May, he was engaged in repeating at the Crown and Anchor the course of lectures he had delivered at the Surrey Institution. He would then willingly have gone to Edinburgh to repeat them once more, but Jeffrey, on being consulted as to this project, told him that Edinburgh was "the worst place in the world for such experiments." From Jeffrey's letter, written on May 3rd, we learn that Hazlitt by this time was feeling ill and over-driven. Jeffrey, who always acted admirably towards his "allies," in money matters, although telling Hazlitt that he was more likely if he came to Edinburgh to be abused "as a Jacobin and a raving blockhead" than to derive any financial advantage from lecturing, accompanied his very plain speech with an act of great and practical kindness. "In the meantime," he wrote, "I am concerned to find your health is not so good as it should be, and that you could take more care of it if your finances were in better order. We cannot let a man of genius suffer in this way, and I hope you are in no serious danger. I take the liberty of enclosing £100, a great part of which I shall owe you in a few weeks, and the rest you shall pay me back in reviews whenever you can do so, without putting yourself to uneasiness. If you want another £100 tell me so plainly, and it shall be heartily at your disposal."

By the end of May Hazlitt's barque, which always seems such a precarious, even such a frail barque, and which yet outrode so many storms, was sailing merrily. His Lectures had been published by Taylor and Hessey shortly after he had finished his delivery of them. Their publication had been accompanied by the publication, also by Taylor and Hessey, of a second edition of *Characters of Shakespear's Plays*, a book which had quickly made for itself a place in the affections of its readers. At the same time, a selection of his dramatic criticism from *The Examiner* and *The Times*, for which he had put in a spell of work in 1817, with a prefatory essay in which he interpreted for his readers his conception of dramatic criticism, and explained the spirit in which he had entered upon his work as dramatic critic, was in the press, and was about to be issued by other publishers. This was full of entertaining material. Presently Miss Mitford would be writing about this selection: "I could not help reading them altogether; though so much of Hazlitt is rather dangerous to one's taste, rather like dining on sweetmeats and supping on pickles. So poignant is he, and so rich, everything seems insipid after him." The indications seemed to be that Hazlitt, with money in his purse, with a good deal of excellent work behind him, with two books just issued and a third about to appear, was entering at last upon a spell of fair weather.

But this was not to endure. In the beginning of June, the belated January number of the *Quarterly*, containing an intolerable review of *Characters of Shakespear's Plays*, made its appearance. Even Crabius, reading the review on the 10th, felt that the book had been "most unjustifiably abused." This is the review, eagerly snuffed up by the "Blackwood" men, in which Hazlitt is told that his knowledge of the English language is "exactly on a par with the purity of his morals." Whatever his knowledge of the English language be, yet 'twill serve. On June 14th, the never entirely unamiable meanderings of *The Examiner* are slashed across, for the first time during this year, by a ribbon of prose, greeny-glittering, dangerous, cool. It is called *The Editor of the Quarterly Review*, and it opens with the words:

"This little person is a considerable cat's-paw; and so far worthy of some slight notice. He is the *Government Critic*, a character nicely differing from that of a government spy—the invisible link, that connects literature with the police. It is his business to keep a strict eye over all writers who differ in opinion with His Majesty's Ministers, and to measure their talents and attainments by the standard of their servility and meanness. For this office he is well qualified. The Editor of the *Quarterly Review* is also Paymaster of the Band of Gentlemen-Pensioners; and whenever an author comes before him in the one capacity, with whom he is not acquainted in the other, he knows how to deal with him. He has his cue beforehand. The distinction between truth and falsehood is lost upon him; he knows only the distinction between Whig and Tory. The same set of thread-bare commonplaces, the same second-hand assortment of abusive nick-names, are always repeated; and the ready convenient lie comes in aid of the lack of other resources, and passes off, with impunity, in the garb of religion and loyalty. He is under the protection of *the Court*; and his zeal for his King and country gives him a right to say what he pleases of every public writer who does not do all in his power to pamper the one into a tyrant, and to trample the other into a herd of slaves. . . . Raised from the lowest rank to his present despicable eminence in the world of letters, he is indignant that any one should attempt to rise into notice, except by the same regular channels and servile gradations, or go about to separate the stamp of merit from the badge of sycophancy."

Here are the "devils and burgundy," as Leigh Hunt would call them, come back to the *Examiner* Office with a vengeance! Leigh Hunt recognised them as devils of quality. "Hazlitt has written a masterly character of Gifford," he wrote to Shelley, "much more coolly done than those things of his in general."

This is Hazlitt's first formal protest against the keeping of "two scores to mark the game, with Whig and Tory notches." His next appearance in *The Examiner* is on July 5th, but this time it is with a mere squib, let off to tease Wordsworth, just as the Westmorland election was drawing towards its close. By the time it had reached Westmorland, however, the laugh was on the Poet's side, and the Peer's. Brougham's progress through the county had been a triumph: Colonel Lowther could barely string together a few sentences in public; Brougham had made himself felt in Parliament: of Lord Lowther and his brother it might be said that they sat there, and no more; Ambleside might illuminate itself in honour of Brougham: but at Appleby on July 4th it was shown once more that Lord Lonsdale must yet be reckoned, in electioneering skill and resource, the "incomparable" of his day. It was noted at the time, that not only the poets, but the spiritual powers of the district, had come handsomely to his aid. Because of the number of clergymen who made their appearance at Appleby between June 30th and July 4th, 1818, the saying went abroad:

"The Lord gave the word and great was the multitude of the preachers."

Here we should say that some of Hazlitt's political writing, always very closely connected with the social phenomena of the day, was devoted during these months to comment on the relationship at this time between the clerical character and Cæsar. In his articles on The Clerical Character,[322] he found that in the course of the distresses of the time the Clergymen of the Church of England were over-ready to render unto Cæsar the things that were Cæsar's, but much less ready to render unto God the things that were God's, and not at all ready to render unto man, or at least to the poor man, the things which the religion they professed commanded them to render unto him. He blamed them, as a body, for being "insolent to those below, and cringing to those above" them, for being, indeed, "the most devoted tools of power." In particular he mentioned with disapproval their readiness to assume towards the poor the functions of the magistrate or the police officer, recently illustrated in the conduct of the officiating clergyman at Derby, when three of the victims of the spy Oliver, poor, confused, wild-eyed Jeremiah Brandreth, "a half-starved, illiterate, and unemployed frame-work knitter," William Turner, a stone-mason, and Isaac Ludlam, also a stone-mason, had been hanged on a platform in front of the gaol, and their heads severed from their bodies, the rest of the sentence, as to quartering, having been graciously remitted by the Prince Regent. Hazlitt wrote in connection with this: "The officiating Clergyman at Derby the other day pestered Brandreth to death with importunities to inform against his associates, but put his hand before his mouth when he offered to say what he knew of Oliver, the Government-spy," and his comment on such conduct was: "Their religion is incompatible with a common regard to justice or humanity; but it is compatible with an excess of courtly zeal." He found that not only the religion but the patriotism of the established clergy of his day was eaten into and made suspect by the worship of Cæsar. "The principle of integrity is gone," he wrote; "the patriotism of the religious sycophant is rotten at the core."[323].

At the same time he found that most of the religious sects at least kept "the principle of integrity" inviolate, and paid tribute to the contribution made to the fibre of the nation by the obstinate political integrity of the Dissenting minister, and of Dissenters in general. He felt that his country, while it tended to congratulate itself on its gift of compromise, had no conception of the extent to which it was preserved, despite its tendency to compromise, from corruption and disintegration by its "no-compromise" men, especially by the obstinate integrity of the Puritan strain in the People. This he regarded literally as the salt of the nation. In his essay On Court Influence he insisted on the integrity of the Dissenters as one of the chief preservatives of the health and strength of the nation, at a time when others were inclined to stand gaping by, not feeling the "blight and the mildew" coming over an England that had once been free, nor the very bones of the country cracking and turning to a paste under "the grasp and circling folds of this new monster, Legitimacy"—and its attendants, servility, compromise with tyranny, class-rancour, and class-selfishness. The different sects in the country seemed to him at the time, the chief depositaries of integrity and the love of truth. "It is hard," he wrote, "for anyone to be an honest politician who is not born and bred a Dissenter. Nothing else can sufficiently inure and steel a man against the prevailing prejudices of the world, but that habit of mind which arises from non-conformity to its decisions in matters of religion." He was ready to admit that Nonconformity bred certain faults, but these he regarded as trifling in comparison with the faults for which it was the corrective. He claimed for it that throughout the life of the country it gave discipline in truth, and in honesty of politics, as well as of religion.

We mention these articles, because they complete his commentary on the immediate post-war troubles of the nation. Apart from these, he did little political writing in 1818. By this time he had had his say on most of what was happening; and lecturing and *belles-lettres* tended to absorb him more and more, together with the developing of that form of the essay which he was gradually making his own.

As to this, he had now realised what he wished to do with regard to it. His ambition had taken the form of wishing to leave behind him, through his essays, a kind of *Liber Veritatis*. About this time he wrote: "I wished to make a sort of *Liber Veritatis*, a set of studies from human life," and again, "I intend these Essays as studies of human nature." He felt that most writers had been too simple in their approach to the nature of man. What they said of it would have been very true if man were only "a simple animal or a logical machine, and all his faculties and impulses were in strict unison," instead of a creature whose faculties and impulses were so eternally at variance with one another that no one could at times hate more what he had done than the man who had done it. Till the intellectual faculty was destroyed, it was impossible for any man to be entirely depraved; till the physical were done away with, it was impossible for any one to be entirely virtuous. As long as man was compounded of two opposite natures, there must be an eternal competition for mastery between the two. From this point of view Hazlitt approached his theme. He might have taken as the text of his discourses Blake's: "Men are born with a devil and an angel," or "I have never known a very bad man who had not something very good in him." He said very much the same thing himself when he wrote that the old theological maxim "the greater the sinner the greater the saint," was not altogether unfounded.

It seemed to him that among the prose-writers even men like Mandeville and La Rochefoucault, whose approach to human nature was not simple, and who assumed the mixed nature of motives in all human action, had yet ended as if they believed that one motive, the lowest, that of selfishness or self-love, was the motive of all human endeavour, thus falling into as great an error as that of the idealists; that among the poets Shakespeare alone had "laid open the reaction or involution of the passions in a manner worth speaking of." Working in the humbler way of prose, and substituting analysis for creation, he was preparing in his essays to do the same kind of work, to show "the reaction or involution of the passions in a manner worth speaking of," all the time showing the play of the mixed nature of man on each, conditioning the ebb and flow of politics and religion, as well as of every passion that stirs within the breast of man. Thus, in a sense, the claim made for him by William Bewick that he was "the Shakespeare prose writer of our country" was not altogether extravagant. His attitude to his subject may be gathered from the words: "Man is an intellectual animal, and is therefore an everlasting contradiction to himself. His senses centre in himself, his ideas reach to the ends of the universe; so that he is torn in pieces between the two without a possibility of its being otherwise. A mere physical being, or a pure spirit, can alone be satisfied with itself."

He was conscious that his work was primarily analytical. Sometimes he spoke of it as "unravelling the web of human life into its various threads." In each essay he usually attempted to unravel only one thread. "My object was to show the latent operation of some unsuspected principle," he wrote, "and I therefore take only one view of that particular subject." Because he was always conscious that he was attempting to show the latent operation of some principle he, claimed that throughout he wrote as a metaphysician; for from the presence of the principle, the root of the matter, the whole essay sprang, much after the fashion of the growth of a plant:

> "So from the root
> Springs lighter the green stalk: from thence the leaves
> More airy; last the bright consummate flower."

3

It is pleasant to find that Hazlitt was sufficiently abreast of the struggle for existence to be able, in the summer of 1818, to return to Winterslow for a spell of peace and quiet and country-life, to be able, in short, to rest upon his oars for a little, if it can be called resting during the summer to be engaged in developing the literary form through which he yet hoped to launch on the world his commentary on human nature, and in preparing for the autumn's work. This was again to be lecturing, and his immediate task was the composition of a second course of lectures to be delivered at the Surrey Institution in the closing months of the year. Living in the Hut, he settled down to a renewal of his old life at Winterslow—walking, meditating, and reading. He was exceedingly anxious to put his best work into his forthcoming lectures, which were to be on a subject very near his heart—the English Comic Writers. Of this quiet interlude in what Procter called "his stormy, anxious, uncomfortable life" he wrote afterwards: "There I returned . . . to finish some works I had undertaken, doubtful of the event, but determined to do my best." In addition to writing the Lectures, he was contributing monthly essays to Constable's *Edinburgh Magazine*, *Blackwood's* rival.

He was not allowed to prolong this spell of rather busy "idleness." In the first days of September the August number of *Blackwood's* reached him. This, with its attack on "the calm, settled, imperturbable, drivelling idiocy" of Keats, is often thought of as the "Keats" number, because the early death of Keats "set a seal upon his reputation," and made him the beloved of all. But it was Hazlitt whom this number had set out to slay. The attack on him was not, like the attack on Keats, confined to one section of the magazine. It sprawled like a fungus from cover to cover. First of all there was the article, *Hazlitt Cross-Questioned*, which we have already noted in connection with the purpose it fulfilled by its two opening queries of bringing out into the light of day the calumny which had been dogging Hazlitt's progress in his literary life. We have no further comment to make on it in this connection. Our concern is now with the attempt made by the remainder of the *questionnaire* to ruin Hazlitt's literary reputation and to cut him off from his chief means of livelihood. The Third Query accused Hazlitt, who was described as "a mere quack" and "a mere bookmaker, one of the sort that lounge in third-rate book-shops, and write third-rate books," of dishonesty in connection with the work he had contributed to the *Encyclopædia Britannica*. The Fourth, which is very long, attempted to poison his relations both with *The Edinburgh Review*, from which it was stated he had been "expelled," and with *The Edinburgh Magazine*, in which, it was stated, he had been forced to take refuge, although he despised it and although he had spoken publicly of its editors "as perfect ninnies" and of the magazine itself as "a millstone." The work he had done for the Magazine was represented as having been contributed with the intention of injuring the reputation of a magazine to which he was bound in contemptuous and reluctant service, while the essay *On the Ignorance of the Learned* was described as a piece of self-congratulation on the part of a man ignorant even of the letters of the Greek alphabet and unable to distinguish between Greek and Latin, on his "never having received any education." Towards the end of this part of the *questionnaire* he was asked: "Do you know what is English, or what is not English, any more than you know that Latin is not Greek?" The Fifth Query contained the attack on his *Reply to Malthus*, which we have already noted in connection with the attack on his character. The Sixth we have also noted already, in so far as it touched on the character of Desdemona, but it assailed also his qualifications for writing *Characters of Shakespear's Plays*. The Seventh attacked his integrity as a dramatic critic. The Eighth is merely a quip: "Do you know the Latin for a goose?" But Hazlitt was assured that as soon as these questions were *anser*-ed "another eight of more complex nature, and worded more gravely," awaited his attention from "an Old Friend with a New Face."

In *Hazlitt Cross-Questioned* the main lines of the attack were laid down. Elsewhere in the Magazine single points of attack were developed and pursued. In an article *On Shakespeare's Sonnets*, the point of attack indicated by the Sixth Query was pressed forward. This article attempted to finish off the work of the *Quarterly*, in counteracting the admiration which *Characters of Shakespear's Plays* had aroused in many readers. An article on The Works of Charles Lamb returned to the attack on Hazlitt's character opened in the First and Second Queries.

Hazlitt recognised at once that *Blackwood's* attack was not a political or critical offensive directed against him but an attempt to cancel his existence as a writer. He seems also to have recognised the impossibility of dealing with such a campaign of lies by any of the ordinary means of exposure: insistence on truth, he knew, could bring no immediate victory in such a warfare. Yet in his first reaction to the attack, the writing of a *Reply*, truth was his only weapon. His manipulation of this weapon, in the immediate circumstances, is all-revealing as to the grain of his nature. He is faithful to it, even when his adherence to it puts him at a disadvantage. Writing constantly as he was, sometimes with no books of reference at hand, he sometimes fell into trivial errors of fact, and he almost always quoted inaccurately. His enemies had taunted him with his inaccuracy, and also with mistranslating a word or two in his work for the *Encyclopædia Britannica*. He admitted his errors at once, but pointed out at the same time that error, which may occur in any work that is not entirely mechanical, was not the literary dishonesty of which he had been accused. This general admission having been made, he met the attack point by point, dealing with it all in the spirit of truth, quietly, gravely, and with a lack of assumption which because of the extreme provocation he had received, is here singularly moving. Hazlitt at least was not of those who were avid of being classed among the Immortals during his lifetime. On the general description of himself as a writer of third-rate books he observed: "you state my pretensions quite as high or higher than I should. It is not everyone who can write third-rate books. There is no work of mine which I should class as even third-rate except my *Principles of Human Action*, a book which I daresay you never heard of, and which I am afraid you would not understand for the same reason that you never heard of it, namely, the abstruseness of the style and matter." With the series of Queries he dealt categorically. As to the First, questioning him as to his dealings with Wordsworth, and asserting: "his genius even you dare not deny," he replied that it would be indeed curious if he were to deny it, seeing he had been the critic who had "gone on the forlorn hope" in praising Wordsworth to an indifferent public. He answered fully the charge of ingratitude towards Wordsworth contained in the Second Query, ignoring only, as we have seen, the element of calumny intertwined with this Query. On the third Query, as to his "playing off" translations on the Editor of the Supplement to the *Encyclopædia Britannica*, he answered simply that he had been asked by Macvey Napier to do some translation from the French, that he had undertaken it while expressing at the same time his belief that he was not specially qualified for the work, had given it up on discovering a blunder he had made, and thereafter had contributed only one piece of translation "at Mr. Napier's particular request." He dealt faithfully with the numerous sub-divisions of the Fourth Query. On the inquiry as to whether he had not been "deservedly expelled" from *The Edinburgh Review*, he remarked: "I leave it to Mr. Jeffrey to answer that question;" as to the insinuation that he had been compelled "to take refuge" in *The Edinburgh Magazine*, he replied: "I answer this is false, seeing that I have at present other resources, though it is your object to drive me out both of this and every other resource;" in reply to the question: "in an essay of yours on *The Ignorance of the Learned*, do you not congratulate yourself, and the rest of your Cockney crew, on never having received any education?" he proceeded to educate his inquisitor, by informing him that the lines which prefaced the essay, and on which the essay was a commentary, were taken from a seventeenth-century poet: "The motto to that article expresses the whole doctrine of it, and is taken from Butler. Was he too of a Cockney crew, or did he wish to depreciate learning from the want of it?" The charge that he was ignorant of the number of letters in the Greek alphabet he dealt with according to its desert, by replying merely: "I do not know the number of letters in the English." To the Fifth Query, as to whether he had not polluted his pages with "obscenities hideous as those of Aretine and dull as those of Cleland," he replied: "I can say nothing to it, for I never read either of these authors." He denied the implication of the Sixth Query: "It is not true that I have insinuated that Desdemona was a lewd woman, any more than Shakespeare has insinuated it, but I have dared to say that he alone could have given additional elegance and even delicacy to a female character from the very disadvantageous circumstances in which Desdemona is placed." He denied also the charge that he had abused his position as a dramatic critic by making a personal attack on an actor he disliked.

The closing paragraph of his *Reply*, directed at insults scattered about elsewhere in the magazine, dealt with that dexterity in lying which enabled *Blackwood's* to insinuate three lies into one sentence. On the nickname bestowed on him he remarked: "Finally, Sir, you call me as a nickname ' pimpled Hazlitt.' And I am *not* pimpled, but remarkably pale and sallow. You were told of this as a false fact, and you repeated and still repeat it, declaring to hundreds of persons individually and to the public that you not only do not care for the distinction between truth and falsehood, but that you are superior to being thought to care about it." On the charges levelled against him of "open blasphemy or, which is as bad, hypocritical piety," he remarked: "I have never written a word of either open blasphemy or hypocritical piety," and added, thus meeting while at the same time ignoring the closing quip of those with whom he did not choose to bandy jests: "Is it answer'd'?"

The next thing we hear about Hazlitt is that he has left Winterslow for London and instituted proceedings against *Blackwood's*. Keats, dining with him one day in September with his publishers, Taylor and Hessey, saw at once how badly he had been wounded, and wrote afterwards to Dilke: "I suppose you will have heard that Hazlitt has on foot a prosecution against Blackwood. I dined with him a few days since at Hessey's—there was not a word said about it, though I understand he is excessively vexed." Keats of course would not understand the nature of the sting the personal calumny contained for Hazlitt, but the silence preserved on the matter was proof sufficient of the keenness of the wound. On September 20th Jeffrey wrote to Hazlitt, agreeing to act as his Counsel. *The Times* gave a lead to public opinion on the matter at issue. In a paragraph in which it mentioned the impending prosecution it described *Blackwood's* as "a book filled with private slander." Even stronger was a paragraph bracketing it along with such periodicals as *The Scourge* and *The Satirist*, and describing it as being "so grossly slanderous on individual character, that a gentleman would blush to have it seen a second time on his table."[324] The attack had been overdone, and public sympathy was with Hazlitt.

Blackwood received Hazlitt's summons for his action in the Court of Session on October 6th, the sum claimed as damages being £2,000. Presently, unable to conceive that a man as poor as Hazlitt was engaging in such a fight unaided, he came to the conclusion that Hazlitt was being financed by and prompted by Constable, whereupon his "friends" decided to approach Scott with a view to securing his intervention with Constable in their favour. As Hazlitt was in no way relying on Constable, the card on which they had relied as a trump did little for them. Blackwood's hope, indeed his expectation, that Hazlitt would give up the action was unfulfilled. In the meantime, circumstances took such a turn with him that he had ever less and less stomach for the action he had provoked. The September number of his magazine had contained a stinging attack on Playfair, the old Professor of Natural Philosophy in Edinburgh University. This "unhandsome" attack was universally condemned. Jeffrey, disgusted by it, wrote to Wilson to dissociate himself from any further intercourse with him in literary matters. Worse still was to come. A few days later there appeared a pamphlet called: "Hypocrisy Unveiled and Calumny Detected"—which summarised in very strong language the activities of *Blackwood's Magazine* during the first year of its existence: "All the venom which these malicious creatures could generate or collect has been spitefully thrown upon Mr. Jeffrey, Mr. Playfair, Mr. Brougham, Mr. Hazlitt, Mr. Napier and others who have been guilty of writing for *The Edinburgh Review*, the *Encyclopædia Britannica*, or *The Edinburgh Magazine*." The signature at the end of *Hazlitt Cross-Questioned*, "An Old Friend with a New Face," came under scathing scrutiny and comment: "The libeller of Mr. Hazlitt avows himself to be an *old* friend with a *new* face,—a face which certainly, whatever features it may at one time have displayed, exhibits only those of a demon. We pretend not to know what Mr. Hazlitt is as a man, but we know that this vilifier of Mr. Hazlitt cannot be a good one. The facts which he insidiously recalls and publishes, whether true or not, are facts which he must have come to the knowledge of under circumstances that either imposed secrecy or implicit trust and confidence. The attack on Mr. Hazlitt comes with a worse grace from these persons, inasmuch as they praised him warmly in the outset, holding him up as the first poetical critic of the day, and afterwards devoting an article to a parallel between him and Mr. Jeffrey; but the secret of all is, that Mr. Hazlitt furnished several very able articles to the *Scots* or *Edinburgh Magazine*; articles which display more original thinking than all that have yet appeared in Blackwood's work." The secret of the enmity of Wilson and Lockhart, who were all but named in the pamphlet, towards Hazlitt, was laid bare in the words: "Hazlitt is an abomination in their sight because he is rising into consequence." The pamphlet was anonymous, but its author was reputed to be powerful, and this rumour was supported by the authoritative tone of the writing. Wilson and Lockhart were threatened with the publication of "A Letter to the Dean and Faculty of Advocates on the propriety of expelling the Leopard and the Scorpion from that hitherto respectable body"—and with further personal consequences arising from the author's displeasure, if they did not mend their ways.

The rough justice meted out in this was approved of by all except by those who were punished by it. Lockhart wrote to Murray professing himself unmoved, but he kept his head no better in the heat of the moment than Wilson, who was known to be *touché*. All in a moment, in their endeavours to get their opponent to disclose his identity, they shattered the anonymity under which up to this time they had lain snug. These men, who had ignored for almost a year all Leigh Hunt's requests to them that they should meet him in the open, wrote to the author of the pamphlet through his publishers, Wilson requesting him to disclose his name, if he did not wish to be regarded as a coward, Lockhart requesting him to disclose it, if he did not desire to annul his claim to the character of a gentleman. Wilson, who had more physical than mental courage, challenged him: Lockhart, who had more mental than physical courage, was more discreet. He confined himself to the demand to know his opponent's identity.

To Murray he had written: "we have, both by writing to the Anonyme and by every other way in our power, done our best to discover the writer. We trust in God he may be *déterré*." The "Anonyme," or Formidable Unknown, as we should prefer to call him, had no intention of being *déterré*, or of engaging in mortal combat with either of a couple of puppies who in his estimation only wanted a lesson in manners, but in forwarding their letters to *The Scotsman*, where they appeared along with his own reply, he made their punishment as public as their offence had been. Cobbett's "sturdy hoofs" could not have kicked them out of action more effectively. To all the victims of *Blackwood's* the triumph must have seemed complete. And as for Hazlitt, we have the impression that through this unexpected turn of events his action had been already won for him. The further article with which he had been threatened did not make its appearance, and it is clear that there was nothing Blackwood desired less, in the atmosphere created in Edinburgh by the publication of *Hypocrisy Unveiled*, than to have to defend himself against Jeffrey's further exposure in the Court of Session of the extent to which *Blackwood's* had carried its slanders against one who was still his coadjutor in *The Edinburgh Review*. At length we find Murray, who was becoming more and more disgusted with the whole matter, complaining irritably of a kind of paralysis on the part of his Edinburgh partner: "even at this late period you omit to send me any one document on which counsel can form an opinion. What is the accusation? What can you prove? . . . To neglect such a thing as this when three-fourths of the talents of the Bar are in hostility to you, and when any jury will be prejudiced against you, is very reprehensible."

4

In the course of these October days we get only one glimpse of Hazlitt, but it is a very characteristic one. We see him, on the 15th of the month, walking towards Covent Garden with Keats, to play rackets on the Fives'-Court in St. Martin's Lane, where he had delighted to witness the great play at Fives of John Cavanagh. Even if Hazlitt had made no impression on his fellows by his writing, he would certainly be remembered by his play at rackets. He liked few things better than to watch cricket, or a strenuous game at Fives, but his passion was for rackets, and there are few of his friends who do not make some mention of him in connection with this. He never claimed to be anything but a "second-rate" player, but he was famous for his volleying, and on the court he drew spectators. This was not surprising, if the various accounts of his ways on it come anywhere near the truth. Equally familiar to his friends was the sight of him crawling about the court "like a cripple," until the moment the racket was in his hand, when the deceptive appearance of languor vanished and he started up and played like a man possessed with a demon. If he played badly, he was capable of giving an exhibition of temperament as picturesque as he had sometimes given in former years when he had felt that he was painting badly, his temper being directed, not against his opponent, but against himself, and tending to express itself in violent action, such as dashing his head against the wall. Of this tendency Procter has written sedately: "he . . . occasionally exhibited impatience if the game went against him." But there was nothing sedate in Hazlitt's performance. Bewick has described the desperation of his play, at times almost distressing to watch, the hint of savagery in his look, the extraordinary speed with which he would run to take what seemed an impossible ball, the string of oaths and ejaculations "that cannot be repeated, but may be imagined," which often accompanied his play, until at last there came the moment when he crawled off the court with his shirt under his flannel jacket as if it had been dipped in water, or shirtless, because it was so wet that he had discarded it.

All this was entirely characteristic of him. He could do nothing that he at all cared to do, without passion. This is why the reader might think when reading some of his descriptions of pictures that he cared for nothing but painting; when reading some of his political essays that he cared for nothing but politics; when reading his descriptions of Mrs. Siddons or Talma or Edmund Kean that he cared for nothing but acting; when reading some of his lectures on poetry that he cared for nothing but this intellectual love; when reading of his loves or his hates that all the life in him must have been poured into loving or hating. Passion was the foundation of his character, and on the Fives'-Court it showed itself in action. What Procter said of him—that "rackets occupied almost his whole existence," and that the racket was "the only instrument with which he desired to conquer"—was not true. Hazlitt did indeed say once that he had a much greater ambition to be the best racket-player, than the best prose-writer of the age, but this was in one of those moments of bitterness in which he felt that all he wrote, no matter what its quality might be, would be calumniated almost out of existence because he was not "a Government tool," that critics of Literature were dishonest, but that in criticism of the game there could be "no juggling." If the stroke was a good one, the hit told. There were not "two scores to mark the game, with Whig and Tory notches."

Procter could not have misinterpreted a moment's petulance thus, had he known his friend at the time when Hazlitt was straining every nerve to obtain mastery over the pen or over the brush, weeping over his paper or slashing his canvas into ribbons; but any one, seeing Hazlitt on the Fives'-Court, might have been excused for agreeing with such a misjudgment. His play was as strenuous as his talk, and there was nothing he liked more, in his play as in his talk, than an opponent who compelled from him every exertion. Above all, on the Fives'-Court as elsewhere, he admired most of all a man who fought a good losing game. This was one of the things that drew him to John Cavanagh: "he was the best *up-hill* player in the world." It was not success that he worshipped, but courage, and the moment the game began to go against a man was for him the test of that. To him the game was not merely a matter of skill and practice and physical effort, although physical dexterity had always fascinated him. It was "subject to all the skyey influences." He played it with his mind as well as with his body. Thus it was that Faith seemed to him as necessary to success in this kind of effort as in any other, and that the courage which goes hand in hand with Faith seemed to him more than skill. He said one day, of someone who had played a disappointing game: "That fellow will never do anything in the world; he never plays well, unless he is successful. If the chances go against him, he always misses the ball: he cries *Craven!*" Of Cavanagh he was accustomed to say that Cobbett and Junius together would have made one of him. Hazlitt understood such up-hill players as Cavanagh; he was far more at home with them than he was with merely bookish men; and he was himself understood and valued by all who, like himself, cared for "the rigour of the game." It was the realisation of this that prompted him to say: "the face of a racket-player is the face of a friend."

On the Fives'-Court, he forgot everything but the game. He said of it that the keeper of it might have inscribed over his door: "Who enters here, forgets himself, his country, and his friends." So perhaps we may take it that on one day at least, of this troubled October, he forgot his enemies too, and the impending action, the nervous fret of which, as we have seen, he sometimes felt would come near to putting him underground.

5

He began to deliver his Lectures on the English Comic Writers on November 3rd. This second course of lectures did not open with quite the glow and glory of the first. Possibly the strain of the impending action had thrown Hazlitt out of his stride somewhat. The first three lectures were somewhat dry and meagre. Nevertheless, his words at times did not lack "bite." Indeed, in the second lecture delivered on November 10th, occurred, when he was speaking on Ben Jonson, the most violent uproar his political intransigeance ever provoked. John Scott, who as an Editor was successful in keeping Hazlitt's politics "in order," said once, when comparing the spirit of *The Quarterly Review* and the spirit of Hazlitt, as the two utmost extremes the age had produced:

"Each of the parties has peculiar merits as well as faults, and we wish we could pick and choose properties from the two, for our own use. What we should most like to cull from the *Quarterly* is, we believe, its *sale*; what we should decline robbing Mr. Hazlitt of, are his *politics*. We do not think that we need have any scruple to mention these latter . . . for the author himself does not scruple to introduce them everywhere, and on all occasions:—they come, like a mastiff, by his side, into all companies he frequents,—whether of old poets, or modern players; and ' love me, love my *dog*,' is his maxim. To this he steadily adheres, in spite of any symptoms of confusion or alarm among silk stockings or muslin petticoats."[325]

They come, like a mastiff, by his side, into all companies he frequents. Nowhere do we see the man and the dark mastiff-familiar more indivisible than in this second course of lectures. They both march boldly into the hall of the Surrey Institution. Sometimes the mastiff-familiar curls up under the lecturer's table, and gives no trouble to the audience. Sometimes he emits a low sympathetic growling at which no one could take alarm or offence. But sometimes mastiff-familiar becomes impossible. He gets up and usurps the lecturer's desk and barks loudly and threateningly at the audience. There are cries of: "Remove that animal." His master refuses either to be parted from him or to silence him, glares round fiercely with: "Love me, love my *dog*." Then indignant gentlemen write to *The Times*: "whatever a lecturer's private political opinions may be, he is wrong in venting them before a mixed auditory, assembled for amusement and instruction in science and literature; it certainly is inconsistent with the impartiality to be expected from a lecture on criticism." Crabius commented sourly on the lecture which called forth this protest: "He raised a tumult by abusing Gifford, which a few hissed at but many applauded." A glance at the press report of the lecture shows at once that here Crabius is reporting imperfectly, or even misleadingly. Canning had been the object of the attack; Gifford had merely been the instrument of it, for it had been introduced by a reference to Gifford's Dedication to Canning of his edition of the Works of Ben Jonson, "in Testimony of the sincerest Admiration of his transcendent Talents," and "of the highest respect for his Public Principles and Private Virtues." The reference to Canning's "Public Principles" was the match set to the gunpowder in Hazlitt, and at this point in Canning's career, the latter part of the troubled year 1818, it would have been provocative to every man in the country who sided with the oppressed rather than with the oppressor. Crabius's account makes it clear that most members of the audience were on Hazlitt's side, and *The Examiner*, the following Sunday, rallied to the lecturer's defence: "Now, if the very mention of Mr. Canning's public principles is a piece of severe irony, which his friends cannot brook, this is not Mr. Hazlitt's fault."[326]

As to the reason why a eulogy on Canning's public principles should at the moment have seemed contemptible not only to Hazlitt, but to almost every man in England at the time, except out-and-out partisans of the Government and ministerial journalists who were endeavouring to cry up Canning into a new lease of popularity, it may be found in the debate on the Indemnity Bill, held on March 11th of this year. The first act of Parliament, when it had reassembled in 1818, in the reaction of feeling caused by the disclosures as to the incendiarism of the spies employed by the Government, had been the repeal of the Suspension of Habeas Corpus. This had been followed by a general outcry against the way in which the liberties of the subject had been abused, and against the treatment of many of those who had been imprisoned under the powers given to the Government by the Suspension Act. Among these was an old and infirm man who had been arrested at Manchester under a charge of High Treason, the charge having been made against him by some unknown informer. In spite of his age and infirmity, he had been loaded with ponderous irons. He had been, at the time of his arrest, suffering from a complaint that in ordinary circumstances was latent, but that had been aggravated by his having been heavily ironed, and kept in irons during his imprisonment, and by the conditions of prison life in general, until a kill-or-cure operation had been rendered necessary. An operation performed on an old man, without anæsthetic, and under prison conditions, might hardly have been thought a matter of jest; but when, during a discussion of the treatment of state prisoners in connection with the Indemnity Bill, the sufferings of this old man had been mentioned, Canning had made them the butt of his wit, in one of the most amusing speeches with which he had ever entertained the House, as he had emphasised the great good-luck of "the revered and ruptured Ogden" in having had such an operation performed at the expense of his Majesty's Government, and described the case as a very fitting one to be brought before the Rupture Society, but a daring imposition on the credulity of Parliament. He had certainly made the Debate his own, and scored a personal triumph in the House. But the following day, when the Debate had appeared in the cooler element of print, the neat alliterative phrase which had thrown the House into an hysteria of mirth had not looked at all pretty. The country as a whole had not been amused, and Canning's only apologists had been the ministerial journalists.

Hazlitt had never thought very highly of Canning, whom he had always seen as a man who went through life as "the head boy of the class" or "a *mere* House-of-Commons man," never passing beyond adolescent cleverness, and invariably tending to consider words rather than actualities. It was this tendency which in his opinion had produced such a phrase as "the revered and ruptured Ogden," itself only a signal instance of the tendency of Canning's mind, of its preoccupation with effective arrangements of words rather than with the realities of human experience, and of its limitations.

The tendency might have passed unchallenged by Hazlitt had it not led to sporting with human suffering. From the moment it did, he made it the object of his attack. It can readily be understood how a man who could never bear to see children kill flies, *for sport*, was affected at seeing the distress of a man who was old, poor, and obscure, on whom extreme suffering had been brought by some nameless informer, who had been peculiarly at the mercy of circumstances and peculiarly abused by circumstances, during an imprisonment that had ended, like so many others, without a trial, canvassed *for sport*. As we have seen, he had always insisted that the danger in all state-imprisonments consisted in the growth of callousness on the part of those who had the imprisoned in their power, merely because it was in their power to inflict suffering with impunity. In the following month he fell upon Canning, referring to him as "the pitiful jack-pudding" that made a jest of humanity in St. Stephen's Chapel, and "the House of Commons' jester," sharpening his wit "on the edge of human agony."

These were the things which had led up to the uproar in Hazlitt's lecture on November 10th, and which make his attack on Canning appear less wanton and irrelevant than it might at first seem. Indeed Hazlitt never showed himself more the true-begotten son of the poor clergyman who at Bandon had risked his security because of his protests against the ill-treatment of state-prisoners, than he did in the anger which Canning's flippancy over the sufferings of Ogden aroused in him. The whole episode is highly illustrative of his principles, temperament and character. He was less attacking Gifford or Canning or any single opponent than the levity in a British statesman which under a Government that was practically independent of public opinion could dare to make the violation of the liberty of a British subject its butt, and the callousness on the part of a British statesman which made the suffering inflicted on a state-prisoner the theme of a series of jests in the House of Commons. The frenzy both of the applause and of the resentment which suddenly turned a quiet lecturing-hall into the likeness of "a one-shilling gallery at the theatre" is in itself sufficient to show that his words were *not* made "of water-gruel."

The second scene of which we hear in these lectures, although different in character, for it had nothing to do with politics, was also occasioned by the pity that smouldered in him. Whatever the mingling of delight, unease, distrust and fear with which he regarded Woman as a sexual being, his patience and forbearance towards such women as were the victims of the social machine, were known to be boundless. On Tuesday, December 15th, when lecturing on Dr. Johnson, he aroused some restiveness in his audience and almost involved himself in a clash with it, by a reference to these, when he proceeded to enumerate Johnson's good deeds, concluding with the words: "and last and noblest, his carrying the unfortunate victim of disease and dissipation on his back up through Fleet Street. . . ." Here he was interrupted not only by a buzz of protest from some members of his audience, who felt that he was introducing into his lecture matter unfit for "Saintly" ears, but by tittering from others, to whom the grotesque element in that sad elephantine progress up Fleet Street made an immediate appeal. The latent touch of the preacher in him rose as he surveyed his audience grimly for a moment, turned back his page as soon as there was silence, "with an air of determination and iron firmness," and read again, deliberately, and in his most impressive manner: "and last and noblest, his carrying the unfortunate victim of disease and dissipation on his back up through Fleet Street." Some of his hearers looked deeply rebuked as he drove home the conclusion of the whole matter: "an act which realises the parable of the good Samaritan!"

Crabius, who found the fourth lecture, on the English dramatists, the first lecture of this course in which Hazlitt recovered any of his "gusto," little to his taste as being "always on the brink of obscenity," dropped off after the fifth. It is from Keats we hear of the fifth, on the English novelists. Although unable to be present at the lecture, he read eagerly the report of it in *The Examiner*, and copied out part of it for his brother and sister-in-law in America, by way of illustrating Hazlitt's "usual abrupt manner and fiery laconicism." This, like the two which followed it, on the works of Hogarth and On the Comic Writers of the Last Century, was regarded as a triumph. In the lecture on Hogarth, when Hazlitt, speaking of the Grand and the Familiar style in painting, illustrated what he meant by the Grand style from the works of Raphael, the hearts of the "Saints," so often estranged from him by what Crabius called his "illaudable" epigrams, must surely have moved within them as they listened to his commentary on Raphael's "speaking" faces, introduced by the words: "We see them, as they were painted, with the eye of faith."

In the eighth and last lecture, the "character" of Sheridan was admired, and justly admired.

Just as Hazlitt was concluding his course with this lecture on the Comic Writers of the Last Century, two of the Writers of the Last Century passed away. They were so celebrated that their passing seemed to make of his last lecture a salute to the passing of an age. The first to go was Sir Philip Francis, popularly reported to be Junius. The second was Peter Pindar. Old Peter, the last of the bards of the past age, still "merry and wise," although old and blind, welcomed the New Year in, and Hazlitt concluded his lectures with a salutation to the poet who had been one of the chief wits in the days that had just passed. His words of praise, uttered on January 5th, 1819, must have been almost the last to reach the old poet's ears, for Peter was even then dying at his apartments in Somers-Town. Just a week after Hazlitt had included him among the Comic Writers of the Last Century there came for him, in his eighty-first year, the summons for which, as Hazlitt said, he had long waited. Thus passed away the one remaining link with the past age. Peter was probably the last man on earth who genuinely preferred taste to genius, and who did not hesitate to say bluntly to any of the volcanic geniuses the new age had produced: "Give me one man of taste and I will find you twenty men of genius." In his time he had made the world laugh somewhat. To Hazlitt, who had visited him shortly before his death, the old gross man, as he poured out his glass of rum from the decanter before him and drank it off neat, looking in the meantime, with his close-shaven crown, not unlike a fine old monk, had seemed "not repenting" any of the mirth he had given to his day and generation, but "like his own Expiring Taper, bright and fitful to the last."

6

The white star on the brow of *The Examiner* of February 7th, 1819, is Hazlitt's beautiful obituary essay on his friend John Cavanagh, the celebrated Fives' player, and "the best uphill player in the world." But this number of *The Examiner* also contains two notices which show us how it has fared with Hazlitt in the meantime, and how it is going to fare.

The first, copied from *The Scotsman* of January 30th, is as follows:

"Mr. Hazlitt's action against the Publishers of *Blackwood's Magazine* has been withdrawn, they having agreed to pay him a certain sum as damages, and all expenses."

The second is given prominence by the heading, *Literary Notice:*

"In the press, and shortly will be published, *A Letter to William Gifford, Esq.*, by an ultra-Crepidarian Critic."

Thus the year 1819 opened for Hazlitt with a battle gained, and a battle about to be fought. The battle gained was perhaps little more than a battle drawn, whereas it might have been a downright victory. All the evidence points to P. G. Patmore, who had been a contributor to *Blackwood's*, who had the reputation of being one of Lockhart's friends, and who by his persistence had insinuated himself into Hazlitt's confidence, as having come in and acted as mediator in such a fashion as to save Blackwood from a downright rout. In December Patmore had been in correspondence both with Blackwood's "agent" and with William Blackwood himself. On the 16th Blackwood had written to John Murray: "I have had two letters from Mr. Patmore, informing me that Mr. Hazlitt was to drop the prosecution. His agent has since applied to mine offering to do this, if the expenses and a small sum for some charity were paid." Blackwood was not satisfied with this suggestion, for he felt that it made him look shabby. His letter continued: "My agent told him he would certainly advise any client of his to get out of court, but that he would never advise me to pay anything to be made a talk of. He would advise me, he said, to pay the expenses and a trifle to Hazlitt himself privately. Hazlitt's agent agreed to this." The "trifle" paid to Hazlitt was £100.[327]

A Letter to William Gifford, Esq., from William Hazlitt, Esq., appeared in the beginning of March. The reason for its appearance was that Gifford, towards the beginning of the year, had given Hazlitt fresh provocation, and very strong provocation. His review on the *Lectures on The English Poets* had appeared about that time. In it Hazlitt is accused of having bound himself to wage everlasting war "against accurate reasoning, just observation, and precise or even intelligible language," of entire lack of originality, and of appearing to regard meaning as a superfluous quality in writing. His attempts to illustrate the nature of poetry are dismissed as throwing "not one gleam of light . . . upon the subject." Such stress is laid upon the total vacuity of the work that we suspect Gifford must have learned in the meantime that the sole thing on which Hazlitt prided himself was being a meta-physician. The reviewer's conclusion is: "His lectures are of that happy texture that leaves not a trace in the mind of either hearer or reader."

Hazlitt caught this accusation neatly on the point of his rapier: "You say that it is impossible to remember what I write after reading it. One remembers what you write—*before!*"

Hazlitt's *Letter*, like his earlier ironical sketch of the Editor of *The Quarterly Review*, is greeny-glittering, but unlike it, it is not cool. The earlier sketch was a piece of prose satire, of the kind from which coolness is inseparable, or in which at least the air, even if it be parching, "burns *frore*." The *Letter* is naked rebuke, in which there is no attempt to disguise the hot indignation which prompted it. It is less like a cool green ribbon of prose than like a river that storms its way along, flecked here and there with dangerous-looking reflections of colour, forming itself into rapids and pouring itself now and again into pools that hiss and sparkle as if warmed by subterranean or subaqueous fires and that send up at times a jet of angry steam or foam "reaching half-way to the stars." Hazlitt's scorn of Gifford's reviewing as a prostitution of literary criticism or a pandering to the prejudices of powerful patrons is compressed into the words: "To crawl and lick the dust is all they expect of you, and all you can do. . . . They know that if you cease to be a tool, you cease to be anything." Step by step he illustrates this accusation by reference to Gifford's conscious dishonesty in dealing with personalities, his conscious dishonesty in dealing with style, his conscious dishonesty in dealing with the reasoning contained in writers whom he is paid to attack, this last dishonesty, however, being partly the result of the frigidity of a mind that had no power to go beyond haggling over verbal points of criticism, or to meet and master any train of thought that was not commonplace or even hackneyed. So much for the matter of his rebuke of that which, calling itself literary criticism, is yet but "a receptacle for the scum and sediment of all the prejudice, bigotry, ill-will, ignorance, and rancour afloat in the kingdom!"

As for the manner of his rebuke, Keats has left nobody very much to say about that. His expression of delight in it and in the man who achieved it is summed up in the words: "the undersigned . . . doth not admire Sheil's play, Leigh Hunt, Tom Moore, Bob Southey and Mr. Rogers; and does admire Wm. Hazlitt." What he says of it is full, final, and satisfying. Writing to his brother and sister-in-law on March 12th, he quoted from "the high-seasoned parts" with such exhilaration that one might think he had read them until he had got drunk on them, adding the comment: "This is the sort of *feu de joie* he keeps up." On the morrow he resumed his scribing, copying not an extract or two from Hazlitt's work, as he often did, but page after page. Then come the all-satisfying words: "The manner in which this is managed: the force and innate power with which it yeasts and works up itself—the feeling for the costume of society; is in a style of genius. He hath a demon, as he himself says of Lord Byron."

Hazlitt's main labours of the winter and spring were now behind him. Between January and March he had repeated his lectures on The English Comic Writers at The Crown and Anchor. Shortly after the appearance of the *Letter* to Gifford they were published. In the early months of the summer he may have been engaged in writing Prefaces to the Plays included in the acting Edition of *The New English Drama* produced by William Oxberry, the comedian. The other work to which we may point with some confidence as having engaged him was the preparation for the press of all that he wished to preserve of his political writing from 1807 onwards.

At the end of June or the beginning of July he returned to Winterslow. He had engaged himself to deliver a third course of lectures in the autumn, this time on Elizabethan literature. Thus far his lectures had been on literature of which his knowledge was deep, but his knowledge of Elizabethan literature, although deep in parts, was sketchy in other parts. This meant that he had a summer's reading

before him, as well as a summer's writing. Armed with advice from
Lamb and Procter, and fortified with so many books borrowed from
them that the landlord of the Hut asked him if he had "any object"
in reading through them all, he set himself to the task. He introduced
into one of his lectures an impression of the quiet summer and autumn
days he spent in composing them, in the company of a few loved books,
his only companions, and his chosen, trusty companions:

"They sit with me at breakfast; they walk out with me before
dinner. After a long walk through unfrequented tracks, after starting
the hare from the fern, or hearing the wing of the raven rustling
above my head, or being greeted by the woodman's 'stern good-
night' as he strikes into his narrow homeward path, I can ' take mine
ease at mine inn,' beside the blazing hearth, and shake hands with
Orlando Friscobaldo, the oldest acquaintance I have. Ben Jonson,
learned Chapman, Master Webster, and Master Heywood, are there;
and seated round, discourse the silent hours away. Shakespear is
there himself, not in Cibber's manager's coat. Spenser is hardly
yet returned from a ramble through the woods, or is concealed behind
a group of nymphs, fauns, and satyrs. Milton lies on the table, as on
an altar, never taken up or laid down without reverence. Lyly's
Endymion sleeps with the moon, that shines in at the window; and
a breath of wind stirring at a distance seems a sigh from the tree under
which he grew old."

7

"I should have no objection to pass my life in this manner out
of the world," he confessed, "not thinking of it, nor it of me; neither
abused by my enemies, nor defended by my friends; careless of the
future, but sometimes dreaming of the past, which might as well be
forgotten." Yet from day to day he could see that, even if all went
well with his own life in Arcadia, all was not well with the lives around
him. And presently, his comment on that went forth to the world he
had deserted.

The Examiner of July 18th, 1819, contains three very arresting, even
if unconscious testimonies as to the state of the country in that summer,
when reform had not yet come, but when reform was so much in the
air that all over the country new hope was stirring in the hearts of the
People. One was in a leading article commenting unfavourably on the
Government's emigration scheme, or, as it was bluntly described:
"Mr. Vansittart's proposal for shipping off paupers to the Cape of Good
Hope." The second was a protest against the driving away from the
homes that had been in the possession of their families in Sutherland-

shire from time immemorial, by the agents of the Marchioness of Stafford, lately Countess of Sutherland, of at least three thousand people who had looked up to her as their protectress, whose cottages had been burnt so that the land might be tenanted by sheep, and who had now to face a world in which they were all forlorn, in extreme poverty and famine. The third was Hazlitt's essay, *Character of the Country People*, which under the motto: "Here be truths"—described the poverty and the degradation of spirit into which the peasantry were falling at the Southern end of the kingdom. This essay, which was written just eleven years after he had come to dwell among them, was also written just eleven years before the agricultural labourers of Wiltshire, those who were determined that rather than remain sunk they would make a last attempt to swim, or in other words, make a last stand for better conditions of life, were shipped off, over a hundred and fifty of them, in convict ships to Botany Bay and Van Dieman's land, leaving behind them a sense of blankness and of loss which had hardly passed from Wiltshire by the beginning of the present century. In the South of England, no less than in the North of Scotland, the vital strength of the country was being drained, although there not because of the eviction of the peasantry for the deer or the sheep, but by heavy sentences of transportation which, passed by magistrates who cared more about the preservation of game than the conservation of the life-blood of the nation, were gradually depleting the country of the manhood which had most fibre, spirit, and resistant quality. The tolerance of such blows at the strength of the nation was one of the things that seemed to Hazlitt symptomatic of "the blight and the mildew" attacking the national life, even as it was one of the manifestations of the class selfishness under which the bones of the country were "cracking and turning to a paste." It was because of such things that from North to South and East to West the country was crying out for a Government which would in some measure represent the people, and which would to some extent be penetrable by popular opinion.

During the opening weeks of August Hazlitt's volume of Political Essays was published. On the last Sunday in January, William Hone the Parodist, in whose sad eyes there was still a wicked sparkle which all the Government prosecutions in the world would never be able quite to extinguish, grave, handsome, undemonstrative John Hunt, and Hazlitt had dined together. This was a memorable meeting of three intrepid spirits. The publication of Hazlitt's series of essays on the distresses of the country and the plight of Europe was in some measure the fruit of this meeting, as it certainly was a lasting memorial to the friendship between these three remarkable men, bound to one another by the compassion for humanity and the love of Liberty which burned in all three of them. The volume, written wholly by Hazlitt, was published by William Hone, and dedicated to John Hunt, whom Hazlitt respected with all his soul as "a friend in need" and "a patriot without an eye to himself, who never betrayed an individual or a cause he pretended to serve," and whom he judged, despite the extreme coldness of his manners, worth a hundred of the charming meteoric Leigh.

The epigraph was: "Come, draw the curtain, show the picture." As to the picture shown when the curtain was drawn, we have already had several glimpses of that. Each of the essays on the state of the country which we have been considering was a momentary drawing-back of the curtain. But the Preface, written in the summer of 1819, adds some new touches to the picture. We could hardly say which section of it is of the more interest and value, that in which he made a statement of his political creed, or that in which he completed his picture of the state to which England was reduced during the years in which the Commoners of the country groaned under the rule of a Tory borough-mongering oligarchy supported by a phalanx of Committee-hacks whose souls had been rotted out of them by Com-mittee-drudgery, an array of Justice Shallows, and a swarming multi-tude of parish-beadles. At the conclusion of his Preface he wrote: "I cannot do justice to the picture but I find it done to my hands in those prophetic lines of Pope, where he describes the last Triumph of Corruption:—

> "Hear her black trumpet thro' the land proclaim,
> That *not to be corrupted is the shame.*
> In soldier, churchman, patriot, man in power,
> 'Tis avarice all, ambition is no more!
> See all our nobles begging to be slaves!
> See all our fools aspiring to be knaves!
> All, all look up with reverential awe
> At crimes that 'scape or triumph o'er the law;
> While truth, worth, wisdom daily they decry:
> ' Nothing is sacred now but villainy.'"

On August 8th *The Examiner* announced that Hazlitt's volume of Political Essays was about to appear. On the following Sunday, August 15th, it quoted a long passage from the Preface. The printer's ink was hardly dry on this when the Corruption of which he had written in his Preface gathered to a head and burst over the crowds assembled at St. Peter's-Field in Manchester on the never-to-be-forgotten August 16th, 1819—with a stench from which the annals of the period have never quite been purified, and leaving behind it a vile creeping fog of hopelessness and a spiritual and physical unease that spread over all the industrial districts of the North like a low fever. The dreadful irony attending this calamity which brought so much hopelessness in its train was that the victims of it had been exposed to it through the hope of Reform which had been very much in the air during that summer of 1819, and especially in the large towns, where many meetings had been held in connection with it. Manchester, although one of the largest towns in the country, was as yet unrepresented in Parliament.

On Monday, August 16th, great crowds assembled in St. Peter's-Field, on the outskirts of the town, to listen to the Bristol demagogue, "Orator" Hunt, as he was popularly called, address them on the subject of Reform. The meeting was perfectly peaceful in intention, and its temper was genial. The men were dressed in their Sunday shirts; most of them had brought their women-folk, in holiday attire; and there were many children in the crowds. Various bands were playing: "God Save the King." Swelled by Reformers from neighbouring towns, the number of people was said to be not less than eighty-thousand, and these were policed by not less than three to four hundred constables on the field. The "Orator" appeared shortly after one o'clock, and took his place, with those supporting him, on the rude hustings, formed of two carts lashed together with boards flung over them. Standing near him on the hustings was the correspondent of *The Times*, who had obtained permission from him to take up that position so that he might be able to report accurately the speeches and the doings of the day, but to whom what actually happened would have been unimaginable, and unbelievable, unless he had actually witnessed it.

It was some time before the "Orator" could subdue the acclamations of the crowds and secure the stillness necessary before he could hope to be heard by the distant members of that vast concourse. He had just succeeded in securing it, and had just begun his speech, when there came riding up to the edge of the crowd a large contingent of the Manchester Yeomanry Cavalry. They paused for a few minutes, and there was some timid and flustered drawing away from the horses by the crowds in their vicinity, which interrupted the speech. At this the cavalry drew their swords and brandished them in the air. Hunt, who although an egregious demagogue, behaved with admirable courage and self-control through that day's fantastic proceedings, called for three cheers, by way of checking panic and assuring the frightened people that the business of the day was going to proceed amicably. No sooner had he resumed his speech, however, than the Cavalry rode into the crowds and straight at the cart from which he was speaking. Realising the danger of the situation, he suffered himself to be arrested quietly—but his effort to preserve the peace was frustrated by the Yeomanry.

No sooner—said the correspondent of *The Times*—had Hunt and his companions been taken, than a cry went up among the Cavalry: "Have at their flags!" Not content with striking at the flags massed on the carts, they presently proceeded to charge through the crowd in any direction in which flags were displayed, "cutting most indiscriminatingly to the right and to the left in order to get at them." The people surged away from them in all directions, and it was then, and not until then, that the first missiles were thrown by the crowds at the armed men who were riding them down. At this the Cavalry lost all command of their temper, and began hacking and cutting at the people like butchers, some of them shouting each time they struck: "Damn you—*I'll* reform you!" Those who attempted to take shelter under the hustings from the reckless sabre-cuts were "jobbed-at" with truncheons and beaten up by the constables, one of whom had exchanged his truncheon for the broken staff of a banner. The correspondent of *The Times* witnessed an attempt made by two of the Yeomanry on the life of the Editor of *The Manchester Observer*, who was on the cart and whom they recognised. Then he sought protection from the police, who insisted on taking him into custody along with all those found on the hustings. As he left the field thus guarded, and horror-stricken at the madness raging around him, he passed a frantic man whose streaming face had been mutilated by a sabre-cut, and a woman lying on the ground, dishevelled, and "with two large gouts of blood on her left breast."

All this happened in less time than is required to describe it. Within ten minutes the vast concourse of people had vanished as if by magic. Nothing was to be seen but the dead or those who were wounded too severely to drag themselves away, and the pitiful finery which had fallen away from them or which had been ripped from them in the confusion, the holiday shawls and bonnets of the very poor—and the Manchester Yeomanry Cavalry, who, reinforced by the Cheshire Yeomanry and the 15th Hussars,[328] were left in possession of the field. In these few minutes two women, a child, and eight men had been killed, one hundred and thirteen women wounded, and almost three hundred men. More than a quarter of the wounds were from the sabre. So dreadful was the fear created, so deep and hopeless the general sense among the people that there was no justice to be found in the hearts of those set in authority over them, that the wounded preferred to crawl away into corners and suffer and die there in silence, than to seek hospital treatment for the sabre-cuts received on the field which from that time ceased to be Saint Peter's, and was known— perhaps because of the crazy crying of one of the special constables on that day: "This is Waterloo for you—this is Waterloo"—by the name of Peterloo. This crawling away of the victims to die in silence seems to us the most terrible of all comments on the nature of that day's work.

From all parts of the country a cry of protest made itself heard. If it had been acknowledged that a terrible error of judgment had been made in placing the lives of the people at the mercy of the untried and badly-disciplined Yeomanry, and if the Yeomanry, most of them the sons of the masters of those whom they had ridden down, had been rebuked or punished for turning a peaceful meeting into a piteous massacre, conduct which might have provoked not a riot but an insurrection in the North, had their victims been taken less unexpectedly and been in any way prepared—feeling might not have run so high; but the magistrates and Yeomanry were thanked by the Government, while Earl Fitzwilliam, the Lord Lieutenant of the West Riding of Yorkshire, who although one of the firmest and sternest supporters of law and order, and one whose combined firmness and prudence were said to have preserved the tranquillity of Yorkshire—was dismissed from his Lord Lieutenancy, because he had attended a great Yorkshire meeting called to protest against the doings of that day. Might it not then seem to every onlooker:

"Nothing is sacred now but villainy!"

Sir Francis Burdett was threatened with a Government prosecution because of the burning words he addressed to his constituents on the outrage perpetrated on their brethren in the North. Such things inflamed public feeling, and the stifled fires kept breaking forth. *The Examiner* of August 29th published Lord Sidmouth's Letter conveying the thanks of the Prince Regent to the Manchester magistrates and Yeomanry, without comment—but published alongside of it Hazlitt's essay On the Regal Character, which had been included in the recently-published *Political Essays*. Placed by the side of the official letter of congratulation, the closing paragraph of this essay takes on the character of a stern indictment: "What is it, then, that makes a great Prince? Not the understanding Purcell or Mozart, but the having an ear open to the voice of truth and justice."

8

On Friday, November 5th, in the hall of the Surrey Institution, Hazlitt gave the first of his lectures on Elizabethan Literature, his subject being the Influence of the Reformation on English Literature. In this lecture, the preaching strain in him, which we hold to be the foundation of his gift as a writer, ran away with him, and in his exposition of the character of Christ, and the way in which the Christian religion is differentiated from all others, he delivered as fine a sermon as we ever remember to have heard preached:

"The very idea of abstract benevolence, of the desire to do good because another wants our services, and of regarding the human race as one family, the offspring of one common parent, is hardly to be found in any other code or system. It was ' to the Jews a stumbling-block, and to the Greeks foolishness.' The Greeks and Romans never thought of considering others, but as they were Greeks or Romans, as they were bound to them by certain positive ties, or, on the other hand, as separated from them by fiercer antipathies. Their virtues were the virtues of political machines, their vices were the vices of demons, ready to inflict or to endure pain with obdurate and remorseless inflexibility of purpose. But in the Christian religion, ' we perceive a softness coming over the heart of a nation, and the iron scales that fence and harden it, melt and drop off.' . . . The gospel was first preached to the poor. . . . It first promulgated the equality of mankind in the community of duties and benefits. It denounced the iniquities of the chief Priests and Pharisees, and declared itself at variance with principalities and powers, for it sympathises not with the oppressor, but the oppressed. It first abolished slavery, for it did not consider the power of the will to inflict injury, as clothing it with a right to do so. Its law is good, not power. It at the same time tended to wean the mind from the grossness of sense, and a particle of its divine flame was lent to brighten and purify the lamp of love!"[329]

What a word was this for a country half-poisoned by the rank gases that had accumulated and exploded on the field of Peterloo, that was still being slowly poisoned by the rank gases being given off by Peterloo! We are told that it probed the conscience of the Christians and the Deists in the audience alike. We are sure it moved Charles Lamb, who although no relisher of lectures, attended these. When it was reported in *The Examiner*, many readers of the paper felt as if it had given them new vision. And there was one, surely, to whom it must have given deeper satisfaction than to any of these. Old Mr. Hazlitt, who had feared that his son might become a "nondescript," must have felt when he read it that the presbytery at Wem had after all had its share in the making of a preacher.

There was much in this third course of lectures that was not quintessential, but hastily thrown together. They are also much less spirited than the two earlier courses had been. Indeed, throughout this set of lectures, we note that the touch of provocativeness which had spiced the others is almost entirely lacking. Crabius says he is "sinking fast," as a lecturer. We hear no more of any "tumults." How is this? Has he succumbed to the atmosphere of the "Saints"? Leigh Hunt says that he lectured on *The Honest Whore* "*mutato nomine*," in deference to their notions of delicacy. All the same, we do not think that the absence of the note of challenge throughout the lectures and the extreme listlessness or sadness of the closing words were in any way conditioned by the audience. A glance at the plight of the mastiff-familiar will do more to explain matters. The mastiff-familiar has been very quiet all this time—too quiet! lies under the table, gives no trouble. You might think he was asleep, were it not that his eyes are open, and gaze into nothingness, hot and sad. He is alert enough, yet he makes no sign, no! not when the *Courier* cur slavers loyally in the expectation of tit-bits from the Treasury Bench, nor when the distant *Quarterly* bloodhound bays. Even when the master of the Court pack threatens all such gaunt and dangerous mastiffs as he with Botany Bay unless they are kept well muzzled,[330] he does not stir. When Mr. Wilberforce, who trusts in God and Ministers, thinks no Parliamentary inquiry into the Manchester butchery is necessary, supports an Address that makes no mention of it and which by many is considered an insult to the People, and washes not only his hands but his eyes of the matter, as he puts his handkerchief up daintily to them, deploring meanwhile the evils of the country, the hackles rise on our honest mastiff's neck; there is the beginning of a growl in his throat; his hot yellow eyes, fixed on the delicate emblem of a pure man's grief, purge "thick amber and plum-tree gum;" you would swear he longed to bear it indelicately to the dust, to worry its spotlessness into filthy tatters; but the moment passes; he has not gathered himself together for the spring.

The truth is, the mastiff-familiar, poor hound! now draws his breath in constriction and pain. The low creeping fog which hangs over the country is choking him. Some quality which is necessary to his vital being has gone out of the air he breathes. This old friend of ours can bark for us no longer. He has fallen very sick. Till he recovers, we must leave him to his repose.

9

This course of lectures, the last given by Hazlitt, ended just before Christmas. Just as it was nearing its close the *Quarterly* appeared, with Gifford's review of the Political Essays. By this time gentle Mr. Gifford has been badgered into picturesqueness. He finds that "the Hazlitt" is an insect of a new species in criticism, black-glittering, somewhat resembling the *sphinx Atropos*, or death's-head-hawk-moth. We would have said rather *greeny*-glittering, but *black*-glittering may pass, as sufficiently descriptive of some of our author's moods, and if we do not agree as to the species itself, or its insect-nature, we may give Mr. Gifford the credit of discerning that the species is new. Hatred has sharpened him into momentary perceptiveness, for from the mouth of the enemy there fall two further grains of truth—that the work of "the Hazlitt" is consistent in character, and that there is something in it which is "rather tragical."

Hazlitt had written nothing since August of this year. If he had put his thoughts on paper they might have been described as "tragical" without the qualification of the "rather." It would be impossible to exaggerate the oppression the events of the autumn had brought to him. Every time he thinks of them the tightness in his breast and the throbbing in his brow warn him that it were better for him not to dwell on them too continuously. There was something in the injustice of them that made the eye start and the brain split. It seemed to him as if the net of tyranny he had seen extending all over Europe had at last included his own country too. That the People should have been offered such an outrage, that the outrage should be justified, that the wrong done the poor should, after the opening of Parliament in November, have been made the pretext for loading them with further repressive measures—seemed to him to indicate that the badge of servitude had been placed upon their brow and the collar of servitude upon their neck, just because the stain of servitude was not in their soul. They were still struggling, but look where he would, their plight seemed day by day to grow worse. In the South, in the agricultural districts, they were "styed," rather than housed, in poverty; in the manufacturing districts they had been trampled under the hoofs of the horses of their masters' sons. It seemed to him that Liberty, driven from country to country in Europe, could now find no rest for her feet, even in his native land.

In Europe there were cities that were still called "free." In these least of all could she find lodging. When Buonaparte had entered Germany, he had declared the Jews citizens, and members of society. Before that time they had been treated as beasts; on passing through many towns they had had to pay the same sum *per head* as was paid for swine. Now the persecution was starting again. In the "free" city of Lubeck that year the Senate had revived the old decrees, forbidding Jews to carry on business in any manner whatever. They were searched in the streets by police officers; they were insulted with impunity. Their houses were entered; their property was wrested from them. Lest there should be found any to pity them, the Senate had decreed that any one found acting for a Jew should be fined for the first offence, should lose his right of citizenship for the second, in addition to being imprisoned or fined; moreover that any one engaging in menial service with a Jew should be first imprisoned and then expelled from the "free" city. What was this but Tyranny?

It was at least all that Hazlitt meant by Tyranny, that any race should be ruled by those who gloried in their power to make life bitter for it. Wherever man was, the spirit of Cain would never be extinct, but when the spirit of Cain showed itself open and triumphant and glorying in its excesses—that was the Triumph of Corruption and the Triumph of Tyranny.

Had the rivers of Europe run blood that this might come to pass! From Valmy to Peterloo, by way of Waterloo, for the Peoples of the earth the way had been bitter.

10

In the first half of 1820 a change comes over Hazlitt's mood, and we are reminded not only how greatly he suffered through public events, but also how much, at times, he rejoiced because of them. The news of the Revolution in Spain came to him like a freshening breeze. Now we see him again in the sun. The gladness in him pours itself into all he does. In the midst of a dramatic article that strayed into *The Examiner* in June, he breaks into a kind of descant not only on his old favourite, Miss Stephens, but on the resurgence of Liberty in Spain, as if he were enchanted by them both:

"Miss Stephens's Echo song seemed sung by a Spirit or an enchantress. We were glad to hear it, for we have an attachment to Miss Stephens on account of ' auld lang syne ' . . . since then, other events not to be named lightly here, but ' thoughts of which can never from the heart ' . . . have stopped our ears to the voice of the charmer. But since the voice of Liberty has risen once more in Spain, its grave and its birth-place, and like a babbling hound has wakened the echoes in the Asturias, in Castile and Leon, and Estramadura, why, we feel as if we ' had three ears again,' and the heart to use them, and as if we could once more write with the same feelings (the tightness removed from the breast, and the pains smoothed from the brow) as we did when we gave the account of Miss Stephens's first appearance in the *Beggar's Opera*."[331]

The note of gladness was due solely to rejoicing over the rebirth of hope in Spain, for in Hazlitt's private life things were not going well. By this time he was a man without a home, that in Westminster having been broken up at the end of 1819.[332] His marriage had long since ceased to satisfy him. A child, born during the London years,[332(b)] had died after a few months of precarious life. William, the child who remained, although loved by both his parents, had become a source of friction between them. We note that from 1816 onwards Hazlitt sometimes wrote from 34 Southampton Buildings, and received letters there. The impression we get of him during the later years in which he lived at 19 York Street is that already he was a man with but half a home. Yet the breaking-up of his London home, such as it was, and the return of his wife and son to the country, left him more or less adrift. We see him in the first months of 1820 passing from place to place. In February he visited Somerset for the first time since he had paid his memorable visit to Nether-Stowey. This time he went to see John Hunt, at the home in which he had settled at Up-Chaddon. Then as he looked out towards Nether-Stowey from a hill near Taunton, the memories of the earlier visit came thick upon him. "How was the map of my life spread out before me," he wrote of this day, "as the map of the country lay at my feet!" There is some indication that from Somerset he passed on to Devon, to visit his parents at Crediton, where they were now settled. His father, who was just approaching his eighty-third birthday, was by this time so frail that his state of weakness amounted to suffering.

By the end of March Hazlitt was back in town. Haydon, when the picture into which he had put so much work, so many prayers, and so many hopes, "Christ's Entry into Jerusalem," was exhibited, felt it an addition to his triumph that at the private view, on Saturday, March 25th, he saw Keats and Hazlitt together in a corner, "really rejoicing." In April Hazlitt was still in town. He was at the Lambs' on the 20th, along with Leigh Hunt. Crabius, who encountered them there, after noting the meeting in his Diary, added: "People with whom I am not cordial."

Shortly afterwards he went to Winterslow to write. It was the first time for years that he had seen the spring come up in the country, and as always, the sense of miracle affected him. The long stretches of hyacinths in the woods flung their joyous colour at him; the birds made the delicate spray of the branches quiver to the joy of their song. There, among the woods and in the Plain, he walked and lingered once more, as he had done in his youth, no longer considering the work of others, but patiently soliciting his own mind, for he was now about to endeavour to enter on his main work as an essayist. He was to "slough" yet another existence, for the Lecturer was about to fall silent, the Table-Talker to come into being.

He returned to London in June, to share in a friend's rejoicing. His old companion of the tight-rope-walking days, Sheridan Knowles, was having a play produced, and this was an event that must not pass uncelebrated by the friend and critic whose word now, in anything connected with Drama, had almost the power to make or mar fortunes, for in the beginning of the year Hazlitt had become the regular dramatic critic of *The London Magazine*, working once more under the Editorship of John Scott. "We heard from good authority that there was a new tragedy worth seeing," wrote "Mr. Drama" the following month in the *London*, "and also that it was written by an old friend of ours. *That* there was no resisting."

One day in the latter half of July, while he was yet in town, Mary

Hazlitt, his niece, came to give him the news of his father's death. He had long known that there was no avoiding this separation: the last time he had visited his father he had seen Death shake him by the palsied hand, and stare him in the faded face in which yet Faith still shone like the trust in the face of infancy. But the grief was no less heavy when it came. Young Mary had been sent to break the news to him, because his life was now so unsettled that his sister had not known where to write to him. Nor would it have been easy for her, in the first pressure of her grief and in the confusion and fatigue of these first few days of bereavement, to have written even had she known. She wrote to him to Winterslow on the 28th of the month, letting him know that although their mother and she were still far from well, being broken down by fatigue and sorrow, they had now "got a bed" to spare for him and that they would be glad to receive him whenever he cared to come—and giving him such details of their father's end as might satisfy his longing mind and ease the pang of his grief. Their father had died on Sunday the 16th at about seven in the morning. He had died as he had lived, making no complaint, showing no fear, no regret for anything he had done in his public life, anything in his private. His death to him was but a release from suffering and weakness—and the hope of entering on a fuller life. He had looked outwards towards something greater than his own personal life, to the last. His words and his thoughts had been, as ever, of glory, honour, and immortality. He had spoken much of his Redeemer, and had repeated the name often to himself. The habit of tender protectiveness towards his womenfolk had been his to the end. When he could no longer speak, with the gesture he had used more than thirty years before, at the time he had left his wife and children on the other side of the Atlantic, he had taken his daughter's hand and placed it in her mother's, thus charging the stronger with the care of the weaker, as he had done on that earlier, briefer, but perhaps even more bitter day of separation. By his upward look, they had both known that he was silently committing them both to God.

The brief notice of his death in *The Examiner* on August 6th touched only on the integrity of his life: "On the 16th of July, at Crediton, in Devonshire, the Rev. William Hazlitt, who was through his whole life a friend to truth and liberty." Yet uncompromising and rugged though he was, there had always been something gentle in his sternness, something graceful and gracious in his whole nature.

To his son William it seemed that this had never shown more than in his last act.

Part Six

THE PASSION

It were better that a man were an angel or a god than what he is; but he can be neither the one nor the other. . . . He must get on by the use and management of the faculties which God has given him, and not by striking more than one half of these with the dead palsy.

HAZLITT.

Chapter One

THE FRENZY (1820-1822)

"Hazlitt . . . wrote an article in the *Edin. Rev.* on the volume of poems I published. I do not know whether he meant it to be favourable or not; I do not like it at all; but when I saw him I could not be angry. I was never so shocked in my life, he has become so thin, his hair so scattered, his cheekbones projecting; but for his voice and smile, I should not have known him; his smile brought tears into my eyes, it was like a sunbeam illuminating the most melancholy of ruins, lightning that assured you on a dark night of the identity of a friend's ruined and deserted abode."

MARY SHELLEY.

I (I)

WE DO NOT KNOW whether Hazlitt, after receiving his sister's letter, went on from Winterslow to Crediton. If he did, his visit must have been a short one, for the theatrical critic of *The London* could not very well spend the whole of the summer in the country, no matter how skilful he might be at writing on the theatre from a distance. By the middle of August he had returned to town—where we can trace him from month to month until the end of the year—and had established himself, not at his old headquarters at 34 Southampton Buildings, but in a couple of rooms at Number 9. His rooms, which were at the back of the house, on the second floor, were like a little flat. A small landing led into the sitting-room, off which the bedroom opened. The windows of both rooms looked on to Staple Inn. He was to regard this small high lodgment as his home, in every essential sense of the word, for almost two years. Secluded as it was from the noise of the street, it was a pleasant enough out-of-the-way corner for a man-of-letters.

I (2)

For the first couple of days he was waited on by his landlady and the maid. The third day, there came into his room with his late breakfast tray a slender youthful creature who moved in minuet time, who walked with as much grace as if she were about to perform some exquisite piece of ritual, who advanced to his table with his tray in a kind of hushed silence much as if she were advancing to an altar. He had not heard her step on the stairs, so that there was nothing but a slight knock to herald her appearance, and it seemed to him as if she had come like an apparition, but an apparition attended by all the graces. While she went about her work, never once looking at him, he gazed at her as if she were an apparition, for it seemed to him as if everything he had ever dreamed or read of grace in Woman were personified in her. Watching her movements he thought that Tibullus must have had some such creature in his mind when he had written: "whatsoever she does, whithersoever she turns her steps, Grace follows her unseen, to order all aright;"[333] that Cervantes, when describing the tread that seemed to scorn the ground, must have remembered seeing someone move like this; that he was watching the lightness of movement which had made old Northcote say of the youthful Marie Antoinette that she seemed to him on one occasion less to have passed through a doorway than to have floated through it as on a cloud; that the Venus de Medici might have moved thus if she had descended from her pedestal. This girl was the embodiment of all he had ever loved in Woman. Surely hers was the face "pale as the primrose" which he had loved in Imogen; surely in the outline of her cheek there was the purity of the angel face of Una. Yet there was no suggestion of severity about her, but rather of a gentleness that had seduction in it. Love seemed to hover round the gentle undulations of her form and walk. He tried to engage her in conversation. Her voice was low, and her words, when she replied, apparently with a touch of reluctance, were very few and simple, but they seemed to him as exquisite in their unstudied grace as her walk. He tried to throw the suggestion of the admiration he felt into his own words. She listened, standing sideways to him, her eyes still downward-looking, her profile as exquisite as that of a Greek statue, and as unmoved. He thought there was something dove-like about her expression as she stood thus, with the soft dark curls falling about her pale face. As soon as he had finished speaking she moved towards the door. His eyes followed her, again fascinated by the undulating walk. There was something about her that reminded him now less of the dove than of the serpent. When she reached the door, to his utter amazement she swayed round and looked him full in the face. For what seemed to him a feverish eternity his eyes sustained the shock of meeting hers, which were the last in the world he would have expected to see in the pale pure face—light, glittering, so fixed or intent in their regard that they seemed to him, as it were, glazed. Then with the very movement which the old artist had described to him as something that might be seen only once in a lifetime and something never-to-be-forgotten once it had been seen, she seemed to be borne or wafted out of the room like a thing of enchantment.

If her movements had appealed to his senses and her gentleness had touched something in his manhood, the shock the unexpectedness of her eyes had given him had almost beguiled him of his reason. The day was to come when it would seem to him that he might have recognised a danger-signal in that strange glazed look: "I might have spied in their glittering motionless surface, the rocks and quicksands that awaited me below." At the moment all he knew was that it had robbed him of himself. His back-sitting-room in Holborn was far enough away from any of the places where the Nymphs are to be encountered. None the less the beginning of that frenzy which poets in olden times associated with the mountains or the waters or the forests was upon him. From this moment he might be said to be nympholept. We say this, but, as usual, his own words best explain the nature of his experience:

"Love at first sight is only realising an imagination that has always haunted us; or meeting with a face, or figure, or cast of expression in perfection that we have seen and admired in a less degree or in less favourable circumstances a hundred times before. Our dream is out at last—Telemachus has discovered his Eucharis."

I (3)

The family in which he had settled was that of a tailor, Micaiah Walker, a hard-working, honest, plain man, simple and strict in his ideas. The mother, whom Hazlitt greatly disliked, was lively, fond of a joke, somewhat inclined to be salacious in her speech, but very hard-working and attentive to the lodgers who represented to her a large part of the family income. She usually kept three or four. Others of the men in the circle of Hazlitt's acquaintances had lodged there, including Robert Roscoe, the fourth son of William Roscoe of Liverpool, who after having lived for several years in the household, had married Martha Walker, the eldest daughter. At the time of his marriage he had been old enough to know his own mind, for he had just passed his thirtieth birthday. His bride had then been six months short of her twenty-first. At the time Hazlitt settled in the house there

were two other lodgers in it, one of them an uncouth Welshman from
Penmaenmawr, called Griffiths, who lived in a back room on the floor
above Hazlitt's, and who, when coming home one night half-drunk,
almost fell over Hazlitt on the stairs. The very unflattering description
Hazlitt gives of him as being half-blackguard, half-quack-apothecary,
may perhaps owe something to this incident.

The members of the family who were still at home were the
youngest daughter Betsy, a girl just old enough to be useful to her
mother in the house and perform little services for the lodgers, a son
Cajah, aged seventeen, who was already a foul-mouthed young lout,
and Sarah, the second daughter. As her eldest sister was at this time
twenty-one years of age, Sarah cannot have been over twenty; she
may have been younger. She helped her mother in a house in which
there was always a great deal to do, and waited on the lodgers, the
heavier work being done for them by a maid. Her life was very
narrow and cramped, and about the time she met Hazlitt she was
beginning to feel that her spirits grew lower every year. She was
too little in the open air, and this had made her rather pale. Were it
not that she was somewhat lacking in the bloom of youth, she might
have been called a pretty girl.

As it was, she looked extraordinarily attractive sometimes in the
house, for she had a very beautiful slender figure, and she moved with
extraordinary grace. Being small in stature and pale in colouring, she
might pass almost unnoticed out of doors, but no one could fail to
take note of her at close quarters. Her forehead had character in it.
It was somewhat rounded, and there was what Hazlitt called "a little
obstinate protrusion" in the middle of it. Because she knew that her
eyes were her worst features—for except in moments of feeling, when
the dilation of the pupils could make them seem gradually to darken as
if with their own lustre, they were somewhat light in colour—she had
formed the habit of looking downwards when talking, and this tended
to give her a curiously innocent or virginal expression, although on the
rare occasions when she looked at any one directly the impression of
innocence was dissipated, for her stare, when she was curious or
puzzled or interested or hostile, could be disconcerting. Because she
knew that her profile was good she usually managed to present it to
the person to whom she was talking, and this too added to her air of
reserve.

Her manner also was reserved. She had learned that many of the
men who took rooms in her mother's house at from 10s. to 15s. a week
would willingly have a little womanhood thrown *gratis* into the
bargain, and she had found that a reserved and formal manner was her
best protection against these advances. At the same time, she had been
trained not to offend, and thus she had become a mistress in the art of
keeping men at arm's length, while not seeming to discourage or

rebuff them. Her manner made it difficult for any one except a ruffian, or a man desperately in love, to penetrate beyond the barrier of her reserved gentleness, while even a man in love, wanting to put his fate to the proof, because of this equivocal gentleness of hers, that in a moment could be merged in what seemed entire indifference, could never fathom her entirely. If she had little power of actual resistance in a direct amorous encounter, she had in a remarkable degree the art of withdrawing herself, before resistance was thrust upon her, so much so that whereas at one moment she might seem to a lover a living being in whose affections he was making some progress, at the next she would have melted into thin air. She was mistress of the art of eluding passion. Because of this, she might well be a torment to a man who loved her, for she not only seemed enigmatical: she had become enigmatical. While she seldom gave a direct rebuff to any man, even under great provocation, her manner was such that no man could ever be sure of her. She was thus the one woman in the world calculated to give a passionate soul like Hazlitt the maximum of torment.

She was largely what circumstances had made her, and considering her circumstances we do not think she was much to blame for her methods of self-defence, although to him they were ruinous. She merely protected herself as best she could. When she was with her family this teasing reserve vanished. To Hazlitt she always seemed rather grave, but there were times when in the kitchen she and her mother and her brother and Betsy all made fun of the lodgers they looked after so well, much as boys laugh at a schoolmaster when they are out of class, or as servants below-stairs sport with the foibles of their masters.

We never see her clearly from any of Hazlitt's descriptions of her, for she is always whirled round on the frantic merry-go-round of his moods; according to him she is fair and foul; she has dove's eyes, and she has the most hypocritical, slimy, glazed, watery eyes he ever saw in a human face; she is an angel, to whom he has been led by a favouring Providence, and she is a bitch to whom he is unlucky enough to be glued, or a she-goat: the one thing he never gives her is justice—the one thing he never denies her, even in his utmost fury, is grace. He referred to Procter's lines:

> "See with what a waving air she goes
> Along the corridor. How like a fawn!
> Yet statelier. No sound (however soft)
> Nor gentlest echo telleth where she treads.
> But every motion of her shape doth seem
> Hallowed by silence,"

as "a description of her." His sense that they conveyed perfectly the suggestion of her personality is more illuminating than are his own descriptions of her.

Procter, who did not like her, has left one direct description of her in his prose: "Her face was round and small, and her eyes were motionless, glassy, and without any speculation (apparently) in them. Her movements in walking were very remarkable, for I never observed her to make a step. She went onwards in a sort of wavy, sinuous manner, like the movement of a snake. She was silent, or uttered monosyllables only, and was very demure. Her steady, unmoving gaze upon the person whom she was addressing was exceedingly unpleasant. The Germans would have extracted a romance from her, endowing her perhaps with some diabolic attribute." We can only conclude from this description that Sarah, sensing his hostility, observed him carefully on such occasions as he came to visit Hazlitt, for Hazlitt voiced his chief complaint of her in the words: "She never looks at you." As to the long strange look she had given him at her first meeting with him—that was not an everyday affair: he did not see anything like it again until he was about to pass out of her life.

The chief value of Procter's description is that it gives, from a dispassionate onlooker, an impression of Sarah's personality which substantiates at least Hazlitt's claims as to her distinction. It leaves on the mind the impression of one who was the reverse of commonplace, and this impression is all the more powerful because the description is designed to do anything but flatter. Sarah—we gather from it—had personality enough for anything, had indeed the gift of fascination or of impressing herself on the imagination, although the impression she made on one man's imagination was primarily that of the dove, on the other's, that of the serpent. The sister who married Robert Roscoe had personality also, for although radical Robert Roscoe might have made a marriage that would have served his ambition, had he chosen to do so, his wife satisfied him so completely that he came to regard his "radical" marriage to the daughter of a struggling Holborn tailor as the best thing that had ever happened to him.

I (4)

But Robert Roscoe was not Hazlitt, and Martha Walker's hap was a good deal easier than her sister's. If Sarah were so closely approximated to Hazlitt's ideal of womanly perfection, in all externals, that inevitably he would be so deeply affected by meeting her that she might be said to be his Fate, he, because he was so desperately genuine, was probably the one man alive whom her ways, although they might enchant him at first, could never entirely subdue to her convenience. This genuineness always made him incalculable. At the outset of his relationship with her we can only watch with pity his wild threshings and plungings. Unhappy in his home life, and despairing of finding happiness without it, he had for some time been deteriorating in his relationships with women. He still preserved his ideal, but he had lost hope of meeting her in the flesh—and of women in general his opinion by this time had become something less than they deserved. Therefore he had interpreted the curious look Sarah had given him as an invitation. In his heart he called it a whore's look; one side of his nature loathed it, but it had set his blood on fire, and filled him with a violent longing to see her again. He was mistaken about it. Sarah's look may have been inspired by many things, by curiosity, by resentment at the fixity of his gaze, or by sheer fascination as she realised its intensity. But it was not a look of invitation. Hazlitt, at the crisis of his life, was making a tragic blunder. The next time Sarah appeared in his room he met what he took to be her invitation as directly as he thought it had been extended to him. The Beast in Madame de Villeneuve's fairy-tale was not more direct in his nightly questioning of La Belle. He was on the brink of falling in love; yet, acting upon what he believed himself, in his reaction from idealism, to have discovered to be truth, that love is "nothing but a lust of the blood, and a permission of the will," a theory which was now to cost him dear, he could find nothing better to do than to ask a girl, dead-weary of men who, cheap though womanhood was on the streets of Holborn, were bargain-hunters in it, and wanted to enjoy it at less than its market value, if he might "go to bed with her," thus cutting away at one blow ninety-nine of the hundred chances that she would ever consider him seriously either as a lover or as a husband, and confounding in her eyes what he was with what he was the furthest thing on earth from being. It not being Sarah's way to make any display of feeling, she replied merely in a toneless voice that her sister slept with her. At this, because his soul and his senses were reeling, Hazlitt leapt to the other extreme. His first impression returned to him with tenfold force. She seemed to him dove-like in innocence. As the rage of the lion was "assuaged with remorse" at the sight of Una's "angel face," the beast in him was rebuked by the simplicity of her answer. Nor were the manifestations of his remorse much different, metaphorically speaking, from those of Una's fierce protector. Turned from his purpose:

> "In stead thereof he kist her wearie feet,
>   And lickt her lilly hands with fawning tong,
>   As he her wronged innocence did weet."

Sarah, possibly touched by his passion and his penitence, or more likely, unwilling to be on disagreeable terms with him, permitted him to kiss her. From that moment all danger to her from Hazlitt was past.

Love was born in him, love which sucked up the element of lust that
had been in his feeling for her, even as the sun calls up the reek of the
marsh.

I (5)

Hazlitt now entered, with a girl less than half his age, on what
seemed to him the sweetest friendship that had ever existed between
man and woman. It is curious to note how rigidly his passion, from
first to last, was governed by the laws he had forged for it through his
own development. We have spoken of the fixed idea with regard to
women, and to his own effect on women, which had taken possession
of him as the result of his early misadventure in Keswick, and of the
extent to which it had shaped his Fate in so far as it had conditioned his
marriage. It conditioned no less the development of the deepest love
of his life. If Sarah had shown any hint of coquetry, or desire to
ensnare him, he would have avoided her in mistrust, like one fearing
a trap; but her reserve and indifference bred trust in him. The
obsession which had never left him as the result of the Keswick incident,
although it had never as yet been whipped into mania, that he was
repulsive to Woman, now fed his love, because he was convinced that
no girl would tolerate the caresses of such a man as he, unless she had
been touched by love. At the same time, Sarah, even in yielding to
these caresses, charmed the Puritan in him: if she had seemed a shade
more passionate, she might have repelled or disgusted him. As it was,
her rare caresses seemed to him as pure as a child's, and this kindled in
him at length what can only be described as a kind of "inflamed
respect."

The scruples which had come to him the moment he knew he loved
her, had made any closer relationship than that of passionate friendship
impossible. Perhaps the friendship was all the sweeter for that. A
relationship of this kind was possible for Hazlitt just because he
loved, for his love, although it had begun in sexual attraction, was of a
quality which made it, as long as he was in sympathy with the object
of his love, almost independent of sexual satisfaction. What meant
more than anything else to him was to feel himself in sympathy with
Sarah. As long as he could do this, it was almost enough for him to
breathe the same air as she did, to live under the same roof, to be
sometimes in the same room. As long as he could do this, the light
caresses she gave him meant more to him than the full possession of
any other woman. If he but touched her hand he felt perfect contentment and peace. He sometimes felt that if the relationship he had with
her were friendship, as she declared it was, it was far sweeter than
anything he had ever known of love. With the curious innocence he

always showed towards her and the complete lack of vanity, the man versed in sexual experience who yet had forgotten what it was to be loved, placed himself at the mercy of a young girl by telling her that hers was the only woman's face that had ever been turned kindly towards him. "You are the only woman that ever made me think she loved me," he said to her one day, worshipping her for what he took to be her kindness.

He said of this experience afterwards, when describing its nature: "The truth is, I never had any pleasure, like love, with any one but her." Even as Beauty had taken away the reproach of Beasthood from the Beast, Sarah had taken away from him his reproach among men, the reproach of his unlovedness, so that he could no longer be said to be "a species by himself." She assuaged too the hunger which had been growing up in him all these years for the contact with youth which he had missed in his youth. For all she gave him he was passionately grateful: it seemed to him not only to fill him with immediate delight, but to cleanse his mind of the memory of the morbid sadness of the past. That she should have come, thus late in his life, to make him realise the possibilities of joy in life, appeared to him nothing short of a miracle, or at least short of the amazing chances of a fairy-tale. "She came (I know not how) and sat by my side, and was folded in my arms, a vision of love and joy—as if she had dropped from the heavens, to bless me by some special dispensation of a favouring Providence—to *make me amends for all,*" he wrote afterwards, when describing the sweetness of the early days of his love.

He was, indeed, entering upon what was for him a new mode of being, the state of happiness. In it he recaptured the bliss of childhood. The days and the nights never seemed too long to him now. During the autumn and winter of 1820 he went about his ways as usual, and was to be found in all his usual haunts, on the Fives'-Court in the afternoon, when he sauntered out after a late and prolonged breakfast, at supper in the Southampton Coffee-House, often surrounded now by a group of friends or cronies who came to hear him talk, in the evenings at the houses of friends, chiefly the Lambs and the Montagus; but wherever he was, always at the back of his mind was the sense that presently he would be returning to the place which had become home for him; and often he had the feeling that although he went here and there, all he really wanted was to get back to the room in which he had found Paradise. When he had returned to it, he slept all night as if on down, for he knew that when day came, the first person he would see would be Sarah, coming in with his breakfast-tray, in her mob-cap and morning-gown. This, because it was the attire that was most closely connected with home, was that in which he liked her best: it pleased him far more than her afternoon or evening finery. It had long been his habit to linger over his breakfast-table, meditating the day's writing. Now he prolonged the hour to detain young Sarah, for she usually remained with him while he was break-fasting. This seemed to him the pleasantest time of the day, when his kettle sputtered on the fire—for he always insisted on having a kettle brought up to him, so that he could make his tea himself—and he drank his strong and acrid brew, and ate his buttered toast, and talked with Sarah, or perhaps it would be truer to say, talked to Sarah, for although she listened "*avec séduction*," she still spoke very little. And she still retained the formality of manner which, although he tried to coax her out of it, was not altogether displeasing to him. He could seldom persuade her to sit while she was in his room; she would re-main standing an hour by his side, until at last he moved to his easy-chair and settled all arguments by folding her in his arms.

It is difficult to believe that the friendship did not mean a good deal to Sarah also, in the first months of it. A life spent in housework or in carrying trays up and down various flights of stairs is not very amusing. At the least her friendship with Hazlitt must have been a new experience. At the most it may have been very near to love. But this she would never acknowledge. It was from her ways towards him that Hazlitt felt sure of her love, for her words always denied that she felt anything beyond sincere regard. The utmost she would acknowledge, and this had to be wrung from her, was that "there was a tie" between them. Even in her "endearments," as she called the rare caresses she gave him (and her name for them was sweet in Haz-litt's ears), she was cool, sometimes torturingly cool. But she seemed happy in his company, and she was with him every moment she could spare. Her father and mother complained that they could not keep her out of his room. Her own explanation of her attachment to him was that she "liked his conversation." At such times as she made this confession, a curious look might be detected on his face. Hazlitt sometimes behaved like a lunatic, but never like a man struck "with the dead palsy." He was fighting now for his one-hundredth share of a chance. His growing hope was that he might persuade his wife to give him his freedom. Then, he promised himself, if Sarah would have him, she should have enough of his conversation—and of *something else.*

I (6)

We note with interest an entry made by Crabius in his Diary towards the end of the November of this year: "I dined with the Wordsworths and Lambs and Mr. Kenyon at Monkhouse's—a genteel dinner and an agreeable afternoon, though I could not help sleeping in good company; Wordsworth and Monkhouse either followed my example or set me one." Crabius put the last touch to his account of this "genteel" and drowsy dinner-party when he added: "and Lamb talked as if he were half asleep." Lamb would not have talked as if he were half asleep if Hazlitt had been of the company, for he was very sensitive towards life, and Hazlitt at the close of this year was alive to the finger-tips. While other men were growing old and dull, for him life had again become young. He will suffer for his new experience, in a world in which every extension of feeling or growth of any kind has to be paid for to the uttermost farthing. Nay! already he has begun to suffer. Already his enchantment is not complete. Now and again he feels

"Blank misgivings of a Creature
Moving about in worlds not realiz'd."

Now and again a word or so denoting self-conflict escapes him: "but let no man fall in love, for from that moment he is ' the baby of a girl.'" Now and again there comes from him a sound that is like a low moan of misgiving. Yet he is still alive to his finger-tips. He still has poignancy as his one perfect and perpetual possession. Now and again, like his moments of self-conflict and misgivings, this, too, finds utterance:

"Thought has in me cancelled pleasure; and this dark forehead, bent upon truth, is the rock on which all affection has split. And thus I waste my life in one long sigh;—nor ever (till too late) beheld a gentle face turned gently upon mine! . . . But no! not too late, if that face, pure, modest, downcast, tender, with angel sweetness, not only gladdens the prospect of the future, but sheds its radiance on the past, smiling in tears. . . . Oh! if I am deceived, let me be deceived still. Let me live in the Elysium of these soft looks; poison me with kisses, kill me with smiles; but still mock me with thy love!"

2 (1)

We can follow the outward movement of Hazlitt's life, easily enough, during the following year. In the January of 1821, when the quarrel bred out of John Scott's exposure of the blackguardism of *Blackwood's*, "the Mohock Magazine," as he called it, had come to its crisis, and Lockhart had come to London with a view to demanding from John Scott "such satisfaction as a gentleman was entitled to," he was at Winterslow Hut, engaged in writing and preparing for the press the group of essays which was to form the first volume of his *Table-Talk*. We get from his own pen a cosy glimpse of him on January 19th, just as he was planning to write his essay, *On Living to One's-Self*:

"I never was in a better place or humour than I am at present for writing on this subject. I have a partridge getting ready for my supper, my fire is blazing on the hearth, the air is mild for the season of the year . . . I have three good hours before me, and therefore I will attempt it."

It cannot be shown that he was in town on Friday, February 16th, the day on which John Scott received his death-wound, not from Lockhart, who had departed in circumstances which take a good deal of explaining, but from Lockhart's friend, Jonathan Christie, innocently involved in a quarrel that was none of his making. On the following Wednesday, however, Hazlitt was certainly in town. This was the day on which John Hunt, charged in the Court of King's Bench with a libel on the House of Commons, pled in a speech every word of which was in the tradition of "the Hampdens, the Sidneys, Russells, Miltons," the righteousness of his cause, and the urgent necessity for the nation of a Reformed Parliament. The sentence passed upon him was a year's imprisonment in Coldbath-Fields Prison, where he had already passed two years of his life.

On the evening of Saturday, April 21st, shortly after the publication of his *Table-Talk*, we see Hazlitt crawling off the Fives'-Court, overwearied with playing at rackets all day long, and settling down to write to Leigh Hunt, who had been galled by the shaft directed at his egotism in the conclusion of *On People with one Idea*.

In the middle of July, a delightful letter from Thomas Pittman, who four years afterwards became All England Rackets' champion, tempted him to leave town for Canterbury, "the true city of God" for racket-players. It is not difficult, as we read this letter, to understand why Hazlitt said: "the face of a racket-player is the face of a friend."

We are accustomed to seeing Hazlitt on the Fives'-Court. At the close of this year, however, we get a glimpse of him delighting in a sport which was unfamiliar to him. We see him on December 10th, hurrying out of town towards Berkshire, like all the rest of the world, as it seems to him, to see the fight between Tom Hickman, the Gas-Man, or "Gas," as he was called, said to be the bravest man in England, and the most cruel, and huge Bill Neate, the Bristol "Bull," at Hungerford, on the morrow; arriving at Newbury to find the inns all crowded out; supping on tea and eggs in the kitchen of the Crown, packed with men who were also going on to the fight on the morrow, and spending the night there in chat; hurrying out to a barber's early in the morning, and then starting on the nine miles' walk to Hungerford (although by this time the light seems to be pressing like bars of solid metal on his tired eyes); seeing the ring at last on a small hill about a mile to the left of Hungerford; threading his way to it through a narrow lane, and securing a good place; watching the champions enter, Bill Neate, a great hulk of a man, but modest and cheerful in his air, the brute Hickman, "too much like the cock of the walk," raking his adversary with cold blue eyes that as they glittered seemed to doom their prey; sharing in the prick of excitement that goes through everybody as the men strip and all eyes are on the ripple and play of muscle in Hickman's back, which glistens in the sun like a panther's hide.

The end of the great fight in which Hickman, although in the first round he seemed by the lightning rapidity of his blows to bewilder Neate and reduce him in a moment to a lifeless lump of flesh and bone, and although to the end he kept him on the defensive, for the first time in his life lost his battle, affected Hazlitt in much the same way as Edmund Kean's great scenes, and for the same reason, the courage of the performance. During the return journey to London, this exhilaration lasted. He seemed to Patmore, who accompanied him, as happy "as a boy or bird." All the way he was the best company in the world. When he got out of the coach at Piccadilly, the evening of the following day, he was still in the highest spirits, and as he set out to walk to Southampton Buildings he felt as if in the crowded life of the last couple of days, years had dropped from his shoulders.

But the exhilaration did not last. Shortly after his return, when writing his account of the fight for *The New Monthly Magazine*, he interrupted a comparison between the life of a prize-fighter and such a life as his own, with the exclamation:

"but I will not libel any life by comparing it to mine, which is (at the date of these presents) bitter as coloquintida and the dregs of aconitum."

2 (2)

These words recall us to the movement of his inward life throughout the year, by no means as easy to follow as that of his outward life, yet not quite unintelligible. The bitter turn in them is referable to the bitter turn Hazlitt's friendship with Sarah had taken at the moment. He had always tended to reject from life all but the perfume and essence of it. John Scott, who although he did not altogether approve of Hazlitt, had understood him to some extent, had warned him almost two years before of the strain he put upon himself by his "practice of living—as it were—upon essences." During the past year this "living upon essences" had been habitual. Indeed, it had not been so much a matter of choice at the moment, as something that had been forced upon him by circumstances. It was no whit less injurious to him for that. By the end of the year it had brought him to a pretty pass.

The state of happiness in which he had been at the beginning of

1821, because of his conviction that Sarah could not have behaved to him as she had done unless she had loved him, because of the feeling he had that a young girl at last had taken away from him his reproach among men, because of his sense that her having done so had made him "amends for all" that had been warped and twisted and frustrated in his life, and because of his belief that although she had come to him at the eleventh hour she had not come too late, seeing that she had come shedding radiance on the past, hope on the future—had endured without much change until the spring of the year. The essences on which he lived at that time were all fragrant. The extent to which he had refined his love into an ideal passion which could sustain him even when he was separated from the object of it, is shown by his indirect references to it in many of the essays written in the opening months of the year. We find one such—although it is carefully disguised so as to seem retrospective in character and thus defeat the curiosity of the uninitiated, Hazlitt's love for a girl being as yet his secret treasure—in his essay *On the Past and Future*, written at Winterslow towards the close of 1820 or the beginning of 1821:

"Without that face pale as the primrose with hyacinthine locks, forever shunning and forever haunting me, mocking my waking thoughts as in a dream, without that smile which my heart could never turn to scorn, without those eyes dark with their own lustre, still bent on mine, and drawing the soul into their liquid mazes like a sea of love, without that name trembling in fancy's ear, without that form gliding before me like Oread or Dryad in fabled groves, what should I do, how pass away the listless leaden-footed hours?"

By this time Hazlitt had come to feel for Sarah much as he might have felt about a little tender flower on which he had come, blooming all by itself in a shabby place, and therefore to be preserved all the more delicately. His relationship with her was altogether an exotic: he never saw her in relation to other people, nor away from the setting in which he had fallen in love with her. No rude breath of comparison with other women could blow upon her, and in her simple setting she was perfect. His relationship with her had thus remained very much what it had become in the first week of his acquaintance with her. It seemed to be something by itself, held suspended in exquisiteness, and unaffected by the passing of time. But it was not in the nature of things that such a relationship could go on for ever unaltered, neither increasing nor decreasing in intensity, as Sarah seemed to wish. Also it was not in Hazlitt's nature to rest contented for ever with such a relationship.

In the beginning of spring, this relationship, passionate yet tenuous, had altered slightly. By this time Hazlitt was making progress in his endeavours to get his wife to divorce him. This in turn had its effect on Sarah. Until then she had taken it for granted that his marriage made any closer relationship than that of friendship impossible. She had felt that her freedom was secure, or rather, that she was mistress of the situation while he was in bonds. No sooner did it dawn on her that he might succeed in freeing himself from these, and that he might then consider her in honour bound to him, than she attempted to make it quite clear to him that she would never marry him even if he were free. It not being her way to give a point-blank refusal, she defined her feeling on the matter by making confession to him of the reason which had made her always refuse to admit in so many words that she loved him. This was an attachment she had had with a man whose rank had made him feel, despite his regard for her, that he could not offer her marriage. The acquaintance had therefore been broken off, but her affection had endured, and this made her altogether averse to the thought of marriage with any other man. Hazlitt, driven by his old fear of being repulsive to Woman, asked her directly whether she was not also affected by some original dislike or repugnance to himself, which no effort on his part could remove. This fear she allayed by a downright denial.

Equivocal though Sarah was, we are inclined to think her confession as to a former attachment was true. It rings true; it was of a kind so unflattering to her self-love that she was not likely to have invented it; it was the most likely thing in the world to happen to a girl, placed as she was placed, for it was not every man who was ready, like Robert Roscoe, to carry his "radical" principles into his marriage; and lastly, in the course of the following year, she had to endure the mortification of an experience almost exactly similar to that which she had here described. Hazlitt at the moment accepted it as truth, but coming as it had done, at the end of that passionate companionship which Sarah called friendship and which he called something for which he would have been ready to forswear what is called love—it was quite powerless to check his passion. Also, even in connection with it, Sarah left the point of equivocation or ambiguity which was inseparable from her. Repulsing him one day when his ardour offended her, she said somewhat angrily: "I had an attachment once before, but that person never attempted anything of the kind," and left him. All that Hazlitt heard in this rebuke was the phrase "once before"—which instantly filled him with the sweet poison of the thought that she was now beginning to be attached to him. Despite himself, he could not keep the hope from stirring within him that she loved him more than she knew and more than she was ready to confess.

But the chief immediate effect of her confession, which was not without its element of pathos, was to intensify the respect which ever since she had declined his dishonourable proposals he had felt for her, until at last it amounted to worship. From "inflamed respect" he passed about this time into a phase of inflamed worship. He said to her afterwards: "It was that which wedded my very soul to you." She had always realised his ideal of physical perfection: now the Imogen-like faithfulness which she had described was just the kind of thing to captivate his spirit completely, and to make him feel that she realised in every detail his conception of the perfection of womanly character. Her gentleness had captivated him from the first. It now seemed to him a grace that had flowered out of strength of character and that crowned the virtues of patience, constancy and fortitude. He was fast reaching the stage when he invested her with all virtues, when he saw everything beautiful in her, and when he saw her in everything beautiful.[334] This tendency of his showed itself in many ways. He now thought the picture of Fanny in his old edition of *Joseph Andrews*, a picture which had always fascinated him, the very image of Sarah. When he read Byron's *Sardanapalus* shortly afterwards, he thought Sarah was like the noble-minded Greek slave Myrrha. He saw in a dealer's one day a copy of an old Italian picture—it might have been one of Guido's lovely fragile women, or perhaps one of Raphael's, for it was somewhat like his St. Cecilia—in oil on a gold ground, bought it, and brought it home to show it to Sarah with more than boyish delight and triumph, because he thought it so like her.

Far from wealthy though he was, he managed to make all the gifts he brought her expressive of his sense of her exquisiteness. He had the books he gave her, some of his own among them, attractively bound. Of these a prayer-book bound in crimson velvet, with green linings, was her special pride and pleasure. On receiving it, she had kissed it again and again, vowing it the prettiest she had ever seen. He asked one day to see her flageolet, saying to her that unless it was itself a pretty one, he wanted to get her one in ivory. Among the gifts of jewellery he gave her was a gold chased heart, which had been fashioned for her so that she could keep a piece of his hair enclosed within it. Nothing he could afford to give her was too good for her. In all ways he treated her as a man might treat one on whom he looked as his bride-to-be. Despite the declaration she had made to him, and although it was for the resigned patience of her attachment to another that he worshipped her, he had the persistent hope that a living man near her might in time overcome an attachment to a man she never saw, and although he never could move her from her coolness, because it charmed him, he was not altogether dismayed by it.

This mood had endured until the autumn. Then once more the relationship had altered slightly, and at the same time Hazlitt had entered on yet another phase of his love. We have seen how he passed from sensuality to tenderness, and from tenderness to worship. In the autumn he began to feel for the first time the corrosion of jealousy, and of a mistrust that began to gnaw at the foundations of his worship. It had never occurred to him to fear, up to this time, that he had any rival in Sarah's affections, except the shadowy lover to whom she still professed herself to be attached. Regarding less the reserve of her words than the sweetness of her ways towards him, he had believed himself loved. His only doubt had been whether he could win her love to the extent of persuading her to enter into a permanent relationship with him, and that—he felt—was an issue he could not put to the proof until he was a free man. His hope had kept him patient.

He had felt no jealousy of either of the other men in the house, the Welshman from Penmaenmawr or a man called Follett, for it had never occurred to him that Sarah could be attracted by either of them. But in the autumn some of Mrs. Walker's rooms were taken by a man who was young, handsome, unmarried, and who had both the look and the manners of a gentleman. Sarah had always professed "to despise looks," but she had owned herself susceptible to charm of manner, and it was with deep misgiving and resentment that Hazlitt saw her thrust into the intimacy of circumstances with this personable stranger, which he well knew might readily be converted, between a girl as attractive as Sarah and a man as attractive as the newcomer, into a real intimacy. Of his own disadvantages of manner he was still painfully conscious. He had talked the language of love to her, but the stranger might also use it towards her. He had thought she had understood something of his character and of the movement of his thought, but it had long been an axiom with him that women cared much less about character and intellect than about external advantages. The new arrival, on the very first night of his entry into the house, had made him aware that there was a new factor to be reckoned with in his precarious intimacy with Sarah. When Hazlitt had been dallying with her on the staircase she had begged him to desist, saying that the new lodger, if he saw them, might take her for "a light character." This had vexed him greatly, for it had seemed to him that there had been a hint of insincerity in it. Did Sarah care more about what she seemed than about what she was? She was very non-committal in her way of talking about the newcomer; she spoke as if she rather resented the increase of work his coming had brought her; and once she had said that she despised the foppery of his red slippers. But to Hazlitt it seemed that she was always running up the stairs to the stranger's room, or chatting with him in the passage or running breathless and blushing to open the door for him, or about the hall or the stairs when he went out.

In her ways to Hazlitt himself she had not altered. She still came in with his breakfast-tray in the mornings, set his kettle on the fire, waited with him while he made his tea and began his breakfast, and sometimes stayed chatting with him throughout the meal—but he thought she now listened for the footstep of the new lodger on the stairs, and once she had coloured violently as the newcomer had passed the door.

An indefinable unrest possessed him, although if he said anything about the matter, Sarah always replied in her most formal way that Mr. Tomkins was nothing to her but a lodger.

A few days before he had gone to Hungerford he had been in Winterslow, and there he had been in morbid dejection. On the first of December he had written to Talfourd from Winterslow Hut: "I seem to have been hurt in my mind lately." Perhaps there had been something at the moment that had particularly vexed him, but depression and unease were beginning to hang over him habitually, for he was beginning to feel that the past year and a half had led him, in his emotional life, to the brink of a precipice. He had realised suddenly that he had become entirely dependent on Sarah for his happiness. When he was out of her sight he now hung in a wretched void, suspended "between tormenting desires" and *ennui* that pressed on him like a horror. Yet he had succeeded in establishing not a shadow of a claim on the girl he loved. In a moment, for all he knew, she might slip out of his hands into those of the first man who had more to give her. He did not know what her intentions were, but he knew now that nothing he could say or do or suffer would cause her to make the slightest alteration in her plans: not for nothing had she the "obstinate little protrusion" in the middle of her forehead. In her gentleness there was something unyielding, and he was in her power, for he had entered into captivity, while she had kept herself free. The moment his trust in her was not perfect, the consciousness of this had swept down on him, showing him that he was on the edge of what—if Sarah had no mercy on his need—might well prove to him a frightful abyss.

2 (3)

After his return from Hungerford, he had only a few more weeks to spend in her company, for at the beginning of the New Year he was going to Scotland to put in the term of residence necessary to bring him within the jurisdiction of the Scottish law of divorce. He spent most of this time in trying to come to some kind of an understanding with her. But as always, she was indefinite. One night he was in a kind of rapture because he had persuaded her to accompany him to Covent Garden—where he had taken a box for the evening—to see Macready play Romeo. He saw little of the play, for this was the first time in which Sarah had appeared with him in public, and he was full of the delight of it. By this time he was so much in love that if she had limped he would have thought her graceful; if she had guffawed in the middle of an act he would have been enchanted by what he would have considered mere girlish gaiety; if she had been awkward to rusticity he would have thought she showed a timidity that in one of her years and graceful appearance was charming. But Sarah's manners in public proved to be as exquisite as in private. In the theatre she looked, if not striking, both modest and sweet. He liked the slight touch of formality in her manner towards him in public, the way in which, as they were leaving the theatre, she hesitated for the fraction of a second before taking his arm, until her mother set her the example of doing so, the way she laughed a little as if it were of no consequence when her cloak almost slipped away from her in the press, and the way she slid into the coach—as gracefully as if she had been stepping in and out of coaches all her life—without displaying even an ankle. When she let her hand rest in his during the drive home he felt as if the slender, exquisitely-turned form beside him held within it all he would ever know of happiness.

Afterwards, when he folded her for a moment in his arms, and she confessed in the softest of voices that she felt there was a bond between them—he was "up to the chin in Heav'n."

That was the highest point of his felicity, for shortly after that, and shortly before his departure from London for Scotland, the thing happened which, whatever it might have been for nine hundred and ninety-nine men out of a thousand, was for this thousandth man, Puritan to the core of him, in the last recesses of his feeling, no matter what his actions might be, nothing less than a horror. It was from this moment that he lost his head, from this moment that all his "mad proceedings," as he afterwards said ruefully, commenced. The incident in itself was slight enough, so slight that Hazlitt's violent reaction against its implications proves in the most conclusive manner that despite the constant conflict between the spiritual and the animal being in him, and the occasional complete triumph of the animal, there were few men who yearned more for "a winnowed purity in love" than did he.

His first quarrel with Sarah was not on account of any withdrawal of her favour, but on a spiritual issue. Passing near the kitchen door one evening he heard Sarah's mother, her brother, and her little sister— all making somewhat rank fun of someone who, he realised, from the mother's calling out: "Oh! he's quite a monster. He nearly tumbled over Mr. Hazlitt one night," must be the Welshman from Penmaen-mawr. As he was passing on he heard Sarah's low voice say something or other which he did not catch, and realised, to his horror, that she was taking part in what he felt to be an abominable conversation. At the same time her brother laughed, and put in: "Sarah says . . ." when Sarah cut him short with the words: "I say Mr. Follett wears straps."

Greasy kitchen-talk it all was, dealing with personalities, canvassing the personal habits of those whom they served, commonplace as kitchen

utensils, on the part of the mother mere she-goatishness. But it dropped
into the inflamed delicacy of the lover like oil of vitriol into raw
wounds. Not only did the talk in itself scarify him and disgust him,
but it flashed across his mind that if they spoke thus of two of the men
in the house, when among themselves, they might canvass his own
peculiarities, sensitivenesses and foibles in the same way: he certainly
had laid himself open to Sarah, trusting in her gentleness. For a
moment he stood there with anger pouring over him like scalding
water, on the brink of walking out of the house, never to set foot in it
again. Then pain got the better of his violent indignation and disgust,
and he went in and confronted them all in a fury which none of them
could in the least understand, to be met by attempts at pacification on
the part of the mother, who said it was a pity if her children might not
indulge in a little harmless levity without calling down such a storm
on their heads, but whose ribald tongue as she proceeded with her
defence, especially when she touched on Sarah and her ways, shocked
and pained him more and more, and made him feel as if some hideous
gulf were yawning beneath his feet. Sarah herself seemed turned into
stone.

Slight though this incident may seem to be, it was for Hazlitt the
major catastrophe of his life. It had done to him something which was
worse than murder. In a sense he never got over the shock of it. All
in a moment the sweet and heady essence he had been distilling from
his love was thrown into a ferment in which it became a burning
poison. Afterwards he realised that this was the moment which had
ruined him. In the days which followed the scene, when Sarah averted
her face from him, he drew near to the threshold of that madhouse-
prison from which he was not to be released until he had been thrust
into its innermost cell and lain there long in weeping and darkness and
captivity, and the mire of sinful thought. Rank and poisonous
imaginings poured through his mind. His soul was undergoing a kind
of scourging. The conception of Sarah's character on which he had
staked his happiness and in which he hoped to find his life's redemption
and his soul's salvation, began to heave and rock. Conventional though
he was, as well as puritanical, in his attitude towards womanly
character, he did not regard chastity as only a physical matter, as the
mere sensualist tends to do. Sarah's caresses, if they had been given to
him out of affection, as he had believed, were to him pure. If, on the
other hand, she had allowed herself to be fondled by him, without
having loved him in any degree, merely because he was a man—they
were wanton, and she was a wanton. She might caress any man in the
same way, might suffer herself to be caressed or handled by any man in
a way which it made his brain rock and his senses reel to think of. His
violent recoil against the whole tone of the conversation in which
she had taken part had destroyed for the moment the strong sense he

had felt of a sympathy, or link, or bond with her, that had seemed to make almost any degree of intimacy perfectly natural and right—for both his temperament and his training made such talk seem mere foulness to him. He could see no half-shades, in this mood, no middle way. If Sarah did not love him, she had yielded to some measure of love-making in mere sensuality, and she might do the same thing with the first newcomer who crossed her path. The thought filled him with violent grief. For the moment, his suffering was spiritual rather than sensual, the suffering of a man who has seen his religion profaned or his idol defiled.

The next time Sarah appeared in his room her face was still stony. He said to her: "You are angry with me?" She replied briefly: "Have I not reason?" at which, with the desperate sincerity that had brought half the troubles of his life to him, he tried to explain to her the doubts of her which were torturing him, speaking to her not as man to woman but as soul to soul, hoping to meet some *virtue* in her which could understand his suffering and reassure him, pouring out his words with vehement grief. Sarah, who understood his feeling so little that she felt he was merely trying to insult her, interrupted him with the formal words: "Let me go, Sir," to which he replied with a passionate appeal to her to prove him mistaken in his suspicions of her. Sarah could or would understand nothing of all this except that all in a night he seemed to have turned treacherously against her to insult her with reproaches for caresses for which but the day before he had worshipped her. What she was beginning to feel most of all was that a vehemence she did not understand was wearing her out. This showed in her brief reply: "Sir, you have no right to harass my feelings in the way you do. I have always been consistent from the first. I told you my regard could amount to no more than friendship." He then made a third attempt to get her to understand how it was that the discrepancy between her actions and her words had suddenly become for him a source of limitless torment. All he could say served him not a whit. Sarah felt more and more that he was making an attack, and a sustained attack, on her character. At last she left him, saying as she went towards the door with something of a flounce, that she was obliged to him for letting her know the opinion he had always entertained of her. His resolution broke down suddenly. His suspicion faded away as he looked at her delicate face and remembered her faithful attachment to her first faithless lover. Protesting that be she what she might, he loved her, he followed her and asked her to kiss him once more. To this Sarah, who had understood more clearly than anything else that he was now distrusting her because she had given her kisses to him too readily, replied with more energy than was her wont: "*Never!*"

She was not very articulate, but in the course of this scene she let fall a few words which show that she felt she was being unjustly treated:

"You sit and fancy things out of your own mind, and then lay them to my charge. There is not a word of truth in your suspicions." Also, the violence of Hazlitt's accusations had offended her. Not only was she harmonious in her movements: she loved harmony of living, and valued it beyond most things. She was not of those who find stimulus even in a lovers' quarrel, and she would have done almost anything to avoid encountering such angry sincerity.

Yet this first quarrel was followed by a reconciliation brought about chiefly by his agony of penitence for having wounded her, and by his very evident suffering. At the same time she gave him fair warning that nothing would tend more to estrange her from him than such violent behaviour. As to the fine shades of distinction in conduct he drew, she was altogether incapable of understanding them. Thus his attempts to explain the measure in which the ambiguities in her conduct tortured him, and her constant equivocations, continued to her to seem insults.

Immediately the reconciliation had taken place, unsatisfactory and patched-up though it was, his thoughts turned again to the future. He was contemplating making an Italian tour, on the commission of his publisher Colburn, once he had finished with the matter which was to take him to Scotland. He talked it over with Sarah, spoke of the possibility of taking her there with him, if he could take her with honour, and of going with her perhaps to see Vevey and the rocks of Meillerie also, and all the places saturated with memories of Rousseau. She seemed to like the idea, although, as usual, she would say nothing definite about it. When he tried, the night before he left town, to come to any definite understanding with her with regard to her future relationship with himself, he came up against a blank wall. He made all sorts of proposals to her, some of them fantastic enough. She would make no promise about anything. All he could get out of her was that he would "find her the same." He thought over her replies in the course of the night, and felt that her ambiguities, at such a moment, had pushed him to the point where he could endure them no longer.

She had kept him on the rack of suspense too long. He was getting to the point where he had no feeling about anything but her. He realised that the thought of her had taken possession of him to such an extent that he might be said to be haunted by her. A little more emotional tension would drive him crazy. Already his faculties were deserting him. He could no longer go on as he had been doing. He had no power to compel Sarah to give him any promise, but he still had it in his power to make a break, at least for a time, with the life of which she had become the centre. Before he left for Scotland he would clear his rooms of his possessions, so that there would be nothing left in them to bring him back to the place. In the morning

he sent for Mrs. Walker and told her so, told her also that his friend
Patmore would be coming for the picture he thought so like Sarah, and
that he was presently going to take his small bronze statuette of
Napoleon—this, which complete with sword always stood on his
mantelpiece, was one of his chief treasures—along to some friends and
to leave it in their care.

This was the second time he had been on the point of quitting the
house for ever. Had he done so, he might have been a happier man,
but he would not have been the writer whose greatest writing, all of it
yet to come, on life and death, love and hatred, and the involution
of all the passions that hold the mind of man in their toils—was
henceforth to be not only gold tried in the fire, but gold thrice-tried.
That he did not there and then take his leave of the house in which
he had experienced both the keenest happiness and the keenest suffering
life had as yet brought to him was owing to Sarah's whim. It did not
please her that he should give up his connection with the household
entirely. Shortly after her mother's departure from his room, Sarah
found occasion to come up to it, found also the means to sap his resolution. As they talked, he said to her among other things that it had
occurred to him that one of the reasons she had shown him so much
favour at the outset of their acquaintance might be that perhaps she
had found some resemblance in him to her lover. She said No, that
there was none, but that yet there *was* a likeness. At this she looked
fixedly at the cherished little bronze figure on the mantelpiece. Hazlitt
asked her: "To whom?" She replied: "To that little image."
"What!" he said, amusement rising in him at this description of his
idol. "Do you mean to Buonaparte?" She said that everything but
the nose was exactly similar. "And was his figure the same?" She
replied that her lover was taller. At this he got up instantly and
placed the statuette in her hands, begging her to accept it. She said
that she would take it into her care, and keep it for him, *till his return.*
He realised that, being incapable of saying to him in so many words
that she did not wish him to sever his connection with her, she had at
last made a gesture in which he could discern her wishes.

Somehow or other, he was utterly charmed by it. It seemed to him
entirely characteristic of her, the one thing in the world she would
inevitably do, and which no other woman in the world would have
thought of doing. It had all her grace, all her ambiguity too, for it
was not quite clear to him in the end whether she was going to keep
the figure for herself, despite her refusal of it, or whether she had only
accepted the custodianship of it. The next moment she made another
gesture of conciliation, for she came over to him and sat beside him
and put her hand in his and her arm round his neck, kissing him. His
heart almost turned over with delight at a token of affection such as
he had very rarely received from her. There followed a parting scene

of the utmost tenderness, and at the end, it seemed to him that he had
to tear himself away from her longing arms.

He left London on the second Sunday of January, 1822, a man half
in heaven, half in hell, but wholly bound, indeed doubly bound, for he
was bound both to the wife who was no wife and to the love who was
no mistress. He was hoping, by the grace of God and the marriage law
of Scotland, to free himself *a vinculo matrimonii*. But who could free
him from the chain he had placed around his own neck? From it was
suspended, over his heart, in a locket of chased gold, the counterpart
of the one he imagined Sarah as wearing over hers, a fragment of his
little *Yes-and-No's* hair.

3 (1)

When Hazlitt drew out of London in January, 1822, he drew towards
that plane of experience—hitherto unknown to him, although, in a
sense, all his life had been a preparation for it—which separated him
for a time from his fellow-men, and which has caused him to be looked
askance at ever since by those who know nothing of the kind of
experience he underwent, and to whom therefore no words, not even
his own, can make it in any measure intelligible. Yet if there is
anything in Hazlitt's life more than another which separates it from
the commonplace, it is this; if there is any one thing of specifically
human interest, which makes this life worth recording, it is the way
in which it arrived at this plane of experience, not in any chance way,
but according to the operation of the law of human nature; if there
is any one thing in his writing which is profound, it is the way in which
he has revealed the operation of law in this plane of experience.

There are few who have done this. Most of those who have known
the secrets of this prison-house are chary of revealing their knowledge.
As for Hazlitt, being a great writer, being a metaphysician to such an
extent that he almost destroyed his own mind in the effort to understand the nature of the frenzy that overtook him (for to experience such
a frenzy as this and at the same time to make it the object of analysis is
almost beyond the strength of any man) and being, above all, a frustrated lover, he had to speak or die. Words were the only points of
light that pierced the darkness in which he lay: "Oh! thou dumb
heart, lonely, sad, shut up in the prison-house of this rude form,
that hast never found a fellow but for an instant, and in very mockery
of thy misery, speak, find bleeding words to express thy thoughts, burst
thy dungeon-gloom, or die!"

We said that sometimes during the year through which he had just
passed, Hazlitt felt that he had come to the edge of a precipice. That
he had, even in the earlier stages of his passion, some dim fore-
knowledge of what the plane of experience towards which he was

drawing might mean, is shown by some words he had written towards the end of the year in which Sarah had first crossed his path:

"The passions intercept and warp the natural progress of life. They paralyse all of it that is not devoted to their tyranny and caprice. . . . By degrees, nothing but this morbid state of feeling satisfies us. . . . The machine is over-wrought: the parching heat of the veins dries up and withers the flowers of Love, Hope and Joy; and any pause, any release from the rack of ecstacy on which we are stretched, seems more insupportable than the pangs we endure. . . . Some idea, some fancy, takes possession of the brain, and however ridiculous, however distressing, however ruinous, haunts us by a sort of fascination through life."

Hazlitt had lived to such an extent in his times, that up to this point his life might be said to be a history, in miniature, of his times. During the year now opening, the natural communion between his mind and all that is to pass around him is to be warped and intercepted. This year thus forms a period entirely by itself in his history. In the beginning of 1820 his heart had overflowed with joy at the resurgence of the spirit of liberty among the Spaniards. By the beginning of 1823 sounds from the outside world will reach him but as the sound of the sea may be heard faintly on a stormy night by a man shut up in an inland prison.

At seven stations in his slow progress along this plane of experience we see him pause—carrying always the ever-increasing burden of his passion, before at last it becomes greater than he can bear, and mercifully for himself he sinks down under it, and at last, even although he is never to be quite free of it, it eases itself on his shoulders. The first of these is Stamford, where he paused on his way North. From Stamford he revisited Burleigh, for the first time since his early painting days. The sense of renewed youthfulness which had come to him in the early days of his love had now passed, and we see him, at Burleigh, suddenly made conscious, by the sight of the things that had meant so much to him in his youth, of the passing of time. No longer is his cry: "I am growing young." As he looks around him, he too now feels, as the other men, his contemporaries, are feeling, that he is well on the way to age. His retrospective mood suddenly brought home to him the consciousness of the extent to which he was becoming the prisoner of his passion, as he contrasted the outward-looking mind of the youth he had been, with the inward-looking mind of the man he had become. It seemed to him that he had been happy when sentiment had played a delicate tune on him, when it had made a day's happiness for him to go to the town of his mother's birth, and visit the home of her childhood, and linger by the gate at which she had stood as a child, watching the setting sun; when he could spend a morning watching the field opposite his window, feeling as he meditated the green, dewy moisture in the tone of it, almost as if he were watching the birth of something new, and something to be rejoiced over, even if it were beyond his pencil's reach; above all, when his thoughts had been coloured by hope, not so much by personal hope, as by hope in the good that was preparing for all mankind.

Yet the realisation of the bonds in which he lay helped him no whit towards freeing himself. On the contrary, while he was at Stamford the powerful irritant of absence began to operate on his passion. He kept going over and over again in his mind the conversations he had had with Sarah, especially the more recent ones. Clear they were, as words scratched on a pane of glass with a diamond—only it was on the "red-leaved tables" of his heart that these words were graven. Perhaps thinking to work them out of his mind, he started to set them down on paper. Everything else took flight, as it seemed to him that he heard Sarah's voice again, in all its sweetness and all its torturing coolness, as he recorded her words. Even his interest in the past and his regrets for it were forgotten. Nothing was clear to him but his own yearning, but his own longing, but his own timid yet imperishable hope: "by her dove's eyes and serpent shape, I think she does not hate me; by her smooth forehead and her crested hair, I own I love her; by her soft looks and queen-like grace (which men might fall down and worship), I swear to live and die for her!" while sometimes, the fear in him, the consciousness that he was near the edge of an abyss, was even greater than the yearning for love which many years of living with a woman of blunted feeling had bred in him.

If Hazlitt, in writing down these conversations, had thought to work them out of his mind, he had gone the wrong way about the matter. By the time he had finished his Book of Conversations, he had merely succeeded in burning them into his mind for ever. Moreover, he had called into being something which had the nature of life in it, something in which he could see Sarah's face as he might have seen it in her child and his, something that was of him and of her, and yet something that was independent of him and of her, something that called out for its own life, as a child might call. He had succeeded perhaps in quieting the eternal restless effort of his mind to reconstruct the ripple and flow of this talk, on the memory of which he lived, but he had made for himself something which, if at times it served him in the stead of a child, served him also at times as a graven image.

As he pulls it out of his drawer, and worships it, or now fondles it, now smiles at it tenderly, because it seems to him to reveal a sublime piece of work on the part of Nature, now laughs a little because he can discern in it too some slight lines of guile or artifice, we remember with misgiving the cool clear words he had uttered, in the years before frenzy had caught up with him, on the effects of any such absorption: "My doctrine is, that the inability to get rid of a favourite idea, when constantly thwarted . . . is likely to drive a man mad. It is this tenaciousness on a particular point that almost always destroys the general coherence of the understanding."

In the meantime, at such moments as his sense of humour is still uppermost, he laughs over his *tour de force*, and tells himself that the Conversations make *very nice reading*.

3·(2)

The next step in his progress was the Renton Inn, Berwickshire. He arrived there towards the beginning of February, and there he remained until the end of March, busy during the greater part of the time in composing the essays which were to complete the second volume of his *Table-Talk*. Because there was still hope in him when he reached Renton he took an immediate liking to this inn, and was at ease in his writing there, much as he had been at the little Winterslow Hut, although the Renton Inn, far from being a small country pot-house, was a large posting inn on the main road to London. It stood high in a lonely place, a mark for all the winds. which seemed to him to beat on it incessantly. Opposite it was a woody hill, looking down on a winding valley across which the thrush and the blackbird flung their jubilant songs. Hazlitt's business, when his immediate task was concluded, was to take him still farther North, to Edinburgh, but his thoughts, his gaze, even his walks, were all Southwards. When telling Patmore that the London road stretched on either side of the inn, "You may guess," he added, "which way I oftenest walk."

He found, awaiting him at the inn, a letter from Sarah, dated January 17th, four days after he had left London. Although it was in reply to one of his, it was stone-cold. The most ardent lover scrutinising it through the powerful lens of passion, could find in it not a crumb of hope whereon to feed. Knowing Sarah's non-committal ways, he could not bring himself to believe that it represented the state of her feelings. In his reply to it, he endeavoured to pick up the thread of the intimacy that had subsisted between them. The opening sentence shows the terms on which they had been, that there had been some real companionship between them, that he had talked to her about his writing, and that she had given him with regard to it the illusion his wife had never given him, of her being in sympathy with it: "You will scold me for this, and ask me if this is keeping my promise to mind my work. One half of it was to think of Sarah: and besides, I do not neglect my work either, I assure you. I regularly do ten pages a day, which mounts up to thirty guineas' worth a week, so that you see

I should grow rich at this rate, if I could keep on so; *and I could keep on so*, if I had you with me to encourage me with your sweet smiles, and share my lot."

This goes far to explain the persistence of Hazlitt's attachment. To a lonely man it is something to have someone who cares whether he does his ten pages a day or not. On another point this letter also sheds light. It shows quite clearly that Hazlitt realised, when he went to Scotland in connection with his divorce, that Sarah had not bound herself to him in any way. It shows also that he hoped, even if he were not united to her in marriage, that their friendship might endure. Indeed, very frequently there is a note in what Hazlitt says about Sarah, which indicates that even if she will not have him as the husband of her youth, he hopes to remain her friend, and to be near her, should she need him at any time, and especially when she might be old and need the companionship which had meant comparatively little to her in her youth: "when all else have forsaken thee, I will creep to thee, and die in thine arms." He urges her to go and see his two favourites, Kean, now returned from his American tour, and playing in *Othello*, and Miss Stephens in *Love in a Village*, saying he will have tickets sent for her and for her mother if they care to go. The rest of the letter is just lovers' chit-chat—the notes of the thrush come up to him from the valley, but they do not move him as once they did; he longs to have again the picture that is so like her, and thinks he must send for it to Patmore, "to kiss and talk to;" he is very sorry that he had made himself so troublesome to her during her last few days in London, for the belief that she had cared for him in some measure, even if it had been an illusion, had given him moments of happiness for which he would ever be grateful to her: "You once made me believe I was not hated by her I loved; and for that sensation, so delicious was it, though but a mockery and a dream, I owe you more than I can ever pay." He concludes with the words: "Oh! if you can never be mine, still let me be your proud and happy slave, W.H."

The terms on which his friendship is held are clear enough. She is the best-beloved. He is the lover who hopes for all, but who is grateful for, and can exist on, such crumbs as she may choose to let fall from her table.

In reply to this Sarah sent him a second communication which, like her first note to him, was stone-cold. Hazlitt was sore perplexed by its tone, so perplexed that he began to wonder whether he were altogether "on a wrong scent," but again he set himself to coax her into some display of human feeling. Writing on the evening of the day on which he had composed the essay, "Whether Actors ought to sit in the Boxes," which had touched on Macready's Romeo, he reminds her of the evening in which they had watched the play together, and of their happiness during the play and after; "you did seem to me, for those few short moments, to be mine, in all truth and honour and sacredness." He tells her that his work is completed, thanking her at the same time for her two poor cold letters, for he is determined not to offend her again by complaints: "You will be glad to know that I have done my work,—a volume in less than a month. This is one reason why I am better than when I came, and another is, I have had two letters from Sarah. I am pleased to have got through the job, as I was afraid I might lose reputation by it (which I can little afford to lose)—and besides, I am more anxious to do well now, as I wish you to hear me well spoken of." He tells her of his walks, and of his longing to have her with him: "I walk out of an afternoon and hear the birds sing as I told you, and think, if I had you hanging on my arm, *and that for life*, how happy I should be—happier than I ever hoped to be, or had any conception of till I knew you. ' But that can never be '—I hear you answer in a soft, low murmur. Well, let me dream of it sometimes—I am not happy too often." Again he asks pardon for his troublesome behaviour in the last few days they had had together, but, he adds: "I hope the *little image* made it up between us." If further apology or appeal to her magnanimity were necessary, he made it in the words: "Do not mock me, for I am a very child in love."

To this he received no answer, not a line. There was no word of business in it, and Sarah afterwards made that the excuse for her failure to reply to it. It did not seem to her, she said, that it required an answer. In her silence he felt in a complete blank. "The rolling years of eternity will never fill up that blank," he wrote on a copy on this letter. "Where shall I be? Where am I? Or where have I been?" The powerful irritant of a bewilderment far greater than any he had as yet endured began to play on his passion.

And what has happened? Why has Sarah done such a thing to him? People do not act out of character, and thus far we have had no suggestion from any word or act of Sarah's that there was any touch of cruelty in her nature. We think the alteration in her mood, occasioning what seemed to Hazlitt like the most cruel caprice, is to some extent explained by a word in her second letter: "Mr. P——— called the day after you left town." Since the day in December when Hazlitt and Patmore had returned to town together after seeing the fight between Bill Neate and the Gas-man, intimacy had sprung up between them sudden as the leaping of a flame. The reason of its growth was that Hazlitt, while desperately in love, was yet conscious that he had little understanding of women, and was very ready, with that genuineness of his which amounted to a kind of wild innocence, to profess himself a child in love, while Patmore, who preened himself on his success with women and on his understanding of them, professed himself learned in the mysteries of love. Hazlitt seems to have taken him at his own valuation, as "a most learned and irrefragable doctor" on the subject. In his bewilderment over Sarah's ways during the last few weeks he had been in London, he had got into the way of asking Patmore, who unlike Procter thought Sarah exceedingly attractive, for advice in his perplexities.

Now Patmore never spoke of Hazlitt without shabbying him. Also, as his sympathy was not real sympathy, but merely an extension of his egoism, he could not help betraying any one who confided in him, not out of malice, but as such creatures do, out of mere vanity. That he betrayed Hazlitt's confidence when he called at 9 Southampton Buildings we think there can be no question. Almost the only thing Hazlitt could get out of Sarah afterwards in explanation of her altered mood towards him, was that it had come to her knowledge that he had discussed her outside the family. Patmore was the only one of his friends who visited Sarah as his emissary. Sarah also told Hazlitt, when he returned to her, that she "could make no more confidences" to him. It would seem, that immediately after she had come into direct contact with Patmore, she had come to the resolution that she would "make no more confidences" to one who discussed her confidences with another. Therefore her letters were such as all the world might read. Therefore she confined them strictly to business. Therefore she refused to make any reply whatsoever to any letter that contained in it no mention of business.

Thus, even as Hazlitt while at Stamford had been borne up and sustained by the elation with which his tender parting from Sarah had filled him, the friendship which was, as he said, his "little all," had had its roots cut by this most disastrous quasi-friend, who intruded everywhere, and who marred everything into which he intruded; who betrayed merely because it was his nature to betray; and on whom the victim of this betrayal came to rely more and more, as his pain and bewilderment increased.

There is a second thing to which we can point as having had its share in occasioning the final hardening of Sarah's heart towards him, and for this his own carelessness alone was responsible. One of the essays he had written at the beginning of 1821, *On Great and Little Things*, contained some references to his passion which were less carefully disguised than the references to it in other essays written about the same time. It was not intended for publication until it had undergone revision, and Hazlitt had not intended it for magazine publication at all, but unfortunately, it had slipped in among other manuscripts forwarded to Henry Colburn, and was published by Colburn in *The New Monthly Magazine* in February. Hazlitt, being in Scotland at the time, had not even seen the proofs of the essay, as was customary with him, before it made its public appearance. In treating of the dangers and difficulties of unequal matches, in this essay, he had added: "But shouldst thou ever, my Infelice, grace my home with thy loved presence, as thou hast cheered my hopes with thy smile, thou wilt conquer all hearts with thy prevailing gentleness, and I will show the world what Shakespeare's women were." The words had been written long before any steps had been taken by Hazlitt towards regaining his freedom. Appearing, most unfortunately at the time when preparations for his divorce were going forward, and made directly applicable to Sarah by the use of the name Infelice, which was known to be one of his love-names for her, they may well have appeared to Sarah as an offence against the terms on which she had parted from him, terms of friendship, passionate friendship indeed, but yet friendship alone.

Moreover, some words which followed, in which he confessed his liking for humble beauties in general, were not flattering to her self-love, as most of his other references had been. We have some evidence as to her resentment of them. When Hazlitt's wife reproached him in the course of the summer for his folly in having published this essay at such a time, said that it had made talk, and that even John Hunt blamed him for its publication, he said quite frankly that no one could be sorrier about the matter than he was himself, for, quite apart from anything else, Colburn's precipitancy in publishing it without having given him the opportunity of revising it in proof, had placed him in the position of seeming to have been careless of Sarah's feelings. The worst thing about the whole matter, in his eyes, was that "it had hurt the girl."

Sarah had begun to cool towards Hazlitt the moment she had been brought into contact with Patmore and had realised, through Patmore's indiscretions, how indiscreet Hazlitt himself, as his passion for her increased, was becoming: but her complete and determined, although characteristically silent and inobtrusive withdrawal from the terms of friendship on which she had parted from him, dates from the publication of this essay. It was after its publication that she discovered there was "nothing which required an answer" in any love-letter he might send to her.

Fortunately for Hazlitt, by the time he realised, in the way which bore on him most cruelly of all, the way of silence, that Sarah, to all appearances, had given him up, he had completed his work, had even completed it, as he justly claimed "magnificently." The essays he wrote at Renton form a group by themselves in his writing. Most of them are universal in their application, but yet highly personal in character. Most of them are also conditioned by, or coloured by, his passion. The only immediate issue which occupied his mind to anything like the same extent as his passion for Sarah, was the happiness of his son, over whom his heart yearned, for he knew that the lot of a child whose parents were divided was likely to be a difficult one, but even the *Letter of Advice* he wrote for his child, whom he had just sent to school, was largely coloured by his consciousness of the extent to which his own life had been ruined by his failure to make anything of love or marriage.

Throughout most of these essays we can distinguish two main currents of thought, each of them blending with and sometimes indistinguishable from currents of feeling. The first of these is applied to what was rapidly being inflamed into an obsession with him, the riddle of Sarah's character. When he met his wife in Edinburgh shortly after this, he told her that he had had at various times two directly opposed opinions of Sarah—the one that she was one of the best girls in the world, and really loving in disposition, the other that she was "a complete designing hypocritical devil who only intended to mislead and make a fool" of him, and who "was playing a game to ensnare" him. But between these two opposites were sufficient intervening conceptions to make what might almost be called a pattern of Sarahs in his work. Not for nothing did he say that one half of his promise to mind his work was "to think of Sarah." In one or another of the Renton essays—even as in some of his letters, where now he suspects there is nothing in her "but a pretty figure and that you can't get a word out of her," where now he cries out vehemently that she is his soul's idol—we can distinguish every conception of her that flitted through his perplexed and tortured mind, from that of her as a lodging-house wench just clever enough to charm a lodger into giving her presents of value, to that of her as gentle Imogen.

It is evident that his mind reels with the effort to understand her. Sometimes various conceptions of her jostle one another within the compass of one short essay. The most notable instance of this may be seen in the essay *On the Knowledge of Character*. In this he wrote: "The greatest hypocrite I ever knew was a little, demure, pretty, modest-looking girl, with eyes timidly cast upon the ground, and an air soft as enchantment; the only circumstance that could lead to a suspicion of her true character, was a cold, sullen, watery, glazed look about the eyes, which she bent on vacancy, as if determined to avoid all explanation with yours." A few pages farther on there comes one of these analyses, not infrequent in his pages from this time henceforth, of what is called *Love at first sight*: "We generally make up our minds beforehand to the sort of person we should like, grave or gay, black, brown or fair, with golden tresses or with raven locks;—and when we meet with a complete example of the qualities we admire, the bargain is soon struck. We have never seen any thing to come up to our newly discovered goddess before, but she is what we have been all our lives looking for. The idol we fall down and worship is an image familiar to our minds. It has been present to our waking thoughts, it has haunted us in our dreams, like some fairy vision." In saying all this, he is but expressing once more his profound sense that Love, which seems so wayward, and which seems, like supreme Art, to be above Law, has yet, like supreme Art, its own laws, and is bound by them, although these lie deep, and never yield up their secret to those who look only at the surfaces of things. He follows up his exposition of the nature of these laws with a lovely invocation of Sarah, in connection with the first moment in which he had set eyes upon her, when it had seemed to him "as if another Imogen had entered:" "O! thou, who, the first time I ever beheld thee, didst draw my soul into the circle of thy heavenly looks, and wave enchantment round me, do not think thy conquest less complete because it was instantaneous; for in that gentle form . . . I saw all that I had ever loved of female grace, modesty, and sweetness!"

The second current of thought is trained, as some of his earlier writing had been, on the nature of the frustration frequently experienced by men-of-letters in their love-life, and particularly on the frustration from which he was himself suffering. This is most noticeable in his *Advice to a Schoolboy*, written for his son. In this he adjures the boy, if unsuccessful in love, to accept his fate, and to turn to other things for consolation, but above all, to avoid letting a sense of sexual frustration eat like a cancer into his life.

The portion of this *Letter* which remained in manuscript and was never published by Hazlitt himself, shows how deeply by this time the idea had sunk into his mind, that preoccupation with the things of the mind or the spirit tended towards debarring a man from having "the necessary advantages of person, confidence, and manner," and thus towards bringing in its train a certain measure of sexual frustration: "Do not place thought as a barrier between you and love. Let not the cloud sit upon your brow: let not the canker sink into your heart. Look up, laugh loud, talk big, keep the colour in your cheek and the fire in your eye, adorn your person, maintain your health, your beauty and your animal spirits, and you will pass for a fine man."

This current of thought merged readily into mingled bitterness and yearning. Thus his advice to his son on this point concluded with the intense bitterness and sorrow of the words:

"A spider, my dear, the meanest creature that crawls or lives, has its mate or fellow: but a scholar has no mate or fellow. For myself, I had courted thought, I had felt pain; and Love turned away his face from me. . . . I no more heard those accents which would have burst upon me, like a voice from heaven. I loathed the light that shone on my disgrace. Hours, days, years, passed away; and only turned false hope to fixed despair. And as my frail bark sails down the stream of time, the God of Love stands on the shore, and as I stretch out my hands to him in vain, claps his wings, and mocks me as I pass!"

The note of yearning in these words is to be found also in a fragment which flits like a ghost from one to another of Hazlitt's manuscripts at this time, as if seeking rest and finding none, and which varies slightly in its form in each. In the manuscript of the *Letter* to his son this appeared in the form: "should you let your blood stagnate in some deep metaphysical question, or refine too much in your ideas of the sex, forgetting yourself in a dream of exalted perfection, you will want an eye to cheer you, a hand to guide you, a bosom to lean on, and will stagger into your grave, old before your time, unloved and unlovely." Yet another version of the words was jotted down on a blank leaf of *Endymion*: "I want a hand to guide me, an eye to cheer me, a bosom to repose on; all which I shall never have, but shall stagger into my grave, old before my time, unloved and unlovely, unless S—— keeps her faith with me." They appear in one form or another so often because he was haunted by the thought. He seems to have been obsessed by a premonition of the loneliness which was to be his portion at the last. In one of the manuscripts of the essay, *On the Fear of Death*, which contains the quintessence of his mood at the moment, this expression of yearning is accompanied also by the cry: "I would have some creature love me before I die."

3 (3)

Edinburgh, the third stage in his progress, he found, and called, a "stony-hearted" city. From it he sent to Sarah yet another letter which went unanswered. Despite this, it may have been from Edinburgh that he sent her a length of plaid silk in which he imagined she would look lovely, and in which he hoped to see her clad on his return. The conflict within himself now absorbed him to the exclusion of almost everything else. In the days of bewilderment which had followed Sarah's silence, the powerful irritant of jealousy had again begun to work on his passion. His unhappiness was steadily mounting in scale. By the time he reached Edinburgh the three irritants, absence, bewilderment, and jealousy—were all eating into nerves which at the best of times were not made of catgut.

Of these the most unendurable was bewilderment. It was this which kept his mind racked by perpetual self-conflict. He would find himself thinking foul thoughts of Sarah, calling her by foul names, jade, bitch, decoy, "little damned incubus." Then would come the reaction and the sense of shame, and he would think, perhaps he would write down the words so that he might have them before him to steady his mind when it began to plunge wildly: "Within my heart is lurking suspicion, and base fear, and shame and hate; but above all, tyrannous love sits throned, crowned with her graces, silent and in tears." He would curse the day he had ever set eyes on Sarah, would make up his mind never to see her again, with his will, while he lived. Then he would realise that the only thing on earth he wanted to do, or cared about, was returning to her. He would feel his mind reeling in these fluctuations of feeling—would catch again at a word as he tried to distinguish between the madness of the mind and of the heart: "I am not mad, but my heart is so; and raves within me, fierce and untameable, like a panther in its den, and tries to get loose to its lost mate, and fawn on her hand, and bend lowly at her feet."

At other times he would feel that the soundness of his mind itself was slowly being sapped. Sometimes, in his inconceivable oppression and "lowness" of mind and body he sat and cried his eyes out, grieving the meanwhile, as an old man might have done, over his own weakness. As his last two letters had drawn no reply from Sarah, he was now reduced to applying to Patmore for fragments of news about her. Rage and rapture jostle each other in his distracted and incoherent letters to this muddling go-between, with whom he is now becoming ever more and more deeply involved. At the end of March he wrote: "I have been in a sort of Hell, and what is worse, I see no prospect of getting out of it." Certainly, if he were not yet in "complete" Hell, he had descended the first three steps thitherwards. In another letter he cried: "Damn her, I could devour her. It is *herself* that I love. . . . I think she would sooner come and live with me than marry me. So that I have her in my arms for life, I care not how. I never could tire of her sweetness. I feel as if I could grow to her body and soul." In this same letter he bombarded Patmore with instructions which in the way they contradict one another are all-revealing as to the weakness of mind to which he had been reduced. At the opening of the letter Patmore is instructed to call at 9 Southampton Buildings, to contrive to see Sarah and tell her how her lover is suffering, and that a letter sent from her to him in Edinburgh would be "a favour . . . greater than an angel's visit;" in the middle of the letter he is told when he calls to ask only for Mrs. Walker, and should Sarah chance to appear, to say only that Mr. Hazlitt "desired his love to her"—but on no account to make any request with regard to a letter. In a distracted postcript both these instructions are contradicted: "Don't go at all. I believe her to be a common lodging-house drab, and that an attempt to move her only hardens her. . . . To think that I should feel as I have done for such a monster."

Yet in a letter written shortly afterwards, his chief wish is that if he were mistaken, and if Sarah, instead of being a woman in whose love he might have renewed his life, were "only a lovely frail one"—he might have lived and died in his fool's paradise of faith in her incorruptibility: "Ours was the sweetest friendship. Oh! might the delusion be renewed, that I might die in it!"

His new surroundings had no power to interest or stimulate him. Edinburgh seemed to him slate-hard. Its Castle and its Crags, Arthur's Seat looking down on it "like a lioness watching her cubs," Princes Street and its tall freckled women, the Firth of Forth glittering "like a broad golden ribbon in the sun"—none of these moved him at all, although he recognised and admitted the sublimity of Arthur's Seat and the character of the Salisbury Crags. The only thing that moved him was the faint glimpse he could get at times of Berwick Law, pointing the way Southwards: "to thee, to thee I turn, North Berwick Law, with thy blue cone rising out of summer seas; for thou art the beacon of my banished thoughts, and dost point my way to her, who is my heart's true home."

Other things too weighed upon him. The chief of these was that he was at the mercy of his wife's indecisions. He could never feel sure for a moment that she would fulfil her promise of coming to Edinburgh. Then he was worried about money. He had now big overhead charges; his son's school fees had to be paid, and his wife's quarterly allowance, before he had any money that he could call his own; there were all the expenses of the divorce to be met. Colborn, his publisher, was in debt to him for the volume of *Table-Talk* which had just been completed. He hoped to make a substantial sum by two lectures which he was going to deliver in Glasgow early in May. But in the meantime he was almost bare. What was worse was, that now, just when he most needed to make money, he felt himself to be totally incapable of writing. Gone were the days when he could settle down to his ten pages a day, and watch the manuscript piling itself up reassuringly. Because he could not rest, because he could not sleep, because his nerves were exhausted by the wear and tear of violent and excessive feeling, he could do no consecutive thinking, and therefore no consecutive writing. This was a distress that was new in kind to him, and it bewildered him. It seemed to him almost as if he had come to a dead-end.

Unhappy though he was, he was still able to command himself in public. Jeffrey, when they met, saw nothing amiss with him. We get glimpses of him at Craigcrook, being very gracious to "the great little man," whom he was presently to salute as "the prince of Critics and the King of men"—and being graciously received both by "the prince of Critics" and by Mrs. Jeffrey. We see him at supper at the house of his friend William Ritchie, of *The Scotsman*, drinking "no wine or fermented liquor, but an enormous quantity of tea." George Combe, the phrenologist and psychologist, who was of the party, noted his fine forehead, the idealism reflected in the eyes, the thin and rather combative lips, not unlike what Pitt's had been, the way in which his features, when he laughed, became sharp, even "cuttingly sharp," his entire lack of ostentation. This lack of ostentation was so complete that while he was speaking the quality of his conversation might almost pass unnoticed, so quiet and inobtrusive was the way in which he said remarkable things. Thus it was only, said the psychologist, when one paused and reflected on what had been said during the past five minutes, that one perceived one had been talking "with an uncommon man." Combe noted that Hazlitt was just as ready to listen as to talk: "He is a well-bred man, does not monopolise conversation, listens with attention to any one who speaks, and affects nothing."

Hazlitt, who was never one to start at the midnight chimes, when in any of his haunts in London, evidently kept up his late hours in Edinburgh too, for Combe, at half-past one, left him "still sitting." We see him too, now and again, at the house of an old acquaintance of his, a certain hard-living, hard-drinking man called Bell, whom he had met by chance in Leith one day, and who had told him that he had settled in Edinburgh. Bell was none too trustworthy, but he was acquainted with Mrs. Hazlitt, and Hazlitt thought he might prove "the very man" to act as an intermediary, should the divorce negotiations develop.

In the course of leaving a trail of evidence as to his marital infidelity, he visited also, at a house kept in James Street by a woman of colour, a woman named Mary Walker. It is proof of all Hazlitt says as to the loneliness of his love-life, that although his wife had for years been complaining of his infidelity, she had not a shred of evidence that she could have produced against him in any court. She could point to no intimacy in which he had found satisfaction: she could not point even to any friendship with a woman, of which she had reason to be jealous, except that with Sarah Walker, and she knew well that Sarah had never been her husband's mistress. Her chief complaints were that he "picked up" girls of the town now and then, that he seemed to like low haunts and low company, and that he preferred the conversation of the low and the fallen to her own. Now Hazlitt left a trail of evidence that could hardly be missed.

Thus he acted. But if Venus Pandemos seemed to claim him, it was yet in the middle of the fevered April of 1822 that he broke forth into his most impassioned expression of yearning towards Venus Urania: "Oh! thou Uranian Venus, thou that never art, but wast and art to be; thou that the eye sees not, but that livest for ever in the heart; thou whom men believe and know to be, for thou dwellest in the desires and longings and hunger of the mind!"

We see him now and again during these months in one unexpected place. He had ignored the clumsy overtures the Blackwood men had made to him since his arrival in Edinburgh, a gesture which John Wilson censured, in his usual jargon, as being notably lacking in "trap." Yet he is now and again to be found, observant if not observed, in their stronghold, The Black Bull at the head of Leith Walk.

There he broke, on the 21st of April, 1822, the most rigid of all his
rules, for as we see him sitting at the table of the tavern parlour, he is
drinking Leith ale. He is as white with excitement as he had been when
as a child he had watched for the curtain to rise on his first play, but
this has nothing to do with the place or its ale. The curtain is now
about to rise on what he regards as the great drama of his life, the
drama of his salvation as a man, of his fulfilment as a man. He has just
heard from Bell that his wife has landed at Leith, and that she is even
now on her way to The Black Bull, where she is going to put up for the
night. He begins a letter to Patmore, telling him of this: "Should this
business succeed, and I should be free, do you think S.W. will be Mrs.
H? If she *will*, she *shall*; and to call her so to you or to hear her called
so by others, will be music to my ears, such as they never heard. Do you
think if she knew how I love her, my depressions and my altitudes,
my wanderings and my pertinacity, it would not melt her? . . . I don't
believe that any human being was ever courted more passionately than
she has been by me;" and again: "when I sometimes think of the time
I first saw the sweet apparition, August 16th, 1820, and that possibly
she may be my wife that day two years, it makes me dizzy with
incredible joy and love of her." He is writing on the table of a tavern
parlour. But his hopes soar upwards until they challenge the felicity of
Heaven: "Oh! is it even possible . . . that she has bestowed her loved
' endearments ' on me (her own sweet word) out of true regard? That
thought, out of the lowest depths of despair, would at any time make
me strike my head against the stars."

In the meantime Mrs. Hazlitt steadily advances upon The Black
Bull, both her sturdy feet very solidly planted upon the earth. Nought
knows she of the stars or of aspirations towards them, nought either
of exultations or of agonies, but she has a very real appreciation of
good eating and drinking, of the value of money, of all the pleasures
that earth can hold for a woman who although now middle-aged is
still good-looking, trim of figure, sound of wind and limb, knowing no
ailment of mind, or even of body, except an occasional twinge of inconvenience or pain when she has eaten or drunk too well. She is
not yet sure that she will go through with the divorce, for she has been
told that the taking of the Oath of Calumny may have very awkward
legal consequences, should it be proved that there had been collusion.
But she is sure that if she goes through with the matter, she will claim
from her husband, who had already agreed to pay all expenses connected with the divorce, an extra quarter's allowance of £37 10s.—on
the plea that her present quarter's allowance had been swallowed up in
preparations for the Edinburgh visit; that in addition she will claim
her travelling expenses to and from Edinburgh together with all
expenses incurred during her visit to Scotland, and that these shall
include the cost of various visits made to beauty-spots in the Highlands

and Perthshire, perhaps too, of a trip to Ireland. She is still the old Sarah, not perhaps as merry as she had been in her youth, but with her appetite for pleasure and capacity for enjoyment unabated by anything life has brought to her, and with as little scruple as ever as to the means by which she satisfies it. There is not a scrap of malice in her. There is also hardly a scrap of feeling.

She goes to work with admirable method. The day after her arrival she consults Mr. Cranstoun the barrister (afterwards Lord Corehouse) as to whether it would be safe for her to take the Oath of Calumny, her English friends having told her that if she took it, and swore that there had been no collusion between her husband and herself, she might be liable to a prosecution for perjury, as Mr. Hazlitt had certainly suggested to her that it would be better for both their sakes to put an end to the misery of their marriage. She was assured that she need have no scruples nor fears. In the course of the week, however, she came to the conclusion that she could not take the Oath, and wrote to Hazlitt to tell him so. This communication brought her a visit from Ritchie, who besought her to reconsider her decision, saying to her "that Mr. Hazlitt was in such a state of nervous irritability that he could not work or apply to anything, and that he thought he would not live very long if he was not easier in his mind." She replied that she herself felt her husband was not likely to survive her, but if he died before his time he had only himself to blame: he would only have reaped the fruit of careless living. Nevertheless she reconsidered the matter; her solicitor drew up for her a Summons of Divorce, in which she claimed the right to retain all her own property, to have provision made for her in virtue of her marriage, and to have payment made by her husband of £100 or such other sums as might be decreed by the Court as expenses; and on Saturday the 27th she forwarded to Hazlitt, through Bell, a paper containing her own private demands for him to sign.[335]

On Sunday the 28th she wrote to Hazlitt to inform him that she had less than £6 of her quarter's money left, and that if he did not send her some money immediately, she would have to return to Winterslow on the Tuesday, while she had money enough to take her home. Hazlitt in the meantime had gone to New Lanark, to see how Robert Owen's schemes were progressing there. On the Tuesday morning Mrs. Hazlitt, having received no answer to her letter, went to Bell, told him of the letter she had written to Hazlitt, and said that she must leave for the South if she had not an immediate sum of money given to her. Bell promised to see Hazlitt on the Wednesday, but on the Tuesday evening she went herself to Hazlitt's rooms in George Street, priding herself on her discretion because she had waited for the dusk to fall, and because she had veiled herself. She found him at tea. He had just come in after walking from New Lanark, some thirty miles, tired, and on the whole ill-satisfied with his expedition, for he had found in all the apparatus of New Lanark nothing but "a desolate monotony." They had a grey kind of conversation together, the kind of talk that only does not develop into a quarrel because those taking part in it feel the futility of any further quarrelling, as they hope to part for ever. He told her that he had at the moment only £1 in his pocket, which she could have if she liked, but that he would satisfy all her demands as soon as he could, and also make her a present of £20 when all was over, as she seemed "to love money." Where money was concerned, he was quite ready to concede to her anything he had it in his power to concede. But on one point he was adamant. He told her that while he was ready to be her friend for life if she gave him his freedom, if she carried out the threat of leaving the business unconcluded, he would never willingly set eyes on her again.

Before he left for Glasgow to give his first lecture there, on Milton, he sent her £4, which was all he could spare at the moment. With this and such money as she had herself, after completing her sightseeing in Edinburgh and its neighbourhood, she took a steamboat up the Firth of Forth, on the morning of May 13th, the day on which Hazlitt was giving his second lecture in Glasgow, on Thomson and Burns; and arrived at Stirling early in the evening. The next day she walked from Stirling to Callander. Hazlitt too that day was on the move. With his friend Sheridan Knowles, who had made all the arrangements for the Glasgow lectures, he set out for Ben Lomond. But the weather was unsuitable for climbing; he was driven by restlessness as by a gadfly, and all his thoughts, now that his lecturing engagements were over, were on getting back to Southampton Buildings. Thus at the close of the day he parted from Knowles, who returned to Glasgow, and took the first steamboat he could get for London.

3 (4)

As his vessel steamed up the Thames on Friday the 17th day of May, the air seemed to him to thicken and in his excitement he seemed to breathe with difficulty, so near he was to all he could now conceive of earthly happiness! But the moment he saw Sarah he knew that there was something badly amiss in her feeling for him. She had no word of welcome for him, no look. She was very unwilling to come up to his room at all, and when she did so she stood by the door, "cold, distant, averse." When he wished to kiss her, she turned her head aside and—it seemed to him—actually shrank away from him, as if he were repulsive to her, or as if she were mortally offended with him. When he asked her what he had done to estrange her, her answers were short, cold and incoherent, but he felt as if her mind were labouring under some sense of injury which she either could not or would not impart. Yet she denied that she had altered in feeling towards him; she denied that she favoured any one else.

Some faint idea crossed his mind, not that Patmore's visits had done him disservice, but that perhaps she was displeased at his having let Patmore know that she had corresponded with him. He asked her if this were so. Once again she replied No! that she had merely thought there had been no need to answer his last letters. He felt that he could hardly bear such a reception. The only thing which gave him any satisfaction at all was to learn that his "rival" had gone, and that there was no one in the house of whom he might reasonably feel jealous. But when he asked her if he were likely to see her on the morrow, she replied indifferently that perhaps he might, but she could make no promise. As soon as she could she slipped away, leaving him wholly unsatisfied, tormented with the feeling that something had gone wrong which he did not know how to right, and full of foreboding. On the Saturday morning she did not appear along with his breakfast-tray. This was a great disappointment to him, as he had been looking forward to breakfasting in her company again more than to anything else, but yet he took heart from seeing that the little Buonaparte, which he regarded as a link between them, had been replaced on his mantel-piece, and tried to tell himself that perhaps her cold behaviour was only coquetry after all. That day one of the first things he did was to order from Taylor and Hessey "prettily bound" copies of three of his favourite books, *The Vicar of Wakefield*, *The Man of Feeling* and *Nature and Art*, which he meant as gifts for her. Once or twice during the day he chanced to see her about the house, and that was all he had of her. On the Sunday morning he took Patmore with him to Coldbath-Fields, to see John Hunt, whom they found walking by the wilted cabbages and lettuces in the depressing prison-garden. Leigh Hunt had sailed on the 13th of the month for Italy and his ill-starred venture of producing (along with Byron) and editing *The Liberal*. Hazlitt seems to have discussed with John at this meeting the possibility of his contributing to this new venture.

In the afternoon he walked out with his son, intending to call with him on one or two friends, but all the time his longing was urging him back to his rooms, and he returned there to tea with his son, although the boy had vexed him by being rude to Sarah. He spoke about this, and William, who for a boy of his years had a remarkable power of taking the offensive, promised not to bear her malice any more. When Sarah came up with the tea-things, Hazlitt told her that his son had something to say to her, whereupon William said in his usual abrupt way: "Sarah, I'm sorry if I've ever said anything to vex you," so they shook hands, and Sarah smiled and said: "*Then* I'll think no more of it." Hazlitt said to her: "I see you've brought me back my little Buonaparte," and she answered softly: "I told you I'd keep it safe for you."

Somehow or other she managed to throw into the simple words the suggestion that this proof of her fidelity was her real greeting to him. Charmed by her manner, he reminded her that he had given it to her, even as he had given her everything he had to give, but at this, with the graceful movement which he had never seen in any one but her, she "waved, like a thing of enchantment," out of the room. Encouraged by the gentleness of her manner, he tried in the evening, after his son had gone, to come to an understanding with her, but the moment she was alone with him, her inaccessibility returned. First of all, she refused to come beyond the doorway, saying that she was busy at the moment, and could hear quite well anything he had to say from where she stood. It was far from easy to speak to her at all, half-poised, as she seemed to be, for flight, but he went over to her, sat down beside her, took her hand, and talked to her for the greater part of an hour, she standing, the meanwhile, with her profile towards him, looking down all the time, her hair curling about her face very beautifully, her expression the perfection of softness and gentleness, her form and attitude, as she stood completely still, like that of some exquisite statue. He would have knelt to her, but that at his movement she drew away as if startled or displeased; he tried to draw her towards him, only to find that she melted away from his embrace; he got up and made as if to kiss her as she left him.

At this she repulsed him most definitely and determinedly. The movement stung him to the quick. He followed her half-way down the stairs as she slipped away from him, but she was out of his sight in a moment or two. At this his control gave way. The calm under which he had been disguising the hysteria mounting within him broke. He tore the locket which contained her hair from his neck, and trampled it under his feet; he hurled the figure of Buonaparte to the floor and stamped on it. From this he fell to shrieking out curses on her name and on her false love. The scream in which his imprecations ended was so piercing and pitiful that it brought the whole household, father, mother and lodgers, every one except Sarah, tumbling into his room, under the impression that murder or rape was being committed. Some one cried: "She's in there! He has got her in there"—thinking that the cries had come from his bedroom, and that he had been offering Sarah violence. "No," he cried vehemently, every suspicion he had ever had about her knocking his brain to pieces and driving him to frenzy, "she's in no danger from me; *I* am not the person." At this he tried to burst from what had become to him a scene of intolerable humiliation, her mother trying to stop him from leaving the house in such a distraught condition, her father crying angrily: "Let him go!" As he sprang downstairs they cried after him, realising at last that he felt himself to have been mortally wounded and injured: "What is it? What has she done to you?" With the cry, "She has destroyed me for ever!" he rushed from the house, leaving his room in possession of a little group of people, half-angry, half-terrified, and because his suffering was of a nature altogether beyond their comprehension, almost stupefied with amazement.

He had rushed headlong from the scene of his shame, but no sooner did he find himself in the darkness and loneliness of the streets, than his passion drove him back to the source from which it had sprung. Her father met him at the door, stern of face and hostile of aspect, as if in two minds about admitting him. Hazlitt asked the old man's pardon for his wild behaviour, said that his madness was over, and requested a few words with him. Mr. Walker at first hesitated, then seeing that the violent fit was indeed over, he followed him quickly upstairs. Hazlitt then did what must have added the last straw to Sarah's discomfiture and her now intense displeasure. Spent now and quiet as a tired child, he explained, white-faced, to her father what it was that had driven him to frenzy, that when his addresses had nothing honourable in them and could have nothing honourable in them, she had given him every encouragement; that now, when he would shortly be in a position to make them honourable, and when he could no longer live without the favour she had shown towards him, she treated him with the utmost coldness, although the only thing he now wanted was to live his life out with her, and to die in her arms. Mr. Walker listened to this with much regret and concern, but said that of course he could not attempt to influence his daughter's inclinations one way or the other. Hazlitt added that perhaps he had brought all this misery on himself by his precipitancy, that he had been advised to leave her quite alone until he was a free man, when he could make her an offer of his hand and when, if she then refused him, he would have to consider the matter at an end. Mr. Walker told him that no one could have given him better advice. Hazlitt took the words as a kind of negative encouragement, and with that they parted.

The next day he was as if stupefied, and Sarah, they told him, was ill. He made up his mind that the best thing he could do would be to go to Winterslow. But first he gathered up the pieces of the locket and of the statue, which were still scattered about the floor, and sent them to her "to be kept in remembrance of the unhappy." Sarah took no notice of this. Nevertheless he sent her the books he had ordered as gifts for her, and wrote a note asking her whether she would accept the three volumes in lieu of three volumes of his own writings, which he had given her from time to time. She sent back to him the three "prettily bound" volumes, with word that she had no value for them, but that he should have those he had asked her to return to him in the course of the afternoon. Thereupon he gave them all to her little sister. When he came in to tea he found the little girl, Betsy, kneeling on the floor packing up his box, and beside her a large paper parcel containing every book he had ever given to Sarah, including the prayer-book in crimson velvet. Touched at this, he asked Betsy to tell her sister that he would be obliged if she would keep them all, except his own works, which he regarded as unworthy of her, whereupon the child rose to her feet and gaped at him, all eyes and wonder, as she blurted out: "*And those are the ones that she prizes the most!*" Hazlitt felt in a moment restored to hope and happiness, by the merest chance word, which might never have reached his ears, and which yet had lifted off his shoulders a load of unbearable suffering. "Childish, wanton, drunk with pleasure," he thrust a twenty-shilling note, which he happened to have in his hand, into that of the astonished child.

"What's this for, Sir?"

"It's for you. Don't you think it's worth that to be made happy?"

He told Betsy that she might stop packing his bag, as he was not going away after all. For a short time he remained in a state of extravagant happiness. As long as he had any sense of being in sympathy with her he could do without seeing her. But when a couple of days had passed, and he had had no word or sign from her, he began again to long for her unendurably. Morning after morning he waited, with a beating heart, for the coming up of his breakfast-tray, for he always hoped that Sarah would appear with it, as of old. But morning after morning he now ate his breakfast alone. The old pleasant companionable meal was evidently a thing of the past. Worse still, he never saw Sarah about the house. She seemed to have vanished completely. As day after day passed thus, the sense of bewilderment began to return. By the Sunday he was almost desperate again. In two days' time he would be gone, as unsatisfied as he had come. If only he could understand what had happened to her, he felt that he could bear it, whatever it was. But his chief torment was that he could not understand. It was like living in a fog. On the Monday, when it looked as if he might have to leave without seeing her again, unless he did something decisive, he sent her a message asking her whether he could have a talk with her. Her answer was ambiguous, but at last she came to his room, very formal and quiet in her manner.

"Did you wish to speak to me, Sir?"

"Yes. May I not speak to you? I wanted to see you and be friends."

"If that's all, I have nothing to say."

Again his heart sank within him. Again he essayed to come to an explanation with one whose sole determination was to avoid any explanation. Yet had he been listening to the few words she uttered during this talk, instead of devouring her with his eyes, he might have gained at least a glimmering of understanding of what it was that had alienated her, for it was now that she said, among other things, that he had not only told her relatives of what had passed between them, but that he had spoken of her indiscretions, which she now realised had been improprieties, "not only in the house, but out of it," so that it had come to her ears from various quarters, as if she were "a light character." Hazlitt seems hardly to have realised how deeply she resented the injury which had come to her reputation through his indiscretion. He let the all-important word pass unnoticed, so absorbed was he in the endeavour to make her realise the quality of his love for her. When he told her, in reply to what she had said, that his esteem for her amounted to adoration, she replied curtly that she did not want adoration. Worship of this kind from a man who had been clumsy enough to injure her reputation, seemed to her but a poor compensation for the reputation she had lost. The extravagance of his protestations only hardened her against him. When his declarations became passionate she moved towards the door, telling him she had heard enough of that kind of conversation. Yet it was not until he began to probe her on the subject of the lodger whom he had considered as his rival, that she checked him with what for her was most unusual bluntness, by saying in so many words that she could and would "make no more confidences" to him. At last, in a running fire of question and answer, she succeeded in getting out of the room without having made any. If she had a secret she was concealing from him she was protecting it well. Never had her reserve seemed to him so impenetrable.

He felt as if he were left for ever alone, without a creature to love him. The room which had become a home to him seemed suddenly desolate. He looked round the place in which he had known what it was to be happy, as if he expected that it could come to his aid, but the table, the chairs, the places in which she had stood, all seemed empty, deserted, dead. Unable to endure his sense of desolation, he went downstairs, despising himself meanwhile, indeed deeply conscious of his own shame, sat with her mother for a time, much as he disliked her, and talked to her of Sarah, much as Sarah disliked that. In the midst of their talk Sarah came bounding in, half-smiling as if with smothered glee as she saw how they stopped short in their talk at her entrance. She looked at him pleasantly enough, but he could get no further talk with her alone.

The next day, on Tuesday the 28th of May, he left the house and took the steamboat on his return journey to Scotland. At the moment of his departure he was still in the greatest self-conflict. He managed to leave the house, apparently gay, careless and unconcerned, almost insolently careless, although despair was tugging at his heart. But on the way to the steamboat he began to think of the time when he was a careless happy child in his father's house, of his early lessons, of what he had looked like when his brother had painted him as a child, of the way in which he had been valued and loved and cherished by all around him. As he thought of the pass to which his life had come, of his loveless existence, and of the waste of loveless years before him, he felt as if his heart would break, and he was on the point of going back, to throw himself on Sarah's mercy, "once more to make a longer truce with wretchedness and patch up a hollow league with love," as he put it afterwards. Then he remembered some of the cool words she had spoken at their last meeting: "I always told you I had no affection for you"—and the memory of her measured tones steeled his resolution. He proceeded on his way, but on slow, reluctant, wounded feet. And at every step that drew him away from her he felt himself approaching so near to frenzy that at any moment the measure of sanity left to him might be merged in it.

3 (5)

On May 20th, the Monday in which Hazlitt had been wearied out by the reaction succeeding his fit of hysteria, Mrs. Hazlitt returned to Edinburgh, after having made a tour in the course of which she reckoned she had walked a hundred and seventy miles. On the Tuesday she "wrote to Mr. Hazlitt for money," only to have her note returned with a message to the effect that he had gone to London and would not be back for a fortnight. In this predicament she called on Ritchie on the Wednesday to inform him that her husband had left without sending her the money she had expected. She had returned expecting to take the Oath of Calumny on Friday, May 24th, but on the Thursday she learned from her lawyer, to her great vexation, that she would not be called upon to take it for about three weeks. With this news she went to see Bell, who regaled her with gossip about Hazlitt's love-affair, which is of some interest as showing that he knew nothing of it, from which we gather that until Hazlitt had left Edinburgh for the first time, his mind had some control over its painful secrets. Bell told Mrs. Hazlitt that her husband and Sarah Walker were at variance with each other, because she had told him she preferred another man to him, but that a mutual friend had written to him telling him to pay no attention to her words, as her heart was devoted to him. Bell claimed also that Hazlitt had shown him some passages of Sarah's love-letters, and said that "they were such low vulgar milliner's or servant wench's senti-mentality, that he wondered Mr. Hazlitt could endure such stuff." On the following Tuesday, the 28th, just as Hazlitt was setting out from London in despair, her immediate anxieties as to money were allayed by the receipt of a £10 note from him. On Friday, the last day of May, she set out on a second tour, taking first of all the steamboat from Newhaven to Burnt Island.

On these days, from the 28th to the 31st of May, Hazlitt was going through the darkest days of his life. Nothing could have been worse for him, in the state bordering on frenzy in which he was, than the time he spent, with a raging fire consuming his heart and brain, pent up on board the steamboat. It seemed a prison to him; the lapping of the water seemed an unendurable repetition of his woes; the sea an abyss into which he longed to leap so as to put an end to his misery. He could not do that, for every time he thought of it the face of his little boy rose before him in appeal. But as the slow hours passed, it seemed to him as if he were enduring the eternity of punishment in this life. All was endurable where there was a limit, but while other people had an end to their woes, he had none. He could escape neither from the one he loved, nor from himself. Nothing lay before him but darkness, and the memory of her scorn.

It was during this journey that his distress began to be open and visible, so that those around him noted it, and pitied it, or despised it, according to their kind. It was during this journey that his suffering took a new and dark and terrible turning. It was during this journey that the first shadow of mania drew near to him, with the return, in tenfold intensity—as the conviction that Sarah had never loved him at last poured over him—of the idea of his own repulsiveness to Woman, from which he had once thought that Sarah's love had rescued him for ever. When he wrote to Patmore: "Would it were quietly over, and that this form, made to be loathed, were hid out of sight of cold, sullen eyes," he was on the very threshold of the madhouse-cell, in which he was presently to find himself in foul and shameful darkness and captivity. We noted the injury done him, in his sensitive youth, by a young girl's wantonness or carelessness; we have noted the sweetness of the healing which had come to him from what he had taken to be a young girl's love for him, making him "amends for all," a sweetness of healing which had put him completely in her power; we have noted how the healing balm, wrought upon by the infinite variety of circumstances which determine human relationships, had turned to poison. We note now, in the terrible rebirth of the idea that he is "the outcast of nature and the scoff of love," the birth also of the mania which was to make him its thrall in the months to come, if that can be called mania which moves forward according to its own laws, and which may be said to be based almost on a refinement of the capacity for reasoning, for Hazlitt being Hazlitt, even

"in the blind and awful lair
Of such a madness reason did lie couched."

Discarding now at last, in view of her treatment of him when he had travelled so far to come to an explanation with her, and especially in view of the indifference with which she had seen him depart in pain, the faith in which up till now, despite all the hurricanes that had come to shake it, he had persisted, that she had at the core of her some genuine spark of love for him, and obsessed once more, in consequence of his rejection of this faith, by his old conception of himself as a man "abhorrent to love," or "a species by himself," he set his mind to a reconsideration of his entire relationship with Sarah. At first his primary feeling was grief for his own fate, regret that he had made himself the man he was: "Is it not that this thinking beyond my strength, my feeling more than I ought about so many things, has withered me up and made me a thing for love to shrink from and wonder at?" He felt, in the sudden intensification of a humility in his estimate of himself as a sexual being, that had always been morbid, that he had become a man quite "out of the ordinary calculation of love." It seemed to him that it was not likely he should ever have met even with the outward demonstration of love from any woman but a lodging-house decoy. Nor, he believed, was there another man alive who would have been used as he had been, even by a lodging-house decoy: "Who is there, besides . . . so vile, so filthy, so abhorrent to love, to whom such an indignity could have happened?"

Presently, dismissing his thoughts of himself and the desolateness of his fate and of this second great humiliation of his life, he brought the whole power of his mind and of his knowledge of character to bear on Sarah. Often enough she had said to him: "You should judge me by my actions." By her actions now she should be judged. Analysing these from the beginning of his acquaintance with her, he now found, on the assumption that they had not been the effect of love, or of friendship so strong and pure that it was sweeter than what was called love, that his judgment of them inevitably had to be exactly reversed. Seeing that she did not love him, he could only come to the conclusion that they had been the effect, not of an innocent tenderness, but of a perversity that had learned to indulge and satisfy itself. It should here be recalled that Hazlitt had a profound understanding of the extent to which human conduct could be conditioned by perversity, and that where women were concerned he was apt to lay too much stress on it as a determining factor of their actions. Had not Desdemona herself come under his suspicions? Now he came to the heart-rending conclusion, on the assumption that Sarah did not love him, that she had in a sense been attracted by him just because he was "abhorrent to love," "a species by himself," and a man "out of the ordinary calculation of love."

From this it followed that she was essentially unchaste. She might act as she had acted with him with any man who stimulated the element of perversity in her. In the entire reversal of his estimate of her she seemed to him no longer what in his thoughts he had called her, his wife, his sister, his friend, his love, his all-in-all, but "a regular lodging-house decoy," leading "a sporting life" with every man who came her way, in succession; her "seraph kisses" became "an itch for being slobbered and felt;" her gentle embraces the effect of "habitual hypocrisy and *lech* for the mere act of physical contact with the other sex:" they were not gentle—they were obscenities designed to stimulate him to the act of lust; her downcast look was the effect not of modesty but of suppressed lewdness, or of a concealment of her habitual gloating over her own hypocrisy. She was clever enough to hide rank thoughts and deadly purposes under angelic looks. Nevertheless, monster of duplicity though she was, at last he could see through her disguise, could see her as she was, no less than "a hardened, impudent, heartless whore." She was a feminine organism lusting for a male one. She had never wanted a lover; she had wanted a man to serve her body. It was almost too much to say that. She was a feminine creature lusting after any male creature. The terms used for human intercourse were more than she deserved. She was a bitch who wanted a stallion.

The foul thoughts that coursed through his mind as to the mingled perversity and unchastity of the gentle equivocal girl in his love for whom he had lost himself, plunged him into limitless torment. Hitherto he had been jealous of a young and attractive man who had been all that a young girl might have required in her lover. The torment there had been in this jealousy now seemed a mercy to him compared to the torment which his reversed estimate of her brought to him. No man who approached her could now be exempt from his suspicions. All might have it in their power to pleasure her caprice. If she were perverse, there was no saying who or what might please her. Men to whom he had never given a thought in connection with her now became suspect in connection with her. There was Griffiths, the tall, stiff-backed, able-bodied quack-doctor from Penmaenmawr. She was small and dainty. She might "take up" with him "merely for bone and measurement and gross manners." Even now the itinerant apothecary might be supplying "her morning's meal of studied wantonness." Or there was the old fellow of sixty who had recently come to the house. Perhaps she might turn to an old man for a change. He was pot-bellied and red-faced. It might seem to her that a slender waist and a pot-belly made a piquant combination, or a red face and a pale one. In his present mood, if there had been a man of colour near her, Hazlitt would certainly have suspected her, as he had suspected Desdemona, of being stimulated instead of being repelled by the contrast in blood and complexion.

There is one hell for the idealist, whose primary longing is that his soul shall meet and know its fellow; there is another hell for the sensualist. There are few men to whom it is given to know the extremity of torment that can be inflicted in both these hells. Hazlitt was indeed almost "a species by himself" in that in one and the same moment he was now subjected to the uttermost pangs of both. Until this time, although his love had been born of an impulse in part sensual, in part spiritual, his had been primarily an ideal passion. Now his suffering was redoubled—for out of the foulness of his thoughts was bred a sudden boiling-up of what might be called retrospective sensuality. When in Sarah's presence day by day, looking at her face, listening to her soft-spoken words, he had known little of its sting. The feeling of being in sympathy with her had once been all but enough to satisfy him. Now, as his sympathy was converted into loathing of her as a spiritual being, his appetite for her as a physical being became a raging hunger. This was intensified in him by his ever-growing and utterly poisonous belief that he had once more been cheated by his idealism, or, as he put it to himself, that he had been cheated out of the one thing he might have had from her by his "worship of her equivocal face." She had just told him that she did not want his adoration. That at least was true. He told himself that "she wanted only a codpiece." No wonder she had in the end tired of his refinements of feeling. If he had handled her like an animal things might have been very different. At least she might have been bound to him by the satisfaction of her lust. The animal in her would have known its mate. His first impression of her had been the true one. She had called to him with a whore's look of invitation. He was filled with desperate regret that he had not ravished her at his first or second meeting with her. After that, it had become an impossibility, for she had bewitched him so that he had become "the fool of love." Yet any one but a fool like himself, or a pedant, after such a look, would have made the experiment, as a matter of life or death, no matter what the cost of the violence done to his own tenderer impulses towards her.

These were the thoughts which ate into his mind like a poisonous mineral as he walked up and down the deck of the boat that was bearing him away from her, feeling as if he were enduring the eternity of punishment in this life, feeling as if the air he breathed stifled him and his own thoughts poisoned him, feeling as if he were pent up not only by the immediate physical confinement of the steamboat, but as if he were "pent up in burning, impotent desires" for which he could find no outlet. Every now and again a sudden shaft of sanity would make him conscious of their foulness. For a moment or two they would be submerged in the cry: "Who is there so low as me?" He would wonder how far he had stepped into madness in his con-jectures, would grieve over what he was becoming. Then as he thought of how he had been once more "hated, repulsed, bemocked," the regret in him at what he had become would be replaced by something he had never known before, a filthy jet of scalding hatred for the woman who had reduced him to such a plight: "Oh God! oh God! The slimy, varnished marble fiend to bring me to this, when three kind words would have saved me!"

He crawled off the boat at Leith like a man who had just been wasted by a severe illness. We have seen that, even before his return to London, absence, bewilderment and jealousy had all inflamed his passion. Absence and bewilderment still inflamed it; the jealousy he was now experiencing was different in degree and kind from any he had experienced before, having become undirected, limitless, universal, and raging like the sea, while in the meantime four new powerful irritants had begun their corrosive work upon him—suspicion, sensuality, anger, and in the end hatred. The seven devils within him contending for mastery over him had so ravaged him that to the friends who saw him shortly after his return to Edinburgh he seemed like a man in a high fever. He felt that the state of his mind separated him from them, sensed that they were beginning to feel ill at ease with him. This drove him still more into himself. He had just enough sanity left to enable him to realise that he was like a man possessed of demons, and that the new irritants to his passion added to the old had seven-devil-yeasted it into frenzy.

It is not surprising that the torment which, he felt, separated him from other men should make him feel that he could not endure the society of man. Yet he no longer had the strength to support solitude. When he was with others, he would feel that if he could only think out his thoughts to the end, he could pierce through the fog that was creeping over his mind. Yet no sooner was he alone than the intolerable procession of thoughts that passed through his mind drove him back again to the haunts of men. He felt that he was so tossed backwards and forwards by his passion as to seem ridiculous to those about him. Indeed, he was like one driven by a gadfly. He could not rest in any one place. He began to understand how it was that mad people never cared to remain long in the same place. They were moving on for ever, *from themselves*. But alas, he could not move on, *from himself*, nor from the hot hell that burned within him nor from the demons which—he felt—surrounded him in his solitude. It was in these days that his mind at last began to slip its cable, so that he was no longer in perfect control of his thoughts, and so that sometimes, like a man in delirium, he babbled of all sorts of things it was urgently necessary he should keep to himself. His consciousness of this was not the least part of his misery. His weakness, not only of mind but of body, grew upon him, for he was unable to eat, having lost all taste or relish of his food because of his feverish distress and anxiety. To the no-friend or half-friend in whom at the time he most trusted he now cried: "Treat me as a child."

3 (6)

It was while Hazlitt was in the height of this grievous sickness of mind, while he felt himself growing spectral in his physical and mental unrest, while he was badly worried, too, by his complete inability to write, although his funds were getting very low, that Mrs. Hazlitt, on the completion of a second visit to the Highlands, bore down upon Edinburgh again. On the Sunday, she wrote to Hazlitt, pressing for a settlement of the money she said he owed her, and, although she had returned to take the Oath of Calumny on June 14th, hinting once more that she might throw up the whole business if the money were not forthcoming. This seems to have been the touch that caused Hazlitt's first complete breakdown, for it is in connection with it that we note the first instance of the way in which his mind had begun to slip its cable. The following day—it was Monday, June 10th— he was in a state of fearful agitation. There can be no doubt that in the height of some such nervous crisis as had come upon him shortly before in London, he showed the letter to Bell, with the result that Bell insulted Mrs. Hazlitt in the course of the evening in his own house, telling her that she was "a pitiful, squeezing, paltry creature to grind a man into the earth for money he did not possess." The next day Ritchie called on her with a message from her husband, simply that he had not got the money she demanded, but that he entreated her not to draw back at this eleventh hour, and that somehow or other he would find her all she needed for current expenses.

In the meantime, Hazlitt, now at his wits' end, found help in Jeffrey, who advanced him £100. Now that he had money in his possession, he sought some relief for his tortured nerves in change of scene. Feeling as if the air of Edinburgh had suddenly become stifling to him, as if he had better be out of the way on Friday the 14th, when the Oath was to be taken, and as if he might recover his power to write if he went where but a few months before he had succeeded in writing magnificently, he set out on the night of the 13th for Renton Inn. Before he left he asked Bell, who in the meantime had made his apologies to Mrs. Hazlitt and had been forgiven by her, to tell his wife that he now had some money, and that he would remit her some when she had taken the Oath. Bell told her that he had raged and stormed at their house before his departure for the country, that he had said he could swear she meant to cheat him, that he had abused her in the grossest way, and said such terrible things about her that Mrs. Bell had thought he was going out of his mind and had herself had a fit of hysterics. Mrs. Hazlitt was ready enough to criticise her husband, but it struck her that conduct of this kind was very unlike him, and she told Bell so, saying that this was not his way, that everybody to whom he had ever spoken of her had always said that he spoke "very handsomely" of her, that he never imputed any fault to her, but made it clear that his only reason for wishing to be divorced from her was that they could not contrive to be happy together. All this was perfectly true. Yet, for once, what Bell said was true also. Hazlitt was not now acting according to the health, but according to the sickness of his mind. He both said and did things which all his friends would have pronounced out of character. He knew well enough what a treacherous rascal Bell was, yet he had raged and stormed about his private affairs in the presence of such a man, worse still, had exposed his wife's indiscretions to the malice of such a man. This is the second instance we note of the way in which his mind was beginning to slip its cable.

The return to the solitude of Renton was a mistake. He was disappointed in his hope of being able to work there. Lovely Renton was still lovely Renton, but all the time he was there he was consumed with disquiet. He could not hear its voice. During the time he was there what was tingling in his nerves and pounding in his blood was the memory of the snatch of kitchen-talk that had been the source of all his unrest: Cajah's laugh, Sarah's low voice, the mother torturing him with the loose suggestions thrown out by her ribald tongue—these had returned to him, and now, instead of merely outraging the idealism in him, they fretted and inflamed the sensuality also. When they had been making game of the Welshman they had called him "quite a monster." Might not the suggestion of this have appealed to the perversity in Sarah, his Sarah, whom he had spared a hundred times from any violence or any suggestion of grossness, just because he had worshipped her and paid her almost divine honours in his inmost heart. His Sarah! No! not his Sarah! Any man's Sarah! More especially any beast's Sarah! In the agony of these thoughts he spent most of the day after his arrival in writing a letter to Patmore, in which he put this kitchen-scene, everything that had been done in it, everything that had been said in it, under the microscope. On the Saturday he could endure the thoughts that rushed in on him in the solitude of the place no longer. The breeze did not cool him; the blue sky did not allure his eye. In the stillness of the country he gazed only on her face, the only face that he had ever felt to have been turned on him in love—now altered, estranged from him not only by her will but by his own polluted thoughts of her, marble-pale, as if murdered by his evil thoughts of her. Before he had had time to hear from Bell what had happened the day before, he rushed back to Edinburgh, and arrived at the Bells' house late on the Saturday night, to have his anxieties at least relieved by hearing that his wife had taken the Oath. In the end she had taken it "manfully"—they said.

Even this does not seem to have allayed the torment he was inflicting on himself by turning over constantly in his mind every word of the conversation that had come nigh to turning his wits at the end of the previous year, that even now was working like madness in his brain. He went walking with the Bells on the Sunday, and Mrs. Bell told Mrs. Hazlitt afterwards that he talked so loudly and gesticulated so wildly that people stood still in the streets and looked after him as he passed, half-inclined to suspect him of being a madman. Especially he had seemed "quite enamoured" of a letter he had just been writing to Patmore, for he had kept fingering it and fondling it and pulling it out of his pocket as if he could not endure to have it out of his sight. He had done this twenty times if he had done it once, wanting to read snatches of it to them and have their opinion of it. This description may have been exaggerated, yet it would seem that Hazlitt must have been behaving for the third time in the course of these seven days of special strain as if his mind were beginning to slip its cable. The one thing he should have done with this letter, one of the most fantastic and piteous of all his outpourings, was to burn it, the moment the writing of it had relieved the pressure on his mind. He knew this himself, knew that what he had displayed in it was the sickness of his mind, and that he had displayed this sickness in the faint hope that his friend might help to heal it. A few days later he voiced this hope: "Oh! answer me, and save me, if possible, *for* her and *from* myself."

He was now up against another crisis. Until the Oath had been taken, he had never regarded his freedom as certain, for he had never felt sure his wife would keep her word to him. But the moment the dreaded Oath had been taken, he felt himself "virtually a free man"— for he had now only to await the passing of the sentence of divorce, in a few weeks' time. This forced him to face the future. And looking into it, he could not disguise from himself that despite the turn his relations with Sarah had taken, the only thing he still cared about was being in some measure of contact with her. If he could not have love, let there at least be friendship. Let them be dear friends to each other, if nothing more. In the earlier stages of his love, he had told himself that his bewilderment about her was the only thing he could not endure. He had, as we have seen, reasoned himself out of this bewilderment, not into peace, however, but into a kind of Hell. It may be thought that the only logical issue of his reasoning would have been that he should have set himself resolutely to put her out of his mind.

But logic could not determine the fluctuations of his passion. The truth is—even in his self-created Hell he was not firmly established. His reasoning faculty, which had led him to the conclusion that Sarah was a perverse and hypocritical young witch, had placed him there; but yet there were moments when the truth in him, operating at a deeper level than that of reason, or in other words, the intuition which was always strong in Hazlitt, told him that his reasoning, unassailable though it seemed, had some flaw in it. Well had it been for him if he had trusted more to such moments, for the reasoning faculty, to any one in such a pass as his, is of all guides the most deceptive, seeing that it can only operate upon evidence, and that evidence, in the complexity of human relationships, is of all things the most deceptive, for there may always be, and indeed there usually is, some piece of evidence concealed or unrevealed which if revealed would in an instant over-throw all the conclusions drawn from what had hitherto been revealed. That is to say, when it is applied to human relationships, it works from treacherous premises.

Hazlitt had reasoned closely from the evidence at his disposal. But the evidence at his disposal was incomplete. There was one thing which, had he known it, would have overthrown all the conclusions he had drawn from such imperfect evidence as he had been able to assemble. Sarah was so far from being the unnatural young witch he had reasoned himself into thinking her, that she had been behaving in the most natural and normal way in the world. In the summer of 1821 she had exchanged looks of liking with a young man then living across the street. This had led to a word or two of conversation between them, and in the end the man, who was none other than the Tomkins of whom Hazlitt had been jealous, had come over to live at 9 South-ampton Buildings. His coming had made no difference to her friend-ship with Hazlitt, which was unique in kind, until Hazlitt had first of all made himself troublesome to her, and had then behaved in a way likely to prejudice her chances of happiness.

These were slender enough at the best, for shortly after Hazlitt's departure, Tomkins, perhaps feeling himself getting so deeply en-tangled in his affections for Sarah that the only alternative would be seduction or marriage (neither of which he wished) if he kept on seeing her constantly, had left the house and gone to live elsewhere. Thus if the story which Sarah had told Hazlitt of her first love were true, it had to a certain extent repeated itself. It must have been sad enough for the girl, who had the grace to attract every now and again the men of rank superior to her own, on whom she attended, but who was finding that there were few to whom the situation in which she was placed was a recommendation, while her family was regarded by most men as a barrier which checked any thoughts they might otherwise have had of marriage with her.

Men who knew their own mind as completely as Robert Roscoe were not to be found every day. Sarah had not broken off her acquaint-ance with Tomkins as completely as she had broken it off with her first lover. She still saw him sometimes. It is easy to understand how distasteful it must have been to her, at a time when the new love which had come into her rather dreary life was frustrated but not yet quite hopeless, to feel that Hazlitt had talked about her so that she ran the risk of being regarded as what she called "a light character." It is easy to understand why, for all his probing, she guarded her secret. There was nothing she wished less than to have this all-but-hopeless love-affair torn to tatters, or at least endlessly analysed, as it certainly would have been by Hazlitt, or even blown upon by his thoughts about it. Her silence plunged him into limitless suffering. The truth, even if it had seemed cruel to him at the moment, would have helped him to regain his sanity. But Sarah dared not risk endangering her secret by revealing it to him. This explains the hardness she showed towards him on his return to London. He was behaving in a way which endangered her little all.

Moreover, his violence may even have caused her to fear for her own safety, or for that of the man she favoured, had she told the truth. It certainly justified some measure of fear, while her strong common sense told her that Hazlitt, who at the time was nothing if not "splenetic and rash," had also in him "something dangerous."

If Hazlitt had known of this entirely normal attachment, all his elaborate and fantastic reasoning would have tumbled down like a pack of cards. But he did not know. Thus his reasoning seemed to him final; but yet his intuition, which was the sum total of every impression that Sarah had made on his underconsciousness, now and again swept like a tide over the structure he had been rearing and washed it clean out of sight. Then he would find himself, after a long succession of rank thoughts had been plying in and out of his brain like worms, falling on his knees in contrition and torturing remorse, with a cry on his lips that was in a very real sense a prayer: "How could I ever have looked upon her little face and thought so of her!"

The crisis of his sensuality, although the memory of it still coloured all his thoughts about her, was now passed, and the yearning to have his idealism justified was again strong. Every thought of her was now a curious compound of suspicion and faith, sensuality and spirituality, love and hatred. There were moments when he would tell himself that although she would have made "the sweetest whore alive," he did not "stomach" the thought of her as a wife. There were moments when he longed to humiliate her: "I hate her for this that she refuses me. Oh! let me be free that I may *not* make her an offer." There were moments when he cried out: "Oh! that I knew she was a strumpet, and that she knew I did." There were moments when the only truth he knew was that he loved her: "I love her as I do my own soul, my heart is wedded to her, be she what she may, and I would not hesitate a moment between her and an angel from Heaven." His only hope of ever knowing a moment's peace seemed to him to depend on recon-ciliation with her. "My state is," he wrote, "that I feel I shall never lie down again at night nor rise up of a morning in peace, nor ever behold my little boy's face with pleasure, while I live,—unless I am restored to her favour;" or again: "I am choked, withered, dried up with chagrin, remorse, despair, from which I have not a moment's respite, day or night;" and again: "I cannot get rid of reflection. I have only that one subject of contemplation in time to come, and the thought stifles me. I cannot even seek relief from its pressure. The bond grows tighter instead of being lightened. . . . I have lost her, myself, Heaven, and am doomed to Hell." Well might he say: "The bond grows tighter." How tight it was, formed as it was of love and hate, of sensual memories and of spiritual aspirations, of resentment and tenderness, of pride and self-abasement, of rage and ruth, how tight it was, how close and how complex, less a bond than a cable against which the hurricanes of opposing passions might all beat in vain, the following confession will show:

"I am dead to all but the agony of what I have lost. She was my life—it is gone from me, and I am grown spectral. If it is a place I know, it reminds me of her, of the way in which my fond heart brooded over her. If it is a strange place, it is desolate, hateful, barren of all interest—for nothing touches me but what has a reference to her. There is only she in the world. . . . If the clock strikes, the sound jars me, for a million of hours will never bring peace to my breast. The light startles me, the darkness terrifies me—I seem falling into a pit, without a hand to help me. . . . Without any fault of mine but too much love, she has vanished from me, and I am left to wither. My heart is torn out of me, and every feeling for which I wished to live. It is like a dream, an enchantment—it torments me, and it makes me mad. I lie down with it, I rise up with it, and I see no chance of repose. I grasp at a shadow, I try to undo the past, or to make that mockery real, and weep with rage and pity over my own weakness and misery. . . . I had hopes. I had prospects to come, the flattery of something like fame, a pleasure in writing, health even would have come back with her smile.—She has blighted all, turned all to poison and drivelling tears. Yet the barbed arrow is in my heart—I can neither endure it nor draw it out, for with it flows my life's blood. . . . I had dwelt too long upon truth to trust myself with the immortal thoughts of love. *That S.W. might have been mine, and now never can*—these are the two sole propositions that for ever stare me in the face, and look ghastly in at my poor brain. I am in some sense proud that I can feel this dreadful passion—it makes me a kind of peer in the kingdom of love. . . . I would die, but her lover, my love of her, ought not to die. When I am dead, who will love her as I have done? If she should be in misfortune, who will comfort her? When she is old, who will look in her face and bless her?"

The outcome of all these fluctuations of feeling was that at last this poor Beast of ours, crying out that on his forehead alone was written the name "Rejected," burdened as he was both with immortal longings and with longings that were the reverse of immortal, although wholly human, crawled back to his Beauty, praying her that the load of his immortality and of his Beasthood might both be lifted from him, and that he might be made altogether man. Back to her he crawled, and once more

> "kist her wearie feet
> And lickt her lilly hands with fawning tong
> As he her wronged innocence did weet."

In other words, in spite of his great dread of a rebuff, of his greater dread of her annihilating silence, he wrote to her, confessing his faults, his unjust suspicions, the folly of the doubts and jealousies with which he had harassed and vexed her. The suspense in which he was locked made his letter very quiet: "Can you not forget and forgive the past, and judge of me by my conduct in future? Can you not take all my follies in the lump, and say like a good, honest girl, ' Well, I'll think no more of them?' In a word, may I come back, and try to behave better?"

In great tension and suspense he waited for her answer for days, until at last he realised that he might as well have cried to a statue. Anything the young frozen Sarah had to say to him now she would say in one way only—her chosen way of silence.

In his great restlessness he kept moving from place to place. On July 2nd he went out to Roslin. He was affected by the exquisite beauty of the scene, and as always, when he came on anything that appealed to the artist in him, by the longing to be looking at it in Sarah's company. The desire to lead her as his wife through all such scenes almost overwhelmed him. Then it seemed to him as if demons were determined to drive him beside himself, for the picture he had drawn to himself of the delight of passing through such scenes with an adored young wife on his arm was immediately succeeded by a distinct and vivid spectrum of Sarah sitting in the room which had been the scene of his happiness, and dallying with some foul and bloated lover. Again he was plunged into the sensualist's special Hell. Although he felt himself to be the victim of some devil's jest, he could not drive from his mind the scene it had conjured up, and the distortions of his polluted imagination continued to inflame him until at length they wrung from him the cry:

"Demoniacal possessions! I see the young witch seated in another's lap, twining her serpent's arms round him, her eyes glancing, and her cheeks on fire. Damn the unnatural hag. Oh! Oh! Why does not the hideous thought choke me?"

No matter what Hazlitt's condition was, he would always go where pictures were to be seen. On the Saturday he went out to Dalkeith House, to see the pictures of the Duke of Buccleuch. Mrs. Hazlitt, who had just returned to Edinburgh after a jaunt to Ireland, had chanced to visit Buccleuch House that same day. Just as she was leaving, she saw her husband drive up in a gig with his friend A. Henderston, who had once been their guest in London. As she was walking home, the two men passed her in their gig. It would have been natural if she had felt a pang at that moment. But she had no need to envy her husband as he drove past her. From the visit to Dalkeith House also Hazlitt had sucked torment. In one of the pictures, "Hope finding Fortune in the Sea," he had seen in the exquisite naked figure floating on the water a picture of Sarah. At the moment he felt as if it had driven him mad.

He was beginning by this time to loathe his rooms in Edinburgh and to feel that he had been "surrounded by demons" ever since he had entered into them. The succession of dreams he was having in them was in itself sufficient to make him associate them with pain. Not only was Sarah's face before him in the daytime. It was with him all the night too. The way in which she had turned it away from him in London had torn at his nerves. Now he dreamed of it perpetually averted from him. He would have in his sleep the most painful sense of bewilderment, would waken in the act of wondering why she had altered so in her demeanour to him. Then the full sense of his desolation would break in on him again. Or he would dream that she was lying beside him, yet not in any sweetness of companionship, but clay-cold and without a heart in her, as if the corpse of love were chilling him to the marrow. Or again, the movement with which she had repulsed his kiss would be the foundation of his dream. He would awaken just as her form was struggling away from him, or vanishing from him—filled with a sense of hopeless, endless sorrow. Yet if sometimes the night seemed longer to him than the day, and if the hours in which his mind could no longer protect itself seemed to him more terrible than the waking hours—when with the morning light there came the piercing sense of a loneliness that shore through his spirit like steel, he knew that his sleep could have for him no torment like the terrible mechanical renewal of a life that had become no life, but only a perpetual endurance of the gnawing of the worm.

Two days after his visit to Dalkeith House, on Monday, July 8th. all the life in him was renewed by a letter he received from Patmore. Hazlitt, who never could understand the depth of the resentment bred in Sarah by his way of discussing her feeling for him and her inscrutability, with other people, had asked Patmore to approach Robert Roscoe, with a view to sounding Sarah's brother-in-law as to her attitude towards the lover who had parted from her in such estrangement, but who longed only to return and throw himself at her feet. Roscoe, who regarded the affair between Hazlitt and Sarah as a most unfortunate one, refused to meddle in it, or to use his influence with Sarah either in the one direction or the other. Her decisions, he said, must rest entirely with herself. It seemed to him that Hazlitt's return to the house after what passed between them would place her in an awkward position, but he did not believe that she would oppose it, or that she would refuse to treat him as a friend if he returned. He believed her to be averse to marriage, but he would not go so far as to say that she might not be won. He thought the man who won her would be fortunate, for he regarded his sister-in-law as "one of the best girls in the world," and as one who would make the husband of her choice very happy. He added that he was the last man alive who should oppose "marrying for love," as he had done so himself, out of the same house, and had had reason to rejoice ever since at what he had done.

It may seem that there was very little encouragement in this for so desperate a lover as Hazlitt, but at least it did not altogether close the door of hope against him. What was special balm to him in it was the reassurance as to Sarah's character. He could bear far more easily to lose Sarah altogether than to believe that she was unworthy of the worship to which she had moved him. Magnifying now all his reasons for hope, even as he had just been magnifying all his reasons for despair, he wrote to Patmore in an almost boyish transport of renewed hope:

"My dear Patmore, I can only say that you have saved my life. If I make enemies with her now, I deserve to be hanged, drawn and quartered. She is an angel from heaven and you cannot pretend I ever said to the contrary! The little devil must have liked me from the first, or she could never have stood all these hurricanes without slipping her cable. What could she find in me? ' I have mistook my person all this while,' etc. Do you know I mean to be the very *ideal* of a lodger when I get back, and if ever I am married, and if I don't make her the best bedfellow in the world, call me *cut*. . . . I will have such a kiss when I get back as shall last me twenty years. Bless her. May God bless her for not utterly disowning and destroying me! . . . I have been thinking of her little face these last two days, looking like a marble statue, as cold, as fixed and graceful as ever statue did, and I could not believe the lies I told of her. . . . I'll never think of another woman, while she even thinks it worth her while to *refuse to have me*."

Nine days later Mrs. Hazlitt made her last appearance in the Court in connection with the business which had brought her to Edinburgh. In the course of her explorations of the city she had had the curiosity to visit James Street one day, and view the brothel which Hazlitt was said to have visited there. She had seen at the window "a woman of colour," with a white turban about her head. On Wednesday, July 17th, this same "woman of colour" was led up to her in one of the private rooms of the Court, was asked: "Do you know this lady?" and replied, "No, I do not." Shortly after this Mrs. Hazlitt heard from Ritchie that her business had been concluded. At two o'clock she called on Hazlitt, only to learn that he was out. At four o'clock she called again, and found him at dinner, but he asked her to stay to tea, and they fell into a long and curious talk in the course of which they compared notes as to much that had been said or done while they had been in Scotland. If it was not exactly an intimate talk, it was such a talk as could only have developed between two people who had long been intimate with each other, and who were still of friendly disposition towards each other, yet who had not a spark of either passion or tenderness towards each other left in them.

She had noted the female figure in the picture of "Hope meeting Fortune in the Sea," and had known that he would like it; and now she said to him that she never could understand how he could admire Sarah Walker's skinny form, that he had always liked plump figures, and that she thought the female figure in the picture at Dalkeith House would have been much more to his taste. To this he replied that it had been very much to his taste and also that he had thought it very like Sarah's. What had been in her mind was that it resembled her own, and she said as much to Hazlitt, pointing out especially the resemblance between "the thighs, the fall of the back" and the entire contour of the figure—and her own. Hazlitt said with indifferent politeness that undoubtedly she was "very well made," and promptly turned the conversation back to Sarah. She told him what Bell had said of the sickly sentimentality of Sarah's letters and he exclaimed indignantly: "What a lying son of a bitch!" She told him that Bell had suggested that Sarah was Patmore's cast-off mistress. Hazlitt said that that too was a downright lie. She told him that Bell had accused him of having spoken of her most abusively the night before she had taken the Oath of Calumny.

Hazlitt made no attempt whatsoever to deny this charge. He replied at once that what had happened was that he had gone to Bell's house, distracted by her threat of throwing up the whole business if he failed to send her money immediately, plagued by other things too, completely at the end of his tether, and that Mrs. Bell had suddenly fallen on him with accusations of using his wife ill, and of giving to the women of the town the money he owed his wife. He had answered that he knew nothing whatsoever about that, but in his intense irritation he had added that whatever he might be his wife was no better, that she had had her own intrigues and that she had been no maid when he married her. The complete candour of this seems to have discomposed Sarah Hazlitt not a whit. The detached friendliness of the terms on which she parted from Hazlitt is shown by the request he made to her, should she chance to visit him after he returned to Southampton Buildings, to show no discourtesy to Sarah. She told him that his passion for Sarah reminded her of "the frenzy" he had once been in about Sally Shepherd, to which he replied instantly: "Oh! that was but a fleabite, nothing at all to this." He went on to explain that Sarah had made him feel—and this was a thing no other woman had done—that she really loved him, and that it was this, and the winning softness and fondness of her manners, such as he had never seen in all his life before, that had ensnared him.

This was touching on a dangerous string, and it was followed by some wild and dangerous words. The remainder of what he said about Sarah, although reported in Mrs. Hazlitt's stolid prose, and in her stolid way, and although she apparently took it with her usual calm, leaves a frightful impression of nerves that had been so racked, jangled, and lacerated by suffering that any mention of Sarah might at any moment produce in them an almost maniacal excitement. He said that when he returned to London he was going to watch her closely and discover what her real character was; that perhaps he might in the end kill her and himself too; that his only regret with regard to her now was that he had not ravished her the first week he was in the house; that he was going to set out by mail that night though he felt as if he might be seized by illness and die on the road; that it was urgently necessary for him to get away from Edinburgh at all costs: above all, he must get out of the rooms in which he had been penned for almost five months. They had become a source of torment to him, for his state during most of the time he had been in them had been that of a man "surrounded by demons."

Perhaps he might kill her and himself too! We do not know what had happened in the meantime to obliterate the surging-up of renewed hope in him with regard to Sarah and to cause such a dangerous reversal of mood. It looks as though he had again begun to torture himself with the vision of her as a "young witch" coiling herself in serpentine embraces around some loathed and loathly lover, her cheeks flushed and her eyes on fire with the joy of her perverse sport. But no matter what had flashed through his mind to disturb it, does not such a violent reversal of mood show that his mind, constantly swinging from one dangerous extreme of feeling to another, has again begun to slip its cable? Only the day before what he had written to Patmore was: "if I once win her consent I shall kill her with kindness"—and when he had spoken of death, it had been of his own: "I wish much to see you, and John Hunt, and my little boy once more; and then, if she is not what she once was to me, I care not if I die that instant."

3 (7)

He has now reached the seventh and last station of his pilgrimage in "that domain which we call the Passions." He did not after all set out by the mail-coach that night, but at eight o'clock of the following morning, Thursday, July 18th, he set out on his return to fawn upon his cold and sullen love. By the beginning of the fourth week in July he was back in the place which he called "home." By the last day of the month his attempt at being "the very *ideal* of a lodger" had ended. It ended in desperate sadness for him, sadly enough for Sarah too.

On the night of his arrival he had to do without the kiss he had promised himself, the kiss that would have set him at peace with himself for twenty years, but he saw Sarah, and she gave him her hand in greeting gently enough. He noticed that she had altered somewhat in appearance: she was very pale; she had been ill; and a look of suffering still lingered about her. He loved her all the more for this, and began immediately to plan to make her life easier, suggesting to Mrs. Walker that he might take most of the rooms in the house at £100 a year, so that Sarah need no longer be everybody's slave, but might have a little time to herself, to get out into the fresh air, or to read or sew in the evenings. Her manner to him was not hostile as it had been at his last parting from her, but though courteous, it was evasive, guarded and cold. Nevertheless, his joy at seeing her again was great. All the time he had been at Edinburgh he had never been at peace. His pillow had seemed like flint to him. But now that he was back in the bed her hands had made, it seemed to him that again he slept on down. There was peace to him even in the thought that he lay again under the roof which sheltered her.

She continued to absent herself from his room, coming up to him only when attendance on him made her presence necessary. But on the third day he sought an interview with her. He saw her sitting on the window-seat of the front parlour, sewing, and now and again looking out into the street. So closely did he observe all her ways that this touched him with a faint surprise, for formerly her thoughts had been so much on what went on in the house that the street might not have existed for her. Her interests had been as narrow and confined as if she had been the denizen of a harem, and this excessive femininity had been one of the things he loved in her. He asked her if he might come in. She gave him no positive welcome, but as she made no positive objection, he entered, sat down beside her, and took her hand in his. Seeing that she suffered this caress, he began to talk to her, quietly and gently, and confining what he said to trivial things. His shirts were needing some new frills: would she see to them for him? "With the greatest pleasure!" Would she add to her kindness by seeing if she could get "the little image" mended? She was cool in her reply to this. It was broken in three pieces, she said, and the sword was gone, but if he wished it, she would try. Would she make up for herself the plaid silk he had sent her: he longed to see her in it, and she had said it would make a very pretty summer gown? She was cool about this too, saying that she had little time to spare at the moment, but perhaps she might. Hazlitt tried to suit his mood to hers, to speak to her peaceably and lightly and to subdue his desire to her will.

But presently, although it was evident that she wished her contacts with him to be formal, he could not resist the temptation of beginning to plead with her that she would receive him again into the relationship of friendship. At this the tears came into her eyes. She stood up and pressed her handkerchief to them. Sarah prided herself on having learned to control her feelings, but it is not difficult to see what was passing through her mind at the moment. Pressed beyond measure by the man whose intensity had wearied her, and towards whom her chief feeling was now one of fear, semi-deserted by the winsome lover towards whom her affection had turned, realising that the man she did not want was ready to risk everything for her, that the man she desired was ready to risk nothing at all, and forced by her position to keep silent about anything she endured from either of them—she must have been overwhelmed for a moment by the sadness of it all. For once in her reserved, equivocal life, she made no attempt to conceal her feeling. Taking her handkerchief away from her eyes she stood, as he pled his passion, with her head drooping, the tears trickling from her eyelashes, a most extraordinary expression of regret, pity, and stubborn resolution on her pale face, and without uttering a word. The expression seemed frozen on her soft features.

Hazlitt caught his breath at the exquisiteness of it. He described it afterwards as being "like a petrifaction of a human face in the softest moment of passion." The artist in him was hardly less moved by it than the lover. Carried away by its strangeness and beauty, and moved by it beyond measure, he told her that again and again he had prayed that he might just once more see that look on her face and then die. He entreated her to speak to him, but in vain. At length, saying merely that she must leave him, she floated away out of his sight with her own peculiar grace, or, as it seemed to him, with the movement less of a woman than of a spirit that was eluding him.

This was now characteristic of her. While she kept out of his quarters, if he came into hers, while not giving him a direct rebuff, she was consistent in quickly finding a pretext for leaving him in possession of them. Yet while she kept out of his sight as much as she could, she was punctilious in fulfilling all his requests. She completed the sewing he had asked her to do for him, and sent it up to him with an inquiry as to whether he wanted any more done. Personal contact alone she evaded. When he sent her a message an evening or two later that he wished to speak to her about some of his arrangements, she did not come. On the Saturday he complained about this to her mother, only to be told that at the moment his message had reached her daughter, Sarah had been dressing to go out to see about getting the little Buonaparte mended, that she had had some trouble about it, as it was so badly broken that no one was eager to undertake the task, but that she had at last found someone to do it, and it was to be brought home that evening. He was then in mingled contrition and delight, for although Sarah's manner had been cool, he persisted in elevating the Buonaparte into the symbol of the "tie" between them, the "tie" that had been broken, but which he hoped to re-establish once more. On the Monday morning she tapped at his door, and when he opened it to her she entered with the little statue in her hand, mended, although some new pieces had had to be put into it. He thanked her, and begged her to shake hands with him. She did so, and he continued to hold in his the only hand in the world he never wished to let go, for he always felt as if the touch of it restored him to peace, beseeching her with his eyes meanwhile, yielding too once more to the temptation to importune her with words: "Have pity on me! Have pity on me! and save me if you can!" To this she made no answer, but she looked him full in the eyes. Then she went "waving" towards the door, as she had done on the first time he had seen her, and as then, when she reached the door she turned round and looked him once more full in the eyes. For the last time in his life his gaze encountered the same long, strange, wondering look as that which she had given him the first day she had entered his room. Then she was gone.

In the evening, unable to rest without seeing her again, he said to her sister that if Sarah would come up to him he would be glad to settle with her for the expense to which she had been put over the Buonaparte: each time he saw her now he had more or less to devise some business pretext. Betsy told him that Sarah had gone out. At this the never-dying worm of suspicion in him reared its head. Formerly Sarah had never watched the street. Now she sat in the window and looked out. Three times in the course of the week, when he had wished to see her, he had been told that she was not in the house. Formerly she had seldom been away from it. She had always been at the beck and call of every one in it. One of the things which had made the place seem like home to him was that usually when he came back to it he could be sure of finding her. In this lay the secret of the charm the house had for him. Why did she now sit in the window that looked on to the street? Why was she always out in the evenings? He asked Betsy where her sister had gone.

"To my grandmother's, Sir."

"Where does your grandmother live now?"

"At Somers-Town."

With some vague idea in his head that he might meet her on her way back he set out for Somers-Town. Just as he had turned into King Street, he saw Sarah coming towards him. He noted how different she looked in the street. So diminutive was she, and so timid in her air, that she was quite eclipsed by the other women passing by. But to him she was Sarah, and he felt a curious pang at seeing her like that, as a stranger might see her, just a slight London girl, pale and rather fragile, with little to distinguish her from any other girl of the same class. Then as some people in front of him moved out of the way, he saw that she was not alone. Walking beside her was a tall, attractive-looking young man, whom at the first glance he did not recognise, but whom the next moment he recollected as the man he had once suspected of rivalling him in her favour. Sarah must have been as if petrified at this unexpected appearance of the lover she wished above all things to avoid, for she passed him without the slightest sign of recognition. He turned round and looked after her. She and her escort turned round at the same moment and looked back at him, and like people in a dream they moved towards him and he towards them, but again, as if stifled by the oppression of the moment, Sarah passed him without either word or sign.

Surely there must have been that in his expression which checked her impulse to try to retrieve and relieve the situation. Hazlitt went home almost choked by the turmoil of his feelings. He felt that there had been something unbearable in that strange passing. Unable to remain in his room, he sought the street again, and saw them both coming towards the door. As soon as he saw that Sarah's companion had parted from her at the door he re-entered the house, and requested an interview with her, sending her the assurance that he was in excellent temper and in good spirits, but saying at the same time that see her he must.

He kept himself well in hand during the interview, in which at last he drew from her the story of the way in which her acquaintance with his "rival" had sprung up and grown. She said that although Mr. Tomkins had thought it better for him to leave the house, as he was not in a position to offer her marriage, they saw no harm in meeting each other occasionally out of doors. Hazlitt told her that Robert Roscoe had not found it necessary to leave the house; that he himself, whose intentions were as honourable and serious as Roscoe's, had not found it necessary to leave the house; and said that he hoped he would not live to see her come to shame through an equivocal lover, after all his love of her. When he tried to put her on her guard against what might prove the corrupting influence of a lover who behaved thus, she thanked him coldly for his good advice and rose to leave him. He begged her to stay a little longer, as this might be the last time they might speak together, but silence fell between them: there seemed nothing more at the moment to do or to say, so presently he bade her Good-night, and asked her to kiss him for the last time. This she refused to do. As she left him, he felt deep grief, but no enmity towards her. She had liked another man better than himself. It was hard hap, but he must just bear it.

As for Sarah, she was no doubt glad to have escaped with her life. But she was not yet out of the wood. All the year her chief dread had been that her lover, through Hazlitt's indiscretions, or in consequence of some violent action bred of his jealous temper, might come to regard her as "light," just at a time when his love for her was warring with his prudence. Hazlitt's genuineness, which made it an emotional necessity for him to understand what had caused the alteration in her feeling for him, was as great a danger to her as the lack of discretion into which he had been betrayed by his suffering. What was best in him imperilled her slender chances of attaining her desire just as much as what was worst in him. Altogether, his temperament made him ruinous to her. Now the one thing she most dreaded came upon her. In the restlessness and dejection which followed upon his explanation with her, Hazlitt presently went out to roam the streets, and whom should he meet, for the third time that fateful night, as he was turning a corner, but her lover.

He spoke to him, and asked for a few minutes' conversation with him. This led to a long talk between the two men. For four hours they canvassed Sarah's relationship to each of them. Sarah, it seemed, for the three months preceding Hazlitt's departure for Scotland, had been in the habit of bringing up his rival's breakfast at an early hour, and of staying with him while he had it. Then she had come in with Hazlitt's tray and given him some of her society. Hazlitt had always risen at such a late hour that the one man had never claimed her attention while the other had had it. Now, as they compared notes, each of them was ready to rend her. Tomkins, listening to Hazlitt's disclosures, felt that the conduct of the girl he had been sorely tempted to marry, despite the dictates of prudence, had been "light."

As for Hazlitt, at the revelation of the favour that had been shown by Sarah to his "rival," the full violence of his suspicions rushed back upon him. In his anger he was quite incapable of doing her any justice. He ignored the extent to which his own passion, pathos, and persistent ardour, or even the attention paid by a man of some distinction and fame to an obscure maiden like Sarah, might reasonably have been expected, in the early days of their acquaintanceship, to have swept so young a girl off her feet, and the steadiness with which afterwards, when she had come to know her own mind, she had resisted his importunity. Ignoring also the light she had thrown on her reason for withdrawing her friendship from him, a withdrawal in which she had persisted since January of the year, he told himself that she had merely made him the victim of her moods, ceasing to write to him because she had been sulking over his "rival's" having left the house, keeping him in suspense while he had been away from her, treating him like something loathsome when he had returned to inquire the cause, showing no desire to shorten the pangs she was inflicting, but wishing his lingering torment to endure to the last moment. Was not this shown by her having pleased him in his tenderest point, by bringing him the beloved Buonaparte on the very day on which she was going out to see her favoured lover!

This last charge—that she had wished "to linger the affair on to the last moment"—seems to us peculiarly unjust. Sarah had done everything to discourage him, since the beginning of the year, except to tell him, with a directness and brutality that were not in her nature, that he had offended against the terms of his friendship with her and that she wished to see no more of him. If to have written to him in the coldest terms, to have discontinued writing to him very shortly after his departure, to have avoided seeing him on his first return, to have ignored his pleading for a renewal of their intimacy in the early summer, to have evaded personal contact with him in every way consistent with courtesy, on his second return, even to the point of finding some pretext for quitting her own room after he had entered it—could be construed into a desire to prolong the affair to the last moment, we know not what action on Sarah's part, if it were not to equal Hazlitt's own in violence, would have been accepted by him as a sure sign that she wished to break it off.

As for her concealment of a love-affair so uncertain in its issue that she did not wish it to be "blown-upon" in any way, was that very surprising, seeing that the moment Hazlitt knew of it he acted in a way that might have blown it out of existence? But we need not insist on this point, for the truth was—it would have been impossible for Sarah to content Hazlitt at this stage, because of the violent reversals of mood which from day to day were shattering him. In one mood he would worship her for an action for which in another mood he would hate her. On the Monday morning he had blessed her for bringing him the Buonaparte. She had not desired the blessing, for she had tried to make it clear to him that what she did for him was a matter of business. On the Monday evening he went to the other extreme, cursing it and denouncing it to the man she favoured as a last piece of duplicity. On Monday evening he had considered her cruel because she had refused him a parting kiss. Before he went to bed that night if she had granted him the kiss for which he had importuned her, he would have been cursing her yielding to his importunity as a crowning act of treachery. The first time he had returned to her Sarah had to some extent resisted him, and the result had been terrifying violence on his part. The second time she had tried to steer clear of his moods by making herself as negative as possible. Both attempts had ended in disaster. But each time she had been doing her best to check his passion; and to describe her conduct on either of these occasions as an attempt to play with it or prolong it was mere injustice. The worst that can be said of her is that she had not in the beginning realised the effect any display of affection and tenderness might have on a man as lonely and as passionate as Hazlitt; the best, that once she understood what she had done, having set her course, she held to it, timid as she was, despite all the hurricanes that blew on her. Of course, from first to last she had never understood Hazlitt; but who could blame her for this? To Hazlitt himself at times, his own personality seemed scarcely credible.

Although he could give her no justice, and although he could make no allowances for her youth, her inevitable limitations, her difficult circumstances, and her defenceless position, Hazlitt continued to give her love in abundance. That night he lay completely sleepless on the pillow which but seven days before had seemed to him of down. Not only his suffering, but his intuitions as to her personality, which continued to strive against his conscious thoughts of her, kept him restless. He could tell himself that she was worthless, yet every now and again his former worship would sweep over him and annihilate his baser thoughts of her. He still felt that were she a saint on earth, she could not have seemed more like one. His grief, his anger, his sense of loss, the discrepancy between his intuition and his reason, the conflict between his love and his hatred—all these gave him no peace. One thing alone he knew, that he had come to an end with Sarah, for even if he could have forgiven her her ways towards him, she would never forgive him for that night's work. "She is dead to me," he wrote to Sheridan Knowles in the course of the summer, "but what she once was to me, can never die! The agony, the conflict of hope and fear, of adoration and jealousy is over; or it would, ere long, have ended with my life. I am no more lifted now to Heaven, and then plunged in the abyss; but I seem to have been thrown from the top of a precipice, and to lie groveling, stunned, and stupefied. I am melancholy, lonesome, and weaker than a child. The worst is, I have no prospect of any alteration for the better: she has cut off all possibility of a reconcilement at any future period."

He had broken himself. If he had remained near Sarah he would have broken her too.

Now the time has come when we may well say of him:

"O! how he longs
To have his passport signed, and be dismissed!"

At Renton he had written with intense yearning of the peace of death. In the following months, as his fatigue and his distress had deepened, this yearning had deepened also. As he had trodden the green mountain turf he had longed again and again to be lying under it; as he had travelled by sea he had longed to find peace beneath the waters whose monotonous plaint had seemed to him to parody his own limitless suffering; as he now traverses the endless streets of London he wishes that his weary pilgrimage were over—for to go on seems to him like continuing in a dreary void. But every time he thinks of making an end of a life which, it seems to him, has come out on nothingness, the face of his little boy, seeking through the world for pity, and meeting only with contempt, comes between him and the water, the cup, or the knife. For him there is nothing to do but to go on. We see him setting out on his quest for other rooms, even while his mind is still falling to pieces, and while he is painfully conscious of its weakness. Once again he is a man without a home; the inability to control his thoughts which we first noted in him in the later months he spent in Edinburgh, becomes more and more marked; presently he finds himself babbling to this or that indifferent stranger about the grief within him that is like to overset his brain, as if he were drunk or in a delirium or in a fever. His distress is now laid bare for all the world to see. He knows himself that the looseness of his tongue is but a symptom of a far more deadly flux of the soul. Cursing himself for a fool, he foamed out his own shame to more or less indifferent people four times in the course of one day's wanderings. He spoke of his misery first of all to an acquaintance who had hailed him just as he was going into a coffee-house; in Regent's Park he met one of Montagu's sons, and when some chance word of concern or sympathy had been spoken, came out again with the tale of his woes; then he went on to Haydon, and finding Haydon out, made a confidant of old satyr-like Sammons, to whom every pretty girl was fair game, and to whom one pretty girl was much the same as another; last of all, he went to look at some apartments in Pimlico. The landlady chanced to say to him: "I am afraid you are not well, Sir," whereupon he replied: "No, Ma'am, I am not well," and on her inquiring further poured forth the whole story, yet once more, from beginning to end.

His friends were appalled at his condition. Haydon, who on the whole was as little qualified to understand the nature of his trouble as old Sammons, but who yet realised that the trouble was genuine, told Miss Mitford that he would "sink into idiotcy" if he could not bring his feeling to a crisis and purge himself of it. Procter felt about Hazlitt's distraction much as Ophelia had felt about Hamlet's. The burden of his lament is:

"O! what a noble mind is here o'erthrown!"

He too did not hesitate to pronounce Hazlitt's love for Sarah "an insane passion." After speaking of the way in which it had entirely subdued Hazlitt's intellect, he wrote:

"He was, for a time, unable to think or talk of anything else. He abandoned criticism and books as idle matters; and fatigued every person whom he met by expressions of his love, of her deceit, and of his own vehement disappointment. . . . To this girl he gave all his valuable time, all his wealthy thoughts, and all the loving frenzy of his heart. For a time, I think that on this point he was substantially insane."

Procter's words are loving, although he too understood nothing of the nature of the frenzy he lamented. On the other hand, Crabius registers stern disapproval of our "murdered" man, as Hazlitt claimed himself to be, or our self-murdered, certainly our all but sunken man; and *the little Crabs all bark* at him. By November good Crabius is able to report satisfactory progress in the process of social punishment:

"I was not sorry to find from Mrs. Montagu that she views Hazlitt as I do, and I infer from what she said that he no longer visits the house. I hope to hear this confirmed. She intimates that Lamb has broken with him."

It would seem that Crabius would not have been sorry to see the man he had once called friend made derelict, or all but derelict. If this were so, his desire was not far from being gratified. Separated from his friends by an experience which few of them could understand, although, in view of his development, it had lain in wait for him all his life, with which few of them could in any measure sympathise, and which all of them deplored, and separated at the same time from the ordinary interests of life by the sickness of mind which made all things nullity to him except his passion, Hazlitt was now in danger of becoming himself a nullity. He had fallen very low, was, in fact, nearing the bottom of the pit he had dug for himself, of which life had long been preparing for him. It is not his way to remain still. No doubt when he reaches the bottom of the pit he will begin to struggle upwards again. But in the meantime, a child or a dog may sense his trouble. As he seizes on this friend or that, and pours forth his story in Ancient-mariner fashion, like one acting under some overwhelming necessity to relate the strangeness of the experience through which he has passed, his mouth works convulsively and his face "twitches all sorts of ways."

Chapter Two

THE RECOVERY (1822-1825)

"The lines of his countenance are regular, but bear evident marks of late and intense application; and there was an habitual melancholy in the expression, as though he had been chewing the cud of past miseries, or brooding on bitter anticipations of the future. His figure was emaciated; and it is evident his mind has preyed upon and consumed much of the vital energies of his frame; and this last, as was said of Shelley, seemed only a tenement for spirit."

MEDWIN.

1 (1)

HAZLITT had told his wife, the day he met her at Dalkeith House, that he meant to go to Winterslow, at the conclusion of the business connected with the divorce, and that if he did so he would take his son with him, as he wished to have the child with him for a little, perhaps until the Christmas holidays, when William could return to school: and that he might go to Devonshire, to his mother's, for a short time. So much for his intentions! As to what he did—our only evidence in the course of the autumn is from the work which now begins to appear again from his pen, after a silence that had lasted since May.

This silence was first broken by an article on Fonthill which appeared in the November *London*. Beckford's famous retreat, which had long been hermetically sealed, as far as the public was concerned, was now thrown open. We might perhaps gather from the appearance of the article at this time that Hazlitt had availed himself of the opportunity of visiting Fonthill from Winterslow. The remainder of his work seems rather to indicate residence in town. In the first mild days of November he went out to see the Dulwich Gallery, which now contained many of the pictures on which he had loved to gaze in his youth, when he had been privileged to visit them in the Desenfans collection. His account of this autumn excursion leaves on the mind a gentle impression both of his sympathy for the "little urchins," the sight of whom at Dulwich College brought memories of his own boyhood thronging thick and fast upon him, and of Dulwich itself before the town had encroached upon it, and its cedar-flanked road. His article, *Mr. Angerstein's Collection*, suggests that he must have visited this collection of pictures at 100 Pall Mall, immediately before writing it. About the same time he visited Cleveland House. In this, the Marquis of Stafford's Gallery, some of the pictures also renewed his memories of the days when life had been young with him.

As we follow him from one to another of the London galleries in the closing months of the year, it is possible for us to see whither he is tending. He is very sick of mind; but to a certain extent he realises the nature of his own sickness. He had for some time been cut off from all the sources of his strength. He had been living, not on his strength, but on his weakness, or on the fever in his nerves. He is now trying to find his way back to the sources of his strength. For him the primary source of strength and of healing was Nature. Very close to it came his love of Art; and close to that his love of literature. He finds his way back to them one by one. His article on the Angerstein collection shows that he is conscious of the extent to which Art can be a balm for "hurt minds," and a cure "for low-thoughted cares and uneasy passions." In his article on the pictures in Cleveland House he is yet more explicit:

"Our intercourse with the dead is better than our intercourse with the living. There are only three pleasures in life, pure and lasting, and all derived from inanimate things—books, pictures, and the love of nature."

There follows a piece of profound analysis on the unchangeable nature of the happiness that arises out of these:

"Marina in *Pericles* complains that ' Life is as a storm hurrying her from her friends!' Not so from the friends above-mentioned. If we but bring an eye, an understanding, and a heart to them, we find them always with us, always the same. The change, if there is one, is in us, not in them. Oh! thou then, whoever thou art, that dost seek happiness in thyself, independent of others, not subject to caprice, not mocked by insult, not snatched away by ruthless hands, over which Time has no power, and that Death alone cancels, seek it (if thou art wise) in books, in pictures, and the face of nature, for these alone we may count upon as friends for life! While we are true to ourselves, they will not be faithless to us. While we remember any thing, we cannot forget them. As long as we have a wish for pleasure, we may find it here; for it depends only on our love for them, and not on theirs for us."

He had almost reached the bottom of the pit. Now he is climbing, but

"long is the way
And hard!"

I (2)

It was probably sheer necessity that drove him back to writing, while his feeling that there was solace in art determined the immediate nature of his writing. In February his money difficulties caught·up with him. This is not surprising. Since March of the previous year he had written very little. Between May, when a short article of his had appeared in the *London*, and November, when his article on Fonthill had appeared, nothing from his pen had been published in any of the periodicals. On February 12th he was arrested for debt. His recovery of the power to write had not been quick enough to enable him to keep the wolf from the door. In this distress he turned for help to the practical resourceful Talfourd. There is something forlorn and helpless about his letter: "I have been arrested for debt this morning, and am at a loss what to do. Would you give me a call to talk the matter over, and see if your influence could procure me any terms of accommodation? I am sorry to plague you about my troublesome affairs." Talfourd's intervention seems to have been effective, for Hazlitt was presently free once more—but this incident, showing him very clearly what would be his fate should he ever let his pen flag, made a lasting impression of pain on him.

I (3)

The financial break-down in February was succeeded by a bad spiritual break-down in the beginning of March. At the close of 1822 it looked as if he were beginning to find his way back to the sources of his strength, and to begin the slow and difficult ascent from the hell into which he had fallen. In this month he fell back again right to the very bottom of the pit. His sickness of mind may be judged from a fragment of a Diary extending over some twelve days in March, from the first Tuesday of the month to the third Sunday. Few pieces of confessional literature make more painful reading. While in Scotland, when tormented by the constant conflict between his intuition and his reason, he had more than once wished that he could get one of his acquaintances to live for a time at 9 Southampton Buildings, and put Sarah's virtue to the proof, an "experiment on character" which, as we saw, he had never made himself throughout the days he had wooed her, because of the strong element of worship in his love for her, and for having desisted from which he blamed himself in his darker moods as for a pitiful folly. In March, 1823, he was again haunted by the idea that if only he could get sufficient evidence to prove that Sarah was "light," he could cure himself of his passion for her, again exalted by the feeling that if only he could get

sufficient evidence to prove that Sarah was all he had thought her, he
could perhaps find peace in the memory of his worship, while all the
time he was racked between two moods, sometimes eager to think her
the one, so that he could burn her out of his thoughts, sometimes
yearning above everything else to find her the other, so that he might
preserve the memory of his ideal.

In the beginning of March one of his acquaintances, referred to in
the Diary as "F.", actually went to live in the house, and, if he did not
get the length of attempting to seduce Sarah, certainly pursued her
with uncommon briskness. Hazlitt's Diary is a kind of commentary
on all F.'s dealings with Sarah during the first two weeks of his
residence there. Each word or look of Sarah, each little thing she does
or even omits to do, is examined through the powerful lens of passion.
There is nothing too trivial to interest him. The things he notes of her,
half in a rapture and half in a rage, show a mortal heart-hunger.
There is very little that F. can tell him of what he wants to know, but
yet even the least pieces of information are to him as precious as drops
of water to a man parching in a desert—what she does, what she says,
how she looks, what she wears, especially if it be something he has
given her, although he is always divided in feeling as to what he hears.
It is better to him to hear that she laughs and chats as usual, than to
hear nothing at all, even although it angers him to know that her
life goes on as usual, while his is broken. "And so she cackled on with
her new gallant," he writes after a conversation she had had with F.,
"and I in hell for this grinning, chattering idiot." Or again: "Damn'd,
treble damn'd idiot! when shall I burn her out of my thoughts"—he
cries, only to follow up the angry outburst with the extreme pathos
of the words: "yet I like to hear about her—that she had her bed-gown
or her ruff on, or that she stood or sat, or made some insipid remark.
. . . Were I in Hell, my only consolation would be to hear of her. In
Heaven to see her would be my only comfort." To hear anything at all
of her was like a boon from Heaven to him, although he extracted
much bitterness from almost all he heard. To know that she was a
wanton, or an idiot, was better than never to hear anything at all. The
complete silence of the past eight months had come near to breaking
him.

Hazlitt's extreme longing to have news of her probably accounted
as much as anything for F.'s residence in Sarah's house. But the Diary
reveals an intense and inflamed suspicion no less than it does an intense
and inflamed longing. Through F.'s prejudiced accounts, prejudiced
because he had gone to the place with some crude idea that she was a
wanton, and Hazlitt's dissections and embroideries on them, we can
see Sarah clearly enough, although always she says little for herself,
still gentle and equivocal, never inviting familiarity, but sometimes,
when she cannot rebuff it without giving offence, suffering it more

tamely than she would have done if she were entirely a free agent; better at eluding than at resisting the impertinences to which her position exposed her; on the whole picking her way as delicately as circumstances permit, among the appetites, of various kinds, of the various men she serves; detached in her thoughts from much that comes her way; and in the last resort, although gentle, inflexible: there is a point beyond which no man alive can intrude upon her reserve.

But Hazlitt sees everything through the microscope of his own morbid suspicion. When Sarah, coming into the back-parlour when F. is there, throws her bonnet and shawl on a chair empty except for his coat which happens to be lying on it, Hazlitt finds some amorous suggestion in the action: "This is her first move, this putting these little matters together and mingling persons by proxy." Surely such a thought is eloquent not only of the extreme laceration of his mind, but also of the extent to which it was becoming poisoned by suffering. It is clear that although now and again he is still moved by her on the other side idolatry, the suspicions with which he is riven make him less than ever capable of giving her justice. She can hardly utter a word into which he cannot read sexual invitation. When F. asks her if she likes going to the play, she tells him that she cares little for comedy, but is fond of tragedy. She says also that she has not been to Drury Lane. Hazlitt's comment is: "This was a hint that she should like to go. We shall see." But when a few days afterwards F. invited her to go to the play with him some time, she told him that she was afraid her mother would object to her going with a stranger. This was not enough for the enterprising F. He renewed his invitation, and then he was met with a direct refusal. Sarah told him at the same time when he asked her if she never went out, that she did so very seldom, and then only to see her sister. These things might seem conclusive evidence as to the injustice of the suspicion with which Hazlitt had tormented himself, yet we find in his Diary no sign that he either recognised or repented his injustice.

The more F. saw of her, the less certain he felt of his ground with her. His crude attempts at forcing more or less amorous or erotic conversation on her had even less success than his attempts at making love, for they were baffled by her colourless or non-committal or even childish replies. Sometimes he thought her a fool, and was ready to swear that her reserve was affected to conceal a lack of intelligence. Sometimes he was not sure that he himself was not the one who was being fooled. She gave neither herself nor others away. He could never succeed, for all his efforts, into drawing her into saying anything indiscreet about Hazlitt, or into any betrayal of Hazlitt's passion for her, while the only one of his friends she mentioned was Procter, who, she said, had "very gentle and pleasing manners." He came to feel that although the position she occupied was not dignified, she herself had some kind of dignity. He was staggered, when she showed him one day Procter's lines, the ones which Hazlitt called "the description of her," by the completeness with which they expressed her personality, as it might appear to one whose mind had not been prejudiced against her in advance. As he looked from the gentle lines to the gentle girl, he could hardly believe his eyes, so exquisitely fitted were they to her fawn-like grace. At length he reported uneasily to Hazlitt that he thought "it would be impossible to offer her rudeness," unless she were to do or say something which positively invited it. Hazlitt's heart sang within him at this, and his thoughts went back to the lines:

"We do it wrong, being so majestical
To offer it the show of violence."

Who knew better than he the feeling of rebuke that something in Sarah could communicate to any one who offered her "the show of violence," who offended against her reserve even with the thought of violence? He had often experienced this tacit rebuke himself, and Sarah's power to communicate it was one of the things he loved most about her, much as he loved Vandyke's portrait of Lady Venetia Digby, with its dove-like innocence and softness, its delicacy, its touch of sadness, because he felt that with such a portrait hanging in the room, "it would be impossible to perform an unbecoming action."

Notwithstanding F.'s scruples, when she came up to his room a few evenings later, to pull down the curtains, he took her in his arms and kissed her. Saying quietly: "Let me go, Sir," she moved to the doorway, from which she asked him tonelessly whether he required his fire to be lighted that night. He felt that her coolness rebuffed him, although she uttered no rebuke or word of complaint. Hazlitt's Diary ends with an entry describing something which took place the following day, when Sarah was at last driven to a rebuke which was downright enough, and only all the more characteristic of her because it was mute. F., "in despair" at her elusiveness, to his delight met her out of doors, on the evening of the third Sunday in March, walking along Lincoln's-Inn Fields by herself in the dusk, small and timid-looking, her little hands in her muff. He followed her and asked if he might accompany her. Quite definitely she refused the offer of his escort. He made as if to take her arm, whereupon Sarah stood quite still, and looked at him.

We see her at this moment more clearly than at any other, except the moment when Hazlitt had importuned her with his love, at a time when it had been only a distress to her to hear his protestations, and when she had stood still for a moment "with the tears trickling from her eye-lashes, her head stooping, her attitude fixed, with the finest expression that ever was seen of mixed regret, pity, and stubborn resolution"—as she stood there in the dusk with her hands in her muff, without speaking a word, but with her soft pale face again hardening into "stubborn resolution." F. felt suddenly that he had behaved like a ruffian in trying to force himself upon her, and in that moment he gave up the chase. Hastily saying that he would press his company on her no further, he held out his hand to her, by way of showing her that he had not meant to behave offensively. She did not refuse this gesture of reconciliation, and after he had shaken hands with her he left her to continue on her way alone. His sense of dismissal was definite, although she had not uttered a word.

Hazlitt was much moved when he heard of this incident. He felt it to be entirely characteristic of all he most loved in Sarah. He could see her very clearly, standing "stock-still," immovable, inflexible, "*like herself*." It gave him a sharp pang, because he felt sure she must have been going to meet the lover she had preferred to himself, and that this had stiffened her into direct resistance of his friend's importunity. Yet he felt a strange pride, both in the firmness she had displayed towards F., and in her faithfulness to the lover of her choice. He had not been altogether wrong about her. Sarah might not be a saint, nor an angel of constancy, but there was some indefinable quality about her that might justify any man's passion, and for him there was some peace in knowing that her love, after all, had some quality in it. His curious morbid vivisection of her ways, looks, words, and personality ends on a note of homage: "I also am her lover, and will live and die for her only, since she can be true to any one."

In this piteous experiment, as in many other things he did in passion, he acted not according to the health of his mind, but according to the measure of its sickness. Yet it is more difficult to understand this treachery against what he himself would have called the *religion* of love, than the publication by him in May of the year of *Liber Amoris*, the book in which he left some record of his frenzy. There are one or two things in connection with the publication of this which, in justice to Hazlitt, should be remembered. The book was published anonymously; it was couched in the form of fiction, purporting to be the record of a passion experienced by a Scot, self-exiled from his own country because he had aroused political enmity and because he had contracted an unhappy marriage; and it was thus supposed to appeal, as an isolated piece of human experience, honestly presented, to the impersonal sympathy or interest of its readers. That its authorship was made a matter of public scandal, and that it was made to seem like a betrayal of a human relationship, was the consequence of the political enmities Hazlitt had aroused, and especially of the hostility of *Blackwood's* and *John Bull*. There is a confusion of thought in regarding Hazlitt, who was of all men the one most deeply wounded by the activities of these, and such as these, as the author of the exposure of which he was the chief victim. As there was nothing showy or derivative in his passion, there was on his part no desire to extend his egoism or his sense of power through the publication of a record of it. Such appearance of knavery as has been given to him in this matter is partly the consequence of the unscrupulousness of his enemies, partly the consequence of his own guileless and passionate sincerity.

These things, which are sometimes forgotten, should be recalled, but it is not on these that we base our explanation of the forces which drove Hazlitt into taking this desperate step, drove him, that is to say, towards the very brink of the precipice he had long been nearing, and over. We base our explanation of this step, defence of it we attempt as little as we attempt criticism of it, rather on what we know of his nature, and on the one indication he has given as to the reason for the action which inflicted on him more self-wounding than he had ever inflicted on himself before, and far more wounding than any of his enemies had ever been able to inflict on him. First of all, we have to remember the extent to which he was driven by his necessity to bring feeling of any kind to a crisis, and the extent to which he had felt stifled because of his inability to bring his passion to any kind of crisis. Not for nothing had he cried: "I am pent up in burning, impotent desires, which can find no outlet." His friends had noted the agony this frustration had caused him, had felt that if he could not "ease his soul" of the burden of feeling it carried his reason might give way. The publication of the book of his love was not a natural crisis, yet some kind of crisis it was. Only Hazlitt knew the extent to which it was necessary to the preservation of his intellect to gain some relief of this kind.

Then he may have been driven by his sense of truth. There are certain overwhelming frustrations, like certain overwhelming fears, which threaten to overturn the brain if they are not met. In the expression of them a half-mastery over them is achieved. What he had experienced was to him a portion of truth, and he was always driven by an almost impersonal necessity to express truth.

He had also evidently the sense that the whole matter had something of the nature of miracle in it. Sarah, so completely had his life and his experience fitted him to feel at the first sight of her that through her he could attain the fulfilment of his manhood, had made for him a new earth, a new Heaven, and a new hell. In each of these phases of experience he had some sense that his life was being wrought upon by something like miracle. Both the nature of the feeling that had come to him in his middle years, and the gradual realisation that feeling of such intensity could awaken no response, had given him the sense that he had in some measure looked below the surface of life, and seen the Hand that moves in the darkness of things conditioning human destiny and weaving the intricate pattern of life which not one tear nor prayer nor sigh of man can alter by a jot. A glimpse of such a thing is like a vision. It is readily understandable that one who was *par excellence* a writer could have no peace until he had attempted to express what he had seen.

And fourthly, he was partly the victim of the creative impulse, to which, once it is aroused, all the other instincts of man must give way. In writing down, innocently enough, at Stamford, to beguile his own loneliness, the conversations he had had with Sarah, he had, unwittingly, called into being something with the spark of life in it, and he had to let it develop its life. No man who has created is henceforth his own master.

All these things, we believe, acted upon him, he being what he was, tossing him now this way and now that, finding him sometimes resisting their pressure, sometimes yielding to it. God knows what struggles he must have gone through before he decided to put his book to the proof, how often he agonised over it, between September, 1822, the month in which he had first thought of putting it together, and May, 1823, when it made its appearance! God knows the extent to which during these months he was racked by mental torments! God knows how often in one mood he thought it a glory, how often in another mood he was ready to throw himself over every bridge he came to at the thought that any other eye than his own should see it! In the end, he ventured it, and took in his own breast the brunt of it. Probably what moved him most of all was the feeling that in not venturing it there was a lack of mental courage.

As we say that we believe all these things may have acted on him, we say at the same time that we believe the only things which had no influence whatsoever on his decision are those which have been imputed to him by certain critics who have talked about his experience with as much insight as a colour-blind man might show who took upon himself to discourse of pictures. Exhibitionism certainly had nothing to do with the publication of this work; neither had the desire to make money.

Hazlitt himself, having done the deed, preserved the fortress of his silence both as to what he had done and what he had suffered in the doing of it. To us it seems as if he gave only one direct indication as to the nature of the impulses that moved him. It may seem fantastic; but there it is—one more of the things which show him to have been in many ways "a species by himself." In one of his letters to Sheridan Knowles, published in the *Liber Amoris*, he wrote: "How then do I console myself for the loss of her? Shall I tell you, but you will not mention it again? I am foolish enough to believe that she and I, in spite of everything, shall be sitting together over a sea-coal fire, a comfortable good old couple, twenty years hence!" This is the heart of his fantasy. Cut off from all communication with Sarah, he went out, as it was his nature to do, on the forlorn hope that if he could make her understand, by the publication of this book, which he believed to be in cipher for the rest of the world, the nature of his love, its heights and its depths, its exaltations and its abasements, its passion and its tenderness, its dignity and its child-like dependence on her—he could win back at least the friendship he had lost, could be near her throughout her life and his, could "look in her face and bless her" when she was old. In this hope there was a touch of madness. Yet there was something sublime in the madness. *Sine dementia nullus Phoebus!*

In another way, too, the publication of this book showed something like madness. It put his peculiar vulnerability at the mercy of his enemies, who at the time were particularly virulent. Wilson, now not only "the slinking Leopard" of *Blackwood's* or "Jack-all of the North," but Professor of Moral Philosophy in the University of Edinburgh, had attacked him in the March number of *Blackwood's*, in a farrago of gutter insult, entitled *On the Scotch Character, by a Flunky*. One of the first essays Hazlitt had published during this year had been *On the Scotch Character*, which had appeared in January in Byron's and Leigh Hunt's joint venture, *The Liberal*. For any Scot to attack this article, which was caustic in the extreme, was not only legitimate, but natural. But for the nature of the mud-slinging by "the Jack-all of the North" or "the sycophantic ruffian," as royal Landor preferred to call John Wilson; for the abuse of a man noted for independence and integrity as a kind of flunkey or valet, because Hazlitt had associated himself with Lord Byron's venture; for the series of questions in it, carefully avoiding statements of fact, but systematically insinuating untruth of a kind designed to humiliate and discredit; and above all, for the attack on old Mr. Hazlitt's memory, there could be no excuse: "Was not your own father an Irish tailor? Did you ever hear him soften down his brogue into a natural gentility of expression? never—never."

Hazlitt had been angered into threatening an action for damages against the London publishers of the magazine. It was therefore no moment for him to publish a book which even if it defied "the world and its dread laugh" yet exposed him to the hoofs of every ass in the kingdom, as well as to the onrush of many animals who had not even the excuse of asininity. For Hazlitt to expose himself thus at such a moment to the enemies his courage, skill and daring in controversy, and his political integrity pushed almost to the point of fanaticism, had gathered against him, had in it some of the violent impulse that leads towards suicide. Indeed it was a kind of suicide. We can only take it that the perpetual torturing movement of his passion had by this time swept him into something like indifference towards self-preservation. Kite, crow and raven might batten on his entrails if they liked. The Scorpion might sting and the Leopard rake him with his "plouthering" paws. He cared not. He was far beyond the caring.

The suffering he had undergone had already almost made worms'-meat of him. Let the man-breakers and the carrion-makers gather to their filthy banquet.

I (4)

Gather they did, and promptly, not only personal enemies, but all who at the time were going almost "black in the face" at the formidable conjunction of Hazlitt and Byron, not to speak of Leigh Hunt, in *The Liberal*, and seeking to discredit that ill-starred but brilliant venture through the indiscretions of the most ill-starred but not the least brilliant of its contributors. In May "lean" Jerdan of *The Literary Gazette* led the public on to hiss; throughout June Theodore Hook, who had already earned the name of "Humbug" Theodore, led the man-hunt in the South, disclosing the identity of the author, accusing Hazlitt of having puffed his own book in *The Times*, which had behaved well in respecting his anonymity, stigmatising him as "a disappointed dotard and an impotent sensualist," and publishing in *John Bull* on the 23rd, for all the world to see, the full text of the love-letter sent from Renton to Sarah, in which he had cried: "Do not mock me, for I am a very child in love." At the close of the month, the "Jack-all" takes up the hue and cry in the North. Not content with fouling the book with the flow of squalid bile which passes with him for literary criticism, he calls down "the scorn and loathing of every thing that bears the name of Man" on the "COCKNEY" and the "L-I-B-E-R-A-L" who because "Sally will not have him after all" has insulted the susceptibilities of every one who had the least "notion" of what "virtue," "honour," "manliness," and "love" mean. The "Jack-all," in fact, is outraged. Nothing as shocking as this, out-Rousseauing Rousseau, has hitherto had the tactlessness to fall in his stainless way.

To yet one more of the voices of the time we would listen, not because it utters the "Out! vile jelly!" with which the coarse thumb and finger of *Blackwood's* ever sought to put out the eye of all that had emotional integrity in the literature of that generation, but because, although perfectly honest and genuine, it is typical of the attitude of all those who, having never learned what Hazlitt had consistently tried to teach his generation, that "men act from passion, and one can only judge of passion by sympathy" discourse of experience like his with as much insight as a colour-blind man might show were he to speak of colours. On the day on which *John Bull* published the love-letter which by God knows what treachery, begging, buying, or stealing had come into its hands, Crabius caught up with the scandal, gulped down the book, as he gulped down everything of Hazlitt's that came his way, and recorded his impressions as follows: "Finished early Hazlitt's disgusting *New Pygmalion*.[333(a)] One can tolerate the passion of a St. Preux or a Werther, as it is set off by the eloquence of a Rousseau or a Goethe, but such a story as this is nauseous and revolting. . . . It ought to exclude the author from all decent society. He has been exposed in *John Bull*, and I should think will feel the effects of his exposure in being slighted by many who tolerated him before."

The chief criticism that can be made of *Liber Amoris* is that it did not achieve what it set out to give to the world, a record of a love-frenzy that had complete emotional integrity. Hazlitt could not give the truth in its entirety, for in the churning up of his mind by agony he had said things of Sarah which it was impossible for him to print. Much in his letters which makes the movement of his feeling intelligible, especially the fearful boiling-up of retrospective sensuality, is omitted, and therefore the book gives but a clouded, interrupted and fitful impression of the tidal wave of feeling of which it was meant to be a record. Much is altered. Thus for the raw cry of tortured sensuality of July 8th, 1822: "I saw a picture of her naked figure the other day at Dalkeith Palace, . . . and it drove me mad," we get something that is turned into a compliment or into a eulogy of Sarah's incomparable grace. There is all the difference in the world between the tone and temper of the two passages. Such alterations flaw in some measure the integrity of the work.

In the meantime, while *Liber Amoris* was drawing all eyes to it, and causing all tongues to wag, there slipped out from the press, almost unnoticed, the book which was flawless in its integrity. This is the little volume entitled *Characteristics*, which also appeared anonymously. In it Hazlitt released the bitter-sweet essence, of good and evil, he had distilled from the experience through which he had passed. What he says on the intertwining of hatred with love, a theme on which his own appalling explosions of hatred had forced him to meditate, is profound, as is also his meditation on the relationship of love to the merits of the beloved. From the theme of disappointment he passed on to the theme of what love can mean to a life that has known it:

"When we hear complaints of the wretchedness or vanity of human life, the proper answer to them would be that there is hardly any one who at some time or other *has not been in love*. If we consider the high abstraction of this feeling, its depth, its purity, its voluptuous refinement, even in the meanest breast, how sacred and how sweet it is, this alone may reconcile us to the lot of humanity."

We would say that this was the conclusion of the whole matter, were it not that he passes on from it to make his confession as to what he feels to be "the religion of love." Even when his passion had been at its most feverish, he had been feeling his way out towards the conception of this. Now he writes:

"It makes us proud when our love of a mistress is returned: it ought to make us prouder that we can love her for herself alone, without the aid of any selfish reflection. This is the religion of love."

What he says in this volume on friendship is bitter. He evidently felt to the full the isolation which the universal disapproval of his conduct had brought on him. In one paragraph he writes: "It is hard to praise those who are dispraised by others. He is little short of a hero, who perseveres in thinking well of a friend who has become a butt for slander, or a bye-word." In the following one he continues:

"However we may flatter ourselves to the contrary, our friends think no higher of us than the world do. They see us with the jaundiced or distrustful eyes of others. They may know better, but their feelings are governed by popular prejudice. Nay, they are more shy of us (when under a cloud) than even strangers; for we involve them in a common disgrace, or compel them to embroil themselves in continual quarrels and disputes in our defence."

Such entries leave no doubt as to the extent of the wounding that came to him. He had dared the publication of *Liber Amoris*, because he had to act according to the law of his nature, but the suffering that came to him in the months that followed was probably greater than he had anticipated. Sometimes it seemed to him greater than he could bear. A prisoner, convicted of some desperate offence, and waiting "for the parting of soul and body as a timely release from its own reflections, and the general enmity of the community," could not have suffered more from the consciousness of "falling in pieces for want of support from the fellow-feeling of a single fellow-creature." In the middle of July when he asked Thomas Hood to explain for him to Taylor why he had not written a promised article for the *London* on the pictures at Petworth, he wrote from Winterslow: "something happened which hurt my mind, and prevented my going to Petworth. I had only the heart to come down here, and see my little boy." This letter shows his continued absorption in Sarah: "I used to think she read and perhaps approved these articles. But whatever I can do, implying an idea of taste or elegance, only makes me more odious to myself, and tantalises me with feelings which I can never hope to excite in others— wretch that I am, and am to be, till I am nothing."

The sense that neither his writing nor anything he could do, could bring him again into sympathetic contact with Sarah, still filled him with pain. The publication of *Liber Amoris* had proved worse than useless in bringing to her any realisation of the quality of his love. Her complete withdrawal from his life was still the deepest source of his suffering. We get from Haydon one glimpse of him, still in the anguish of estrangement, still feeling that the morning brought him no life, nor the evening any peace, nor any moment of the day any respite from his longing. He was like a man perishing by inches in a dreary void. When he came up to town from Winterslow in September, according to Haydon he passed most of the night watching the door of 9 Southampton Buildings. Friendship, love, and life—all seem to him to be receding from him. He is obsessed by the feeling that to him alone, among men, "the gates of life are closed." Once more, after a year spent in sore struggle, he has slipped back to the bottom of the pit. Once more he lies in darkness.

I (5)

It was just after this that the hand which had helped him to make his first start in journalism was again stretched towards him, with assurance of continued affection and regard. John Wilson, who had perpetually assailed his relationship with Jeffrey, was blaring out to the world the lie that Craigcrook and the Prince of Critics would receive Hazlitt no more; Crabius and others who had grudged his friendship with Lamb were prophesying that even Lamb would be among those who would henceforth cut his acquaintance. What Wordsworth had said of Hazlitt, "the Fellow" is not fit for decent society, was being echoed on all sides. Just then Lamb, whom Hazlitt had been avoiding for some time, in the course of a public rebuke which he delivered to Southey, was moved to take action on behalf of the friend on whom all the world seemed inclined to turn its back, and make a public profession of his faith in Hazlitt's value both as a man and as a writer. In the course of an article in the January number of the *Quarterly*, Southey had made an affectionate reference by Lamb to little Thornton Hunt in one of his essays an instrument for wounding the child's father, then enduring adversity in Italy.

Lamb hated this gesture. In his *Letter of Elia to Robert Southey*, which appeared in the October number of the *London*, after asking, "Was it worth your while to go so far out of your way to affront the feelings of an old friend, . . . for the pleasure of reflecting upon a poor child, an exile at Genoa?" and vindicating his friendship with Leigh Hunt, he passed on to his friendship with Hazlitt. There had been no direct reference to Hazlitt in the article which had stung Lamb into rebuke, but for many years Lamb had suffered from "being complimented" at the expense of Hazlitt by one and all of the Lake Poets. He chose this moment, when Hazlitt had lost faith in his friendship, and when all the world had lost faith in Hazlitt himself, for making a public profession of his inalterable regard for the friend who was being rapidly driven into the wilderness. In the course of this profession he warmed into such passion as he rarely allowed himself to show. His words, quite different in quality from those he had used in speaking of Leigh Hunt, borne along as on a high tide of feeling, and interpenetrated both with regret and with sympathy, are profound in their understanding of Hazlitt, and leave on the mind of the reader a profound impression of Hazlitt's personality. Many of Hazlitt's contemporaries have described his eccentricities. Not one of them has described, as Lamb did, the flame which never ceased to burn clear in Hazlitt's spirit, despite the eccentricities, oddities, and waywardnesses, which made of him a man separate from others, yet not a man to be driven into the wilderness because of this natural separateness of spirit, but a man whose leavening influence on the mind of his generation placed him among the finer spirits of the age:

"What hath soured him, and made him to suspect his friends of infidelity towards him, when there was no such matter, I know not. I stood well with him for fifteen years (the proudest of my life) and have ever spoke my full mind of him to some, to whom his panegyric must naturally be least tasteful. I never in thought swerved from him, I never betrayed him, I never slackened in my admiration of him, I was the same to him (neither better nor worse) though he could not see it, as in the days when he thought fit to trust me. At this instant, he may be preparing for me some compliment, above my deserts, as he has sprinkled many such among his admirable books, for which I rest his debtor; or, for any thing I know, or can guess to the contrary, he may be about to read a lecture on my weaknesses. He is welcome to them (as he was to my humble hearth) if they can divert a spleen, or ventilate a fit of sullenness. I wish he would not quarrel with the world at the rate he does; but the reconciliation must be effected by himself, and I despair of living to see that day. But, protesting against much that he has written, and some things which he chooses to do; judging him by his conversation, which I enjoyed so long, and relished so deeply; or by his books, in those places where no clouding passion intervenes—I should belie my own conscience, if I said less, than that I think W.H. to be, in his natural and healthy state, one of the wisest and finest spirits breathing. So far from being ashamed of that intimacy, which was betwixt us, it is my boast that I was able for so many years to have preserved it entire; and I think I shall go to my grave without finding, or expecting to find, such another companion."

These words reached Hazlitt at Winterslow. Goaded by his suffering, by the sense that no one understood it, and that to a certain extent he was being punished for his irregularities by social ostracism, so nervous and ill that he was ready to shy at his own shadow, as sensitive to criticism on his strangeness[336] [b] as a man that had been flayed alive, he had retired for the autumn to the asylum of Winterslow Hut, in the greatest depression of body and mind, to purge his soul of its bitterness in the great and characteristic group of essays[337] through which we can follow the movement of his mind and feeling throughout the closing months of this year. In the most powerful of them all, *On the Pleasure of Hating*, which asserts the activity of hatred as one of the great driving forces of the universe, he states his theme in the words: "Pure good soon grows insipid, wants variety and spirit. Pain is a bitter-sweet, which never surfeits. Love turns, with a little indulgence, to indifference or disgust: *hatred alone is immortal*."[338] This great essay is an expansion of the most powerful and the most hopeless of all his surveys of human life and of the ways of man to man, flung off in a paragraph contributed by him to *The Examiner* in this year:

"Happy are they that can say with Timon—' I am Misanthropos, and hate mankind!' They can never be at a loss for subjects to exercise their spleen upon: their sources of satisfaction must hold out while the world stands . . . if they take pleasure in the distresses of their fellow-creatures, they have their wish. Let them cast an eye on that long disease, human life, on that villainous compound, human nature, and glut their malice. There is madness, there is idiotcy; there is sickness, old age, and death; there is the cripple, the blind, and the deaf; there is the deformed in body, the weak in mind, the prisoner and the gaoler, the beggar and the dwarf; there is poverty, labour, pain, ignominy; there is riches, pride, griping avarice, bloated luxury; there is the agony of suffering or the lassitude of *ennui*; there is the sickness of the heart from hope delayed, and the worse and more intolerable sickness from hope attained; there is the gout, the stone, the plague, cold, fever, thirst, and nakedness, shipwreck, famine, fire and the sword, all are instruments of human fate, and pamper the dignity of human nature: there are the racking pains of jealousy, remorse, and anguish, the lingering ones of disappointment, sorrow, and regret; there is the consciousness of unmerited, hopeless obscurity, and ' the cruel sunshine thrown by fortune on a fool;' there is unrequited love, and—marriage."

But Hazlitt was not Timon. Neither was he as good a hater as he thought. He loved more than he hated. Indeed it might be said of him that he hated much because he loved much. Therefore he suffered. Therefore, "lest his courage fail," he lashed himself into anger, because "any state is better than despair;" would fain lash himself into hatred too, if he could. It is on this note that *On the Pleasure of Hating* closes:

"Seeing all this as I do, and unravelling the web of human life into its various threads of meanness, spite, cowardice, want of feeling, and want of understanding, of indifference towards others and ignorance of ourselves—seeing custom prevail over all excellence, itself giving way to infamy—mistaken as I have been in my public and my private hopes, calculating others from myself, and calculating wrong; always disappointed where I placed most reliance, the dupe of friendship, and the fool of love; have I not reason to hate and to despise myself? Indeed I do; and chiefly for not having hated and despised the world enough."

But in the middle of writing *On the Pleasure of Hating*, he remembered Lamb, and the sweetness of Lamb's gesture of friendship towards him in his forlorn condition fell on his dejection like rain on mown grass. Earlier in the year he had written: "To be capable of steady friendship and lasting love, are the two greatest proofs, not only of goodness of heart, but of strength of mind." Now he paused in the midst of his bitter train of thought to reflect: "I think I must be friends with Lamb again." There had come to him, unsought, full and ample and public evidence that one friend at least could keep faith with him in his hour of weakness and need. The first sign we have of his emergence from the pit into which he had once more fallen, and of his returning to "all the cheerful ways of men," is that on the last Monday of January, 1824, he sought out Lamb at his new home in Colebrooke Cottage, Islington. Crabius was there, but we get the impression that he did not add to the joy of the evening. His entry as to his meeting with Hazlitt ends with the words: "we did not speak." A sour Crab now, rigorously withholding, at least from the one whom he would fain continue to see an Ishmaelite, all evidence that his juices were "pure golden pippin."

2 (1)

Hazlitt had found that he was not "the dupe of friendship" to the extent he had thought. Whether or no he was to remain "the fool of love" had yet to be put to the proof. It is from William Bewick, now portrait-painting in Edinburgh, that we learn of his new bid for life. Bewick tells us that he received in April, 1824, an invitation from Hazlitt, who had returned to Scotland, had married again, and who was now on his "marriage-tour," to visit him at Melrose. If it should seem strange to the reader, remembering how Hazlitt had spent some of the nights of the previous autumn in watching for a sign of life in 9 Southampton Buildings, that his passion for Sarah, a passion which had almost cost him his reason, should terminate in his marriage with another woman in the spring, we can only say that this new bid for life occasions no surprise in any one who has watched the fluctuations of his mind and mood during this passion. Even in the height of it, he had known, although his one desire was to marry Sarah, that should she refuse to have him, he would attempt to re-create his life by entering on some new human relationship.

Few men might have felt in this fashion, but Hazlitt did. Both the ravenous heart-hunger which had grown upon him during the years of a marriage which had never satisfied him and the terrible yearning for a woman's tenderness which had been bred in him by years of living with a woman who had neither sensibility nor tenderness, made it inevitable that he should. He knew, too, that the power to form a new human relationship was a matter of life and death to him. He had felt himself, in his utter isolation, to be perishing by inches. He realised that his only chance of life was in the formation of some new human tie. Having realised this, he was likely to act on it, it not being his way to live his life like one "struck with the dead palsy." The energy in him drove him on. Our knowledge as to his "wooing weather" is slight, but we know that even before July, 1822, he had met a woman whom he both admired and liked, and about whom he could feel none of the torturing doubts he felt about Sarah, doubts which increased in their power to torment him in proportion to the waxing of the passion which had wasted and shattered him. On July 8th, when one of Patmore's letters had reawakened in him the hope that Sarah might have him, he was instant in repudiating any thoughts of this quiet attachment, in favour of the more vehement one. "I had begun a new amour," he wrote to Patmore, "but it's all off, God bless you." Then followed the declaration that he would never think of another woman as long as Sarah thought him even worth the trouble of refusing him.

In his conversation with his former wife on the evening of July 17th, just as he was preparing to leave Edinburgh, he was more guarded, but some words of his, reported by her, seem to point towards the lady who was his second choice as one whom he had met in Edinburgh, either at Jeffrey's or at Ritchie's, or among the circle of their friends: "He wished he could marry some woman with a good fortune, that he might not be under the necessity of writing another line; and be enabled to provide for the child, and do something for John, and that now his name was known in the literary world, he thought there was a chance for it; though he could not pretend to anything of the kind before."

Now Ritchie was a lawyer. Most of those Hazlitt met through him, and through Jeffrey, were connected not only with letters but with the law. The few pieces of information we have as to Hazlitt's second wife, Isabella Bridgwater, from the friends to whom he spoke of her or who met her about this time or in the years immediately following their marriage, indicate that she was likely to have acquaintances in legal circles, that she had some money, and that she was one to whom his fame "in the literary world" was not a matter of indifference. The first of these is contained in a letter written by John Hunt to his brother in Italy, on August 31st of this year. As it was written just after John Hunt had seen both Hazlitt and his bride, in London, we take it that he had his information from Hazlitt himself. "This Mrs. Hazlitt . . . was the widow of a Barrister," he wrote, "and possesses an independence of nearly £300 a year." Many years afterwards the second of these details was confirmed by J. Payne Collier: "His second wife I never saw, but he told me one day she was worth £300 a year." Charles Armitage Brown, who saw a good deal of her in Florence in 1825, told Crabius shortly after Hazlitt's death, that the lady had fallen "in love with him on account of his writings." These, along with Charles Cowden Clarke's statement, that he had heard the lady was Scottish, are the chief hints given as to the connections and circumstances of Hazlitt's second wife by those with whom he was in contact at the time of his second marriage,[339] that she was the widow of a barrister, that she had an income of her own, and that she had fallen in love with him on account of his writings. At last, it would seem, Hazlitt had found what he had despaired of finding, a woman who could care for a man because of the immortal part of him. He had viewed Desdemona over-critically, but now he has himself his chance of seeing what he can make of life with the kind of woman who could genuinely say:

"I saw Othello's colour in his mind."

2 (2)

Although Isabella Hazlitt seems rather to have avoided than to have courted notice, there are certain things which we can gather as to her personality from the chance remarks of those who met her during the years she lived with Hazlitt and entertained his friends. There can be little doubt that her appearance was delightful. There is some evidence that she had been, in her first youth, very lovely. Her acquaintance, George Huntly Gordon, on the one occasion on which he had met her in her youth, had thought her "one of the loveliest girls he had ever seen." From what he says of her we gather that she was a good deal younger than Hazlitt. All his life he retained a very vivid impression of her charming personality, and in his old age he still insisted that he had seldom seen a lovelier woman than she had been. Her colouring was very delicate and fine. From Hazlitt himself we get only one indication as to her appearance, but it is striking enough to atone for the lack of any further details. He tells us that when they spent a night in Lyons, in January of the following year, the dark-skinned, sun-baked girl who waited on them seemed so dazzled by his wife's complexion that she

HAZLITT AT THE TIME OF HIS SECOND MARRIAGE

forgot everything she was supposed to fetch them, and kept exclaiming every time she entered the room: "*Ah! Que Madame a la peau blanche!*" behaving, in general, as if she were gazing on a creature from another planet. He adds that the contrast between his wife's appearance and that of the rough, dingy-hued, gipsy-like daughter of the South of France, who in this uncouth fashion paid her tribute of homage to it, was indeed great.

Every impression we get of Isabella Hazlitt seems to point to a gracious and winning personality. John Hunt wrote of her to Leigh as being "a very pleasant and lady-like person." Leigh Hunt when he met her was captivated by her. Haydon felt that she had quality. Charles Armitage Brown testified to her breeding. When grumbling to Crabius against Hazlitt as "the worst-tempered man" he had ever known, he spoke very highly of the second Mrs. Hazlitt "as a gentle-woman." George Huntly Gordon found her no less delightful when he visited her in Paris and made the acquaintance of the great writer who had become her second husband than she had been in her first youth. In almost all her personal qualities, she seems to have been the exact opposite of Hazlitt's first wife. We note, too, that she made her husband's fireside delightful to his friends, and that some of them, who had always been glad to come to listen to his "strenuous talk," now felt that the evenings they spent with him took on another character. The "strenuous talk" was still there, but Hazlitt's asperities were softened by the presence of a very gracious woman, and the evening's entertainment had not only stimulus, but charm and ease.

Indeed, it is not too much to say that every man who met her had nothing but praise for the woman who had fallen in love with Hazlitt "on account of his writings;" nor is it too much to say that this woman might have made any man happy except the troubled and troubling man of genius to whom she had ventured to ally herself. To make Hazlitt happy she would have needed magic, or that special intuition of his special sensitiveness which would have been far more to him than magic of any kind, if he could but have found it in any woman. She was gentle, but it is to be doubted whether, where he was concerned, she possessed this special gift.

2 (3)

Hazlitt and his bride left Melrose shortly after Bewick's visit to them. Our next glimpse of them is in London, where they were in rooms in 10 Down Street, Piccadilly. A word in one of John Hunt's letters seems to indicate that he saw something of Hazlitt in town in June, while a letter written by old Mrs. Hazlitt to her grandson Willie, seems to indicate that the child had seen something of his father and his stepmother, and had reported that they were happy together. "We were all very glad to hear from you that you were well and happy," she wrote, "and also that your Father and Mrs. Hazlitt were comfortable together." From her letter it is evident that Hazlitt is at last about to put into effect the plan of visiting France and Italy which he had formed as early as 1821, when he had hoped the journey would be financed by Colburn: "Tell Father to write to me by you, and now and then besides, and before he goes abroad; I don't like his going; so many die there; such stagnant waters surrounding the towns, and all over the country." There was another who wanted news of Hazlitt. Willie's mother, who had been in Paris since the beginning of July, and had found it "very amusing," wrote to him on July 26th, rather reproaching him with not having given her the kind of news of his father she wished to have, such as who the booksellers were who had commissioned him to write for them and who were financing his travels; whether he was to be at 10 Down Street until his departure from England; what his plans were and how long he expected to be abroad.

In August Hazlitt was getting ready for his journey. He had lost his chance with Colburn, and he had failed to come to terms with any other publisher for the book he proposed to write, but he meant to pay his way by newspaper articles as he went along, and to make the best terms he could for his book when he returned. He left London for Brighton on the last day of the month. The journey on which he was now to embark was one which he had already made many times in his imagination—with Sarah. He had written over two years before to Patmore of the journey with which his dreams had been playing perpetually: "It is . . . what I proposed to her to do—to have crossed the Alps with me, to sail on sunny seas, to bask in Italian skies, to have visited Vevai and the rocks of Meillerie, and to have repeated to her on the spot the story of Julia and St. Preux, and to have shewn her all that my heart had stored up for her." Now at last he is about to make this journey, is about to show all these things to a woman worth many Sarahs, yet not the woman for whom he had stored them in his heart, nor the woman to whom his imagination was wedded, nor the woman who possessed the magic to which alone the core of him responded. Procter married this year the love of his youth, sweet Psyche-like Anne Skepper, Mrs. Basil Montagu's daughter. Their friend Edward Irving gave them his blessing, and along with it a large Bible, in the fly-leaf of which, together with his wishes for the happiness of the journey they were to make together, he had written: "But as for me and my house, we will serve the Lord."

For that journey everything was fresh and fair and clear. No dangerous cross-currents were likely to meet the voyagers. No clouds hung over them at the outset of their journey. Hazlitt set out on his quest for the recovery of health and happiness, leaving behind him in England the one woman who could have turned every inch of it to joy for him, having before him in Paris, waiting to press her financial demands upon him, the wife who had blunted for him what should have been the best years of his life, and who still retained the power to press upon his life, to lacerate his sensitiveness, and to sap his strength, having beside him a charming woman and a loving one, who yet had never touched his imagination, and having among his books a certain volume bound in crimson velvet, which, if we mistake not, was either the prayer-book which Sarah's lips had kissed,[340] or the counterpart of it, which he had had bound for himself at the time he had charmed her with his beautiful gift, to be, like the duplicate of the heart-shaped locket he had given her, a link between his life and hers.

3

He arrived at Paris by way of Dieppe and Rouen, on September 4th. It was perhaps an error of judgment on his part, or a defect in imagination, to expect that because he had been happy in the France of 1802 and 1803 he could recapture that lost happiness in the France of 1824. As he drove into Paris he was assailed by the memory of former days and former hopes. When he visited the Louvre the longing for the days that had been, deepened into passion. In the years following upon the return from the Louvre in 1803, his pillow had been haunted by the dream that he was revisiting it, but that everything was confused and changed, and that on looking round for his favourite pictures, he found them all faded or defaced or vanished. Many a time he had wept himself awake from this dream. On reaching Paris he could not rest until he had put it to the proof. Then he found that many of his fears as to the changed appearance of the Louvre had been unfounded. Instead of the Republican doorkeepers with their rough voices and homely provincial French he found, to be sure, a servant in court-livery at the gate, but the galleries themselves were not so much altered externally as he had feared. Although most of the pictures Buonaparte had reft from the kingdoms subjugated by him had been restored to the countries which had produced them, nothing could be better managed than the way in which the remaining ones were arranged, and there were enough remaining to plunge him once more into that state of luxurious enjoyment which he regarded as the highest privilege of the mind of man. There was little of which the eye had to complain. Yet he was conscious of a change which altered for him the character of the place. The soul of it seemed to him to lie in captivity. His account of his visit gradually becomes an impassioned descant on

the passing of the hope for the brotherhood of man which had flushed
the skies of his youth:

"There . . . were the 'Transfiguration,' and the 'St. Peter Martyr,'
with its unrivalled landscape background. There also were the two
'St. Jeromes,' Domenichino's and Correggio's—there 'stood the statue
that enchants the world'—there were the Apollo and the Antinous,
the Laocoon, the Dying Gladiator, Diana and her Fawn, and all the
glories of the antique world. . . . But Legitimacy did not 'sit squat,
like a toad,' in one corner of it, poisoning the very air, and keeping the
free-born spirit aloof from it."[341]

It galled him to see the white flag waving over the Palace of the
Tuileries, reminding him of all that had supplanted all in which he had
hoped, and to miss the splendour of the Brazen Horses on its gates;
it wounded him to see the white flag flapping over Buonaparte's Pillar,
in the Place Vendôme, while many people were still asking who
Charles X was; it put him beside himself to see those who were left of
"the pale band of warriors" that had so often conquered "in the name
of liberty and of their country," wearing, like a badge of servitude, the
white ribbon. One day, in going to view the Champ de Mars, when he
passed the old "Invalid Hospital," restored by Napoleon himself to
shelter the veterans bruised in his wars, he saw, with rage and grief,
a band of these, the men who had given their limbs for the Revolution,
"with a bit of white ribbon sticking in their button-holes." That
seemed to him a mutilation and crippling of the mind more grievous
than the mutilation of body they had suffered in fighting the battles of
the Revolution. Surely that little piece of white silk must gnaw into
their souls more deeply than ever enemy steel had bitten into their
flesh. The fine weathered faces and the old eyes that seemed to hold in
them "defeat and victory, the eagle and the lilies," had surely deserved
a better fate.

Yet if at times a glimpse of the "accepted hells" in these men's eyes
filled him with rage and pity, there were times when his rage was
turned against the French just because the hells had been accepted too
easily. It would have been impossible for his own countrymen, he
judged, to have shown such acceptance in similar circumstances.
The French, in his opinion, although they had overrun Europe like
tigers, had "defended their own territory like deer."

Sometimes he pondered the riddle of Paris, the glory it had been in
the days of its heroic energy, the city of shallow pleasures it had
become. One day he watched two young students making a sketch
of a ruined hovel near the top of Montmartre. They were quite dis-
regarding the reality, the drooping moss, the crumbling walls, the
traces of the winter's flaw. Everything in their sketch had been

repaired; not a stone was out of place; every suggestion of age or decay had been tidied away. It struck him that this refusal to face reality was typical of the age that had set in, and he found himself exclaiming: "Oh Paris! it was indeed on this thy weak side . . . that thy barbarous and ruthless foes entered in."

He found the same tendency in the exhibitions of painting and statuary he saw. They were typical of a world in which the extinction of Liberty had left in its place a curious shallowness of feeling against which his spirit fretted: "the Senses, like a favourite lap-dog, are pampered and indulged at any expense; the Imagination, like a gaunt hound, is starved and driven away. Danger and death, and ferocious courage, and stern fortitude, however the subject may exact them, are uncourtly topics and kept out of sight; but smiling lips and glistening eyes are pleasing objects, and there you find them."

The Theatre, too, apart from French comedy, which was a delight to him, and the acting of Madame Pasta, the integrity of whose art charmed him, gave him little pleasure. As for French dancing, it seemed to him elaborate and mechanical contortion, and sent his thoughts flying back to Southampton Buildings and the days when the one who was "all grace" had moved "in measured steps" before him and wafted him "into Elysium."

On the whole we get the impression that he was restless, irritable, ill and perhaps a trifle homesick throughout his stay in Paris. The things in which he found most peace were the things in which he found least change. He still delighted to walk in the gardens of the Tuileries on those bright days in which Paris "dazzles the eye like a steel mirror." "This and the ' Man in Black,' by Titian, in the Louvre close by (whose features form a *sombre* pendant to the gay parterres) are the two things in Paris I like best," he confessed. "I should never tire of walking in the one, or of looking at the other." Another thing which he still loved was "the barrier of Neuilly, like a thing of air, diminished by a fairy perspective." One day he walked beyond it, to see if he would suddenly come, as he had come over twenty years before, on the "smooth life" of flock and shepherd in old time. The flock was still by the roadside, as if it had remained there browsing peacefully throughout all these changeful years, with the ever-watchful dog beside it. But its old guardian, with his crook and his sheepskin cloak, was gone. Age had given way to youth. Instead of the old shepherd a boy grinned up at the meditative stranger, with a flash of white teeth, looking just like one of Murillo's beggar-boys.

He was fortunate in finding in Paris an old fellow-student of the Hackney days (now a scientist of some distinction) whom he had not seen for thirty years, but whose sympathies had remained as his own, and with whom he could grumble to his heart's content at the change that had come over men and things. When this friend, Dr. Edwards, who was also a friend of Laplace, looked in on him in the evenings, after having called on the great astronomer, Hazlitt, who had a great respect for Laplace, said that he felt as if he had been visited by a man who had just called on a star. Apart from anything else, Laplace had a claim on his interest as having been one of the examiners in mathematics of the youthful Napoleon Buonaparte, and Hazlitt could never be indifferent to any one who had ever had any kind of contact with Napoleon. It had never ceased to be a bitter chagrin to him that he had missed the opportunity of meeting Talma, who idolised Napoleon, in London in 1817, when the great actor of the "dumb eloquent" gestures had had a season there. Even at the moment he was regretting that he was again being defrauded of intercourse with Talma, who had gone to Lyons in the autumn of this year.

Sympathy with Napoleon probably conditioned the one new and vital friendship Hazlitt formed in the Paris of 1824. This was the friendship with Henri Beyle, better known by his pen-name of Stendhal. Hazlitt may have met Stendhal through Dr. Edwards, who was acquainted with him, but Stendhal had for some years been an admirer of Hazlitt's work, the force and fire of which appealed to him; had written to him in terms which had given him exquisite pleasure; and had wished to see *Characters of Shakespear's Plays* translated into French. It is not surprising that these two men should have been congenial to each other. To some extent they were alike in temperament, being both of them, although intellectual rebels, men of extreme sensibility, which they sometimes concealed under "a cruel way of talking."[342] They were both of them "nothing if not critical;" they had deep literary sympathies in common, having been both of them profoundly influenced by Rousseau, while they were both of them lifelong students and worshippers of Shakespeare; they were both of them lovers of Italian art.

Also, as writers, their preoccupation was the same, their main study the reaction or involution of the passions; Stendhal in *De L'Amour* had done the kind of work Hazlitt had attempted to do in his *Liber Amoris*, and had actually achieved in his *Characteristics*. They had in common certain antipathies, detestation of cant, detestation of the reign of mediocrity, and detestation of the persecution of the free and independent mind by certain "legitimate" Governments. But the primary bond must have been the sympathy felt by them both towards Napoleon. To Hazlitt at this time, although his work as a writer was already three-quarters done, it was beginning to seem that all he had thought and suffered would have been in vain, if he could not interpret the trouble and the struggle and the defeated aspirations of his age in terms of a *Life* of Napoleon.

It is not difficult to understand all it must have meant to the man in whom this purpose was growing, to come into contact with one who had served under Napoleon, who had accompanied the Emperor to his coronation as King of Italy, who had seen Napoleon at Berlin in 1806, riding down Unter den Linden, who had heard the cannon at Wagram, who had looked upon the flames at Moscow and shuddered amid the snows of the retreat, who had watched the Empress and the little King of Rome drive out of the Tuileries for the last time, who had mourned most passionately the agony of St. Helena. Napoleon "radiant under the sun of Austerlitz," pale under the snows of the Russian winter, dying at St. Helena! Such reminiscences had a poignancy beyond compare for the man who had always gone against the tide in his championship of his country's enemy; whose love for Napoleon, although he sometimes sought to ascribe it to political causes, seemed to most of his friends to be "a passion and a gallantry;" and who, although often driven by lack of means into the writing of what he regarded as "Ephemerides," frittering his energy and making it all but impossible for him to concentrate all his powers on one great task, meant his crowning work and the apology for his life to be a biography of Napoleon into which he would pour every gift he possessed—of mind, soul and spirit.

When Hazlitt left Paris for Italy, he carried a copy of *De L'Amour* with him. Nor did he forget its author, during his Italian wanderings. In an essay which he sent to *The Examiner* from Rome, he mentioned "Mr. Beyle's . . . charming little work, entitled *De L'Amour*," and translated from it, by way of illustrating the implacable nature of Italian jealousy, the story of La Pia, just touched on in Dante, which Stendhal had told very beautifully, and in full. The words with which he closed his essay show the extent to which he had responded to the quality of Stendhal's work:

"One such incident, or one page in Dante or in Spenser, is worth all the route between this and Paris, and all the sights in all the post-roads in Europe."

4

When Hazlitt left Paris for Italy at the end of the second week of January, 1825, he was looking forward not only to seeing Leigh Hunt, who was now more or less languishing in Florence, but to making the acquaintance of Landor, who, although as bitter in hatred of Napoleon as Stendhal was ardent in love, interested him perhaps even more as a writer and a force than did the author of *De L'Amour*. In the course of the spring of 1824 he had reviewed the first volume of *Imaginary Conversations* for the *Edinburgh*. According to Julius Hare, the general impression left by Hazlitt's review of the book was: "How famously the *Imaginary Conversations* have been cut up in *The Edinburgh Review*!"

Nevertheless, Hazlitt's friends knew that "the book was one after his own heart" and that he considered some parts of it "finer than anything else from a modern pen."

At Fontainebleau, where he and his fellow-traveller spent the first night of that journey, he viewed the plain round piece of mahogany on which Buonaparte had signed his abdication, or as Hazlitt put it to himself in his excess of bitterness, had signed *the abdication of the human race in favour of the hereditary proprietors of the species.* All the world came to see that, while even Paris, he thought, had forgotten the house in the Rue de Chantereine at which Buonaparte had alighted when he had returned after the battle of Marengo. At Lyons they decided to cross into Italy over the Mont Cenis. Hazlitt's thoughts during this stage of his journey were dominated by Rousseau and Buonaparte. At Lyons they saw the inn at which the youthful Rousseau was said to have stopped on his way to Paris, "when he went to over-turn the French monarchy by the force of style." Hazlitt let his imagination play freely with this moment.

When they arrived at Chambery in the dusk of the following evening, he felt that there was a charm in the name, and in that of Charmettes near it, "where he who relished all things more sharply than his fellows . . . alone felt peace or hope." When he caught sight of the peaked tops of the Grande Chartreuse, his heart beat faster at the thought of Buonaparte moving among such scenes: "It gives one a vast idea of Buonaparte to think of him in these situations. He alone (the Rob Roy of the scene) seemed a match for the elements, and able to master ' this fortress built by nature for herself.' Neither impeded nor turned aside by immoveable barriers, he smote the mountains with his iron glaive, and made them malleable; cut roads through them; transported armies over their ridgy steeps; and the rocks ' nodded to him, and did him courtesies! '" The heights seemed to him the fitting dwelling-place for Buonaparte, and Marengo had always seemed to him the most poetical of Napoleon's battles, because of the way in which he had "given wings to war, hovering like Perseus in the air with borrowed speed," and falling "upon his adversary from the clouds, from pathless precipices—and at the very moment of being beaten, recalled victory with a word." If a poet, or "if a magician had planned a campaign, it could hardly have been fuller of the romantic and incredible."

As they descended the Mont Cenis, he found Buonaparte's signature writ large on the road that wound "its inconceivable breathless way" down the side of the mountain, "like the circumgirations of an eagle, gallery seeing gallery sunk beneath it." If Marengo was such a battle as a poet might have planned, this was such a road as an eagle might have designed. The scene acted and re-acted on the beholder, at first stunning the sense like a blow, and then giving the imagination strength to contend with a force that seemed to mock it. Hazlitt's description of it makes stirring writing, especially his description of the last stages of the descent, in which it seemed as if they were being hurried from one yawning depth to another, ' into the regions of Chaos and old Night,' until they seemed to see "the building-up and framework of the world." As they rode down the winding, circuitous path, and whirled round the various turnings of it in rapid, mechanical flight at the end of this day's journey, he felt that there was "something like witchcraft" in the scene and in their progress through it.

When Victor Emmanuel had been restored to his capital at Turin, one of the first acts by which he had signalised his return to power had been the forbidding his subjects to use Napoleon's eagle road over the Mont Cenis. Hazlitt, on the day he crossed by it into Italy, was in no very gracious frame of mind towards the present Sardinian Majesty. When he had reached Pont Beau-Voisin, the frontier town of the King of Sardinia's dominions, two days before, he had been badly jarred by a piece of petty tyranny. He had been travelling with two trunks, one of them containing his clothes, the other the books which were his companions during his travels. His first trunk had passed unchallenged at the *douane*, but when he unlocked the second, it could not have created more of a sensation if it had been filled with gunpowder. The names had been taken down with the greatest care; then the books, along with all the periodicals and newspapers from home he had with him, had been corded and *leaded*, and the trunk itself made a prisoner of state. All this had been done not only with great seriousness but with great politeness, but Hazlitt had been not a little startled at thus finding himself, for the first time in his life, "within the smooth polished grasp of legitimate power," and at having been thus made to realise, by a piece of practical inconvenience, on the threshold of Italy, the nature of the "conspiracy for the suppression of light and letters," in which most of the Governments of Europe at the time were involved.

The incident had brought home to him painfully the power of arbitrary Governments not only to dispose of the bodies but to cripple the souls of those in their power. It had seemed to him symbolic of the eternal warfare between Tyranny and the Mind of Man, and had brought home to him sharply the realisation that in countries which were not free, books were always suspect as being "the corrosive sublimate" eating out despotism and priestcraft, "the artillery that battered down castle and dungeon-walls—the ferrets that ferreted out abuses, the lynx-eyed guardians that tore off disguises—the thumping make-weight thrown into the balance that made force and fraud, the sword and the cowl, kick the beam." Therefore they were the special dread of tyrants and knaves. He did not for a moment doubt the issue of this kind of warfare. No power on earth had been able to prevent

Rousseau's works from reaching the peoples of the earth. Nevertheless Hazlitt's anger against the attitude of mind that expressed itself in tyranny aimed at the mind was bitter. "Go on, obliging creatures!" he wrote when commenting on this incident. "Blot the light out of heaven, tarnish the blue sky with the blight and fog of despotism, deface and trample on the green earth; for while one trace of what is fair or lovely is left in the earth under our feet, or the sky over our heads, or in the mind of man that is within us, it will remain to mock your impotence and deformity, and to reflect back lasting hatred and contempt upon you." He had no doubt that books were "the future rulers of the world." But this experience, coming to him just as he was about to enter into Italy, sharpened his sympathy with the stirring towards Liberty which could be sensed throughout the country.

They travelled the next day (it was Monday, January 24th) to Turin, and there Hazlitt found that his trunk of books would be forwarded to any address he cared to give the authorities, provided only the combustible material within it were "out of his Sardinian Majesty's dominions." In Paris, as we saw, he had felt that "the black ox" trod on his forehead. When he walked out in Turin after getting rid of the dust of the journey and getting into a change of clothes, he experienced a genuine moment of intoxication or exhilaration. There was something in the air of this city of Palaces that carried off *the blue devils*. From a terrace outside the town he saw the chain of the Alps they had left behind them, "rising like a range of marble pillars in the evening sky," Monte Viso and the Mont Cenis resembling "two pointed cones of ice, shooting up above all the rest." The previous day, near the summit of the Mont Cenis, he had seen a young peasant-woman, a soldier's wife, whose face had seemed to him of the kind that would have called forth all Raphael's powers, not so much because of its grace, or of its colouring, though that was "fresh as the winds," but because of its expression, which was "pure as the mountain snows." Now, in Turin, he felt deeply "the fine, serious grace" of the women who passed him. He imagined that in their graceful downcast looks one might read the soul of the *Decameron*. He noted on the trees the "deep sad foliage"—which had taken on, from being prolonged into the depth of winter, a mellow tone which hitherto he had only seen in pictures. This added to his sense of being in a world new to him, and vividly pictorial. But perhaps what added as much as anything else to his sense of well-being was that at last he was warm. He had been feeling the cold bitterly ever since he had left Paris. Now the air was soft and balmy; he felt transported to "another climate—another earth—another sky." The winter had suddenly become spring—he felt as if he were beginning his life anew.

After a couple of days' stay at Turin they set out for Parma, which they reached on Saturday, January 29th. There he saw, restored to its native soil, the first of the pictures now returned to Italy on which formerly he had loved to brood in the Louvre. This was Correggio's "St. Jerome." At Bologna, he was both stimulated and deeply moved by some "old and curious pictures" of Giotto and Ghirlandaio, in which it was evident that the aspiration of the artists had far outstripped their powers of execution. At Bologna, too, he found "the shattered cords of memory" beginning to vibrate of themselves again, for he saw there the "St. Cecilia" of Raphael, "with looks commercing with the skies," which—as it had seemed to him some years before—might have been the original of the small and delicate copy of an Italian picture whose "soft looks" had made it dear to him, owing to the resemblance he had traced in them to some of the expressions of the woman he had hoped to have by his side when one day he made a pilgrimage to the original.

They reached Florence at the beginning of February. As they stood on the brow of the hill overlooking it Hazlitt thought it enchanting. It seemed to him like a city planted in a garden. In the midst of it the Duomo and other churches raised their heads. The hills opposite it were covered with vineyards and olive-grounds "till they joined a snowy ridge of Appenines rising above the top of Fesole," one planta- tion or row of trees after another fringing the ground "like rich lace." The olive-trees, being still in leaf, gave to the scene the appearance of "a grey summer." Yet he shivered as he looked at it. The cold, which had returned, seemed to push its way through his body as a rough hand might push itself through a piece of thin paper. "From the thinness of the air," he wrote, "there was a feeling of nakedness about you; you seemed as if placed in an empty receiver. Not a particle of warmth or feeling was left in your whole body: it was just as, if the spirit of cold had penetrated every part; one might be said to be *vitrified*."

The first thing he did on reaching Florence was to go to the Post Office for letters—probably he was, as usual, longing very much for one from his son—and to grumble, we gather, at distant friends, when he found none, although consoling himself to some extent, still grumblingly, with the reflection that if they had had any bad news to send him, they would doubtless have been quick enough in writing. Then he sought out Leigh Hunt, who was living at Maiano. When he spoke of going to the Palazzo Medici to call on Landor, he was warned that the author of *Imaginary Conversations* was not a man whom it was advisable to approach without due form ànd ceremony.

Leigh Hunt was not at that time acquainted with Landor. Charles Armitage Brown, who had been Keats's friend and who was now Landor's best friend in Florence, offered him a letter of introduction, but he preferred to take his own way, and to base his acquaintanceship on intellectual sympathy. Accordingly, saying that he would "beard the lion in his den," he walked up to Landor's quarters one winter morning clad in such a manner as to make a lasting impression on Mrs. Landor and on another of Landor's friends, J. Seymour Kirkup, the artist. The descriptions we have of his attire on this occasion help us to understand in some measure why he felt the cold so bitterly. Mrs. Landor's impression, as reported by Mr. Edward Wilson Landor, one of Landor's relatives who afterwards spent some time with him in Italy, was that Hazlitt was wearing that morning "a dress-coat and nankeen trousers half-way up his legs, leaving his stockings well visible over his shoes." Kirkup gives an impression of attire which seems still more exiguous when we consider that at the moment Hazlitt was finding the cold *vitrifying*. He says that Hazlitt was attired "in nankeen shorts and white stockings." However, the meeting went merrily. Kirkup says that Hazlitt in his nankeen shorts was "made much of by the royal animal."

And as for Hazlitt, who had *discerned* his man accurately, within a short time he could say as truly of Landor as of his favourite Orlando Friscobaldo: "I became only of late acquainted with this last-mentioned worthy character; but the bargain between us is, I trust, for life. We sometimes regret that we have not sooner met with characters like these, that seem to raise, revive, and give a new zest to our being." Landor, who had the manners of a prince, and the heart of royal Lear, often went about looking like a beggar. He was little likely to notice whether Hazlitt was clad in nankeen shorts or in velvet—but he knew well enough when he was stimulated and amused. We get the impression that Hazlitt, whose own laugh, as Bewick said, was like a brief hysteric shout, liked to provoke Landor's, which although also a thing by itself, was a much more thorough affair. Leigh Hunt said of it that it was "in peals, and climbing," for each peal seemed to be fetched from a higher storey.

The pleasure Hazlitt took in this performance could alone account for the outrageous travesty of the proceedings leading up to his divorce which Kirkup[343] says he gave to a greedily-listening Landor. Kirkup's recollections were put together more than forty years after his meeting with Hazlitt. It is more than likely that the story is garbled: for one thing, it is untrue, and while there was much in the forms connected with Hazlitt's divorce that might have drawn his raillery—it was most unlike him to exaggerate what was fantastic in these forms to the point of untruth. The only comment on the matter we know him to have made was that the whole business had been an infinite distress to him. But the description of Landor, all eyes and ears, throwing out "signs of the most lively interest," seems authentic, and seems to indicate that Hazlitt, in some reference he made to his divorce, contrived to play upon his host's idiosyncrasy or "humour."

At any rate, it was evident to every one very quickly that Hazlitt and Landor heartily enjoyed each other's "wilfulness and caprice," and that "a strong personal liking characterised their brief acquaint-ance." It is not hard to understand how these two men, each of them reckoned incommonly capricious, prejudiced, violent, and "difficult" by the onlookers, found it so easy to get on with each other. Although there was one subject on which they would never agree, Buonaparte, on almost every other point they were in sympathy with each other. They were, in the main, in agreement on contemporary politics: thus they had both steadily fought, since 1815, against reaction, and against the tendency towards the repression of the liberties of the Peoples, in every country in Europe; they both deplored the effect that Pitt's ministry had had on the development of England, and they both held that the strong Anti-Gallican bias it had given to English sympathies and politics had been hardly less a disaster for Europe than for England herself; they both despised Canning; and they both sympathised with every liberal movement, in Italy, Spain, and Greece. Their personal tastes were alike. Nature, books and pictures made up half the life of each. Also, they were both devoted to children, Landor's love for his little brood being as marked as Hazlitt's for his one son. In temperament they were alike in many ways. Although each of them was formidable in attack, each of them attacked only the strong. Each of them had his own chivalry. At the core of the formidableness in each was gentleness. Hazlitt could never bear to see even a child hurt anything weaker than itself. Landor grieved because he could not prevent his children from taking the birds' nests. He could say of himself: "I never took one in my life, though I have found many."

And even in connection with Buonaparte, Landor had memories which he could share with Hazlitt, and which would be of interest to a man whose thoughts were settling on a biography of Napoleon as the crown of his life's work. He, too, had been in Paris in the autumn of 1802, before his initial worship of Napoleon had changed into intense hatred; he too had walked among the statues and the orange-trees and the fountains playing in the gardens of the Tuileries; he too had spent hours every day in the Louvre, and had wished that he could spend years instead of hours. He had had a much nearer view of Buonaparte at that time than Hazlitt had had, had been near enough to see that his face, although touched with melancholy and reserve, was beautiful, and that with its rich olive complexion and clear outline, it was at that time "as youthful as a girl's."

It was usually at night that they met. In the daytime Landor was out of doors in all weathers. Like Wordsworth, he composed when walking alone, and like him, he was often to be seen among the hills, muttering his thoughts when he walked. Hazlitt actually found some resemblance between the nature of his friend's writing and the structure of these hills, and expressed his feeling in some words all-revealing as to the quality of his understanding of Landor: "his work resembles his own Fesolan hills near Florence, (his favourite haunts, where wandering, his hurried steps keep time to the beatings of his heart)— volcanic structures, pointed, bare, fanciful; with wild flowers for ornament, with castellated ruins to attract the eye of memory, with fiery furnaces of burning indignation and of enduring wrongs sleeping in their bosom, and golden seats for Truth and far-sighted Humanity crowning their tops."

Hazlitt, although not usually out of doors in the morning, was usually busy enough in the hours that followed his breakfast, during the six weeks he spent in Florence, in bringing his newspaper work up to date. For the rest, sightseeing took up a good deal of his daytime leisure. At the Pitti Palace he found four favourite pictures he had missed at the Louvre, the Ippolito de' Medici, Giorgione's Music-piece, Raphael's Leo X, and the Cardinal Bentivoglio. The Venus de' Medici had also been restored to its old place.

He left Florence just as the coming on of the milder weather had begun to make it enchanting to him. Towards the end of February the days had begun to be like April days in England, and the "balmy lightness" and "vernal freshness" in the air had made him feel that if ever he might see the coming-on of spring as he had erst seen it in the spring-time of his life, it would be in Tuscany. In the course of his journey to Rome the weather turned colder again, cold enough to freeze the milk they carried with them so that they could make their own tea in the inns they passed by the way. They travelled by Siena, which Hazlitt felt to be so much a place of the past rather than of the present, of the dead rather than of the living, that he said "it was" might justly be inscribed on its entrance; by Radicofani, where they spent the night by the fort, "resting on its red right arm" two thousand four hundred feet above the sea, an experience which was "like being lodged in a cloud," so much did the place seem "the very rocking-cradle of storms and tempests"; by Aquapendente situated over the running stream from which it took its name, and San Lorenzo, also on the summit of a hill, which seemed to Hazlitt like a town that had run away from the plague and stopped suddenly on the brow of a hill to see if the Devil were following it. Now and again as they journeyed they passed the ruinous haunt of some bandit chief perched on the top of a cliff, as if still "watching for its long-lost prey," and sharing in the desolation it had made. Near the inn of La Scala were two of these which rose "in lonely horror from the very point of two hills, facing each other, and only divided by a brook." Hazlitt felt that the effect they produced might well have baffled the pencil of the boldest artist.

At Rome he lived, for the second time in his life, in a house that had sheltered a man of great fame, none other than the house which had been Salvator's, in the Via Gregoriana. As he lay in bed of a morning he could see St. Peter's; without stirring from his room he could view the whole city at a glance. This he did "without passion." He had been told by an enthusiastic friend that Rome was to all other towns what London was to a country village, and he had believed the report. Now he felt that it was not justified. Somehow or other Rome failed to move him. Perhaps he had expected too much; perhaps he was becoming weary of antiquity, beginning to feel it as something that in Italy was stifling the life of the present; perhaps he had expected to feel an enthusiasm of which no man is capable except in youth. At any rate, his imagination declared against it: "No! this is not the wall that Romulus leapt over: this is not the Capitol where Julius Cæsar fell: instead of standing on seven hills, it is situated in a low valley: the golden Tiber is a muddy stream." He found St. Peter's "not equal to St. Paul's." Rome had neither, he felt, the beauty of Florence on its mountain-side, nor the splendid background of Turin or Edinburgh. It had no picture gallery that equalled the Louvre. It was great only in ruins. The Coliseum, the Pantheon, the Arch of Constantine, Nero's Golden House (now very still) where myriads had shouted in honour of a man, as if he were a God, the Baths of Titus, with the grass and the poppy, the flower of oblivion, growing over them—these all had their own word, or their own silence, by which they could move him; but they would have moved him more in a desert. The present offended against their dignity; and they seemed to him to offend against the life of the present. Tombs were impressive; but who that wanted to live would take up his abode among tombs, even among the tombs of the mighty dead? There was something about the air of the city that tended to stifle energy and sap life. It seemed to him as if the dead, or the memory of the dead, had touched the living "with the dead palsy."

We do not wish to suggest for a moment that Hazlitt found little to enjoy in Rome. There he found again the "Transfiguration" and Domenichino's "St. Jerome," which he had missed from the Louvre, on revisiting it, and in the gallery of the Vatican, Raphael's "Crowning of the Virgin," which he had never seen before.

But on the whole, the energy in him made him react against what he felt to be the oppression of its antiquity.

While at Rome, he had a letter from Landor, who had read *The Spirit of the Age*, which had just been published. He was greatly pleased that Landor had found some good in his attempt to illustrate the Spirit of the Age from the lives of some of the foremost men the age had produced. On April 9th (it was the day before his forty-seventh birthday) he wrote in reply to this new friend's word of praise with the lack of assumption habitual with him when he spoke of his own work: "I am much gratified that you are pleased with *The Spirit of the Age*. Somebody ought to like it, for I am sure there will be plenty to cry out against it. I hope you did not find any sad blunders in the second

volume; but you can hardly suppose the depression of body and mind
under which I wrote some of these articles."

When Hazlitt wrote to Landor, he was thinking of moving from
Rome to Albano for a month, and he hoped, if he did so, that Landor
would come and spend part of it with them. Such an invitation from
Hazlitt was a marked sign of the pleasure he found in Landor's company. "I should be glad, if I settle at Albano, if you could manage
to come over and stop a little," he wrote. "I have done what I was
obliged to write for the papers, and am now a leisure man, I hope, for
the rest of the summer." He did not, after all, settle at Albano. Instead,
he returned to Florence in the second half of the month. Florence,
when they reached it, was now bathed in sultry heat. Gone was the
suggestion of "a grey summer" which it had given them when they
had first glimpsed it. Now it deserved its name, for it had blossomed
into "the city of flowers."

Their second visit to it was brief. Hazlitt wanted, before leaving
Italy, as he proposed to do, at the end of May, "to make a pilgrimage"
to see once more the last of the very great pictures of which the Louvre
had been shorn since his first visit to it. The "St. Peter Martyr" was now
at Venice. There too, although he had no desire to see them in their
new setting, were the Brazen horses that had stood on the gates of the
Tuileries. For Venice, then, he set out with his fellow-traveller before
the freshness of spring had yet passed from the Italian air. Their first
night's journey brought them to Traversa, where they spent the night
in a tiny inn, almost a hovel, on the roadside. At Bologna they were
just in time to get a second glimpse of the fine semi-frustrated pictures
which had moved Hazlitt so strangely when he had first seen
them. The Guidos and Domenichinos gleamed dark and beautiful
through the twilight. On the third morning they set out early for
Ferrara, and enjoyed a delightful day's travelling. When they reached
Ferrara Hazlitt fell in love with its melancholy grace. It moved him
much as the face of one of Guido's women might have done. This
seemed to him a city that had already been translated into history or
poetry. He found in it the one place in Italy in which he would have
chosen to make his home.

The pleasantest part of their journey was now over. At Padua
Hazlitt's eye was offended by the "vulgar and flaunting statuary."
Soon after leaving it they began to cross the canals and rivers intersecting this part of the country. Then they followed the course of the
Brenta, along what Hazlitt called "a flat, dusty, and unprofitable road."
The sun, which was now very hot, beat down upon them, and cast an
unpleasant glare on to the sluggish slimy waters. Hazlitt was beginning to feel very irritable and very uncomfortable, when suddenly,
as he raised his tired eyes to a glaring wall, he noticed a sundial, with
the inscription on it: "*Horas non numero nisi serenas.*" This moment

made a profound and lasting impression upon him. "I cherish no hours save the serene!" Who had left the stray gift of this thought upon the dusty way? Some monk of olden times, perhaps, who had made of his life one long dream of quietude! *Horas non numero nisi serenas*—he might have said to himself one night, when the heavens were clouded and the gathering storm was scattering the fallen leaves. At least in this exquisite device he had left to minds less tranquil the secret of his own golden store of peace. It would be difficult to describe the effect of this moment on Hazlitt, the way in which the words with their "impassioned repose" recalled him to quietness and restored to him that inner peace which temporary irritations so often banished from him but from which he never willingly suffered himself to be alienated. All in a moment he was wafted into a region "of pure and blissful abstraction," into a world of *ideal* voluptuousness that no disquiet could mar, a world in which the consciousness of self was left behind, and with it all the things that tortured self—accidents of time and place, irritations and disappointments, heat and cold, and all that makes man "the idle prey of the most petty and annoying circumstances." This was to be at peace.

Yet if Hazlitt had numbered only his serene hours the record would have been a meagre one. To be thus completely at peace was rare with him. "The only true leisure," he wrote, "is the repose of the passions." This kind of leisure was seldom his, for passion was his element. On the first day at Venice he was again the child waiting for the curtain to go up at the play. The whole of the first morning at every fresh landing or embarkation he teased his good-natured guide with the question: "But when are we going to see the 'Saint Peter Martyr'?" It was true that the first sight of Venice rising from the sea, crowned as if with "crimson conquest," had been like a miracle, affecting him with mingled awe and incredulity, that he felt he had never seen palaces until he had come to Venice and viewed the architectural or poetical miracles that seemed literally to be suspended in the water—those at Rome were but dungeons to them—that it seemed to him he had at last come to a place in which the practical was identical with the poetical: but he had waited for two and twenty years to find out whether the "Saint Peter Martyr" was still as he constantly saw it in his mind's eye, "with the dark, scowling, terrific face of the murdered monk looking up at his assassin, the horror-struck features of the flying priest, and the skirts of his vest waving in the wind, the shattered branches of the autumnal trees that felt the coming gale," above all, with the *soul of faith* revealed through every detail of the picture. Had its brightness been impaired by the long perspective of the years? Had time had power over its colours?

When at last they reached the Church of Saint John and Saint Paul the light was bad, and he found himself rebuked like a child by the priest, for the impatience which made him fuss and fidget and even turn his back on the host, in his anxiety to see the picture properly. But when he returned to see it again in the afternoon the light fell full on it through a high-arched Gothic window, and there it was "in all its pristine glory, with its rich, embrowned, overshadowing trees, its nobly-drawn heroic figures, its blood-stained garments, its flowers and trailing plants." There too was the convent-spire which he had so often remembered in his dreams, "rising in the distance amidst the sapphire mountains and the golden sky." There were the cherubim "bringing the crown of martyrdom with rosy fingers." Everything was just as he remembered it. And the colour in the faces was exactly as it had been twenty years before. Time had had no power over it. He looked at it, with the memories of his former impressions thronging thick upon him. Yet he felt sure that he did not only see this picture through his former impressions. He had seen it for the first time when he had been young and sensitive to impressions. But he felt sure that if he were viewing it now, in his forty-seventh year, for the first time, it would have commanded his entire homage, for he felt the picture to be a world in itself, and one that filled the mind without an effort. He had previously said of its background that while the distance between Claude's landscapes and those of all other painters except Titian was immeasurable, Claude, Gaspar Poussin, and Salvator among them could not have painted the background of the "Saint Peter Martyr." In the course of this summer, after his visit to Mont Blanc and Chamouni, he once more witnessed to its greatness: "I have it present with me ' in my mind's eye,' and swear, in the wildest scenes of the Alps, that the ' St. Peter Martyr' is finer."

From Venice they returned to Padua, and thence went by way of Verona to Milan, which was busy and bustling and full of visitors. The Emperor of Austria was there at the moment, and the town seemed to feel "the presence of its lord." In passing through Lombardy, and noting everywhere the signs of work and careful husbandry which made it "one continued and delightful garden," Hazlitt had felt that the Northern Italians were as fine a race of people as walked the earth, and that all they wanted to make them happy was freedom from the Austrian yoke. He wished that the Government of England would say three words to the power that oppressed the Northern Italians: "Let them alone." Ever since he had entered Italy and had had, on the borders of the Sardinian domains, his initial experience of "the smooth polished grasp of legitimate power," he had pitied the country because he had been sensitive to the way in which its life was being crippled by what was called the "settlement" of it, and especially by the menace of Austria hanging over it, ever ready to extinguish the flame of freedom wherever it appeared. It seemed to him shameful that the country should be left at the mercy of "protection"—as it was called—which would fain strike the name of Italy out of the map, which attempted to suppress the publications of its finest historians, which suppressed systematically any movement of spiritual or intellectual life, which would, if it could, not only leave Italy without a name, a body, or a soul to it, but make it forget that it ever had any of these.

But his last impression of Italy, like his first, was neither of his Sardinian Majesty's handiwork, nor of the Emperor of Austria lording it over Milan—but of the grandeur of the handiwork of the one who once had seemed to wear, by natural if not by hereditary right, upon his brows, the iron crown. Having crossed into Italy by the Mont Cenis, he now wished to cross into Switzerland by the Simplon, the road over which had been raised "by the same master-hand."

As they ascended by the side of the brook Simplon he had one of his old-time wishes fulfilled. Precipices and mountain-torrents enough there were. The eagle screamed overhead, and the chamois looked startled round. But to him the greatest wonder of all, in these wild solitudes, was to see the hoary rocks still covered with snow, while the clefts in their sides were filled with the fragrance of spring shrubs and flowers. It was as if the mountain were dallying with vernal sweetness and at the same time with the austere graces of winter up to the last moment.

5

For over a week, after what Hazlitt called their "jaunt through the air," they rested at Brieg. Then they proceeded on their way to Vevey. Once or twice Hazlitt had been tempted to stop at some beautiful place and spend the summer at it. But still, something whispered him on to Vevey. "In travelling, we visit *names* as well as places," he said, "and Vevey is the scene of the *New Eloise*. In spite of Mr. Burke's philippic against this performance, the contempt of the Lake School, and Mr. Moore's late *Rhymes on the Road*, I had still some overmastering recollections on that subject, which I proposed to indulge at my leisure on the spot which was supposed to give them birth." Their first sight of Lake Geneva, when they arrived at Vevey in the beginning of June, was through a drizzle of rain. They were lucky enough, the day after their arrival, to be accommodated with a set of rooms in a farmhouse, a mile out of Vevey, "so ' lapped in luxury,' so retired, so reasonable, and in every respect convenient," that they remained there until the third week of September. The house stood on a bank sloping down to the brook that passes by Vevey, and was so "entirely embosomed in trees and ' upland swells,'" that Hazlitt said it might well have been called "the peasant's nest." Although, or perhaps because, Hazlitt's life was such a "stormy, anxious, uncomfortable" one, he often felt that all he wanted was harmony and quiet.

"The golden mean is an exact description of the life I should like to lead," he once confessed, but he never had much hope of realising this desire.

He seems to have attained it, however, during the fifteen weeks he spent at Vevey. This was the most easeful spell in his life for over twenty years, indeed we might say the only easeful spell. He wrote a few essays, and did a little newspaper work, but he had not yet made a start on the work on Napoleon which was presently to absorb all his energies. He read a little, usually out of doors. In a wood near Clarens he re-read the *New Eloise*, finding it, if not the miracle it had seemed to him in his youth, yet not the worthless performance some of its critics would have it to be. If he admired the sentiment less, he perhaps relished even more keenly than before, the perfection of the style in many passages, the imagination and the poetry of single words. He had time to linger on them now, for he could read, not as he had read for many years, with an eye to reviewing, but slowly, lazily, now and again pausing to look at the lake or the rocks of Meillerie, or the green hills over Clarens with the Dent de Jamant sticking out of them, as he said, "like an iron tooth." He could get enough books to amuse him, including the Scotch novels, from the library at Vevey. Occasionally, he wrote out of doors also. *Merry England* was composed in this way. At the close of the essay he gives us an impression of the author, in the midst of his task:

"As I write this, I am sitting in the open air in a valley near Vevey: Clarens is on my left, the Dent de Jamant is behind me, the rocks of Meillerie opposite: under my feet is a green bank, enamelled with white and purple flowers, in which a dew-drop here and there still glitters with pearly light. . . . Intent upon the scene and the thoughts that stir within me, I conjure up the cheerful passages of my life, and a crowd of happy images appear before me. No one would see it in my looks—my eyes grow dull and fixed, and I seem rooted to the spot, as all this phantasmagoria passes in review before me, glancing a reflex lustre on the face of the world and nature. But the traces of pleasure, in my case, sink into an absorbent ground of thoughtful melancholy."

We have said very little for some time of his "fellow-traveller." During their time in Paris she drops entirely out of Hazlitt's record of his journey. We have the impression that during these months he lived in memories which entirely absorbed him, but from which of course she was excluded. In his record of his journey to Italy and his various journeyings in Italy, he makes mention of her occasionally, and always in some pleasant connection or other. We get glimpses of her, making tea for Hazlitt's breakfasts, sometimes giving hospitality at her breakfast-table to other travellers, receiving the compliments of a Spanish artist who travelled with them for a time, on the excellence of her fare, being gracious to a Frenchman whose platitudes on Alpine scenery were beginning to make her irritable lord throw out signs of restiveness, seeing to the little comforts that made a difference to him in travelling, as when she took care to provide herself with milk for his beloved tea, in districts where the inns were so poor that they might be unable to get milk on their arrival. In fact, we see her as one of the best fellow-travellers in the world, and in her relations with her fellow-beings harmonious, at Florence, winning Charles Armitage Brown's respect and admiration, hospitable towards Landor, charming Leigh Hunt. We would say that she was one of the most perfect of companions in such a holiday as Hazlitt and she were now enjoying. They were neither of them people to be bored by its quietude. They walked when they liked, read when they liked, slept when they liked, and if Captain Thomas Medwin, Shelley's untrustworthy biographer, who visited them at Vevey, is to be believed, Hazlitt also shaved when he liked, and only when he liked. They enjoyed throughout the summer the simple but excellent food of the farm, including delicious trout caught in the lake, and abundance of grapes. It was the go-as-you-please life which Hazlitt, at least, needed more than anything. He wrote of the pleasant idleness of the time spent at Vevey:

"Days, weeks, months, and even years might have passed on much in the same manner, with 'but the season's difference.' We breakfasted at the same hour, and the tea-kettle was always boiling (an excellent thing in housewifery)—a *lounge* in the orchard for an hour or two, and twice a week we could see the steam-boat creeping like a spider over the surface of the lake; a volume of the Scotch novels . . . or M. Galignani's Paris or London *Observer*, amused us till dinner time; then tea and a walk till the moon unveiled itself, 'apparent queen of night,' or the brook, swoln with a transient shower, was heard more distinctly in the darkness, mingling with the soft, rustling breeze; and the next morning the song of peasants broke upon refreshing sleep, as the sun glanced among the clustering vine-leaves, or the shadowy hills, as the mists retired from their summits, looked in at our windows."[344]

That he did not forget his "little boy," as he continued to call his son, although Willie, who had been settled at a school in Devonshire before his father's departure from England, was now shooting into a lad with something of his father's self-will and obstinacy, is shown by the first letter he sent his son from Vevey. This pleasant little letter shows that Hazlitt made a companion of his son, and talked to him about his feelings and his work. In it he tells the boy what has happened to the *Letter of Advice to a Schoolboy* which he had written from Renton, when Willie had just begun his school life at a preparatory school in Hunter Street:

"Dear Baby,—We are got as far as Vevey in Switzerland on our way back. I propose returning by Holland in the end of August, and I shall see you, I hope, in the beginning of September.

"The journey has answered tolerably well. . . . I hope Grandmother and Peggy are both well. I got your letter at Florence, where I saw Mr. Leigh Hunt and Mr. Landor. I have a very bad pen.

"The *Table-Talk* and the *Spirit of the Age* have been reprinted at Paris; but I do not know how they have succeeded. The *Advice to a Schoolboy* is in the first. If you should be in London, remember me to all friends, or give my love to my Mother and Peggy.—I am, dear Baby, your ever affectionate father, W. HAZLITT.

"We are stopping here. Write to me, and tell me all the news."

The journey has answered tolerably well. We take it that Hazlitt, in saying this, is trying, although every one who met him at the time testifies to his worn look, to let his son know that he is recovering to some extent his health and spirits. Was he happy at Gelamont, as their farm-house was called? As happy, we would say, as a man can be who is not happy, or, to put it a little differently, as happy as a man can be who has everything to make him happy except the one thing needful to make him happy, having which one thing, he might have dispensed with everything else, a man, moreover, in whom, by this time, joy itself tended to sink into "an absorbent ground of thoughtful melancholy." In the solitude of Vevey, as he read Rousseau and dreamed of the hopes of his youth, and thought of the dreams of his youth, he knew that the one thing needful to him was lacking. Ease, and quiet days, and pleasant, tranquil, affectionate companionship, were all good things, none of them to be rated lightly: yet these were not happiness. Very specially for a man of Hazlitt's temperament, they were not happiness. They were but its accessories. Long had he dreamed of the rocks of Meillerie. Now he could look on them every day of his life. But the one to whom he would fain have shown them, the one without thinking of whom he could never look at them, the one to whom he could have spoken of all he felt about them, the one who would have been to him as the soul of the place, she, alone, was denied to them and to him.

At times, the ease he enjoyed served but to sharpen his sense of the felicity which had passed him by, and which he now knew he would never know.

He liked Vevey so well, however, that they remained at it almost a month longer than they had at first intended to stay. On September

20th they left it with many regrets. Yet they were looking forward to the tour in Holland of which Hazlitt had written to his "dear Baby." In a "char-aux-bancs" which they hired they spent four days in travelling to Basle. What meant most to Hazlitt in this journey was the glimpse he got of "one little dark speck, the Isle of St. Pierre, where Rousseau had taken refuge for a few months from his sorrows and persecutions," for, said he, "the widest prospects are trivial to the deep recesses of the human heart, and its anxious beatings are far more audible than the 'loud torrent or the whirlwind's roar'!" At Basle they thought of floating down the Rhine in a small boat, but gave up the idea as the boats seemed neither safe nor comfortable—and travelled by coach to Cologne. Their tour throughout Holland, which Hazlitt described as "perhaps the only country which you gain nothing by seeing"—so exactly similar was it to the Dutch landscapes of it—seems to have been somewhat disappointing, or perhaps Hazlitt was by this time tired of travelling. He said that all the way from Utrecht to Amsterdam "you might fancy yourself on Clapham Common." Amsterdam itself he pronounced a kind of paltry Venice. He was told there that Rembrandt was the finest painter in the world, but the Rembrandts he saw were inferior to those in England. At The Hague, however, he saw some of his favourites by Rembrandt, Vandyke, and Paul Potter, those which had been removed from the Louvre. At Antwerp he was told that Rubens was the greatest painter in the world, and that "The Taking down from the Cross" was "the finest picture in the world." To this, remembering a picture he had gone to Venice to see, he replied curtly: "One of the finest"—an answer with which his guide was little satisfied.

They reached London on October 16th, having travelled by Ghent, Lille, St. Omer and Calais. London looked to him on his return "like a long, straggling, dirty country-town," and he was struck by the surliness of the manners of his fellow-countrymen, by their insularity, and by their unconscious assumption of their superiority to all the rest of the world. He warned them that they must not merely take this superiority for granted, but must make it a reality. "Let us take care," he wrote, "that by assuming an insolent local superiority over all the world, we do not sink below them in everything, liberty not excepted. While the name of any thing passes current, we may dispense with the reality, and keep the start of all the rest of mankind, simply by asserting that we have it, and treating all foreigners as a set of poor wretches, who neither know how, nor are in truth fit to live! Against this post, alas! John Bull is continually running his head, but as yet without knocking his brains out." Whom Hazlitt loved he certainly delighted to chasten, for this was his first admonitory greeting to his countrymen on his return, in an article which appeared in the *Chronicle* in the beginning of November. Yet all the time he had been abroad, not only

in Paris but in Italy and in Switzerland, he had meditated with a kind
of obstinate and surly pride on the strength and resistant fibre in these
same countrymen of his which had made them wrestle their way
through the long war to final victory. The English were slow to be
moved: he had declared them to be all the better fighters for that.
They did not storm out all their strength in the beginning of a tug-of-
war, but they held on. They fought neither in cruelty nor in malice;
he had declared them all the better fighters for that: cruelty was a
confession of fear, but those who fought as they boxed, for "the
rigour of the game," were as obstinate in defence, where the courage
of most nations failed them, as they were courageous in attack. Above
all, they were good fighters, because it was in difficulty and danger that
they realised their personal identity most keenly. His essay on Merry
England, which he had written in a valley near Vevey, appeared in
The New Monthly shortly after his return. In it we find the following
estimate, which at least does ample justice to his own countrymen,
although it shows that lack of sympathy towards the French which
had been habitual in Hazlitt ever since they had, in his opinion, failed
themselves in their hour of their greatest need:

"I think the reason why the English are the bravest nation on
earth is, that the thought of blood or a delight in cruelty is not
the chief excitement with them. . . . The English are led to the attack
or sustain it equally well, because they fight as they box, not out of
malice, but to show *pluck* and manhood. *Fair play and old England
for ever!* This is the only bravery that will stand the test. There is the
same determination and spirit shown in resistance as in attack. . . .
There is . . . always a certain degree of effeminacy mixed up with any
approach to cruelty, since both have their source in the same principle,
an over-valuing of pain. This was the reason why the French, having
the best cause and the best general in the world, ran away at Waterloo,
because they were inflamed, furious, drunk with the blood of their
enemies, but when it came to their own turn, wanting the same
stimulus, they were panic-struck, and their hearts and their senses
failed them all at once."

The bravest nation on earth! Yet all his life he had criticised it for
being purblind to the movements of thought and feeling outside its
own country. All his life he had felt its great strength to be that of a
half-blinded giant. His first action on his return to it was to try
to open its eyes to what went on beyond "the white Alps" and among
"the castellated Apennines," where the inhabitants crawled about the
mouldering relics of former greatness, while the genius of Italy, even
as Despair was beating on the gates, brooded over the remains of
virtue, glory, and Liberty.

Chapter Three

THE END OF THE WAY (1826-1830)

"It was finely said one day in my hearing by Mr. Hazlitt, when asked why he could not temporise a little now and then, or make a compromise with an untruth, that it was *not worth his while*."

LEIGH HUNT.

I

THERE seems no reason to doubt that Hazlitt shortly after his return fulfilled his intention of going to see his son at his school at Tavistock, or that he visited his mother and sister at the cottage at Crediton into which they had moved in the autumn of 1824, and enabled the old lady to see with her own eyes that the "stagnant waters" surrounding the towns and "all over the country" in the places he had visited, had not been the death of him; but his headquarters during his stay in England were again at 10 Down Street, Piccadilly. His intention was to make but a short stay, for he was about to embark on what he regarded as the great work of his life, and he felt that the place in which to do it was Paris. As early as the spring of 1822, he had recorded, in the essay *On the Fear of Death*, the terms on which he would be willing to resign life: "I confess I should like to live to see the down-fall of the Bourbons. . . . I should like to see some prospect of good to mankind such as my life began with. I should like to leave some sterling work behind me. I should like to have some friendly hand to consign me to the grave. On these conditions I am ready, if not willing, to depart. I could then write on my tomb—Grateful and Contented."

It is evident from this, that his work as an essayist, or his putting together of what he regarded as a kind of *Liber Veritatis* in his essays, had not completely satisfied him. The range of his essays was very wide, reaching from such descants on the human mind as: "How high it can soar in faith! How nobly it can arm itself with resolution and fortitude! How far it can surpass itself in cruelty and fraud! How incapable it seems to be of good, except as it is urged on by the contention with evil!"—to what he frankly admitted were mere prose satires, the fruit of the moments in which he felt that the web of human nature in its ultimate unravelling resolved itself only into the various threads "of meanness, spite, cowardice, want of feeling, and want of understanding, of indifference towards others, and ignorance of

529

ourselves." He was conscious that the thoughts in many of them were "founded as the rock," that the tone was like that of an Italian picture, and that the colour was "of virgin tints," bright, pure, profound. He was aware, too, of the quality of his style. While he always held that "the passions make antitheses and subtle distinctions, finer than any pen," he knew that he had not been altogether unsuccessful in delineating their fine and subtle play, in writing that was "done with a brilliant's point." Yet he was not altogether satisfied as to the permanence of the form. He knew that his work was organic. But he knew also that most of his readers did not understand this, and he felt at times as if he had squandered or at least scattered the fruit of his mind carelessly, as if all that he had written might be regarded as "Ephemerides," and pass out of the memories of men, like the amusements of an idle hour.

The "sterling work" he now wished to leave behind him, the work through which he believed that he could achieve what he understood by immortality, that is to say, a sure place in the hearts and thoughts of men, through what he had bequeathed to the world, was his *Life* of Napoleon. In the completion of this book he saw the climax and the crown of his career as a writer. He felt that if only he could achieve what he wished to do in it, much as he had suffered, he would never grudge the pang, for he would not have "thought and suffered in vain:" through it he would have left a covenant between him and the world for ever.[345]

Although he is reported by Captain Medwin as having said at Vevey, while admitting that he intended to write this Life, that the time was not yet ripe for the undertaking of such a task, he was now as much on fire to begin the work as if he had some premonition that the time remaining to him would be short. Now he felt that if the work were to be done by him, it must be entered on without further delay, and his desire was to proceed to Paris, where he would have at his disposal not only all the available published material on the subject, but such information as he could gather from Stendhal and others in Stendhal's circle who had in one way or another come into contact with Napoleon or who had some special knowledge of him, and where at least he would be writing on the scene of Napoleon's greatest triumphs and humiliations, and able to reconstruct the life in the setting in which it had been lived. Already he had noted carefully any trace of Napoleon or Napoleon's doings on which he had come in his travels.

At 10 Down Street he was visited by his friends, and from some of them we have pleasant impressions of his establishment there. Haydon spent some time with him there shortly after his return, and reported on the meeting to Miss Mitford, whose interest in Hazlitt, now that she was a dramatic writer, was tempered by a feeling that "one had as soon provoke Satan as that man." "Hazlitt looks ill," he wrote, "but his jaunt has done him great good, and his present wife a greater." He told Miss Mitford how they had "roared with laughter" together, "and made more noise . . . than all the coaches, wagons, and carts in Piccadilly." Hazlitt seemed to him better-groomed and better-kept than of yore, and to have been subdued to civilised ways of living: "He was breakfasting to-day as a gentleman should, and seemed to be living ' cleanly ' as a gentleman ought. I like Hazlitt, in spite of all; everybody must."

The Lambs came to see him also. Patmore, shortly after the publication in May of his anonymous *Rejected Articles*, called on Hazlitt one day when they were with him, and saw the book lying on his table. Patmore, who had not met the Lambs before, says that Hazlitt pointed to the book, saying to Mary: "There's something about Charles and you. Have you seen it?" and that Mary immediately took it up and began to read the opening imitation of an Essay of Elia, with a somewhat dissatisfied air. This is not surprising, as she, no less than her brother, was a taster of fine literature, and as Patmore shabbied everything he touched on, in literature as in life.

Another visitor was Leigh Hunt, who like Hazlitt himself had arrived home in the course of the preceding autumn, and who had now settled at Highgate. One of his notes to Hazlitt is of interest because of the impression it leaves as to the part played by "this" Mrs. Hazlitt, as she was sometimes called, in putting her husband's visitors at their ease: "I know but one thing that would take me to town sooner than the pleasure of passing an evening with your masculine discourse on one side the table, and ' the calm of pleasant womanhood ' which you have on the other. Pray forgive my saying this, and let Mrs. Hazlitt forgive me, but I am more at ease with you in your own house than anywhere else, and have felt so comfortable there both at Florence and in Down Street, that I trust to please you by saying what I do, and think you should be pleased because it is true."

It is from Leigh Hunt that we learn also of Hazlitt's departure for Paris in July—*to write Buonaparte*.

2

Much of Hazlitt's work had been done out of necessity, to supply the needs of the moment. It would be pleasant to think that his marriage with a woman of means had set him free, during the last years of his life, when he was ripe for a task of this kind, for the long unbroken mental effort which alone could have brought this cherished project and labour of love, to the conclusion he would have wished for it. But we cannot see that this was so. He seems to us, even during the years in which he was engaged on this very heavy task, to have had to struggle continuously to keep his head above water financially, with the writing which he regarded as ephemeral in kind. He had already in the first part of the year published enough, we would have thought, to keep him on his feet for the remainder of the year. In January the exquisite essay describing an evening's talk at the Lambs', *Of Persons One Would Wish to have Seen*, had been published in *The New Monthly*. At the same time he had been engaged in the composition of a number of essays he required to complete two volumes, somewhat similar in kind to his *Table-Talk*, and in preparing for the press his articles on his journey through France and Italy, with some supplementary material. In April he had contributed to *The Examiner* and *The New Monthly*.

The year was not a good one for publishing, Constable's failure in January having sent a tremor through the publishing and bookselling world, but in May his new collection of essays had been published by Colburn, under the title of *The Plain Speaker*, and his book on his travels was published by Charles Cowden Clarke. It had been his intention to sell his travel-sketches to the best bidder, and one would have thought that the money he received for *The Plain Speaker* and for them would have been sufficient to carry him on to the end of the year. Yet shortly after he had taken a house in Paris with a view to devoting himself to his main task, he was in money difficulties which compelled him to devote at least part of his time to writing for the English periodicals. On August 7th he wrote to Patmore: "My dear Patmore, I am damnably off here for money as I have taken a house and garden (No. 58, Rue Mont-Blanc) and have been disappointed in remittances which I ought to have received. If you could by any possibility raise £20, I will send you back manuscript to that amount by return of post, written on the spot since I have been here. . . . I shall be glad to hear from you *tandem-wise*." Surely this suggests either that he was supporting his own establishment, and that he was at his wits' end when his own resources failed him, or that his expenses in connection with his former wife, his son, and perhaps his mother and sister, were keeping him poor. At any rate, it is clear both that he was not free from financial anxiety, and that he was not free to devote himself unreservedly to his main task. In August, 1826, he began a series of "Conversations" in *The New Monthly*, giving some impression of the themes on which he had touched in his various talks with Northcote, under the title of *Boswell Redivivus*. These ran monthly, with but two omissions, until the spring of the following year. In December, 1826, he contributed again to *The Examiner*. In January, 1827, his essay *On the Want of Money* appeared in *The Monthly Magazine*, to which this was his first contribution; in March *On the Feeling of Immortality in Youth*.

For recreation, in the first couple of months at Paris, he turned again to painting. In his letter to Patmore he touched on this merely in a couple of words: "I have made a rough copy of the Titian." In one of his essays, however, he has told how the making of this copy became for him an unforgettable experience. The passage is one which enables us to see him very clearly as he was at this time of his life, to see very clearly too, how in the man of forty-eight the boy of eight who was apt to make himself ill by his absorption in Latin grammar can still be discerned. There has come no alteration of temperament with the years, but only the application of a temperament that was never anything but passionate, to an increasing range of subjects and interests. No doubt in returning to the Louvre to paint he had thought to plunge himself once more into the rich sensations he had experienced when copying Titian over twenty-three years before. The result was one which he would never have anticipated, the plunging himself into a misery which would have something ludicrous in it, so disproportionate is the magnitude of the distress to the occasion for it, were it not that it was sufficiently intense to bring him within measurable distance of a break-down. The picture which he had selected was one of which he had formerly made an excellent copy, "The Young Man with a Glove."[346] It was not long before he discovered that he had rashly challenged the ghosts of his youth. To many the anguish he suffered will seem fantastic, but in reading his record of it we draw very near to the hot heart of Hazlitt. "To those who knew him best he was the greatest marvel," said the friend who wrote in *The Atlas* after his death, of the strange combinations and perplexing contradictions of his character. While we read Hazlitt's record of his suffering, even if we do not cease to marvel, we feel that it is entirely characteristic of him, and that here he fell into a kind of distress into which no other man of his time would have fallen. Satan had indeed digged a pit here which would have caught no other man, but which was the perfect trap for this one. His own account of what he suffered can alone make his experience credible:

"I lately tried to make a copy of a portrait by Titian, after several years' want of practice. . . . I failed, and floundered on for some days, as might be expected. I must say the effect on me was painful and excessive. My sky was suddenly overcast. Every thing seemed of the colour of the paints I used. Nature in my eyes became dark and gloomy. I had no sense or feeling left, but of the unforeseen want of power, and of the tormenting struggle to do what I could not. . . . The only relief I had was in the excess of pain I felt: this was at least some distinction."

We have here once more a trace of the sense Hazlitt had shown when in the agony of love, that at least in the excess of his pain there was some distinction, that in the kingdom of feeling, if in none other, he was a kind of Peer. Now as then he felt that he must turn his thoughts away from the object of his desire, or they would "lead to madness." But the worst thing of all to bear was, that he felt the work in which he had thought to renew his youth had almost interposed itself like a barrier between him and his youth, and all that he had most loved. It had even come between him and the places in Paris which had meant most to him:

"Why did I think of attempting such a thing without weighing the consequences of exposing my presumption and incapacity so unnecessarily? It was blotting from my mind, covering with a thick veil all that I remembered of these pictures formerly—my hopes when young, my regrets since, one of the few consolations of my life and of my declining years. I was even afraid to walk out of an evening by the barrier of Neuilly, or to recal the yearnings and associations that once hung upon the beatings of my heart. All was turned to bitterness and gall."

The adventure did not end as tragically as he had feared. "I did not cut a hole in the canvas, or commit any other extravagance," he said afterwards, with a touch of sober approval of his self-control in an experience which had been to him as "a phantasma or a hideous dream."

A glance at the essays written by him at this time shows at once why any experience that seemed to him to mar or obliterate the past was to him such a deep distress. As he touches on the past in one essay after another we realise that it is gradually growing in upon him and catching up with him, indeed absorbing the present into it and becoming the more substantial part of his life. He looks backwards now rather than forwards. Whatever his marriage has done for him, he has not taken root in it, nor has this new human relationship built up for him any real and substantial new world. His writing about this time is saturated with longing for the past. "After a certain period," he wrote in one of these essays, "we live only in the past." In an essay on the Sun-Dial he had seen near Venice he wrote: "I confess, nothing at present interests me but what has been—the recollection of the impressions of my early life, of events long past . . . the only wish I can form, or that ever prompts the passing sigh, would be to live some of my years over again—they would be those in which I enjoyed and suffered most!" Again, in his essay *On Knowledge of the World*, he wrote: "As we advance farther in life, we are naturally inclined to revert in imagination to its commencement." In his essay *On the Feeling of Immortality in Youth*, he spoke of himself as turning to the past for "consolation."

At the same time, in the work of these years, no matter what their theme, we often get glimpses of fretfulness towards or impatience with the passing show around him. Not without some measure of self-knowledge had he written: "We are at best but humoured children to the last." He behaves rather like a "humoured" child towards the Parisians and their ways, which were not his ways, and some of the essays he sent home from Paris are full of what Haydon would call his "croaking." "People endure existence even in Paris," he wrote in one of them; "the rows of chairs on the Boulevards are gay with smiles and dress: the saloons, they say, are brilliant; at the theatre is Mademoiselle Mars—what is all this to me?" He gibes at the French for their lack of sentiment, "the precious link that connects together the finer essence of our past and future being by some expressive symbol." He gave it as his opinion that no Frenchman, even one with a million years in which to meditate, would ever have conceived of such an inscription as the one which had charmed him on the way to Venice: "*Horas non numero nisi serenas.*" The "impassioned repose and *ideal* voluptuousness" of this were as much beyond the sympathies of any Frenchman as the poetry of the line:

"How sweet the moonlight sleeps upon this bank!"

Poetry—he held—compounded as it was of will and passion and high fantasy, was beyond the reach of the French, although it was the element of the English mind. In yet another of these essays he contended that any understanding of Milton's Satan, of his unrelenting pride and "courage never to submit or yield", would have been beyond the capacity of the French, for they would only have thought Satan "a very ridiculous old gentleman for adhering so obstinately to his original pretensions, and not making the best of circumstances, and giving in his resignation to the ruling party." He contrasted this limitation on their part with the temperament of his own countrymen: "An Englishman will go to the devil sooner than yield to any odds. Courage is nothing but will, defying consequences; and this the English have in perfection." The truth is—he could not forgive the French because their wound, as it seemed to him, had closed; because they seemed to him to prefer shallow pleasures to deep griefs; because their lightness of temperament had cancelled the dignity of their sorrows. It was in this mood that he wrote:

"They forgot the reign of terror under Robespierre in a month; they forgot that they had ever been called the *great nation* under Buonaparte in a week. They sat in chairs on the Boulevards (just as they do at other times) when the shots were firing into the next street, and were only persuaded to quit them when their own soldiers were seen pouring down all the avenues from the heights of Montmartre, crying, ' *Sauve qui peut!* ' Then they went home and dressed themselves to see the *Allies* enter Paris, as a fine sight, just as they would witness a procession at a theatre. This is carrying the instinct of levity as far as it will go."[347]

In the letter on his money difficulties he had sent to Patmore shortly after his arrival in Paris he had written: "I get into nothing but rows and squabbles." If he talked as he wrote we cannot very much wonder at his finding himself in perpetual hot water. Yet he seems to have enjoyed his occasional excursions into society, sponsored by Stendhal or Dr. Edwards. The pleasure he took in the conversation of the Parisian women is sufficient to account for this. He never ceased to relish the way in which the women in the circles he frequented made of conversation not only a fine art but an intellectual gymnastic.

We have one glimpse of him in his home at 58 Rue Mont Blanc. George Huntly Gordon, who had admired Mrs. Hazlitt so much in her first youth, paid a visit to her in the course of 1827, and was delighted not only with his "former flame of one day," but with Hazlitt, whom he found pleasant and hospitable, and of whose *ménage*, ways, and talk he has left an account the truth of which is self-evident: "Once when I dined with them, and he drank three or four basins of Tea, he dissertated most charmingly from six o'clock till two in the morning." He has given us a glimpse of Hazlitt, too, expatiating on the treasures of the Louvre: "he . . . was my cicerone in the Louvre one day from ten till four. His conversation on that day I thought better than any book I had ever read on the art pictorial. He was more striking and eloquent even than his printed pages. In the Louvre it was not a *sederunt* but a peripatetic dissertation, and most admirable it was."

But no matter what Hazlitt did, whether he went out or stayed at home, whether he painted or expatiated on pictures to his friends, whether he wrote for the periodicals or rested for a time from bread-and-butter writing, he pushed on with his main task so steadily that by the summer of 1827 he had a considerable portion of his *Napoleon* ready for the press. In June, 1827, he returned to London and placed this in his publishers' hands.[348] When he returned to Paris to complete the task, he took his son with him, as he had now a home in it. Indeed, the desire to have William with him is likely to have been the chief reason for his flying visit to England. It is not difficult to imagine the delight he would have in taking the boy with him to see all that had meant so much to him in his own youth, or the kind of guide he would have been, the eager interest with which he would accompany his son to the Louvre, the Garden of the Tuileries, the Barrier de Neuilly and the Bois de Boulogne; to Versailles and Fontainebleau and the site of the Bastille and the Champs de Mars, and all the places specially associated with the Revolution and the life of Napoleon, not forgetting the little house in the Rue de Chantereine unknown to tourists, forgotten even by the Parisians themselves, where the young First Consul had alighted after the battle of Marengo.

Charles Lamb, in a letter to Hazlitt's brother-in-law, who in the meantime had been knighted for his services to the Government and had returned to Malta as Chief Justice, touched on William's holiday in Paris with his father: "Hazlitt is resident at Paris, whence he pours his lampoons in safety at his friends in England. He has his boy with him." During this summer Lamb began to make waggish complaint of the difficulties that came to him from the multiplication of Mrs. Hazlitts. When asked by his friend Edward White to forward a letter which had come for "Mrs. Hazlitt," he wrote to Patmore: " *which* Mrs. Hazlitt I don't yet know, but Alsop has taken it to France on speculation. Really it is embarrassing, there is Mrs. present H., Mrs. late H., and Mrs. John H., and to which of the three Mrs. Wigginses it appertains, I don't know. I wanted to open it, but its transportation!"

Lamb's jesting, on this as on some other occasions, proved luckless for his friend. In the autumn of 1827 "Mr. H." returned to England without any "Mrs. H." at all—either "Mrs. present H." or "Mrs. late H." Yet another ill-starred bid for life was over. All we know of Hazlitt in the days that followed is that he buried himself in Winterslow Hut to push on with the "dogged prose" of his *Napoleon*, supporting himself in the meantime up to the end of the year not only by essay-writing but by weekly journalism. Presently he fell very ill. "I have been nearly in the other world," he wrote on December 7th to his publisher. "My regret was ' to die and leave the world *rough* copy.' Otherwise I had thought of an epitaph and a good end."

3

We hear nothing from either of the principals in this matter as to the reason of Hazlitt's desertion by his second wife. There is only one contemporary comment on it, and it does not blame Hazlitt. Crabius, after a conversation with Charles Armitage Brown at Florence, on October 7th, 1830, less than a month after Hazlitt's death, jotted down in his Diary, among other things: "We talked about Hazlitt." There follows Brown's commendation of the second Mrs. Hazlitt, and a word on her desertion of her husband: "she parted on account of the ill-conduct of the boy." Now Brown disliked Hazlitt, and tended to do him less than justice. We may therefore be sure that if he had felt Hazlitt was open to criticism on the score of his treatment of his second wife, he would have had no hesitation in saying so. Thus there is little reason to doubt his word when he exonerated Hazlitt from blame and pointed to "the boy" as the troublemaker.

Hazlitt's son made no mention of the matter, which, after all, is not very surprising, if he were generally regarded as the author of the separation; his grandson, on the other hand, made a brief statement on it which confirms Brown's account of the marked hostility shown by "the boy" towards his stepmother.

Here we would point out that William, at the time he joined his father and stepmother in Paris, was not a child any longer, but a boy nearing his fifteenth birthday. He was of an age at which he could make his hostility felt very effectively: he was also by nature both critical and censorious. Keats's reference to him, while he was yet a child, as a "little Nero," seems to indicate anything but an easy disposition. We have little doubt that he made himself excessively disagreeable to his stepmother, just as, a few years before, when it had looked as if Sarah Walker might have become his stepmother, he had made himself odious to Sarah.

Nevertheless, we think the sole responsibility for the failure of the second marriage should not be laid on him. His rudeness was probably the pretext through which his stepmother effected her inobtrusive withdrawal from a position she was beginning to feel untenable, and a life which she was beginning to feel intolerable, rather than the source of irritation which had made her position untenable or her life intolerable.

Probably one of the primary reasons for the failure of the marriage was the blighting effect of the melancholy which by this time had become habitual with Hazlitt. He had married partly to cure himself of this melancholy, or, to put it a little differently, because he had felt himself to be "falling in pieces for want of support from . . . a fellow-creature." In yielding to this impulse, although it was a very natural one, he invited disaster. The moment for linking his life with that of another should have been the moment when he had recovered his strength sufficiently to stand alone. Then there might have been some hope of the union. But in clutching too quickly at what he regarded as a renewal of his life, although he followed his temperament, he jeopardised his chance of securing permanent happiness. It would have been better if he had waited until "the shattered cords" had ceased to vibrate of themselves, before he had attempted to draw new music from them.

He seems to have realised, himself, the withering effect of his melancholy. " Happiness, like mocking, is catching," he wrote. "At least none but those who are happy in themselves, can make others so. No wit, no understanding, neither riches nor beauty, can communicate this feeling—the happy alone can make happy. Love and Joy are twins, or born of each other." But apart from this, the marriage had contained within itself from the beginning the seeds of disruption. First of all, while the lady had fallen in love with Hazlitt "for his writings"—that is to say, while she valued him for what was deepest and best in him, Hazlitt—although he liked her, although her delicacy and refinement must have had a strong appeal for him, and although, little mercenary though he was, he was not entirely insensible to the advantage of being married to a woman who had means of her own, had never fallen in love with her, nor had she ever touched what was deepest in him.

The proof of this is contained in his writing. Any one who touched the deeper levels of feeling in Hazlitt inevitably left some trace on his writing. Those who did not touch these levels of feeling, no matter how great a part they played in his life, how much they affected his fortunes, how constantly he saw them, made no appearance at all. The matter was not primarily one of liking—indeed it was not dependent on liking or disliking—but of depth of feeling. Some, with whom he was at constant variance, like Coleridge and Wordsworth, appear constantly in his writings, because they had touched the deeps in him. Others with whom he was at variance, do not. Thus, although he was constantly attacked by *Blackwood's*, there is hardly a reference in his work to Lockhart or Wilson. They were not of the quality of mind with which he could make contact. Of Crabius, who literally peppered his Diary with references to Hazlitt, Hazlitt, in all the many million words of his works, had not a word to say. In a sense, Crabius did not exist for him. He never mentions Miss Mitford or her work, although she took the liveliest interest in him and in his. There is no reference to his first wife. Even of many of his friends, whom he liked heartily, and by whom he was himself loved and admired, like intrepid jesting William Hone, he has little to say, because they never touched the deeps in him. Of others, like Charles Lamb, because they had touched the deeper levels of feeling, he wrote constantly. In his ways towards his family we see the same tendency. He loved his mother, but he never met her at the level of feeling at which he was accustomed to meet his father; therefore while his references to his father are constant, he refers to his mother, in the course of all his writing, only in connection with the one thing in her which disturbed the spring of feeling in him, which, being touched, forced him into expressiveness. This was her habit of retrospective tenderness for places.

To say all this is but to say that in a certain sense those only existed for Hazlitt who through reaching the feeling in him had become part of his imagination.

Isabella Hazlitt, although very different in grain from Sarah Hazlitt, had come no nearer to doing this than Sarah Hazlitt had done. If she had hoped to win his love, she must have realised, as the years went by, and his absorption in a past in which she had no share

increased from day to day, that there was lacking in her life with
Hazlitt something which was necessary to vital and essential union.
Moreover, the love for Sarah Walker was now part of this past.
Hazlitt's wife must have known of it at the time of her marriage with
him; but she could not have known that instead of fading into the
background when he had formed a new union, it would have been re-
created in sentiment, and it must have been a heartbreak to her, if she
continued to love Hazlitt, to see this happening. There are those who
write of Hazlitt's love for Sarah as if it were transitory. Hazlitt himself, being no mean psychologist, knew better. "These bargains are for
life," he wrote, because he knew that when feeling has gone deeper than
a certain level it becomes part of the man himself. Our proof as to
the enduring character of Hazlitt's love for Sarah is again from his
writing. While his wife made no appearance in it, his love for Sarah
coloured the writing of his last years and conditioned it almost continuously. There is no saying when some memory of this passion will
sharpen his work into poignancy, soften it into pathos, or quicken it
into flame. Again and again some chance word shows that he is
turning over in his mind the bitter-sweet of memory, or living over
again the exaltation, the sweetness, the agony and the folly of the years
in which he had enjoyed most and suffered most.

Thirdly, there was the passion for Napoleon and the frenzied
absorption in the *Life of Napoleon* during these Paris years. Any one
who has ever lived with any writer, poet, painter or musician, absorbed
in creative work as Hazlitt was now absorbed in the work which he
believed was going to be the justification of his existence, will realise
the power of work like this to drain the from day-to-day existence of
its vitality. There must have been times when Isabella Hazlitt felt as if
she were living with the mere husk of a man, or with a man who put
all the substance in him into something that was quite unconnected
with his relationship with her.

Lastly, there was "the boy." But even here we feel that what may
have affected Mrs. Hazlitt more than her stepson's rudeness was her
husband's excessive tenderness towards his son. Of the tenderness he
had showered upon William, from his son's infancy onwards, there can
be no question. Every one who saw the father and son together noted
it. When Mrs. Montagu first saw young William the child was nestling
in his father's lap as many a child nestles only in his mother's. If the
house in Westminster could be called a home, if was Hazlitt's love for
his son that made it so. He was never too deep in meditation, as he
sat in Milton's room, to hear the child when William, still on all fours,
came scrabbling at the door. Bewick has left an account of the kind of
welcome the little boy received when he came to seek his father:
"Upon hearing a noise at the door, and perceiving his only child
creeping in upon all fours, he jumped up from his seat, ran to him,

and clasping his boy in his arms, hugged and caressed him, like some ardent mother with her first-born." The almost feminine tenderness shown to the little boy on all fours was extended also to the schoolboy. The *Letter of Advice* Hazlitt had written at the time of his son's first entrance into school life shows the most anxious tenderness in the attempt it makes to correct anything in William's character which would tend to set him at variance with his fellows. On every point on which a boy could be guided or helped by advice, Hazlitt gave it in full. What he was trying to do was to shield his son from learning too roughly from experience—in the greater things as well as in the day-to-day contacts of a schoolboy's life. He was trying, in fact, to anticipate the boy's needs through his tenderness, trying to provide for them in advance. His understanding of his child's difficult tempera-ment was deep, and already he was endeavouring, very carefully and gently, to train and discipline it so that it should not be a trouble to the boy himself and an annoyance to others. In Biblical phrasing, he was *preventing* with his tender mercies his child's way. If Hazlitt could not do much else for his William, at least he loved the boy well, which was much.

The evidences of this prodigal tenderness are more likely than her stepson's humours to have made Mrs. Hazlitt come to the conclusion that the substance had been spilled out of her married life. Her pang would be twofold. It would consist partly of the realisation that Haz-litt was capable of a far deeper tenderness than any she herself had been able to awaken in him, partly of dismay that her husband should lavish it on one who was showing open hostility towards herself. Any one of the things we have mentioned would have made her life difficult. The joint effect of them must have made it all but impossible. The boy's coming, no doubt, served to bring her sense of dissatisfaction with it to a climax. She had married Genius and she had found that the feast to which she had been bidden was but a feast of shells. Being a well-bred woman, she resigned her claims on Hazlitt quietly, in favour of "the boy," slipped out of his life inobtrusively, and made the break final. Hazlitt's grandson says that she went to Switzerland with her sister and wrote to him from Switzerland saying that she had parted from him for ever. He never saw her again.

Our sympathy with her is deep, for her position with regard to Hazlitt was from the beginning all but impossible. But our deeper concern is for him. For him it had been a vital matter to recreate himself in a new human relationship. His failure to do so left him without root in life. He had not loved her in the deepest degree, because he loved another in the deepest degree. But she had represented human companionship to him, pleasantness, a link with the everyday world of social relationships, in which she moved with such ease, and he with such difficulty. The shipwreck of this third relationship with a woman, with a woman, too, of whom every one of his friends who met her had some good to say, must have made him feel, more than ever, in his love-life, a species by himself. Once more he might cry: "On my forehead alone is written—*Rejected*." The best proof of the extent to which he suffered, as he withdrew himself into his keep, is that before the year was out he had almost slipped out of life. Of course there was an immediate physical reason for his illness. He had got into a coach when hot after walking fifteen miles, and had caught cold because an old lady had insisted on keeping the window open. There is always a physical reason for every illness. But it was always when something had preyed on Hazlitt's mind, and brought him low, that his body had no power of resistance to any minor physical ailment.

Shortly afterwards, while yet at Winterslow, he wrote *A Farewell to Essay-Writing*. The theme of this, together with the brooding over the past, not now fitful but continuous, a conscious gathering-up, "like drops of honey-dew," of the moments in his past existence when the sense of life had filled him most strongly, shows his consciousness of having come to an end of some portion of his life. So does the fragile beauty of the opening of the essay: "Food, warmth, sleep, and a book; these are all I at present ask—the *ultima thule* of my wandering desires. Do you not then wish for

> ' A friend in your retreat,
> Whom you may whisper, solitude is sweet?'

Expected, well enough:—gone, still better. Such attractions are strengthened by distance. Nor a mistress? 'Beautiful mask! I know thee!'"

In these words there is a note which we have never heard sounded by Hazlitt before. He is not now tempestuously breasting the Hill Difficulty. He is no longer steering uphillward. For the first time, as he crawls back to life "with half-strung nerves and shattered strength," his gaze is along the downward slope.

4

Still he is, if not "a jolly candidate" for 1828, as Lamb would put it, yet a candidate for her favours. He has one strong reason for continuing to live. He is only half-way through his *Napoleon*; according to his own theory of life, the will to finish it is likely to carry him on until it is completed, if not much longer.

At the close of 1827, just as he was crawling back to life after his sharp attack of illness, his main preoccupation had been the seeing

of the first two volumes through the press. This had been accomplished
not without stormy weather. As Scott had published in 1827 a *Life of
Napoleon* in nine volumes, which had been reprinted within the year,
Hazlitt felt that it would be an impertinence to appear at the moment
before the public with a second *Life*, if there were not some special
justification for its appearance. The justification, in his eyes, was that
his book approached Napoleon from a totally different point of view,
and interpreted very differently the career of Napoleon as a gesture on
the part of History. In his Preface he had endeavoured to explain his
conception of Napoleon as the child and champion of the Revolution,
as the bulwark that had been reared by Nature between the Peoples of
Europe and hereditary despotisms, and as a ruler who, if he had been
a tyrant, had become one less out of lust of domination than under the
compulsion of circumstances, seeing that the dissensions within France
herself could only have been repressed and the aggressions of her foes
repelled by one who had had the daring and energy to make himself a
military dictator. To a certain extent his career had been predetermined
for him by the events which had preceded his coming. This Preface,
Hazlitt tells us, had been acclaimed in Paris as a masterpiece. But his
English publishers, Charles Cowden Clarke and Henry Leigh Hunt,
John Hunt's son, felt it to be what Leigh Hunt would have called a
"gunpowder text," and Hazlitt refused to alter it. "Shall I retract my
opinion altogether, and forswear my own book?"—he wrote indignantly to Cowden Clarke, and again : "I thought that all the world
agreed with me at present that Buonaparte was better than the
Bourbons, or that a tyrant was better than tyranny. In my opinion,
no one of an understanding above the rank of a lady's waiting-maid
could ever have doubted this." No doubt he wished that he had to deal
with John Hunt, rather than with Henry, the less-valiant son of a
valiant father. But perhaps his publishers, twelve years after Waterloo,
were justified in regarding this Preface as "a gunpowder text."

In the January of 1828 he continued to tease both his publishers and
himself with a nervous anxiety as to the reception of this cherished
book of his, such as he had shown with regard to no other of his works.
Because he feared that his enemies would unite to crush it out of
existence, he was eager that his friends should assist it, by noticing it,
preliminary to its publication. In one of his notes to Cowden Clarke,
he wrote: "Do you think it would be amiss to give Buckingham the
first vol. for next week's *Athenæum*, though Hunt, etc. do not write in
it? The public are to be won like a widow—

> ' With brisk attacks and urging
> Not slow approaches, like a virgin.'"

The book was noticed by anticipation both in the *Athenæum* and in

The London Weekly Review, in the first week of January, yet Hazlitt seems to have felt his publishers lacking in enthusiasm over the pre-publication advertising. To Henry Hunt he wrote on January 18th: "Don't you think an account in *The Examiner* would tell in just now, after *The London Review* and *The Athenæum*?" and, apparently in reply to some criticism passed on the Editor of *The Athenæum* by Hunt: "I am not surprised at what you tell me, but drowning men catch at Buckinghams." One of his letters to Cowden Clarke has a hint of desperateness. After reproaching Clarke for having failed to send him the "puff" of the book which had appeared in *The London Weekly Review*, he reproached him almost bitterly both for being half-hearted, finical, and over-scrupulous about preliminary advertisement and discouraging about the "puff" which had appeared in *The Athenæum*. "When the house is beset with robbers, are we to leave the doors open, to show our innocence and immaculateness of intention?" he wrote, and again: "There is a puff of Haydon in *The Examiner*, like blue ruin, *out of pure generosity*. But with respect to ourselves we shut up our mouths like a maidenhood, lest it should look like partiality." He felt, as he had done on many other occasions, that the Tories knew their enemies, but that the men of his own party were half-hearted in serving their friends. At the close of the letter he added: "Do not suppose I am vexed; I am only frightened." The undertaking was a big one; the book challenged popular opinion; it required strong support if it were to be floated successfully. Hazlitt felt, rightly enough, as the sequel showed, that the energy which would have been necessary to make so ambitious an undertaking a success was not being shown. He was like a man with a premonition of disaster. Most of his letters about the *Napoleon* show such tension and irritability, that it must have been a relief to the publishers no less than to the anxious author, when early in the spring of 1828 the first two volumes of the biography, leading up to the Peace of Amiens, were shipped over safely.

In March Hazlitt came up to town to engage in weekly journalism and to take up once more the office of dramatic critic for *The Examiner*. It is interesting to note with what natural power he now deals out again such rough justice as it is possible for a writer in weekly papers to deal to his contemporaries. We note this power specially in three instances, once, when he taught the public what it owed to Edmund Kean; a second time, when he intervened between Leigh Hunt and the angry pack who sought to run him down after the publication of his *Lord Byron and some of his Contemporaries*; a third time when he commented on the quality of the *aqua vitae* which Landor this year produced from his very remarkable "private still." In the past few years Kean had suffered greatly. His career had never recovered from the blighting effects of the prosecution to which he had been subjected in 1825, when his enemies and his disparagers had been "glad to see him brought to the ordinary level in a vulgar *crim. con.*" When he had returned to Drury Lane in 1827 his course had been neither too prosperous nor too untroubled. The first thing Hazlitt did, on returning to dramatic criticism early in 1828, was to rend Kean's persecutors, to plead once more the cause of the man of genius, to recall the public to the debt it owed to a genius like Kean's, and to rebuke the newspapers (he mentions *The Times* by name), who when an actor of genius dominated the English stage could find nothing better to do than to *send him to Coventry*. In this article Hazlitt did almost as much service to Kean, at a critical moment of his career, as he had done when, in writing his account of Kean's first appearance, in 1814, he had hailed the advent of an actor of genius. The passion, pity and indignation he poured into it made it as electrifying as Kean's acting, although now a little the worse for wear, could at times still be.

It was in May that he rallied to the defence of Leigh Hunt, who had been "under a cloud" ever since the *Lord Byron* had appeared. The book had some faults of taste, as no one knew better then Hazlitt, who indeed rated both Hunt and Byron among coxcombs, but it was not all "compact of jars;" it had sincerity to recommend it; and it contained some very fine witing. Some of its faults arose out of its sincerity, for Hunt had the special knowledge of Byron that only a man, or a woman either, could have, who had been unfortunate enough to be at his mercy and in his power. It was natural that it should be criticised. It was not fair that it should be slain, and then vilified as being carrion. Even before its appearance Moore had attacked it in *The Times*, in a cutting, contemptuous, and rather foul-mouthed set of satirical verses called *The Living Dog and the Dead Lion. Blackwood's* attacked it in March in an article which Scott feared would provoke a duel. It was primarily the tone of this review which rallied Hazlitt to Hunt's defence. There is little new in the forty-six closely-printed pages in which Wilson unpacked his heart of its insincerity, sordid malice, and vulgarity, except that he now trains his jet of squalid bile on Mrs. Hunt and the Hunt children. In his gutter idiom, "dear little Thornton Hunt," as Lamb called this sensitive child, and his brothers and sisters are metamorphosed into "bold brats," and described as "a litter of small, squeaking cockneys, all afrisk, with tails atwist, to the ineffable delight of the parent grunters."

Hazlitt's defence of Hunt's book is highly indicative of character. He had little reason to be satisfied with Hunt over Byron. When in the autumn of 1826 he had allowed some refractions of Hunt's talk about Byron to appear in the first of his "Conversations" with Northcote, in *The New Monthly*, Hunt had complained to the Editor although he knew that Campbell was Hazlitt's enemy. He had here done Hazlitt a definite disservice, for Hazlitt had more or less relied, when he had gone to Paris, on the "Conversations" with Northcote, designed to be serialised in *The New Monthly*, as pot-boilers, while he pushed on with his *Napoleon*. There can be little doubt that the irritation aroused in Campbell by Hunt's complaint was one of the things which inclined him towards discontinuing the series at the first opportunity.

Nevertheless, when Hunt's own indiscretions were being universally attacked, what was uppermost in Hazlitt was the genuine indignation of a man-of-letters who saw a work of real literary merit unscrupulously vilified. He was one of those who realised what a writer Hunt might have been, had he not been too successful in his youth, too facile, and too much involved in journalism—and he found that in this book, for the first time, Hunt had given his gifts "fair play," and "done himself common justice." Therefore in his defence he ignored all Wilson's raucous nonsense, and merely gave himself up to pointing out the beauty of certain passages, which the reviews had found it convenient to ignore, especially the account of the Sea Voyage. In a few words he gives an impression of the quality of the writing. His comment on the description of the storm at sea is: "Now this is not fresh-water description—cock-boat sailing." He quoted the "bright and breathing" pages in which Hunt had described the voluptuous sensations and fine movements of feeling he had experienced on entering the Mediterranean, remarking on the style of these enchanting passages: "It is here bright and quick as the first feeling of truth, or light as the foam, just severed from the parted wave."

This was the one perfect defence. In producing and pointing such passages Hazlitt defeated, in the course of a few pages, any attempt to make Hunt's work appear one long sordid indiscretion.

The article on Landor appeared in June, in salutation of the third volume of *Imaginary Conversations*. Hazlitt never wrote anything more highly charged with the true *vivida vis* which is inseparable from what is best in his literary criticism. In this article he bates not a jot of the criticism of Landor he had previous expressed. The violence, the extravagance, the eccentricity, the perversity, and the whimsy—all receive their comment, and perhaps above all, the literary incendiarism: "Mr. Landor's conceptions are all glowing, ardent, untractable, formidable from their power or splendour. He might dream he had been delivered of a firebrand instead of a book; Aetna and Vesuvius glare in the margin." The perversity is dealt with in the words: "to say to Mr. Landor, *Do not do this*, is to say to him, *Do it*!" But now even the censure is interpenetrated by affection for the man, and feeling for the idiosyncrasy of the man; and when Hazlitt comes to explaining what is best in Landor, he is incomparable. The strength, and the gentleness that springs out of it like a white lily, the pride and the purity, the scorn of "broad rumour," the worship of that which is high, all receive their due. He says that Landor "enters into the style and character of the ancient poets, bringing out their freshness and beauty, like roses newly washed in the dew;—utters sentiments of patriotism worthy, both in style and matter, of an old Greek or Roman; and draws pictures of domestic manners and the tenderest affection, that seem actually taken from ' the red-leaved tablets of the heart.'" He touches on the pride and aloofness in the words: "Seeing how fast modern wits live,—how soon their reputations wear out, like the hasty shower that spangles the grass for a moment and then sinks into the ground for ever,—he keeps aloof from the vain and noisy strife, retires to the sanctuaries of ancient fame; wraps himself in the garb and mantle of ancient genius, and by becoming prematurely obsolete, hopes to win a reversion of immortality."

It is clear that the two dialogues on Liberty touched him to the quick. The one between Ferdinand the Seventh and his Confessor drew from him the cry: "Venom, venom: the very essence of prussic acid." The one on Judge Wolfgang and Henry of Melctal hurled him back into the sorrow and anger with which in 1816 he had contemplated the silences of the poets. The "aching dark root of fire" which the negations of these had implanted in him flared up in him suddenly as it had not done for years, at the nature of the oppression related in this dialogue, and the words in which he commented on it have, like Landor's own, the scalding of tears:

"Heart-breaking, both in the incidents and expressions. Our writer's style glows among the snows, melts among the rocks of the lonely Helvetia. He takes the bleeding patriot's part, but has no sympathy with the blood-thirsty oppressor—unlike some of our pensioned sonneteers, who cant about Schill and Hofer, but are struck dumb at the names of Francis or Ferdinand. Ours is an honest railer: he does not sell sentiment, does not traffic in indignation, does not go to market with exclamations and interjections; his rage boils over and scalds himself, having none of the crafty qualifications of the *Lake School*. He does not say to it, *Hitherto shalt thou come, and no farther*—that is, as far as his interest, hypocrisy, and servility permit it to float him into a snug place, but not out of it again for the world."

It is stirring, as we read this review, to sense the recognition of one master-spirit by another. One fragment of dialogue alone in the book would have crowned it, for Hazlitt:

Polycrates: I wonder that liberty can exist in any country where there is one resolute and determined man.
Anacreon: And I that tyranny can exist in any country where there are two.

This was the last article but one which appeared from Hazlitt's pen in 1828, before he gave up his newspaper work for the summer and withdrew himself once more into the obscure travail of the *Napoleon*. There is some evidence to show that his desire was to return to Paris for the summer to complete his work; there is none to show that he was able to fulfil his desire. It is true that on the day following the appearance of his review of Landor's work, June 15th, there appeared in *The Examiner* an article on Kean in Paris, but we find no indication in it that he had seen any of Kean's performances in Paris in May or the beginning of June, but rather every indication that he based what he said on the reports which had reached him of the impression Kean had made, and on his knowledge of the average Frenchman's reactions to Kean. He thought the French as little capable of doing justice to the merits of tragic acting like Kean's, as they were of doing justice to the merits of English tragic poetry. Even in Stendhal's feeling for Kean there was as much amazement as admiration. Hazlitt did not need to go to Paris to know that the primary reaction of the Parisian audience to Kean would not be: "Here at last is the genuine tide of passion once more let loose in the theatre," but the exclamation: "*Mon Dieu, qu'il est petit!*" or to retort, in proud defence of Kean: "He is diminutive, it is true: so was the *Little Corporal*: but since the latter disappeared from the stage, they have ceased to be the *Great Nation*."

It seems likely that between the middle of June, when his last theatrical article was written, and October, when we find him at Winterslow, complaining to the Post-Master at Salisbury of delay in the delivery of his mail, and of over-charging, he lay *perdu*, deeply engaged in pushing on with the second half of his *Napoleon*. Nothing further appeared in the magazines from his pen until the late autmun. Nor did he return to weekly journalism until the end of November. In December he contributed to *The London Weekly Review* and *The Atlas*. There was nothing in the production of this scanty winter-harvest of essays which required his presence in town, and in the absence of any indication as to his whereabouts except the letter of complaint he had written to the Postmaster in Salisbury, which suggests that his residence at Winterslow was continuous, we are probably safe in believing him to have been at Winterslow until the end of the year.

5

Early in 1829, although the *Napoleon* was not yet complete, he returned to town. It is not difficult to understand why he did this. Any respite he took from journalism was always followed by financial difficulty. Having done little writing for the monthlies, or weeklies, since June, he was now hard put to it to keep his head above water. There was also another reason for his immediate difficulties. It had

long been his custom to supplement the income he made by writing
for the periodicals, by publishing each year a volume or a couple of
volumes of collected essays or articles. In 1827, being much occupied
with the *Napoleon*, he had published nothing in book form. In 1828 he
had published the first two volumes of the *Napoleon*, but he had not yet
been paid for them. In the beginning of 1829 he was faced with the
prospect of never being paid for them, for his publishers, Hunt and
Clarke, were sharing in the vicissitudes that had come to many
publishing firms in the wake of Constable's bankruptcy. Their
financial position was very precarious. It was doubtful whether he
would ever receive from them any of the £200 for which he had
contracted.

This forced him once more into a vigorous from-day-to-day effort,
throughout which he continued work on the difficult closing volume
of the *Napoleon* as well as he could, while writing in the meantime to
meet his from-day-to-day expenses. The work he did this year was
different in kind from any he had done for many years. Gone was the
leisure in which he could meditate his essays. He had neither time nor
mind, while he was finishing his work on Napoleon, for producing the
kind of sustained meditation which John Scott, when editing the
London, would have called "a *chef d'œuvre* of a Table-Talk." He was
back to the elements of journalism, and to the conditions of his early
days as a journalist, writing for dear life, chiefly for the weekly newspapers, with what remained over of his mind from his paramount
task. Most of the work was a cross between the essay and the paragraph.
Some of it comes nearer the essay than the paragraph; some of it
comes nearer the paragraph than the essay. One pungent contribution
to *The Atlas* consisted of a single sentence: "The science of Political
Economy means the *divine right* of landlords." He resumed also, at the
beginning of this year, the publication from week to week of the
Northcote "Conversations." Altogether, more than seventy contributions in the course of this year can be traced to his pen. He looked
on all this work, except perhaps the "Conversations," as ephemeral.
Indeed it was but the surplus of his mind, like the chippings flung away
by the hand of the sculptor from the main block on which he was
engaged. But then, the surplus of such a mind! Much of it is gold-
dust of history. The historian of these times may find here, not tinsel-
spangling, but many particles of fine gold for the illumination of the
pages of history. Such is the description with which he opened the
year's work, of the youthful Charles Fox, at the time he was regarded as
"the greatest coxcomb in Europe," as he first burst upon the astonished
gaze of Grattan, like an apparition, at three in the morning, looking
like some young *débutante* in the part of Rosalind in *As You Like It*,
laughing like to kill himself as he shook the water off the plume of
feathers in his hat, while the rain poured off his blue-and-white silk

coat and waistcoat into his sodden shoes. This, which Hazlitt had heard from Grattan's eloquent lips, has a kind of enchantment, a *bouquet* or perfume, as it were, of youth and careless gaiety and high spirits, rare even in Hazlitt's spirited evocations of personality. Or there is the impression given of Sheridan in his old age, still with something in him that life had left uncorrupted: "No one could pass him in the street, even in his decline, without being struck by him as one of the brightest and bravest of men. His eye, though quenched, was like a sword;" and the curious hint, only to be found in Hazlitt, that Sheridan was a Cromwell *manqué*: "He had a nose and a mouth like Oliver Cromwell's." Or there is the no less interesting impression of the crowds at Yarmouth jostling Nelson when he went to take possession of his ship, and breaking into grumbling which might have reached his ears and which certainly denoted dissatisfaction with his appointment: "What! have they made that little insignificant fellow a Captain!"

There is gold-dust of poetry too, to be found in this weekly journalism, and gold-dust of literature. Here we find Coleridge's Memorabilia recorded, the "unction" of old Peter Pindar's talk, and the opinion of Lamb that Scott's novels, as well as old Peter's jokes, were *below par*— for they had never a memorable word or phrase in them, and nothing to carry the reader's mind on except the story—together with Hazlitt's own outcry against this heresy. Again, the brief essay on Poetry, contributed to *The Atlas* on March 8th, except for the injustice shown to Shelley, is fine gold.

In what Hazlitt flung out of his mind as to politics also, in the course of this year, there are to be found some uncommonly fine sparkles. From among these we reclaim the moment when, struck by a sudden questioning or self-questioning, he pauses to compare the faces produced by a Republican and an aristocratic society:

"I am by education and conviction inclined to republicanism and puritanism. In America they have both; but I confess I feel a little staggered in the practical efficacy and saving grace of *first principles*, when I ask myself, 'Can they throughout the United States, from Boston to Baltimore, produce a single head like one of Titian's Venetian nobles, nurtured in all the pride of aristocracy and the blindness of popery?'"[349]

The Northcote "Conversations" ran throughout the year from its opening to its close. At first Hazlitt used, in *The London Weekly Review*, under the title of *Real Conversations*, some of the material he had prepared in 1826, before setting out for Paris. When this periodical ceased to appear in April, he began a new series in *The Atlas*, under the title of *Conversations as Good as Real*. For this he drew from week to week on his meetings with Northcote in the course of this year. His friends got accustomed to hearing him saying: "Well, I think I'll see if I can get another conversation out of Northcote," as the prelude to his taking his departure from them. Some of them could not understand his liking for Northcote's company. "What, do you still stand up for that little withered old wasp!" he was asked sometimes, for Northcote's tongue had not grown less bitter with the passing of the years. Hazlitt did not view Northcote in this light. The old man's entire absorption in his art, the satisfaction he seemed to draw out of it, the memories connected with it which would pour out of him from time to time, made his studio seem one of the most peaceful places in the world to his visitor. Long before Hazlitt had asked him for permission to record some of the "Conversations," the talks with Northcote had been one of his chief delights. Now he not only went constantly to see Northcote; he liked to take his son with him as often as he could, so that William could see something of the full contentment a painter might find in his art, and imbibe something of a painter's passion and of the spirit in which a painter worked.

Patmore declared that the "Conversations" which Hazlitt reported might be said to be entirely his own creation, to such an extent did he suggest the fine things which were afterwards in the dialogue attributed to Northcote. There is some truth in this. At times Hazlitt even goes the length of putting into Northcote's mouth opinions which were peculiarly his own. At the same time, there is much in the "Conversations" which could only have come from Northcote, like the "divine chit-chat" about Johnson and Burke and Goldsmith and Sir Joshua Reynolds, in which Hazlitt delighted. Northcote knew Sir Joshua not only as friend knows friend, or as artist knows artist, but as a biographer knows the subject of his biography. Thus it was often with a word from Sir Joshua that he met any situation or even commented on any mood. One day he rebuked Hazlitt, who was railing at his calumniators, by a reference to Sir Joshua's strength: "Sir Joshua always despised malicious reports; he knew they would blow over: at the same time, he as little regarded exaggerated praise. Nothing you could say had any effect, if he was not pleased with himself. He had a great game to play, and looked only to the result."

If Northcote did not talk of the world that had passed or that was just passing, like this, to others, it was because they had not Hazlitt's sympathy with it. Apart from this, Hazlitt and he talked endlessly about the processes of creation, the processes of painting, and the painters. Of this kind of talk Hazlitt could never have too much. Titian was of course a standing subject of conversation between them, as Hazlitt had a passion for him, and Northcote held that no man could ever have done what Titian had done unless he had had the devil to help him. Northcote, moreover, had gathered a great huddle of material for a *Life* of Titian, and Hazlitt from time to time gave him a hand in getting it into order. They talked also, to their hearts' content, of others among the Old Masters, and of the painters of the day, their gifts, defects, foibles and eccentricities. And if no other subject engaged them, there were always the queer turns and twists of human nature to discuss. Northcote knew as much about these as any man. He liked to gossip, and Hazlitt, as Procter tells us, "when in good spirits and good humour, was the most delightful gossip in the world."

For some time Hazlitt had contributed nothing to the *Edinburgh*. In July, 1829, when Macvey Napier undertook its Editorship, he approached his old "ally" with an invitation to resume his reviewing for it, with the result that Hazlitt's articles on Flaxman's Lectures on Sculpture and on American Literature appeared in the October number. In the article on American Literature we find, when he writes on Washington Irving's failure to bring to his writing either the grace or the grandeur that might have been plucked "from the bosom of this Eden-state, like that which belongs to cradled infancy," the words, few but vivid, which seem to suggest that Hazlitt retained to the end of his life impressions, if not actual memories, of the vast tracts of virgin country through which he had wandered in his childhood. We note also with interest that he takes here the opportunity of expressing the charm of one of the favourite books of his childhood, the *Letters from an American Farmer*, which had accompanied his family out to America and had been brought back with them to Wem. This was characteristic of him. Hazlitt never lost his love of the books which had pleased him when life was young with him. To the end he could read *Goody Two-Shoes* and *Little Red Riding-Hood* with the feelings of a child.

Well was it for him that he had resumed his contributions to the *Edinburgh* in the autumn of this year, for the *Edinburgh*, even if it "came up like a coal-barge," as Hazlitt had said of it in a moment when the heaviness of some of its prose had irritated him, paid its contributors as handsomely as any pleasure-yacht that ever sailed the summer seas. This was now of great consequence to him. All his continuous writing, since the beginning of the year, for the smaller fry of periodicals, had barely kept him afloat. When he forwarded his article on American Literature in the early autumn he had to bring himself to ask for "a small advance" on it: "I would not thus early appear *in forma pauperis*, but the loss of £200 on my *Life of Napoleon* through the failure of Messrs. Hunt and Clarke has driven me to great straits at the present moment."

6

For some time, in his restless, homeless, and now semi-impoverished life, he had been drifting from one set of poor rooms to another. We can follow him from Half-Moon Street, where he lived in 1828, to Bouverie Street, in 1829. At the close of 1829 he drew into the last of these he was to know on earth, a small back upper room in 6 Frith Street, Soho, with a still smaller closet-like bedroom opening off it.

We have seen him now, at most of the various stages of his life—as a child, padding along by the side of his father on the New England roads, on eager clattering feet; as a round-faced boy, on the eve of the first anniversary of the Fall of the Bastille, intent both on his work and his play, but with a vague sense, as he saw this or that, and particularly as he saw the press-gang at work in the streets of Liverpool, that all was not well with the world yet, although he believed the new doctrines of Liberty, Equality and Fraternity would yet prove the solution for all man's troubles; as a lad in his teens with the sensitiveness and thought-fulness becoming marked in his expression; as a young man, vulner-able but resolute; as a rebel against the prevailing values and the modes of thought current after Waterloo, with the first frosting coming into his dark locks and a hint of pain in his expression suffici-ently marked to catch the eye of the observer. Then years later, the dark locks, though still curling, were thinning and almost grey; the expression of pain had become habitual, and a touch of desperate-ness had been added to it. Haydon spoke of his face at this time as "hard, weather-beaten and saturnine." Saturnine and weather-beaten it was, and it was fast becoming lined or even furrowed with passion and feeling, but it was never hard. Wistfulness was still its characteristic.

Our eyes linger on him once more as he draws into what was to be his last resting-place in the journey conducting him to his "native dust and final home." Let us see him clearly while we can, before the shadows have quite closed on him. By the time the leaves are changing colour on next autumn's trees his countrymen will be saying of him: "Napoleon and his biographer both belong to an era which has passed away,"[350] and it will be as difficult to get an undistorted impression of the one as of the other. Nay! the distortion has already begun. The Mohawk reviewer is already telling us that he is "a small, fetid, blear-eyed pug," or assuring us that his is "the face of a satyr," and although the Mohawk reviewer lacks an eye, and a brain behind the eye, and a soul informing the brain, there are many to whom it is only necessary to repeat a lie of this kind often enough, to win their credence for it. Let us then examine the fine features while we can.

At first sight he seems unfamiliar to us. This is because we see him without the flowing locks which had always been reckoned his chief beauty. His hair is now short, and it is iron-grey. None of his friends liked this change. "He cut it off as if in spite," said Leigh Hunt, "and suddenly appeared with docked grizzled hair, to the great resentment of his friends, and (what he could not easily believe, or pretended not to believe) of the ladies."

There is another difference. The look of suffering, which had first become noticeable in 1815, which was far more noticeable after the frustration of the great love of his life, is now more marked than ever. It has become accentuated almost to hopelessness. This accentuation may have been caused by this time partly by physical pain, but it is primarily the effect of mental suffering. We have already tried to trace the things which thrust Hazlitt's life into the shadowed side of the road, and gradually imposed on him the habit of suffering. We note, towards the end of his life, as one of the main sources of his suffering, an intensification of his sense of the malignity of his fellow-men. It is true that by this time he had had many evidences, public as well as private, of the way in which his writing was valued. John Scott had testified to its rare quality. We have seen that Lamb had witnessed to it in the autumn of 1823. In the spring of 1826 Sheridan Knowles had testified to it both by word and by deed, for he had dedicated his *Alfred* to Hazlitt, and accompanied the Dedication of the play with a letter of passionate gratitude and devotion. On July 26th, 1829, there had appeared in *The Examiner* an article on Hazlitt, interesting as showing the way in which Hazlitt's writing was beginning to fire the blood of youth, and evidently written by a hero-worshipper so passionately admiring that he had compared his attempt at praise to the impulse of "a youthful disciple crowning Aristotle with a garland of field flowers." Hazlitt was no longer neglected. He was universally read. But this could not compensate him for the bitter consciousness of the inflamed enmity his work provoked. He had tried to leave the world better than he had found it. He was now beginning to feel as if it had all but fallen upon him and crushed him. He had fought, ever since he had begun to write, against tyranny, against class selfishness carried to a point where it sapped the strength and integrity of the nation, against vested interests that excluded care for the good of humanity, against servility and the spirit of lying. He could justly make, as he approached the end of his journey, the proud claim, one of the very few claims he ever made for his work: *I never wrote a line that licked the dust.* Those who battened on the things against which he had fought had not indeed had the better of him; his mind had triumphed in that he had contrived to pour out to the world "the spirit of that mind;" he had won his footing, and he could keep it against all comers. Yet they had seemed to him for the past few years, all they whose constant efforts were *to slay the mind*, or to slay *the better mind*, of their generation, to have "straddled quite over the whole breadth of the way"—so as to bar the future to his further progress in life. In England Weasel-Gifford in his day had sucked, or attempted to suck, all the life-blood out of his work. *The Literary Gazette* and lean

Jerdan "of the artificer's face," *John Bull* and its "flash" editor, were still indefatigable in their attempts to poison the mind of the greater part of the public against him, so that, although he was at the height of his fame, it was beginning to be more difficult for him than it had been to "place" his books. In Scotland there was the Mohawk reviewer. Wilson, who had lived richly for years by instructing the youth of his country in Ethics, was insistent in attempts that, like Theodore Hook's, were not *nice, were not very nice*, to cut off the man who had no means of subsistence except what he earned from his writing, from a livelihood. His attempt to hack Hazlitt off from the *Edinburgh* had failed. But Campbell of *The New Monthly* was known to be Hazlitt's enemy. Therefore the attack was continued in that quarter. "Why is not Hazlitt kicked out of the concern?" he had blared at Campbell in November, 1826. In the previous year this *nice* "Professor of Morality" had described the man whose integrity the world had failed to corrupt as "a scamp of the lowest order." In March, 1828, while trying to force upon the world by sheer lung power his own estimate of Stendhal as a literary quack, he had also bellowed forth the lie that Hazlitt, whose influence was just beginning to work upon his generation, might already be regarded as worse than dead: "So infamous, it appears, had Hazlitt been rendered by some able articles in this work, that he had been excommunicated from all decent society, and nobody would touch a dead book of his, any more than they would the body of a man who had died of the plague."

Hazlitt's first admission of his consciousness that the campaign against him was beginning to drive him backwards, had appeared in 1827, immediately followed by the confession that seeing the future was barred to his progress he had turned to the past. His essay *On Public Opinion*, published in January, 1828, had been coloured by the sense of organised injustice done towards himself, and of the acceptance of the injustice in many quarters as justice, merely because it had been pushed to such an extreme. At times it seemed to him that all the world agreed only in agreeing with those who set up a hue-and-cry against any one they had determined to destroy. Some words of his published in the following month, in his essay *On the Causes of Popular Opinion*, throw light on the nature of his suffering:

"To have all the world against us is trying to a man's temper and philosophy. It unhinges even our opinion of our own motives and intentions. It is like striking the actual world from under our feet: the void that is left, the death-like pause, the chilling suspense, is fearful. . . . To what purpose write a good book, if it is sure to be pronounced a bad one, even before it is read? If our thoughts are to be blown back stifling upon ourselves, why utter them at all?"

Again and again in his later essays he touched on this theme—the effect on a man of the consciousness of having all the world against him. At the end of 1829, when told by Northcote that there was something wild and reckless about the way in which he was turning his back on the world, he replied with a bitterness that yet did not exclude the truth:

"When one is found fault with for nothing, or for doing one's best, one is apt to give the world their revenge. All the former part of my life I was treated as a cipher, and since I have got into notice, I have been set upon as a wild beast."

Doubtless his sense of being hunted down as a wild beast was accentuated in these years by the decline in his physical strength, itself accentuated by the effort he was making to complete the long *Life of Napoleon*. We find here and there in his work evidences of the consciousness that he is not working under the conditions required to bring his work to the fruition he would have desired for it. Shortly after he had embarked on this task, he had written of the author, his task and his requirements:

"He has a task in hand, a vow to perform: and he cannot be diverted from it by incidental or collateral objects. All the time that he does not devote to his paramount duty, he should have to himself, to repose, to lie fallow, to gather strength and recruit himself."

Here he enumerated all the things which were lacking to himself, as he set out upon what he believed to be his paramount task. As he drew towards the last year of his life, he was inclined to look with especial wistfulness towards those who having done some good towards the world, were suffered to lie fallow for a time. This wistfulness appears very clearly in the review, written between sharp bouts of illness, which he did for the *Edinburgh*, of Godwin's *Cloudesley*. He did not find Godwin's latest work good, but he found sufficient excuse for its faults in the circumstances in which Godwin worked. What Hazlitt says of these is even more applicable to his own difficult life, supporting itself by writing from day to day, than to Godwin's, and the note of passion with which he speaks of the life of "an author by profession," who has no benefice, no pension, no fortune of his own to enable him to rest at times from his labours, is personal:

"His is only ' the iron rod, the torturing hour.' He lies ' stretched upon the rack of restless ecstacy :' he runs the everlasting gauntlet of public opinion. He must write on, and if he had the strength of Hercules and the wit of Mercury, he must in the end write himself down. . . . With all his efforts, he builds no house, leaves no inheritance, lives from hand to mouth, and though condemned to daily drudgery for a precarious subsistence, is expected to produce none but works of first-rate genius."

Hazlitt had not always written like this of an author's life. There had been times when he felt that a prince could not have led a much easier one, when he felt he had "no great cause to complain," when the liberty it had left him had seemed to him sufficient compensation for all its difficulties. "I rest when I please, breakfast *at length*, write what comes into my head, and after taking a mutton-chop and a dish of strong tea, go to the play, and thus my time passes," he had written of it not long before. But now with his strength failing him, and with sickness gaining upon him, knowing that he must write until the shadows close in on him, if the wolf is going to be kept from the door, there are moments when he sees it thus. This is the first time we have heard from him the admission: "*he must in the end write himself down.*"

He does not ask for much now. If he "can slip out of the world without notice or mischance," it is as much as he can expect. We have no doubt that he realised the nature of the slope he had begun to descend, had indeed for some time realised it. Otherwise how should he have written:

"We do not in the regular course of nature die all at once: we have mouldered away gradually long before; faculty after faculty, attachment after attachment, we are torn from ourselves piece-meal while living; year after year takes something from us; and death only consigns the last remnant of what we were to the grave. The revulsion is not so great, and a quiet *euthanasia* is a winding-up of the plot, that is not out of reason or nature."

Not only was the look of suffering greatly accentuated. The look of fatigue was greatly accentuated also. Yet we have two descriptions of him as he was about this time, which we would not readily be without, because they show that, despite suffering and fatigue, he retained to the end the power of sudden conflagration when anything stirred him. The flame within him was burning low, but it was never quenched. The first of these descriptions is from Charles Cowden Clarke and his wife, who called on him one evening at his rooms, and saw one of his copies of the Ippolito de' Medici, a mere stretched canvas without frame, on an old-fashioned couch in one corner of the room, leaning against the wall. As they stood looking at it Hazlitt took a candle and held it high up so as to throw the light well on to the picture, forgetting everything else in the world as he launched forth into an impassioned discourse on the merits of the original. Charles and Mary Cowden Clarke never forgot the impression made upon them by his face as he talked thus, holding the candle high, and utterly forgetful of self as he spoke of Titian: "The beam from the candle falling on his own finely intellectual head, with its iron-grey hair . . . and eyes of earnest fire, formed a glorious picture in itself, and remains a luminous vision for ever upon our memory." This is our last glimpse of Hazlitt as he was wont to look when translated in memory to the place to which he had once gone "to dream and be an Emperor." The second description is the one given of him by the friend who wrote on him in *The Atlas* after his death:

"There was not a particle of energy about him ordinarily. His face, when at repose, had none of the marks of extraordinary intellect, or even of animation. The common expression was that of pain, or rather the traces left by pain. . . . But when he kindled, a flush mantled over his sunken cheeks, his eyes lighted up wildly, his chest expanded, he looked like one inspired, his motions were eloquent, and his whole frame partook of the enthusiasm."

7 (1)

In January, 1830, he was still in the coil of journalism. Indeed he entered on new schemes of work in the beginning of the year. Ever fertile in resource, he started on January 3rd a new series of articles in *The Atlas*. On January 9th he began a new series of Northcote "Conversations" in *The Court Journal*. He continued also to contribute to the *Edinburgh*. On January 15th he forwarded a review of Walter Wilson's *Memoirs of the Life and Times of Daniel Defoe*, along with a letter to Macvey Napier showing once more the curious lack of assumption with which he always spoke of his work when dealing with friends: "I have done as well as I could. I hope it will do. I hope you will let me know soon . . . but though I have put some strength and truth into it, I fear there is little discretion." His necessity forced him at the same time to ask for speedy payment: "If it is inserted, I shall be glad of a remittance for it as soon as convenient."

On February 20th the third of his new series of "Conversations" appeared in *The Court Journal*. Then came a complete interruption to both his series of articles, which lasted for six weeks. From this we would gather that towards the end of February he had the first of those attacks of illness which gradually, in the following months, wore down his strength. For years he had suffered from a chronic irritability of the stomach, of which he speaks, in his rare references to it, as "indigestion." It is not difficult to see how this may have originated in the early days of poverty and hard and careless living, when coffee, tea and sausages seem to have constituted most of his diet. It had not been improved by the years of hard drinking from 1812 to 1817. He confessed as much to George Combe in Edinburgh in May, 1822, when he said that he had "hurt himself by drinking too freely," and therefore had "given up all strong potations." Yet the excessive addiction to very strong tea, which followed upon his abstention from alcohol in any form, may have been almost as injurious to his health. At all events, he was subject to attacks of what he called "indigestion," making him at times "abhor" himself and everybody and everything else. While he had been travelling abroad, the irritability or sensitiveness of his stomach had made much of the foreign food served up to him abhorrent to him, so that it had been a matter of the first importance to him to stay at places where he could get simple cooking, and English cooking. He cannot have been too well when he returned to England at the close of 1825, for the first thing he did was to go on a "regimen." About this time he wrote of his "indigestion" in terms which indicate that it inflicted on him a heavy toll of suffering: "Suppose a man to labour under an habitual indigestion. Does it not oppress the very sun in the sky, beat down all his powers of enjoyment, and imprison all his faculties in a living tomb?" His trouble, whether it were indigestion or inflammation of some kind,[351] evidently affected his spirits very much, when it was at its worst, for he spoke of it as having the power to interfere with all his pleasures, to tarnish the face of nature, and throw a gloom over everything. It passed from the stage of being a dull discomfort to the stage of acute inflammation during his illness at the close of 1827. He spoke then of having had "a violent spasm." In the course of 1830 such crises of pain and sickness became more and more frequent with him. Some of his friends thought his doctor was not treating him judiciously in these, and that "the last remnants" of his strength, at a time when he was "excessively worn and low," were being "wasted" by a drastic course of treatment which served only to reduce him further, and to exhaust him, when he needed above everything to have his strength conserved first of all, and then rallied and built up again by "port wine, brown soup, and the like generous regimen." Whether this be so or no, although he recovered from several attacks of illness, his weakness grew upon him week by week and day by day. What he needed more than anything else in the course of the summer was someone to take care of him. Probably by this time he lacked the energy to betake himself to his mother's cottage in Devonshire. Or perhaps he may have remained in town because he felt that his work constrained him.

Towards the middle of March he was hoping to be at work again shortly. On the 19th he wrote to Macvey Napier promising to forward the review on which he was engaged, in a fortnight, if he had had no relapse in the meantime, or, as he put it, if not "prevented by accidents." His letter contains one reference to money, showing how much his work for the *Edinburgh* now meant to him financially: "I received your remittance and am thankful for that."

He seems to have timed his recovery very accurately—probably by this time he knew the turns and twists of his illness—for we note that in exactly a fortnight's time he resumed his work for *The Court Journal*. The fourth of his "Conversations," appeared on April 3rd. On April 11th, 18th and 25th he contributed articles to *The Atlas*. Then the life in him ran down again. His work both for *The Court Journal* and *The Atlas* ceased, this time never to be resumed. Of all things there is an end. Hazlitt's long toil as a journalist is now over.

By this time he had completed the text of the *Napoleon*, although the Index still remained to be done, and a Preface had to be written instead of the "gunpowder text" which had been rejected by the publishers of the first two volumes, and which, refusing to give it up for any publisher, he had quietly slipped into the text, disguised as the opening of volume three. The friend who in the end wrote the Preface said of him: "He lived to complete *The Life of Napoleon*, and then laid down his own. He intended to add an Index, which it has been necessary to supply from another hand, for his was stiff and cold before he could accomplish it. He contemplated a Preface." We take this to mean that Hazlitt completed the text of the book early in 1830, just before his bouts of illness or "accidents," as he was wont to call them, incapacitated him for the continuous labour in which the compilation of the Index would have involved him. It seems likely that the two concluding volumes were in proof by April, for an advance notice of the complete *Life* appeared in *The Atlas*[352] on May 2nd. We gather from this that as soon as the text of the concluding volumes was in print, he had placed them, although they were incomplete in their details, in the hands of one of his friends or of the Editor of *The Atlas*, with a view to securing a notice of them which, in anticipating the publication of the work as a whole, would revive interest in it and prepare the way for its appearance. Doubtless at the time *The Atlas* notice was prepared he was hoping to complete the Preface and Index quickly and to see the publication of his work early in the summer. The renewal of his illness must have frustrated this hope.

I should like to leave some sterling work behind me! In one sense, he may be said to have realised his wish; in another, to have "left the work unfinished when he died."

7 (2)

In May, 1830, it is no longer in the haunts of men that we must look for him, at the theatre or the Fives'-Court or the Southampton or the Office of one or another of the weeklies to which he contributed or of one or another of his publishers, nor even at Northcote's studio nor the houses of some of the friends left to him—but in the small closet-like bedroom, the "dark unwholesome dungeon," which opened off his room at 6 Frith Street. His world has shrunk to a nut-shell. The air of his room seems to him thick and close. Even in imagination he cannot go an inch beyond his prison-house. His chief misery is that he cannot conceive of any state of existence beyond the oppression of the moment. He is "shut up and spell-bound in that." Even "the curtains of the mind" seem to be drawn close, and his soul, like his body, to have been flung like lumber into a corner of his solitary room.

He still speaks of having been laid low by "an indigestion," but the "leaden grasp and giant force" of the pain point to some source of trouble more serious. Now he knows the solace of opium, for the doctor gives it to him to drug his pain. It gives him moments of bodily ease, but it plays strange uneasy tricks with his brain. He hardly knows at times whether it is morning or evening. When he wakens from his drugged uneasy slumbers he does not know whether a beam of gold on the wall opposite his bed is a ray from the rising or the setting sun, whether he has the day to face, or the night to endure. Scarcely he knows whether time has advanced, or gone backward, or stood still.

After what seems to him an eternity of suffering the pain at last ebbs. At once he begins to think of other things. He looks at his physic-bottles, longs to throw them out of the window, thinks of his sitting-room, the arm-chair by the fire, a copy of the new novel, *Paul Clifford*, which has been lent him, his paper and pens. For a time the thought is sufficient. Then one day he makes the effort to get up, crawls into his sitting-room, feeling as if he were making a long journey. When at length he has seated himself in his arm-chair by the fire he feels as if he has really begun to live again, for this is part of his "re-introduction to the ordinary modes of being." He looks round the room, counts the stars or diamond figures in the carpet, perhaps notes with a touch of displeasure the violent contrast of the red and yellow in the crude wreaths of flowers twined round them. These things are not amusing; neither are the joint-stool and the fire-screen in the corner, nor the tongs, but his observation of them makes him conscious once more of his own identity. He stretches out his hands to the fire, as a man stretches his hands after sleep, to assure himself that he is awake, picks up a book, realises that he is enjoying himself. Now he has left his illness behind him. The memory of his pain becomes unreal. It seems to him something he has done with for ever, something which can never hold him in its clutch again. How should a man who can still enjoy *Tom Jones* ever again "labour under an indigestion"? But there is the new book in his room. *Paul Clifford* too looks interesting. He begins it, gets fairly embarked on it, is struck by the vitality of the characterisation, presently is galloping across the heath with the three highwaymen, with the moon shining full upon them. The sense of his weakness drops from him: he feels a touch of exhilaration. Once more the curtains of his mind are thrown open. His thoughts pass beyond his little room. His friends will be gathering for supper at the Southampton. The thought of joining them—even the thought of food, is pleasant.

Soon the sitting-room loses its novelty, and he longs to be out. There is nothing in it to tempt a man to prolong his convalescence. When recovering from his illness in Winterslow two years before, he had been wakened in the morning by the rich notes of the thrush, that seemed to "startle the dull ear of winter," and to "have drunk up the full draught of joy from the very sense of contrast." The thrush would now be sending its clear pure notes into the grey of the summer dawn, but not in Frith Street. In Winterslow the thin warbling of the robins on the leafless spray had given him a sense of companionship and of continuity in his life, for the sound had followed him wherever he had been and had always made music for him. Now, as likely as not, the sound that comes in at his back-window is one that is sufficient to jar his nerves for the rest of the morning, that of "a man beating his wife and calling her names." In Winterslow he had loved to linger over his morning tea, and watch the clouds come sailing from the West, and think of the coming of spring. Here brick walls left him in possession of little even of the sky. As soon as he can, he gets out into the open air again. To his surprise, everything seems to him to wear what at first he calls "a very questionable and spectral appearance." What has happened to the people during the time in which he has been immured in his dungeon? They are sadly fallen off. They seem to him to resemble flies crawling about, torpid, scarce half-alive. Then he realises that it is he who is crawling. They are brisk enough, but he is viewing them through the haze of his own sensations, seeing them much as Lazarus might have seen his fellow-men, when summoned forth from the darkness of the tomb. It is he who has become half a ghost. He feels unprotected, almost a man without a skin, or like one issuing for the first time into the dangerous world. He feels everything with a new sensitiveness. We saw him in the opening years of his journey through life, a child in a nankeen dress, marching along the bright New England roads, by his father's side, with bright open looks, *like one that never could be tired*. Now the journey, it would seem, has been almost long enough, for—as he crawls along the streets of London, slow in his walk; careless to the point of slovenliness in his dress, almost insignificant in appearance, seeing that the distinction of his brow is concealed by the large slouching hat over his eyebrows—the pavements weary him like a succession of blind toils; and when he climbs the flights of stairs to his upper room, his feet falter and drag; on the landing he pauses like a man who has to gather his strength for a fresh effort. His hands had always been sensitive and fine. Now, as he rests one of them on the railing of the narrow staircase, you can see that they have become thin, too thin, and that his features, which had always tended to look "cuttingly sharp" when contracted in laughter, seem "cuttingly sharp" even when in repose. Life certainly has spared him none of its chiselling. In returning to it, shorn of half his strength, he is like one entering upon it with purpose as yet all uncertain and faltering aims. What is he now to do with himself? Dimly he is conscious that he is entering upon a new phase of being, or loss of being. The business of adjustment is none too easy. He sees everything from a new angle, and for a time this is confusing. "The machine has received a shock, and it moves on more tremulously than before, and not all at once in the beaten track."

7 (3)

The actual world is insubstantial, but the mimic world remains, the enchanted mirror, in which he can still see, "not darkly, but in vivid hues and bold relief, the struggle of Life and Death, the momentary pause between the cradle and the grave." One of his notes to the Manager of Covent-Garden, requesting a couple of free passes, is dated June 14th of this year. Even without this indication as to his doings, we might have known that as soon as he was able to get out of doors, he would have found his way to the theatre. Two years before he had declared that when the play-bills ceased to interest him he might be regarded as a candidate for the other world: "Ill will it fare with us, when we do not cast a sidelong glance at those pregnant abridgments, the play-bills, and when their flaunting contents, that unfold to us the map of our life, no longer excite a smile or a sigh. Any one who pleases may then write our epitaph, though it will not be worth writing." When he could no longer close "the vista of the day" with the mimic scene, his name might be written out of the book of Life. His writing to request a couple of gift-tickets need cause no surprise. He enjoyed the theatre most when he had "a free admission," for he felt then, not like one of the public, but as if he were part and parcel of the scene. Then he marched to the theatre "like a favoured lover," which was as it should be, for in the world of Theatre he both was, and regarded himself as, one of the *privileged* class. "A free admission" was something to which he had earned a right, because of his long connection with the theatre. He wrote a little later this summer: "A free Admission is the *lotos* of the mind: the leaf in which your name is inscribed as having the privileges of the *entrée* for the season is of an

oblivious quality—an antidote for half the ills of life. I speak here not
of a purchased, but of a gift-ticket, an emanation of the Managers, a
token of conscious desert." He certainly had deserved something of the
Management of Covent-Garden, for in the autumn of the previous
year, when its fortunes had been tottering, he had pled its cause with
passion: "We sincerely hope that this theatre will not only open, but
keep open. That is the point at issue. Sorry should we be to see the Muse
of Tragedy blind of an eye, to see comedy limp on one leg, and to find,
in sporting phrase, one of the *day-lights of the town darkened*—no longer
to witness the rival playbills flaunt it at one another in the pastry-cooks'
or oil-shops, or the shrill cry of 'a bill for Covent-Garden or Drury-
Lane?' mingle with the last summons of the postman's bell, or
penetrate the thick vapours of the fog, as we took our way to either in
the winter-evenings of each revolving year!" On the Monday following the appearance of these words "young Kemble," as he named her,
her heart fluttering under her dress like a caged bird, had made her
first appearance on the stage. After that there had been no question
as to whether Covent-Garden would *keep open*. Her Juliet had saved her
father's fortunes. For Hazlitt, this first night of *Romeo and Juliet* had
meant that the sun of his theatre-world had set for him with a soft
radiance that was hardly less enchanting to him than the piercing glory
of its first uprising. Fanny Kemble was not Mrs. Siddons. No one was
Mrs. Siddons. It was out of the course of Nature that there should be a
second Mrs. Siddons. But Fanny Kemble was Fanny Kemble. That was
enough. He had not prostrated himself before her as he had prostrated
himself before the genius of Mrs. Siddons. The critic in him had
detected here and there flaws in her performance. But he had gone to
see her night after night. What had moved him most of all had been
the music of the young voice, as yet not quite certain of its own
cadences. On December the 9th he had been present at the first night
of Belvidera. That too had moved him strangely. Night after
night had found him in his "favourite niche" or "beloved corner" in
the second circle of Covent-Garden. "I would, if I could, have it surrounded with a balustrade of gold," he wrote of it, "for it has been to
me a palace of delight. There golden thoughts unbidden betide me,
and golden visions come to me. There the dance, the laugh, the song,
the scenic deception greet me; there are wafted Shakespeare's winged
words, or Otway's plaintive lines; and there how often have I heard
young Kemble's voice, trembling at its own beauty, and prolonging its
liquid tones, like the murmur of the billowing surge on sounding
shores." In the beginning of 1830 "young Kemble" played in other
parts and recalled vividly to him the wonder and awe with which Mrs.
Siddons's rendering of them in other days had filled him. On April
28th she played Isabella in *The Fatal Marriage*, the part which had made
Curran say that when Mrs. Siddons had played it, all he had wanted was

a couple of *pails* on either side of him, to catch his tears. Whether Hazlitt was well enough to go to see her as Portia in March we do not know. He speaks only of the first nights of Juliet and Isabella and Belvidera when he had watched "the big tear trickle down the cheek of sensibility" and had thought the boxes filled with innocence and beauty "like beds of lilies." In June he would no longer be able to see her, for her season had closed on May 25th.

But although the appearance of Fanny Kemble was the last vivid delight of his theatre-life, and affected him especially because it made for him "a precious link" connecting the present with the finer essence of the past, he did not go to the theatre only to see Fanny Kemble. The Theatre itself was more to him than any actor or actress. He could be content with its more humble entertainment, looking at it now, not with any intent of criticism, or for any professional purpose, but with the simple pleasure of the years in which play-going had been a rare treat to him, as he had been able to afford to go to the theatre only once or twice a year. He went to it again now, although he went to it night after night, almost with the feelings of his youth. In the last year of his life, even as he could still relish the books that had been part of his childhood, he could still watch the pantomime with the glad eagerness of a child, feast his eyes with the coach in which Cinderella rode to the ball, recalling meanwhile the fairy visions of his childhood, or delight in Little Red Riding-Hood, as it recalled to him the innocence of his childish thoughts. When he could he would be present at Juliet's wooing, and gaze on Juliet's tomb. But when that was not possible, he could enjoy farce or romance. He tells us that he laughed so often over "Teddy the Tiler," a one-act farce on the 'scapes and scrapes of an Irish workman, which had come out at Covent-Garden in February, 1830, that by the summer it had become part of his existence. When *Robert the Devil*, a musical romance showing the strange punishment that had come to the wicked duke Robert for the betrayal of his former love Matilda, had come out, also at Covent-Garden, in February, it too cast its spell over him. He says that he went to see both of these pieces at least thirty times, and that he would willingly have sat them out thirty times more.

There is a new note in Hazlitt's writing on the theatre this year. He had always loved it. Now it seems to be almost more an obsession than a passion with him, or at least, that as he had occasionally to drug his body with morphia, so he now tended to drug his mind with "the mimic scene." To see Fanny Kemble constantly was one thing; to see a Monk-Lewis affair like *Robert the Devil* more than once, was another. To use his own words, he had become "a tippler of the dews of Castaly—a dram-drinker on Mount Parnassus." His favourite seat in the theatre was like a little fortress to him, where he could win release from loneliness and care, "bid defiance to mischance," and leave duns and debts, calumny and the malice of his foes far behind him. But it was even more than this. The finishing of the *Napoleon* had left him very tired, more tired than any man should be, tired not only in body but in mind —and in his "beloved corner" he had found a place in which his brain could be free from its own restless motion. Here he could no longer think. Here he could no longer "torture a sentence or strain a paradox." Here the mind was "full without an effort, without asking why." Other men in such a state of fatigue have often turned to drink or drugs. Dram-drinking on Mount Parnassus was far less dangerous to him than the dram-drinking which had injured the membrane of his stomach. Nevertheless, dram-drinking of any kind, mental as well as physical, is dram-drinking. What had been merely a pleasure in other years was now becoming a habit. We feel this when we read the words:

"The custom of going to the play night after night becomes a relief, a craving, a necessity—one cannot do without it. To sit alone is intolerable, to be in company is worse; . . . It is not that perhaps there is any thing new or fine to see—if there is, we attend to it—but at any time, it kills time and saves the trouble of thinking. O Covent Garden! ' thy *freedom* hath made me effeminate'! It has hardly left me power to write this description of it. I am become its slave. I have no other sense or interest left. There I sit and lose the hours I live beneath the sky, without the power to stir, without any determination to stay."

Yet there were certain things about the theatre which in the sensitiveness of his last response to it, and in this last phase of his love for it, wearied him and troubled him and jarred on him more than they had ever done before. He had always deplored the tide of prostitution which poured through the streets of London, and had hated to see it surge into the theatre. Of recent years it had done this to such an extent that it seemed to him to have fouled the Temple of the Muses. When Shakespeare or Otway was being played, the Muses might preside over the stage, but Venus presided in the lobbies—not a Venus who still had "something of the sea" about her, nor even Vulcan's love, but the poor trull of Mammon. The stage might dally with the innocence of love, but the lobbies were full of half-naked women, "planted against the pillars . . . or marching up and down arm-in-arm with *Tom-and-Jerry* admirers." Hazlitt had not been wont to speak harshly of these women. More than once he had protested indignantly against the treatment of them as if they had ceased to be women, or even human beings. In the real sense of the word, rather than in the equivocal sense in which Patmore had once applied it to his relations with them, they had been his *protégées*. The box-lobby dandy demonstrating his mettle by "hectoring over some luckless woman," or the moralist exploiting his virtue at their expense, received short shrift from him. His exquisite delicacy towards the feelings of "the lowest and vilest," not only of man but of womankind, was noted by his friends as a rare and beautiful thing, by others as an eccentricity. Now there are moments when he speaks of the women of the lobbies with sharp impatience, even with a touch of contempt, as if he had wearied utterly of the spectacle of the stale treadmill of prostitution. But what troubled him most of all was to see young girls about the theatre in the clutches of the old Jew-women (who in their "long duffle cloaks, rusty black bonnets, and coloured handkershiefs," haunted the landing-places) from whom they had hired their poor finery for the evening. For them his pity was profound. If "the clothes, the curls, and bracelets" were not making their *per centage*, as likely as not the lobbies would ring presently with screams, sobs and curses, as these old hags set upon some poor young thing, and seemed ready to rip the clothes off her back. This was an abuse of recent origin, and feeling that the toleration of it by the public was a sign of degeneracy, he protested against it in the strongest terms. It vexed him beyond endurance to see a young creature "dragged in and out of the boxes every five seconds" by a couple of these "Old Cloaks."

7 (4)

I confess I should like to live to see the downfall of the Bourbons.

At the end of June the King of England died. At the end of July the King of France was driven from his throne. The death of one whom he had ever considered but as "the head-cypher of a Court" made no ripple in Hazlitt's life and work. "The news of the Revolution of the Three Days," he said, was to him "like a resurrection from the dead," and indeed, almost it called him back from the gates of Death. Our old friend, the mastiff-familiar, who for some time has been lying gaunt and stiff, with glazing eyes, once more starts up and gives tongue. The eyes that had purged "thick amber and plum-tree gum" over the fate of half the countries of Europe are once more alight and clear. Is he then fully restored to life? Nay! this is but the last leaping of the flame.

Yet in Hazlitt's heart hope for mankind was renewed. A second of the terms on which he had professed himself ready to resign life had been fulfilled. The battle had not been lost, as he had thought in his despair. It had taken a longer time to win than he or any of those who, fevered with hope, had dreamed when they had seen the towers of the Bastille crash on a July day forty-one years before, but it had not been lost. Almost half a century had passed before a great nation had succeeded in throwing off the coils of a dynastic tyranny that had strangled its strength. Yet in the end it had thrown them off. Hazlitt felt that he would never again despair. Liberty had still a spirit of life left in it; the hatred of oppression was after all still the unquenchable flame in the heart of man. The wheel had come full circle. A Bourbon monarch had sought once more to put a yoke on the neck of France, and the result of the attempt had been that he had been driven out of his kingdom. The issue had been fairly joined; and the day had passed when the other nations of Europe would think it worth their while to send him back again at the cost of millions of lives. This was a fateful hour in the history of the struggle of mankind for Liberty. It deserved to be blazoned in letters of flame. The news of the work done in Paris on these three days, July 27th to July 29th of 1830, was communicated to all France within the space of a few hours by the "wonderful contrivance" of the new telegraphs. "Wonderful" though the contrivance was, it was not picturesque. Hazlitt thought half-regretfully of the chain of beacon-fires which, lighted from hill-top to hill-top, had branded into the imagination of the watching people the news of the taking of Troy. The fire-messenger, vivid, appalling, would have been the fitting sign.

As dying by inches in his back-room in Soho, he sang his last "*Io paean* to Liberty," his thoughts turned back once more to the poets whose fellowship had made the glory of his youth. Believing as he did that not one of them had kept faith with his own soul in the years that had followed Waterloo, that Southey had been so shrill largely in order to drown the deep warnings of his own conscience, that Wordsworth had been silent because he had preferred his own security to the Liberty of other men, that Coleridge had rotted his soul out with casuistries designed primarily to cheat his own despair, he wondered whether, now that the grievous wrong done to the country whose early struggles for Liberty they had all sung had at last succeeded in righting itself, they would again feel themselves free men. He thought of Southey. Would the Laureate once more hail France in his verse? He thought still more of Wordsworth. Would the fire return to Wordsworth's dimming eyes, and the song to his lips? He thought most of all of Coleridge: "what shall we say to *him*—, the sleep-walker, the dreamer, the sophist, the word-hunter, the craver after sympathy, but still vulnerable to truth . . . because not sordid or mechanical?" Now that tolerance of the Bourbon tyranny was no longer tied about his neck, might he not again soar and once more dazzle the souls of men with the glory of his flight! Might he not once more bless "the paeans of delivered France!" Might he not be able to exclaim, like his own Ancient Mariner—as he returned from the wastes of despair and scepticism to the simplicity of his first faith:

> "The self-same moment I could pray;
> And from my neck so free
> The Albatross fell off, and sank
> Like lead into the sea."

Alas no! It was too late. The hope was but bred of his own yearning! How could they return upon their footsteps, when "every note of exultation at restored light and freedom would recall to them how their hearts failed them in the Valley of the Shadow of Death!"[353]

Injustice done by one country to another had a way of coming home to roost. The coils of the Bourbon belly had not strangled France—yet they had strangled the song in the throat of the greater poets in England, had stretched across to the cloudy and poetical side of the Channel, and flung the Soul of England back stifling upon itself.

7 (5)

I should like to see some general prospect of good to mankind, such as my life began with.

At the end of August there was a stirring in the Southern counties of England herself in which many saw the beginnings of a revolutionary rising, and which was stamped out with more severity than has sometimes been provoked by revolutionary risings. It was, in fact, the breaking of the long endurance of the peasants and agricultural labourers, whose plight by this time was desperate. When Hazlitt had visited Fonthill in the autumn of 1823, his own unhappiness had not prevented him from noting, nor from being shocked by, the extreme inequalities and contrasts of fortune within a very small district. In Fonthill Abbey even the servants, thirty of them, had sat down to dine "on Westphalia hams boiled in Madeira wine, and other luxuries of the same stamp," while among the cottagers in the neighbourhood he had seen old age stagger under its load of labour, or sickness fainting for want of a glass of wine, or even from sheer insufficiency of bread. On his return to Winterslow in the autumn of 1827 he had been profoundly troubled by the distress he found everywhere prevailing in Wiltshire. When he had gone there in 1807 he had thought the living conditions of the agricultural labourers hard. Yet the living conditions of 1807, compared with the living conditions of 1827, were luxurious. In 1807, if the labourers had not much meat in their diet, they had occasionally bacon, cheese, and butter, and other vegetables than potatoes. In 1827 the diet which was almost universal consisted of bread and potatoes, and even of these there was not enough. Men who were "absolutely ground into the earth with toil," as Hazlitt put it, could not earn enough with all their labour to keep body and soul together in themselves and their families, so low was the price of a man's work. Their petitions to Parliament produced no effect. The only sign that cognizance of their poverty was being taken by the governing classes was the constant increase in the severity of the penal statutes against such crimes as might be dictated by poverty, in the country especially, against poaching; the peppering of country estates with man-traps and spring-guns; the vindictive enforcement of the game-laws; and the preoccupation of the magistrates with the efficacy of punishment. Between 1827 and 1830 there were over eight thousand criminal convictions under the Game Code. Heavy sentences of transportation were frequent. Hazlitt looked on at these things in indignation and dismay. The writing of his last three years is charged with the indignation he felt both at the conditions under which the countryman worked, and at the Code which, administered as it was by game-preserving magistrates, was recklessly depleting the country of its best blood, for the countryman, after all, who poached for his family when it was starving, was the countryman who had the will and the nerve to refuse to let himself be *sunk* by the conditions of his life. The country was thus gradually being robbed of its life-blood for the preservation of the game. He thought that things could not go on much longer as they were doing, without bringing in their train disaster of some kind. Thus he wrote: "as the game laws . . . produced a revolution in one country, so they are not unlikely to produce it in another."

The summer of 1830 was one of such distress that for many the dread of starvation was changed into grim experience of the actuality. Labouring men and women were frequently driven in that hard year into supplementing their scanty diet by roots and sorrel. There were times when some had nothing else to eat, while the glint of the pheasant's wing or the scurrying hare tempted them almost beyond endurance to help themselves from the forbidden plenty of the countryside. If they yielded to the temptation they risked being sent away from all they knew and loved to break their hearts in penal settlements overseas. Some preferred to die. In May four harvest-labourers were found dead under a hedge from starvation, or, as Cobbett put it in his blunt, angry prose: "men were found dead . . . lying under a hedge, and when opened by the surgeons nothing but sour sorrel was found in their stomachs." In the course of the year the sighing grew to a murmuring, and the murmuring changed at last into action. On August 29th, exactly a month after his Most Christian Majesty had been driven from his throne, the first riot began in Kent, and presently the movement spread along the South. Some of the more hated workhouses were attacked. Some of the more hated overseers were taken and set punctiliously beyond the confines of the parishes in which they had long wounded the spirit of the poor, a gesture not without "dumb eloquence." What this widespread rising betokened was something more than the desire of the peasants to protect their lives from the torpedo touch of extreme poverty. It was nothing less than the determination of the English peasantry to regain the status of Man.[354(a)]

Although Hazlitt is one of the few writers of the day whose work gradually paints the development of the conditions which had resulted in this, the last forlorn uprising of the peasantry of England, he has left no comment on the rising itself. At the date of the first disturbance in Kent he was too ill to write. But we have his assurance on all such matters: "As to myself, any one knows where to have me!"

7 (6)

His weakness was altogether physical, not mental. He had been writing until the middle of August, and the flame had never burned more brightly and clearly than at the last. All the writing he had done in his room at Frith Street in the course of the summer, in the shadow of illness, shows, if anything, an intensification of all the qualities which we associate especially with his work, a certain bitter-sweetness, a certain bitter-strength, protest against prejudice and injustice, and the passion for truth.

He had always loved the gay-bizarre effect of flowers "stuck in the girdle of old winter." Three of the essays he wrote this summer, *The Free Admission*, *The Sick Chamber*, and *The Letter-Bell*, are like flowers flung in the face of "the ugly Customer," as he had once named Death, so bright and clear are they.

The bitter-strength is shown in two sets of "Maxims" which he left in manuscript. One of them concludes with some words in which we have the quintessence of his scorn both towards his calumniators and his half-friends:

"If there is a prejudice against any one, believe and act upon it as if it were true, though you know it to be false. If he is weak and dis-spirited, depress him still more: if he is in danger of ruin (through the fault of others or even your own), stretch out your hand, not to save him but to push him over, and then say it was impossible to help him."

In the other set we find his "I believe" on his life-long study, Man— the bitter laconicism of which corners in one terrible nutshell all the conflicting impulses of man's nature:

"I believe in the theoretical benevolence, and practical malignity of man."

The protest against injustice and prejudice is shown exercised on a new theme. For the French, the Italians, the Spanish patriots, the Greeks, the dumb helpless masses of his own countrymen, he had protested often enough, as well as for all those enslaved by the white race. The pattern of his work would not have been complete if it had not included the Jew. This, too, was necessary. Jew or Gentile, Greek or Hebrew, black man or white—all were alike to Hazlitt when they were the victims of "the practical malignity of man." His writing is, as was usual with him, practical in purpose, for it was occasioned by the introduction in the House of Commons of the first Jewish Disabilities Bill in May, 1830. Hazlitt at the time detested the sight of the "old Jew-women" in the theatre, making their profit out of the need and the shame of young girls, yet the justice in him compelled him to admit the conditions of life which had driven the Jews into making a living by means which "nicer hands" would scorn:

"We throw in the teeth of the Jews that they are prone to certain sordid vices. If they are vicious it is we who have made them so. Shut out any class of people from the path to fair fame, and you reduce them to grovel in the pursuit of riches and the means to live. . . . You tear up people by the roots and trample on them like noxious weeds, and then make an outcry that they do not take root in the soil like wholesome plants. You drive them like a pest from city to city, from kingdom to kingdom, and then call them vagabonds and aliens."

But what is most typical in his essay is the way in which he delves at once to the principle conditioning the persecution of the Jews. As always, in his writing on political abuses, he gives, not an explosion of humanitarian feeling, but "the steady pressure of an intellectual criticism based on fundamentals." Thus, as once, in writing of the treatment of State prisoners, he had explained the nature of the persecution to which they were apt to be subjected, past, present, and to come, he now accounts for all persecution of the Jews, past, present, and to come. In barbarous states, he says, bugbears had always been as necessary to men as idols, and in many of them the common stock of ill-humour had tended to find a safe vent for itself in hatred of the Jews, the strangers within the gates. The pleasure of hating had thus been indulged in without prejudice to or disruption of the peace or interests of the rest of the community. Ill-humours that might have been troublesome within the State had thus been safely discharged. Nations in a primitive state of civilisation, or nations that had reverted to a primitive state of civilisation, inevitably tended to concentrate their evil humours on "some object of national antipathy, as in country places they get a strange dog or an idiot to hunt down and be the bugbear of the village." The conclusion Hazlitt drew from this train of reasoning was that even as the persecution of the Jews was a sign of barbarism or retrogression in a nation, so the emancipation of the Jews was but "a natural step in the progress of civilisation."

The passion for Truth shows in the noblest of all his essays, that on *The Spirit of Philosophy*, which, like the "Maxims" from which we have quoted, he left in manuscript. The theme of this essay, which is full of reflections from his early struggles as a thinker and writer, is the patience which is needed for the discovery of truth. Often in reading Hazlitt's work, we are conscious of the desperate patience he showed throughout his life in the midst of what looked like desperate impatience. In this essay we have the expression, in phrasing that returned to the idiom of a childhood nourished on high thoughts, faith in good, and the spirit of the saints and martyrs, of the faith that sustained him.

7 (7)

In the beginning of September, giving up the hope he had cherished, ever since he had read *Paul Clifford* in May, of writing an article on Bulwer's novels, he desired to return to the publishers of the *Edinburgh* some books he had borrowed from them, with this purpose in view. On September 6th his son wrote the following note for him:

"Mr. Hazlitt is very sorry that he has been obliged to keep the *Pelham*, etc. but he was not quite sure as to whether he had to write an article respecting them. He has for some time been confined to his bed, dangerously, and is consequently unable to take them himself or to see about sending another with them. If Messrs. Longman would direct any of their persons passing in this neighbourhood to call for them, Mr. Hazlitt would feel much obliged: he is already so for the loan of them."

William was by this time in constant attendance on his father. Between these two there was in these days, as there had been, from the time Mrs. Basil Montagu had first seen the child William perched on his father's knee, deep affection. Yet there was also a point of discord as to the choice of a career, which, like the affection between father and son, would seem to have been hereditary in the Hazlitt family. As old Mr. Hazlitt had in his time vexed his father John Hazlitt, *mercator*, of Shronell, County Tipperary, by embracing Unitarianism, as William Hazlitt had vexed his father by turning away from preaching to writing and painting, so William Hazlitt the younger vexed his father by refusing to allow himself to be made a painter. It had long been one of Hazlitt's main desires that the pain of his own frustration as a painter might be healed by the delight of seeing his son become a great painter. William Bewick reports him as having said in the days when young William was wont to come in at the door, creeping "upon all fours," to see his father, that "if he had to express his greatest ambition, it would be that his son should become a great painter, as he himself had unfortunately not become." Hazlitt had done everything he could to encourage his son to take an interest in painting. No doubt the boy's visit to Paris and the glories of the Louvre, in 1827, had been part of this plan, just as it was so that his son might see how "beautiful and free" the life of the artist could be, even in old age, that he had taken William so often to Northcote's studio. But all his effort was in vain. William, who had always had a very fine ear for music, wished nothing so much as to adopt the career of a professional singer. Even as to the William Hazlitt whose life-work it had been to preach Christ, and him crucified, a poet or a writer had seemed but a trifler and nondescript, so to William Hazlitt the Essayist a singer seemed a kind of nondescript. The mere idea that his son should adopt the career of a public entertainer threw him into violent distress. For years he had tried to get this desire out of the boy's mind. Now he could not bear to hear it spoken of. In the course of the summer Sarah Hazlitt tried to approach him on the matter through Lamb and Martin Burney, with the result that Martin Burney refused to interfere, and that Lamb, after having had a word with Hazlitt about it, was dismayed by his violence and distress, and wrote to William's mother in terms that put an end to her hopes of any further effort on his part: "I named your thought about William to his father, who expressed such horror and aversion to the idea of his singing in public, that I cannot meddle in it directly or indirectly."

So William, who was now nearing his nineteenth birthday, although with vague leanings towards literature and journalism, was without a profession. Despite the uncertainty as to his son's future, Hazlitt was pleased when William told him of his attachment to Catherine Reynell, the daughter of an old friend of his, C. H. Reynell, the printer, whom he had known ever since he had been associated with *The Examiner*. He told Lamb in these last days that he was glad William was engaged to "Kitty."

We said that the little group of essays Hazlitt wrote in the setting of the sick-room were like flowers thrown in the face of "the ugly Customer." But "the ugly Customer" is not to be cozened with flowers. By this time poor William was almost the only person who refused to recognise his presence on the threshold of the sick-chamber. "No young man believes he shall ever die," Hazlitt had once written. William in his young strength went further than this: he refused to believe that death could take the life which was so close to his own. So often had he seen his father start up from extreme languor into sudden life that he expected the miracle to be once more repeated. He told everybody that he had good hopes of his father's recovery. Those who had not seen Hazlitt for some time, and who also were used to his languors and recoveries, may have believed his report. The friends who were about Hazlitt judged for themselves. Chief of these was Lamb, who had come in from Enfield to spend some time in town early in July, and who was still at 34 Southampton Buildings. Among others whom we know to have visited him were Montagu, Lamb's friend Edward White, Hessey, William Hone, Charles Cowden Clarke, W. H. Reynell, and Patmore. Doubtless there were others of whose visits no mention has been left. Sometimes his visitors wearied him in his weakness, although he was sensible of their kindness. He asked Cowden Clarke one day to go into the adjoining room and sit there for a little, as he could not bear talking at the moment, nor any sound at all. He may of course have been in pain at the moment, but weakness grew upon him from day to day. There came a day when Procter called and was shocked at the sight of it. He had heard that Hazlitt was very ill, but words pass very easily over the surface of the mind. Hearing that Hazlitt was very ill was a very different thing from seeing him gasping and struggling, in vain! it would seem, on the threshold of the grave, as his words came in a faint whisper; from seeing the one who often, after a madly-contested game at rackets, had bounded from the ground in the excess of energy and thrown his racket high up to the roof, waving his right hand over his head to catch it, unable to raise that same right arm in a gesture of greeting; from seeing how *small* he had become in his weakness:

"I saw him . . . as he lay, ghastly, shrunk, and helpless, on the bed from which he never afterwards arose. His mind seemed to have weathered all the dangers of extreme sickness, and to be as safe and strong as ever. But the physical portion had endured sad decay. He could not lift his hand from the coverlet; and his voice was changed, and diminished to a hoarse whistle, resembling the faint scream that I have heard from birds. I never was so sensible of the power of Death before."

"The ugly Customer" is now no longer on the threshold. Now he is well within the room itself.

Hazlitt's son's description of the illness as one of the attacks of "cholera" to which his father had for some time been subject, gives some idea of the nature of the pain which had thus wasted Hazlitt, although the description of the illness as "cholera" is in itself perhaps hardly more accurate than Hazlitt's references to "an indigestion" had been. At times the crises or spasms of suffering were acute. In one of these Hazlitt was also in distress of mind because anxiety about money matters overwhelmed him. Talfourd wrote afterwards of this with curious imperceptiveness: "In a moment of acute pain, when the needless apprehension for the future rushed upon him, he dictated a brief and peremptory letter to the Editor of *The Edinburgh Review*." This is written from the point of view of the man who knows that the struggle is over, and that there will be no further charges. But Hazlitt, when the "apprehension for the future rushed" upon him, did not know that the struggle might not continue. If he did not die "to save charges," as he had once said many an old actor and painter did, he certainly saved "charges" by dying. But while he lived he had to provide against "charges." A glance at the work he had done this year will show how reasonable his anxiety was. While he could work, he could always keep his head above water; but as soon as his strength failed, he was in difficulties. Between April 25th, when his weekly journalism had ceased, and July he had published nothing. In July his essay, *The Free Admission*, had appeared in *The New Monthly*; in August, his essay on the illness he had had, *The Sick Chamber*.354 (b) His collected "Conversations" of Northcote, published towards the end of August, may have brought in some money,354 (b) but his completed *Napoleon* was not out yet, and he had never recovered, financially, from the loss that had come to him in the preceding year, when the bankruptcy of his publishers, in depriving him of the sum due to him for the first two volumes, had bereft him of the greater part of a year's income, while his illnesses must have brought him additional expenses. He had work in manuscript, but he was too ill and helpless to dispose of it. His anxiety was therefore anything but "needless." The letter he dictated was not to the Editor of the *Edinburgh*, but to Jeffrey. Whether there was any confusion in Hazlitt's mind at the moment, whether his thoughts had gone back to the days when Jeffrey had been Editor, and had often supplied him in advance with money which had been repaid in articles written for the *Review*, we do not know. Possibly there was, for the letter was written by Martin Burney. If his son had approved the writing of it, and had thought his father's mind quite clear, surely such a letter would have been written by him.

As to its being "peremptory," Carlyle, with whom Jeffrey happened to be staying when he received Hazlitt's last letter, described it as being "sternly brief," and although he quoted it from memory, felt sure that these were almost the very words of it: "Dear Sir, I am dying; can you send me £10, and so consummate your many kindnesses to me?" The impression it made on him was that Hazlitt was worn-out, and was dying "like a worn-out soldier."

To Jeffrey also, who knew his man, it did not seem "peremptory"— but desperate rather, and he lost no time in consummating his many kindnesses by sending five times the amount Hazlitt had requested him to send, with a letter of sympathy which might have meant more to Hazlitt than the money, had he but lived to receive it.[355]

We think it possible that William may not have seen eye to eye with his father about the sending off of this letter, although Hazlitt knew well enough where he would find, not only generousness, but what is far more valuable, the kindness that makes it sweet. We feel sure that he could neither understand nor sympathise with the pang that came to his father on his last night on earth, that it shocked, stunned and bewildered him rather, and left him without any power to help. We discern the nature of the pang ourselves but dimly, partly through William's horrified but guarded words, partly through the small grain of truth that can be sifted from the legend that began to grow about Hazlitt's last moments before his body was in the grave, and had assumed fantastic proportions within a few years of his death.[356] The more Hazlitt's strength decreased, and the more the actual world retreated from him as he lay in the twilight of illness, the more did he live in his memories. As he lay on his bed, motionless, hardly able to move hand or foot, shrunken, weak, with closed eyes, more than ever his mind was a kingdom to him. While he looked desolate, dried up, lifeless as a branch fallen from a tree when the sap has gone out of it, the shadow of all he had been, he had yet a keen life of his own of which those around him, because he could no longer speak of it, knew little. The garden at Wem and the happy cherished little boy watering the cabbages as earnestly as if not only their life but his own depended on it, his father's movements and quaint ways, the line of the Welsh hills, the leaves on the dwarf-oaks at Wem, the sights and the sounds that had stirred him when he had first come up to London, the mail-coaches pouring along Piccadilly and the sound of the Letter-Bell, the play-bills and the hushed expectancy of the theatre before the entry of Mrs. Siddons, Coleridge looking like Saint John, Wordsworth's eyes as they watched the streaming light of the setting sun turning the green of a bank to yellow, the first sight of the "Jacob's Ladder," the Louvre and the "Saint Peter Martyr," Kean's Othello—on these and on such memories as these his thoughts lingered. Sometimes there were later ones, of Winterslow and its woods, or of the days at Southampton Buildings, and of Sarah coming into the room "like soft music." Sometimes later memories still, of his Italian journey, of the distant hills of Perugia and the fort of Radicofani, resting on its "red right arm!" At the end some "sudden turn of memory" brought him back again to the days in which he had suffered most and yet enjoyed most, and to the one who had given him the most exquisite moments of happiness he had ever known, the sweetest of all his friends, of all his loves, although the love who had never been to him either wife or mistress, the one in whom he had found all grace—and memory ceased to be mere memory because all his memories became transmuted into longing so intense that it obliterated everything but its own sharp pang. Once more he is in "the blind and awful lair" from which, seven years before, he had barely escaped with his reason. To his son, who probably had not heard him mention Sarah's name for years, this "sudden turn of memory" must have seemed the last fearful twist of that old madness. Little as he understood it, he realised that it was killing his father. On the morning of Friday, September 17th, he had thought that his father was better; in the evening hours, he knew that his father would die if the obsession which had taken hold of him could not be driven away. Hazlitt at this point was beyond trying to interpret himself. We can only interpret what he felt at the moment when speech failed him by what he had said in the days when he had been able to interpret the movements of his feeling. If it were madness, at least he understood the nature of his own madness. Only a short time before, he had written: "No person who is in love can ever be persuaded the passion is not reciprocal;" and "the lover, from the strength of his attachment, almost always believes that there is a secret sympathy between them;" and again: "What lover would ever acknowledge a flaw in the character of his mistress, or would not construe her turning her back on him into a proof of attachment?" This is the spark of madness in the strength of love. He could recognise it: he could not prevent its consuming him—to the end. Frustrated though his passion for Sarah had been, he had never quite got rid of the belief that there had been between Sarah and himself some bond of sympathy which was indestructible, let them hack at it how they would. In his faith in the indestructibility of this bond, he had promised himself that he would be with her in his last moments: "When all else have forsaken thee, I will creep to thee, and die in thine arms." Is then his hope so surprising that at the moment when he was dying this sympathy should be of a force to bring her to him again? Or is his longing so surprising when we remember the yearning that had flitted ghostlike from place to place in his writing eight years before, charged with the premonition of the loneliness which would be his portion at the last, or his crying: "I would have some creature love me before I die. Oh! for the parting hand to ease the fall!" He had said: "When she is old, who will look in her face and bless her?" How should he not long to look in her face and bless her before he died? Once, when treading the green mountain-turf in Scotland, in the strength and elasticity which had enabled him to cover thirty miles a day, his thought had been that it would be sweet to be laid beneath it, with her, to sleep with her in that cold bed, if in no other, his hand in hers, his heart for ever still. How, when going to his long home, alone, should he not wish for the touch of her hand before he lay still! Once he had cried that if he could not be at peace with her, he would never rise up in a morning without corroding thoughts, nor ever lie down at night with quiet in his heart. How then should he not long to feel at peace with her at the last! Once he had felt that he could not live without her. Now he felt that he could not release his hold on life until the touch of her hand had set him free to go on his last journey. He had needed her in life to give him peace. He needed her far more at the gates of death. "These bargains are for life"—he had cried. Now he knew that they were for Death also. Hers was "the parting hand" that alone could "ease the fall."

It would have been all but impossible for any young man to understand this last uncoiling of the long twist of passion and longing! His son could only hope that the madness which had come with the night would pass away with the shadows of the night. On the Saturday morning William was still hopeful that it might pass before it had sapped the last remnants of his father's strength. He told W. H. Reynell that he did not think his father was in such danger as was supposed, but "that he had something on his mind which would kill him if he did not dispel it." Lamb called in the course of the afternoon, and Hessey, and Edward White.[357] Hazlitt was now very still. While his friends and William, who was sitting by his bedside, thought him resting, about half-past four in the afternoon, he breathed his last. William, whose desperate hope had sustained him until this time, remained watching by his bed for some moments before he realised that his father had ceased to need his care.

I should like to have some friendly hand to consign me to the grave.

This wish, too, was granted. When Hazlitt was buried on Thursday, September 23rd, at five o'clock in the afternoon, in the churchyard of St. Anne's, Soho, Charles Lamb was there, to fulfil the father's wish and comfort the son. He had always done all he could for Hazlitt. This is the last service. Now Hazlitt needs him no more.

Nor any man! No! nor woman either, they who granted his need or they who denied it. Our traveller has had a *forte journée* to perform. He bears upon his vestments deep spots and stains from his journey. Yet we hold that in the last recesses of his mind he kept himself unspotted from the world in his passage through it. Now at last the hard journey is over. All his life he has battled his way along. Never since he left the shelter of his father's house at Wem, and saw the road to Shrewsbury stretching out before him, his pathway into the world, like something in *The Pilgrim's Progress*, had he known a moment's security or safety, in a world and a social order against which his spirit was in perpetual protest. Now he lies *snug, out of harm's way*. Who would waken him for the unwinding of the remainder of that autumn's story, to see, ere the year had passed, the peasants crushed and their claims denied with the now habitual: "Down, wantons, down!"—to see that the first act of the Reform Government for which he had long waited would be to send special Commissions from County to County, not to examine into the sources of the trouble and to deal out help, but to deal out punishment, to hear Lord Camden say that the discontent among the agricultural labourers was due to the French spirit, and the Iron Duke deny that any distress existed among them, to see the "ship-loads to Botany Bay" for which Southey had long been clamouring set out on their sad voyage, to see the New Year come in with weeping and wailing at Salisbury and Winterslow and all along the Wiltshire downs, the weeping of men torn from the things they know and love and sent overseas, the weeping of the women and the children left behind, sunk, without hope, as the *Eliza* and the *Proteus* and the *Eleanor* set sail for New South Wales and Van Dieman's Land, with over four hundred and fifty of his distressed fellow-countrymen, those who had yet to be taught, if they survived the heartbreak of their lot—and many did not—that men were "born to bear fardels!" Who would have him return from his long home to go once more to what for him was ever the Holy War! Where he lies fierce anger can no more lacerate the heart. Who would have him hear once more of "the thickening phalanx of the foe" or his lady's waning love! Or who, for this, would rob him of his soft mantle of dust!

Or to listen to the controversy as to whether he had died in poverty or no, and all the talk about the awards and punishments meted out to men of genius in his day and generation! Does he not know it all? Who is there among the disputants who felt such things as he did, who found such words for them as he? This is a tale that he has already told:

"Such is the fate of genius in an age, when in the unequal contest with sovereign wrong, every man is ground to powder who is not either a born slave, or who does not willingly and at once offer up the yearnings of humanity and the dictates of reason as a welcome sacrifice to . . . power."

Or to return to hear what *They Say*! The winds blow upon his grave, from North, South, East, and West. Some of them are gentle; some of them are sneaping enough:
"He had the heart of a child."—"He had a demon."
"He was gentler than a woman."—"He spared no one."
"He was every inch a man."—"He was a monster."
"He was the greatest critic on art that ever appeared, (his writing on the subject cast a light like a painted window) exquisite in his relish of poetry."—
"He was a painter who knew no painting, a critic who knew no literature, a writer who knew no English."

"He was the most fearless writer of his day."—"He was a coward."
"He loved much."—And in reply to this a gust comes coldly, creakingly, although from the City of Flowers, where Crabius is now among the poets: "He was a gross sensualist."

On this see-saw of claim and counterclaim, the inevitable heritage of all such writers as he, did he not also leave his word! "I agreed that they were seldom spoiled by flattery, and had no reason to complain *after they were dead.*"

Pain is a bitter-sweet that never surfeits.

Yet he has drained the cup. Who then would have him linger! But the mail-coaches pouring down Piccadilly, the postman in his scarlet coat and the sound of the Letter-Bell, the flaunting contents of the play-bills, the theatre and the "beloved corner" in the second circle, the evenings with the cronies at the Southampton, who listened to him as to an oracle, the Fives'-Court, the going on a journey to the South-West, the arm-chair at an inn and the partridge on the fire, the falling of the leaves, the rich notes of the thrush in winter, and the robin redbreast "pecking the crumbs at the door or warbling on the leafless spray"—all these were yet left to him. What of it! They are now part of him even as he is part of them. Death cannot rob him of the past. And see the gift it has brought him. Did he not long to *sleep o' nights*? Now he lies, *in a sleep deeper and calmer than that of infancy.* Who would disturb such repose!

Any one who pleases may then write our epitaph, though it will not be worth the writing.

One there was, an "old and attached friend," [358] who judged it worth writing, and who had it engraven on his tombstone. If it be not Literature, it is at least History in the rough:

Here rests

WILLIAM HAZLITT

Born April 10, 1778. Died 18 September, 1830.
He lived to see his deepest wishes gratified
as he has expressed them in his Essay
' On the Fear of Death.'
Viz.:
" To see the downfall of the Bourbons,
And some prospect of good to mankind":
(Charles X
was driven from France 29th July, 1830).

" To leave some sterling work to the world":
(He lived to complete his ' Life of Napoleon ').

His desire
That some friendly hand should consign
him to the grave was accomplished to a
limited but profound extent; on
these conditions he was ready to depart,
and to have inscribed on his tomb,
" Grateful and Contented."

He was
The first (unanswered) Metaphysician of the age.
A despiser of the merely Rich and Great:
A lover of the People, Poor or Oppressed:
A hater of the Pride and Power of the Few,
as opposed to the happiness of the Many;
A man of true moral courage,
Who sacrificed Profit and present Fame
To Principle,
And a yearning for the good of Human Nature.
Who was a burning wound to an Aristocracy,
That could not answer him before men,
And who may confront him before their Maker.

He lived and died
The unconquered Champion
of
Truth, Liberty, and Humanity,
" Dubitantes opera legite."

This stone
is raised by one whose heart is
with him, in his grave.

If his night were "perceable with power of any starre"—this might reach it.

There was another who was pleased to arrange[359] an epitaph for him, the Poet whom he had pronounced in what were perhaps the last words ever penned by him: "still vulnerable to truth . . . because not sordid or mechanical:"

Obiit, *Saturday Sept. 18, 1830.*
W. H. Eheu!
Beneath this stone does William Hazlitt lie,
Thankless of all that God or man could give.
He lived like one that never thought to die,
He died like one who dared not hope to live.

"O most loving Soul! placed on this earth to love and understand and from thy presence shed the light of love," on thee, too, have the years thus avenged themselves? *Hatred alone is immortal!* Was he then justified of his bitterness? Even when the cup of love has once been drunk between man and brother-man, is the Pleasure of Hating all that remains for him who lingers over the lees?

Eheu!

NOTES

BIBLIOGRAPHICAL NOTE:

The following abbreviations have been used for books to which frequent reference has been made:

Coleridge Letters: *Letters of Samuel Taylor Coleridge.* Edited by Ernest Hartley Coleridge.

Coleridge, Unpublished Letters: *Unpublished Letters of Samuel Taylor Coleridge.* Edited by Earl Leslie Griggs.

Lamb Letters: *The Letters of Charles and Mary Lamb.* Edited by E. V. Lucas.

Morley: *Henry Crabb Robinson on Books and their Writers.* Edited by Edith J. Morley.

Sadler: *Diary, Reminiscences and Correspondence of Henry Crabb Robinson.* Edited by Thomas Sadler, 1872.

Southey Letters: *Selections from the Letters of Robert Southey.* Edited by John Wood Warter.

Southey, Life and Correspondence: *The Life and Correspondence of the late Robert Southey.* Edited by Cuthbert Southey.

Wordsworth Letters—The Early Years:
The Middle Years:
The Later Years: *The Letters of William and Dorothy Wordsworth.* Edited by E. de Selincourt.

Works: Hazlitt's Works, Centenary Edition. Edited by P. P. Howe.

1. Of this censure we know from Dr. Price's letter to the Rev. William Hazlitt, dated June 28th, 1782. Margaret Hazlitt says in her Diary that it was in consequence of her father's intervention the regiment was changed.

2. *Letters from an American Farmer,* by G. Hector Saint John de Crévecoeur London, 1782.

3. To his American friends Hazlitt remained "Billy," and they wrote of him afterwards to his father by the name by which he had been known in America in his childhood. In one of these Letters, quoted by Mr. Hazlitt, we find the words: "I read Billy's letter to Fanny, and she was delighted with it. . . . The letter does Billy much credit. He has uncommon powers of mind, and if nothing happens to prevent his receiving a liberal education, he must make a great man." *The Hazlitts:* 1, 391.

4. cf. "The majority of the Boston ministers, and a great number of those who are dispersed throughout the country, are already Arians but are yet generally afraid to avow their sentiments." *Letters to and from Dr. Price* (1767-1790) (reprinted from the Proceedings of the Massachussets Historical Society, May, 1903), page 64.

5. cf. "In twenty or thirty years there will probably be here as much

freedom of thinking upon religious subjects as there is at present among the Dissenters in England." *Letters to and from Dr. Price:* page 64.

6. *Letters to and from Dr. Price:* page 76.
7. *Letters to and from Dr. Price:* page 64.
8. *The Hazlitts:* 1, 378, and *Letters to and from Dr. Price:* 64 and 76. Mr. Hazlitt, in a letter to Dr. Price, dated November 15th, 1785, described him as "as worthy a man as any in America . . . friendly, generous, and without guile."
9. *Letters to and from Dr. Price:* 64.
10. *History of the Rise, Progress, and Establishment of the Independence of the United States,* 1788.
11. *Works:* 5, 147.
12. W. C. Hazlitt suggests "others" for the missing word. *The Hazlitts:* 1, 377. "Indians" seems more likely.
13. *Works:* 8, 259.
14. *Works:* 8, 53.
15. *Works:* 16, 319.
16. *Works:* 20, 343.
17. *Works:* 1, 95, and 14, 241.
18. *Prospectus of the New Academical Institution, London,* April 24th, 1787.
19. *Works:* 5, 2.
20. *Works:* 12, 296.
21. *Works:* 12, 305.
22. John Hazlitt's contributions to the Exhibition that year were: "284, Frame with four miniatures," and "297, Portrait of a Lady." *The Royal Academy of Arts: A Complete Dictionary of Contributors,* by Algernon Graves: Vol. 4, page 52.

W. C. Hazlitt adds to these, a Portrait of Dr. Kippis. *The Hazlitts:* 1, 334.
23. He is probably referring to a portrait of Peggy done by her brother. Yet Peggy herself, according to Hazlitt's son, sketched and painted "with very considerable ability." John Hazlitt exhibited portraits or miniatures of his sister in 1804 and in 1810. His portrait on ivory of Peggy is a delightful piece of work.
24. These lines are from an early draft of *The Excursion.* By the time the poem was published they had been altered to:
"And from the pulpit, zealously maintained
The cause of Christ and civil liberty."
On November 4th, 1789, Dr. Price, an old man drawing towards death, could say with complete faith: "What an eventful period is this! I am thankful that I have lived to it: I could almost say, *Lord, now lettest thou thy servant depart in peace, for mine eyes have seen thy salvation.*"
25. *Works:* 14, 241.
26. This was an old favourite. It had first been produced at Drury Lane

on January 19th, 1771. Hazlitt would be already acquainted with one of its scenes from Enfield's *Speaker*.

27. It is nowhere stated that the Miss Shepherd who travelled from Wem to Liverpool was of the family of the Rev. William Shepherd of Gateacre, but it seems very likely that she was. What is quite certain is that she was not the "Sally Shepherd" who was one of Hazlitt's "flames."

28. The value of these letters as giving a continuous record of Hazlitt's development at this time has not always been realised, because some of them were misdated by his son, and the misdating was only partially corrected by his grandson. Thus the way in which they reveal the relationship between the father and son has been very much obscured.

29. This was a very generous supporter of Unitarian dissenters.

30. *Works:* 13, 96-97.

31. *Works:* 20, 262.

32. Hazlitt's reminiscences show clearly that his first visit to Wisbeach and Peterborough occurred when he was a boy. There is no other year, except this, to which we have any clue enabling us to date the visit, and there is no year in which there is so much likelihood that he visited it as this. His sister never saw her grandmother again after old Mrs. Loftus visited them at Walworth in 1787.

33. Mr. Hunter became a friend of the Hazlitt family when some years after Mr. Hazlitt's retirement from the ministry the family was for a time at Bath. He does not actually say that he gained his information as to Hazlitt from them. What he says is that having "some particular friends here who were members of Mr. Hazlitt's congregation at Wem," he had put together such information regarding the Essayist as he had gained from the lips of "a lady not at all given to embellishing." This seems to point to Margaret Hazlitt, and it is difficult to see how such details as those given could have been gained except from a member of Hazlitt's family.

   The dates in the short biographical sketch need to be revised. What Mr. Hunter says of Hazlitt at the age of nine applies to him at the age of twelve; what he says of him at the age of twelve or thirteen applies to him as he was between fifteen and sixteen.

34. *Works:* 8, 311-312.

35. cf. Virgil, *Eclogues:* 2, 58-59.

36. He quotes this from "the great and admirable Robinson," as he calls Robert Robinson, of Cambridge, whose *Life*, by George Dyer, Wordsworth thought one of the best books of biography in the English language.

37. This is Coleridge's phrase.

38. "as a mere pretext." Of course Burke never hesitated to confess this. To him from the beginning the war was ideological: "It is with an armed doctrine that we are at war." *Letters on a Regicide Peace:* 1. cf. also *Letters on a Regicide Peace:* 4. *Letter to the Duke of Portland*, and *On the Conduct of the Minority*.

39. *Letter to a Member of the National Assembly.*
40. Thomas Chubb's *Tracts and Posthumous Works* were published in 6 volumes, 1754. Chubb was a deist.
41. *A Discourse Delivered at the Commencement of the Manchester Academy,* September 14th, 1786, by Thomas Barnes, D.D.
42. *Reports relating to Hackney College,* No. 2, January 17th, 1787.
43. *The Evidence of a Future Period of Improvement in the State of Mankind* ... represented in a Discourse delivered on Wednesday, 25th April, 1787, at the Meeting-House in the Old Jewry, London, to the Supporters of a New Academical Institution among Protestant Dissenters, by Richard Price, D.D.
44. *The Proper Objects of Education in the present State of the World:* Represented in a Discourse delivered on Wednesday, the 27th of April, 1791, at the Meeting-House in the Old Jewry, London, to the Supporters of the New College at Hackney, by Joseph Priestley.
45. *The Rise and Progress of Popular Disaffection. The Quarterly Review,* January, 1817.
46. *An Evening Walk* and *Descriptive Sketches.*
47. *Le Souper de Beaucaire,* July, 1793.
48. *On the Policy of the Allies,* October, 1793.
49. *Lines at a Vacation Exercise,* Milton.
50. The passage in the letter is: "I like Dominie (that is the name by which Dr. Rees goes here) and his lectures very much." In *The Hazlitts,* 1, 401, this is altered into: "I like Dominie (that is the name which Dr. Rees gave him) very much." Consequently the name "Dominie" has sometimes been taken to apply to Corrie. Elsewhere Mr. W. C. Hazlitt altered it into Damien.

    In one of the letters also he expands Hazlitt's contraction "Dr. Pr." into "Dr. Price," although Dr. Price was dead before Hazlitt entered the College. "Dr. Pr." is evidently Dr. Priestley.
51. He was always ready, perhaps too ready, to stake all on reason.
52. cf. *William Pitt and the Great War,* by J. Holland Rose.
53. Advertisement to *Die Räuber,* 1781.
54. *Fears in Solitude.*
55. cf. *Works:* 6, 362.
56. *Works:* 8, 152.
57. *To the Supporters of Hackney College,* April 28th, 1790.
58. *Works:* 1, 46.
59. *Works:* 8, 64.
60. *Works:* 9, 51.
61. *Works:* 9, 58.
62. *Aeneid,* 6, 95. "Yield not thou to ills" ...
63. *Works:* 12, 373.
64. *Works:* 17, 88.
65. *Works:* 20, 373.
66. *Works:* 20, 372.
67. *Works:* 12, 276-277.

68. This letter is dated only Sunday, October 23rd. October 23rd was a Sunday in 1796. In 1795 it was a Friday. This, of course, is slender evidence for dating the letter 1796 rather than 1795, as it has formerly been dated, but the tone of the letter, and the account given of the work Hazlitt has been doing, show him to have left his College days a good deal behind him, and to be midway in the struggle of writing. We therefore date it 1796, and regard it as one of the chief clues for Hazlitt's development between the time he left College and the time he met Coleridge in January, 1798.

69. *Works:* 12, 279.

70. *A Letter to a Noble Lord.*

71. *Works:* 12, 228-229.

72. *Lamb Letters:* 1, 54.

73. *On the Present War.* (*Conciones ad Populum.*)

74. *Works:* 8, 92.

75. *Works:* 10, 63-64.

76. *Works:* 1, 56.

77. "about this time" refers to 1799. By "my sister," Crabb Robinson means his sister-in-law, Mrs. Thomas Robinson.

78. *A Treatise of Human Nature.*

79. *An Essay towards a New Theory of Human Vision.*

80. John Wicksteed married Bethia Swanwick of Wem, a direct descendant of Philip Henry. Their son was Charles Wicksteed. In February, 1836, Crabb Robinson wrote of John Wicksteed as "the only *home* acquaintance he had ever heard Hazlitt praise warmly.

81. *Coleridge, Unpublished Letters:* 1, 104.

82. cf. *Letter* to the Editor of *The Courier,* December 9th, 1809. (*Essays on his own Times:* 2, 613.)

83. *Conciones ad Populum.* (*Essays on his own Times:* 1, 17.)

84. cf. *quia non est pura voluptas,* etc. *De Rerum Natura:* 4, 1081-1083.

85. It is not possible to fix with absolute precision the date of Hazlitt's arrival at Nether Stowey or of his departure from it, but it may be regarded as all but certain that he went over to Nether Stowey on Saturday, May 26th, or Sunday, May 27th. May 27th to June 17th are the dates suggested for his visit by Thomas Hutchinson in his edition of the *Lyrical Ballads,* page 248.

86. Knight and Dr. de Selincourt both give the date as May 16th. A comparison of the details of Dorothy Wordsworth s *Journal* with Coleridge's *Letters* of May, 1798, shows that there is error here.

87. *Coleridge Letters:* 1, 247.

88. *Coleridge, Unpublished Letters:* 1, 105.

89. *Coleridge Letters:* 1, 248.

90. *Coleridge Letters:* 1, 249.

91. *Coleridge Letters:* 1, 253.

92. Hazlitt gives the title thus.

93. We gather this from a few words in ·Coleridge's Letter to Poole, May 7th, 1802, referring to "the miniature which Hazlitt promised

to Mrs. Coleridge: but did not give to her, because I never finished my sittings." *Coleridge, Unpublished Letters:* 1, 195.

94. Afterwards he was inclined to regret that he had passed over this second opportunity of hearing Coleridge preach.

95. Hazlitt may have met Northcote at his brother's house or at Godwin's while yet he was a student at Hackney.

96. Perhaps this is because he usually discussed his training as an artist with Northcote, who would be familiar with the details of it.

97. *Works:* 20, 52.

98. It was feeling of this kind which moved him vicariously when one day, seeing Lamb running along the top of a high wall in the Temple, he called out in what Leigh Hunt described as a sort of rage and cruel transport of sympathy: "Lamb, if you don't come down I shall push you over."

99. This is one of Hazlitt's versions of the lines:
"Yet ne'er so sure our passion to create
As when she touched the brink of all we hate."
                                        Pope, *Moral Essays:* 2, 51-52.

100. Letter to Rowan Hamilton, September 26th, 1830.

101. *Works:* 8, 14.

102. *Works:* 8, 14.

103. *Works:* 10, 32.

104. It would not have been easy for any painter to have satisfied Hazlitt with his conception of Venus. The "Venus Anadyomene" is only one of many Venuses which he found, for one reason or other, "not quite the thing."

105. In "The Nursing of Bacchus," Hazlitt does not seem to have realised that this was a copy. The Original is in The National Gallery.

106. *Works:* XI., 99-100.

107. *The Royal Academy of Arts: A Complete Dictionary of Contributors,* by Algernon Graves, vol. 4, 52.

108. *Works:* 17, 99 and 395.

109. It has been suggested that he did this copying at his brother's house, but it is certain that he could not have had the original paintings of the Old Masters before him there.

110. James Sheridan Knowles was named after his father's cousin, the dramatist. His father had been a schoolmaster at Cork, and there may have been acquaintance between his family and the Hazlitt family during the Bandon days. However that may be, after the Knowles family had settled in London in 1793, devoted friendship developed between Hazlitt and young Sheridan. Hazlitt took a keen interest in the boy's work at this time—one of Sheridan Knowles's poems had already been published—and was rewarded by hero-worship.

An account of the friendship between Hazlitt and Sheridan Knowles in its earliest stages is given in the *Life of Sheridan Knowles,* privately printed by his son, R. B. Knowles, in 1872.

111. Hazlitt's grandson associates this picture with Manchester, but gives no evidence for this attribution. Also he says that Hazlitt painted it in 1803. This cannot be true, as he took the picture to Paris with him in 1802.

We prefer to take such indications as to its inception and progress as are given by Hazlitt himself.

112. This is entered in the list of exhibitors under the name of John Hazlitt as "839. Mr. Coleridge."

113. *Unpublished Letters:* 1, 195.

114. In his letter to his father of October 16th, 1802, Hazlitt writes of the "five" copies he is to do for Railton.

115. This sonnet is dated August 7th in the *Poems* of 1807. We take this to be an unnoticed printer's error, for the sonnet is dated August 1st in the manuscript of the poem.

116. "Supper at Cana of Galilee." Hazlitt calls it the "Marriage of Cana."

117. The father of Prosper Mérimée.

118. Hazlitt often refers to both these portraits as "A Man in Black," and this, when the details are not given, makes the reference obscure. In his later writing he usually, but not always, refers to the first as "The Young Neapolitan Nobleman" or "The Young Man with a Glove," and keeps the title "The Man in Black," for the second portrait, which grew upon him when he visited Paris in 1824, whereas "The Young Man with a Glove" did not seem as splendid as his memory of it. One of his copies of "The Young Man with a Glove" is in the Museum at Maidstone.

119. "I knew that all my gift arose only out of a certain warmth of soul aroused by that of which I had to treat." Rousseau, *Confessions*, Book 10.

120. *Works:* 10, 164.

121. In his letter of October 21st, Hazlitt wrote to his father: "Mr. Mérrimée came to look at the black and the old woman, which he liked very much, although they are contrary to the French style." *Literary Remains:* 1, 42.

W. C. Hazlitt altered this to: "Mr. Mérimée came to look at the [young man in] black and the old woman. . . ." *The Hazlitts:* 1, 414.

This conjectural addition is obviously erroneous, for Hazlitt could at that time have no copy of "The Young Man with a Glove" in his room. On October 21st he was at work on it, and was hoping to finish it the following week, but he attempted so many things that only on January 7th does he mention finishing it.

The reference is obviously to two of the paintings he had completed before coming to Paris.

122. cf. the Dedication "au premier consul Bonaparte" of the second edition of *La Génie du Christianisme.*

123. We say this because Hazlitt made no reference to French acting until Talma and Mademoiselle Georges came to London and he admired their acting in 1817. His passion for French comedy was later.

124. These lines are adapted from the lines:
"Learn to read slow; all other graces
Will follow in their proper places."
William Walker's *Art of Reading*.

125. The Man with the Glove.
Ippolito de' Medici.
Titian's "Mistress."
The Death of Clorinda.
Sketch of a Head.

126. cf. The Certificate as to his work quoted in *The Hazlitts:* 1, 116.

127. Coleridge seems to admit that it was a stratagem when he called it "the experimental truce of Amiens" and wrote of its value in uniting all parties in favour of war. Letter to the Editor of *The Courier*, December 21st, 1809. (*Essays on his own Times:* 2, 643.)

128. *Works:* 14, 197.

129. It is not clear why Coleridge should have excepted Longman and Rees. It is interesting to note that they were the publishers of Hazlitt's fifth book, four years afterwards, *A Reply to Malthus*.

130. *Coleridge, Unpublished Letters:* 1, 265.

131. *Coleridge, Unpublished Letters:* 1, 266.

132. *Coleridge, Unpublished Letters:* 1, 268.

133. *Coleridge, Unpublished Letters:* 1, 267.

133. (*b*) If, as De Quincey suggests, Hazlitt made an offer of marriage to Dorothy Wordsworth, it must have been in this year, for he would hardly have ventured to propose marriage to any woman in 1798, when he was penniless and prospectless; and he saw nothing of Dorothy in later years. Yet there is no positive evidence to confirm the suggestion, and all of what we might call negative evidence seems to point to its falsity. If Hazlitt had proposed marriage to Dorothy Wordsworth and had followed up his proposal with the escapade which drove him from the Lake District, Wordsworth would have dropped acquaintance with him there and then, instead of continuing on "very affectionate" terms with him for some years afterwards.

134. "While yet a child and long before his time
He had perceived the presence and the power
Of greatness and deep feelings had impressed
Great objects on his mind with portraiture
And colour so distinct that on his mind
They lay like substances and almost seemed
To haunt the bodily sense. . . ."
For the final version of the lines, cf. *The Excursion:* 1, 134-139.

135. This he remembered almost to the day of his death, for there is an echo of it not only in his earlier work but in the phrase "that fine madness in them which our first poets had" in the essay on Poetry he contributed to *The Atlas* on March, 1929. *Works:* 20, 209.

136. *The Prelude:* 5, 120-140. It is not surprising, seeing the poem was never published during Hazlitt's lifetime, that by the time he came to

write of this dream his memory had become confused as to some of its details. But if he was confused as to the details, there was no confusion in his mind as to the quality and purport of the dream.

137. cf. *The Borderers:* 1539-1544. Traces of Hazlitt's memory of these lines may be noticed in Hazlitt's *Works:* 4, 231; 11, 92; 12, 258; 14, 235; and 17, 107. Wordsworth noted how Hazlitt had retained them in his memory for over twenty years, although they had only been "read" or "recited" to him.

138. *Coleridge, Unpublished Letters:* 1, 279.

139. *Biographia Epistolaris:* 1, 275.

140. It seems likely that it was of this portrait, rather than of the first "side-portrait," that Southey made game towards the end of the year.

141. *Works:* 14, 207-208.

142. *Free Thoughts on Public Affairs. Works:* 1, 98.

143. *Works:* 14, 210.

144. *Works:* 14, 122. The italics are the biographer's.

145. *Moral and Political Philosophy, Principles of.*

146. *Works:* 12, 347.

147. This portrait was never finished. After Hazlitt's death Wordsworth replied to an inquiry by his son about it as follows: "At his desire I sat to him, but as he did not satisfy myself or my friends, the unfinished portrait was destroyed."

148. As his letter arrived in the course of Dorothy Wordsworth's illness in February, 1804, it must have reached Wordsworth some time between February 13th and February 22nd.

149. We gather this from a letter he wrote early in 1807 to his father: "I am going to dinner at Hume's to-morrow, where I also was on Christmas day, and had a pleasant time enough. It was much such a day as it was two years ago, when I was painting your picture."
    But it is just possible that "two years ago" may mean two Christmases ago, thus referring to the Christmas of 1805, when we know Hazlitt to have been at Wem. John Hazlitt had portraits of his father and sister in the Exhibition of 1804.

150. *Works:* 1, 116.

151. *Works:* 1, 114.

152. Christopher Wordsworth's review of it, in *The British Critic*, appeared about this time. This review was merely galling to Hazlitt, not only because the reviewer failed to understand his argument, had indeed confessed this failure to his brother the Poet, but despite this, had found the Essay an attempt to undermine the Christian religion.

153. Procter in *The Athenæum*, January 20th, 1835.

154. *The Hazlitts:* 1, 421.

155. *The Hazlitts:* 1, 423.

156. *Works:* 7, 306.

157. *Works:* 7, 315.

158. Afterwards, as bitterness grew upon him, he found that some of them had to be *craftily qualified*.

159. *Works:* 7, 297-298.
160. *The Hazlitts:* 1, 422.
161. *The Hazlitts:* 1, 423.
162. *Works:* 1, 186.
163. *Works:* 1, 283-284.
164. "starve"—altered in the 1817 edition to "suffer."
165. Appendix to the Fifth Edition, 1817. It is here that Malthus is most explicit as to this, but it had been touched on even in the First Edition, and had been, even as he claimed, implicit throughout his work.
166. *Works:* 1, 189.
167. *Works:* 1, 357.
168. *Works:* 1, 289.
169. *Works:* 1, 181-183.
170. *Works:* 1, 283.
171. *Mr. H———,* Act 1, Scene 1.
172. *Works:* 12, 303-304.
173. *Works:* 10, 237.
174. *Works:* 6, 105.
175. *Works:* 12, 227.
176. *Works:* 16, 45.
177. Lamb told Manning that after her mother's death it would be £120. *Lamb Letters:* 2, 48.
178. *Lamb Letters:* 1, 359.
179. *Lamb Letters:* 1, 359.
180. *Lamb Letters:* 1, 360.
181. *Lamb Letters:* 1, 367.
182. *Lamb Letters:* 1, 426.
183. *Lamb Letters:* 2, 11.
184. *Lamb Letters:* 2, 23.
185. *Lamb Letters:* 2, 38-39.
186. This letter is given in the *Lamb Letters,* vol. 2, pages 37-39. It is not dated, but it was endorsed, probably by the late Mr. W. C. Hazlitt, October, 1807. The course of events suggests that this date is impossible, but the letter may be provisionally dated by the reference to Godwin's tragedy, which Mary Lamb says was produced at the end of the following week. Godwin's *Faulkener* was produced on Friday, December 16th, 1807. Thus the letter is likely to have been written between December 4th and December 10th. The contents of the letter also, and its relationship to the succeeding one of December 21st, 1807, indicate the early part of December as the likely date.
187. *Lamb Letters:* 2, 37-38.
188. *Lamb Letters:* 2, 40.
189. *Lamb Letters:* 2, 39-40.
190. *Works:* 17, 98.
191. *Works:* 8, 96.
192. Published in *Lamb and Hazlitt.*

193. The italics are the biographer's, as also on page 379.
194. *The Hazlitts:* 1, 425.
195. *The Hazlitts:* 1, 426.
196. *The Hazlitts:* 1, 425-426.
197. *Lamb Letters:* 2, 45.
198. *Lamb Letters:* 2, 167.
199. *The Hazlitts:* 1, 426-427.
200. *Works:* 20, 134.
201. *Works:* 10, 54.
202. When he saw the original he was greatly disappointed with the colouring, and wrote: "This is not the picture, the print of which we used to gaze at enamoured—there is another somewhere that we still shall see!" *Works:* 10, 54.
203. Letter of January 12th, 1808. Even allowing for the "funning" of this letter, this must be accepted as throwing light on Hazlitt's ways. Its truth is borne out by many passages in his works.
204. *Works:* 9, 204.
205. It has been suggested that Wordsworth comes under the suspicion of having taken the opportunity, when in town in 1808, of alienating Sharp, of whom he saw a good deal during this visit, from Hazlitt, and that it was the withdrawal of Sharp's support which wrecked the prospects of the projected *magnum opus* of Hazlitt's youth.

   There are so many instances of Wordsworth's coming in the wake of the friendships Hazlitt formed, and endeavouring to ruin them, that when one of Hazlitt's friendships with one of Wordsworth s acquaintances terminates mysteriously, Wordsworth cannot be acquitted of suspicion.

   Hazlitt's own quarrels usually arose out of political differences. He is unlikely to have had any such with Richard Sharp. We know that such financial dealings as he may have had with Sharp had nothing to do with the termination of his friendship. We know that his feeling towards Sharp did not alter. In *On the Want of Money* he wrote: "I am not ashamed of such patronage as this, nor do I regret any circumstance relating to it but its termination."

   There remains the possibility that some one may have been at pains to alter Sharp's feeling towards him, and there is the possibility that Wordsworth acted here as he did on other occasions. At the same time, there is no evidence that he did so on this occasion, wherefore we make no mention of this in the text.
205 (*b*). Possibly Hazlitt had tended to seek the patronage of Windham for his *History of English Philosophy* out of the knowledge that Robinson's friend Amyot was Windham's secretary. Possibly also in the appearance of a review of his *Reply to Malthus* in *The London Review*, in May, 1809, almost two years after the appearance of the book, Robinson's hand may be discerned.
206. His letter, endorsed by H. C. R., December 4th, was written on Sunday, December 3rd.

207. It was published in November.
208. Lamb's letter to Manning of January 2nd, 1810: "Holcroft had finished his life when I wrote to you, and Hazlitt has since finished his life—I do not mean his own life, but he has finished a life of Holcroft, which is going to press."
209. "I believe by accident," Godwin acknowledged, albeit somewhat acidly, when commenting to Mrs. Holcroft on this omission.
210. Kegan Paul's *Life of Godwin:* 2, 176.
211. Kegan Paul's *Life of Godwin:* 2, 177.
212. William Nicholson—once a great friend of Godwin—was at the moment estranged from him and was not on speaking terms with him.
213. *Lamb Letters:* 2, 98.
214. His letter to Henry Robinson of December 3rd, 1809, shows this. He realised that some of the stories related by Holcroft of Cumberland would not render the editor of Holcroft's Diary any more acceptable in Cumberland's eyes.
215. On March 6th.
216. *Lamb Letters:* 2, 97-98.
217. *The Hazlitts:* 1, 433-434.
218. *Lamb Letters:* 2, 72-73. This letter was dated by the late Mr. E. V. Lucas, conjecturally, "Probably 3rd June, 1809." A comparison of its contents with Hazlitt's postscript and with the happenings of 1810 shows that it belongs to 1810 rather than to 1809. Its attribution to 1809 has caused some confusion as to the Lambs' intentions and movements in that year.
219. The references Hazlitt makes are obviously to this midsummer visit of the Lambs, rather than to the autumn one of the preceding year.
220. *Works:* 17, 320.
221. *Works:* 12, 42.
222. *Works:* 17, 66.
223. *Works:* 8, 188.
224. "I received Mr. C.'s letter and transmitted it to Hazlitt," Lamb wrote to Mrs. Clarkson on September 18th.
225. H. C. R. wrote of it: "And certainly this is the only painting by Hazlitt I ever saw with pleasure." *Sadler:* 1, 192.
226. Up to the present day this is the usual line of defence taken by the apologists of Malthus. We are still being told that he did not say that which reference to his books immediately shows him to have said.
227. "Miss W."—Dorothy Wordsworth. She returned to the Lambs from her visit to the Cooksons at Binfield, on October 19th.
228. *Lamb Letters:* 2, 112.
229. Hazlitt's quotation is, as usual, inaccurate. As this obscures the sense, the lines from *The Somnour's Tale*, that were running in his mind, have been here restored.
230. *Morley:* 1, 25.

231. *Morley:* 1, 23-24.
232. *Morley:* 1, 30.
233. *Works:* 12, 57.
234. *The Hazlitts:* 1, 448-449.
235. "six lectures." Letter to Crabb Robinson, October 29th, 1811: "I have written six."
236. *Coleridge, Unpublished Letters:* 2, 56.
237. Letter to Henry Crabb Robinson, October 29th, 1811.
238. Note on "Call not the royal Swede unfortunate," in the 1827 Edition of Wordsworth's Poems, vol. 3, page 235.
239. Southey to Landor, February 9th, 1812. *Southey Letters:* 2, 254.
240. "How the King of Rome sucks and sleeps seem to him of more importance than the fate of armies and of kingdoms . . . should this puny being, for its own repose, and the future happiness of mankind, dwindle and drop into an early grave, we verily believe it would afflict his father more than the desolation of ten kingdoms: yet if he lives he may probably by his idiotism or his ingratitude, avenge the wrongs of many a childless parent on his father's head."
   The Courier, May 23rd, 1811. (*Essays on his own Times:* 3, 785.)
241. *Life and Letters of William Bewick:* 1, 109.
242. Patmore took these to be the pencilled names of all sorts of visitors who had come to pay homage to Milton's memory. William Bewick took them to be Hazlitt's own jottings-down of ideas around which essays might be built. *Life and Letters:* 1, 118-119.
243. *The New Monthly Magazine,* October, 1830.
244. As to the gross rumour of the time that Hazlitt had received £1,500 from the management of Drury Lane for the articles on Kean (L'Estrange, *Mitford:* 2, 47) this might justifiably be dismissed without examination, for it would have been impossible for a man of Hazlitt's temperament to have written as he had done, for any other reason than that Kean's genius had brought him a sudden intensification of life. He had indeed been told by Perry to give "as favourable an account" as he could, but he was not amenable to such hints, and it was partly because he was not amenable to them that he lost his work on the *Chronicle* in the spring of this year. But if any practical evidence is needed by way of refutation of this gossip, it is supplied by Hazlitt's poverty at this time. Such gossip was set afloat by those incapable of understanding such a genuine movement of the mind as he had experienced. Criticism of the kind Hazlitt gave to Kean is never found for sale in the markets of the world.
245. We have been helped in the difficult task of attempting to describe the character of Hazlitt's political writing in this year by Sir Herbert Grierson's *Milton and Wordsworth, Poets and Prophets*, and especially by the definition of the prophetic poet, as "a poet putting into the language and pattern of poetry, his deepest intuitions as these have been evoked by a great political or religious experience."
246. *Works:* 7, 33.

247.   *Works:* 7, 30. *The Bourbons and Buonaparte.* Hazlitt says this also in his third reply to Vetus.

247 (*b*).   *Works:* 7, 50.

248.   *Works:* 7, 61, and 7, 55-56, The italics are ours.

249.   *Works:* 7, 68.

250.   *Works:* 7, 31.

251.   *Works:* 7, 32-33.

252.   *Works:* 19, 127-128.

253.   *Works:* 7, 73. *On the late War.* The italics are Hazlitt's.

254.   *Morley:* 1, 142.

255.   *Works:* 7, 386.

256.   Procter's *Autobiographical Fragment: William Hazlitt.*

257.   One of these may have been a touch of jealousy. Perry liked to feel that the whole paper was written by himself, and it may have been annoying to him to see Hazlitt striding with such ease from one department to another, and seeming to make each peculiarly his own as he took it in his stride. Then Perry's way of claiming all the good things in his paper as his own sometimes had awkward consequences for him. He came in for a good deal of admiration no doubt, and basked in it; but sometimes he found himself challenged by readers of the *Chronicle* as to opinions which were assumed to be his own and which were very far from being his own. He sometimes complained that Hazlitt fouled his chances of social success. Also there were differences in matters of taste. Lastly, Hazlitt was not complaisant. He would not take a hint, nor even a command, as to the tone of what he wrote. The immediate provocative action on his part, as matters drew near to a crisis, was the insertion of a mordant paragraph on Sir Thomas Lawrence, whom he had been told to praise, in an article on the Royal Academy Exhibition of 1814.

   If in addition to the difficulties caused by "imperfect sympathies" between Hazlitt and his Editor, Hazlitt had been guilty of causing friction and disorganisation in Perry's "team" of reporters by neglecting to take his turn in reporting a debate that bored him, the coolness that led to the termination of his work for the *Chronicle* is readily understandable.

   Altogether, he was far too temperamental a recruit to suit Perry.

258.   This was Hazlitt's view. In the Fenwick note to *The Excursion*, Wordsworth recounts gossip to the effect that Fawcett's death had also been hastened by intemperance.

259.   *Works:* 19, 18.

260.   *Works:* 5, 217. *The Examiner*, August 7th, 1814.

261.   The study of Tamora in *Titus Andronicus* and the contrast it presents to the study of womanly nature in Desdemona is one of the things which convinces us that Shakespeare had a hand in *Titus Andronicus.* The play completes his presentation of human nature.

262.   *Works:* 7, 82.

263. *Works:* 7, 85.
264. *Works:* 4, 365.
265. *Morley:* 1, 164-165.
266. *The Examiner,* December 1st, 1816.
267. *Works:* 15, 229-230.
268. *Lamb Letters:* 2, 167.
269. This vivid word is taken from *The Examiner,* April 12th, 1818: " What of those enormous multitudes, who shadowed the seas when Napoleon stood on the deck of the *Bellerophon,* like the King of the very world that had conquered him!"
270. *Life:* 1, 316.
271. *Southey, Life and Correspondence:* 4, 121.
272. " No one will compare Shaw—the Life-Guards'-man with the celebrated Coup-Tête; the one was a gallant soldier, the other a sneaking villain; yet the one cut off as many heads in a day as the other; it is not the blood shed then, but the manner and motive; the one braved a formidable enemy, in the field, the other gloated over a helpless victim." *Works:* 13, 167.
273. *Works:* 12, 136.
274. *Baron Grimm and the Edinburgh Reviewers.* cf. *Works:* 4, 131, and 20, 398-399.
275. *Works:* 4, 133-134.
276. *Works:* 20, 401.
277. *Works:* 20, 401.
278. *The Examiner,* February 4th, 1816.
279. *Works:* 7, 151-152.
280. *A Lay Sermon,* 1816. Appendix C.
281. *Works:* 7, 98.
282. *Works:* 7, 259-260.
283. *Works:* 7, 287.
284. *Works:* 19, 156.
285. *Works:* 19, 181.
286. *Works:* 7, 149.
287. *Works:* 19, 186.
288. *Works:* 7, 208-209.
289. *Works:* 19, 199.
290 (*a*). *Works:* 7, 214. The italics here are the biographer's.
290 (*b*). *Works:* 19, 252.
291. *Works:* 7, 189.
291 (*b*). The injunction was refused for the reason that the play was considered of so pernicious a character as to deprive the author of any rights over it.
292. *Works:* 7, 185-186.
293. *Works:* 7, 143.
294. *Works:* 7, 124.
295. *Works:* 7, 128.
296. *Works:* 7, 137.

297. *Works:* 7, 181-182. The italics at the end of the quotation are the biographer's.

298. *Works:* 7, 152.

299. *Lamb Letters:* 2, 146.

300. *Memoir:* 1, 110.

301. *Wordsworth Letters—The Later Years,* Appendix 3, 1349-1350. This letter was printed *for the first time* in 1939. It is of the utmost importance in helping us to distinguish between truth and falsehood in this matter. In itself it warrants a reconsideration of all the evidence brought against Hazlitt.

302. This letter was printed in its entirety *for the first time* in *The Times Literary Supplement,* December 27th, 1941.

303. *Wordsworth Letters—The Middle Years:* 2, 781-782.

304. *Lamb Letters:* 2, 163. Mr. E. V. Lucas dated this letter May, 1815.

305. "Dr. W.

   ". . . Thursday is our club night—the evening I told you I expected W. H., so we must defer our meeting till you can name another open evening. I almost fear I can scarce reckon upon any particular one, I am so busy, but I hope to see you somehow soon. . . .

                    "Yours truly,
                         "C. L."

306. *Coleridge, Unpublished Letters:* 2, 189. This letter, of September 25th, 1816, follows one to Rose of September 17th, in which Coleridge claimed that Southey and he had saved Hazlitt "from infamy and transportation," to which he had exposed himself "by the most loathsome conduct . . . the excess of which would perplex Belief while the Detail outraged Modesty." *Unpublished Letters:* 2, 178-179.

307. If this review were Hazlitt's it would indeed be a deep stain on his critical record. But we do not think it can be called his. The conclusion we have come to after considering all the evidence is that Jeffrey, or more likely one of his deputies, "cut up" both Coleridge and Hazlitt most foully. The article is all that is the reverse of characteristic of Hazlitt. Moreover, there are three specific points in which it differs from anything Hazlitt would say:

   (a) The tone of the references to Byron is utterly contrary to the tone of all Hazlitt's references to him.

   (b) What is said of *The White Doe* is characteristic of Jeffrey but not of Hazlitt.

   (c) The reference to "the new school" of poets is so unlike Hazlitt that it seems to us a conclusive piece of evidence as showing that the review was altered out of all recognition by the time it appeared in print. The Lake poets might be "the new school" to Jeffrey or one of his deputies. To Hazlitt they were the classics of his youth.

   Moreover, the tone and quality of the prose is utterly unlike Hazlitt's.

308. Evidently "3" has been omitted from the letter.
309. *Coleridge, Unpublished Letters*: 2, 196-197.
310. *The Examiner*, April 12th, 1818.
311. *The Examiner*, June 28th, 1818.
312. Charles Cowden Clarke reports Hazlitt as saying of the *Blackwood* type of criticism, aimed at personal oddities, blemishes, or infirmities: "To pay those fellows *in their own coin*, the way would be to begin with Walter Scott, and *have at his clump foot*." *Recollections of Writers*, 147.

    Hazlitt's scorn was justified; it is perhaps needless to add that he never fouled his pen with the *have at his pimples* or *have at his lameness* or *have at his greasy hair* or *have at his clump foot* type of criticism.
313. *Les Dieux ont Soif*, Chapter 19.
314. Possibly *The Edinburgh Magazine*, to which it was sent, flinched at being involved in a fray as bloody as this promised to be.
315. "But I am bound to declare that their treatment of him on this occasion was not the cause of his subsequent feelings towards these distinguished men, or his treatment of them as arising out of these feelings. It was not the petty anger arising out of a sense of some trifling personal injustice (even if he entertained any such, which he scarcely could in the case in question) that could make Hazlitt either blindly insensible to the claims of such men as Wordsworth and Southey, or wilfully unjust to those claims, whether personal or intellectual." *My Friends and Acquaintances: William Hazlitt*.
316. *A Tale of a Tub*: Section 9.
317. This is William Bewick's description.
318. Enfield's *Speaker*: Select Sentences.
319. William Bewick's Life and *Letters*: 1, 147.
320. *Works*: 19, 257.
321. This consists of a few words from an attack on Wordsworth which had appeared in *The Examiner*, over a year before, on December 22nd, 1816, and which he now, most unjustifiably, for they are polemical fireworks rather than serious criticism, tacked on to a genuine interpretation of the conditions in which the poetry of the Lake School had its origin. With characteristic honesty, he practically disowned these afterwards, as serious criticism, for he went out of his way to point out that they consisted of "mere epigrams and *jeux d'esprit*, as far from truth as they are from malice." They may be forgiven for their energy. The passage is the famous one which takes "He hates" as its key-phrase. They are an impertinence in this lecture in which the remainder of the material is on a higher plane; and they are the only blot on this lecture.
321 (*b*). Byron—says Leigh Hunt—regarded Hazlitt with a touch of fear. He probably felt that Hazlitt alone among contemporary critics saw him as he was, "a *sublime* coxcomb."
322. *The Yellow Dwarf*, January 24th and 31st and February 7th, 1818.

323. *Works:* 7, 253.

324. That Hazlitt noted this paragraph with appreciation we know from his reference to it in one of his last Essays, *On Editors*, published in *The New Monthly Magazine*, after his death, in November, 1830: "We know only one Editor who openly discards all regard to character and decency, and who thrives by the dissolution of partnership, if indeed the articles were ever drawn up. We shall not mention names, as we do not wish to advertise a work that ' ought to lie on no gentleman's table.'" *Works:* 17, 363.

325. *The London Magazine*, February, 1820.

326. *The Examiner*, November 15th, 1818.

327. The amount is stated in a letter from William Blackwood to Cadell, in April, 1823, when Hazlitt was again threatening a prosecution.

328. More than one witness at the inquests which followed testified that the Hussars had kept their heads and tried to check the madness of the Yeomanry.

329. *Works:* 6, 183-185.

330. Castlereagh in November brought in a Bill which would have made Transportation the punishment for any one convicted a second time of libel.

331. *Works:* 18, 342-343.

332. The bitterness with which Hazlitt afterwards spoke of Bentham's having "philosophically put an execution" in his house suggests that his tenancy of 19 York Street was brought to an end against his will, and that he left this "classic ground" reluctantly. cf. his letter to Leigh Hunt of April 21st, 1821.

332 (*b*). John Hazlitt. Born November 28th, 1815. Died June 19th, 1816.

333. From the first of the Sulpicia poems in the fourth book of the Elegies. Hazlitt took it to be the work of Tibullus.

334. This was the stage of what his friend Stendhal, in his brilliant metaphor, would have called complete "crystallisation."

335. These demands were:

1. William Hazlitt to pay the whole expense of board, clothing, and education for his son William Hazlitt by his wife Sarah Hazlitt.

2. William Hazlitt to pay board, lodgings, law and all other expenses incurred by his said wife during her stay in Scotland on their divorce business, together with travelling expenses.

3. William Hazlitt to give a note of hand for £50 at six months. . . .

336 (*a*). The alternative title of *Liber Amoris*.

336 (*b*). William Bewick, although some of the things he says about Hazlitt cannot be relied on too implicitly, understood well both the naturalness of Hazlitt's "strangeness," and the inevitability of the isolation it brought him. The following passage seems to us to throw as much light on the nature of Hazlitt's isolation as any with which we have met:

"William Hazlitt was one of the most unaffected men I have ever met with, undisciplined and unrestrained by the rules and usages of society. . . . What was remarkable in Hazlitt was the simplicity and spontaneity of all his strangeness, and if he gave way to vehemence of passion or irritation, or was melted into moods of softer and even amatory emotions, he never attempted to conceal in the least his feelings, or repress the expression of them, just as if he believed all the world sympathised with his indignation, his jealousy, his romantic attachments, or his wrongs. It excited sorrow and pain to see a man of such intelligence, with features so capable of expressing the varied emotions of his too sensitive nature, lash himself into terrible bursts of uncontrollable rage, the effect of his excitable nervous temperament, where the slightest discord vibrated to his inmost soul, while it found no echo in the breasts of others, who could only gaze with wonder as at a frenzied being, amazed by the violence of the physical action which followed the phases of his mental excitement, at the expression of his features, and at his burning language." *Life and Letters:* 1, 107-108.

This was what made Hazlitt seem so strange to the men of his generation, that many of the feelings which moved him most profoundly "found no echo in the breasts of others." This was also the secret of his value. He awakened the men of his generation to feeling with which they had been unacquainted. But until he had created the taste by which he was enjoyed, he was inevitably regarded as "some beast of strange and forraine race."

337. *On the Spirit of Obligations.*
On the Pleasure of Hating.
On Application to Study.
And, we think:
On Reason and Imagination, which was certainly written before Byron's death in the following April. In it he pleads for the discernment of truth through passion, as well as through reason.

338. *Works:* 12, 128. The italics are ours.

339. We prefer to follow their suggestion, slight though it be, than to rely on what was said of her in later years. What Hazlitt's son said of her is to some extent demonstrably inaccurate. What he said of her was: "In 1824 my father married Isabella, widow of Lieut.-Colonel Bridgwater, a lady of some property, with whom and myself he proceeded on a tour through France and Italy." Hazlitt's grandson was supplied with some information by her acquaintance G. Huntly Gordon, and his account is a paraphrase both of that given by Hazlitt's son in 1834 and by G. Huntly Gordon in 1866. He added the detail that his grandfather had met the lady "accidentally in a stage-coach, in the course of his numerous excursions."

340. This was the only book bound in crimson velvet of which Hazlitt ever spoke. Hazlitt's grandson suggested that the volume bound in crimson velvet, which was the companion of Hazlitt's travels, was

Liber Amoris. To have had *Liber Amoris* thus bound would have
been as unlike Hazlitt as the touch of affectation or coxcombry once
imputed to him, of sitting near a crimson curtain to set off his dark
curls.

341. *Works:* 10, 107.

342. Hobhouse, who had met Stendhal in Italy, noted that he had sometimes
"a cruel way of talking."

343. Kirkup's story is as follows, that Hazlitt, after describing how he
had called in a woman from the streets and put her in his bed for
form's sake, had continued: "down I lay, and the folding-doors
opened, and in walked Mrs. Hazlitt accompanied by two gentlemen.
She turned to them and said: ' Gentlemen, do you know who that
person is in that bed along with that woman?' ' Yes, madam,'
they politely replied, ' 'tis Mr. William Hazlitt.' On which, sir, she
made a curtsey, and they went out of the room, and left me and my
companion *in statu quo.* She and her witnesses then accused me of
adultery, sir, and obtained a divorce against me, which, by gad, sir,
was a benefit to us both."

344. *Works:* 10, 287.

345. He was of course wrong in this. His *Napoleon* has been left undisturbed
on the shelf along with much other Napoleonic lumber while his
"Liber Veritatis" is now beyond the reach of time. Through it his
spirit has passed, as he would have wished, into the minds of men.
It is safe to say that *the better mind* of his country would not have
been what it is to-day, had Hazlitt not been Hazlitt.

346. It would not be possible from Hazlitt's references to it to identify it.
He calls it merely " A Man in Black." (*Works:* 17, 220.) Our clue is
the statement that he had copied it before, and copied it well. The
copy of a portrait by Titian he had made during his youth was that
of "The Young Man with a Glove."

347. *Works:* 17, 217-218.

348. Our authority for this statement is the following paragraph in *The
Examiner* of June 17th, 1827: "Napoleon.—A literary gentleman of
high attainments, who has been residing in Paris for some time
for the purpose of collecting authentic documents and facts to
enable him to write the Life of Napoleon, is just returned with a
considerable portion of his manuscript, ready for the press. We
understand the work will extend to four octavo volumes." This
was copied from *The Morning Chronicle.* It may perhaps be regarded
as a "puff" of the *Napoleon,* the only one of his books Hazlitt was
eager to advertise in advance of publication.

349. Hazlitt, of course, could not have foreseen the answer to this question:
"No—but they will yet produce the head of Abraham Lincoln."

350. *The Examiner,* September 26th, 1830.

351. The article on Hazlitt in *The New Monthly Magazine,* October, 1833,
called it "a depravation of the stomach."

352. The circumstances of the publication are debatable. It has been

suggested, because of the appearance of this notice, that the work may have been published at this time. It would be such a strange thing for Hazlitt's publishers to issue the book without the Preface and the Index he was contemplating, at a time when there was no reason to believe he would be unable to complete them in the course of the summer, that we would not believe they did such a thing, did we not have some positive proof of it. We have come on no such proof. Not a single copy of any edition lacking the Preface and Index has been found.

The first advertisement of the book on which we have come refers definitely to the publication of the two concluding volumes as "posthumous." It appeared in *The Examiner* of September 26th, 1830, without any indication as to the price of the book, and is as follows:

"Hazlitt's *Napoleon* is now completed in 4 volumes. The first and second volumes of this admirable piece of biography have met with a rapid sale. . . . The third and fourth volumes, now first presented to the public, assume the character of a posthumous publication. Napoleon and his biographer both belong to an era which has passed away.

"The death of William Hazlitt on the eve of the publication of his greatest work is a coincidence which adds to its interest, and the public will feel the claim which such a work, at such a period, independently of its intrinsic merit, has on its protection and support."

This advertisement was repeated in *The Examiner*, October 17th, 1830, with the addition of the price, £2 10s., for the completed work, and the statement that the third and fourth volumes would "be sold separately for a limited time at 30s."

353. To the modern reader, these words in their passion may seem excessive. They will not seem excessive to students of the social history of the times. These poets in their youth had all expressed the most sensitive sympathy for the People. In the years following Waterloo, when the People were without guidance, the Poets gave them no leadership; when they were inarticulate in their trouble, the masters of words kept silence; when they suffered, the Poets, at the worst, joined their oppressors, or at the best, passed by on the other side of the road. For the People, the years when, suffering from the aftermath of a long war, unrepresented in Parliament, and caught between the Agricultural and the Industrial Revolution, they went through a period of bitter, and for the most part inarticulate suffering, were indeed, even as Hazlitt had said, "the valley of the shadow."

354 (a). The effect of the silent Agricultural Revolution on the status of the peasantry of England was at the time summarised in the saying that in 1760 the agricultural labourer had been a "man;" in 1830 he was a "pauper."

354 (*b*). A writer in the *Athenæum*, repudiating the report that Hazlitt died
"in a state of destitution," stated that he had received "within two
or three months" of his death sums "of consequence in the aggregate,
for his writings in the periodical press." This claim seems exaggerated, in view of the fact that Hazlitt, in the course of four months,
had contributed only these two essays. The same writer claimed that
Hazlitt had also received "considerable sums for his *Conversations
of James Northcote* and other works. . . ."

  The controversy as to his poverty which sprang up immediately
after his death tended to make some of his friends exaggerate his
resources, even as it tended to make others exaggerate the degree of
his poverty.

355. It was because he died without having received Jeffrey's letter and its
enclosure that rumours of his utter poverty at the moment of his
death went abroad so swiftly. The day after Hazlitt's death there
appeared in *The Examiner* the following statement: "We are
informed on good authority that Mr. Hazlitt has died in poverty,
and that the peremptory requirements of the moment render the
immediate interference of friends necessary. Those who sympathise
with the fate of men of genius will be quick in understanding this."
Those of Hazlitt's friends who had seen to it that he lacked nothing
felt, very naturally, that this public statement made them appear in
a false light. The statement was taken exception to in *The Court
Journal*, and reasserted in *The Examiner* on September 26th. Thus
from the outset of the controversy two issues were confused:
(1) whether Hazlitt had died in poverty or no, and (2) whether in his
poverty he had been neglected by his friends or no. Procter, writing
in *The New Monthly* in November, did not distinguish between these:
"It has been said that Hazlitt died forsaken and in poverty. *This is
not the fact.* He was as well off as he generally was, and he had
friends who provided all that was necessary for him, and stood by
him to the last." This statement, like Talfourd's later one, makes it
clear that Hazlitt was not forsaken by his friends, yet in the very
claim that his friends provided for him we have the admission that
he died in poverty.

  The impression that he was "forsaken" by his friends, however,
although false, was not easily driven out of men's minds. We see a
reflection of it in Carlyle's words: "He seemed to have no *old* friends
about, and to have been left in his poor lodging to the humanity of
medical people and transient recent acquaintances." Also, the
"poverty" was fantastically exaggerated in the course of time by
the "rumour" which followed Hazlitt after his death as relentlessly
as it had pursued him during his lifetime.

356. Thomas Holcroft and Crabb Robinson between them enable us to get
some impression of the nature of this legend. In an article by
Thomas Holcroft, entitled *Hazlitt's Death-Bed*, which appeared in
The Monthly Magazine in March, 1833, not only was Hazlitt's

poverty exaggerated, and the amount Hazlitt had requested Jeffrey
to send him magnified into £100, but the story of his request was
prefaced by a reference to "some sudden turn of memory" which
"had caused a pang in the dying man's bosom."

Holcroft said no more than this, but undoubtedly there had
been some talk, by which this reference would be interpreted by
most of his readers, about some "pang" suffered by Hazlitt on his
death-bed in connection with his feeling for a woman, for we get
the final brew of fact and fiction, as usual, and as usual, served up in
a form injurious to Hazlitt's memory and tending to show him in an
ignoble light, in the report of a conversation on this article, given
by Crabb Robinson. After giving some account of a dinner at J. P.
Collier's on April 6th, 1833, at which Reynolds and Sheridan Knowles
had been present, he wrote: "The talk was literary and desultory;
I incidentally heard that Thomas Holcroft was the author of a
scandalous article entitled *Hazlitt's Last Hours*, in which Basil
Montagu is attacked for refusing to Hazlitt just before £50 which
Hazlitt wanted to give a worthless woman by whom Hazlitt was at
last fascinated."

Crabb Robinson knew nothing of Hazlitt's emotional life. What
he says of it has the usual touch of distortion and prejudice. For the
rest, even what he says of the article is garbled. Basil Montagu had
not been attacked for refusing to lend money, although it had been
mentioned that he had refused to lend, not £50, but £40; there had
been no suggestion of criticism of him in Holcroft's narrative. Nor
had there been any reference whatsoever in the article, which is
passionately sympathetic towards Hazlitt, to a "worthless" woman,
to Hazlitt's having been fascinated by her, or to Hazlitt's having
wanted the money for her. What is "scandalous" is not the article,
but the garbled report, to some extent based on the conversation to
which he had just listened, given of it by the recorder.

So much for H. C. R.'s reporting! In itself it is all but valueless.
Yet it shows that the poverty, the request to Jeffrey, "the sudden
turn of memory," the painful nature of this "turn of memory," and
the connecting of it with a woman assumed by those inimical
to Hazlitt to be "worthless," in fact, all things that had ever
been acknowledged about Hazlitt by his friends or used against
him by his foes, were by this time becoming so inextricably confused that they might be said to be matter of legend rather than of
fact.

357. The most reliable material relating to Hazlitt's death is as follows:
    1. Sarah Hazlitt's memorandum on it.
    2. W. H. Reynell's letter informing his sister of it.
    3. The brief account of it given in *Literary Remains*.
    4. Procter's article in *The New Monthly*, November, 1830.
    5. Carlyle's account of the arrival of the letter to Jeffrey. These
       are all accounts by those who were either eye-witnesses of that

of which they wrote, or who had intimate knowledge in connection with it.

W. C. Hazlitt added one or two details in his *Memoirs*, such as Hazlitt's desire to see his mother, and the statement that his last words were: "Well, I've had a happy life." We record these, but we do not feel justified in including them in the text of the book. They seem to us to have a touch of *panache*, very foreign to Hazlitt. We therefore content ourselves with mentioning that they were attributed to him .

·Although we do not know whether he uttered them, we know how he would have gone on to justify or qualify them, if he had uttered them:

"Good and ill seem as necessary to human life as light and shade to a picture. We grow weary of uniform success, and pleasure soon surfeits. . . . The wretched are in this respect fortunate, that they have the strongest yearnings after happiness; and to desire is in some measure to enjoy."

358. Said variously to have been R. H. Horne and Charles Wells.

359. We say "arrange" because this was first composed by Coleridge as an "Epitaph, on a Bad Man." It was twice adapted by him to contemporaries. The date is given as "September 10th" in the *Poems*, edited by E. H. Coleridge.

INDEX

Albano, Hazlitt's desire to spend a month at, 520.

Alexander I. (of Russia), 322.

Alfoxden, Hazlitt and Coleridge at, 119-120, 122.

Alsager, Thomas M. (of *The Times*), Hazlitt at dinner with, 318.

American Farmer, The, accompanies the Hazlitt family to America, 12; Hazlitt's lifelong liking for, 552; 585.

Amsterdam, Hazlitt sees the Rembrandts at, 527.

Antwerp, Hazlitt sees "The Taking down from the Cross," by Rubens, at, 527.

Aquapendente, Hazlitt at, 518.

Aspland, Robert, on the classing of truth as seditious, 57-58.

Athenæum, The, advance notice of Hazlitt's *Life of Napoleon* in, 543.

Atlas, The, on Hazlitt after his death, 533, 558; advance notice of his *Life of Napoleon* in, 560.

Baillie, Joanna, her "grace" as a writer praised by Hazlitt, 378.

Bandon, The Rev. William Hazlitt's ministry there, 9, 10; his protests against the ill-treatment of American prisoners from, 11.

Bannister, Jack, Hazlitt's pleasure in the acting of, 80; as Autolycus, 156.

Barbauld, Anna Letitia, Hazlitt's first preceptress, 21; Hazlitt's liking of her *Ode to Spring*, 51; her verses on Warrington Academy, 61; his salute to her in his Lectures on the English Poets, 378.

Barnes, Thomas, dramatic critic of

The Examiner, 313; his challenge to Hazlitt on his interpretation of Iago, 317.

Beaumont, Lady, Coleridge on, 183.

Beaumont, Sir George Howland, visit to Keswick of, 183; Hazlitt's attack on Coleridge before, 184; Hazlitt's portrait of Coleridge for, 185, 189.

Beauty and the Beast, 366, 421.

Beckford, William, 138.

Bedford, Grosvenor, 324.

Bell, Mr. (intermediary between Hazlitt and his wife during the divorce negotiations), 451, 453, 460, 466-467, 468, 475.

Belsham, The Rev. Thomas, at The New College, Hackney, 64; his dismay at the trend of its development, 65; lectures to Hazlitt on Hebrew, 71-72; on the tendency of the students to "give up" Christianity, 76; an admirer of Hartley, 77; his "Buy the *truth*," 85.

Bentham, Jeremy, 293.

Berkeley, George (Bishop of Cloyne), discussed by Hazlitt with Coleridge, 102; Hazlitt's study of, 104; Hazlitt's intention to lecture on, 287.

Bernadotte, Jean Baptiste, Hazlitt on the Crown Prince of Sweden, 317.

Bewick, William, his drawing of Hazlitt, 44; one of Haydon's pupils, 295; his report on Hazlitt's London home, 295, 597; his impressions of Hazlitt's lectures, 373; given a ticket for them by Hazlitt, 375; his estimate of Hazlitt as a writer, 375, 386; on

THE AUTHOR'S ACKNOWLEDGMENTS

THE deepest debt of which I am conscious, now that this biography of Hazlitt is about to be published, is to the work on Hazlitt, both biographical and editorial, of Mr. P. P. Howe. I acknowledge this debt most gratefully, and I desire at the same time to pay the work the tribute of my profound respect and grateful admiration. Among other books, published in recent years, in which light has been thrown on Hazlitt, and to which I am therefore indebted, are: *The Correspondence of Henry Crabb Robinson with the Wordsworth Circle*, *Henry Crabb Robinson on Books and their Writers*, *Unpublished Letters of Samuel Taylor Coleridge*, *The Letters of William and Dorothy Wordsworth*, *Leigh Hunt*, *Contribution à l'histoire du Romantisme anglais*, by Louis Landré, and Mr. Edmund Blunden's *Leigh Hunt*. I wish also to express my gratitude towards and admiration of *The Village Labourer*, *The Town Labourer*, and *The Skilled Labourer*, by John and Barbara Hammond, books which do much to explain the emergence, in the social and economic conditions prevailing in England between 1780 and 1830, of such a writer as Hazlitt. I am glad, at the same time, to have this opportunity of expressing my indebtedness for material used in this biography to earlier work on Hazlitt, especially to the works of the late Mr. W. Carew Hazlitt, to whose daughter, Miss Hazlitt, I am grateful for sanctioning my use of this family material, which must ever be the primary source of knowledge as to Hazlitt's childhood.

I am indebted in various ways to those who have been kind enough to read the proofs or assist the work by their care: Sir Herbert Grierson, K.B., whose *Milton and Wordsworth, Poets and Prophets*, has assisted me in estimating the character of Hazlitt's political writing; Mr. Nowell Smith, for giving the work the benefit of his exquisite scholarship; Mr. Lawrence Hanson, for sympathy extended towards the work when it was carried on in circumstances adverse to it; and to Mr. Milton Waldman for his helpful and penetrating criticism. There are others, close friends and kin, whom I do not name, but to whom my debt is greater than I can express. I trust they will know that they are named, one by one, in my grateful thoughts.

Other debts, which I acknowledge with thanks, are: to Captain H. P. Chichester Clark for permitting me to examine the manuscript of a Diary kept by his great-grandmother, Mrs. Clark of Efford Manor, which gives a very vivid impression of the excitement in and around Plymouth in 1815, when Napoleon "stood on the deck of the *Bellerophon*"; to Mr. and Mrs. Morris of Wem for permitting me to take photographs of Hazlitt's home, now theirs; to Alderman Richard

Mansell, J.P., of Shrewsbury, for the loan of the photograph of the Unitarian Chapel, Shrewsbury (taken before the interior was renovated in 1903), which is reproduced in this book; and to Mr. E. T. Sloane, the Editor of *The Shrewsbury Chronicle*, for checking from his files the text of Hazlitt's first journalistic venture, which appeared in *The Shrewsbury Chronicle*.

I am indebted to the Trustees of Dove Cottage for permission to examine the early manuscripts of *The Prelude* and of the opening of *The Excursion*, an investigation which, although undertaken with another end in view, has given me many a clue as to the nature of Hazlitt's early intercourse with Wordsworth; to the Committee of the Maidstone Museum for permission to reproduce some of the portraits of the Hazlitt family in their care; to the Trustees of the National Portrait Gallery for permission to reproduce portraits of Coleridge and Lamb; to the Librarian of the Morgan Library, New York, for permission to quote from certain Lamb letters; to Messrs. J. M. Dent & Sons, Limited, not only for permission to quote from the text of their Centenary Edition of Hazlitt's Works, Edited by Mr. P. P. Howe, but to reproduce the frontispieces of Volumes 5 and 19 of this Edition, and to make quotation from *The Letters of Charles and Mary Lamb*, Edited by E. V. Lucas, and from *Henry Crabb Robinson on Books and their Writers*, Edited by Edith J. Morley; to Messrs. Constable & Co., Limited, for permission to quote from *Unpublished Letters of Samuel Taylor Coleridge*, Edited by Earl Leslie Griggs; and to the Delegates of The Clarendon Press, Oxford, for permission to quote from *The Letters of William and Dorothy Wordsworth*, Edited by E. de Selincourt. I make acknowledgment here also of my debt to *Lamb and Hazlitt*, by W. Carew Hazlitt, published in 1900 by Messrs. Elkin Mathews & Mar ot, Limited, from which I have drawn some material. Finally, I offer my thanks to the publishers for the care with which the work has been produced, despite the difficulties of the times.

London,
April 11th, 1943.